Teamwork & Teamplay

A Guide To Cooperative, Challenge and Adventure Actvities that Build Confidence, Cooperation, Teamwork, Creativity, Trust, Decision Making, Conflict Resolution, Resource Management, Communication, Effective Feedback and Problem Solving Skills

Jim Cain, Ph.D.
Barry Jolliff

Teamwork & Teamplay
468 Salmon Creek Road
Brockport, NY 14420
www.teamworkandteamplay.com

KENDALL/HUNT PUBLISHING COMPANY
4050 Westmark Drive Dubuque, Iowa 52002

ISBN 978-0-7872-4532-0

Printed in the United States of America
10 9 8

Contents

Introduction

One of the most fascinating things about challenge and adventure education is the vast knowledge possessed by some of the outstanding educators in this field. The more we listened, and learned, and shared, and eventually taught, the more often folks began to ask the inevitable question, "How do you guys know all this stuff?"

It is our sincerest intention to try to answer that question with this publication. In the following pages, you will find a variety of challenge and adventure activities which we feel are the best for bringing a group together. Not just the familiar activities, but some simple and excitingly new activities. Techniques for planning a challenge program are provided, as are instructions for creating some of the most basic and useful equipment for these challenge activities. There is also an extensive list of references and resources that we have found useful—if we know about them, so should you! Finally, and possibly most importantly, throughout this book you will find hints, insights, tricks, and rare pieces of our philosophy that we feel are necessary to turn a typical challenge and adventure program into an outstanding challenge and adventure program.

We know this stuff, because we were curious. We inquired, read books, called people on the phone, researched magazine articles, cruised the internet, attended workshops, visited professionals in the field, volunteered at summer camps, traded ideas with other facilitators and program leaders, built tons of equipment from PVC tubing, lycra, and rope. We found out what ERIC/CRESS, and AEE, and ACA, and ACCT, and PA are. We have racked up substantial long-distance phone bills, faxed letters around the world, ordered books in foreign languages, received packages from places we have never heard of, and generally have become a curiousity to our local postal service workers and UPS delivery personnel. We have complete rooms in our houses filled with storage boxes full of tennis balls, nylon webbing and rope. We have traveled hundreds of miles with our cars filled with challenge course equipment. We have learned the value of Rubbermaid® storage containers, and can stuff enough equipment in a backpack for a whole days worth of programming.

If these characteristics seem familiar to you, or you find this type of behavior perfectly normal, then you are probably on your way to becoming an excellent challenge and adventure programmer. And it is for you that this book is written.

Jim Cain
Barry Jolliff
1998

Some Information about Jim Cain

Dr. Jim Cain is the Director and creative force behind Teamwork & Teamplay - the Adventure-Based Training Company, a former Executive Director of ACCT and Senior Consultant to the Cornell Teambuilding Program. He makes his home in Brockport, New York. For 15 years he worked as a senior research engineer for Eastman Kodak. He holds a Bachelor degree, two Master degrees and a Ph.D. in Mechanical Engineering from the University of Rochester. He frequently serves as a visiting professor on subjects ranging from experiential education to challenge and adventure-based activities, and from recreational dancing and games leadership, to structural engineering, chaos and powder mechanics. Jim recently received the Karl Rohnke Creativity Award, presented by the Association for Experiential Education, for his work on the book Teamwork & Teamplay.

Jim began teaching dance and games as a 4-H camp counselor in 1973 and has assisted with more than 450 camping programs since then. He is a third generation square dance caller, plays guitar and mandolin, and has recorded with the ensemble Thistledown performing Celtic acoustic music on guitar, fiddle and hammered dulcimer. His first CD *The Hills of Lorne* has sold over 9,000 copies. Jim's next musical project is a digital recording entitled *Barn Dance Tonight* featuring music of traditional and contemporary country dancing.

Some of Jim's experience in adventure-based leadership comes from his 20 year involvement with the Ohio-based Buckeye Leadership Workshop. In recent years, he has presented workshops, staff training events, seminars and keynote presentations in 35 states and 6 countries, including AEE Regional and International Conferences, NCI, ASTD events, 4-H Conferences in 8 states and recreation workshops in a dozen states. In 1996 Jim helped create and facilitate a team building program for the NASA Lunar-Mars project to prepare personnel for extended missions. Jim also assists with the staff training of many summer camps, collegiate adventure programs, and corporate teambuilding organizations each year. Most recently his work includes facilitating challenge and adventure activities, writing award winning adventure-based activity books, and the analysis, design and construction of portable, ground-level and permanently installed adventure equipment. Jim has designed and constructed his own barn which holds an extensive woodworking shop and space for adventure activities. In 1998, Jim traveled twice to Nagano, Japan to construct a high and low element challenge course near the site of the 1998 Winter Olympic Games. The high element ropes course was only the second ever constructed in that nation, and received extensive media coverage.

In addition to challenge and adventure education programs, Jim has created a series of corporate teambuilding activities that have been used with technical teams, managers, sales teams and assembly workers. These activities have also been applied in academic, therapeutic recreation and other professional settings. Jim has also worked extensively to create fully accessible adventure programs and challenge course equipment for organizations which include participants with specialized needs.

Jim has presented workshops for a wide variety of challenge course organizations in North America, and has assisted in the construction of several ground-level and high element adventure courses for these groups. During his graduate studies he mechanically tested the strength and physical properties of many types of adventure equipment and ropes course hardware. He has worked extensively with the Association for Challenge Course Technology and many of the reviewed vendor members of this organization, including Project Adventure, Inner Quest, Adventure Experiences and Alpine Towers. In addition to challenge and adventure activities, Jim also makes a variety of boomerangs, 2 liter bottle rockets, rain sticks, tin whistles, sundials, and generally has more toys than many developing nations. As the owner and director of Teamplay, Jim frequently consults with schools, colleges, youth centers, camps and corporate clients regarding the use of adventure-based activities. He has created a multitude of portable, ground-level initiatives and challenge activities in addition to designing and building equipment for these activities. His publications include contributions to the *Bradford Papers, The Book of Metaphors Volume II* edited by Michael Gass, *50 Ways to Use Your Noodle* by Chris Cavert & Sam Sikes, *Adventure Programming* by Miles & Priest, and the new classic *Teamwork & Teamplay*. Watch for a new book, *Teambuilding Hardware,* a second volume of *Teamwork & Teamplay,* and *The Book on Raccoon Circles.*

Jim Cain, Ph.D.
468 Salmon Creek Road, Brockport, New York 14420
Phone (585) 637-0328 Fax (585) 637-5277
Email: jimcain@teamworkand teamplay.com
Website: www.teamworkandteamplay.com

Some Information about Barry Jolliff

Barry Jolliff makes his home near Wooster, Ohio, with his wife and three children on a small farm, where he raises a variety of vine crops, especially gourds, and enjoys his vegetable garden. He is currently in the teaching profession, as a sixth grade science teacher in a public school. In the classroom he has used the teamwork approach to teach activities from math to science to small group projects where teamwork was needed. He has led many workshops teaching teachers how to incorporate teamwork activities into their classroom. He has a Bachelor's degree and a Master's degree, both in education, from the Ohio State University.

Barry has worked extensively with the Ohio State University Cooperative Extension Service in several 4-H and youth development positions over many years. During this time, he directed summer camp programs, counselor training sessions, and adult training seminars. He has also worked as a program director for a city community center and as a district youth coordinator for the Methodist Church.

Barry began his outdoor adventures as a 4-H camper in 1966 and as a camp counselor in 1971. Through the leadership skills taught in 4-H and responsibilities given to counselors, he was soon leading indoor and outdoor recreation and camp dances. These recreation skills were soon put to use as Barry began working with local church groups and 4-H clubs. In 1976, Barry bought a few records for line and square dances and a portable P.A. system. Since then he has won countless records completely smooth and frequently transports a whole truck load of equipment when he is on the road to lead recreation programs.

Barry's real inspiration for becoming a recreation specialist, which was not self proclaimed, came from attending the annual Ohio-based Buckeye Leadership Workshop. Barry first attended the workshop in 1975, and has been actively involved since then. He is currently serving on the BLW permanent planning committee. At BLW over the years, Barry has taught recreational dancing, social recreation, games without props, mime, woodworking, boomerangs, and a challenge and adventure activities class entitled Teamwork & Teamplay with co-author Jim Cain.

Barry's challenge and adventure related activities have changed over the years from building a small permanent, ground level initiatives course in the woods beyond his home to his more recent totally portable challenge course programs (have truck-will travel). His initial challenge activities enlightenment happened the first time Barry strapped on a seat harness and ascended forty feet into the trees on the Scarlet high ropes course at the Adventure Education Center near Columbus, OH. Eventually he took their instructor's certification course for both ground-level and high-ropes courses.

Barry has led recreation in one form or another to youth of all ages throughout Ohio and neighboring states to places as far away as Montreal, Florida, Louisiana, and Seattle. He has worked with a diverse audience, from 4-H and church camps, to training camp counselors, to entertain high school and college clubs, to corporate leadership training seminars, and "kick-off" programs for national and state youth meetings such as National 4-H Congress, National Youth of Unity, National Dairy Conference, Ohio 4-H Exposition and the Ohio State 4-H Leadership Camp. Often times you can find Barry leading activities at birthday parties for six to sixty year olds. He has also presented programs at recreation and leadership workshops and conferences in Ohio, Michigan, Indiana and Florida.

Barry Jolliff
760 East Hutton Road
Wooster, OH 44691
Phone: (330) 345-8492
Email: bjolliff@sssnet.com

Disclaimer

Writing this guide to share our challenge and adventure experiences has been a labor of love. We have at times however, considered the element of risk involved in these types of activities and wondered just how much to share. In the modern world, any author worth their salt is aware how difficult it is to ensure that their intent is properly followed—and we share that concern. The results of this concern are presented in this disclaimer:

Challenge and adventure activities can present elements of physical and emotional risk. The information presented in this guide is for your reference and you as the user are ultimately responsible for judging the suitability of an activity and safely supervising the activity. The authors assume no responsibility or liability for the use of the information presented in this manual. This includes errors due to misprinting or omission of detail.

No single book can substitute for practical experience and education. While this guide serves as an introduction to the use of challenge and adventure activities, it is only an introduction. There are several outstanding organizations that professionally train challenge instructors—See Chapter 8 for a list of some of these organizations. Learn from the best and be the best!

You are strongly encouraged to lead activities with a "challenge by choice" philosophy. Allow each individual to communicate their comfort level with the activity and to join in rather than be coerced into participation. Challenge and adventure programs are an opportunity for participants to experience growth, and as such should be the result of an invitation, rather than a requirement.

Good luck, play hard, learn much and be careful!

The Concept of Basic Training

The books that tend to be the most useful, those wonderful copies with the torn corners, tattered pages, partially destroyed covers, highlighted paragraphs and paper clips on all the really good pages, are the ones that contain just the right amount of information in an easy to find format. The quicker a reader can find that critical section, that basic activity instruction, that definition, that vital piece of information, the more valuable the text.

Knowing that you are no doubt just as busy as we are, we have decided to include a section known as *basic training* in many of the following chapters. The concept of basic training is fairly simple: within the boundaries of the basic training blocks in each chapter can be found the essence, the concise definitions, the critical mass of the content that follows. Some of the following chapters contain more than 25 years worth of research, and as such contain lengthy lists of resources and information. If you are pressed for time, try reading the basic training block first. This should give you the greatest amount of information in the minimum amount of time. Then, when you have time to leisurely enjoy reading the remainder of each section, you will already know some of the information contained in each section.

Basic training blocks in the following chapters look like the one shown below. Within the block can be found a variety of concise information based on the subject of the section the block is contained within.

Basic Training

- Basic training blocks can be found in nearly every section of this book.
- These blocks contain a very concise listing of the information presented within the following section of the book.
- If you are quickly scanning a section, the basic training blocks provide the greatest amount of information for the least amount of invested time.
- In some cases, the basic training block points out vital pieces of information that can be found within the section.
- Don't forget that there is more to life (and this book) than basic training!

Comments

Your comments regarding the information presented in this manual are **extremely** important to us. We would really like to know your opinion of this material. Please take a few minutes to complete this comment sheet and mail it to the address shown below. Tell us your experiences with this material, which activities are best for your group, your ability to follow the instructions for making your own props, variations for activities, photographs of your gang at play and any other information that you would like to share. Thanks.

The best part of this manual is:

Improvements I would suggest to this manual include:

I would like to see additional material presented on the topic of

I have used the following chapters of this manual the most

I found the following parts of this book the least valuable to me

I typically use the following resources (reference books, organizations, individuals) for these types of activities

I plan to use this material with the following groups (corporate groups, schools, camps, church youth groups, etc.)

From what organization, store or location did you purchase this book?

Please score the following attributes of this manual— 1 = OK 3 = Good 5 = Great!

The written text was clearly presented	1	2	3	4	5
Photographs and sketches were helpful	1	2	3	4	5
I liked the format of this manual	1	2	3	4	5
Subjects and activities are easy to find	1	2	3	4	5
Many of the activities presented are new to me	1	2	3	4	5

Mail to: Jim Cain & Barry Jolliff
Teamwork & Teamplay
468 Salmon Creek Road
Brockport, NY 14420

Chapter One

"Why Are We Doing This?"

The use of challenge related education and training has increased dramatically in the past decade. While previously encountered only in classrooms and summer camps, corporations are finding that what works in the classroom also transfers to the board room. The ability to work as a group, to effectively communicate, to collectively solve problems, to foster a sense of empathy and respect for other team members, to provide honest and useful feedback, to resolve conflicts, to effectively manage resources and to share in a group experience builds a sense of community that, when properly accomplished, translates effectively back to the work environment. Challenge and adventure activities also just happen to provide an interesting and fun method for learning and applying these skills.

Sooner or later however, someone is likely to ask the inevitable question, "why are we doing this?" And this question does not just occur in the corporate setting but has parallels in every segment of society that attempts to employ challenge related programs to accomplish specific goals within their organization. In the following chapter, recent viewpoints on the effective use of challenge and adventure activities are explored. Just a brief explanation of "why we are doing this."

What Is Going On Here?

In the most basic of terms, challenge and adventure activities provide the opportunity for participants to push past their own comfort zones (physically, emotionally, intellectually, spiritually) and to enter a region of unknown outcome, which is often referred to as the growth zone. The step beyond the comfort zone of the individual is generally conservative, especially early in the program, to acquaint the participant with the process. If the step beyond the comfort zone of the individual is too great, the participant jumps beyond the growth zone and lands firmly in a zone of anxiety known as the panic zone.

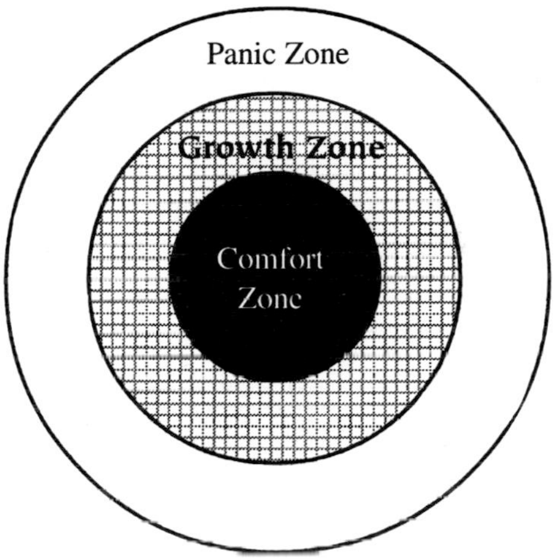

Mihaly Csikszentmihalyi presents this information in a slightly different format when discussing the ability to achieve flow during a personal growth activity or learning event. In the 1990 Harper & Row publication entitled "Flow" Csikszentmihalyi discusses the flow region as the optimal learning environment between boredom from lack of stimulation or challenges and anxiety from an overabundance of stimulation or challenges.

Providing an opportunity for an individual to experience growth in a supportive environment, using skillfully planned activities, is one of the most attractive features of a challenge and adventure program. Challenge activities provide the opportunity for individuals and groups to reach beyond the typical, the normal, and experience the unique as they attempt to utilize new skills, apply these skills to new problems and situations, and internalize how their efforts helped achieve their goals. The retention of skills learned during such events are typically higher than other learning events involving only lecture, reading or writing assignments, because the individual has participated in the experience at a higher level.

Graphically, the relationship between the learning technique and the retention of the skills looks like this:

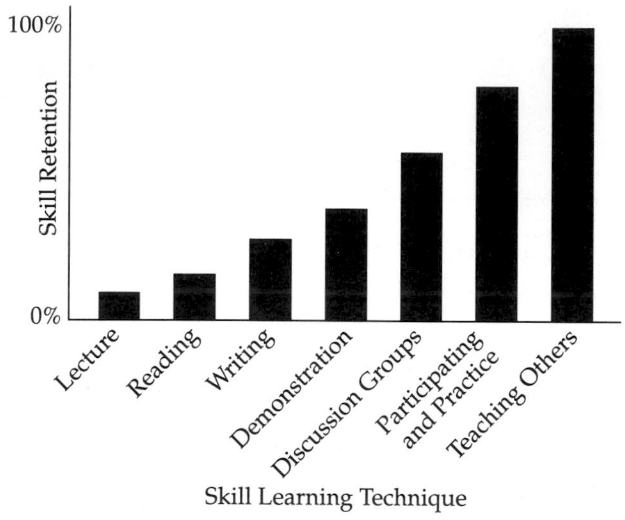

In other words, the more immersed the individual is in the learning process, the greater their ability to retain the skills and lessons learned. While participants typically only retain about 10% of what they read, their retention jumps to 50% if they are actively engaged in the learning process with discussion and demonstrations. This retention increases even further, to more than 70% if the participant has the opportunity to participate and practice what they learn, and to 90% if they are given the opportunity to experience, reflect, internalize and then share what they have learned.

Challenge and adventure activities not only involve the participants at the highest level of learning technique, they also address an additional concern frequently encountered in education—that different individuals can learn best in different ways.

While there are a variety of individual learning techniques, at least seven distinct methods are commonly discussed. These learning methods include: linguistic and word related teaching, logical or mathematical structures, spatial or geometrical recognition, kinesthetic or body related awareness, musical awareness, self knowledge, and finally the perception of others.

If you have ever tried to explain to someone how to bounce a basketball, you'll quickly find that this is typically an opportunity for a kinesthetic or body centered teaching technique. Learning the names of the members in the group is a word centered talent. Trying to decide how best to arrange the ropes to retrieve the Pot of Gold has a geometric content.

The good news here, is that the challenge and adventure activities presented in this book provide the opportunity for participants to experience many of these learning styles. Marching to the Beat of a Different Drum utilizes musical and kinesthetic abilities. Plenty of Room at the Top has a distinctive geometrical challenge to it. Understanding how the 25 film canisters can group participants 4 different ways with none of their previous partners is certainly centered in the mathematical/logical field. Being able to provide effective feedback or anticipating the needs of other members in the group allows participants to exercise their perception and knowledge of others.

Ok. So challenge and adventure activities utilize the experiential techniques and learning scenarios that are known to optimize the retention of skills learned by the participants. And so these activities can be presented in a variety of methods that utilize at least seven known and distinctive learning styles. What skills can be learned from these techniques?

Learning the Ropes with Challenge and Adventure Activities

On the front cover of this book you'll find eleven skills that can be explored using the challenge and adventure techniques in this book. If you want to check your learning retention at this point, see how many you can name without looking. Given that you are probably reading this text, you'll probably remember about three of the skills mentioned. If you remember more, you'll need it. There is a ton of great information yet to come.

Let's begin this section by quickly exploring a few of the skills mentioned, and see how challenge and adventure programming activities can be applied.

Problem Solving. No question about it, of the 83 activities listed in Chapter 4 alone, more than half of the activities listed require a solution to a challenge. Specific activities such as 2B or KNOT 2B show a variety of problem solving techniques. These skills are exactly the type that can be taken back with the participants to their work environments and applied there.

Creativity. When the group is confronted with a visual, geometric or physical challenge, the solution may not be immediately apparent. Most of the activities in this book were chosen because they have several acceptable solution techniques. The ability to think creatively, both individually and within a working group, are essential skills. The opportunity to see a unique solution technique, such as that possible with Plenty of Room at the Top, and Villages and Wells, provides the participant an opportunity to learn new ways to creatively solve problems.

Effective Feedback. While effective feedback may not be the first skill you consider when embarking on a challenge and adventure activity, the opportunities are clearly there. Several of the activities in this book are specifically chosen so that the success of the group is clearly an indication of the group's ability to communicate, to openly discuss the situation, and to provide accurate and helpful feedback as participants accomplish the activity.

Confidence. Having the opportunity to reach outside our comfort zone in an atmosphere of support certainly provides the right setting for success. Some of the activities presented in Chapter 4 are going to be completely unfamiliar to many of the participants that experience them. Learning how to apply skills to new and unfamiliar problems successfully, builds confidence in both individuals and teams. Being impowered to make decisions, to allocate resources, to choose their level of participation and involvement, and to share in the outcome certainly provides more opportunities for building confidence than many real-life situations.

Other useful skills not mentioned on the cover, but also included in the activities presented in Chapters 4 and 7 of this book include: exploring diversity, achieving group consensus, coordination and balance, motivation, timing, focus, non-verbal communication, and visualization.

OK. Now that we see what skills are involved, where can these activities be presented, and to what audience?

Who Benefits from Challenge and Adventure Programming Activities?

Challenge and adventure activities certainly are not the only technique for building useful skills in both individuals and groups. But these activities have an appeal that goes beyond many traditional teaching methods. After realizing the power in these techniques, the next step is to identify where to use these techniques. Here are just a few suggestions:

Corporate Meetings for building team spirit, team unity, loyalty. Church Youth groups as a method for introducing new members to the group in a non-threatening environment. Staff Training Session as a means of creating ownership for the facilities, familarity with available adventure resources, and building staff spirit and unity. College Orientation Programs for encouraging cooperation, not competition. Physical Conditioning Classes, to encourage fitness of mind, spirit, and body, and as an alternative to competitive sports. Leadership Conferences as a technique for providing participants with opportunities for leadership, participation, setting goals and achieving them. Programs for Youth-At-Risk to show that there are ways to break out of patterns that do not work, and create new patterns that will lead to success.

For more suggestions of suitable audiences, see the lower front cover of this book.

So What Is the Real Goal of Challenge and Adventure Activities?

By this point, you may be beginning to see how you can employ challenge and adventure activities for your own group. We just want to mention however, that there are two levels to these activities that are quite different. Level 1 is typically defined by the challenge listed for each activity in Chapter 4. Place the ball in the target zone. Move the object from here to there. Transport everyone through the web. Try to get the ball in the bucket.

Level 2 is not interested in whether the ball ever reaches the bucket. Level 2 is interested in the process that takes place within the group. How did the group plan? How were the opinions of each member valued? Who made the final decision to start? Which technique was chosen, and why? Level 2 is not necessarily a higher level than level one, it is simply a different place to be.

The lessons learned in Level 1 reinforce the ability to set a goal and achieve it. In Level 2, the process of achieving the goal is considered. Both levels have value. Both levels are part of the challenge and adventure experience. Any challenge and adventure program without both of these levels is, in our humble opinion, incomplete. The real goal then, is to not only to successfully complete the challenge, but also to complete the challenge using skills and techniques that bring the group together.

Why All This Research?

You may be wondering why so much effort has been extended in this publication to researching this field and creating such an extensive database of information. Initially, so did we. But recently, a personal conversation between author Jim Cain and Richard Wagner of the University of Wisconsin, put all this work into perspective. Wagner is an outstanding authority on the evaluation of training programs, and has written several journal articles of merit on this and other challenge program subjects.

The point made by Wagner is that the quality of the facilitator is one of the most significant factors in the overall perception of a challenge and adventure program. Let us say this again in a slightly different fashion so that the point is not missed:

Of all the elements in a challenge and adventure program, the facilitator has the greatest impact on the ultimate success or failure of the program.

This is why we have spent the last five years of our lives creating this book. So that you, the leaders and facilitators of challenge and adventure programs can make sure that you are prepared to have a great, positive impact on the groups for which you facilitate these activities. If that is your desire, we encourage you to read not only the pages in this book, but also those of the journal articles, books, and resources we have referenced. Incidently, a summary of Wagner's comments on the four critical elements for success in a challenge and adventure program can be found in the May 19, 1991 New York Times article by Claudia H. Deutsch entitled "Back From the Great Outdoors." This is just one of the hundreds of articles referenced in the following pages of this chapter. If you have limited time, at least try to read the first five articles presented in the Basic Training section. We are sure you'll find these interesting.

Finally, if you would like to learn as much as you can about this field, try reading our suggestions in the Free Advice section of Chapter Nine. You'll probably

Basic Training

Challenge and Adventure Programming in a Nutshell

Challenge and adventure programs create situations that challenge the abilities of individuals and groups. These situations are metaphors for the problems and challenges faced by many individuals and groups during a typical day. By being part of such an event, participants learn skills that can be used in their daily activities. By discussing their performance during these events, participants learn how to improve their application of these new techniques to obtain positive results, while in an atmosphere of trust and cooperation. The end result is a more confident and capable individual and a more cooperative team.

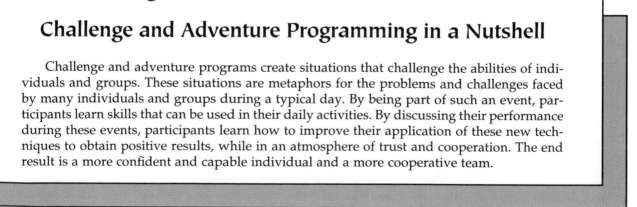

find a few suggestions there that are worth trying. We have collectively spent more than 50 years leading challenge and adventure programs, and each time we lead a new group, we learn a bit more. The process never ends.

The next section in this chapter is a literature review of some recent and significant challenge and adventure programming related journal, newspaper and magazine articles. Chapter Eight provides an extensive list of books published in this field.

References from Recent Publications

Some significant articles on challenge and adventure education and programming can be found in journals, periodicals, microfilms, magazines and newspaper articles. Many libraries have facilities for locating these articles using keywords such as: teamwork, teambuilding, outdoor education, ropes course, challenge education, experiential education, recreation, groupwork and outdoor training. Some of the most outstanding articles are presented here. Chapter Eight contains a bibliography of books, references and sources for equipment and some additional information available on the internet.

Sample Entry:
Lead Author's Name, "Title of Article," *Title of Publication*, Volume, Number, Month Year, pages.

Basic Training

Basic training for this chapter includes reading the following five articles and as many of the additional articles as possible. Ready, set, go!

- Buller, Paul F.; Cragun, John R. and McEvoy, Glenn M., "Getting the Most Out of Outdoor Training", *Training and Development Journal*, Volume 45, Issue 3, March 1991, pages 58–61.
- Gass, Michael; Goldman, Kathy and Priest, Simon, "Constructing Effective Corporate Adventure Training Programs", *The Journal of Experiential Education*, Volume 15, Number 1, May 1992, pages 35–42.
- Roland, Christopher; Summers, S.; Friedman, M.; Barton, G. and McCarthy, K., "Creation of an Experiential Challenge Program", *Therapeutic Recreation Journal*, Volume 21, Number 2, 1987, pages 54–63.
- Wagner, Richard J. and Roland, Christopher C., "How Effective is Outdoor Training?", *Training & Development*, Volume 46, Number 7, July 1992, pages 61–66.
- Wagner, Richard J., Baldwin, Timothy T., and Roland, Christopher C., "Outdoor Training: Revolution or Fad?", *Training & Development Journal*, Volume 45, Number 3, March 1991, pages 50–57.

Significant articles from the world of challenge and adventure information

Adair, B., "The Role of Recreation in Assessing the Needs of Emotionally Disturbed Youth," *Journal of Leisureability*, Volume 1, Number 4, 1974, pages 25–33.

Adams, Michael, "The Woodstock of the Meetings World," *Successful Meetings*, Volume 38, Issue 12, November 1989, pages 32–39.

Allen, Stewart and Meier, Joel F., "Let's Take a Risk with Adventure Recreation," *Parks and Recreation*, Volume 17, Number 2, February 1982, pages 47–50.

American Alliance for Health, Physical Education and Recreation (AAHPER), "Rope Activities for Fun, Fitness and Fonics," ERIC Document ED 160586, May 1978.

Anonymous, "Confidence Course Instructor's Guide," Montgomery County Public Schools, 1984, ERIC Document ED 249033.

Anonymous, "How One Company Trains in the Great Outdoors," *Business Week*, July 24, 1971, pages 40–41.

Anonymous, "Outdoor Education Directory: Organizations Involved in Outdoor Experiential Education," March 1993, ERIC Document ED 357944

Anonymous, "Outdoor Education, A Bibliography of ERIC Documents," Supplement Number 8, November 1978, ERIC Document ED 164168.

Anonymous, "Outdoor Lessons in Managerial Risk-Taking," *Business Week Magazine*, April 21, 1980.

Anonymous, "Teambuilding Workshops at NatWest Life", *Industrial and Commercial Training*, Volume 27, Issue 10, 1995, pages 20–21.

Anonymous, "Teamwork Taught in an Outdoor Environment," *New Jersey Business*, October 1990.

Anonymous, "Welcome to Hell Camp," *Time Magazine*, March 7, 1989.

Argyris, Chris, "Teaching Smart People How To Learn," *Harvard Business Review*, May-June 1991, pages 99–109.

Arkell, R. and Paice, V., "Personal Change and Involvement in Outdoor Education," *Saskatchewan Journal of Educational Research and Development*, Volume 4, Number 2, pages 29–30.

Arkin, Anat, "Breathing Fresh Air into Training", *People Management*, Volume 1, Volume 15, July 27, 1995, pages 34–35.

Armour, Norton L., "The Beginning of Stress Reduction: Creating a Code of Conduct for How Team Members Treat Each Other", *Public Personnel Management*, Volume 24, Issue 2, Summer 1995, pages 127–132.

Association for Experiential Education, "Programs Granting Academic Credit and/or Degrees," *Journal of Experiential Education*, Volume, Number 1, Spring 1979, pages 17–27.

Attarian, Aram, "Artificial Rock Climbing Walls—Innovative Adventure Envionments," *Journal of Physical Education, Recreation and Dance*, Volume 60, Number 7, September 1990, pages 28–32.

Attarian, Aram, "Research Update: Research on Adventure (Risk) Education," *Parks and Recreation*, Volume 26, Number 5, May 1991, pages 19–23,65.

Austin, D.R., "Recreation and Persons with Physical Disabilities: A Literature Synthesis," *Therapeutic Recreation Journal*, Volume 21, Number 1, 1987, pages 36–44.

Bacon, Stephen, "The Conscious Use of Metaphor in Outward Bound," Colorado Outward Bound School, Denver, CO, 1983.

Backus, Laurie, "Outdoor and Adventure Programs: Complementing Individual Education Programs and Treatment Plan Objectives," *Practical Pointers*, AAHPERD, Volume 4, Number 1, July 1980.

Bahin, Fikry S. and Chesteen, Susan A., "Executives Contemplate the Call of the Wild," *Risk Management*, Volume 35, Issue 7, July 1988, pages 44–51.

Bales, K.B., "Experiential Learning: A Review and Annotated Bibliography," *Journal of Cooperative Education*, Volume 16, Fall 1979, pages 70–90.

Bank, John, "Outdoor Development: A New Perspective in Management Education," *Leadership and Organization Development Journal*, Volume 4, Number 3, 1983, pages 3–44.

Barker, Julie, "The Great Outdoors", *Successful Meetings*, Volume 44, Issue 11, October 1995, pages 91–94.

Barrett, Jon, "A Reading List," *Proceedings of a National One-Day Conference "Adventure-Based Interventions"*, April 1994, Ambleside, England, ERIC Document ED 378027.

Barrett, Jon, "Directory of Outdoor Activity Provision for Yound People in Trouble or At Risk," North Basecamp and Adventure Education, Penrith, England, 1993.

Barrett, Jon, "Report on a Survey of Outdoor Activity Provision for Young Offenders and Young People At Risk," North Basecamp, Dumfries, Scotland, 1992.

Barry, Maude, "Training in Team Building," *Industrial & Commercial Training* (UK), November 1980.

Beckhard, R., "Optimizing Team Building Efforts," *Journal of Contemporary Business*, Volume 1, Number 3, 1972, pages 23–32.

Beeby, M. and Rathborn, S., "Development Training Using the Outdoors—A Pilot Program," *Journal of European Industrial Training*, Volume 6, 1982, pages 12–15.

Beeby, M. and Rathbourne, S., "Development Training—Using the Outdoors for Management Development," *Association of Teachers of Management Journal*, Autumn 1983.

Bennet, D.B., "Four Steps to Evaluating Environmental Education Learning Experiences," *Journal of Experiential Education*, Volume 20, Number 2, 1988, pages 14–21.

Berman, D.S. and Anton, M.T., "A Wilderness Theraphy Program as an Alternative to Adolescent Psychiatric Hospitalization," *Residential Treatment for Children and Youth*, Volume 5, Number 3, 1988, pages 41–53.

Bialer, Emily, "Outdoor Challenge Energizes Team Spirit," *The Practical Accountant*, August 1993, page 9.

Bickerstaffe, George, "How to Survive a 'Leadership' Course," *International Management*, Volume 37, Number 4, April 1982, pages 40–41.

Blanchard, Charles W., "Experiential Therapy with Troubled Youth: The Ropes Course for Adolescent Inpatients," *Proceedings of the International Conference of the Association for Experiential Education*, October 1992, Banff, Alberta, Canada, ERIC Document ED 353116

Blythe, Chris, "Site Inventory for Outdoor Education Facilities and Recreation Camps," *Pathways: The Ontario Journal of Outdoor Education*, Volume 7, Number 1, December 1994, pages 28–30.

Bolt, James F., "How Executives Learn: the Move From Glitz to Guts," *Training & Development Journal*, Volume 44, Issue 5, May 1990, pages 83–87.

Brackenreg, Mark, 'Theories, Practices and Benefits of Debriefing in Outdoor Education," *Journal of Outdoor Education*, Volume 26, 1993, pages 3–11.

Braham, James E., "Outward Bound to Your Outer Limits," *Machine Design*, October 20, 1983, pages 216–222.

Brauchle, Paul E. and Wright, David W., "Fourteen Team Building Tips," *Training & Development*, January 1992, pages 32–36.

Braun, Joseph A. and Brown, Max H., "Challenging Student Teachers," *Phi Delta Kappan*, Volume 65, Number 9, May 1984, pages 601–602.

Braverman, Marc, et. al., "Three Approaches to Evaluation: A Ropes Course Illustration," *Journal of Experiential Education*, Volume 13, Number 1, May 1990, pages 23–30.

Broadwell, Laura, "Business Games: They're More than Child's Play," *Successful Meetings*, Volume 36, Number 7, June 1987, pages 36–39.

Broderick, Richard, "Learning the Ropes," *Training*, Volume 26, Issue 10, October 1989, pages 78–86.

Broida, D., "Gaining Awareness Through Adventure," *Parks and Recreation*, Volume 13, Number 6, June 1978, pages 30–34.

Broida, David, et. al., "Gaining Awareness Through Adventure," *Parks and Recreation*, Volume 13, Number 6, June 1978, pages 30–34.

Bronson, Jim, et. al., "Evaluation of Team Development in a Corporate Adventure Training Program," *Journal of Experiential Education*, Volume 15, Number 2, August 1992, pages 50–53.

Brown, Michael H., "Transpersonal Psychology: Facilitating Transformation in Outdoor Experiential Education," *Journal of Experiential Education*, Volume 12, Number 3, Fall, 1989, pages 47–56.

Buchanan, D., "Outward Bound goes to the Inner City," *Educational Leadership*, Volume 50, Number 4, 1992–1993, pages 38–41.

Buller, P.F. and Bell, C.H., "Effects of Team Building and Goal Setting on Productivity: A Field Experiment," *Academy of Management Journal*, Volume 29, 1986,pages 305–328.

Bunting, Camille T., "Group Initiatives—Make a Game Out Of Problem Solving," *Camping Magazine*, February 1988, Pages 26–29.

Burdett, John, "Teambuilding: A Manager's Construction Guide," *Canadian Manager*, Volume 14, Issue 4, December 1989, pages 16–19.

Burnett, Donna, "Exercising Better Management Skills", *Personnel Management*, Volume 26, Issue 1, January 1994, pages 42–46.

Carden, B., "Design and Use of Ropes Courses," *North Carolina Journal of Outdoor Education*, Volume 1, Number 1, 1979, pages 44–48.

Carey, Robert, "Go Take A Flying Leap (for the Company)," *Successful Meetings*, Volume 41, Issue 7, June 1992, pages 59–62.

Cash, Robin, "Outdoor Training—Can You Afford Teamwork?," *Financial Executive*, Volume 7, Issue 3, May/June 1991, pages 4–6.

Cason, D. and Gillis, H., "A Meta-Analysis of Outdoor Adventure Programming with Adolescents," *Journal of Experiential Education*, Volume 17, Number 1, 1994, pages 40–47.

Chapman, A. and Lumsdon, C.A., "Outdoor Development Training: A New Tool for Management," *Leadership and Organization Development Journal*, Volume 4, 1983, pages 28–31.

Chase, Penelope and Paul, Sara, "Integrating Assistive Personnel: A Teambuilding Approach", *Nursing Management*, Volume 26, Issue 6, Jun 1995, pages 71–73.

Chaudron, David, "Organizational Development: How to Improve Cross-Functional Teams", *HRFocus*, Volume 72, Issue 8, August 1995, pages 1–4.

Chenery, M.F., "Effects of a Summer Camp on Child Development and Contributions of Counselors to those Effects," *Journal of Leisure Research*, Volume 13, Number 4, 1981, pages 311–322.

Chesteen, S.A., Caldwell, L.G. and Prochanka, L.J., "Taking Legal Risks Out of Adventure Training," *Training and Development Journal*, Volume 42, Number 7, 1988, pages 42–46.

Chipkin, Harvey, "A Team Builder's Guide to the Galaxy," *Business Month*, Volume 135, Issue 3, March 1990, pages 66–69.

Chu, Lantien, "Insurance and Risk Management at the National Outdoor Leadership School," *Outdoor Network Newsletter*, Volume 1, Number 7, Fall 1990, pages 6–7. ERIC Document EJ424947.

Cicchino, Angelo A., "Sales Organizations—The Need for Teamwork and the Art of Building it," *Broker World*, Volume 13, Issue 8, August 1993, pages 58–62.

Cinnamon, Jerry, "Artificial Climbing Wall Design and Use," March 1985, ERIC Document ED 256538.

Clements, Christine, et. al., "The Ins and Outs of Experiential Training," *Training and Development*, Volume 49, Number 2, February 1995, pages 52–56.

Cline, F.B. and Seibert, P.S., "Help for First-time Needs Assessors," *Training and Development Journal*, Volume 47, Number 5, 1993, pages 99–101.

Cockrell, David, "The Fragmentation of Outdoor Leadership," *Proceedings of the National Conference for Outdoor Leaders*, 1991, ERIC Document ED 335193.

Coffee, J.V. and Ferree, J.,"Buddies, Backpacks and Blisters," *School Counselor*, January 1974, pages 230–232.

Cook, K.V., "The Effectiveness of an Outdoor Adventure Program as a Training Method for Resident Assistants: A Thesis in Parks and Recreation," Unpublished Masters Thesis, Pennsylvania State University, May 1980, ERIC Document ED 210142.

Couch, Robin L., "Outdoor Training—Can You Afford Teamwork?," *Financial Executive*, Volume 7, Issue 3, May/June 1991, pages 4–6.

Cousineau, C., "The Nature of Adventure Education," Oakland County Schools, Pontiac, Michigan, 1977, ERIC Document Number ED 174 474.

Covell, Geoff, "Further Portable Adventure Programme Elements," *Journal of Adventure Education and Outdoor Leadership*, Volume 8, Number 3, Fall 1991, pages VI-VIII.

Crawford, Norman, "Outdoor Management Development: A Practical Evaluation," *Journal of European Industrial Training*, Volume 12, Issue 8, 1988, pages 17–20.

Crocker, J. and Wroblewski, M., "Using Recreational Games in Counseling," *Personnel and Guidance Journal*, Volume 53, Number 6, 1975, pages 453–458.

Currie, Graeme, "Teambuilding Training in a Clinical Environment", *Journal of Managerial Psychology*, Volume 9, Issue 3, 1994, pages 8–12.

Darling, John R., "Team Building in the Small Business Firms," *Journal of Small Business Management*, Volume 28, Number 3, July 1990, pages 86–91.

Dattilo, J. and Murphy, W.D., "Facilitating the Challenge in Adventure Recreation for Persons with Disabilities," *Therapeutic Recreation Journal*, Volume 21, Number 3, 1987, pages 14–21.

Dawson, R., "An Alternative Feedback/Evaluation Model for Outdoor Wilderness Programs," October 25, 1980 *Proceedings of the 8th Annual Conference of the Association of Experiential Education*, ERIC Document ED 207745.

Deutsch, Claudia H., "Back from the Great Outdoors," *New York Times*, May 19, 1991.

Dickey, H.L., "Outdoor Adventure Training," *Journal of Physical Education and Recreation*, Volume 49, Number 4, April 1978, pages 34–35.

Duggan, Joe, "Challenge Course Runs from Fear to Elation," *Lincoln Journal-Star*, September 11, 1994, page 1C.

Durgin, Carolyn and McEwen, Douglas, "Troubled Young People After the Adventure Program: A Case Study," *Journal of Experiential Education*, Volume 14, Number 1, May 1991, Pages 31–35.

Durst, M.E., "Experiential Learning: Its Meaning and Value," *North Carolina Journal of Outdoor Education*, Volume 2, Number 1, Fall 1980, pages 18–23.

Eder, S., "Learning on the Rocks," *American Education*, Volume 12, Number 3, 1976, pages 16–21.

Eisman, Regina, "Incentive's Excellent Adventure", *Incentive*, Volume 169, Volume 9, September 1995, pages 32–34.

Eisman, Regina, "Leap of Faith", *Incentive*, Volume 169, Issue 9, September 1995, pages 28–31.

Eisner, E.W., "Reshaping Assessment in Education: Some Criteris in Search of Practice," *Journal of Curriculum Studies*, Volume 25, Number 3, 1993, pages 219–233.

Ellis, G., Witt, P., and Aguilar, T., "Facilitating Flow Through Therapeutic Recreation Services," *Therapeutic Recreation Journal*, Volume 2, 1983, pages 6–15.

Elsner, Gary, et. al., "Education Requirements for Natural Resource Based Outdoor Recreation Professionals," *Proceedings of the National Conference for Outdoor Leaders*, 1991, ERIC Document ED 335191.

Erickson, Susan and Harris, Buck, "The Adventure Book: A Curriculum Guide to School Based Adventuring with Troubled Adolescents," Wilderness School, Goshen, Conn., 1980 ERIC Document ED 200381.

Evans, Will, "Administering Safety—Challenge courses and climbing walls," *Camping Magazine*, May/June 1996, pages 39–48.

Ewert, Alan, "Adventure Education: What's the Law?," *Outdoor Communicator*, Volume 11, Number 3, Spring 1981, pages 18–21.

Ewert, Alan, "Managing Fear in the Outdoor Experiential Education Setting," *Journal of Experiential Education*, Volume 12, Number 1, Spring 1989, pages 19–25.

Ewert, Alan, "Outdoor Adventure Recreation: A Trend Analysis," *Journal of Park and Recreation Administration*, Volume 5, Number 2, pages 57–67.

Ewert, Alan, "Theoretical Foundations of Outdoor Adventure Activities," *Outdoor Recreation Research Journal*, Volume 2, 1987, pages 3–16.

Falvey, Jack, "Before Spending $3 Million on Leadership, Read This," *Wall Street Journal*, October 3, 1988.

Farbman, A.H. andEllis, W.K., "Accessibility and Outdoor Recreation for Persons with Disabilities," *Therapeutic Recreation Journal*, Volume 21, Number 1, 1987, pages 70–76.

Fersch, Ellsworth and Smith, Mary, "Final Quantitative Evaluation for 1971–72, Year 1 of Project Adventure," ERIC Document ED 173059.

Fischesser, Mike, "The Evolution of the Ropes Course," *Adolescent Counselor*, July 1991, pages 23, 43.

Flor, Richard, "An Introduction to Research and Evaluation in Practice," *Journal of Experiential Education*, Volume 14, Number 1, 1991, pages 36–39.

Flor, Richard, "Building Bridges Between Organization Development and Experiential/Adventure Education," *The Journal of Experiential Education*, Volume 14, Number 3, November 1991, pages 27–34.

Flynn, Gillian, "Smooth Sailing for Teamwork", *Personnel Journal*, Volume 74, Issue 6, June 1995, page 26.

Ford, Phyllis, "The Responsible Outdoor Leader," *Journal of Outdoor Education*, Volume 22, 1988, pages 4–13.

Forrester, R.A., "How Outward Bound Training Can Lead to Better Buying," *Retail and Distribution Management*, Volume 15, Issue 5, September/October 1987, pages 21–23.

Fortman, K.J., "Counselor Training Manual for Resident Environmental Education Camps," Ohio State Dept. of Natural Resources, Columbus, Ohio, 1981, ERIC Document Number ED 211 362.

Forum, Volume 7, Number 3, Fall 1981, ERIC Document Number ED 215 481.

Foster, Herbert L., "A Personal and Professional Challenge: Socially Acceptable Risk Taking, Challenge and Adventure," *The Forum*, Volume 8, Number 4, Winter 1982, pages 24–28.

Fowler, Alan, "How to : Decide on Training Methods", *People Management*, Volume 1, Issue 25, December 21, 1995, pages 36–37.

Fox, Carla, et. al., "Project Ranger Curriculum Guide," Portland Public Schools, June 1978, ERIC Document ED 187485.

Frakt, Arthur N., "Adventure Programming and Legal Liability," *Journal of Health, Physical Education, Recreation and Dance*, Volume 49, Number 4, 1978, pages 49–51.

Frant, R.D., "Learning Through Outdoor Adventure Education," *Teaching Exceptional Children*, Volume 14, Number 4, February 1982, pages 146–151.

Froiland, Paul, "Action Learning—Taming Real Problems in Real Time," *Training*, Volume 31, Number 1, January 1994, pages 27–34.

Gall, Adrienne L., "You Can Take the Manager out of the Woods, but . . . ," *Training and Development Journal*, Volume 41, Number 3, March 1987, pages 54–59.

Garren, Ric, "Wheelchair Etiquette," *Challenge Magazine*, Volume 2, Issue 3, 1995, page 15.

Gass, Michael, "Programming the Transfer of Learning in Adventure Activities," *The Journal of Experiential Education*, Volume 8, Number 3, pages 18–24.

Gaw, Beverly A., "Processing Questions: An Aid to Completing the Learning Cycle," *The 1979 Annual Handbook for Group Facilitators*, University Associates, pages 147–153.

Geber, Beverly, "Let the Games Begin", *Training*, Team Supplement Issue, April 1994, pages 10–15.

Gibson, P., "Therapeutic Aspects of Wilderness Programs: A Comprehensive Literature Review," *Therapeutic Recreation Journal*, Volume 8, Number 2, 1979, pages 21–33.

Gilbert, Jim and Bruner, Eric, "Life Beyond Walls—Proceedings of the National Conference on Outdoor Recreation," November 1988, Fort Collins, Colorado, ERIC Document ED 357935, 273 pages.

Gillen, L.M., Davie, R.S. and Beissel, K.R., "Evaluating the Progress of Australian Engineering Graduates," *Journal of Cooperative Education*, Volume 20, Number 3, 1984, pages 53–70.

Gillis, H. Lee, "Adventure, Wilderness, Outward Bound, Therapeutic Camping, Experiential Learning, Ropes Courses & Games," Thesis Bibliography, University of Georgia, Fall 1984, ERIC Document ED 267935, 32 pages.

Gillis, H. Lee and Gass, Mike A., "Bringing Adventure Into Marriage and Family Therapy: An Innovative Experiential Approach," *Journal of Marital and Family Therapy*, Volume 19, Number 3, 1993, pages 275–288.

Goff, Leslie, "Managing at Warp Speed", *Computerworld*, Volume 28, Issue 43, October 24, 1994, page 93.

Gomolak, Lou, "Over the River and Through the Woods to Self Awareness," *College and University Business*, Augusut 1972, pages 43–45.

Goodstein, Carol, "Outdoor Adventure Schools Need Specialized Coverage," *Rough Notes*, Volume 134, Issue 12, December 1991, pages 38–39.

Goodstein, Carol, "Outdoor Adventure Schools Need Specialized Coverage," *Rough Notes*, Volume 134, Issue 12, December 1991, pages 38–39.

Gray, Tonia and Patterson, John, "Effective Research into Experiential Education: A Critical Resource in its Own Right," *Proceedings of the 22nd Annual AEE Conference*, Austin, Texas, November 1994, pages 138–145.

Grenier, Jacques, "Directory of Outdoor Education in Canadian Universities," May 1981, ERIC Document ED 209054.

Guadiano, M.G., "High Risk Activities in Physical Education," *Physical Educator*, Volume 37, Number 3, October 1980, pages 128–130.

Hagen, Robert P., "Team Building," *Manage*, Volume 37, Number 1, First Quarter 1985, pages 26–28.

Halliday, Nancy, "Playing it Safe—Risk management for games play," *Camping Magazine*, May/June 1996, pages 31–34.

Hallowell, Kirk; Vincere, Tom and Sweda, Ashley, "From Cowtails to Corporate Adventure—Training for Business Clients," *Proceedings of the 22nd Annual AEE Conference*, Austin, Texas, November 1994, pages 282–283.

Hamilton, F., "Experiential Learning Programs for Youth," *American Journal of Education*, Volume 88, February 1980, pages 178–215.

Hammel, H., "How to Design a Debriefing Session," *Journal of Experiential Education*, Volume 9, Number 3, 1986, pages 20–25.

Hammerman, Donald R., et. al., "Teaching in the Outdoors," Thrid Edition, 1985, ERIC Document ED 282718.

Hanchalk, D., "Interpersonal Trust and Experiential Education," *Journal of Outdoor Education*, Volume 16, Number 2, Spring 1982, pages 15–18.

Hanna, Glenda, "Overcoming Barriers to Implementing Outdoor and Environmental Education," *Pathways*, Volume 6, Number 1, December 1993, pages 24–28.

Harrison, David, "Outdoor Training Exercises: More Fresh Air than Hot Air", *People Management*, Volume 1, Issue 7, April 6, 1995, page 51.

Hartley, Mike, "Questioning Tradition: Alternative Safety Techniques and Procedures for Ropes Course and Climbing Programs," *Proccedings of the International Conference of the Association for Experiential Education*, October 1992, Banff, Alberta, Canada, ERIC Document ED 353119

Harvey, Judy, "Challenge Education at New Garden Friends School," *Phi Delta Kappan*, Volume 65, Number 9, May 1984, pages 604–605.

Havens, Mark D., "Make the Experience Accessible for Everyone," *Outdoor Network Newsletter*, Volume 1, Number 5, Spring 1990, pages 6–7.

Hazel, William M., "Win/Win—Developing the Skills to be Truly Competitive," *Pennsylvania Recreation and Parks*, Spring 1995.

Helesic, Terri and Priest, Simon, "Outdoor Adventure and Legal Liability," *Pathways*, Volume 3, Number 6, October 1991, pages 4–10.

Helesic, Terri and Priest, Simon, "Outdoor Adventure and Legal Liability," *Pathways*, Volume 3, Number 6, October 1991, pages 4–10.

Hendee, John C. and Brown, Michael H., "How Wilderness Experience Programs Facilitate Personal Growth: The Hendee/Brown Model," *Renewable Natural Resources Journal*, Volume 6, Number 2, Spring 1988.

Hendricks, Bruce, "Improving Evaluation in Experiential Education," *ERIC Digest*, EDO-RC-94–8, November 1994. (Cross referenced as ERIC Document ED 376998)

Herdman, Paul, "Adventure in the Classroom," *Journal of Experiential Education*, Volume 17, Number 2, August 1994, pages 18–25.

Hezman, Scott and Connors, Eugene, "Avoid Legal Pitfalls in Non-traditional Training," *HRMagazine*, Volume 38, Issue 5, May 1993, pages 71–74.

Hilton, Phil, "Alien Rope Tricks," *Personnel Management*, Volume 24, Issue 1, January 1992, pages 45–46.

Hoffman, Lou and Ritrovato, Lou, "Kids, Wildlife and Their Environment: An Elementary Teacher's Guide to Wildlife Activities," 1978, ERIC Document ED 156478.

Hogan, R., Curphy, G. and Hogan, J., "What We Know About Leadership," *American Psychologist*, Volume 49, Number 6, June 1994, pages 493–504.

Hollandsworth, J.G., "A School-Based Outdoor Adventure Program," *North Carolina Journal of Outdoor Education*, Volume 2, Number 1, Fall 1980, pages 24–26.

Hollee, Actman, "Outward Bound", *Sporting Goods Business*, Volume 29, Issue 1, January 1996, pages 70–75.

Honey, Peter and Lobley, Roger, "Learning from Outdoor Activities: Getting the Balance Right," *Industrial & Commercial Training* (UK), Volume 18, Issue 6, November/December 1986, pages 7–12.

Horn, M.E., "Lessons in Adventure, NOLS," *Parks and Recreation*, September 1966, pages 704–705.

Huberstone, Barbara and Lynch, Pip, "Girls Concepts of Themselves and Their Experiences in Outdoor Education Programmes," *Journal of Adventure Education and Outdoor Leadership*, Volume 8, Number 3, Fall 1991, pages 27–31.

Huffman, Michael G. and Harwell, Rick, "Park Managers Attitudes Toward Climbing: Implications for Future Regulation," *Association for Experiential Education International Conference Proceedings*, Lake Junaluska, October 24–27, 1991.

Humphrey, J.H., "Active Games as a Learning Medium," *Academic Therapy*, Volume 5, 1969, pages 15–24.

Hundley, W., "Overcoming Obstacles to Trust," *Dayton Ohio Daily News*, January 6, 1990.

Hynes, Kevin, "Challenge Accepted," *Prarie Soldier*, October 1994, Page 5.

Jackson, B., "Debunking the Mystique of the Ropes Course," *The OTRA Journal*, Volume 1, Number 1, 1992, pages 2–3.

James, Thomas, "Kurt Hahn and the Aims of Education," *Journal of Experiential Education*, Volume 13, Number 1, May 1990, pages 6–13.

Jenkins, Carri P., "Empowering—The Expanding Role of Followers," *BYU Today*, September 1990, pages 28–63.

Jenkins, Peter, "Technical Tree Climbing," *Proceedings of the 1988 National Conference on Outdoor Recretaion*, Fort Collins, Colorado, November 1988, ERIC Document 357940.

Johnson, Cynthia Reedy, "An Outline for Team Building," *Training*, Volume 23, Number 1, January 1986, pages 48–52

Johnson, Jon A., "Adventure Therapy: The Ropes-Wilderness Connection," *Therapeutic Recreation Journal*, Volume 26, Number 3, Fall 1992, pages 17–26.

Kazemak, Edward A. and Albert, Bruce M., "Learning the Secret to Teamwork," *Healthcare Financial Management*, Volume 42, Number 9, September 1988, pages 108–110.

Kesselheim, A.D., "A Rationale for Outdoor Activity as Experiential Education: The Reason for Freezin'," paper presented to the Conference on Outdoor Pursuits in Higher Education, Boone, North Carolina, ERIC Document Number ED 148 530.

Kezman, Scott W. and Connors, Eugene K., "Avoid Legal Pitfalls in Nontraditional Training," HRMagazine, Volume 38, Issue 5, May 1993, pages 71–74.

Kilcourse, Tom, "Management Team Development: A Problem-Centered Technique," *Journal of European Industrial Training*, Volume 8, Number 2, 1984, pages 3–38.

Kimball, R. and Ratliff, S., "Readings in Experiential Education: A compendium of Model Programs," ERIC Document ED 099281, 1974.

Klocke, D.J. andWichern, D.L., "Mountain Bound: A Test for Counseling Techniques," *School Counselor*, Volume 28, Number 2, November 1980, pages 105–108.

Knapp, Clifford E., "Designing Processing Questions to Meet Specific Objectives," *Journal of Experiential Education*, Volume 7, Number 2, 1984, pages 47–49.

Knapp, Clifford E., "Lasting Lessons: A Teacher's Guide to Reflecting on Experience," 1992, ERIC Document ED 348204.

Knapp, Clifford E., "Reflection Re-Examined: A Hard Look at a Sacred Cow," *Proceedings of the 22nd Annual AEE Conference*, Austin, Texas, November 1994, pages 289–293.

Knapp, Clifford E., "Thinking in Outdoor Inquiry," August 1992, ERIC Digest EDO-RC-92-3, ERIC Document ED 348198.

Knapp, J. and Sharon, A., "A Compendium of Assessment Techniques," Cooperative Assesment of Experiential Learning, Columbia, Maryland, January 1975, ERIC Document Number ED 148 842.

Kozlowski, J. D., "A Common Sense View of Liability," 1988, *Parks and Recreation*, Volume 23, Number 9, pages 56–59.

Kozlowski, J. D., "Causation, Assumed Risk, and a Failure to Warn in Sports Suits," 1988, *Parks and Recreation*, Volume 23, Number 9, pages 18–21.

Kozlowski, J. D., "In Search of the Adequate Warning Sign: Communication is the Key," 1988, *Parks and Recreation*, Volume 23, Number 10, pages 20–25, 63.

Krouwell, B., "Management Development Using the Outdoors,"*Training Officer*, Volume 16, Number 10, October 1980, pages 262–265.

Kuntz, R., "A Directory of Adventure Alternatives in Corrections, Mental Health, Special Education and Physical Rehabilitation," *Journal of Experiential Education*, Volume 2, Number 2, Fall 1979, pages 19–26.

Laabs, Jennifer J., "Team Training Goes Outdoors," *Personnel Journal*, Volume 70, Number 6, June 1991, pages 56–63.

Lais, Gregory J., "Toward Fullest Participation—Suggested Leadership Techniques for Integrated Adventure Programming," *Bradford Papers Annual*, Volume 2, 1987, pages 55–64.

Larson, Jane P., "A Ropes Retreat: Fun, Adventure and Personal Growth," *Perspectives in Education and Deafness*, Volume 13, Number 5, May/June 1995, pages 12–17.

Lefebure, Jane B., "In Search of Adventure," *Currents*, Volume 17, Number 5, May 1991, pages 27–28.

Len, James, "Add a Little Adventure: An Introductory Adventure Program," *Pathways*, Volume 3, Number 4, June 1991, pages 24–29.

Little, C., "Developing a High School Adventure Program—Persistance and Innovation," *Journal of Outdoor Education*, Volume 10, Number 1, 1975, pages 22–25.

Long, Janet W., "The Wilderness Lab Comes of Age," *Training & Development Journal*, Volume 41, Issue 3, March 1987, pages 30–39.

Lorber, Laura, "People Learning to Work Better Together by Surmounting Challenges Together," June 25, 1991.

Loynes, Chris, "The Outdoor Trainer and Developer: Collaborative Learning," *Journal of Adventure Education and Outdoor Leadership*, Volume 11, Number 1, Spring 1994, pages 6–7.

Luckner, John, "Effective Skills Instruction in Outdoor Adventure Education," *JOPERD*, January 1994, pages 57–61.

MacDonald, Wayne, et. al., "Safety in Outdoor Adventure Program (S.O.A.P.) Safety Policy," May 14, 1979, ERIC Document ED 180728.

MacDonald, Wayne, et. al., "Safety in Outdoor Adventure Programs (SOAP) Safety Policy," May 14, 1979, ERIC Document ED 180728

Malone, Gregory A. and Mashek, Bill, "Planning Therapeutic Outdoor Programs," *Parks and Recreation*, Volume 18, Number 9, September 1983, pages 47–48.

March, Bill and Wattchow, Brian, "The Importance of the Expedition in Adventure Education," *Journal of Adventure Education and Outdoor Leadership*, Volume 8, Number 2, Summer 1991, pages 4–5.

Matthews, B.E., "Adventure Education and Self Concept—An Annotated Bibliography with Appendix," December 17, 1976, ERIC Document Number ED160 287.

Matthews, B.E., "Group Cooperation in Outdoor Education," *Communicator*, Volume 9, Number 2, Spring-Summer 1978, pages 46–47.

Matthews, Bruce E., "Adventure Education and Self Concept -- An Annotated Bibliography with Appendix," December 7, 1976, ERIC Document ED 160287.

Mazany, P., et.al., "Evaluating the Effectiveness of an Outdoor Workshop for Team Building in an MBA Programme," *Journal of Management Development*, Volume 14, Number 3, 1995, pages 50–68.

McAvoy, L., "Outdoor Leadership Training," *Journal of Physical Education and Recreation*, Volume 49, Number 4, April 1978, pages 42–43.

McCleary, Iva Dene and Chesteen, Susan A., "Changing Attitudes of Disabled Persons Through Outdoor Adventure Programmes," *International Journal of Rehavbilitation Research*, Volume 13, Number 4, December 1990, pages 321–324.

McClenahen, John S., "Not Fun in the Sun," *Industry Week*, Volume 239, Number 20, October 15, 1990, pages 22–24.

McEwen, Cynthia, "Creating Organizations that Work," *Training & Development*, March 1991, page 52.

McNerney, Donald J., "The Facts of Life for Teambuilding", *HRFocus*, Volume 71, Issue 12, December 1994, pages 12–13.

McNutt, Brendan, "Adventure as Therapy: Using Adventure as Part of Therapeutic Programmes with Young People in Trouble and At Risk," *Proccedings of a National One-Day Conference "Adventure-Based Interventions"*, Ambleside, England, April 1994, ERIC Document ED 378016.

Meier, Joel F., "Is the Risk Worth Taking?," *Journal of Physical Education and Recreation*, Volume 49, Number 4, April 1978, pages 31–33.

Meier, Joel, "Minimizing Accidents and Risks in High Adventure Pursuits," *Paper Presented at the March 30, 1984 AAHPERD Conference*, Anaheim, California ERIC Document ED 252500.

Meier, Joel, "Risk and Hazard Management in High Adventure Outdoor Pursuits," ERIC Document ED356934

Meier, Joel, "Risk and Hazard Management in High Adventure Outdoor Pursuits," *Proceedings of the 1984 Conference on Outdoor Recreation*, Bozeman, Montana, November 1–4, 1984 ERIC Document ED 356934.

Mendel, Werner, "Corporate Training by Adventure Learning," *Cornell Hotel and Restaurant Administration Quarterly*, June 1993, pages 31–33.

Mendell, Werner, "Corporate Training by Adventure Learning," *Cornell Hotel and Restaurant Administration Quarterly*, Volume 34, Issue 3, June 1993, pages 31–33.

Metcalfe, John A., "Adventure Programming," New Mexico State University, March 1976, ERIC Document ED 118336.

Metzger, Devon J., "Practicing What We Preach: Involving Student Teachers in Their Own Learning," *Action in Teacher Education*, Volume 10, Number 4, Winter 1989, pages 15–18.

Meyer, Dan, "The Management of Risk," *Journal of Experiential Education*, Volume 2, Number 2, Fall 1979, pages 9–14.

Miles, J.C., "The Value of High Adventure Activities," *Journal of Physical Education and Recreation*, Volume 49, Number 4, April 1978, pages 27–28.

Miller, Doug, "Group Facilitating," *Camping Magazine*, Volume 67, Number 5, May/June 1995, pages 28–32.

Millward, Robert, "Attitude Development Through Outdoor Education," Student thesis, Penn State University, University Park, PA, 1972.

Miner, J.L., "My Most Unforgettable Character: Kurt Hahn," *Reader's Digest*, December 1975, pages 127–131.

Miner, Todd, "Safety Issues for Experience-Based Training and Development," *Journal of Experiential Education*, Volume 14, Number 2, August 1991, pages 20–25.

Mingie, Walter, "Outdoor Education: Opening and Closing Activities," 1981, ERIC Document ED 241249.

Mitchell, C., et.al., "Outdoor Training Companies," *Training and Development Journal*, Volume 45, Issue 3, March 1991, pages 63–65.

Mobley, Michael, "The Role of Risk and Risk Management in Experiential Education," May 1981, ERIC Document ED 241213, 179 pages.

Morrisey, J.T., "A Historical Survey of Outdoor Education 1861–1978," November 28, 1979, ERIC Document Number ED 215 801.

Moss, Jim, "Avoiding a Lawsuit, Outdoor Network Newsletter," Volume 1, Number 9, Spring 1991, pages 6–7. ERIC Document EJ424948.

Moss, Jim, "Lawsuits: The Ins and Outs of Outdoor Education Cases," *Outdoor Network Newsletter*, Volume 1, Number 7, Fall 1990, page 7. ERIC Document EJ424946

Neffinger, G.G., "Real Learning in Unreal Circumstances," *Innovative Organisation Development Practices Part II* (UK), pages 27–31.

Newman, B., "Want to Buy a Climbing Wall?," *Mountain*, November-December 1984, pagess 44–45.

Nice, Trish, "Project Exploration: A Ropes Course Curriculum Guide," Project Exploration, Townsend, Mass., ERIC Document ED 183314.

Ogilvie, K., "The Management of Risk," *Journal of Adventure Education and Outdoor Leadership*, Volume 6, Number 4, 1989, pages 30–34.

Ogilvie, K., "The Management of Risk," *Journal of Adventure Education and Outdoor Leadership*, Volume 6, Number 4, 1989, pages 30–34.

Ongena, J., "Adventure Education: An Opportunity to Teach Youth Self Confidence and Respect," *NASSP Bulletin*, Volume 66, Number 454, May 1982, pages 71–78.

Ongena, J., "Adventure," *Outdoor Communicator*, Volume 11, Number 3, Spring 1981, pages 12–17.

Ongena, J., "Should our Schools Offer Adventure Education?," *Canadian Association for Health, Physical Education and Recreation*, Journal, May/June, 1984, pages 4–7.

O'Neil, J., "Rx for better thinkers: Problem-based learning," *ASCD Update*, Volume 34, Number 6, page 1.

Osborne, J.E., "Turning to Team Building to Tackle Tough Times," *Supervisory Management*, Volume 37, Issue 5, May 1992, pages 1–3.

Overhold, Miles H., "Games People Play," *Executive Excellence*, Volume 7, Number 7, July 1990, pages 9–10.

Owens, Thomas, "Business Teams," *Small Business Reports*, Volume 14, Number 1, January 1989, pages 52–58.

Peterson, C., "The Right to Risk," *Journal of Physical Education & Recreation*, April 1978, pages 23–24.

Petrini, Catherine and Thomas, Rebecca, "Team Building for Humanity", *Training and Development*, Volume 49, Issue 10, October 1995, pages 13–14.

Petrini, Catherine M., "Over the River & Through the Woods," *Training & Development Journal*, Volume 44, Issue 5, May 1990, pages 25–36.

Petrus, E.F., "Teaching Group Dynamics in an Intensive Small Group Laboratory in a Wilderness Setting," 1977, ERIC Document ED 152–604.

Phipps, Maurice L., "Definitions of Outdoor Recreation and Other Associated Terminology," *Proceedings of the National Conference for Outdoor Leaders*, 1991, ERIC Document ED 335189.

Phipps, Maurice L., "Group Dynamics in the Outdoors—A Model for Teaching Outdoor Leaders," ERIC Document ED356935.

Ping, Ki, "The Group Tree of Experience," *Journal of Adventure Education and Outdoor Leadership*, Volume 11, Number 1, Spring 1994, pages 19–21.

Pollak, Timothy R., "An Annotated Bibliography of the Literature and Research on Outward Bound and Related Programs," June 1976, ERIC Document ED 171476.

Potts and Knowlton, "Outdoor Program Eases Racial Tension," *N.A.S.S.P. Bulletin*, Number 59, October 1975, pages 108–110.

Priest, Simon and Clark, Donald, "Help Yourself! A Guide to Getting Grants," *Journal of Experiential Education*, Volume 13, Number 1, May 1990, pages 31–37.

Priest, Simon and Lesperance, Mary Ann, "Time Series Trends in Corporate Team Development," *Journal of Experiential Education*, Volume 17, Number 1, May 1994, pages 34–39.

Priest, Simon and Naismith, Mindee, "A Model for Debriefing Experience," *Journal of Adventure Education and Outdoor Leadership*, Volume 10, Number 3, Fall 1993, pages 16–18.

Priest, Simon, "A Model of Group Initiative Facilitation Training (G.I.F.T.)," *Outdoor Communicator*, Volume 20, Number 1, Fall/Winter 1988/89, pages 8–13.

Priest, Simon, "An International Survey of Outdoor Leadership Preparation," *Journal of Experiential Education*, Volume 10, Number 2, Summer 1987, pages 34–39.

Priest, Simon, "Shopper's Guide to Corporate Adventure Training," *Personnel*, Volume 68, Issue 7, July 1991, pages 15–16.

Priest, Simon, et. al., "Pass Keys to Locked Doors," *Journal of Experiential Education*, Volume 16, Number 2, 1993, pages 11–20.

Project Adventure, 15 Year Safety Study, February 1992 Report from Project Adventure.

Project Adventure, Teaching through adventure: A practical approach, 1976, Hamilton, Mass, ERIC Document ED 148548.

Prud'homme, Alex, "Executive Retreats: Let's Get Physical," *Business Month*, Volume 135, Issue 3, March 1990, pages 60–66.

Quinsland, L.K. and VanGinkel, A., "How to Process Experience," *Journal of Experiential Education*, Volume 7, Number 2, 1984, pages 8–13.

Rademacher, Craig and Watters, Ron, "Proceedings of the 1991 International Conference on Outdoor Education," Idaho State University, Pocatello, Idaho, October 1991, 155 pages, ERIC Document ED 370721.

Raiola, Ed, "Outdoor Adventure Activities for New Student Orientation Programs," 1984, ERIC Document ED 242446

Raiola, Ed, "Teaching Students to Work with Special Populations," *Journal of Experiential Education*, Volume 5, Number 3, Winter 1983, pages 39.

Rankin, J.S., "The Legal System as a Proponent of Adventure Programming," *Leisure Today*, April, 1978, pages 28–29.

Raudsepp, Eugene, "How to Build an Effective Team," Machine Design, November 24, 1983, pages 61–64.

Reece, Carolyn, "Meeting New Challenges—Making New Friends," *Children Today*, Volume 7, Number 4, July/August 1978 pages 16–21.

Reter, Jessie L., "Orientation Groups—Bring New and Old Staff Together," *Camping Magazine*, Volume 67, Number 5, May/June 1995, pages 22–23.

Richardson, Diana, "Outdoor Adventure: Wilderness Programs for the Physically Disabled," *Parks and Recreation*, Volume 21, Number 11, November 1986, pages 43–45.

Richardson, Michelle and Simmons, Deborah, "Recommended Competencies for Outdoor Educators," ERIC Document EDO-RC-96-2, January 1996.

Riggins, R.D., "Effective Learning in Adventure-Based Education: Setting Directions for Future Research," *Journal of Environmental Education*, Volume 18, Number 1, 1986, pages 1–6.

Riley, Cheryl L., "Ideas the Work for Outdoor Teachers and Leaders," *Proceedings of the National Outdoor Education Conference*, October 1985, Potosi, Missouri, ERIC Document ED 259863.

Ringer, Martin, "Leadership Competence for Outdoor Adventure: From Recreation to Therapy," *Proceedings of a National One-Day Conference "Adventure-Based Interventions"*, Ambleside, England, April 1994, ERIC Document ED 378018.

Robb, Gary M. and Ewert, Alan, "Risk Recreation and Persons with Disabilities," *Therapeutic Recreation Journal*, Volume 21, Number 1, 1987, pages 58–69.

Robb, Gary M. and Ewert, Alan, "Risk Recreation and Persons with Disabilities," *Therapeutic Recreation Journal*, Volume 21, Number 1, 1987, pages 58–69.

Robb, Gary M. andShepley, Stuart G., "Forging Partnerships: The Real Challenge," *Camping Magazine*, Volume 61, Number 2, Nov-Dec 1988, pages 18–22.

Robb, Gary M., et. al., "Special Education . . . Naturally," 1983, Indiana University, Bloomington, Indiana.

Robertson, Sue, "Gloucester Youth Action Scheme," April 1994, ERIC Document ED 378020

Robottom, I., "Social Critique or Social Control: Some Problems for Evaluation in Environmental Education," *Journal of Research in Science Teaching*, Volume 26, Number 5, 1989, pages 435–443.

Roden, Iain, "Outdoor Training for Employee Effectiveness", *Personnel Management*, Volume 26, Issue 9, September 1994, page 69.

Roland, Christopher, "Outdoor Management Training Programs: Do They Work?," *The Bradford Papers*, Volume 5, 1985.

Roland, Christopher C., "Ropes Courses: Facing the Accessibility Issue, The Bradford Papers, pages 42–46.

Ross, Janet, et. al., "Idea Notebook," *Journal of Experiential Education*, Volume 9, Number 1, Spring 1986, Pages 34–39.

Rottenberger, Kerry, "Meetings Don't Have to Be All Work to Be Productive," *Sales and Marketing Management*, Volume 14, Number 7, June 1989, pages 84–86.

Rourke, Tom, "Who Benefits from Experiential Therapy?," *Adolescent Counselor*, July 1991, pages 41–42.

Rynders, John E., Schleien, Stuart J. and Mustonen, T., "Integrating Children with Severe Disabilities for Intensified Outdoor Education: Focus on Feasibility," *Mental Retardation*, Volume 28, 1990, pages 7–14.

Sakofs, Mitchell S., "Certification of Adventure Program Leaders—A Future Reality?," *Communicator*, Volume 19, Number 2, 1979, pages 35–36.

Savoy, Gordon, "Voyageurs '72: An Adventure Program for Eigth Grade Pupils, ERIC Document ED 085150, 1972.

Schafermeyer, H., "Adventure Programming—Wilderness and Urban,"*Journal of Physical Education and Recreation*, Volume 49, Number 1, January 1978, pages 30–32.

Schein, Edgar H., "What to Observe in a Group," from the book *Reading Book for Human Relations Training*, edited by Lawrence Porter and Bernard Mohr, 1982, NTL Institute.

Schroeder, C.C., "Adventure Training for Resident Assistants," *Journal of College Student Personnel*, Number 17, January 1976, pages 11–15.

Schroeder, C.C., "In Support of Adventure Training: A Rejoiner,"*Journal of College Student Personnel*, Volume 17, Number 6, November 1976, pages 518–519.

Schwartz, Gil, "What your Competitors are Reading Now", *Fortune*, Volume 129, Issue 1, January 10, 1994, pages 110–111.

Scott, Andrew, "Outward Appearances," *Accountancy*, Volume 102, Issue 1140, August 1988, pages 109–110.

Scovel, Kathryn, "Executives Take to the Hills," *Human Resource Executive*, August 1990, pages 28–31.

Secunda, Dave, "An Overview of Professional Organizations," *Outdoor Network Newsletter*, Volume 1, Number 4, winter 1990, pages 6–7.

Serlen, Bruce, "Put Your Company Over the Top with Teambuilding Programs," *Corporate & Incentive Travel*, January 1994, pages 12–15.

Shroyer, G.F., "Legal Liability of Outdoor Camps," *Journal of Physical Education and Recreation*, Volume 52, Number 6, June 1981, pages 62–63.

Siedenberg, J.M., "A 'Come from Behind' Victory for Cooperative Education," *Journal of Cooperative Education*, Volume 76, Number 4, 1986, pages 232–236.

Sills, Robert, et. al., "When Teachers Are the Students," *Vocational Education Journal*, Volume 70, Number 2, February 1995, pages 24–29.

Simmons, G.A. and Cannon, E.C., "It Is Outdoors: A Guide to Experiential Activities," AAHPERD Publication, 1991, ERIC Document ED 330694.

Smedley, Lee, "Experienced Based Training and Development—What is Corporate America Looking For?," *Proceedings of the 22nd Annual AEE Conference*, Austin, Texas, November 1994, pages 47–49.

Smith, Charles A., and Prather, S., "Group Problem Solving," *Journal of Physical Education and Recreation (JOPER)*, Number 46, September 1975, pages 20–21.

Smith, Kemper D. III, "Beyond Wilderness Skills: Education for Individual and Group Development," April 1984, ERIC Document ED 252368.

Smith, Thomas E., "Alternative Methodologies for Processing the Adventure Experience," 1986, Raccoon Institute, Cazenovia, WI 53924.

Sokolic, William H., "Teamwork in the 'Jungle'," *The Philadelphia Inquirer*, October 14, 1991.

Sorohan, E.G., "We Do: Therefore We Learn," *Training and Development Journal*, Volume 47, Number 10, 1993, page 55.

Spacht, Roger H. and Hirsch, Jude, "Adventure Programming—Keeping it Safe," *Camping Magazine*, Volume 67, Number 6, July/August 1995, pages 20–23.

Spitzer, D.R., "20 Ways to Energize Your Training," *Training*, June 1985.

Sproul, Susan and Priest, Simon, "The Ropes Course as an Educational Tool," *Pathways: The Ontario Journal of Outdoor Education*, Volume 4, Number 2, February 1992, pages 9–12.

Stahl, A., "Bridging the Gap Between Research and Teacher Education," *Journal of Education for Teaching*, Volume 17, number 30, 1991, pages 293–299.

Steele, T.W., "Add Some Adventure to Your Physical Education Program," *New York State Journal of Health, Physical Education and Recreation*, Volume 33, Spring 1982, page 6.

Stein, Scott, "The Wonderful World of Corporate Teambuilding: Myth vs. Reality," *Proceedings of the 22nd Annual AEE Conference*, Austin, TExas, November 1994, pages 110–112.

Stevens, Peggy Walker and Richards, Anthony, "Changing Schools Through Experiential Education," March 1992, ERIC Digest EDO-RC-91–13.

Stitch, T. F. and Gaylor, M. S., "Risk Management in Adventure Programs with Special Populations," *Journal of Experiential Education*, Volume 7, Number 3, 1984, pages 15–19.

Strutton, James L., "Why Training Usually Fails: What Can Be Done About It", *Manage*, Volume 45, Issue 3, January 1994, pages 14–15.

Stutz, J.P. and Knapp, J., "Experiential Learning: An Annotated Literature Guide," CAEL Project Report, ERIC Document Number ED 148 859.

Sudore, Gail M., "Learning Excitement," *Outdoor Communicator—Journal of the New York State Outdoor Education Association*, Volume 18, Number 2, Fall/Winter 1986/87, pages 34–41.

Suttenberg, E. and Poppenhagen, B., "Current Theory and Research in Experiential Learning for Adults," *Journal of Experiential Education*, Volume 3, Number 1, Spring 1980, pages 27–31.

Symons, John, "Understanding and Analysing Outdoor Management Development Programmes," *Journal of Adventure Education and Outdoor Leadership*, Volume 11, Number 3, Fall 1994, pages 6–12.

Szwergold, Jack, "When Work has You Climbing Trees," *Management Review*, Volume 82, Issue 9, September 1993, page 6.

Tarullo, Glenn Martin, "Making Outdoor Experiential Training Work," *Training*, Volume 29, Number 8, August 1992, pages 47–49.

Taylor, Barry, "Learning by Adventure", *Association Management*, Volume 46, Issue 11, November 1994, pages 26–27.

Teaff, Joseph and Kablach, John, "Psychological Benefits of Outdoor Adventure Activities," *Journal of Experiential Education*, Volume 10, Number 2, Summer 1987, pages 43–46.

Temme, Jim, "Calling a Team a Team Doesn't Mean that it is: Successful Teamwork Must be a way of Life", *Plant Engineering*, Volume 49, Issue 1, January 9, 1995, page 112.

Tholkes, Ben, "Anxiety and Outdoor Adventure: A Study of State Anxiety and Activity Performance," *Coalition for Education in the Outdoors Second Research Symposium Proceedings.*

Thomas, S.E., "Experiential Learning and the Handicapped: Reports from the Field,"

Thompson, Brad Lee, "Training in the Great Outdoors," *Training*, Volume 28, Issue 5, May 1991, pages 46–52.

Tindall, Barry S., "Beyond 'Fun and Games'," *Parks & Recreation*, Volume 30, Number 3, March 1995, pages 87–93.

Unthank, K.W., "Falling into Good Company," *American Education*, Volume 17, Number 6, July 1981, pages 6–10.

van der Smissen, Betty and Brookhiser, Judy, "Bibliography of Research: Organized Camping, Evnironmental Education, Adventure Activities, Interpretative Services, Outdoor Recreation Users and Programming." A bibliography listing more than 2000 university theses and additional references on the above topics. ISBN 0–87603–068–8 American Camping Association, ERIC Document ED 304268.

van der Smissen, Betty, "Legal Liability—Adventure Activities," March 1980, ERIC Document ED 187500

van der Smissen, Betty, "Legal Liability—Adventure Activities," New Mexico State University, March 1980, ERIC Document ED 187500.

van der Smissen, Betty, "Minimizing Legal Liability Risks," *Journal of Experiential Education*, Volume 2, Number 1, Spring 1979, pages 35–41.

Veal, Bob, "Developing Teams Outdoors," *Executive Excellence*, Volume 8, Issue 12, December 1991, page 16.

Vissers, Naomi and Priest, Simon, "Protecting the Adventure Organization from Risk," *Pathways to Outdoor Communicator*, Volume 3, Number 1, Spring 1993, pages 14–17.

Voight, A., "The Use of Ropes Courses as a Treatment Modality for Emotionally Disturbed Adolescents in Hospitals," *Therapeutic Recreation Journal*, Second Quarter, 1988, pages 57–64.

Wagner, Richard J. and Fahey, D., "An Empirical Evaluation of a Corporate Outdoor-based Training Program," *Proceedings of the Midwest Academy of Management*, St. Charles, IL.

Wagner, Richard J. and Lindner, J.M., "Data on Outdoor-centered Training: Who's Doing What?" *Sales & Marketing Management*, Volume 145, Number 2, 1993, pages 39–40.

Wagner, Richard J. and Roland, Christopher C., "Facilitators: One Key Factor in Implementing Successful Experience-Based Training and Development Programs," *Coalition for Education in the Outdoors Research Symposium Proceedings*, Bradford Woods, January 17–19, 1992.

Wagner, Richard J. and Weigand, R., "How Effective is Outdoor-Based Training in Improving Management Behaviors: A Healthcare Application," *Journal of Healthcare Education*, Volume 7, Number 3, 1993, pages 1–4.

Ward, Mark, "Are You a Team Killer?," *EDN*, August 8, 1991, page 1,52.

Warner, Alan, "How to Creatively Evaluate Programs,"

Wartik, N., "Wilderness Adventure,"*Venture*, Volume 6, Number 1, January 1984, page 88.

Watters, Ron, "Historical Perspectives of Outdoor and Wilderness Recreation Programming in the United States," *Proceedings of the 1984 Conference on Outdoor Recreation*, November 1984, Bozeman, Montana, ERIC Document ED 356933.

Webster, S.E., "Project Adventure: A Trip into the Unknown," *Journal of Physical Education and Recreation*, Volume 49, Number 4, April 1978, pages 39–41.

Wernel, Bradford, "Managing the Great Outdoors," Crain's Detroit Business, June 11, 1990, pages 1, 36–37.

Wernel, Bradford, "Where ropes go, vertigo: an exercise in humility," Crain's Detroit Business, June 11, 1990, pages 1, 37.

West, June, "Team Building through Wilderness Activities in Eighth Grade Special Education," *Conference Paper presented at Western States Communication Association Annual Meeting*, February 1993, ERIC Document ED 371514, 35 pages.

Whittaker, Tom, "Danger, Adventure Education and Schools," *Journal of Physical Education, Recreation and Dance*, Volume 52, Number 9, November/December 1981, pages 53–54.

Wichmann, Ted, "Of Wilderness and Circles: Evaluating a Therapeutic Model for Wilderness Adventure Programs," *Journal of Experiential Education*, Volume 14, Number 2, August 1991, pages 43–48.

Wiesendanger, Betsy, "Games Managers Play," *Sales & Marketing Management*, Volume 145, Issue 2, February 1993, pages 36–41.

Winterdyk, J. Albert, "A Wilderness Adventure Program as an Alternative for Juvenile Probationers: An Evaluation," Master's Thesis, Simon Fraser University, September 1980, ERIC Document ED 200348.

Witman, J., "Almost Anything Goes: Cooperative Competition," *Programming Trends in Therapeutic Recreation*, Volume 1, 1979, pages 14–16.

Wolff, Michael F., "Before you Try Teambuilding," *Research-Technology Management*, Volume 31, Number 1, January/February 1988, pages 6–8.

Wood, D., "Analyzing Adventure Education: Behavior Patterns, Relativing Objectives, Sequencing Activities, and Discovering Student Perceptives," Unpublished Doctoral Dissertation, Boston University, 1978.

Wurdinger, Scott, "Examining the Learning Process Used in Adventure Education," *Journal of Adventure Education and Outdoor Leadership*, Volume 11, Number 3, Fall 1994, pages 25–27.

Yaffey, David, "Outdoor Pursuits and Adventure Experiences," *Journal of Adventure Education and Outdoor Leadership*, Volume 8, Number 2, Summer 1991, pages 22–25.

Yaffey, David, "The Value Base of Activity Experience in the Outdoors," *Journal of Adventure Education and Outdoor Leadership*, Volume 10, Number 3, Fall 1993, pages 9–11.

Yerkes, Rita, "What About the Young Child?," *Journal of Experiential Education*, Volume 11, Number 2, Summer 1988, pages 21–25.

Zenger, John H.; Musselwhite, Ed; Hurson, Kathleen and Perrin, Craig, "Leadership in a Team Environment: the New American Manager," Zenger-Miller, Inc., 1991.

Chapter Two

Planning a Challenge and Adventure Activity

ac·tiv·i·ty (ăk-tĭv'ĭ-tē) *n.*, A planned or organized thing to do.

Creating a successful challenge and adventure program is similar to creating a good book. First you grab the reader with a good title, an interesting cover, or a topic that is of interest to many readers. Once the reader has opened the book, you have a few quick pages to really grab them, so that they can hardly put the book down. Next you add in a variety of ideas, changes in plot, a bit of excitement here, some irony there, and eventually a climax that leaves the reader exhausted, but happy.

Challenge and adventure programs require the same forethought and planning. They also need some flashes of color, an exciting beginning to really pull in the participants, some innovative new ways to look at the world, some changes in plot, and a gradual building of spirit that takes each participant a little higher than they thought possible, often leaving them exhausted, but happy at the end of the program.

In this chapter, and throughout the remainder of this book, the elements of a successful challenge and adventure program will be discussed.

Basic Training—Part I

Preparing for a Challenge and Adventure Program

Visit the location before the event if possible. Know where key landscape features are that can be used to enhance the experience (a quiet place for processing, a level place for A Balanced Life, an inclined place for Marble Tubes). Know where the telephone, bathrooms, parking lot, water fountain and registration areas are.

Double check your equipment before the event begins. Use a checklist if you find this technique helpful. The same checklist also works at the end of the program, when you are packing your equipment for the trip home.

Know as much as you can about your audience before the program. How many participants? What are their physical abilities? Are there any participants with special skills or needs? What are the ages of the participants? What is the ratio of women to men, supervisors to personnel, teachers to students?

For the duration of the program, you are the leader of this group—look and act like you are! Dress appropriately for the event, and in a manner that will add credibility to your profession and gain the confidence of the group. Avoid wearing sunglasses unless absolutely required—participants benefit from having direct eye contact with their leaders. Learn the names of group members and use them. Be enthusiastic, confident and prepared.

Pack a few extra things that some participants may have forgotten (sunscreen, an extra water bottle, insect repellent, some hair scrunchies, an extra hat, a dry pair of gloves in the winter months). Always, always bring a first aid kit—just in case.

Basic Training—Part II

Preparing for a Challenge and Adventure Program

Take a few minutes to observe the group before the program begins. What is the mood of the group? Are they properly prepared for the event (footwear, clothing, enthusiasm)? If possible, talk informally with some group members. Try to identify their expectations for the program.

Have a plan in case the weather does not cooperate. What if it rains or snows? What if high winds and lightening are present? What if there is a heat advisory or temperatures drop well below the freezing point?

Have a variety of activities ready in case the entire group does not arrive at the same time.

The elements of a successful challenge and adventure program can be grouped into five specific categories:

1. Evaluating the needs and goals of the group
2. Planning the specific challenge activities to address these needs and accomplish these goals
3. Presenting the challenge and adventure program
4. Processing and debriefing the experience with the group
5. Post event follow-up and extension of lessons learned to the participant's environments

The first two elements will be presented in this chapter. Activities for challenge and adventure programs are presented in Chapter 4 and 7. Chapter 6 discusses processing and post event activities. Chapters 1 and 8 present references which address all of these elements in even greater detail.

Step 1-Evaluating the Needs and Goals of the Group

Some of the first steps in creating a successful challenge and adventure program happen well before the day of the event. The first step in planning a successful challenge and adventure program is evaluating the needs and goals of the group. In the simplest terms, this means understanding why the group would be interested in experiencing a challenge and adventure event. In some cases, the leadership or managment has made the decision for the group. For school and camping programs, the administration, teaching faculty or program staff may have included these program elements within their curriculum plan. For some self-directed work teams, the decision may have come from the participants themselves. Behind the decision however, there is usually a desire within the group to accomplish something by participating in a challenge and adventure activity program. The first step, is to find out what this desire is.

Consider the needs of each of the following four groups:

"We have 14 new student directors for our freshman college mentor program this fall. They'll be meeting each other for the first time, and we would like them to get to know each other quickly."

"We have a brand new project at work, and the goals of this project are very demanding. We would like the team to have the opportunity to build some excellent communication skills and really begin this project on a solid foundation."

"We have a camping weekend planned for the adult leadership of our local youth development program. Our youth will be experiencing challenge and adventure programs during their summer camp, and we just wanted the adult leadership to understand what this experience is all about."

"We have a work group that has been together for about 11 years. There is quite a bit of tension and a definite lack of communication between some members of the group. We'd like to use teambuilding as a means of repairing this relationship and turning this dysfunctional team back into a high-performing work unit."

In each case, the needs of the group are slightly different. In many cases, the needs of the group will be to experience a structured series of activities that teach and encourage good community building skills. No problem there, the challenge and adventure activities in this book alone provide a wide range of these experiences. For programs that desire an improvement in the communication between group members, challenge and adventure activities are also suitable.

In some cases however, the needs of the group may fall outside the realm of challenge and adventure activities. While the fourth scenario above does involve some elements which can be addressed by challenge and adventure activities, this group has identified some long-standing problems that may require significantly more effort to resolve than can be conveniently addressed during a challenge and adventure program.

In this first step however, the effort is only to identify the needs and goals of the group, without filtering these needs based on what we believe challenge and adventure programming activities can accomplish. If this makes you feel a little uncomfortable, especially considering the needs of the group in the fourth scenario above, it should. But the decision to proceed with the development of the challenge program can only come after the needs have been accurately established. If we filter what we hear, because of what we already know we can do, two opportunities will be lost. First, we'll miss the chance to accurately understand what the true needs of the group really are. Secondly, we'll miss the chance to reach out of our own comfort zone, and take on a project that will extend what we do into a new area.

Some challenge programs may choose to present what they can accomplish right up front, and say, "here is what we do. If you want this type of program, we are here to assist you." Two things about this approach cause some significant amount of alarm. First, this places the decision to participate in a challenge and adventure program directly on the leadership of the requesting organization or group, when in reality, the challenge program provider is probably in a better position to judge the suitability of this group to the challenge program they can provide. Secondly, the challenge program provider has lost a valuable opportunity to see inside the group that desires this experience. If you happen to lead challenge activities that utilize communication skills, and you contract to present a program for a group that has some communication issues, you might want to know just exactly what those issues are. Consider this hypothetical scenario, based on a recent true-life event:

The administrators for a college-based challenge program were contacted by a local law enforcement agency to see if they could provide a challenge experience for two groups of participants approximately 19 to 21 years of age. Yes, was the answer. This was the typical age of the college population they served. This was all the information communicated during this initial program assessment. Two days later, the local court heard the case of two rival gangs that were involved in a violent event. As part of their sentence, the Judge required these two rival gangs to simultaneously participate in a challenge event at the college-based program site.

In this example, there was no opportunity for the challenge program to adequately identify the needs of the group. The amount of information provided was too general and neglected to provide some important information. This scenario however serves as an example of what can happen when an accurate needs assessment is not performed. The college-based program did manage to survive the event however, but only thanks to their talented and quick-thinking staff. An accurate needs assessment, conducted without filtering any information, would have given this group a much better understanding of the participants and allowed them to either create an even better program, or to decline the opportunity based on their ability to provide such a program.

Basic Training

Needs Assessment

Listen to every detail of what the client discusses without filtering any information. Keep asking questions until you know exactly what the client is expecting from the challenge and adventure program.

The reason for listening in such detail, is that the contact person or client is likely to provide not only the needs of the group, but also the goals they wish to achieve during the challenge program. If the needs in the second scenario concerned communication issues, the goals of the group may be to have each member be able to communicate effectively with at least two other members of the group. This is useful information in the planning stages of a challenge and adventure programming event. Now you have not only identified the needs of the group (communication), you have also identified the criteria for which the group will judge the success of the program (each participant can communicate effectively with at least two other members of the group). Techniques for quantifying just how well this goal was met are presented in Chapter 6.

At the end of this chapter, a sample needs assessment form is presented. This is not intended to be the optimal needs assessment tool for every program, but it does suggest some of the essential information that you need to know when performing a needs assessment for a group interested in a challenge and adventure programming event.

Step 2—Planning Challenge Activities to Address Specific Needs and Goals

The second element of a successful challenge and adventure programming event is selecting the activities that will provide participants with the experiences they need to accomplish their goals. Here is the first opportunity the challenge program provider has to evaluate whether or not the activities they can provide will meet the needs and goals of the group.

Near the beginning of Chapter 4, there are several pages which list the activities presented in this book, the intensity level of each activity, and the skills or themes which these activities can provide to the group. In addition to this list, each of the activities in Chapter 4 is individually presented, providing an even more extensive presentation of the skills that can be exercised with these activities.

Remember however, that even an activity that has a large problem solving component or theme can be modified to focus the effort of the group on communication or resource management issues. The skills and themes presented at the beginning of Chapter 4 are merely suggestions of what is possible.

Creating the Blueprint

The final element of the pre-event planning process is for the facilitator to have all the essential information about the event available to them prior to the event. Such details as where, and when, and how many participants, and what does the location look like, are as important to the challenge and adventure program as a set of building plans are to the successful construction of a home or office building.

At the end of this chapter, you'll find an example of a program planning sheet and a blank planning sheet that can be used to provide the facilitator with essential program information.

It may be appropriate to share this information with the client prior to the challenge and adventure programming event. This provides one more opportunity for the client to review the plan against the needs and goals of their organization. Chances are, they will appreciate the thoroughness of your planning, and your communication with them.

Needs and Goal Assessment Sheet

Name of Organization or Group
Contact Person
Date of the event
Event time and duration
Location of the event — Map Needed? Yes No
Number of Participants
Major Reason for Event
Are there participants with special needs?
What happens if it rains?

The Needs. Which of the following elements are important to this group?

Resource Management	Coordination	Balance
Effective Feedback	Confidence	Cooperation
Exploring Diversity	Decision Making	Motivation
Conflict Resolution	Timing	Group Focus
Problem Solving Skills	Team Spirit	Visualization
Play / Fun	Trust Building	Creativity
Achieving Group Consensus	Communication	Teamwork
Environmental Studies	Spirituality	Peer Respect

Others ______________________________

The Goals. How will we know if we have met the needs of the group?

____
____
____
____
____
____
____
____

The most challenging detail of this event will be:

____

Needs and Goal Assessment Sheet

Name of Organization or Group
Contact Person
Date of the event
Event time and duration
Location of the event — Map Needed? Yes No
Number of Participants
Major Reason for Event
Are there participants with special needs?
What happens if it rains?

The Needs. Which of the following elements are important to this group?

Resource Management	Coordination	Balance
Effective Feedback	Confidence	Cooperation
Exploring Diversity	Decision Making	Motivation
Conflict Resolution	Timing	Group Focus
Problem Solving Skills	Team Spirit	Visualization
Play / Fun	Trust Building	Creativity
Achieving Group Consensus	Communication	Teamwork
Environmental Studies	Spirituality	Peer Respect

Others ______________________________

The Goals. How will we know if we have met the needs of the group?

____

____

____

____

____

____

____

____

The most challenging detail of this event will be:

____

Teamplay Planning Sheet

Event	*Teamplay Staff Training and Picnic*
Event Date	*Saturday, August 16, 1999*
Length of Program	*9:00 am till 4:00 pm with a 1 hour break for lunch at 12:00 noon*
Location	*Teamplay Headquarters 468 Salmon Creek Road Brockport, NY 14420*
Contact Information	*Barry Jolliff 760 East Hutton Road Wooster, OH 44691*
	Phone / Fax (330) 345–8492 Email: bjolliff@aol.com
No. of Participants	*30*
Reason for Event	*Staff Training and Picnic—begin learning Teamplay activities*
Special Needs	*One key staff member on crutches*
In Case of Rain	*Activities and picnic will be held in the picnic shelter*

Activity	Equipment	Approximate Time
Get Acquainted—Autographs	*35 copies of handout, pencils*	*10 minutes*
Funderbirds	*3 Funderbirds*	*15 minutes*
Handcuffs and Shackles	*30+ sets*	*10 minutes*
Group Formation with Film Canisters	*30 Film Canisters*	*10 minutes*
2B or KNOT 2B	*1 complete set of four puzzles*	*30 minutes*
Wing It	*6 Wing It Rods with Wingnuts*	*20 minutes*
Magic Carpet	*3 Plastic Sheets*	*20 minutes*
Danger Zone	*1 Large Plastic Sheet*	*20 minutes*
Raccoon Circles	*3 Raccoon Circles*	*45 minutes*
Lunch / Break		
Different Drum	*Battery Cassette Tape Player*	*20 minutes*
The Water Tube	*2 Water Tubes*	*30 minutes*
Waterfall I	*2 different length PVC tubes*	*20 minutes*
Surfing the Web II	*Inclined Web using Trees*	*35 minutes*
Boardwalking	*4 sets of Boardwalkers*	*20 minutes*
Move It or Lose It	*50+ boxes*	*15 minutes*
Lycra Tube	*3 Lycra Tubes*	*20 minutes*
Closing Activity—Popsicle Sticks	*100 Sticks, markers, tape*	*20 minutes*

Additional Activities if Needed	Equipment	Approximate Time
63 / 64 / 65	*3 sets of Puzzles*	*15 minutes*
Marble Tubes	*30+ tubes and marbles*	*30 minutes*
Midnight Sun	*Magic Carpet sheet*	*15 minutes*
Monumental	*30+ Monumental Dice*	*30 minutes*
Not Knots	*30 pieces of rope*	*20 minutes*
Right Where I Belong	*30+ blindfolds*	*20 minutes*
Under the Doormat	*15 carpet squares*	*20 minutes*

Comments about activities (filled in after the event)

Under the Doormat was well received by the group. Probably need to have several different sizes of carpet squares for different sizes of people!

Needed a closer source of water for Water Tube and Waterfall.

One participant was able to juggle three boxes during Move It or Lose It, pretty amazing!

Good comments from the staff during Raccoon Circles. Need to allow more time for this activity in the future. It could easily fill a whole hour.

More set-up time needed for Surfing the Web. Only two trees were available.

The Lycra Tube was a big hit.

Notes

Consider having a slightly longer morning session, and a shorter afternoon session. Some folks were pretty tired after a full day's worth of running around.

Need to replace several missing wing nuts and one Wing It threaded rod with bad threads.

Map of Activity Area

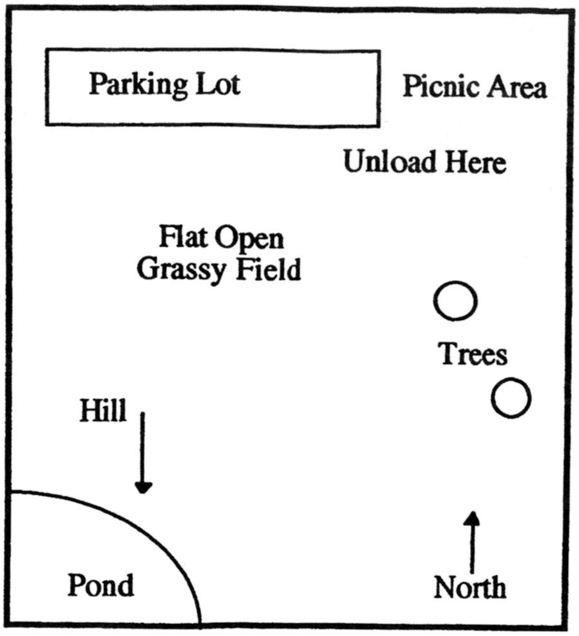

Teamplay Planning Sheet

Event
Event Date
Length of Program
Location
Contact Information

No. of Participants
Reason for Event
Special Needs
In Case of Rain

Activity	Equipment	Approximate Time
Get Acquainted Activity		
Lunch / Break		
Closing Activity		

Additional Activities if Needed | Equipment | Approximate Time

Comments about activities (filled in after the event)

Notes

Map of Activity Area

Chapter Three

The Beginning of Teamplay

Ok, you have 15 minutes before the session begins, and you need two activities suitable for starting your group . . .

Basic Training

- Participants may not arrive at the same time. Plan an activity so that participants can be involved from the moment they arrive. Perhaps instruct the first two participants that arrive, and have them teach the next to arrive, and so on.
- Maintain a personal list of name games and group formation activities that require no props at all.
- Select get acquainted activities that encourage new participants to join in.
- Remember what it was like when you were first new to a group.

Even Before the Adventure Experience Begins . . .

While challenge and adventure activities are often used with teams, do not expect every group to arrive as a cohesive team. In fact, do not expect groups to arrive together at all.

It is a good idea to have a few activities ready for when the very first participants arrive. This gives the facilitator immediate contact with group members, and begins the process of building a working relationship immediately. Here are a few ideas that can be used in the time just before the program begins.

Handcuffs and Shackles. This simple rope puzzle for two or more can be found in Section 4.28 of Chapter 4. If you teach the first two arriving participants how to initiate this activity, you'll give them an immediate opportunity for a leadership role. Not a bad reward for showing up a little early.

Plenty of Room at the Top. Finding a way to stack 20 nails on the head of another nail is no easy task—but there are creative ways to do it. See Section 4.48 of Chapter 4 for this activity. This is a great activity for the board room, the classroom, the meeting room or the play room.

Funderbirds. These simple hand toys are unique to most audiences, and can be used for name games and other fun activities. See Section 4.26 of Chapter 4 for more information about making and using this unique bird.

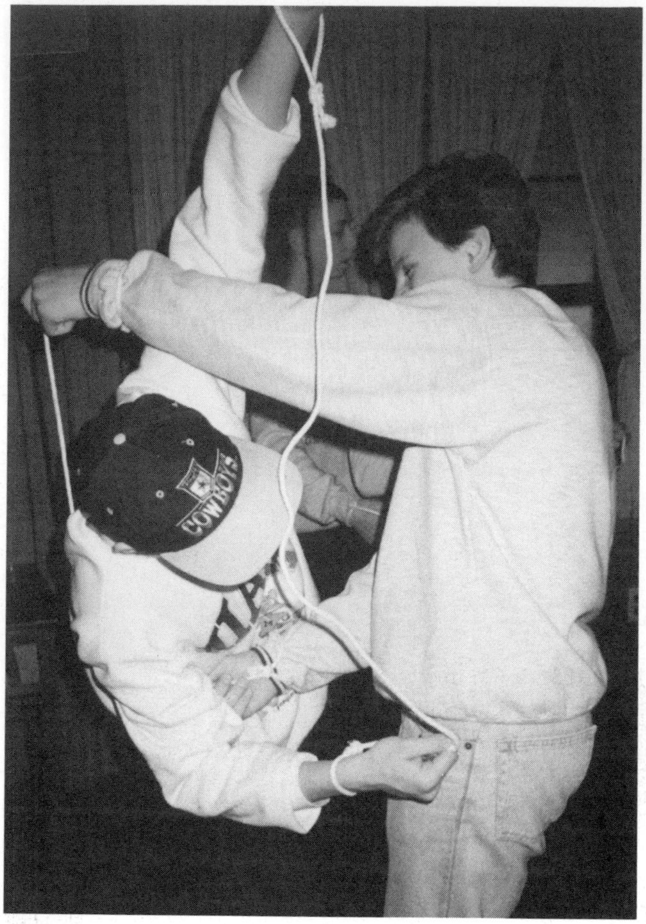

John Hancock.

Near the end of this chapter you'll find several pencil and paper activities that can be used as get acquainted activities for the group. John Handcock can begin even before all the members of the group have arrived. There are two variations of this activity presented. Autographs is best used when the entire audience has arrived. You may want to make copies of these original sheets before writing on them.

Nametags.

Provide some unusual supplies for making name tags. The more colorful and creative the better. Provide pipe cleaners, paper, paint swatches, magazines and newspapers, small wooden boards, headbands, string, markers, crayons, caligraphy pens, old photographs and postcards, safety pins, index cards, glue, glitter. . . .

The Puzzle Table.

This has been a favorite table at several conferences we have attended in the past few years. It also serves as a location where participants tend to congregate between programs. Simply supply a variety of wood, metal, plastic and paper puzzles for participants to work on individually or in groups. Since many challenge and adventure activities incorporate problem solving skills, these puzzles make excellent warm up exercises.

Doodles.

For those times when the first activities are performed with participants seated in small groups, Doodles provides an interesting get-acquainted activity. While there isn't much scientific content to the validity of the interpretations, the light-heartedness of the activity generally encourages group members to tell about themselves through stories and personal experiences. The amount of information provided generally exceeds that obtained by saying, "please stand and tell us a little about yourself."

Frontloading the Challenge and Adventure Experience

front·load·ing (frŭnt-lōd-ĭng) *n.*, Information presented before the program begins.

No question about it. Frontloading is essential in a challenge and adventure program. It is here that the expectations of the participants and the knowledge of the facilitator come together. This is the time when the tone of the program will be set. This is the time to encourage participants to be vocal about their opinions throughout the program, to ask questions, to help each other. This is the time to demonstrate that you are prepared to meet the goals and challenges with the group. That you are going to push them outside their comfort zone. That you will never ask them to do anything that you wouldn't be willing to do yourself. It is your chance to explain to the group what choices they have in participation, and that they can always choose how

Basic Training

Frontloading

- Welcome to the program! We have a very unique experience planned for you today, and before we begin, I just wanted to tell you a little bit about what is about to happen to you . . .

- Today, we are going to make every attempt to offer you the opportunity to try something really new. It is our hope that at least once today, we will give you the chance to work a little outside your comfort zone, to try something you have never tried before, or to be a part of an experience that is new, unusual or unique for you. For some of you, this may mean that you'll experience a problem for which you can see no immediate solution. For some, you may become frustrated by the pace at which the rest of the group is working. For some, you may be encouraged to stretch beyond what you think you can do, with the full support of the group behind you.

- In each and every one of these cases, as an individual, you have the right and duty to decide for yourself just how you are going to participate. We encourage a policy of "challenge by choice," which simply stated means that you always, always have the option and choice of how you will participate. Your facilitator and fellow group members may encourage you, may provide support for you, may even challenge you to go beyond your traditional limits, but you always have the choice to participate at whatever level you feel is appropriate.

- As a facilitator, I will never ask you to perform a duty or task that I myself would not be willing to perform. The goal is not to make you look silly out here, the goal is to help this group perform as a championship team.

- As a facilitator, my duties today are to provide you with the safest, most exciting, most challenging program that I can. I will instruct you on the basic components of each adventure activity and listen carefully to any comments, questions, or concerns you may have. I am here to assist your group, but ultimately, the challenge is yours.

- As members of your group, I need to make sure that you are committed to this program. That you are willing to consider new ideas, some of which may come from surprising sources. That you will respect not only my opinions and suggestions, but the opinions and suggestions of each member of your group. I need you to ask questions when you do not understand, to indicate that you are willing to fully support a plan, even if you are not entirely sure of the outcome, and to assist me in watching for opportunities where risk can be reduced, and an improvement made to the techniques employed by this group.

Are you ready? Are you willing to try? OK, then let's begin!

they are going to participate. Let them know that you will encourage them to try new things, but will never, never force them to.

Many of the interpersonal conflicts that sometimes arise during an intense challenge and adventure program can be traced back to the expectations of both the participants and the facilitator, which are forged in the frontloading stage of the adventure experience.

A few years ago, we probably would not have written these previous paragraphs. We just assumed participants came to the program because they wanted to, and that was an adequate place to start. In retrospect, quite a few of the problems encountered during challenge programs could probably have been avoided had a conscious effort been extended to frontloading the challenge and adventure experience. This step, which we now know is essential to the success of the experience, is simply a method for voicing the expectations of both the group and the facilitator, and an excellent technique for creating a working relationship between the group and the facilitator.

One of the last topics typically explained in a Teamplay program is the concept of "creative cheating." This simple phrase has some amazing complications unless immediately defined to the group. For the purpose of the challenge and adventure activities ahead, the concept of creative cheating is really very simple. For any activity where the facilitator asks for the group to be in smaller groups of three, and there is an extra person or two, then you can creatively cheat and use groups of two or four people. For any activity where the facilitator suggests going clockwise, the group can ask about going counterclockwise. The goal here is to create an atmosphere between the group and facilitator where communication, creativity, brainstorming and playful ingenuity is always at work. By encouraging creative cheating, participants will always be looking for an idea that is new, and potentially unique. Participants will be looking outside the obvious path, engaging in discussions with other group members, and pressing the facilitator for more information. This is exactly the kind of behavior you want to encourage in a group. As a facilitator however, you must be willing to suggest activities and techniques which are suitable for the impact of creative cheating. If you really need four participants in a group, say so.

The only time when creative cheating is never employed, is when there is an issue which pertains to the safety of the group. If the facilitator requests two spotters for an activity, there is no room for the group to creatively cheat and use only one spotter. This important exception to the creative cheating rule will also elevate the interest of the group in looking for potential risks and safety concerns in the techniques they propose. This is another valuable product of the creative cheating approach.

Beginning the Challenge and Adventure Experience

Even before a challenge and adventure activity begins, participants have already begun to form an opinion of the program. Hopefully some of the activities presented earlier in this chapter will make those first moments positive for each participant.

Frontloading then provides a chance for the facilitator and the group to begin building a relationship that will continue throughout the program. This step reinforces the goals and expectations for both the group members and the facilitator.

At this point, the preparation is complete. Now it is time to begin the challenge and adventure experience with the group. So what will you do with these 12 people to start the program?

The Warm Up

Certainly one of the most obvious places to start a challenge and adventure activity that is sure to have some physical components, is with some physical warm up and stretching. Here are a few ideas for performing this task in some creative ways:

The Stretch Wave. Begin with the group standing in a large circle. A leader from the group begins the Stretch Wave by assuming a stretching position, such as raising their arms high above their head. The next person to their right then creates the same position, and this pattern continues around the circle to the right as each new member of the group creates this stretching position. After the wave returns to the original leader, the next person to the original leader's right begins a new stretching position, and the wave again travels around the circle in this new stretching position.

Encourage participants to use slow, gentle movements at first, and to consider the abilities of the rest of the group when selecting a stretching position.

Who's In Charge Here?. Using the same large circular formation from the previous activity, allow one leader from the group to select an exercise for the group, and to lead this exercise from the center of the circle. They begin by saying with great enthusiasm, "I'm In Charge!" And then proceed to say the name of the exercise and begin. At any time, another group member has the choice of running into the circle and saying, "I'm In Charge!", and selecting a new exercise to lead.

For example, this activity may begin with a leader

selecting arm circles to warm up. After a few moments, another group member runs to the center of the circle and yells, "Hey, I'm in charge!" and says, "OK, neck rolls to the right—go," and begins leading this exercise. When a group member runs up and says, "I'm in charge!" and selects squat thrusts, back flip or some other strenuous activity, you'll be surprised how quickly another group member will jump in with a more suitable choice. When this activity has run its course, the facilitator can jump in to lead one last exercise, and then take the focus of the group to the next activity.

Marching to the Beat of a Different Drum. This is certainly one of our favorite activities, although you may have to judge for yourself whether or not this activity is appropriate as one of the first activities for your group.

Marching to the Beat of a Different Drum can be found in Section 4.22 of Chapter 4. This activity involves each participant of the group leading any dance movement to a rather short selection of music. The types of music vary greatly, and the activity level of the group can grow progressively more intense. This is an energizing activity, and typically leaves the group excited and ready to move on to the next activity.

Each of the above warm-ups provide an opportunity for all member of the group to take a very brief leadership role. This opportunity will be presented again and again within the context of the challenge and adventure activities which are to follow.

Other Techniques for Beginning

Raccoon Circles. Dr. Tom Smith graciously allowed the presentation of a few of his innovative Raccoon Circles techniques to be included in this book. You can find more information on these in Section 4.51 of Chapter 4. A Raccoon Circle is a 12 foot (3.6 meter) long segment of 1 inch (25 mm) tubular webbing that has been tied into a loop with a water knot. This simple prop can be used for get-acquainted activities, warm up activities, challenge and adventure activities, processing and facilitation and closing activities. A very versatile performance from such a humble piece of challenge equipment.

Beginning with Raccoon Circles. If you plan to use a Raccoon Circle approach for processing and debriefing throughout the challenge and adventure program, you may find it helpful to begin using these props right from the very start. First have members of the group all take a hold of the Raccoon Circle with both hands, palms down. Hands should be about shoulder width apart, as should the feet of each participant. Now have each member back up until the Raccoon Circle forms a tight circle. From this position it is easy to demonstrate that a single pull from one participant has an immediate effect on every member of the group. If a participant lets go of the Raccoon Circle quickly, this too has an immediate effect on the group. For the group to stay in balance, and to function as a team, all members need to support each other, and to do their share. See Chapter 4 for more activities that can be accomplished with Raccoon Circles.

Funderbirds. These unique challenge props are presented in Section 4.26 of Chapter 4. The goal is simply to keep these objects aloft using only hands. Once the group has perfected the skill to keep the Funderbirds aloft, try incorporating some name games into the activity. First say you own name whenever you hit the Funderbird. Next, say the name of anyone else in the group when hitting the Funderbird. This second variation is considerably harder as one side of your brain focuses on hitting the Funderbird, and the other side of your brain focuses on trying to remember a name of another member of the group.

Wing It. As a physical warm-up, Wing It is not a very strenuous activity, but it does work well as a warm-up activity. You'll find the directions for Wing It in Section 4.81 of Chapter 4. This is an ideal activity to demonstrate to the group just what a problem solving activity really is. The goal here is for each member of a group to place a wingnut on a threaded rod, and as quickly as possible, spin this wingnut to the other end and off the rod. Several signficant elements of the challenge program can be processed with this event. First, it is completely inclusive. All members of the group are included. Secondly, it involves some problem solving, planning and execution of a plan. Thirdly, groups typically change techniques during the activity, so the elements of change and continuous improvement surface. Finally, this is a speed activity which typically raises the excitement and energy level of the group.

2B or KNOT 2B. As a final warm-up activity, 2B or KNOT 2B is one of the most positive activities presented in this book. You'll find instructions for this activity in Section 4.3 of Chapter 4. The goal is for the group to collectively decide which segment of a rope puzzle is holding all the other rope segments together. The solution of the puzzle is not significant, but the necessity for achieving group consensus is. This single activity demonstrates the need for working together as a group in a very visually convincing way. Save this best one for last.

Other Activities

You can find a variety of other games and activities in Chapter 7 that can also be used to begin a challenge and adventure program. If you are looking for some creative ways to form groups, see the suggestions provided following this section. For groups where members may be unacquainted with each other, activities such as Autographs and John Hancock can be useful name recognition activities. Instructions and sample sheets are given for each of these activities at the end of this chapter.

For groups that wish to experience a more in-depth introduction to the other members of the group, Doodles provides a pencil and paper project that brings out some interesting personal facts. Instructions and sample sheets for this activity can be found at the end of this chapter.

Basic Training

A Summary of Chapter Three

- ♦ Engage the participation and involvement of group members from the moment they arrive.
- ♦ Frontloading is not an option, it is an essential method for establishing a working relationship between the group and the facilitator.
- ♦ Challenge by Choice is not an option, it is the rule!
- ♦ Be inclusive from the very start.
- ♦ Secure the committment of each member of the group. This is the glue that will hold your group together when the going gets really tough out there.
- ♦ Encourage creative cheating, but never, never when the safety of the group is at risk.
- ♦ Learn the names of the members of your group, and use them.

Basic Training

Creative Techniques for Group Formation

Go Fly an Airplane. Half the group writes their name on a paper airplane, and then sails it away. The person who finds the airplane from the other half of the group becomes their partner.

Thumbs Up. To split into two groups, clasp your hands with the fingers and thumbs of both hands interlocking. Those with the right thumb on top move to the right, those with the left thumb on top, move to the left.

Film Canisters. Fill plastic film canisters with different objects to organize groups. Choose objects which will create different sounds inside the canisters. See the activity in Section 4.24 of Chapter 4 for more ideas about how to use film canisters for group formation.

Blindfolds. If you happen to be using blindfolds for an activity, you can organize the members of a group by the color of their blindfolds.

Nuts and Bolts. See the activity in Section 7.20 of Chapter 7 for a way to use a variety of metal nuts and bolts to organize and form smaller groups from larger ones.

Playing Cards. Grouped by suit, number, card deck pattern, all red cards, all black cards, etc. Here is an activity for those card decks that are missing a few cards each.

Autographs

Find someone in the group who has done any of the activities listed below, and have them sign their name in that block.

Can speak a foreign language	Has been on TV	Has traveled to at least 10 other states	Would bungie jump if the chance occurred
Grew up in farm country	Has traveled by train	Has an unusual hobby	Likes to read books
Has traveled far and wide	Worked at a gas station	Has bought a lotto ticket	Knows how to dance the tango
Has seen a major play in a big city	Voted in the last election	Looks the most like you	Plays a musical instrument
Likes rollercoasters	Likes to ride horses	Has performed on stage	Knows someone famous
Has many siblings	Has been to Mount Rushmore	Has a nickname that they like	Owns a neat toy
Likes their dentist	Has not been on an airplane	Has a collection of some kind	Has ridden a camel or unicycle

John Hancock

Here is a get-acquainted activity that involves some handwriting analysis, memory skills, name recognition, and penmanship (or rather the lack thereof). This activity can be performed in two different ways.

John Hancock—Version I

As the group is arriving, have a copy of the following page available for each person to quickly (in fact, very quickly) autograph with their signature. When the entire audience has arrived, make copies of this signature page for everyone. Then have the group try to identify each person with their signatures. When the correct identification is made, have this person stand and tell a little bit about themselves.

John Hancock—Version II

Provide name tags for each member of the audience. A very quickly drawn, and typically illegible, signature is appropriate for this activity. Then provide each member of the audience with a copy of the following page, and have them obtain these same signatures from each member of the group. Also have the owner of the paper write down the real name of this person and what they like to be called. By engaging both participants in writing down the names of the people they are meeting, they are using verbal, visual, kinesthetic and cognitive skills to learn names, which typically reinforces the ability of the audience to remember these names. While nametags can be extremely useful, this activity encourages the audience to actually learn the names of their fellow members, since their nametags are generally illegible!

# Fast Signature	
Full Name	Please call me...

# Barry Jolliff (signature)	
Barry Jolliff	Barry

1	

2	

3	

4	

5	

6	

7	

8	

9	

10	

11	

12	

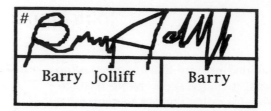

Doodles

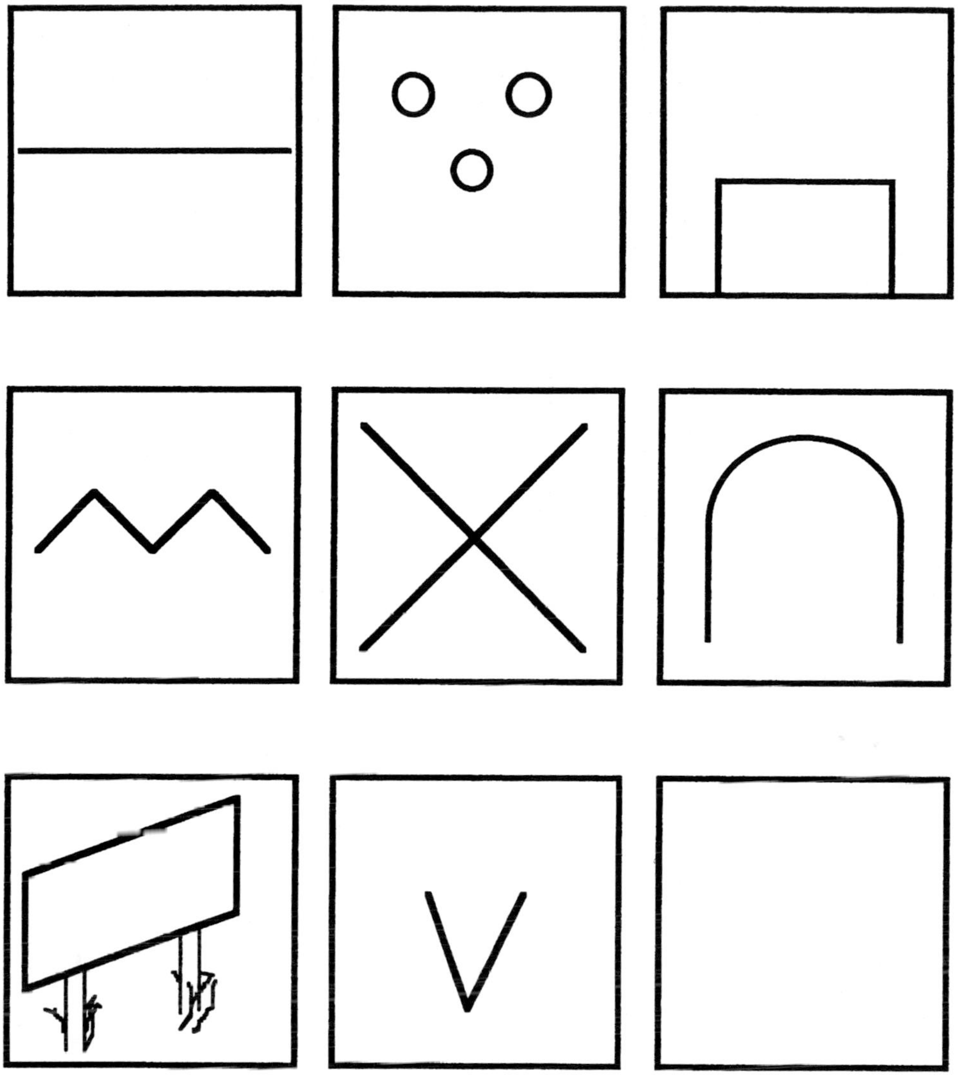

Instructions Draw, sketch, write, doodle or scribble something in each of the nine squares.

Doodles—Evaluating the Results

The following information has little or no scientific basis. The real purpose of this exercise is more in the conversation surrounding the evaluation of your doodles than in the actual evaluation. In other words, have fun, and don't take the answers (or yourself) too seriously.

Instructions Have each member of the group read one of the following subjects. The question at the end of each paragraph can be answered by the reader and then by the other members of the group. Take time for participants to share their personal stories and experiences surrounding each subject.

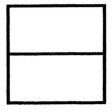

Confidence The line at the middle of this block indicates your confidence with the world around you. Items drawn above the line are objects which you have a command over. Items drawn below the line are things which are generally out of your control. Question: Name one thing that you can do really well.

Imagination Life is full of circles. We travel, and we return. We learn, and we forget. This block illustrates how you use your imagination. If you draw the face of an animal or person, you show a liking for pets or friends. If you draw an object, such as a bowling ball, you are inventive. Question: What is your favorite day dream?

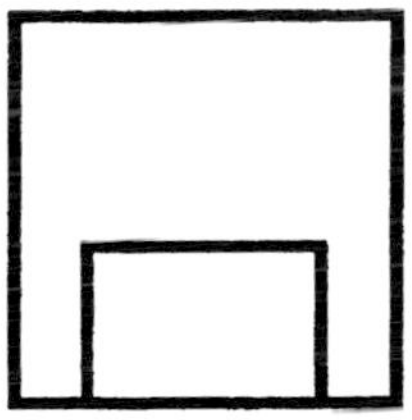

Home This box strongly identifies with your home. If you draw inside the box, your interests are within your home. Not surprisingly, if you draw outside the box, you have interests outside the home. Home symbols such as a fireplace, house, windows, or doors indicate a strong desire for a home atmosphere. Question: What is your favorite memory of home?

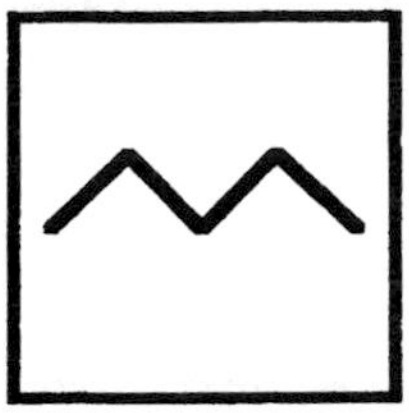

Aspiration If you make this shape into a mountain range you have high aspirations and goals. You enjoy challenges and solving problems. If you make geometric patterns from this design, you are able to add creativity to solving the challenges in your life. Question: What is a goal you have set for yourself to accomplish in the next five years? Ten years? Twenty years?

Decision Making Skills This block describes your decision making skills. If you draw lines or arrows that intersect or point to the center, this indicates that you are focused on your decision. If you draw non-linear shapes, such as circles or irregular wavy lines, it indicates that you are not overly concerned with making decisions. Question: What is the biggest decision you have had to make recently?

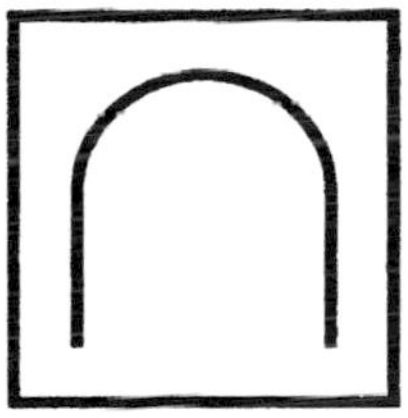

Plans for the Future The arch in this block indicates a passage way to your future. If you draw a dark tunnel, this indicates that you may be expecting some stormy times ahead. If you draw a rainbow, rose trellis or doorway, you are looking forward to your future. If the door is open, opportunity lies ahead. If you happen to draw a refrigerator, you are probably hungry. Question: What is the one thing you would most like to do in your future?

Personal Motto What you draw on this sign suggests a personal motto for you. If the sign is positive, you generally have a pleasant outlook on life. If the sign is a warning—watch out! If the sign indicates directions, you are likely ready for a change in your life. Question: If you could have any bumpersticker on your car, what would it say?

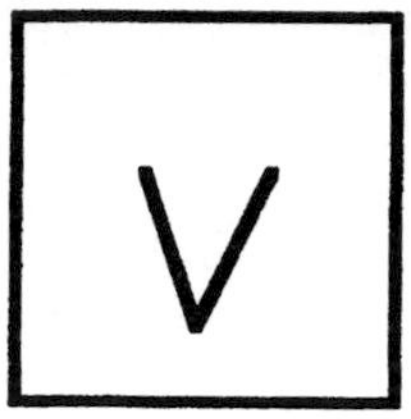

Creativity If you draw an ice cream cone, the V-neck of a shirt or sweater, or the tip of a pencil you have average creativity. If you used the V shape as part of a more complex pattern or object, you are a complex thinker, and probably know how to program your VCR without using the manual. Question: Have you ever created a better way to do something? Have you ever invented something?

The Great Unknown This block illustrates what is filling up your thoughts these days. Chances are the item in the square is important to you. If the drawing shows a person, it may be a friend or acquaintance that you would like to know better. If it shows an object, it may indicate a new hobby or interest for you. Question: What is your favorite thing to do when you have lots of free time?

Chapter Four

Activities for Teamwork & Teamplay

Chances are that this is likely to be the most used chapter in this book. Here are the activities for which the preparation, planning, construction, facilitation and follow up are designed for. Try to remember however, that as a facilitator, if all you do is "play" these activities, then your teambuilding session is likely to be just a series of games. These activities are but a single building block of any team or community building program. Equally important, if not more so, are the planning and debriefing stages (see Chapters 2, 3, and 6) which help to reinforce the activities found in this chapter.

Basic Training

The Equipment for These Challenge Activities

Each of the activities in this section is complemented by a similarly numbered section in Chapter 5, where instructions can be found for constructing the equipment used in these activities. For example, the equipment required for the Bull Ring activity described in Section 4.14, can be assembled using the instructions presented in Section 5.14 of Chapter 5.

What's Here

Here is a list of the activities that you'll find in this chapter, an idea of the intensity level of the activity, and the major skills needed or theme of each activity.

No.	Activity	Intensity Level	Skill or Theme
4.01	100 Words or Less	Moderate	Verbal Challenge, Feedback
4.02	20 / 20 Vision	Low	Visual Challenge
4.03	2B or KNOT 2B	Low	Consensus Building
4.04	63 / 64 / 65	Low	Geometrical Challenge
4.05	A Balanced Life	Moderate	Balance, Problem Solving
4.06	A Collection of Knots	Low	Movement, Problem Solving
4.07	A Work of Art	Low	Communication, Visualization
4.08	All Aboard	Moderate	Balance, Problem Solving
4.09	Alphabet Soup	Moderate	Problem Solving
4.10	Alphabetically	Low	Non Verbal Communication

No.	Activity	Intensity Level	Skill or Theme
4.11	Bag It	Low	Tactile Skills
4.12	Blackout	Moderate	Problem Solving, Proximity
4.13	Boardwalking	Moderate	Problem Solving, Teamwork
4.14	Bull Ring I	Low	Problem Solving, Teamwork
4.15	Bull Ring II	Low	Problem Solving, Teamwork
4.16	Bull Ring III—Write On!	Low	Problem Solving, Teamwork
4.17	Bull Ring Golf	Moderate	Problem Solving, Teamwork
4.18	Cave In	High Emotionally	Reality, Decision Making
4.19	Community Juggling	Low	Communication, Focus
4.20	Community Jump Rope	Low	Timing, Problem Solving
4.21	Danger Zone	Moderate	Problem Solving, Proximity
4.22	Different Drum	Moderate	Diversity, Fun, Energizer
4.23	Expansion and Contraction	Low	Working as a Group
4.24	Film Can Group Formation	Low	Group Formation, Change
4.25	First Contact	Moderate	Problem Solving, Proximity
4.26	Funderbirds	Low	Coordination, Teamwork
4.27	Gridlock	Low	Problem Solving, Risk
4.28	Handcuffs and Shackles	Low	Creativity, Problem Solving
4.29	Human Knot	Low	Conflict Resolution, Proximity
4.30	Inch by Inch	Moderate	Cooperation, Teamwork
4.31	Just One Word	Low	Creativity, Problem Solving
4.32	Life Raft	Moderate	Problem Solving, Resource Mgmt.
4.33	Line Up	Low	Communication, Problem Solving
4.34	Linearity	Low	Creativity, Decision Making
4.35	Living Ladder	Moderate	Teamwork, Resource Mgmt.
4.36	Log Rolling	Moderate	Balance, Trust, Problem Solving
4.37	Lycra Tube	High Physically	Trust, Energizer, Cooperation
4.38	Magic Carpet	Low	Problem Solving, Proximity
4.39	Marble Tubes	Low	Problem Solving, Cooperation
4.40	Midnight Sun	Moderate	Problem Solving, Cooperation
4.41	Mine, Mine, Mine	Moderate	Trust, Communication, Feedback
4.42	Missing Page	Low	Communication, Creativity
4.43	Monumental	High Physically	Spotting Techniques
4.44	Move It or Lose It	Moderate	Problem Solving, Resource Mgmt.
4.45	Moving Towards Extinct	Low	Problem Solving
4.46	Not Knots	Low	Problem Solving, Creativity
4.47	Parade	Low	Problem Solving, Resource Mgmt.
4.48	Plenty of Room at the Top	Low	Creativity, Problem Solving
4.49	Popsicle Sticks	Low	Creativity, Problem Solving
4.50	Pot of Gold	Moderate	Problem Solving, Communication
4.51	Raccoon Circles	Low / Moderate	Trust, Communication, Teamwork
4.52	Real Estate	Low	Problem Solving, Communication
4.53	Right Where I Belong	Moderate	Communication, Trust
4.54	River Crossing	High Physically	Problem Solving, Strength
4.55	Shark Attack	Low	Teamwork, Cooperation
4.56	Simply Amazing	Moderate	Trust, Problem Solving
4.57	Strange Attraction	Low	Problem Solving, Teamwork
4.58	Stretch It	Low	Problem Solving, Teamwork
4.59	Stretching the Limit	Low	Problem Solving, Teamwork
4.60	Stump Jumping	Moderate	Communication, Cooperation

No.	Activity	Intensity Level	Skill or Theme
4.61	Surfing the Web I	Moderate	Problem Solving, Teamwork
4.62	Surfing the Web II	Moderate	Problem Solving, Teamwork
4.63	Surfing the Web III	Moderate	Problem Solving, Teamwork
4.64	Surfing the Web IV	Moderate	Problem Solving, Teamwork
4.65	Surfing the Web V	Moderate	Problem Solving, Teamwork
4.66	Target Specifications	Low	Teamwork, Communication
4.67	Tennis Ball Mountain	Low	Creativity, Problem Solving
4.68	The Boardroom	Moderate	Problem Solving, Creativity
4.69	The Paper Chase	Low	Teamwork, Cooperation
4.70	Time Tunnel	Moderate	Cooperation, Communication
4.71	Tower Building	Low	Creativity, Resource Mgmt.
4.72	Traffic Circle	Moderate	Problem Solving, Communication
4.73	Tree of Knots	Low	Problem Solving, Proximity
4.74	Under Cover	Low	Cooperation, Teamwork
4.75	Under the Doormat	Low	Cooperation, Trust, Proximity
4.76	Universe	Low	Creativity, Learning Experience
4.77	Villages and Wells	Low	Creativity, Problem Solving
4.78	Water Tube	Moderate	Problem Solving, Cooperation
4.79	Waterfall I	Moderate	Problem Solving, Cooperation
4.80	Waterfall II	Low	Problem Solving, Cooperation
4.81	Wing It	Low	Problem Solving, Teamwork
4.82	Worm Hole	Low	Problem Solving, Cooperation
4.83	Yada Yada Yada	Low	Communication

The New Stuff

If you are looking for the "really new stuff" that you may not have seen before, try the following activities:

4.01	100 Words or Less	4.45	Moving Towards Extinction
4.02	20 / 20 Vision	4.46	Not Knots
4.03	2B or Knot 2B	4.49	Popsicle Sticks
4.04	63 / 64 / 65	4.50	Pot of Gold
4.06	A Collection of Knots	4.51	Raccoon Circles
4.11	Bag It	4.52	Real Estate
4.12	Blackout	4.53	Right Where I Belong
4.14	Bull Ring I	4.57	Strange Attraction
4.15	Bull Ring II	4.58	Stretch It
4.16	Bull Ring III	4.59	Stretching the Limit
4.17	Bull Ring Golf	4.60	Stump Jumping
4.21	Danger Zone	4.66	Target Specifications
4.22	Different Drum	4.68	The Boardroom
4.24	Film Can Group Formation	4.69	The Paper Chase
4.26	Funderbirds	4.70	Time Tunnel
4.30	Inch by Inch	4.72	Traffic Circle
4.31	Just One Word	4.73	Tree of Knots
4.32	Life Raft	4.74	Under Cover
4.34	Linearity	4.75	Under the Doormat
4.37	Lycra Tube	4.76	Universe
4.38	Magic Carpet	4.77	Villages and Wells
4.40	Midnight Sun	4.78	Water Tube
4.42	Missing Page	4.79	Waterfall I
4.43	Monumental	4.82	Worm Hole
4.44	Move It or Lose It	4.83	Yada Yada Yada

At the end of this chapter, you'll find a section entitled "More Ideas for the Future," that has a few suggestions for several very unique challenge and adventure activities, how to use them, and where to find them.

Before We Get to the Good Stuff

Generally speaking, the activities in this book were not created in a vacuum. As life-long participants in the challenge and adventure programming field, we have been truly blessed to have been a part of a variety of organizations and experiences that have enhanced our knowledge in this field, and gained some wonderful friends in the process.

But before we get to the good stuff, we just wanted to let you know that, while we are both pretty creative guys, some of the activities mentioned here have been shared with us by friends and colleagues. A few of these activities are truly original, written just for this publication. Others have had a long life, and are a classic part of the challenge and adventure programming system. Still others are adaptations of games and activities that have been modified to be a challenge and adventure activity.

In every way we possibly could, we have tried to keep appropriate records of who shared with us what and when. You'll find reference to several sources throughout Chapter 4 that have shared their ideas with us, and graciously allowed us to include their thoughts and ideas here for you the reader to enjoy.

In some cases, our research included so many "original" activities that were simultaneously recorded in several places, that it was difficult to know exactly where the concepts first originated. We have attempted to competently acknowledge those original sources where possible, and for any cases in which our research fell short of adequately acknowledging the appropriate source, we sincerely apologize.

The authors would personally like to thank the following groups and individuals for sharing their tremendous enthusiasm and knowledge surrounding the field of challenge and adventure programming. We have enjoyed learning from you, and are pleased to call you our mentors, our partners, and our friends.

Brenda Malone, Tim Borton, John Fark, Bill Henderson, Mike Currence, Chuck Wurth, Warren Elmer and the Gang at Cradlerock, Chris Cavert, Dr. Tom Smith, Gary Moore, Randy Smith and the Gang at Inner Quest, Mike Fischesser and the Gang at Alpine Towers, Dick Prouty and the Gang at Project Adventure, The Members of Young Farmers in Ontario Canada, The Buckeye Leadership Workshop Committee, The Management and Staff of 4-H Camp Ohio, The Staff of Easter Seal Camp Fairlee Manor, The Adventure Education Center, Dr. Denny Elliott, Glenn and Paula McClure, Paul Lintern, Susan Michalakes, Ruth Moe, Martha Hampton, Jack and Rosie Harting, Chris Miller, Tony Miller, David Sobotka, Debbie Jackson, Kirk Weisler, Karen Ward, Richard Wagner, Jim Wall, the Gang at Bradford Woods, and to the many, many others that have touched our lives, we thank you.

In addition to these groups and individuals with which we have personally worked, several important individuals and resources are so outstanding in challenge and adventure programming that we are genuinely compelled to thank them for their contributions. So much of the information that is available today on challenge and adventure programming exists because these sources have shared their knowledge with us. We appreciate their contributions, and willingness to share their knowledge with every new generation. You can find additional information about these folks, and the references they have authored, in Chapters 1 and 8.

Karl Rohnke, Joel Goodman, Michael Gass, Simon Priest, Carmine Consalvo, Benjy Simpson, Geoff Sanders, Christopher Roland, NOLS, Outward Bound, The American Camping Association, and the staff and volunteers of The Association of Experiential Education

With these accolades complete, let's get on to the subject at hand. Chapter 4 contains the best activities we know. All the challenges, activities, initiatives and games that have worked so well, especially those that are also very portable.

Activity 4.00

Sample Activity Description

The activities in this chapter are presented in the following format. This first paragraph is just a quick description of the activity and generally gives some suggestions on the effective presentation of the activity and the audience for which the activity is suitable.

Equipment

Here is where you will find all the props required for the activity. In some cases the equipment consists of standardly available balls, ropes and other typical sports equipment. In other cases, specialized equipment is required, and for these cases, a complete description of how to construct this equipment is presented in Chapter Five.

The Challenge

Here, a very brief description of the challenge or problem is presented.

Typical Presentation, Storyline or Metaphor

The use of effective metaphors, scenarios and stories can often enhance the experience of the participants during the activity. This paragraph presents various stories which can be edited or altered to suit the needs of your participants.

Variations

Nearly all of the activities presented in this chapter have more than one possible solution. A good facilitator will also vary the activity to challenge the group. For these reasons, this paragraph is used to acquaint the reader with potential variations, alterations and adaptations that can be used to modify the activity. In some cases, the physical abilities of participants need to be identified so that appropriate adaptations and challenges can be provided. In other cases, the size of the group may necessitate some modifications.

Important Points

While all the activities in this chapter have been chosen because of their simplicity, utility and low risk, this paragraph identifies any potential problems which may be encountered by the facilitator or participants. This paragraph also identifies specific information which is necessary for the facilitator to present, so that participants can maximize their experience during the activity.

Discussion and Debriefing Topics

At the completion of the activity, a discussion of the experience is typical for many challenge related events. This paragraph presents potential topics, techniques and methods for bringing out the fine points of the activity, and for exploring the experience of the participants during the activity.

Sequence

The location of this activity within a group of activities, or within the context of an adventure program is discussed in this paragraph. Some activities work well as opening events, others bring about specific skills, such as problem solving, trust building, decision making, etc., while others require skills which should be developed prior to the activity, such as communication between team members. A few of the activities in this chapter are also idea for the final challenge in a day's worth of activities.

Activities Using Similar Skills and Follow-on Activities

While many of the activities in this chapter are unique, this paragraph identifies other activities found in this book which utilize similar equipment, skills, or solution techniques.

Notes

We thought you might appreciate a little space to include your own variations, ideas, and suggestions for each of these activities.

Activity 4.01

100 Words or Less

This is not so much an activity, but a variation that can be used to modify the preparation time used for other activities in this chapter. Simply give a pencil and a copy of this page to the group, and ask them to write down each word spoken by team members as they plan how to accomplish the challenge confronting them. When the group is ready, or when all 100 words are filled in, the activity begins. This is an interesting device for encouraging the group to use clear, concise terms during planning.

1 ____	18 ____	35 ____
2 ____	19 ____	36 ____
3 ____	20 ____	37 ____
4 ____	21 ____	38 ____
5 ____	22 ____	39 ____
6 ____	23 ____	40 ____
7 ____	24 ____	41 ____
8 ____	25 ____	42 ____
9 ____	26 ____	43 ____
10 ____	27 ____	44 ____
11 ____	28 ____	45 ____
12 ____	29 ____	46 ____
13 ____	30 ____	47 ____
14 ____	31 ____	48 ____
15 ____	32 ____	49 ____
16 ____	33 ____	50 ____
17 ____	34 ____	

51 ______________________
52 ______________________
53 ______________________
54 ______________________
55 ______________________
56 ______________________
57 ______________________
58 ______________________
59 ______________________
60 ______________________
61 ______________________
62 ______________________
63 ______________________
64 ______________________
65 ______________________
66 ______________________
67 ______________________
68 ______________________
69 ______________________
70 ______________________
71 ______________________
72 ______________________
73 ______________________
74 ______________________
75 ______________________
76 ______________________
77 ______________________
78 ______________________
79 ______________________
80 ______________________
81 ______________________
82 ______________________
83 ______________________
84 ______________________
85 ______________________
86 ______________________
87 ______________________
88 ______________________
89 ______________________
90 ______________________
91 ______________________
92 ______________________
93 ______________________
94 ______________________
95 ______________________
96 ______________________
97 ______________________
98 ______________________
99 ______________________
100 ______________________

Activity 4.02

20/20 Vision

Every now and then you might have a group that you really want to challenge every step of the way. Here is a visual challenge that can be used to modify any of the activities in this chapter.

Equipment

On the following page, you'll find several geometric patterns to copy onto a transparency or clear piece of graphic film or plastic. Instructions for using these patterns are presented here and in Chapter 5. This patterns can be placed directly over a computer generated text document, effectively blocking the reader from seeing the text.

The Challenge

For the group to find a way to read through the distortion, and solve the problem written underneath.

Typical Presentation, Storyline or Metaphor

Having reached the site of the treasure, you find an ancient sign with unusual markings. Time and weather have scarred the face of the sign, and the important information written there. Can your team find a way to read this sign?

Variations

Other variations, such as only being able to read half the instructions, smudging the text, having the words fade in and out, creating some of the instructions in a foreign language, and using extremely light text in fading light all provide visual challenges to the group. The object here is not to frustrate the group, but to additionally challenge them to comprehend something, when the techniques for doing so are available.

Important Points

Chapter 5 provides instructions for creating a wooden box to hold the activity instructions, and the transparency overlay. The activity instructions are fastened to the back of the box, but the transparency is free to move about ½ inch (12 mm) inside the box. By shaking the box, the transparency allows different portions of the document to be viewed. Thanks to the eye's ability to sustain an image, the brain can perceive all the text without distortion, enabling the document to be read, simply by shaking the box.

Discussion and Debriefing Topics

Was the group perplexed by this challenge? Are there any experiences you've had which prepared you to solve this challenge? Did you discover a solution accidently or was the group able to creatively suggest a solution?

Sequence

20 / 20 Vision is simply a way to additionally challenge a group, any time they need to read the instructions for an activity. This variation is probably best suited to those groups that can appreciate the nature of such optical trickery.

Activities Using Similar Skills and Follow-on Activities

Some suitable activities to be included behind the 20 / 20 Vision transparency are: simple instructions for 2B or KNOT 2B, a description of what to do with the boxes for Move It or Lose It, an explanation of what to do with the nails in Plenty of Room at the Top, or a description of what to do with the tennis balls in Tennis Ball Mountain.

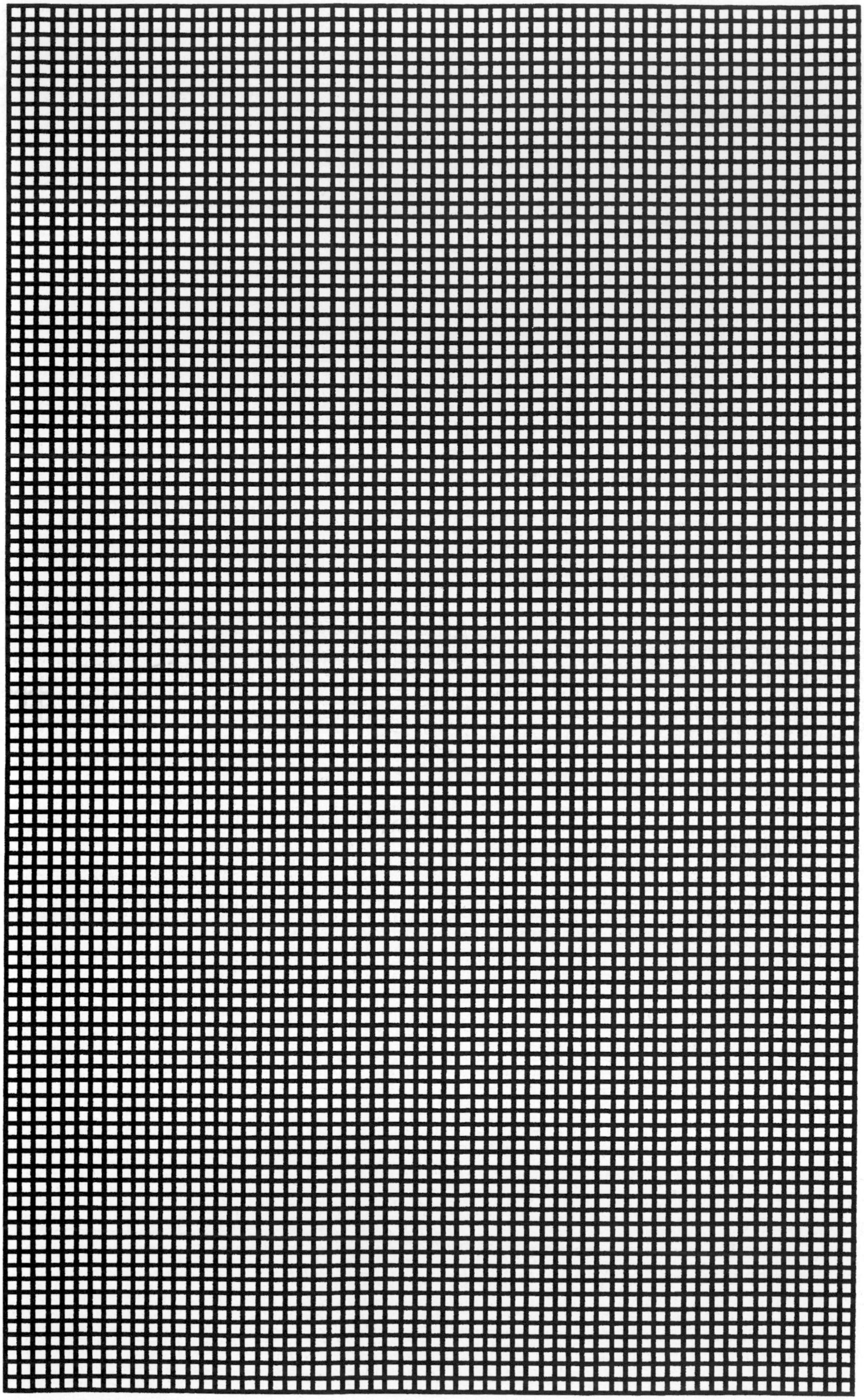

Activity 4.03

2 B or KNOT 2 B

2B or KNOT 2B is a super activity for building group consensus. It is a simple activity that builds useful skills. 2B or KNOT 2B encourages group members to participate and it is an excellent introduction to problem solving techniques. It is also an activity for group problem solving and decision making that requires little or no physical activity, making it available for populations with limited mobility and high mobility alike.

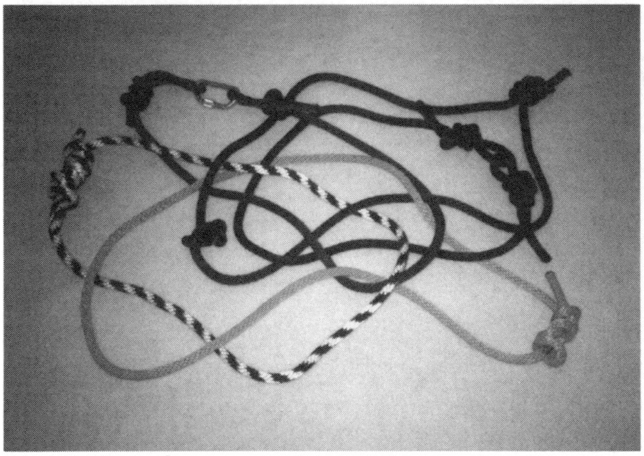

Equipment

A series of 4 independent rope rings held together by a fifth rope ring. Tubular webbing, climbing ropes, shoe laces and even belts can also be used in place of ropes.

The Challenge

For the group to decide as a whole, which rope loop is holding together all the other rope loops, without touching any of the ropes.

Typical Presentation, Storyline or Metaphor

One of the skills most admired by the king and queen of your kingdom, is the unity of the people that live here. Your leadership informs you that there is a magical treasure to be found in the enchanted woods to the north. The king and queen are going to select the finest team they can to retrieve this treasure, by proposing a series of puzzles, and selecting the team or group that shows the most cooperation and unification. The rope puzzles before you are the challenge. See if you can decide as a group which rope is holding together the other four.

Your rescue team has been called for a mountain climbing rescue. The equipment has been flown in to assist your efforts, but your climbing ropes have been badly knotted. Since time is limited, you must determine, as a group, which single knot to untie, so that all the remaining ropes are unconnected.

Variations

One variation in 2B or KNOT 2B is the number of ropes that can be included in the puzzle. Three ropes are generally not enough. Five ropes seem about right. Seven or eight ropes can be very challenging.

The length of the ropes used for 2B or KNOT 2B is typically somewhere between 7 and 15 feet (2.1 and 4.6 meters). If you choose to use 165 foot (50 meter) climbing ropes, you can cover a much larger area, and include more twists and turns in the rope. This size may be appropriate if you happen to have more than 15 people in a single group.

Color or pattern changes in the ropes can also provide additional challenges to the activity. The Teamplay version of 2B or KNOT 2B uses four varieties of increasing difficulty. The first puzzle has five ropes that are different solid colors (blue, red, green, etc.) The second version has five ropes with different striped colors (blue and white, red and white, etc.) The third version has five ropes that are all the same solid color (blue). And the final version has five ropes that are all the same striped color (red and white).

If you happen to tie more than one knot in any single rope loop, you can add some difficulty to the challenge, and probably confuse the group a bit in the process. Another challenge would be to include a rope without knots, by splicing the rope to form a single, seamless rope loop. Both of these variations are meant to unfocus or distract the group from their true mission, and as a result, provide excellent opportunities for discussion during debriefing.

For improved visability, the collection of 2B or KNOT 2B ropes could be mounted to a wall or placed on a large table. Another adaptation would be to present this activity in dim light, so that most group members will experience some level of being visually impaired. Bright colored ropes are useful in this scenario, so that when light is provided, the difference will be significant.

Important Points

Although many challenge and adventure initiatives require some physical attributes, such as strength, balance, flexibility or mobility, here is an activity that requires no physical exertion and yet successfully helps a group understand their own problem solving and decision making skills. The ropes used in this activity can be thought of as metaphors for difficult tasks, computer networks, the information superhighway, the members of a group or team or even the individual tasks of a much larger project.

One of the first skills that 2B or KNOT 2B provides, is the opportunity for the group to reach a consensus as a whole. It is important early in a challenge and adventure program for participants to realize that their comments and opinions are valued. Secondly, 2B or KNOT 2B provides a very visual method of identifying problem solving techinques to the group. If you happen to have five ropes and ten partipants, you can ask groups of 2 to analyze a single rope. Their objective is not to determine which rope is the right one, only whether or not the one rope they are reviewing is the correct rope. This demonstrates that a large problem can be broken into a series of smaller, more manageable pieces.

Two other problem solving techiques go hand in hand. First the group can decide as a whole which rope is the right one, or they can attempt to identify any ropes that are NOT the correct rope. This process of solving a problem by elimination be a useful point to discuss during the debriefing stage of this activity.

Another variation is to have teams working on individual ropes, and then to have various teams check each other's work, before reporting back their findings. This type of support encourages the group to watch out for each other.

Finally, by using a series of increasingly complex ropes (varying the color, adding more ropes), the group learns how to use a simple skill learned early in the process, for attacking even more difficult problems. If you want to reinforce to the group that this process has actually occurred, try repeating the original solid colors version after the most difficult version with all ropes of the same striped color. Typically the group has acquired an advanced technique, and some consensus "speed" in the process.

It can be beneficial to use a visual prop to explain how the one rope is holding the other four together in the 2B or KNOT 2B puzzle. A key chain ring with 4 additional rings makes a good model. It is best to place the 2B or KNOT 2B puzzle on the ground before the group arrives. This insures that the puzzle is visible, and that group members will not be able to observe which rope is the correct rope during the construction of the activity.

Discussion and Debriefing Topics

Did you find this activity easy or more difficult than you initially thought? Were you able to judge for yourself which rope was holding the others together? Were you willing to bet your next paycheck that you were right? Were you able to accomplish this task quickly? Did you experience any frustration as other group members struggled to identify the correct rope for themselves? Which series of ropes were the hardest to solve?

Sequence

The opportunity to demonstrate that group consensus and communication between group members is valued and encouraged should happen early in the challenge experience. This activity is also a good activity for beginning the introduction to the problem solving techniques.

Activities Using Similar Skills and Follow-on Activities

Not Knots is also an activity that utilizes ropes to encourage communication, problem solving and group consensus building. Bull Ring is a slightly higher level activity which fits well after 2B or KNOT 2B.

Notes

Activity 4.04

63 / 64 / 65

Here is a group puzzle that has been stumping folks for more than 80 years. If you like this sort of puzzle, you might want to try reading the *Scientific American* article by A. K. Dewdney on page 116 of the April 1989 issue. You too can be an expert with the Banach-Tarski paradox.

Equipment

Four puzzle pieces cut from a checkerboard or grid pattern. Each square on the board or grid should be at least one inch (25.4 mm) long.

The Challenge

When cut apart, the puzzle pieces form a square that measures 8 squares by 8 squares, for a total of 64 squares. In the first variation, these same four puzzle pieces can be placed in a rectangle that measures 5 squares by 13 squares, for a total of 65 squares. In the second variation, these same four puzzle pieces can be placed in the shape shown below that consists of two rectangles 5 squares by 6 squares (for a total of 60 squares) and a 3 square "bridge", bringing the total area of this configuration to 63 squares. What is the true number of squares in the puzzle?

Typical Presentation, Storyline or Metaphor

An otherwise intelligent king and queen are visited one day by a traveler who proposes that he can take any of the gold plates in the royal vault (which just so happen to be in square plates, 8 units by 8 units), cut them three times, and make even more gold! The king and queen are interested, but still wary of the idea, so they allow the traveler one plate of gold to try. After making the three necessary cuts, the traveler reassembles the gold plates in the rectangular pattern shown below, and claims that there is now more gold. An advisor to the king and queen stops by at just this time, and assembles the four pieces of the plate into the third pattern shown below—and promptly throws the traveler into the dungeon. What was the true area of the gold plates? Why?

Variations

Instead of presenting the puzzle in the above format, you could simply provide the group with the four puzzle pieces and ask them to determine the area that these pieces will cover. An alternative story for this version is that you installing floor tiles in a building that has three different areas, two rooms and a hallway. Your assistant claims that he can complete each of the three spaces with exactly the same amount of tile, even though each space has a different area. Can he really do it?

Important Points

The objective of this activity is not only to solve a puzzle, but for the group as a whole to collectively agree on a solution. Building group consensus is essential for many of the activities in this book, and this activity encourages the active involvement and agreement of the group.

In the case of the king and queen above, things which seem to good to be true, generally are! There is only one true area for these four puzzle pieces. Since the four pieces were originally cut from the 8 by 8 square, the true area for this puzzle is 64.

In order to actively involve the entire group, it may be necessary to have a paper version of this puzzle for everyone to work with. Then use a larger version for the final presentation by the group.

Discussion and Debriefing Topics

How easy was it for your group to come to an agreement on what the true area of the puzzle was? Would it have made any difference if the puzzle were made of gold, or paper, or aluminum, or glass, or wood? Is it possible to cut something apart and end up with more?

Sequence

This problem is a good warm-up activity for building group consensus before trying other activities that will require the agreement of the entire group.

Activities Using Similar Skills and Follow-on Activities

Nearly all of the activities in this book encourage group participation and the agreement of the entire group. 2B or KNOT 2B utilizes some of these same skills.

Notes

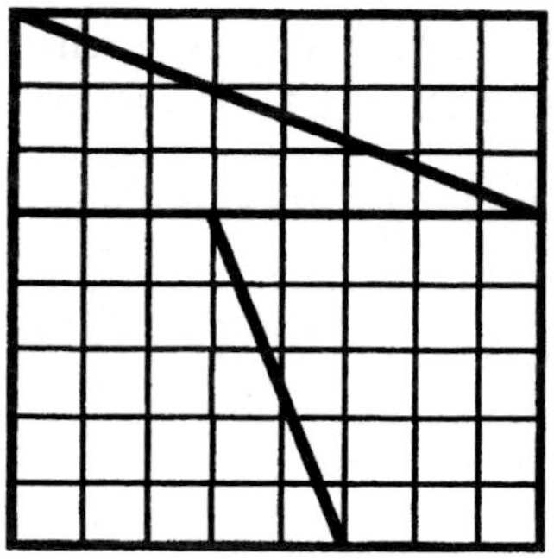

64 Squares

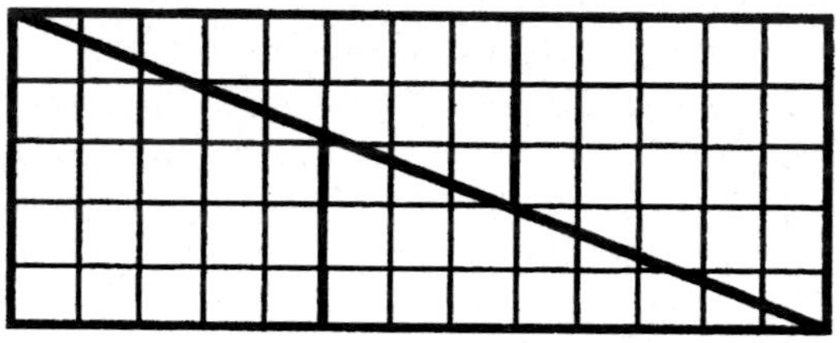

65 Squares

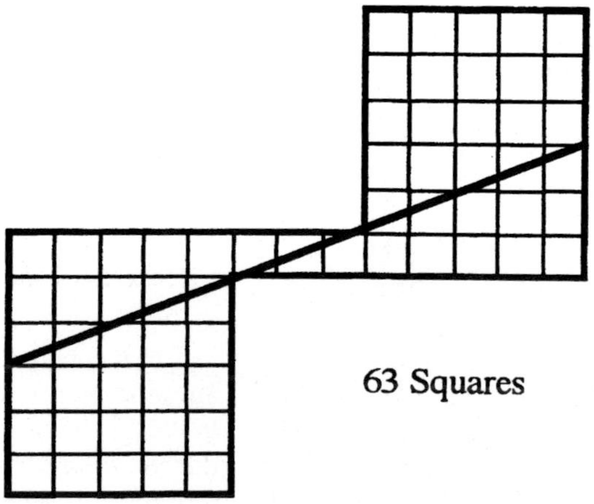

63 Squares

Activity 4.05

A Balanced Life

Here is an activity that simply screams a variety of metaphors surrounding the issue of balance. This can be a personal balance, or the balance within a group, or a balance of priorities, or a balanced diet, or . . . . . .

Equipment

The directions given in Chapter 5 for the construction of this activity are not flexible! You'll need two rough cut oak planks that are 2 inches (51mm) thick, 12 inches (305 mm) wide and 10 to 12 feet (3.0 to 3.7 meters) long, joined together at the ends with carriage bolts. You will also need a fulcrum constructed of a hardwood block, 12 inches (305 mm) square and 8 inches (203 mm) tall. The equipment for A Balanced Life looks roughly like a children's playground teeter-totter, except that a block of wood has replaced the pivot at the center. The balance on this board is only stable if exactly equal weights are placed on both sides of the central block.

This activity should be conducted on a smooth, horizontal surface. This equipment can support the weight of 10 average sized adults.

The Challenge

For the entire group to mount the balance, one at a time, without tipping the balance, or causing the planks to ever touch the ground. The second part of this challenge is for participants to dismount the balance, again without tipping the planks, or causing the planks to touch the ground.

Typical Presentation, Storyline or Metaphor

Well, it rained, and rained, and rained, and now your office is flooding. You've managed to get the computers and other essential office equipment to higher ground, but now your brand new shoes are getting soaked. Phil, the Vice-President in charge of risk management, brings in a long plank and a single block to set the plank on (the other block was let go during a recent down-sizing event that most of the group would rather not discuss right now). Can your group find a way to stay dry by keeping the plank from tipping on the block?

Variations

One variation that greatly increases the anxiety of the group is to place an egg beneath each end of the plank. Any downward movement would be likely to crush the egg. If however one egg is broken, the group may decide to leave that end down, and complete the activity with the board tilted, to protect the remaining egg.

Important Points

It is possible for the ends of the planks to touch the ground, forming a pinch point. Be cautious when spotting in this region not to place your foot below the planks at any time.

Participants must board the planks at the center fulcrum position. Even if the planks tip, this central region will not move appreciably.

Discussion and Debriefing Topics

Was the group able to create a plan and then carry this plan out for the entire activity, or were modifications made to the plan along the way? Was there a definite order in which the participants boarded the planks? Was the loading or unloading of the planks more stable? Was the balance easier to achieve with many participants on the planks, or only a few?

Sequence

This activity is likely to involve contact between participants. It should ideally come after some spotting practice, and after some introductory proximity activities, such as All Aboard or Magic Carpet.

Activities Using Similar Skills and Follow-on Activities

The balance and proximity found in A Balance Life are also useful in Magic Carpet and All Aboard.

Notes

Activity 4.06

A Collection of Knots

There are a variety of activities for which a single piece of rope is an essential prop. While the activity Tree of Knots teaches some basic knot tying skills, only a portion of the total group is needed to complete the activity. A Collection of Knots extends the skills learned in Tree of Knots, and involves everyone in the group.

Equipment

A single length of rope, ⅜ inch (9mm) in diameter or greater, at least 30 feet (9 meters) long for a group of 6–12 participants.

The Challenge

Challenge I—After tying a series of different styles of knots in a long length of rope, participants are asked to pick up the rope, and then to untie each of the various knots without letting go of the rope.

Challenge II—Participants are asked to pick up a long rope and without letting go of the rope, to tie a knot between each of the group members.

Typical Presentation, Storyline or Metaphor

While surveying a new section of farmland, your team is asked to utilize a historically significant technique known as "chaining" to determine the amount of land in the tract. Before measuring the land however, it is necessary to untangle the "chain" so that an accurate determination can be made.

Variations

Allowing participants to use one hand for working the rope while the other hand stays in one position on the rope is usually helpful for both challenges. If you happen to use the phrase, "your right hand must stay in whatever location it touches the rope," creates an opportunity for some folks that immediately realize that never touching the rope with their right hand allows them complete freedom during the activity. This is obviously a case of creative cheating at its best.

Important Points

Make sure that participants do not attempt to tighten a knot that still has a person inside of it!

Discussion and Debriefing Topics

Was this activity easier or more difficult than you imagined? What was the most challenging about this activity? Even though the entire group was connected to the challenge, how many participants were actually involved with any particular knot?

Sequence

This activity works well following a session in basic knot tying techniques.

Activities Using Similar Skills and Follow-on Activities

Tree of Knots and Pot of Gold require some basic knot tying capabilities. Hoopla and Worm Hole require similar body movements.

Notes

Activity 4.07

A Work of Art

Here is a visual version of the children's game Telephone, using challenge and adventure props.

Equipment

Two sets of nearly identical equipment consisting of tennis balls, short segments of colorful rope, webbing, climbing hardware, marble tubes, and other available challenge equipment.

The Challenge

At both ends of a long line of people, two artists stand poised, ready to begin their work. One artist arranges the available equipment in any style they choose. An observer then verbally describes what they see the artist doing, and passes this information along the line to the other group members. Eventually the description reaches the other artist at the far end of the line, and they begin to construct a copy of the original artwork using the pieces in front of them.

Typical Presentation, Storyline or Metaphor

The use of effective metaphors, scenarios and stories can often enhance the experience of the participants during the activity. This paragraph presents various stories which can be edited or altered to suit the needs of your participants.

Variations

One challenging variation is to only allow communication to pass down the line, from the original artist towards the copying artist. This can be frustrating especially for group members in line, because they cannot express any need for more information from the participants in front of them.

A slightly more devious variation is to use two sets of equipment that are only somewhat identical. Perhaps all the objects are the same, but the color varies. Or perhaps both artists have a rope, but it is a different size.

A third variation that always causes frustration for the communication transfer line participants, is to limit their communication to verbal techniques only. No hand or arm motions and no body language. This variation can be taken a step further by blindfolding every other participant along the communication transfer line.

Important Points

The distance between the two artists should be at least 35 yards (32 meters), and group members should be standing at least 3 yards (about 1 meter) apart. Encourage the original artist to use simple shapes and patterns initially, so that the group can experience some level of success, before other artists create unusually difficult patterns. You may want to encourage the group to carefully choose a group member with excellent verbal skills as the first person to view the artists work.

Group members standing in the communication transfer line, should only give instructions based on what they have heard, not based on what they can see of the artist's creation at either end of the line.

At the completion of the activity, have the group members from the communication transfer line run a final quality check to ensure that the copy is as close as possible to the original. Then have them first view the original, and then the copy.

Discussion and Debriefing Topics

Were you able to effectively communicate the original artists intent? Does the copy look like the original? Were you able to visualize what was being communicated to you? Were you able to express what you saw using only verbal techniques? Did the person you were talking to give you positive feedback that they understood what you were telling them? How much of our communication is strictly verbal? What other techniques do people use to communicate?

Sequence

A Work of Art is a challenge activity with a very strong emphasis on communication. Using this activity early in the adventure program illustrates that not all participants communicate in the same way. A valuable point to make before starting a program where problem solving and communication issues are sure to surface.

Activities Using Similar Skills and Follow-on Activities

Other activities which have a strong communication emphasis include 2B or KNOT 2B and Target Specifications.

Notes

Activity 4.08

All Aboard

While many of the activities in this book are hopefully new to the reader, this one (including the name) is adapted from Karl Rohnke's classic text, Silver Bullets. It is simply a great activity, and while earlier versions are also possible, such as cramming into telephone booths and Volkswagons, and under tiny umbrellas during rainstorms, not to mention the 'Team on a T-shirt' version, the All Aboard version remains our favorite.

Equipment

In Chapter 5, directions are given for creating a series of stacking All Aboard platforms. As an alternative, this activity can also be performed with various size carpet squares, plywood panels, non-skid throw rugs or tarps. There is also another version of this activity in this chapter entitled Shark Attack which uses a boat shaped plywood panel to keep the participants from becomming shark bait.

The Challenge

For all group members to stand aboard the platform long enough to sing one verse of Row, Row, Row Your Boat, without touching the surrounding ground. Begin with the largest platform and repeat the activity with increasingly smaller platforms.

Typical Presentation, Storyline or Metaphor

Global warming has melted the polar ice caps and the surviving members of your group must take residence on an island which continues to shrink as the water level rises.

You are on a ship at sea that has suddenly begun to sink. The only safe place is the crow's nest. As participants continue to mount part of the crow's nest breaks off, leaving smaller and smaller available space for the members of your crew.

Variations

If the stacking variety of All Aboard platforms are not available, try using non-skid carpet squares, rugs, or various plywood shapes including circles, ovals, and squares.

Try passing a ball, balloon or penny around the group after they have mounted the platform. You can also have participants try to change places on the larger platforms.

Important Points

As a facilitator and spotter, instruct participants that only their feet may touch the All Aboard platform. Participants may stand on their own foot, but not on the feet of other participants. Do not lock elbows with other participants. All participants must be touching the platform with at least one foot.

Participants will typically find some method of connecting arms across the platform and standing up together.

Discussion and Debriefing Topics

What techniques worked well? Which techniques did not work? What if we had twice as many people? What is the smallest size island we could fit on? Did you feel that other members of the group listened to your ideas? What if part of the group had been blindfolded? Could you do this activity without talking? What if there was no gravity? What if it was very windy?

Sequence

All Aboard is clearly a proximity activity—that is, it brings participants very closely together. Use this activity with other proximity activities, such as Magic Carpet.

Activities Using Similar Skills and Follow-on Activities

Other proximity activities include: Magic Carpet, Danger Zone, and Cover Up.

Notes

Activity 4.09

Alphabet Soup

Here is a parlor activity that has recently been reincarnated for challenge and adventure programming under such titles as Speed Spelling, Calculator and most recently Keypunch. Although the number of keys, shape of the playing area, and end challenge are different for all these activities, the basic concept is similar. This version is called Alphabet Soup, and uses alphabetical keys. Project Adventure sells some very nice equipment for a somewhat similar numerical version of this activity under the title of Keypunch.

Equipment

26 paper plates or "keys" on which to write each letter of the alphabet. A long rope to outline a boundary around the 26 keys.

The Challenge

To create a method so that each of the letters of the alphabet are contacted by a member of the group, in order, with only one participant inside the circle at a time. This activity is typically timed.

Typical Presentation, Storyline or Metaphor

On your first day of the job at the soup factory, your work group has been asked to perform a quality check on the alphabet soup line. There are many bowls of soup to check, so you'll need to work fast. Your group needs to determine if all of the letters are present as quickly as possible. For quality control reasons, you'll need to actually contact each letter in some way.

Variations

One of the first variations that is typically encountered by the group, is to decide who touches which letter. It may be useful to have a single person touch all letters. Another variation would allow everyone to touch those letters closest to them

Rather than touching all the letters in order, try including additional letters and vowels, and have the group spell out a few seven letter words by touching the letters in order to complete the activity. Another variation would be to send the group to the boundary circle to collect the letters they need to complete a sentence, word or phrase. You might try creating a phrase that has significance to the group.

It can be startling to the group if several letters are omitted entirely, creating gaps in the sequence. This is a great point to process later.

This is a quick activity which can be used several times. Try telling the group that you are going to give them 5 chances to achieve the best time they can. For some groups, this will mean taking several minutes the first time, sort of a practice round, just to get the feel of the activity.

How about using keys with pictures of hands forming sign language letter, words or phrases. Another version would be to use Morse Code sequences instead of the more common letters or numbers. Yet another version would be to use a foreign alphabet—how's this for an opportunity in diversity and cultural education?

For elementary students, how about a version of this activity where each of the disks has the face of a clock, with various times illustrated. Students must touch the disks in the correct order according to the times displayed. As a history lesson, the disks can be labeled with the names of important historical events, and the students asked to touch each of the disks in the correct chronological order.

Rather than playing for speed, how about a slow motion version where each plate shows a scene from a story, and the person touching that key has the opportunity to invent that portion of the story.

For corporate settings, how about keys that show a sequence in the manufacturing operation of the business, or in the marketing/distribution channel. Perhaps the keys can illustrate all the steps in correctly filling a purchasing requisition. For medical groups, or EMT's, WFR's, etc., how about keys that depict the correct sequence in providing care for an injured patient.

If you happen to like the numerical version of this activity, consider using a large tarp or plastic sheet with a variety of shoeprints or footprints scattered about. Number the footprints upwards from 1. You can call this version "The Dance Studio." Yet another version using numbers would be to paint a series of lines dissecting the tarp, and number each of the spaces. This could be the "Painting by Numbers" version.

Important Points

This is an activity where establishing a time goal can be useful. The problem is very simple. The directions for accomplishing the task are simple too. The execution of the plan however, can be filled with human errors.

Initially, tell the group about the activity without letting them see the letters and boundary rope. Ask them to set a time goal for the group. Begin timing when the first person leaves the planning area, and stop when the last person has returned. It can be useful to place a straight rope line to act as a starting line, in the planning area.

Some creative groups may establish a goal of several minutes, in which case they can leisurely complete the task, and then have the last person wait to cross the finish line at precisely the correct time. This group would gather big points in this example for accuracy, but not for hustle.

Discussion and Debriefing Topics

Was your initial goal accurate? Were your successive goals more accurate? What changed? Did familiarity with the activity make your group a better judge of the time required to complete the activity? Did you try different techniques? How different was your first time and your best time?

Sequence

Alphabet Soup is a great beginning activity for establishing goals within a group. It also provides some problem solving opportunities, and some frustration in trying to plan the solution of a problem they have not personally experienced on the first round. Use this activity early in the program to establish goals within the group.

Activities Using Similar Skills and Follow-on Activities

The goal setting skills used in Alphabet Soup can be used in such activities as Bull Ring Golf, Surfing the Web, and Wing It.

Notes

Activity 4.10

Alphabetically

Some activities are so simple they are hard. This is one such activity. You can find a similar activity using numbers in Karl Rohnke's book *Silver Bullets*.

Equipment

Nothing, although it does help to have a working knowledge of the local alphabet. Blindfolds are an optional prop.

The Challenge

Begin with group members sitting or standing in random positions, and with eyes closed. The challenge is to have a single participant say the first letter of the alphabet (A if you happen to be saying the English alphabet), and to have other participants say the remaining letters in order, without ever having two participants saying the same letter at the same time.

Typical Presentation, Storyline or Metaphor

Some activities are so simple that they require no story at all. You are on your own for this activity.

Variations

Any sequence can be used for this activity (numbers, days of the week, months of the year, holidays throughout the year, ingredients in a recipe, etc.) It can be interesting to see if performing this activity with eyes open increases the success rate.

Important Points

Standing in any random positions is a good way to begin this activity. If the group happens to be in any organized line or circle, some solutions will immediately pop up.

Discussion and Debriefing Topics

Did your group try to use any non-verbal clues to determine the order within the group? What makes this activity so difficult? Once you had created a pattern, was the rest of the activity easy to complete?

Sequence

This is a brief activity that can be used at nearly any time during the day's events.

Activities Using Similar Skills and Follow-on Activities

This activity encourages eye contact, non-verbal communication and a sense of what the other group members are thinking. Another activity that requires these same skills is Stump Jumping.

Notes

Activity 4.11

Bag It

This activity is similar to a party game we played as children. Who knew back then that it would grow into a full fledged challenge activity?

Equipment

A drawstring stuff sack, filled with about six or eight small objects. The objects inside the bag should be unique, and have no sharp edges or corners.

The Challenge

To pass the bag once around the group without talking, while group members feel (but not look) inside the bag and attempt to guess what it contains.

Typical Presentation, Storyline or Metaphor

During the recovery of treasure from a sunken vessel, a variety of items have been gathered and stored in a special storage vessel. Many of these artifacts will degrade in sunlight. Your group has been selected to inspect the contents of the vessel (the stuff sack) and to determine the items it contains, without exposing these objects to sunlight.

Variations

There are a fair number of challenge related props such as z-balls, carabiners, figure 8 descenders, building blocks, ping pong balls, a rope with a square knot tied in it, half a tennis ball, etc. that will be familiar to the group. Consider using some not-so-familiar objects, such as turn of the century kitchen equipment (eliminate any items with sharp edges), an 8-track tape, a pet rock, a child's toy, etc. If you want to use a teachable moment, try filling the bag with small pieces of rope tied into various knots, and then asking the group to decide which knots are present.

If your space and time permits, have two bags ready. For the first bag, do not allow the group to talk as the bag is passed just once around the group. Then have the group collectively decide what is in the bag. If you really want to draw out the group process, have the group try to decide what color each object is.

For the second bag, with different objects from the first, allow the group to openly discuss the contents of the bag as it is passed from person to person. As an additional challenge, ask the group to rank the objects from most expensive to least expensive, or from hardest to softest.

Important Points

Each of the objects in the bag must be smooth, soft and free of any sharp edges, points, or potential for pinching the probing fingers of each investigator. Accuracy and not speed is important for this activity.

Discussion and Debriefing Topics

Which items were the most familiar? Were there any unusual items in the bag? Did the facial expressions of others in the group alert you to the presence of anything unusual in the bag? Which method was more difficult, the first round where talking was inhibited, or the second round where conversation was encouraged? Why?

Sequence

This is a fairly low energy activity, and should be used as a cool down activity after a high energy event, or when the group just needs to slow down a bit.

Activities Using Similar Skills and Follow-on Activities

Other activities which modify our senses includes Mine-Mine-Mine, and the adapted version of Community Juggling where participants wear large cotton gloves.

Notes

Activity 4.12

Blackout

Here is another activity that uses the same props as Magic Carpet and Danger Zone.

Equipment

The plastic sheets or tarps from Magic Carpet or the sheets or ropes from Danger Zone. A Lycra Tube will also work in a pinch.

The Challenge

For the group to completely cover up the Magic Carpet using only their bodies.

Typical Presentation, Storyline or Metaphor

During a archeological expedition your group discovers a rare painting of an advanced computer architecture on the floor of a prehistoric cave. (Hey, if you are going to make up a story, might as well make it a whopper!) Anyway, the painting turns out to be extremely light sensitive, so in the interest of preserving this unusual work, your team needs to cover up the painting immediately, before any additional deterioration occurs. You look around and discover that all that remains in the cave to cover up the painting are the group members themselves. Being careful not to disturb or scratch the surface of the painting your group begins to place themselves in a comfortable, but effective light blocking pattern over the painting.

Variations

Changing the shape of the Magic Carpet will require the group to use various configurations to successfully cover the changing surface areas of the carpet. You can also try circles, triangles, letters and other significant shapes or symbols.

After shadowing the carpet, have the group then attempt to move the carpet, and the shadow too!

A completely different variation of this activity that requires almost no props at all is to have the group completely block out all the light between a well lit room and a closet or adjoining room with no windows, by blocking all the light coming through the entrance doorway. You may want to give the group a few pieces of foam to use as light insulation.

Important Points

It takes a fair amount of contact to keep holes from opening up between participants. Encourage participants to gently place themselves, so as not to disturb the painting and so that they do not pulverize the other members of the group. Be prepared for participants to utilize any available clothing to assist them in their shadow casting efforts.

With activities such as this one, it is typically best to let a member of the group determine if the team has met the desired goal, rather than putting the facilitator in the role of judge and jury. Participants know when they have done a good job, and are generally capable of knowing for themselves when they have successfully completed the task.

Discussion and Debriefing Topics

Was this activity easier or more difficult than you imagined? Were you able to plan your approach completely, or did you need to make adjustments after the activity was begun? How much of a factor is the total size of the painting?

Sequence

This and other types of proximity activities (activities where participants are brought physically very close together) require some preliminary lead-in activities so that group members can become acquainted with each other, before their personal space is invaded.

Activities Using Similar Skills and Follow-on Activities

Other types of proximity activities include Knots, First Contact, Danger Zone, All Aboard, and Magic Carpet.

Activity 4.13

Boardwalking

Boardwalking is certainly one of the most clever ideas ever invented. Getting an entire group to walk in a synchronized manner is not an easy task.

Equipment

Eight and ten foot long boards are not the easiest thing to carry around in your car if you happen to be conducting a portable program, so we recommend the jointed system of boardwalkers shown here and described in Chapter 5. They require a bit more work to create, but can be used for a variety of other activities. The directions for constructing simplified non-jointed boardwalkers are also given in Chapter 5.

Typical Presentation, Storyline or Metaphor

While visiting the boardwalk at the beach on one of the hottest days of the year, your group has encountered an incredibly hot patch of sand on the way back to the ocean. Your entire team ends up cooling their heels on some rather unusual looking boards, that just might be able to transport you to the cool water, just 20 yards (or meters) away. But you'll have to maneuver these boards around the various sunbathers, sandcastles and other beach debris that you encounter along the way.

A series of new high speed team sleds are being designed for the next winter athletic games. Your team has been chosen to test drive the new concept.

The Challenge

For the group to create a method for successfully moving the boardwalkers through a planned space. This can be a short distance to retrieve an object, or simply to coordinate the synchronized movement of the group through a winding path.

Variations

One of the most unique variations for this activity is to begin by placing each participant on some of the wooden platforms used for All Aboard and River Crossing. With participants scattered in this manner, place one complete line of the boardwalkers near at least one of the platforms, and the other line near a close but different set of platforms. The challenge of the group is now to find a way to pull the boardwalkers together, and then to collect all of the various participants scattered about on the different wooden platforms. A storyline for this version might be that your intergalactic taxi has been called to collect the inhabitants from a variety of different planets for the first ever intergalactic summit meeting.

A reverse version of this variation would be to begin the activity with all participants on the boardwalker, and then to drop off "passengers" at various places, like a school bus returning students to their homes.

Another variation involves providing the group with individual boardwalkers and a supply of quick links, and having them create the most efficient configuration they can to transport the entire group. Be sure to mention that a safety inspection of the "vehicle" will be required before the journey can begin. This variation adds some construction activity to the event, and an additional level of problem solving as the group attempts to define the best way to join the boardwalkers together.

The path that the group takes can add many elements of challenge to this activity. Generally going around some objects is better than going over them, although slight inclines can be interesting. Having the group turn a corner, or even backing up, provides some additional challenges.

Participants often try to call out "left-right" or "one-two" to indicate which one of the boardwalkers they wish to move. As a facilitator, you can limit their choices, or perhaps more appropriately, encourage their creativity by asking them to use phrases other than "one-two" or "left-right."

If a member of the group happens to accidently touch the ground during the movement of the boardwalkers, have them turn around so that they are now facing backwards. Be sure that their is adequate spotting for this variation by both the facilitator and other group members in the vicinity of this person. If the group has been keeping a cadence or using words to indicate which boardwalker they are about to move, the position of this inverted participant will now be the opposite of the rest of the group. A point for debriefing at a later time.

If any of the boardwalking ropes happen to touch the ground during the activity, you can request that these ropes not be used for the remainder of the activity. This will typically encourage a greater level of contact between group members in this region of the boardwalkers.

If you happen to have two sets of boardwalkers, try having the two groups pass each other with the right side boardwalkers of the first group going between the legs of the second group. Very challenging.

Still another activity involves using two boardwalkers with a rope between them to travel and retrieve a bucket filled with water, or some other easily hooked object.

Finally, you can also begin this activity with participants facing in different directions.

Important Points

Boardwalking is an excellent activity for discussing the occurence of "breakdown." Breakdown is the process by which a working technique suddenly falls apart. Establishing a method for successfully keeping in step is one thing. Keeping this technique going is quite another. Typically breakdown occurs because the technique or method does not allow for any small variations from the plan. A slight overstep or an error in timing can make the difference between moving the group forward, and going nowhere.

Discussion and Debriefing Topics

How did your group decide on the technique they were going to use? Was this technique useful for keeping the group in step with each other? Did your group experience breakdown? What happened then? Which was easier, going straight, turning, or backing up? Did your group find it harder to turn to the left or the right? Did your group's technique require a change when you recovered the object? Did your group begin and end with the same technique? Are there any other techniques for using the boardwalkers.

Sequence

As a challenge and adventure activity, Boardwalking is one of the few activities that necessitates the exact timing of the groups effort for success. Community Juggling also requires this level of synchronization.

Activities Using Similar Skills and Follow-on Activities

You can use the same portable equipment for Life Raft, although you may not want to facilitate both activities during the same event because of the similarity between these two activities. Community Juggling is an appropriate activity to come either before or after Boardwalking.

Activity 4.14

Bull Ring

Bull Ring has to be one of the simplest portable challenge activities ever invented. It also has many variations that allows the same equipment to be used for a variety of activities.

Equipment

The Bull Ring is made from a 1½ inch (40 mm) diameter metal ring, available at most hardware stores, and several pieces of string or twine. You'll also need a tennis or golf ball.

The Challenge

The challenge is to carry a small ball using a metal ring and twine Bull Ring through a series of obstacles and place the ball into a goal, such as a tin can, plastic bucket or onto a segment of PVC tubing.

Typical Presentation, Storyline or Metaphor

The newest Mars probe returns to Earth with several new rocks from our closest neighboring planet. The re-entry on Earth however, was a little bumpier than Mars, and a few of the precious stones end up bouncing around the salt flats of the western United States. Your team has been assembled to retrieve these stones, using a new prototype Bull Ring Retrieval System—Mark 1. First you must elevate the stone, and then carry this to the awaiting containment cylinder.

Variations

This activity can be made more difficult by transporting the ball around objects such as trees, tables, chairs and fences. Gentle slopes, stairways and narrow doorways also provide additional challenges. Heavier and larger balls are more difficult to transport and harder to keep on the metal ring. Smaller balls such as golf balls fit further into the metal ring and are easier to transport. Ping-Pong balls can also be used, but are greatly affected by wind. You can accommodate more participants, and include the additional element of trust building by blindfolding the participant holding the string and assigning a sighted person to assist them while moving. If you have less participants than strings, just allow participants to hold more than one string. You can increase the difficulty of the goal by placing the container at an angle, or attaching the container at a higher elevation (such as on a fence, doorknob or wall hook). You can substitute a PVC plastic tube (1 inch in diameter, 15 inches long, pressed into the ground) instead of a container, as the final goal. For this goal, the ring needs to be carefully dropped over the tube so that the ball rests on the tube. For

additional difficulty, try placing the goal under a table or near a wall. The most impossible location for placing the goal is in the corner of a room. Try this sometime, and ask the group to brainstorm ideas for reaching the goal.

Additional Bull Ring variations include using a rubber band instead of the metal ring. Using various lengths of string attached to the Bull Ring may also allow the group to successfully navigate some more interesting and challenging obstacles. Participants should hold only the very ends of each string.

If your group has any participants in manual wheelchairs, you can use a short segment of shock (bungie) cord to tie the Bull Ring string onto a railing of the wheelchair. This will leave both of this participant's hands free to maneuver the chair.

A final variation is to replace the string or twine with dental floss. Because the floss is easily broken, participants must not be overly aggressive or they will physically eliminate themselves from the activity.

Important Points

Do not allow participants to tie the string around their fingers or wrists, because a sudden movement may cause rope rash rather quickly. Make sure to choose an appropriate ball for the location. Using heavy billiard balls or metal ball bearings on a gymnasium floor not only produces a loud thump if the ball is dropped, it also produces a rather large dent! It can make for an interesting discussion to ask the group what minimum number of strings are required to keep the ball from falling off the Bull Ring.

Discussion and Debriefing Topics

Did your group have a single leader, or was everyone part of the leadership? What techniques did you use to overcome the obstacles? What if the tennis ball was replaced with a bowling ball? If you were blindfolded, did you trust the person assisting you?

Sequence

Bull Ring utilizes physical movement and cooperation. It also takes a little coordination to keep the ball on the ring. This is a great activity for early in the challenge program.

Activities Using Similar Skills and Follow-on Activities

Bull Ring II, Bull Ring III, Bull Ring Golf, Stretch It, and Pot of Gold utilize similar formations and skills.

Notes

Activity 4.15

Bull Ring II—Table Tops

This first variation of Bull Ring replaces the transportation of a ball with the acquiring of various objects while participants are in a seated position. This version of Bull Ring was originally used for a group with limited lower body movement, but plenty of upper body mobility.

Equipment

The Bull Ring is made from a 1½ inch (40 mm) diameter metal ring, available at most hardware stores, and one piece of string for each participant. You'll also need a variety of magnets, cones, marbles and other small objects to move around on the surface of a large table at the center of the group. Chairs are needed for all participants.

The Challenge

The challenge is to capture various objects on the table, and move them to a collection place, using only the Bull Ring. Begin this activity with participants holding the midpoint of each string. This will allow everyone to pull or release a little string, without losing their connection with the rest of the group.

Typical Presentation, Storyline or Metaphor

One of the rarest fishing devices ever invented is the Bull Ring Fish Acquisition System—Mark 2. This unique device requires the assistance of several fisherman at one time, and always brings back the limit. As you gaze out over the table sea today, you can see a vast variety of the wonderful things there to catch. Using the Bull Ring, your group tries to acquire as many fish (including the elusive magnetic fish), treasures, and other valuable objects as possible. These object can then be collected at the nearby bait shop.

Variations

A variety of objects present difference challenges for the group. Marbles are best contained by the Bull Ring as it drags along the surface of the table, and can be moved to the collection can by pulling on the strings at one side of the group, and releasing the strings on the other side. Cone shapes made from wood or plastic can be captured by the Bull Ring, and then slid towards the collection can. Magnetic objects can be picked up by the metal ring, and removed by the bait shop owner. Challenge the group with several higher difficulty objects, such as a crumpled piece of paper, a suction cup dart stuck to the table, a brand new pencil, a paper clip, a piece of duct tape, or a magazine. Perhaps, in this case, picking up the piece of tape might enable the group to pick up the paper clip more easily. Producing what is commonly referred to as "complex tool-building behavior" within the group.

You can also add some obstacles by spacing two tables almost together, so that a small gap is present. Any obstacles reaching the gap must be carried, or forever lost to the depths of the sea. Folded duct tape can also be used to create barriers or fences.

Important Points

Do not allow particpants to tie the string around their fingers or wrists, because a sudden movement may cause rope rash rather quickly. Use of a larger diameter string or rope may be more appropriate for the dexterity level of your group. Visual perception skills may also require the use of a larger ring, or high contrasting colored objects. If gross motor skills in the group are limited, using all shock cord or elastic for the Bull Ring strings produces some interesting effects. With this system, a single quick pull or erratic movement has less effect on the group than with non-elastic strings.

Discussion and Debriefing Topics

Did your group have a strategy for which objects they would retrieve first? Which object was the hardest to obtain? Which objects were the easiest to acquire? Was there a leader in your group, or did the leadership role change often?

Sequence

Bull Ring II utilizes physical movement, visual perception and cooperation. It is an interesting activity for many audiences, including those with limited mobility.

Activities Using Similar Skills and Follow-on Activities

Bull Ring I, Bull Ring III, Bull Ring Golf, Stretch It, and Pot of Gold utilize similar formations and skills. Expansion and Contraction uses some large scale body movements in contrast to the small motions used in Bull Ring II.

Notes

Activity 4.16

Bull Ring III—Write On!

Yet another activity you can accomplish with a Bull Ring. This version eliminates the balls entirely, and adds a pen or marker to the center of the Bull Ring.

Equipment

A Bull Ring (see description in early activities and in Chapter 5), a wide tipped marker, some masking tape, a few rubberbands, and a large piece of paper taped to the floor or the top surface of a table. First attach the marker to the Bull Ring using the masking tape and rubber bands. Your group can then use this apparatus to write on the paper. For balance reasons, it is best to center the marker in the Bull Ring.

The Challenge

Using the Bull Ring Universal Writing Tool—Mark 3, the group will make marks, color in spaces, answer test questions, and play games by writing with the Bull Ring.

Typical Presentation, Storyline or Metaphor

Your newest work of art is finally on display at the national art museum. Your fans are thrilled. But that joy turns to disbelief when you realize that you forgot to sign your precious work of art, and now it is roped off in the main showroom of the museum. You gain access to the museum after hours, and with a group of your friends, and the Bull Ring Universal Writing Tool—Mark 3, you attempt to draw your signature onto the artwork.

Variations

One of the simplest challenges is to have the group fill in a coloring book page with different color markers, or to completely fill in a geometric shape without going outside the lines. Another activity is to have groups quickly spell words and for an observer to guess what they are spelling. A third challenge could be a king-sized tic-tac-toe game using two different teams. A fourth activity would be for the group to create a visual work of art, either in the form of a painting or perhaps a poem. A fifth variation would be to allow one, two or three people to control the motion of the Bull Ring, and for others in the group to simply allow the Bull Ring to move easily about.

A final activity would be to create a king-sized computer graded test sheet, with squares for answers (A) (B) (C) (D) and (E), and to have the group read a short quiz question and then mark the correct answer using the Bull Ring Universal Writing Tool—Mark 3.0.

Important Points

Probably the most important point is to find a way to adequately fix the marker or pen to the Bull Ring. Next, try to use a thick enough piece of paper so that the marker or pen does not soak through, or puncture the paper, causing damage to the table or floor surface below. If your group will be coloring a page from a coloring book, be sure to fashion a quick way to replace the marker, and to have a variety of colors available.

Discussion and Debriefing Topics

How was your group's penmanship? What grade would you give your group on their art project? Did you find that you had control of the marking pen, or not? Which method produced a better result, when you fought the group for control or the motion of the pen, or when you went along with the others in the group? Was the result better when everyone was in control of the Bull Ring, or when only a few participants controlled the motion of the Bull Ring?

Sequence

Some familiarity with the Bull Ring is important, so playing one of the other variations of Bull Ring is probably best prior to this activity.

Activities Using Similar Skills and Follow-on Activities

Bull Ring I, Bull Ring II, Pot of Gold, and Stretch It use similar equipment and skills.

Notes

Activity 4.17

Bull Ring Golf

It is simply amazing how many things you can do with a Bull Ring. Here is a nine hole golf course plan using a variety of balls and golf course green designs. This activity might be interesting to corporate and athletic groups.

Equipment

A Bull Ring with enough strings for every member of the group. A variety of balls, tubes, cans, cups, buckets, and obstacles. See the section on variations below for different hole ideas.

The Challenge

To take a ball and place it in the appropriate destination. The group scores one stroke for every time the ball is dropped or fails to reach the right destination.

Typical Presentation, Storyline or Metaphor

In an effort to introduce golf as a team sport, an international sports promoter has created an interesting new golf course design. Your team is the first to ever play on this course.

Variations

Hole Number 1—The Enchanted Forest
Begin with a golf ball on the Bull Ring. The hole is a large plastic bucket on the ground, about 40 feet (12 meters) away, through some narrowly spaced trees.

Hole Number 2—The Stadium Cup
Begin with a tennis ball on the top of a vertical PVC tube 1 inch (25 mm) in diameter and 12 inches (305 mm) long, pushed into the ground. The Bull Ring is around the PVC tube, also on the ground. Lift the ball off the tube, and then take it to the hole, which is a stadium sized plastic cup, tacked to a pole or fencepost about 3 feet (1 meter) off the ground.

Hole Number 3—The River
Begin with a Ping-Pong ball placed on the Bull Ring. The hole is a 2 inch (51 mm) horizontal PVC tube 12 inches (305 mm) long, lying on the ground next to a tree. The ping pong ball must be placed inside the horizontal tube without touching the ground.

Hole Number 4—The Switch
Begin with the Bull Ring lying on the ground. Three vertical PVC tubes 1 inch (25 mm) in diameter and 1 foot (305 mm) long, are located about 3 feet (1 meter) apart. One top of one tube is an orange golf ball. One top of the second tube is a white golf ball. The third tube is empty. Exchange the position of the orange and white golf balls. This hole will probably produce a few strokes on the scorecard.

Hole Number 5—8 Ball
Allow the group to elevate the Bull Ring, and then place a billiard ball or steel ball bearing on the Bull Ring. Don't attempt this variation on a wooden floor. The hole is a large tin can next to a wall.

Hole Number 6—Home Plate
Begin with the Bull Ring around a 1 inch (25 mm) diameter by 5 foot (1.5 meter) long vertical PVC tube that has been pushed into the ground. Place a baseball at the top of the tube. Have the group remove the baseball using the Bull Ring, walk to first, second, and third base, and finally come back to home to replace the baseball back on the tube.

Hole Number 7—The North Pole
Begin with Bull Ring around a vertical PVC tube 1 inch (25 mm) in diameter and 12 inches (305 mm) long, pushed into the ground. Use a frozen ice cube as the ball for this hole. The hole is a tilted ice bucket, 100 feet (30 meters) away. Better hurry on this one.

Hole Number 8—The Water Trap
Activity begins with a Bull Ring placed over a tire that is lying flat on the ground. A tennis ball is placed on the Bull Ring, which is on the ground, inside the tire. The attached twine is allowed to drape over the edge

of the tire. The hole is a 5 feet (1.52 meter) tall Water Tube behind some nearby trees or bushes.

Hole Number 9—The Dilemma
The group must pick up a golf ball lying on the ground, using only the Bull Ring. The final hole is a small cup located about 5 feet away from the inside corner of a room or building.

Other Variations

Another Bull Ring Golf variation involves using a wide rubber band instead of the metal ring. With this prop you can play a more traditional version of golf. Begin with a golf ball placed on a golf tee. Stretch the rubber band Bull Ring over the golf ball, and either capture or cradle the ball. Every time the golf ball hits the ground counts as one stroke. The various holes can be tin cans placed around strategic obstacles. Each hole can still use a different ball. Suitable choices include, golf balls, tennis balls, Ping-Pong balls, super bounce balls, whiffle balls, baseballs, etc. This activity can even be played inside by placing the golf tees into small blocks of wood.

Here is a final variation that can be used during a Bull Ring Golf game. Any time the ball is dropped, one participant must let their string go slack, or let go completely of their string, until the ball reaches the hole.

Important Points

This is a championship course, and it is unlikely that any team will score a perfect round. Collecting a few strokes provides the opportunity to discuss difficulties encountered during the game.

Discussion and Debriefing Topics

Which hole did you find most challenging? Why? Did your score improve or decline as you went from the first hole to the last? If you could remove any score from your scorecard, which hole would it be for? What kinds of comments did you hear during the activity from other players in your group? Did you receive any constructive criticism during the activity?

Sequence

Bull Ring Golf can come after some familiarity with the Bull Ring. This activity might be perfect for the group to enjoy casually after a lunch break. As participants arrive back, let them begin at any hole they like.

Activities Using Similar Skills and Follow-on Activities

Bull Ring I, Bull Ring II, and Bull Ring III use similar skills. Pot of Gold and Stretch It use similar, but more advanced skills.

Notes

Activity 4.18

Cave In

Cave In can be an emotionally intense experience. This activity is intended for groups that have a long-term relationship and have intimate knowledge and respect for each other.

Equipment

It is useful to have a tarp, tablecloth or blanket that is large enough to completely cover the group. Use a material that is open weave and allows air movement. Plastic cloth is not a good choice.

The Challenge

For participants, playing roles as either themselves or imaginary personalities, to take part in a simulated cave-in, where only one member of the group is guaranteed survival. The group must collectively decide which member of the group is the best choice to leave and seek rescue assistance, knowing that the fate of the remaining group members is uncertain.

Typical Presentation, Storyline or Metaphor

The cavern you have been exploring is suddenly flooded, causing massive walls to collapse. The situation is extremely dangerous. Only a portion of the original opening to the cavern is still passable. Who from within your group should you send for help, if only one person can be assured a safe exit?

Variations

Other critical survival situations, such as a lifeboat at sea, a frozen tent in the Arctic, or a shrinking desert oasis, provide backdrops for similar simulations.

If having participants play themselves is considered too realistic, consider creating imaginary profiles for each of the participants, based on common stereotypes. Joe is a computer programmer with a wife and four children. He is the only source of income for this family. Paula is a medical doctor that is likely to create an essential vaccine in the next five years. Using roles that provide some detachment from reality allows a group to participate in this simulation, without having to prioritize the actual qualities of real-life group members.

Important Points

The best place to facilitate this activity is to be beneath the covering with the group. Encourage decisions to be made based on logical processing, but take into account the emotional comments made by members of the group. Only choose the first person to escape safely from the disaster. Ranking the remaining group members is unnecessary, and, if using real life participants, can have the same effect as being chosen last for a baseball game.

It is essential, when completing this activity, to simulate a complete rescue of ALL group members from the survival situation. This reinforces that no matter what the priority of the group member chosen to leave, all participants have value and are worthy of rescue.

Discussion and Debriefing Topics

During the decision making process, ask the group what qualities our society values. Are there any behaviors that are less accepted than others? Is there really a best choice for this simulation, or given the right set of circumstances, could anyone be acceptable? For those that choose to remain behind, are you comfortable with your decision? Are you comfortable with the decision of the group? What did you learn about the members of your group?

Sequence

No question about it, Cave In is an activity that can have an extremely significant effect on a group when using real-life participants. This activity requires significant lead-in work, to prepare the group for open discussions. Make sure that the group is capable of sustaining a discussion, and offering their opinions before attempting this activity.

Activities Using Similar Skills and Follow-on Activities

Danger Zone is a suitable activity to use before Cave In. Follow-on activities should be playful and energetic to restore the enthusiasm and lightheartedness of the group.

Notes

Activity 4.19

Community Juggling

If your group has ever felt like they were juggling too many jobs at one time, this activity is probably ideal for them.

Equipment

A variety of soft, colorful, diverse objects that can be tossed without hurting anyone. Useful objects include: tennis balls, hoseplay balls, beanbags, plastic fruit, flying disks, pieces of upholstery foam, stuffed animals, inflatable pool toys, rolled-up socks, pillows and balloons.

The Challenge

To pass an increasing number of objects between group members using a somewhat random but established pattern.

Typical Presentation, Storyline or Metaphor

Well, it is the end of the month, and there are still forty things left to do before the close of business today. You have a mountain of paperwork, which needs signatures from many of your co-workers, managers, and supervisors. Your work group begins the traditional end-of-the-month crunch session as they massively attempt to complete all the tasks before them in one tremendous orchestrated finale of effort.

You have a cool piece of e-mail that you pass on to your best friend, and they pass it on, and they pass it on, and somehow in the process you get it back, read it, and pass it on again.

It takes concentration to keep all of your most important projects going. See how many of these critical projects you can keep moving for 2 minutes. You may want to prioritize which projects are the most important and protect these the most.

Variations

In addition to varying the size, shape and texture of the objects, this activity can be greatly altered by having the participants wear gloves. Provide a variety of gloves such as new medical examination gloves, cotton work gloves, knitted mittens, slick ski gloves, cycling gloves, welding gloves, etc. Even the best athlete will be humbled by their performance using gloves. Playing with your non-dominant hand is also a challenge.

Another variation includes having the participants say their name as they receive the object, or say the name of the person they are passing the object to. Players may also make a unique sound as they catch the object.

After establishing a pattern, add in a "switch." In this case, the switch is to reverse the pattern, and send the objects back the other way. See how often you can can switch and still keep control of the objects.

Playing this activity in waist-deep water is challenging. If you wish to slow down the speed of play, try using light objects such as air filled balloons or beachballs.

Important Points

It is important to establish a pattern by passing a single object across the circle of participants. Make sure participants know that they are passing the object to the same person each time. This means that there are only two people the each person has to watch, the person they are receiving the object from, and the person they are passing the object to. Start a single object randomly across the circle of participants, passing it to every participant before returning it back to the starting position. It is sometimes helpful to have group members hold up their hands until they have received the object. This helps to identify which members still need to receive the object.

Try to use objects which vary by size, shape and texture. Begin with a single object passed around the circle until everyone has had the chance to catch and throw it several times. Then continue this object and add additional ones. Players should not try to recover dropped objects.

You might want to consider the members of your group before attempting to juggle anything unusual, like a giant plastic spider, rubber snake or other icky object.

Encourage participants not to toss objects near the face of the receiver. Introduce additional objects only when the group has demonstrated proficiency with a single object.

Instead of tossing an object, try bouncing it to the next person.

Discussion and Debriefing Topics

Which objects were the easiest to catch? Which objects were the most often dropped? What is the maximum number of "projects" your team could handle at one time? Was it easy to concentrate during this activity? What was most distracting during the activity? Were you pleased with the performance of the person tossing the objects to you, and the person receiving the objects thrown by you? What would have improved your efficiency in this task? If you tried the switch, was it difficult to change the pattern you were used to following? Were there any problems associated with switching?

Sequence

Community Juggling ends with participants in a circle, the perfect position for a debriefing or processing session, or for another circular activity.

Activities Using Similar Skills and Follow-on Activities

Funderbirds use some similar eye-hand coordination skills.

Notes

Activity 4.20

Community Jump Rope

Here is a way to turn a familiar playground activity into a challenge and adventure programming opportunity.

Equipment

One rope at least 30 feet (9 meters) long, suitable for twirling as a jump rope.

The Challenge

To move everyone in the group from one side of the jump rope to the other, without touching the rope. Each person must jump the rope at least twice during their journey.

Typical Presentation, Storyline or Metaphor

After working all summer to build a community playground, your group has been asked to be the guest of honor at the opening day celebration. A local group of children has asked your group to join them in a double-dutch jump rope demonstration, and you'll need to practice. Each member of your group needs to be able to jump twice over a twirling jump rope. You can either accomplish this one at a time, with partners, in small groups, or with the entire group at one time.

During the peak of the holiday shopping season, the power goes out in the large department store you are in. A battery back-up unit continues to power the revolving door. You must lead everyone in your group outside, through this revolving door.

Variations

If you explain that the challenge of the activity is simply to move from one side of the rope to the other, without touching the rope, some creative folks will simply walk around the two participants twirling the rope. A perfectly logical and acceptable solution. Now you can additionally challenge these folks by including that they must jump the rope twice at some point in their journey.

Allowing participants to pass individually, with partners, or in groups also changes the difficulty of this activity. Requiring participants to be in contact with another person during their jumps is also a way to alter this activity.

Rather than having each person perform two jumps, you can establish a progression from zero to 10 jumps for the group. Here the first person can run under the rope as it twirls. The next person jumps once, and so on.

Consider sending participants through two at a time from opposite directions and have them pass an object such as a ball or balloon. If the group is small, the facilitator can tie one end of the rope to a tree or post and twirl the other end without requiring another person to assist.

Important Points

Asking for volunteers to twirl the rope gives some participants the opportunity to participate, even if they would rather not jump. Encourage group members to give other participants hints on how best to jump the rope. The goal here isn't really to jump the rope, the goal is to bring participants together for a common purpose, and communication between participants meets that goal.

Participants often try some form of rhythm (singing, chanting, etc.) to establish good timing. You may want to encourage the best jumpers to go last, so that the least time is lost if early jumpers fail and the team has to begin again. Let the entire group decide on the jumping technique they wish to use. If they are unable to decide as a whole, encourage individuals to demonstrate different techniques and let the group decide which approach is most likely to succeed.

Discussion and Debriefing Topics

When your group decided how they were going to pass through the rope, did you think you could do it? Did you know exactly what you were going to do before you started? Once your group had a plan that worked, do you think they could have gone for more than 2 jumps in a row? Which did you prefer, going through the ropes by yourself, or with others?

Sequence

Community Jump Rope requires a rope, and fits well next to other rope activities. It is also a problem solving and carefully timed activity.

Activities Using Similar Skills and Follow-on Activities

Stump Jumping requires the same level of concentration and timing as Community Jump Rope. Tree of Knots can use the same rope for a much different activity.

Notes

Activity 4.21

Danger Zone

This is a simple proximity challenge that generally requires a great deal of contact between participants. Use this activity after the group has had a chance to know and work with each other. Since this activity finishes with participants in relaxed, reclined positions, there is an opportunity for a brief rest, processing or group discussion at the completion of this activity.

Equipment

A long rope can be used to create an irregular boundary, or a large blanket, tarp or plastic sheet can be used to define the limited space available. Some additional "equipment" such as plastic containers, boxes, or other adventure stuff can be used as examples of expedition equipment that also must be stored on the ledge.

The Challenge

With participants standing within the limited space available, have everyone assume a position that they could sleep in for the entire night.

Typical Presentation, Storyline or Metaphor

During a climbing expedition, a sudden storm requires that a camp be immediately set up for the evening. Wind levels are substantially less near the surface of a flat ledge nearby, but the space available is fairly small for the group. Your goal is to create a comfortable sleeping space for each member of your group, on the small ledge. You must take into account the needs of each group member, and also provide room for your equipment. No one in the group is allowed to "hang over the edge."

Variations

By using a rope, a variety of irregular shapes can be made for the ledge. Ropes also allow for modifications depending on the number of participants in the group.

Optional equipment that must also be accomodated provides an additional challenge to this activity. Large plastic containers, inner tubes, camping gear, water jugs, beach balls and other challenge or sporting goods make good choices for this equipment.

If this activity is used indoors, try placing the ledge near a wall, or even in a corner. This produces additional variations since participants can now lean against the walls.

After participants are in place, have them all turn over (as many people do when they are sleeping) one person at a time. A second variation would be to have all participants turn over at the same time (slowly!) After order is restored, ask for a volunteer to be a "snorer", and have this person change places with another person in the group.

Important Points

The issue of personal space can be explored through this activity. This activity should not be used with a group where the participants are unfamiliar with each other, at least until other lead-in activities have been used. When the final participants are finding their space, encourage everyone to be careful where they are stepping, so that no one is stepped on.

Discussion and Debriefing Topics

It is a risky question, but asking if anyone "claimed" their space quickly, without taking into account the needs of others in the group, certainly gives the opportunity to process the needs of the group above the needs of the individuals. Ask how many participants are actually in the same position they would normally sleep in. For those that are not, ask why they chose this new position rather than a more familiar one. Ask those participants that are on the edge of the ledge what will keep them there if a big wind comes up.

Sequence

This and other types of proximity activities (activities where participants are brought physically very close together) require some preliminary lead-in activities so that group members can become acquainted with each other, before their personal space is invaded.

Activities Using Similar Skills and Follow-on Activities

Other types of proximity activities include Knots, First Contact, Blackout, All Aboard, and Magic Carpet. If the intent is for the group to further explore personalities of each group member, the very intense Cave In initiative can be used after this activity.

Notes

Activity 4.22

Marching to the Beat of a Different Drum

This simple activity builds energy within a group. It offers the chance for every participant to take the leadership role, even if only for a short time. It works well as the first activity of a session, or as an energizer.

Equipment

The most simple equipment is a cassette tape player and a cassette tape with a variety of musical segments, each approximatly 30–60 seconds long. Use a variety of music styles, and have at least as many segments prepared as the number of participants in the group. Records can also be used effectively, but the transition between songs is generally less subtle.

The Activity

Participants can begin the activity seated in chairs that have been arranged in a circle. A person is chosen to go first, followed by the participant to their right, and so on around the circle. The first leader is instructed to interpret the first musical segment using movement or motions. Suggest that leaders use motions that are appropriate for the mobility level of the group. The other participants are to imitate the movements of the leader. The second leader interprets the second musical segment, and so on.

Variations, Modifications and Recommendations

Choose musical segments that are appropriate for the group. Marches and dance music usually produce bold movements, while classical and folk music typically produce smaller, quieter movements. For children, consider using cartoon music or songs from children's programs. For a western theme, consider using a collection of cowboy tunes, country and western music. For an audience discussing diversity issues, consider using music from a variety of countries. Occasionally include an energetic musical selection, such as a march, college fight song, or national anthem.

The length of the musical selection should be approximately 30–60 seconds, with a short pause in between segments. If you wish to use this activity as an energizer, the last musical segment should be a high energy selection. If you wish to address the group and hold their attention after this activity, the final two segments should be more reflective and peaceful, so that the participants complete the activity in a refreshed, but relaxed mood. Music is a great motivator for many populations, and the choice of music selected for this activity will directly affect the energy level of the group, and their response to this activity.

Important Points

One of the most significant experiences that challenge and adventure activities provide is the opportunity to move participants outside of their comfort zone into an area of growth and self discovery. For some participants, movement to music is not an easy thing to participate in, let alone provide a leadership role. By simply asking participants to be willing to try new things at the beginning of a challenge and adventure programming session, a facilitator can set the stage for this activity. And remember, if a participant is self-conscious about their movements, they can simply close their eyes, and everyone else can watch them.

One of the most powerful uses of this activity is to expose participants to a diverse variety of other cultures, through their music. By choosing rhythms, musical styles, historically significant selections, and culturally diverse musical segments, the participants of this activity can begin to understand other populations.

For large audiences (i.e. more than 50 people), try breaking into smaller groups of 8–12 people. This allows for a more intimate interaction between participants, and reduces the total length of the activity to 5 to 10 minutes in length. Longer programs are possible, but be aware that some dance forms are strictly aerobic, and it is important to pace the participants with the music segments chosen.

When the physical abilities within a group vary dramatically, it is important to encourage all leaders to utilize motions and movements which are suitable for the entire group, and to consider the capabilities of other group members before leading a difficult or strenuous motion.

Discussion and Debriefing Topics

Debriefing can include asking participants which role they enjoyed more, the leader or follower. For school populations, discuss the origins of each musical selection, and also the instruments that were used in each selection. If a foreign language was spoken during the selection, have the participants discuss what the language was. Process the thoughts experience by participants as each new musical segment was played. Were some selections more memorable than others? Ask leaders if they enjoyed their musical segment. If not, ask each leader what it was about their segment that made it difficult to interpret.

Using a piece of graph paper, plot the energy level of the group based on the musical segments played. Using a world map, draw a line connecting the countries of origin for each of the musical selections.

Sequence

Marching to the Beat of a Different Drum is an ideal opening activity for a large group or audience. It also works well as an energizer to improve the energy level of a group after a lunch break.

Activities Using Similar Skills and Follow-on Activities

Since this activity utilizes listening skills and movement, other activities using these same skills are natural follow-ons. If processing is not used at the completion of this activity, it is important to choose the energy level of the final musical selections to match the energy level the group needs for the next activity.

Notes

Activity 4.23

Expansion and Contraction

Here is an activity that can be used to metaphorically discuss limitations on flexibility, flexible thinking, turning a problem inside out, and being pushed to the very limits of your ability.

Equipment

If you happen to have some Marble Tubes that are cut squarely at both ends, you can use one of these for each participant. If you don't happen to have PVC tubes about 15 to 20 inches (391 to 508 mm) long, you can use ⅜ or ½ inch (9 or 13 mm) dowel rods about 18 inches (457 mm) long. Again, you'll need one dowel rod for each participant.

The Challenge

For the group to experience being linked together by the connecting rods (the dowel rods). Beginning first with a circle, then trying to create the smallest possible shape with the group, turning this circle inside-out, and finally expanding the circle to the very limit of the group.

Typical Presentation, Storyline or Metaphor

It isn't just the fact that we are all humans that ties us together. There are many things that we share, the air we breathe, our interests, our hobbies, our goals and dreams. In this activity, we are all connected not only to our neighbors, but to the entire group as well. In order for the group to succeed, we all need to help it move. Let's explore that concept, by staying in contact with each other as we experience some rapid downsizing and also some internal growth in our organization.

Variations

Choosing suitable connection rods is very important. Smooth ended marble tubes work well, so do smooth dowel rods, and even the smallest diameter foam pool sticks now available.

Asking the group to form different configurations, such as circles, squares, modern art, a beating heart, or an orchestra can be an expressive experience. Shrinking or contracting the size of the group is a good first activity.

The expansion of the group, which can be interpreted as an event of rapid growth, should push participants to hold both hands well away from their bodies. If the group simultaneously reaches their complete limit, all the connection rods should drop at exactly the same moment.

You can ask the group to create a goal for the size of circle they can create. Another goal may be the total number of connection rods dropped during the activity.

Important Points

It is easy, even for athletic groups, to experience arm fatigue after only a few minutes of this activity. Move quickly from the contracted to the expanded position. Encourage the group to be in constant communication during the expansion portion, so that as few connection rods are dropped as possible. Also encourage participants to respect the connection or bond between themselves and their neighbors. Slow, gentle hand movements are suggested. Never use marble tubes that have a pointed or angled end cut, this style of tube is just too sharp for Expansion and Contraction.

Discussion and Debriefing Topics

Did you feel connected to your neighbors? Were you in constant verbal contact with them? Did you feel that they respected the bond between you? When you reached the limit of your abilities, did you drop the connecting rod? Who dropped it? Was there any effort after the drop to reunite the bond? Are there any real life situations where you feel tested to the limits of your abilities? Did the world look (and feel) different to you when you turned the circle (the problem) inside-out?

Sequence

Expansion and Contraction is a lower energy, reflective activity. You can use this activity after a high energy initiative, to bring the level of the group down so that processing or debriefing can occur in a quiet setting.

Activities Using Similar Skills and Follow-on Activities

Other activities which bring participants into close proximity, like the contraction portion of this activity, are Handcuffs and Shackles, Human Knot, and All Aboard. Another activity which expresses the expansion portion of this activity, would be Around the World, with a Lycra Tube.

Notes

Look for a version of this activity entitled DNA on page 124 of the book, 50 Ways to Use Your Noodle, by Chris Cavert and Sam Sikes.

Activity 4.24

Forming Groups With Film Cannisters

If you happen to have the same large group throughout the day, or perhaps over the course of several sessions, and you want to be sure that each participant has the opportunity to work with a variety of group members, here is a simple technique for dividing the large group into several unique smaller groups.

Equipment

You'll need a collection of film cannisters and a stuff sack to hold them. Directions are given in Chapter 5 for making a film cannister group formation kit. There are a variety of methods for making the film cannister kits. So far, five variations have been identified.

The Challenge

To break into into smaller groups by finding other group members with similar qualities, such as possessing a film cannister with similar sounding contents, or similar smelling contents.

Typical Presentation, Storyline or Metaphor

This is an adventure in group formations. It is also a simple technique for forming multiple groups with no repeated partners in any formation. Effective metaphors for this activity include exploring the diversity of the group and the opportunity to explore the possibilities of working with others in many different combinations.

Variations

Chapter 5 presents instructions for making and using this simple prop.

Important Points

Using the technique presented in Chapter 5, it is important to have approximately the same number of film cannisters, as participants. If you happen to have too many left over cannisters, your group sizes are likely to be uneven.

If you use spices for separating the group, encourage group members not to talk during the smelling process. Having a group member shout out, "I've got pepper," will quickly encourage group members to use speach and hearing skills, rather than simply using their sense of smell.

Discussion and Debriefing Topics

Were you able to hear what other members of your group heard inside of their cannisters? Did you choose the right group to join? Were there any techniques that made your decision easier, such as trading cannisters with other members of your smaller group? Which process was easier to find your group members with, hearing or smell? Why? Could you identify the source of the aroma in your cannister?

Sequence

This activity employs skills in listening, and using other less often used senses, rather than the more often used talking and hearing. This activity generally comes just before those adventure programming elements that require smaller groups.

Activities Using Similar Skills and Follow-on Activities

Once you have formed the appropriate size groups, you can begin the activites for which these groups were formed.

Notes

Activity 4.25

First Contact

For some audiences, the element of physical contact can be reassuring, as when the sure hand of a spotter helps a participant maintain their balance during a challenge activity. For others, physical contact is not the first thing that comes to mind when challenge related programs are discussed, and the personal space of these individuals needs to be valued and assured. For those willing to risk a minimal amount of contact, here is a simple activity that requires no equipment, and that has a variety of solutions.

Equipment

None!

The Challenge

Each member of the group must be in physical contact with each of the other members of the group at the same time.

Typical Presentation, Storyline or Metaphor

One of the attributes that distinguishes a culture, or a community, or a family is the connection between members of these groups. To illustrate this connection, your goal is to successfully connect yourself to each of the members of your group simultaneously. Be sure to respect the personal space of each individual by first planning your connection points before initiating contact.

Variations

This activity can be modified to allow contact only with hands (probably the least intimidating approach), or only contact below the knees, or only with extremedies (heads, arms and legs). Another variation is to begin the activity by placing two participants in contact, and then adding a single person at a time, completing the necessary links to keep everyone connected at all times. After achieving contact with the whole group, disassemble this collection of people and have them quickly try to regain their whole group connection again.

Important Points

In the past few years, challenge facilitators have become aware of not only the physical safety issues of participants, but also the potential for emotional risk. Before attempting this activity, it is best to know if any participants have concerns about physical contact. One potentially easy way of accomplishing this is to initiate the activity known as Human Knot, where group members are closely linked by hands in a large knotted clump. During the post activity processing of Human Knot, identify any concerns within the group regarding the proximity of participants to each other. If there is any concern regarding this issue, First Contact is probably not the right activity for your group, even if you are only using hand contact.

Discussion and Debriefing Topics

When you first heard the directions for this activity, did you imagine a mass of people looking like a Twister® game gone wrong? Was it difficult to connect with everyone in your group? What is the maximum number of people that you believe could accomplish this activity simultaneously?

Sequence

This activity has worked very well during programs between foster care families and their children. It does utilize a significant amount of contact however, and should be introduced after some additional activities, such as Human Knot, All Aboard or Magic Carpet.

Activities Using Similar Skills and Follow-on Activities

Knots, All Aboard and Magic Carpet all use proximity (the closeness of participants) to their advantage.

Spider's Web is another activity that typically has a fair amount of personal contact.

If participants happen to be lying down for this activity, it could be the perfect time for a game of Ha!

Notes

Activity 4.26

Funderbirds

One of the finest days ever spent by author Jim Cain was working in the woodshop of Bill Henderson of Lima, Ohio. Bill is a 4-H specialist in Northwestern Ohio, a wonderful songleader, woodworker, dulcimer player, and a good friend.

Equipment

You'll need one of the unique inventions that Bill Henderson calls a Funderbird. Directions for making these can be found in Chapter 5.

The Challenge

Funderbirds provide a hand version of hacky-sack, or becomes a suitable replacement for beach ball and balloon games. The challenge here is simply to keep the Funderbird up in the air as long as possible.

Typical Presentation, Storyline or Metaphor

Successfully learning a skill, and then applying that skill is valuable. The ability of the group to learn and demonstrate their mastery of the Funderbird has a direct relationship to their abilities to learn and master other skills.

Variations

Variations for the Funderbird include several different hitting styles. Underhand typically works best. You can invoke the basic volleyball rule that no participant can hit the Funderbird twice in a row. While playing name games, you can encourage participants to say their own name when hitting the Funderbird. A more difficult variation, and one that typically produces even more problems, is to have participants say someone else's name in the group as they hit the Funderbird. Trying to get both sides of your brain working at the same time can be challenging. Using your non-dominant hand to hit the Funderbird typically produces a greater number of misses and misguided hits. If you want to additionally challenge some talented players, give them a cotton glove or pair of mittens to wear.

Important Points

For those that are not especially skilled in hacky-sack playing, this includes the authors, Funderbirds provide another opportunity to participate, and still hide our less-than-coordinated talents. This activity can also be performed with a seated audience.

Discussion and Debriefing Topics

Were you able to successfully control the Funderbird? Did you manage to learn any techniques from other members of the Group?

Sequence

Funderbirds work well to pull a group together at the beginning of a program, or after a mid-program break.

Activities Using Similar Skills and Follow-on Activities

Having used Funderbirds for an informal name game, you can now progress to some more elaborate name games.

Activity 4.27

Gridlock

Sometimes the best way to solve a problem is just to keep trying until you get it right. This is an exercise in group memory, as well as some ordinary trial-and-error problem solving techniques.

Equipment

Gridlock requires a giant checkerboard pattern with each grid approximately 1 foot (305 mm) square. This can be accomplished by taping a grid pattern to a floor with masking tape, or marking a pattern on a tarp or cloth, or creating a grid with either ropes, flat webbing or a large open-weave net. You can even create a stepping stone pattern for Gridlock. See Chapter 5 for details.

The Challenge

To determine a path across the grid network of spaces. A participant is allowed to move as far as they can, until they make an error. At this point, a new participant begins the journey, and attempts to make a better choice at the site of the last error. Allow the group a few minutes to plan before the activity begins.

Typical Presentation, Storyline or Metaphor

Ok, here's the drill. You work for a very competitive delivery company. You have the best trucks, the friendliest drivers, the best computerized technology at your fingertips, and right now you have a vital package that is needed on the other side of town. It is 5pm, rush hour, and you need to find the best way across town. Main roads, side streets, back alleys, any way you can find. Anytime you come to a deadend or traffic jam, you'll need to change drivers. When you find the correct route to take you through all the traffic, you can alert the company and have the rest of the drivers follow you.

Variations

The directions for creating the gridlock pattern in Chapter 5 show square, rectangular, circular, and a stepping stone version. You can modify the length of the rectangular pattern by folding some of the grid underneath the rest of the tarp.

You can allow two groups to simultaneously work towards each other. This approach however, increases the difficulty of the activity, as participants now have to observe the movements of two other participants, rather than just one.

If you happen to use a continuous path, participants know that they can only step on a space that is touching the space were they are now standing. It is also typical to only move forward or sideways on the Gridlock pattern.

More difficult combinations might allow jumping blocks, backward and foreward motions, and diagonal movements.

As a facilitator you can always allow participants to place an object on acceptable places to step, rather than memorizing each location. This visual clue however may allow waiting group members to pay less attention to the active member of their group.

Important Points

There is a critical moment in preparing to solve a problem where no amount of additional planning will produce any better quality result. Sooner or later, you just need to give it a try, and see what happens. Gridlock encourages trial-and-error problem solving techniques, and also keeps the group focused on the active participant, so that each person will know the correct route to take when their turn arrives.

Discussion and Debriefing Topics

What type of things did you discuss during your planning time? Were there any penalties associated with a wrong choice? Are there penalties in real life for wrong choices? Were there any errors made from spaces where the path was already known? How could these types of mistakes be avoided in the future? Were there any spaces or movements that surprised you? Why?

Sequence

Gridlock is a problem solving activity, and can be used after some initial group play.

Activities Using Similar Skills and Follow-on Activities

Gridlock is one of the few challenge and adventure activities that encourages the simple technique of trial-and-error for isolating a solution. Switching solution techniques for the following activity will expose the group to a variety of methods for problem solving and decision making.

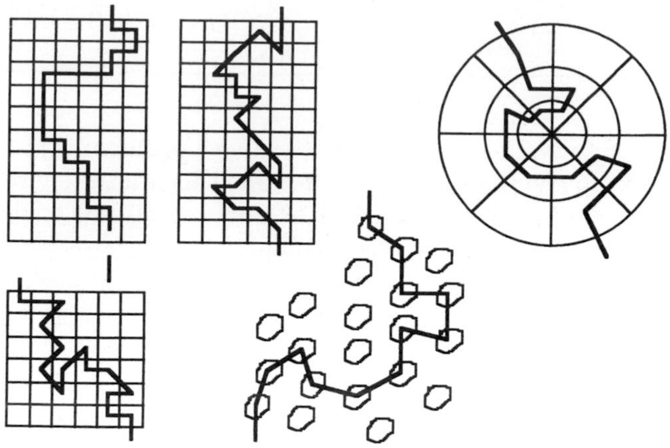

Notes

Handcuffs and Shackles

Handcuffs and Shackles are certainly one of the easiest get acquainted activities ever invented. An easy way to include new members of the group instantly, and also to provide an opportunity for participants to take a leadership role. This "parlor trick" has been around for quite a while. You can find versions of this activity in some turn-of-the-century magic books, a variety of books on knot making and rope tricks, the Klutz Book of Magic by John Cassidy & Michael Stroud, and in Silver Bullets by Karl Rohnke. Don't be surprised if some folks have still not experienced this activity yet. Even the most familiar activites are new to every generation.

Equipment

Handcuffs and Shackles are constructed from 5 feet (152 cm) of soft clothesline rope. The Handcuffs and Shackles are identical, so that the same rope can be used for either activity. You'll need one piece of rope for every participant.

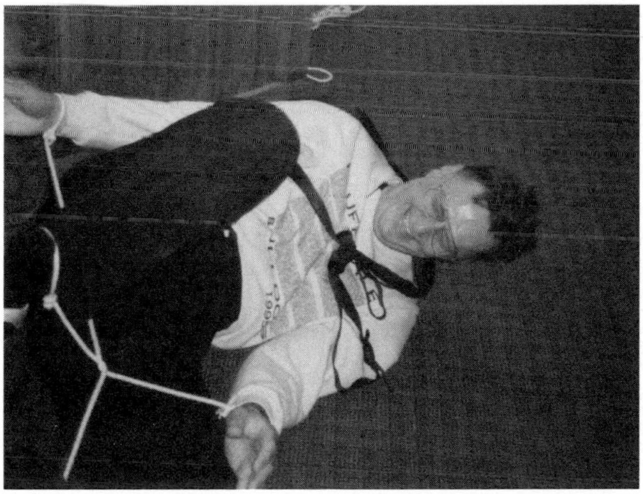

The Challenge

While handcuffed or shackled to a partner, become disconnected from this other person without removing your hands (or feet) from your own handcuffs (or shackles), and without untying the knots in the rope loops.

Typical Presentation, Storyline or Metaphor

As a beginning activity, handcuffs and shackles needs little introduction, although the title provides some interesting metaphors. If you need a story try this one. . . .

In order to complete their research on time for a highly prestigious foundation, four scientists have been handcuffed together by the head of the department until their work is completed (this hardly ever happens in real life). Because of their immense knowledge in the highly specialized field of nuclear phrenology (the study of predicting human character by reading the bumps on your head with laser beams—no kidding!) these scientists must occasionally converse with each other. Not wanting to alarm their department head by simply cutting their handcuffs off with the laser beam, these four scientists have figured out a way to detach themselves from one partner, and quickly join another. See if you can do the same.

Variations

Handcuffs are simply that. Rope loops tied loosely around both wrists of a single participant, with one partner's handcuffs passing through the other's.

Shackles were invented much by chance, by some rather creative folks at the Black Hills Recreation Leaders Laboratory. For those that have already experienced handcuffs, shackles provides a new experience with a similar solution. You can also handcuff and shackle a person to themselves, or shackle one partner and handcuff another.

Some folks may figure out a solution fairly quickly. For these folks, there are two additional challenges that are easily presented using the same segment of rope. The first is to see if they can reattach themselves to another person or group. The second step is to see if they can make a single overhand or figure-eight knot in their own rope, again without untying the knots or removing the rope from their wrists. A knot on a bight is fine, but an actual overhand or figure-eight knot takes a little creativity to figure out.

For a real variation to this activity, try joining three, four or even the entire group together. You can even make one large circle with the group, and have them achieve their freedom together. If you begin with partners, and have them reassemble themselves in a large circle, you'll have them in a configuration from which you can begin your next activity. By the way, these same ropes can be used as "extensions" between hands for the Human Knot.

From a magician's point of view, one of the most interesting methods for accomplishing this task is when two participants are handcuffed together with their rope handcuffs passing through a 2 inch (51 mm) hole in a door. A more readily accessible prop might be to use a chain link fence that typically surrounds a baseball field, but only with populations that aren't likely to try and pull the other person through the fence! This version removes much of the personal contact, but focuses the solution of the activity on the ropes themselves.

Important Points

The most remarkable effect of this activity is not so much in getting the handcuffs separated, but in the process by which two people work closely together to accomplish what seems to be a difficult task. One of the best ways for using this activity is to have about a dozen sets of handcuffs available at the beginning of an event. When the first two participants arrive, show them the activity, and have them instruct others how to do it. This immediately gives those arriving early the chance to be involved, and also provides an opportunity for informal leadership from these folks.

Encourage those that may already know the solution to allow their partner to figure it out, rather than being told the solution. As a facilitator, try to lead participants to figuring out the solution by encouraging them to consider the rope, not their partner.

Discussion and Debriefing Topics

Did you think this activity would have an easy solution? Did you find that you or your partner did more of the work? Would it have helped if the ropes had been twice as long? Which was easier, handcuffs or shackles? Was the solution something you expected, or totally different than you expected? Were you able to help anyone else during the activity?

Sequence

This activity easily fits into the get acquainted category. It can also be used prior to a trust building sequence. For programs focused on couples or partnered activities, Handcuffs and Shackles is a low risk activity that is ideal for the initial stages of a program.

Activities Using Similar Skills and Follow-on Activities

Now that pairs have successfully completed this activity, try a larger version with the entire group. You can handcuff or shackle an entire group together in a circular formation. The ropes can also be used to join partners together for the Human Knot.

Notes

Activity 4.29

Human Knot

For many people, Human Knot is one of the first challenge and adventure activities they have ever seen. If you check the variations section, you'll find some interesting alternatives to this classic activity.

Equipment

Nothing, unless you plan to use this activity with a population with limited mobility or limited upper arm movement. Then you might want to consider the variation mentioned using the ropes from Handcuffs and Shackles.

The Challenge

For a dozen or less participants standing in one large circle to reach across and take the hands of two different persons, and then to unwind this knotted mess, without letting go of hands, to create a single circle again.

Typical Presentation, Storyline or Metaphor

As an exercise to understand the method in which DNA strands are so tightly wrapped together, your group has been assembled. To unlock the gene sequence, and to see who your neighbors truly are, you merely need to unwind this knotted strand to form a single circle.

Variations

This activity can require the need for an immediate variation or alteration if you happen to work with populations that may only have the use of a single arm or hand. Forming a line instead of a circle is appropriate, or perhaps a series of smaller straight lines.

Sometimes you'll need a visit from the Knot Doctor to "operate" on a particularly difficult knot. This visit is allowed to unjoin and rejoin two hands, and then the unwinding process continues. You should also mention to participants as they begin to unwind their knots, that they can rotate their hands relative to the other hands they are holding. This will avoid any unnecessary stress to the hand, wrist, elbow and shoulder joints as the Human Knot unwinds.

If you use ropes or other devices to extend the reach of each participant, several good things happen. First of all, the mobility of the group is greatly increased, giving each participant more room to maneuver. Secondly, you can choose to use ropes, webbing or other objects that are flexible and colorful. Now participants can offer advice based on the color of the rope that need to move. This adds some additional assistance during the problem solving portion of this activity.

Another variation when using ropes, which slows down the rate of movement during the unwinding process is to only allow one rope at a time to go slack. The opposite effect, which may be helpful with a rambunctious group, is to only allow one rope to be taut at a time. This will probably reduce arm stress during the event.

At the end of the activity, you will more than likely have some participants facing outward, while others are facing inwards. For an additional challenge, and without letting go, have the group reverse the direction they are facing, by turning the entire circle inside out.

Important Points

Prior to beginning the unwinding process of Human Knot, passing a "pulse" through the group will alert the facilitator if a single continuous circle is present, or possibly two or three smaller circles (which may be linked or unlinked to each other). By selecting a single person to gently squeeze their right hand, and for the receiving person to squeeze their other hand, the pulse is passed around the group. When the pulse returns to the originator, any participant not receiving the pulse must be part of a circle that is unconnected from this main part.

If you happen to have more than 10 or 12 participants, it can be almost impossible to maneuver within the group. Using short segments of rope, possibly from Handcuffs and Shackles, can allow greater mobility for the group, and also for more participants to join.

Often time, participants may offer additional comments such as "don't cross your arms," or "make sure to grab the hand of someone directly across from you." These comments are fine, but you'll probably have some greater challenges if you offer no additional constraints to the knotting process. The most obvious of which is that some participants will be facing outward, while others are facing inward.

Discussion and Debriefing Topics

Did you feel that the other members of this group respected your abilities during the unwinding process? Was there a single leader helping the group, or a variety of leaders during the process? Did the leadership change during the activity? Was there a moment when you thought the whole thing was impossible? Were some participants able to unwind themselves very easily, while others were more difficult? Does this situation seem similar to any in your life?

Sequence

Human Knot brings everyone in the group close together. It is ideal for a preliminary proximity activity, prior to All Aboard for example. If you happen to use Handcuffs and Shackles prior to this activity, you can use the same ropes for an extended version of Human Knot.

Activities Using Similar Skills and Follow-on Activities

Human Knot is an activity where each participant is in a close proximity with other participants. Other activities with this same configuration are Magic Carpet, All Aboard, Handcuffs and Shackles, and the Lycra Tube.

Notes

Activity 4.30

Inch By Inch

The ability to effectively search a limited area is a useful and often commendable skill. Whether the intent of the search is to find a lost contact lens, an injured hiker, a lost piece of equipment, the car keys, or the remote control for the television, the ability to quickly and effectively locate the hidden or missing object is often a test of both skill and patience. Inch By Inch turns the search into a team-based activity.

Equipment

A method for identifying the boundary of the search area. This may include a rope boundary, wooden stakes or simply the walls at the edge of a room.

The Challenge

To find an object as quickly and efficiently as possible.

Typical Presentation, Storyline or Metaphor

Debris or a foreign object (FO) on the landing deck of an aircraft carrier can cause severe damage to the tires and landing gear of a high speed aircraft. Inspection of this surface is necessary on a daily basis to insure safe conditions for both the pilots and deck personnel. In order to certify the condition of the landing deck, it is necessary to inspect this area on an inch by inch basis. In order to facilitate a safe landing area, and to be ready as quickly as possible, your team must determine the quickest method for successfully searching the landing deck, and recovering any debris found there.

Variations

Consider using an audio transmitter, such as a beeping pager or transistor radio, and finding this device with the group blindfolded. This encourages the use of listening skills.

If you happen to select a metallic object, such as a paperclip in the grass, you can consider giving the group some extra equipment, such as a few magnets. Use other familiar objects that participants will clearly recognize, such as keys, plastic toys, and coins. Do not use any sharp objects.

Rather than placing an object, consider spraying a perfume or cologne on a tree and having the group use their sense of smell to find it.

Important Points

Blindfolded searches should only take place in an environment free from obstacles. The size of the search area should be fairly small initially. After the group has perfected their searching techniques, larger areas can be used.

Discussion and Debriefing Topics

Do you see a similarity between this activity and "finding a needle in a haystack?" Did anyone happen to go right past the object on the first pass? What skills do your think are important in finding a missing object? Did members of your group communicate effectively while searching? Was there a clear pattern to your search, or a random wandering?

Sequence

The ability of a group to look for something that is out of place is a good lead into trust and spotting activities where identifying and resolving an unsafe condition is the responsibility of each group member.

Activities Using Similar Skills and Follow-on Activities

You'll find an activity entitled Camouflage in Chapter 7 that utilizes some of these same searching skills in an environmentally educational manner.

Activity 4.31

Just One Word

Some activities are so simple they are difficult! Here is a classic puzzle that groups often have difficulty solving, even when the solution is right in front of them.

Equipment

You will need 11 pieces of blank paper. Print just one of the following letters in bold print on each of the 11 pages: D, E, J, N, O, O, R, S, T, U, W.

The Challenge

For the group as a team to use these letters to spell out just one word.

Typical Presentation, Storyline or Metaphor

You receive a garbled email transmission from a friend on vacation. You remember that they said they would send you a message containing just one word, so that you would know how their vacation was going. Now can you unscramble the message.

Variations

You can probably fool even the most experienced puzzle player if you were to use a foreign alphabet or language for the translated phrase, "just one word." Another version might be to use Morse Code rather than alphabetical characters, or perhaps even photographs of hand gestures from sign language.

Rather than using letters that form the phrase "just one word," consider using letters to form the phrase, "only a single word," or "only one word." In addition to spelling out just one word, try seeing how many other words the group can form. The group can even try creating a cross-word puzzle arrangement of words using these letters.

Rather than having a trick solution, you can use letters that form a word of significance to the participants, such as quality, integrity, honor, creativity, etc.

Important Points

It is important to make sure that each member of the group has the opportunity to participate in both the handling of the letters and in creatively solving the problem.

Discussion and Debriefing Topics

Was the explanation given to your group sufficient for the group to solve the problem? Should the solution have been obvious from the start? What kept your group from seeing the obvious solution? Are there any other problems you've faced that turned out to be easier to solve than you first imagined?

Sequence

Just One Word is largely a mental challenge, unless you happen to make the letters from giant wood or concrete slabs. This type of activity is perfect before a creative problem solving activity or other initiative that requires the use outside the box thinking.

Activities Using Similar Skills and Follow-on Activities

Other activities which use similar skills include: Not Knots, 2B or KNOT 2B, Handcuffs and Shackles, and River Crossing.

Notes

Activity 4.32

Life Raft

Here is another activity that makes use of the jointed boards from Boardwalking.

Equipment

The four inner Boardwalking boards (the ones with screw eyes at both ends), joined together to form a square, with four quick links. The four remaining Boardwalking boards are placed parallel to the four outside edges of this square. This forms the Life Raft. Four hoops or rope circles are used as islands. Four objects, such as flying disks, stuff sacks, etc. are used for supplies. A long rope to mark some dangerous channel currents in the ocean. A few nautical props, such as a life preserver or a sharks fin add some comical realism.

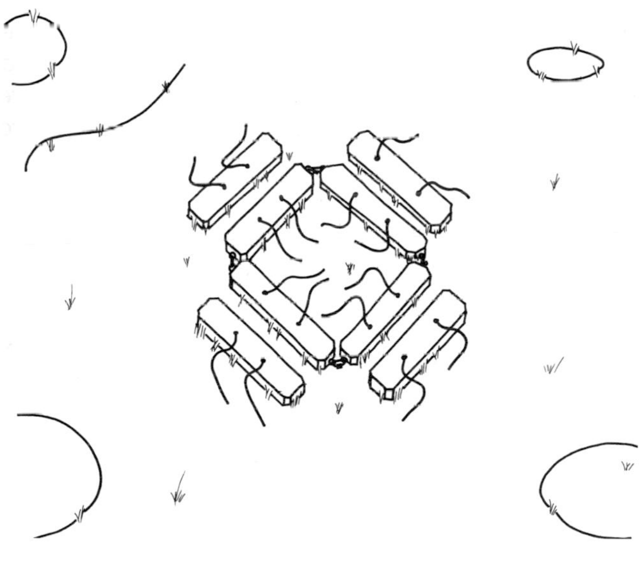

The Challenge

To assist group members in gathering as much equipment as possible from the nearby islands, and then maneuvering the Life Raft and all participants to safety before a typhoon hits.

Typical Presentation, Storyline or Metaphor

What started out as a peaceful afternoon aboard your yacht has quickly become a disaster. The good news is that your sinking ship had a Life Raft. The bad news is, it wasn't a very sturdy one, and all of your essential supplies have washed up on different nearby islands, and, oh by the way, a typhoon is coming your way. You need to retrieve as many supplies as you can and still make it to safety on the islands before the storm hits.

Variations

One of the first variations encountered is the way in which the participants use the life raft. Often some participants will use the outer four boards to quickly obtain objects from the island, leaving the inner four boards behind, and stranding those participants left onboard. Encourage the group to have a plan that includes these participants before beginning the activity. The four inner boards of the Life Raft must stay connected to each other.

The standard kinds of essential equipment include food supplies, communication equipment, medical supplies, clothes and shelter. If you include such additional equipment as an ultralight airplane, or a shark-proof cage, or a canopy covered rubber raft, or a weather station, you may generate some additional creative solutions to the group's predicament.

The spacing of the islands to the Life Raft will contribute to the total amount of time needed for this activity. The rope channel marker cannot be crossed, and depending on where it is placed, can also lengthen the time required to navigate around it.

There may be no need to bring any items back to the life raft. If you happen to use flying disks, and have participants stationed on all four islands to sit out the typhoon, they can attempt to share possessions, by flying the disks to each other. This is certainly risky, especially in the middle of a typhoon.

Important Points

The element of time in a challenge activity seldom provides a useful challenge, and typically encourages the group to hurry through the planning stage. Do not overplay the need for speed in this activity. As a facilitator, you may be surprised to know that some groups can spend half an hour or more on this activity.

Discussion and Debriefing Topics

Before anyone left the life raft, was there a definitive plan? Did everyone know what their contribution to the effort was? Did you encounter any difficulties? If you could begin this activity again, what would you do differently the next time? What is the difference between a typhoon and a monsoon?

Sequence

If you happen to use Life Raft after Boardwalking, your group is likely to try to use the four outer boards as miniature Boardwalkers. You may encourage more creative uses for these boards if you do not use Boardwalking prior to this activity. One such variation is to simply place the boards end to end and have the whole group walk to the islands.

Activities Using Similar Skills and Follow-on Activities

Boardwalking certainly uses similar skills and equipment. Danger Zone and Magic Carpet also use some of the same basic problem solving and solution generating techniques used here.

Notes

Activity 4.33

Line Up

Here is a simple activity that can be accomplished with no additional equipment.

Equipment

None, although blindfolds can be useful.

The Challenge

To have the entire group line up according to a variety of criteria, using only limited communication methods.

Typical Presentation, Storyline or Metaphor

A noble King and Queen have asked that all their royal subjects visit them and they will determine the taxes they will pay by their ability to pass several challenges.

Variations

A beginning variation without blindfolds is to instruct participants to line up accoring to birthday, from January 1st to December 31st, without talking. Verify the accuracy of the group by having participants say their birthdays in order. Next, instruct participants to line up alphabetically by the first initial of their middle name, without using their hands or arms, and without talking. For a third version using blindfolds, instruct participants to line up by height from tallest to shortest. Talking is optional in this version, and you may want to instruct participants where you want the line to be, before they put on blindfolds. Another version of this third variation, is to have particpants line up by height while kneeling.

Participants can line up by age, zip code, family size, clothing color—using various challenges such as blindfolds, no speech, limited use of hands, etc. If balance is a concern, have players close their eyes—then if any difficulty occurs, players can quickly regain their sight and balance, without removing a blindfold.

Important Points

For birthdates, hand gestures or even wrist watches (12 hours = 12 months) can be used to indicate the date. Height usually requires some physical contact between participants. Alphabetic line-up can be frustrating at first, but some inventive methods, such as writing in the dirt or a traditional or invented sign language usually occur.

Whenever blindfolds are used, have at least two spotters available to keep players from wandering off or reaching the boundary of the playing area.

Discussion and Debriefing Topics

Discuss the techniques used to overcome the various challenges. Which challenge was the most difficult? Which ability is the easiest to give up (speech, sight, hearing, mobility, etc)?

Sequence

Line Up is a low risk activity, but may be the first blindfolded experience some participants have had. This can be a useful activity before more difficult blindfolded tasks are experienced.

Activities Using Similar Skills and Follow-on Activities

Stretching the Limit is another line activity. Additional trust activities, such as a blindfolded trust walk with a partner, can build on the skills used for Line Up.

Notes

Activity 4.34

Linearity

This activity is basically a puzzle that can be used to demonstrate the power of building group consensus, and accepting the consequences of that consensus as a group.

Equipment

The plastic cloth from Magic Carpet, or the largest All Aboard platform, or a single section of the Boardwalking boards. A 5 foot long rope, and a 10 foot long rope. Both ropes need to be the same color. See Chapter 5 for directions on how to place the equipment for this activity.

The Challenge

Decide as a group which rope, 2 or 3, is the continuation of rope 1.

Typical Presentation, Storyline or Metaphor

One of the most important elements in successfully completing a challenge activity is the ability of the group to function together. To think together, to discuss problems freely, to make suggestions, and ultimately to agree on the course of the group. As a team, see if your group can agree on this simple puzzle. Determine which of the ropes on the right side of the carpet (or box, or board) is a continuation of the rope on the left side.

Variations

If you would like to adapt this activity to a series of increasingly difficult puzzles, begin the activity with two different color ropes. This is obviously pretty easy to solve for most groups, but the discussion of how the group reasons the answer is valuable. Next try two ropes of the same color, but slightly different in diameter or texture. Then move on to two identical ropes, as mentioned above. Then for an even more difficult challenge, try 3, 4 or even 5 ropes exiting from the right side.

Important Points

You'll need to pull the long rope tightly, so that it forms a straight line. The upper rope generally looks like the continuation of the rope on the left, when in fact, it is the lower one. As a facilitator, you can decide if you'll let the group use any outside resources to check the straightness of the lines. It is probably best not to allow them to touch either the ropes or the covering carpet, box, or board.

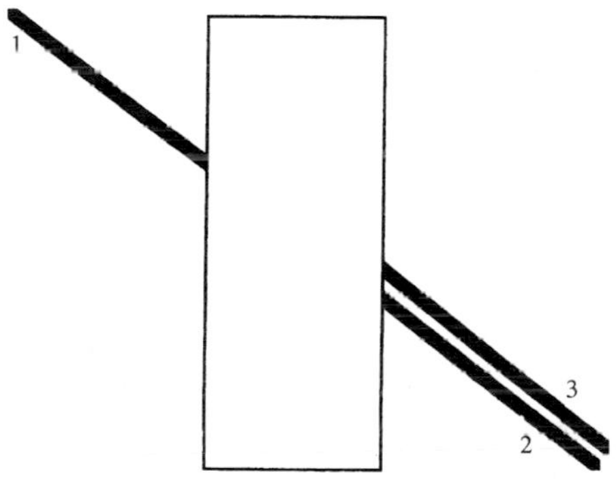

Discussion and Debriefing Topics

Was it immediately obvious for some group members to decide which rope was the correct one? Did anyone change their mind during the decision making process? Is it hard to make someone change their mind? What techniques did you use to gain the consensus of the group? Do you think that having consensus within a group is important?

Sequence

This is a quick activity that reinforces the need for group consensus. It would be ideal just prior to an activity that requires communication and total agreement of the group.

Activities Using Similar Skills and Follow-on Activities

Another activity that requires group consensus is 2B or KNOT 2B. All Aboard and Magic Carpet also utilize group consensus in a much more physical way.

Notes

Activity 4.35

Living Ladder

Living Ladder is an excellent technique for showing how a group can support a single person in their efforts without overburdening any single member of the group. It also shows that the most important component of a successful project is the people involved.

Equipment

Six to eight hardwood dowels, 1½ to 2 inches (38 to 51 mm) in diameter and 36 inches (about 1 meter) long. Oak or ash hardwood dowels are recommended. These materials are typically used for traditional wooden ladder rungs. Other equipment, such as broom handles, smaller dowels or even 2 inch (51 mm) PVC tubing is not recommended.

The Challenge

For one member of the group to climb along the horizontal ladder which is being supported by the rest of the group.

Typical Presentation, Storyline or Metaphor

Your exploration team has fallen into a giant pit. Try as you might you are not able to find a way out. There are however, a series of tree roots leading towards the top of the pit. Your group must choose their best climber and help them reach the top safely.

Variations

For their first exposure to this activity, it is best to allow a single participant to "climb" the ladder. As this person climbs past the last ladder rung, the two persons holding this rung can move to the front of the ladder, creating an infinitely long ladder.

This version also allows the group to select the best candidate for climbing, based on body weight, strength and personal choice.

Important Points

The technique for holding the hardwood dowels is important. Participants should hold the dowel firmly in one hand, and use the other hand to support this hand. Allow the shoulders and elbows to drop, so that the dowel is comfortably held with arms in an extended and relaxed position. Feet should be shoulder width apart, and participants should be standing vertically or leaning slightly backward. The next two partners should stand as close as possible to these first two partners. At any time when a climber is present on a dowel rod should partners attempt to move. Once the climber has gone past the last partners in line, they may carry the dowel rod to the front of the line, and again form another rung of the living ladder.

The technique for climbing is very much a matter of individual taste and preference. One simple technique is to crawl on hands and knees over the ladder rungs. For some participants, this may be a little difficult. Another technique involves using the hands to pull the lower body over the ladder rungs. A different technique is to sit on the first set of rungs, and then pull yourself backwards over the remaining rungs in a seated position. Encourage the climber to distribute their own weight over several dowels at a time.

Discussion and Debriefing Topics

Did you feel supported by the other members of the group? What was the most difficult task during the climb? As a partner holding the dowel, did you work well with your partner? Do you feel that they held up their end of the work? Do you think you could probably support an even heavier person?

Sequence

Living Ladder depends on the focused attention of the group. Be sure that the group displays outward signs of appropriate spotting and respect for all group members before attempting this activity. In many ways, the safety of the climber is in the hands of the rest of the group.

Activities Using Similar Skills and Follow-on Activities

Another very physical activity is River Crossing.

Notes

Activity 4.36

Log Rolling

Another classic activity that can be a permanent or portable element for your challenge and adventure program. This activity requires contact and balance.

Equipment

For a portable challenge event, several boards or planks at least 7 inches (178 mm) wide can be placed end to end on a flat surface, although a single continuous board works best. You'll need at least 12 inches (305 mm) of board length for each participant. See Chapter 5 for instructions on creating both a portable and a permanent Log Rolling element.

The Challenge

For a beginning activity, have participants at both ends of the log change places. Then, with each half of the group standing on the board and facing the center, all participants are to change ends with the other half of the group without touching the ground.

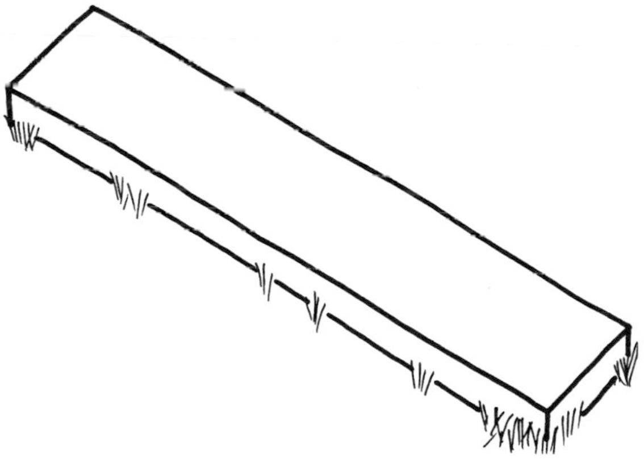

Typical Presentation, Storyline or Metaphor

Log Rolling in the Yukon is an important historical tradition. Your group has been selected to participate in this year's Klondike Derby, which features a parade of logs down the river, filled with log rollers both old and young. It is a custom for the participants on each floating log to stand stationary and face the mayor as they pass by the town square on their logs. Unfortunately, the letter did not specify what order the participants should be standing in on the logs. Your team must be ready to float down the river, and arrange themselves in any order stated.

Your exploration team is crossing a bridge high above a great waterfall in the South American rain forest. Another team is coming from the opposite direction. You must pass this team, keeping both your own members and the members of the other team safe and dry.

Variations

It can be challenging to adapt some of the Line Up activities, such as having participants line up according to height, age, birthday or the first letter of their last name, and perform these on the Log Rolling board.

Important Points

This is an activity that requires two spotters, one on each side of the board. Encourage participants to only make one trade at a time, so that spotters can be present and ready. Additional contacts along the length of the board are useful and encouraged.

Encourage participants whose balance becomes unsteady, to step off the board rather than falling to the ground. Spotters should be ready to assist at all times.

Discussion and Debriefing Topics

Were you able to use the same passing technique for all participants, or were several techniques utilized during this activity? Did anyone experience a loss of balance that was saved by one of the spotters? How did it feel to have them there? What was the biggest problem you encountered during this activity?

Sequence

Log Rolling requires a fair amount of balance and one-on-one personal contact between participants exchanging positions. This is a useful activity to try after All Aboard and before Windmill.

Activities Using Similar Skills and Follow-on Activities

Windmill, by Chris Cavert, is another variation based on the theme of Log Rolling. River Crossing also requires balance and contact between participants.

Notes

Activity 4.37

Lycra Tubes

Thanks to Barry Jolliff, Lycra Tubes made their first appearance at the Buckeye Leadership Workshop around 1989, after having been used in some modern dance settings. Barry incorporated the dance elements of movement and balance, with these useful, active and occasionally thrilling activities. Here are a few things you can do with a Lycra Tube.

Equipment

5 yards (4.6 meters) of 36 to 60 inch (0.9 to 1.5 meters) wide nylon lycra material sewn into a tube. See Chapter 5 for directions. You'll want a large flat grassy area for using the Lycra Tube.

The Challenge

There are a variety of movements that combine teamwork, support, balance and timing, using this unique piece of challenge equipment. You can also use this prop for directing the focus of the group, and during processing and debriefing sessions.

Typical Presentation, Storyline or Metaphor

A variety of metaphors can be used with the Lycra Tube. The tube can represent the boundaries of the group, the limits of understanding, the norms of a society, a surface to bounce ideas off of, a support system, a wave of excitement, and a vehicle for trying something totally new.

Variations

Here is a sample of just a few of the many things that can be done in a lycra tube:

LEAN ON IT Have participants stand inside the Lycra Tube facing the center. Slowly back up until the Lycra Tube is completely stretched tight. At this point, participants can lean outward slightly and feel the support of the Lycra Tube.

SIT IN IT Beginning with a moderately stretched Lycra Tube, have all participants sit on the Lycra Tube, with their legs extended towards the center of the circle, and the top of the Lycra Tube above the shoulders of each participant. Each participant should now be able to lean backwards and be fully supported by the tube. This is a great position for processing. You can even create a "wave" motion by having a single participant lean backwards and then forward, followed by the person to their right, passing a wave around the circle.

ROUND UP CIRCLE With the Lycra Tube well stretched around the group, have participants hold the top of the tube, and pull the lycra to the top of their shoulders. From this position, the group can now skip sideways to the left and the right. This is a useful activity for teaching observation and empathy for other participants. By watching others in the group, the speed of the movement can be tailored to the abilities of the group. Encourage participants to move only as quickly as other members of the group are comfortable with.

AROUND THE WORLD or ROCK AND ROLL With the group standing inside a very limp Lycra Tube, have a single participant back up, stretching the Lycra Tube in the process. This participant will now roll to the right completely around the inside perimeter of the Lycra Tube, until they reach their original starting position. The next person to the right then begins their journey. Encourage participants to stand near the center of the tube, so that they do not contact the person rolling around the perimeter. This activity has been known to make some participants dizzy. Proceed with caution, and encourage participants to stay in control during their journey around the tube.

THE GIANT ROLL This activity is the same as Around the World except that all participants roll at the same time and in the same direction. Encourage participants to keep adequate space between themselves to minimize contact during this activity.

4×4 CROSS OVER No question about it, this is "the activity" to do in a Lycra Tube. It is also the most energetic activity, and one that requires some appropriate safety considerations.

Begin with four participants of nearly the same weight in the Lycra Tube, equally spaced around the perimeter. Assign two opposite participants to be partners for Group 1, and the other two opposite participants to be partners for Group 2.

Safety tip: Proceed through these next few steps at a walking pace, before attempting these same movements at a faster pace. Also, ask participants to hold up their right hands about shoulder high, during each passing event. This simple reminder really helps participants remember on which side they are to pass their partner. Equal weight participants are encouraged, because this activity has been know to launch some lightweight participants that were joined by heavyweights.

Begin by asking Group 1 partners to back up. As they do, they pull the Lycra Tube tighter. The Group 2 partners now walk forward, almost touching right hands, changing places with their partner, and then backing up. As Group 2 partners back up, Group 1 partners come forward, almost touching right hands, changing places with their partners, and begin backing up. Walk this section of the activity at least four times before speeding up the cross overs. This cross over process continues indefinitely. As each group backs up, the Lycra Tube gives a firm push forward to the other group. The harder each group backs up, the stronger the push forward for the other group.

This particular activity requires an awareness of other group members, so that all participants are able to stay in control at all times. It is critical that group partners remember on which side to cross with their partners.

6×6 CROSS OVER This activity is similar to the 4×4 Cross Over, except that it requires six participants, working as two groups of three. Every other person around the perimeter of the tube is a member of the same group. Group A members push back against the Lycra Tube as Group B members move to the position of their next group member to the right. Group B members now push backwards as Group A members move to the position of their next group member to the right. While not as energetic as the 4×4 Cross Over, this activity does require balance, grace and timing. Sometimes encouraging a group to select a song or chant helps to create a tempo or rhythm for the group to follow as each set of cross overs are made.

POPCORN Here is an activity for small children. With three or four adults acting as fence posts, the Lycra Tube is fully stretched. Children now inside the Lycra Tube are said to be kernels of popcorn inside a frying pan. As the temperature warms up, the kernels begin to pop, and the popcorn bounces around the inside of the Lycra Tube. Explain to participants that they should bounce off the Lycra Tube, not other children!

PROCESS IN IT The Lycra Tube can be a great place for processing and debriefing after another challenge activity.

INSTANT SHADE If it happens to be a sunny day, and there are few trees in sight, the Lycra Tube can be used to provide shade for the group. Just stretch the Lycra Tube into a large circle, and lift the top of the Lycra Tube over the heads of all participants by about 24 inches (610 mm). The stretch within the Lycra Tube will create a canopy that blocks the sun.

SCAVENGER HUNTS Pile the entire group into a Lycra Tube and send them off on a scavenger hunt. They'll need to stay inside the Lycra Tube for the whole event. If they stop for a drink of water, they'll need to work together.

FACE IT Have three participants stretch the Lycra Tube into a large triangle. With all remaining participants, except one, facing one of the sides of the triangle. From the center of the Lycra Tube, the remaining "unknown" person then presses only their face against the Lycra Tube, and the members of the group outside the Lycra Tube attempt to recognize this person, only by their facial imprint. When guessed correctly, this participant joins the outside group, now standing with eyes closed, and taps the next person to participate.

GET SOME PRIVACY Sometimes when you are leading a single group in a large area with many other groups nearby, it can be helpful to use the Lycra Tube to block out some of the surroundings that can distract the group. The Lycra Tube won't block much sound, but it can be used as a visual barrier, and allow the group to focus on the challenge confronting them, rather than the distractions coming from all directions.

Important Points

Always keep the Lycra Tube above the shoulders and below the hips of all participants. Sometimes tubes have a tendency to bunch up, looking more like a rubber rope than a wide rubber band. If this happens, stop the activity and resume again with the Lycra Tube spread fully open.

Lycra Tube activities are best supervised at all times. You shouldn't leave a Lycra Tube lying around for unsupervised play any more than you would a climbing rope or similar piece of challenge equipment. It is a useful tool in the hands of a skilled facilitator, but can be a major risk if left for unsupervised activities.

Lycra is a fairly expensive material. You can often find it on sale during the fall and winter months. Color is really unimportant, although darker colors will hide grass stains better than lighter colors. Patterns are fine too, but try to avoid vertical stripes (these tend to make participants dizzy). 36 inch (0.9 meter) width lycra is perfect for young children. 48 to 60 inch (1.2 to 1.5 meter) width lycra is fine for adults, but for some activities, the 60 inch (1.5 meter) wide fabric is almost too wide. 5 yards (4.6 meters) is an ideal length for groups of 7 to 10 participants. Additional fabric can be added for larger groups, but the spring-like bounce of the Lycra Tube will certainly be affected by this additional length, making the cross-over activity a little less thrilling (which may be a good thing after all!)

If you happen to have any left-over lycra, try making blindfolds using 7 by 21 inch (178 by 534 mm) pieces. Directions for lycra blindfolds can be found in Chapter 5.

Discussion and Debriefing Topics

Did you notice that any time you bounced against the Lycra Tube, it had an immediate effect on the rest of the group? Were you able to upset the balance of the group with a single motion? Were you able to stay in control as you traveled around the tube in Around the World? Was the Cross Over a challenge for you personally? What could the Lycra Tube represent for you?

Sequence

Lycra Tubes can be used to teach teamwork, cooperation, safety, balance and coordination building activities. They are especially useful for processing and debriefing sessions. These props can be used for activities that range from quiet and reflective to fast moving and high energy. Lycra Tubes are often used as a means of energizing a group.

Activities Using Similar Skills and Follow-on Activities

Both Lycra Tubes and Raccoon Circles can be used for focusing the attention of the group within the circle. They are ideal for processing sessions, and can be used as a wonderful group energizer. This activity can also be used at the beginning of a challenge program. Participants just joining the group will want to come forward and see what the interesting blur of color really is.

Notes

Activity 4.38

Magic Carpet

Magic Carpet requires a minimal amount of equipment and provides a challenging initiative to solve. Several of the variations presented make this activity adaptable to many audiences.

Equipment

The Magic Carpet consists of a single piece of tarp or plastic cloth. Other options include a plastic shower curtain, plastic tablecloth, or blanket. For groups of 8–12 participants, the Magic Carpet should be approximately 4 feet by 5 feet (1.2 meters by 1.5 meters).

The Challenge

To turn the Magic Carpet over, without touching the ground surrounding the Magic Carpet.

Typical Presentation, Storyline or Metaphor

Your group is on a Magic Carpet ride, high above the fields of the surrounding countryside. You suddenly realize that you are going the wrong direction, because the carpet you are riding on is in fact, upside-down! Since you are no longer touching the ground, you must turn the carpet over, without stepping off the carpet.

Variations

In order to limit the risk in this activity, request that all participants must maintain contact with the Magic Carpet at all times. This eliminates the option of carrying participants on shoulders and other balance related concerns.

One variation which greatly increases the difficulty, and time required to accomplish the activity, is to only allow participants to touch the Magic Carpet with their feet. For this technique, participants will typically scuff the carpet to turn it over. Make sure to use a tough material if you choose this method. Thin plastic sheets have been known to tear during this variation.

For large groups, provide three Magic Carpet sizes, and place these near each other before participants climb on board. If you mention that the whole group is one team, they may decide to combine resources, and transfer to another Magic Carpet while turning over their own empty Magic Carpet. Once the group has accomplished this task by combining resources, encourage them to repeat the activity, this time without sharing space or carpets with the other members of their group. If the three Magic Carpets are placed further away, participants may choose to shuffle the carpets closer together rather than working alone.

Using a plastic cloth or tarp that is a different color on each side makes it easy for a group to see when they have accomplished their goal.

Consider using a series of decreasing size Magic Carpets to increase the difficulty level. If you happen to be using the inexpensive plastic table coverings available at many party stores, you can even cut off a portion of the Magic Carpet after each successful inversion.

Another variation using a single Magic Carpet is to begin the activity with a single person, and gradually add additional team members each time the carpet is flipped over.

A substantially different solution is possible if the facilitator mentions that each participant's feet must be touching the Magic Carpet, but yet allow other parts of the body to touch the ground surrounding the carpet. This method works well for very small carpet sizes.

Another variation involves using different shapes for the Magic Carpet. In general, rectangles are easier to flip than squares. Triangles are easier to flip than circles. Perhaps alphabet shaped Magic Carpets could be used. Each new geometry is likely to produce a slightly different solution technique.

Finally, rather than calling this activity Magic Carpet, you can call it Surfing the Web, and make up your own metaphors regarding the flip side of data and anti-data in the computer world.

Important Points

The size of the Magic Carpet and the size of the group greatly effects the difficulty in accomplishing this initiative. Minimize risk by requiring all participants to be in contact with the carpet at all times.

Typical solutions for this activity involve crowding a majority of the group towards one edge or corner, and having a few group members attempt to twist or fold the Magic Carpet over. For a rectangle, twisting a corner of the Magic Carpet, somewhat like a bow-tie, provides the greatest amount of area for movement.

From a mathematical viewpoint, the fundamental problem with Magic Carpet is that many of the techniques available to turn the carpet over result in reducing the area of the carpet to approximately half the original area. An optimum solution then, is one that would allow the carpet to be turned over, and yet maximize the total area of the carpet throughout the activity.

Oddly enough, carpet is not a good choice for the Magic Carpet initiative. It is difficult to fold and is generally too thick to twist easily. Plastic sheets are a better choice, and take up much less space in the equipment storage container.

Discussion and Debriefing Topics

An interesting question to ask participants during this initiative is what their role is with regard to the solution. Were they active or passive in their contribution to the final solution? Who did the most work?

One debriefing method, known as *Both Sides Now,* uses the Magic Carpet as a tool for conflict resolution. Using a light colored plastic material, allow participants to write their feelings, or expressions, or supporting evidence for their side of the conflict. Participants with opposing views are then asked to write their comments on the other side of the material. The activity proceeds just as Magic Carpet does, but with participants reading these comments out loud during the struggle to turn the material over.

Another therapeutic technique for Magic Carpet, known as *Turning Over a New Leaf,* uses this metaphor for audiences with dependencies. The struggle to overcome adversity and turn over a new leaf can be assisted by other group members, and occasionally some outside support—all of which can be processed during the activity.

Sequence

Magic Carpet requires all participants in a group to work within a tightly constrained space. As such, it is important to build up to this level of proximity.

Activities Using Similar Skills and Follow-on Activities

The tarp or plastic sheet used for Magic Carpet can also be used for Cave In, Danger Zone, and Blackout. The proximity of this initiative is similar to All Aboard.

Notes

Activity 4.39

Marble Tubes

To a challenge education programmer, PVC tubing is worth it's weight in gold!

Equipment

You'll find directions for two versions of marble tubes in Chapter 5. The simplest style involves cutting 15 inch (381 mm) long pipes from 1 inch (25 mm) diameter cold water PVC tubing. Another style uses 1½ to 2 inch (38 to 51 mm) diameter PVC tubing that has been cut to length, and then split into two pieces lengthwise.

You'll need at least one Marble Tube section for each participant, along with a few marbles, golf balls, and other small rolling objects.

The Challenge

To relocate several marbles from Position A to Position B using only the PVC tubes. Participants that are holding a marble in their segment of PVC tubing are not allowed to move their feet.

Typical Presentation, Storyline or Metaphor

During the annual spring walk of the local bird watching society, your group notices a bird's egg that has rolled downhill away from a nest on a low branch. Knowing that many animals are wary of human scent, you attempt to relocate this marble-sized bird egg back to the nest, without touching it.

Variations

For a truly unique experience, try passing a collection of marbles up a flight of stairs, or up the incline of a hill.

Allowing participants to hold near the ends of the tubes make this task a little easier. For a more difficult challenge, only allow participants to touch their own marble tube. For an even harder task, participants can touch any tubes they like, but the tubes cannot touch each other.

Attach a variety of colored tape to the ends of the marble tubes, so that only similar colors can be partners. You can also add some of the various connections found in hardware stores, such as elbows, tees, Y sections, etc.

Drilling a few holes in some marble tubes will additionally challenge the participants having those tubes. We call these the "swiss cheese tubes."

Try passing other objects, such as foam balls, which make little or no noise. Passing water is also fun. See Waterfall II.

One of the hardest variations is to only allow participants to touch their tube with one hand.

Important Points

Choose a reasonable distance to transport the marbles or balls. For a group of 12 participants, 50 to 70 feet (15 to 21 meters) is adequate.

Discussion and Debriefing Topics

Do you think your group worked together well, or were there fine points that could be improved upon? How did your group decide on the plan? Did the execution of your plan change during the activity? Did the order of participants change during the activity? How many of your marbles (goals) did you achieve?

Sequence

Marble Tubes require just a bit of problem solving, but quite a bit of activity, especially if the marble is going uphill. This activity has a lower energy level, and may be useful in between a high energy activity and a processing or reflective moment.

Activities Using Similar Skills and Follow-on Activities

Waterfall I and Waterfall II use similar equipment.

Notes

Activity 4.40

Midnight Sun

Midnight Sun requires what can sometimes be an unreliable piece of equipment—the sun itself. This activity is a variation of Blackout.

Equipment

You'll need something to place on the ground, such as a large beach towel, or the plastic tarps from Magic Carpet and Danger Zone, or a long rope to create an outline or a large familiar shape.

The Challenge

For the group to create shadows using their bodies that completely shade the surface of the object or space in front of them.

Typical Presentation, Storyline or Metaphor

While exploring in the polar region of the earth, your group experiences the Aurora Borealis, the northern lights (or in the southern hemisphere, the Aurora Australis, the southern lights). Your group just happens to have some large scale, long exposure photographic paper that can record this event. You place this paper on the ground, but suddenly you are reminded what time of year it is, as the Midnight Sun makes an appearance. Before your photographic paper is ruined, your team unites to block out the sunlight reaching the paper.

Your corporation has decided to create a giant holiday light display on the side of their 30 story headquarters. The last light is put in place at about noon, but the display is controlled by a large light sensitive patch, which only switches on after the sun sets. Your group would like to check to make sure that all the light bulbs are working, and since the control eye is nearby, you try to block the sunlight reaching it, so that it will turn on the display.

Variations

Depending on the location of the sun, the size of the object that the group can cast a shadow over changes dramatically. By sunset, a 12 person group can probably cast a shadow over a whole bus. Using a large tarp works well for this activity, because you can fold it to create the most appropriate sized challenge for the group. Using a rope also works well, because you can create objects and shapes that have meaning to the group. How about a sunlight sensitive polar bear that forget their sunblock?

After the group creates a way to completely block the sunlight reaching the object, have them move back about 20 yards and then come forward quickly to recreate the shadow again. If the object really was a photographic paper, the time between shadows would be similar to the exposure setting of a camera.

A slightly more difficult challenge would be to have participants block the sun without touching each other. This typically involves several rows of participants, but can add an interesting and substantially more difficult variation to the process.

A completely different variation, and one that doesn't require any additional props, is to split the group into two parts, and have them create shadows in the shapes of various objects, such as animals, vehicles, buildings, trees, etc. The other group then tries to guess what they are creating. We call this version Shadow Art.

Yet another no prop version that is most effective in the very early morning or near sunset, is to have the first group sit on the ground with their backs to the sun. The second group stands behind them, casting their long shadows over their seated companions. The seated group must now guess which shadow is being created by which group member behind them. We call this version, The Shadow Knows.

One final version that also works well for this activity, is to have the group estimate the number of participants that they will need to successfully cast a shadow over the entire target. Processing this estimate can be useful with corporate groups.

Important Points

It takes a fair amount of contact to keep holes from opening up between participants and allowing sunlight to reach the object. Encourage appropriate contact or even no contact between participants.

Discussion and Debriefing Topics

Was this activity easier or more difficult than you imagined? Were you able to plan your approach completely, or did you need to make adjustments after the activity was begun? Does is matter what time it is? Could you use this same approach at 9 am or 7 pm? Was it easier to complete this task when you were allowed to be in contact with other participants?

Sequence

You'll need to use this activity in the early morning or late afternoon, so that shadows are fairly long. If you happen to be inside, you can use bright spotlights to create the same effect.

Activities Using Similar Skills and Follow-on Activities

Other types of proximity activities include Knots, First Contact, Danger Zone, Blackout, All Aboard, and Magic Carpet.

Notes

Activity 4.41

Mine, Mine, Mine

Don't let the title of this activity fool you. This activity has nothing to do with military weaponry, but rather to do with the elation expressed by an individual when they find their own personal object in an area filled with many impostors.

Equipment

You will need one blindfold for every two people. As an outdoor activity, a grove of similar trees is ideal. For an indoor version, or when a grove of trees is not immediately accessible, try using potatoes.

The Challenge

This activity is accomplished working in pairs, with one partner blindfolded. The sighted partner leads the blindfolded partner to a single tree (or to a potato) and instructs the sightless partner to inspect the tree (or potato) completely, taking care to remember any distinguishing features, dimples, bumps or otherwise identifying markings. The blindfolded partner is then lead away from the tree, their blindfold removed, and then asked to visually go and find their tree (or potato), without touching it. When they locate their original tree (or potato), they are free to yell, "mine, mine, mine!"

Typical Presentation, Storyline or Metaphor

During a visit to the Yukon territories one year, you identified a unique object late one evening just as darkness was setting in. Now after 5 years you have returned to again search for this object, but this time in the bright summer light. Can you find the object which has haunted your imagination for so long?

Variations

One of the most significant variations in this activity would be to have the blindfolded participant also wear any type of gloves (surgical, rubber, household cleaning, cotton gloves, mittens, an oven mitt, welder's gloves, or (my favorite) the chain mail gloves worn by workers handling scrap metals and other sharp objects (typically sold only in specialty equipment stores—but really cool).

The difficulty level can be substantially raised by increasing the number of trees (or potatoes) available, and the distance from which the blindfolded participant is lead prior to contacting the tree initially, and away from the tree after the first stage of this activity.

Nearly any objects that are similar, but unique will work for this activity. Pumpkins in the fall are another good choice. Tennis balls however, would not be easily discernible. Rocks from a creek bed might make an interesting activity. What about a sighted version of this activity where participants study a leaf, and then try to identify their leaf when it is mixed with other (numbered on the back) leaves? There is even another activity called Naturally Mine, where participants study a natural object, such as an orange, leaf, twig, blade of grass, pebble or wood chip, and try to recover this same object when it has been placed in a pile with other similar objects.

If you want to include other senses, why not have the blindfolded partner sample (by smell) some common household spices (such as cinnamon, pepper, sage, rosemary, etc.), and then see if they can identify the same smell again when the blindfold is removed.

Finally, how about a taste version of this activity, where participants each bring their own recipe of chocolate chip cookies to see if blindfolded participants can find the same baker when the blindfold is removed. Better have some cold milk on hand for this version.

Important Points

Any time a participant is blindfolded, it is a necessity to have another sighted person working directly with this individual during every phase of the activity. Wooded areas are typically filled with uneven footing, roots, rocks and other objects which can additionally challenge a blindfolded participant. If there is any concern about the risk involved, simply have participants close their eyes rather than blindfolding them. Then if the terrain becomes unsteady, the participant can simply open their eyes to regain their footing.

Discussion and Debriefing Topics

What information did you use to locate your tree (or potato)? Were there any other clues (location of a bird singing, road noise, direction of sunlight) that assisted you in your search?

Sequence

Working with partners is a good place to begin a trust building sequence with challenge and adventure activities. The use of the blindfold requires some familiarity and trust with the sighted partner, so a few lead in trust activities would be useful here.

Activities Using Similar Skills and Follow-on Activities

Activities which utilize other senses, such as Bag It.

Notes

Activity 4.42

The Missing Page

Try to imagine that you are reading through your favorite collection of challenge activities when you suddenly realize, right in the middle of the description for a terrific activity, that one of the pages in the book is missing! The partial directions in front of you lists some interesting equipment, but absolutely no idea what to do with this stuff. Your job is to write the rest of the activity.

Equipment

Provide a collection of some standard challenge and adventure programming equipment (such as tennis balls, hoola hoops, rope, pvc tubing, short segments of 2×4's, carabiners, beach balls, blindfolds and anything else you typically carry with you) and some unique props (rubber chicken, mouse traps, a plastic Halloween pumpkin, a birthday candle, dice, balloons, 100 feet of string). Be sure to include a clipboard, paper and pencil for the group to write down the activity (you never know what wonderfully creative activity may occur).

The Challenge

Devise a challenging activity using any of the props provided. You can encourage the group to create an activity on a certain theme (such as trust building, problem solving, communication, etc.)

Typical Presentation, Storyline or Metaphor

The missing page description in the first paragraph easily applies to this activity. For corporate, technical or academic groups, explain that a computer virus has destroyed a portion of the system which retained the information for this activity. Using sophisticated recovery techniques, only the equipment list was salvageable.

Variations

Rather than using typical challenge equipment, you might consider using some simple household items that could easily be recycled. Plastic milk jugs can be cut to create funnels, scoops and storage containers. Cardboard boxes can become signs, stepping stones or obstacles.

By identifying a theme for the activity, planning time can typically be shortened, allowing more time to actually attempt the challenge. Some groups may attempt to create the world's longest challenge activity, so stay tuned in to the group.

Be sure to keep a few unusual props ready, just in case the group needs some additional ideas to get going.

Important Points

This type of free-form challenge requires the group to be familiar with challenge activities in general. Obviously this is not one of the first activities to present to your group. If you choose to include familiar objects that the group has seen used before, don't be surprised to see them using these props again in a similar way.

One of the most important moments in this activity comes when the group is asked to identify any safety related concerns with their proposed activity. It is a unique experience to watch a group work together to identify safety concerns, and then to work to eliminate any unnecessary risks.

Discussion and Debriefing Topics

Creative activities, and especially the ideas for a new activity, typically begin with the comments made by a single person, and then branch out in many directions as the thoughts of other participants generate more possibilities. See if the group can identify the initial thought which lead to the final activity. Discuss the selection of props used and those which were not used. Discuss any modifications which were made due to safety concerns. Discuss any modifications which were made during the actual demonstration of the activity, after the planning stage was completed. Have the group evaluate the effectiveness of the activity.

Sequence

This activity should come after the group has been exposed to a variety of challenge activities, so that they have some experience on which to base the invention of their new activity.

Activities Using Similar Skills and Follow-on Activities

Based on the equipment chosen by the group, other challenge activities using this same equipment can be explored, so that participants can see other potential uses of these same props.

Notes

Activity 4.43

Monumental

Monument + Mental = Monumental

The purpose of Monumental is to provide a structured method for learning spotting techniques within a group. Making spotting the responsibility of the group, and encouraging participants to be watching for opportunities to avoid risks and to provide assistance where necessary, is essential in group challenge activities where climbing, lifting and balance issues are present.

Equipment

You'll need one of the dice presented in Chapter 5 for each of the participants. These dice have various body positions on each face, plus a few marked with an "S," for Spotter. A blank face on a die indicates that a participant can assume any position they like.

The Challenge

All members of the group roll one of the large wooden dice to see what body position they must assume in a living monument they are creating as a group. Any time an S is rolled, that person becomes a spotter, and one other person may be elevated. Each group member, except for spotters, must be in contact with two other group members at any time.

Typical Presentation, Storyline or Metaphor

An international artist has been commissioned to create a monument displaying group cooperation and involvment. Your group has been selected to be the subjects of this artwork. You have been given a method (the Monumental Dice) for developing various poses that will be reviewed by the artist.

Variations

It can be helpful to throw all the dice at the same time, so that spotters can be identified early in the Monumental building process. If you choose to throw dice one at a time, you can build the monument one participant at a time.

You can allow participants to trade dice after they have thrown them. This would allow one person to assume a lifting position, while their dice trading partner becomes the person to be lifted. This transfer of responsibility should not be a result of stereotypes, but rather of personal preference. You can even roll all the dice and let the entire group choose which position they are best suited to assume.

Important Points

Effective spotting is no game. This activity is simply a structured method for teaching participants how to correctly support someone during a challenge activity. Encourage spotters to always keep light contact with the person they are spotting. Hands up at all times, feet apart in a stable stance, eyes on the person at all times, focusing on the upper body at the shoulders and head. Spotters should anticipate where a person may move to and be ready to assist immediately. Encourage verbal communication between the spotter and the person they are spotting. Spotting begins with the elevation of any participant, and continues until that person has both feet back on the ground.

The most important benefit of this activity is raising the awareness of participants for risks which are avoidable, for situations that are unstable, for positions that may be uncomfortable, and for techniques that may possess some real physical risk if not properly spotted. Monumental provides the opportunity to increase the number of eyes watching for risk.

Discussion and Debriefing Topics

Were you able to create some artistic poses, even without spotters? What role does a spotter play? Were you able to incorporate the spotters into the monument? What is the first priority of a spotter? When do you need one? How many spotters are enough?

Sequence

Monumental is an excellent activity to proceed any challenge and adventure activity which requires effective spotting, such as a the Wall, Surfing the Web, and even All Aboard. It is an opportunity to increase the group's awareness to risk, and to participate in the reduction of that risk by their own efforts.

Activities Using Similar Skills and Follow-on Activities

Activities that can benefit from spotting include: all the varieties of Surfing the Web, Under the Doormat, and All Aboard found in this book. And such activities as The Wall, Willow in the Wind, and Trust Falls, which are found in many of the additional challenge and adventure related references in Chapter 8.

Notes

Activity 4.44

Move It or Lose It

Why should challenge instructors be the only ones to carry a ton of equipment to the program? Here is an activity that combines some low cost props with what many folks consider a very practical life skill—the ability to haul a bunch of stuff at one time.

Equipment

You'll need quite a few identical lightweight containers. Some of my favorite are empty 2 liter soda bottles with the caps (you can use these later for making terrariums or bottle rockets—see Chapter 7), copier paper boxes and their lids (always useful for storing your stuff), or plastic film canisters with lids (which can also be used for holding small items, and for organizing large groups into smaller groups—see Chapter 5). In many places, all of these items are generally low cost or even free—but you need to start saving them now, to insure that you'll have enough when the date of your challenge program rolls around. You'll need about 100 containers total for a group of 10–12 participants. It is also helpful to have three ropes to mark the boundaries of the present container location, a transfer location, and the final destination location.

The Challenge

Working as two teams, your group needs to transport the containers from their present location to a transfer station about 30 feet (9.1 meters) away, where the second half of the group will take over and carry the containers to their final destination, an additional 30 feet (9.1 meters) away. Any containers touching the ground are lost.

Typical Presentation, Storyline or Metaphor

During a cold winter storm, a train carrying supplies to a remote village is stopped by an avalanche. The train crew (the first half of the group) can bring the supplies to the end of the train in a single trip, but does not have the necessary equipment to carry them over the snow. The avalanche has also interrupted electrical power inside the train, and any dropped containers cannot be seen in the darkness. While all this is happening, a helicopter has landed to pick up the supplies. The helicopter crew (the second half of the group) has the necessary snow equipment, and can pick up the supplies from the train crew in a single trip, but only if the train crew hands the containers directly to them. Snow blindness keeps them from finding any containers dropped into the snow.

Variations

You can additionally challenge a group by only allowing each person to touch the containers with one hand. You can also limit the total number of hands touching the containers at any one time. For each of the containers listed above, you can decide whether to allow the participants to remove the lids or caps during transport or not. If there is a narrow doorway available, have the transfer point located near this doorway. Instead of containers, consider using large pieces of foam, partially inflated beach balls, foam noodle pool toys, or any soft, lightweight objects.

In addition to the boxes or containers, try offering the group one very long rope to help tie the boxes together. This may not help, but provides something new for the group to consider.

Important Points

By choosing lightweight objects the risk of injury is minimized. The corners of the boxes are probably the most likely risk in this activity, and a few spotters watching the stack of swaying boxes is a good idea. These same spotters can also remove any dropped film canisters or bottles from the path of the group as they move towards the next location. Encourage participants to pick up as many containers as they can before leaving the train, transfer zone, or the final helicopter location. If you make the rope surrounding the containers fairly small, participants will need to be more careful not to drop the containers outside the storage space.

This activity takes on a completely different character on a windy day!

Discussion and Debriefing Topics

Did you choose a safe number of containers for your first try, or did your group go for the maximum number? What percentage of containers did your group successfully transport? Did your group modify the carrying technique during the activity, after initial planning was complete? Which of the three zones was most difficult, the pick-up zone, the transfer zone, or the final destination zone?

Sequence

This activity can be used early in a problem solving sequence. The activity itself is not difficult, and brings into discussion many of the topics generally associated with successful problem solving methods. It also helps participants identify their roles during the activity (spotter, transporter, transfer agent, solution inventor, etc.)

Activities Using Similar Skills and Follow-on Activities

Any group which successfully completes this activity is probably adequately skilled to help you collect and transport all your challenge equipment back to your vehicle or storage location at the end of the program.

Notes

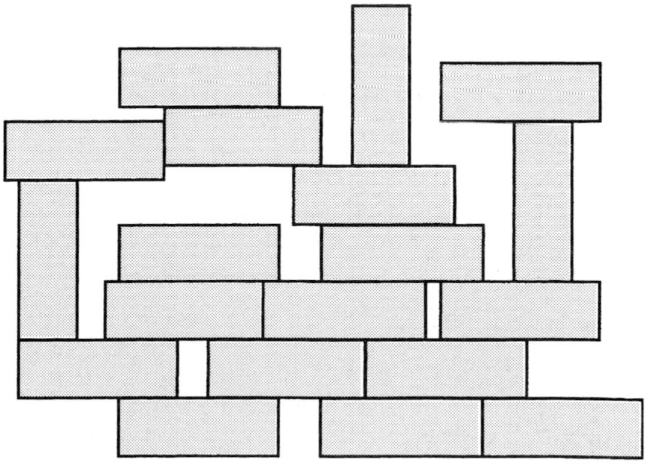

Activity 4.45

Moving Towards Extinction

Moving Towards Extinction provides a very visual technique for understanding what happens when a much needed resource is exhausted. This activity also illustrates the difficulty that an organization or a society experiences when the environment changes, but the culture or methods do not.

Equipment

A dozen rope hoops, plastic hoops, carpet circles, Raccoon Circles or plywood disks of various diameters from 1 foot (305 mm) to 3 feet (about 1 meter).

The Challenge

For all group members to have both feet inside any circle at various times during this activity. Begin the activity with about a dozen circles, and remove at least one each turn, until only one circle remains. Each time the facilitator calls, "check-in," group members must place both feet inside a circle. After this, participants begin to mingle about in the general area of the circles, waiting for the next check-in time. Reinforce the basic requirement that both feet must be within the circle every so often.

Typical Presentation, Storyline or Metaphor

Your team has been assembled to review a startling occurrence in the rain forest. It appears as if a vital link in the food chain is becoming extinct. A blue-green moss which provides food for much of the local wildlife is starting to disappear. Your team arrives and immediately begins to look for the circles of this moss growing in the surrounding area. At specific times, your group pauses to check in, and to count the number of moss patches observed. During each check in time, each scientist must have both feet within one of the moss circles.

Variations

Several different types of ropes can be used to create the various size circles. Perhaps the most dramatic way to demonstrate the extinction of this plant, is to use circles made with chalk, and then to erase a circle each round, until there is only one left.

Important Points

Participants quickly realize that the number of circles is diminishing. Typically however, they begin this activity by standing in the circles, and will continue this technique until there is no room left. By the time there are only three circles left, some participants may not have a place to stand. At this point, it is ideal to discuss what is happening with the group. Ask them to anticipate what is going to happen next. And finally, ask them what the basic rules are for this activity. Having them focus on the phrase "both feet must be inside" rather than their preconceived notion that their entire body must be inside the circle. The element of discovery, and opportunity for change here, is the moment when participants realize that they can sit down on the ground, with their feet inside the perimeter of the circle, and still satisfy the basic rules of the activity.

One of the most important concepts that can be extended by this activity, is that in order to stop the extinction of something on our planet, we have to do something different! If we continue doing the same thing, we are likely to get the same results. Momentarily we adapt to the changing environment, but in the end our behavior must change, or we too become extinct.

Discussion and Debriefing Topics

When did you realize that the circles were going to continue vanishing? Were you worried about your other group members, or just concerned about whether there would be a place for you? Be honest. Did it occur to you to try something different so that everyone in your group would have a chance to succeed? What is something in your life that you have always done the same way?

Sequence

Moving Towards Extinction encourages the group to fully understand the rules of the activity, and often to question them to see how rigid they really are. This is also an environmentally based activity, that can be followed or preceded by other environmental activities.

Activities Using Similar Skills and Follow-on Activities

All Aboard, Magic Carpet and Worm Hole bring participants close together, just as this activity does. Plenty of Room at the Top involves some creative thought to solve.

Notes

Activity 4.46

Not Knots

After hauling around the tons of equipment used in challenge and adventure programming, it can be very refreshing to find a new activity that requires equipment that can also be used for other activities. In this case, the ropes used in the activity 2B or KNOT 2B can also be used for Not Knots. Several more activities for these ropes can be found within this chapter and in the Rope Kit presented in Chapter 9.

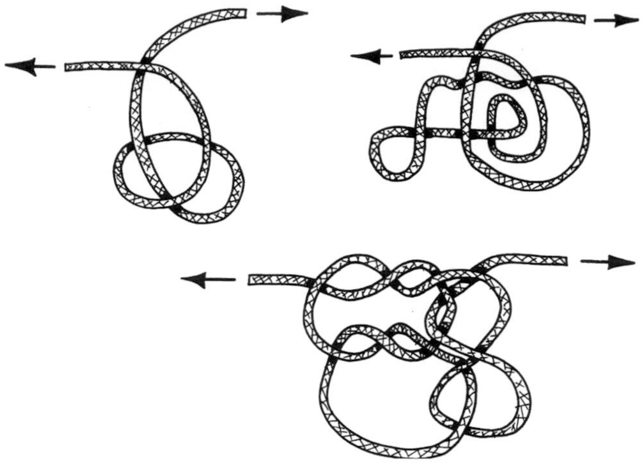

Equipment

Several colorful ropes, each 5 to 10 feet long.

The Challenge

Using a single piece of rope, create a series of loops, twists and turns in the rope, and place the rope on the ground so that it is not immediately obvious whether the rope will create a knot when the two ends of the rope are pulled in opposite directions. The challenge is for the entire group to decide, without touching the rope, whether a knot will be formed when the rope is pulled, or whether the loops, twists and turns in the rope will simply unwind, leaving a straight piece of rope. Achieving group consensus is the ultimate goal of Not Knots.

Typical Presentation, Storyline or Metaphor

Decision making is more than a series of lucky guesses. It is defined by making good choices and understanding the information available. The rope puzzles here are designed to fool you. See if you and your group can successfully decide which ropes form knots when the ends of the rope are pulled.

Variations

The length and number of knots formed along a length can easily be varied. If you use a very long rope, more participants can be included in the activity as they wander around checking the path of the rope. You can use this activity either before or after a teachable moment where you instruct the group on a variety of knot tying techniques.

Important Points

Building consensus within the group is the primary goal of this activity. What is important is that the group agrees as a whole before pulling on the rope. The second opportunity for this activity is to make sure that all participants sense that their comments are listened to by the group, and that their voice counts.

Discussion and Debriefing Topics

Did you find this activity interesting or frustrating? Why do you think it is important to have everyone in the group in agreement? How often were you correct in your estimates of which ropes were knots, and which ones were not?

Sequence

This activity is ideal early in the program, so that participants can experience the need and desire for group consensus and participation.

Activities Using Similar Skills and Follow-on Activities

Handcuffs and Shackles utilizes some rope work, and potentially some knot tying skills. 2B or Knot 2B requires this same level of group consensus.

Notes

Activity 4.47

Parade

Parade is a ground level challenge activity that requires no equipment at all. It provides a challenge of getting from here to there with various constraints on the group. The information shown here was developed during a visit to Easter Seal Camp Fairlee Manor, where groups typically have both feet and wheels touching the ground at any one time.

Equipment

None!

The Challenge

To move the entire group from Point A to Point B, a distance of about 6 meters (20 feet), with a decreasing number of contact points with the ground each time the journey is made. All participants must be in contact with the rest of the group.

Typical Presentation, Storyline or Metaphor

Part 1. Your group has been asked to participate in an annual holiday parade to be held in New York City. Using only the participants now present in your group, you must construct a parade float, with no more than 20 points of contact with the ground. Parade judges particularly enjoy musical floats, so you might want to consider having live music (humming, singing, percussion, etc.) on your float.

Part 2. The organizers of a European festival happened to see your New York City parade float and have invited you to attend their celebration this year. However, the streets of the town where the parade is to be held is quite a bit smaller than New York City, so for this parade only 15 points of contact can be made with the ground.

Part 3. Well, your group obviously knows how to make the finest parade float in the world. While you were parading in Europe, another foreign nation saw your float and have invited you to their country. This country is known for their festivals and exceptionally narrow streets. For this parade you can only have 10 points of contact with the ground, and will need to provide very loud music to overcome the roar of the crowd that is expected to view the parade.

Variations

Rather than simply counting the number of contact points with the ground, the facilitator can prescribe the number of feet touching the ground. This will encourage participants to use some form of transportation rather than walking to move the float. If there are wheelchairs in the group, see if participants can find a safe method for reducing the number of wheels touching the ground.

If the number of feet touching the ground become the criteria for the size of the float, reduce the number of feet each time until participants are able to complete the parade with no feet touching the ground (rolling, on hand and knees, etc.)

Important Points

This is an activity in which participants sometimes find themselves locked into a single mode of thinking, and try to use several walking or hopping participants to move or steady the rest of the group. As the number of feet touching the ground decreases, such groups will generally think that the minimum number of feet touching the ground cannot possibly decrease below a fairly high number. By asking participants what the minimum number of feet touching the ground is for the parade, the facilitator can help the group move away from their locked thinking and focus on the task of reducing the number of feet (but not necessarily contact points) touching the ground.

If participants are likely to crawl or roll for this activity, an appropriate playing surface is necessary. A flat grassy lawn is ideal when outdoors, or a carpeted room inside. Try to avoid driveways and other hard surfaces.

Discussion and Debriefing Topics

Debriefing issues include discussing if there were any group members with special needs during the movement of the parade float. Discussing the leadership roles during the activity (i.e. was there a music director, someone chanting a cadence, a dance choreographer, etc.)

Sequence

Parade works well as a beginning proximity activity.

Activities Using Similar Skills and Follow-on Activities

By having participants in contact with each other, moving in unison, and spotting each other, this activity provides many of the skills necessary for All Aboard, Boardwalking, and Moving Toward Extinction.

Notes

Activity 4.48

Plenty of Room at the Top

Sometimes the most difficult problems can have the simplest and most elegant solutions. We know a few carpenters that have earned quite a few free cups of coffee, just by knowing a solution to this fascinating puzzle. If you ever needed a simple way to show your group that even something that seems impossible, is not, this is it. Be sure to check out the two rather unusual solutions to this problem shown at the end of Chapter 4.

Equipment

20 large nails and a piece of wood.

The Challenge

To place as many nails as possible on the head of a single nail that has been hammered into a piece of wood.

Typical Presentation, Storyline or Metaphor

Two urban radio enthusiasts decide to put a new antenna on the roof of their urban apartment building. Even though there really isn't much room up there, they figure out a way to balance all the various components to the antenna on top of a single pole. Can your group do the same?

Variations

Varying the size and quantity of nails does little to change the basic solution to this unique problem, but having several sizes of nails present at the same time can certainly add a degree of confusion. Consider using knitting needles rather than nails. Also, rather than completing this activity with the entire group at once, consider allowing groups of two or three participants to work together at a time, and then each presenting their technique to the entire group for evaluation.

One of the most unique variations to this now classic problem is to present the group with a variety of bolts, screws, and nails (with and without heads), and ask them to stack as many of these items on the head of a single nail as possible.

If you really want to boggle the minds of your group, give them about 70 decking nails (the really long variety), and challenge them to place all of these on the head of the single nail.

Several wild variations are presented here and at the end of this chapter. In addition to the classic roof truss solution to this problem, rings can be formed from the nails to create a chain that can be hung off the solitary straight nail. Technically speaking, this solution works. It doesn't involve any external adhesives. A single ring can also be used to bundle the remaining straight nails. Finally, even without attempting this solution on the day of the equinox, one group was able to balance two large nails on the head of another, and then pile most of the remaining nails upon these two. Well done.

So if you are thinking that there is only one solution to this problem, think again. And we haven't even considered some really fun ideas like magnetizing the nails, or melting them down, or splitting the head of the single nail to form a cradle. What else can you do?

Important Points

Try to encourage each member of the group to become involved with both the creative problem solving of this problem, and the handling of the nails. Sometimes a solution becomes evident just by manipulating the elements of the puzzle. In this case, that means handling the nails.

When using this activity outdoors, use very large nails. They are easier to find than small nails if dropped in the grass!

Discussion and Debriefing Topics

Did you think that this challenge was impossible? What is the difference between an impossibility and a possibility? What methods helped you find your solution? Were you surprised with the solution you created? When you see solutions involving rings and balancing acts, do you consider these a) cheating, b) creative cheating or c) just another version of a correct answer?

Sequence

Plenty of Room at the Top is an interesting puzzle to challenge a group with as they are arriving for an adventure program. Having several small nail puzzles available, and one very large version for illustration purposes, works well. Consider using this activity early in the program to illustrate that creativity and hard work can solve a challenge, even when it seems impossible.

Activities Using Similar Skills and Follow-on Activities

There are a variety of puzzles that can be used to illustrate that groups can accomplish more than individuals. It is a great idea to have a few of these on hand. Other problem solving and puzzle related activities in this book include: 2B or KNOT 2B, Not Knots, Linearity, 63 / 64 / 65, Villages and Wells, and Handcuffs and Shackles.

Notes

Activity 4.49

A Closing Activity With Popsicle Sticks

Having a simple activity for bringing some closure to the group experience is essential. Here is an activity which has both a group challenge, and then an interesting closing technique for illustrating the effectiveness of a group. Kirk Weisler of Orem, Utah added some of his own comments, and made this an even more interesting activity.

Equipment

Two or three popsicle or craft sticks for every participant. Something to write with such as a pen, marker or pencil. A roll of masking tape.

The Challenge

For groups of about 8 participants to make a flying object from two of their popsicle sticks using only the sticks and 12 inches (305 mm) of masking tape. Save the third popsicle stick for the closing activity. The goal for this object is to fly as far as possible, or as Kirk would say, "they'll be given a chance to throw this sucker for a gold medal!" Have groups line up behind a clearly defined line, and each throw their creation individually, with all the appropriate cheering and hoopla typically accompanying the launch of a new vessel.

Typical Presentation, Storyline or Metaphor

It is not enough to simply experience life and all it holds. We need to take what we have learned and let it make us soar. Each of the challenges your group has met today added to what you can do. Let's take these pieces of our experience, and let them fly.

Variations

Craft and popsicle sticks work terrific for this activity and are not very expensive. You can probably substitute other kinds of tape, or string, but masking tape works just fine.

If you want to insure that the group doesn't focus only on the object that flies the farthest, try using another line to define "the next level." This line, fairly close to the throwing line, is a goal that can be met by all groups, and illustrates that everyone has made an advancement.

Important Points

Make sure that participants take pride in the workmanship of their creation. It is a reflection of themselves. You can invite the person that had the least contact with the masking tape to throw the object.

The Closing Activity

After seeing how far each of the flying objects have gone, ask each of the participants to take a writing tool, and write a single word on their popsicle stick expressing how they feel about the challenge activities they have experienced. After writing on their own stick, pass this around the group, and have other members also add their words.

Now take a single stick, and toss it in the direction of the other flying objects. This is the power of one. It doesn't go very far. Next show that two sticks working together goes a little farther, but still isn't all that powerful. Now take at least 12 of the word sticks from the group, and wrap them together in a brick using the masking tape. It doesn't look very much like a flying object, but when you give this brick a throw (and remember, you are trying to illustrate a point here), you'll see that it often will go as far as any of the other flying objects. That is the power of sticking together and working as a group.

Sequence

This activity should be used before a major break or at the end of the program.

Activity 4.50

Pot of Gold

Like several other object retrieval initiatives, Pot of Gold involves the use of available props or objects to retrieve the Pot of Gold which is located within a region that cannot be walked upon. Many variations are possible to modify the difficulty level of this activity.

Equipment

A plastic pot or bucket to use as the Pot of Gold. Some tennis balls or brightly painted rocks for the gold in the Pot of Gold. One 100 foot (30 meter) rope for a boundary circle. Six or more ropes roughly 6 to 20 feet (2 to 6 meters) long, that can either reach across the diameter of the boundary circle, or be tied together to reach this same distance. A variety of additional props can be used, such as plastic hoops, dowel rods, rubber deck rings, short boards, etc., although these props are typically of little value to the solution.

The Challenge

To retrieve the Pot of Gold from the center of the boundary circle, without touching the interior of the circle, and without spilling the contents of the Pot of Gold.

Typical Presentation, Storyline or Metaphor

While on a hiking trip, your group encounters not only a rain shower, but also a rainbow, and the Pot of Gold at the end of the rainbow. Although this mythical object is nearby, it floats on a thin mist, which cannot support the weight of any human. Using only the objects you have available, you must retrieve the Pot of Gold, without spilling any of the contents.

A second variation is possible if the Pot of Gold is filled with water rather than gold nuggets. During an intense forest fire, your firefighting team runs dangerously low on water to stop the raging fire coming in this direction. A local source of water is nearby (the Pot of Gold filled to the brim with water), but is surrounded by ashes too hot to walk on. Using any of the equipment available, recover this water source, spilling as little water as possible.

Variations

Once during the presentation of this activity, a facilitator mentioned that the group could not touch the region inside of the boundary circle, but not that the circle was stationary. As a result, a very creative group decided simply to kick the rope into the center of the circle, and grab the Pot of Gold directly, without using any additional props. A very effective method of creative cheating.

Given that the group has several pieces of equipment which are probably of little value to the solution of this problem, consider mentioning to the group that anything touching the ground inside the circle is lost, this includes the ropes. However, items that are lost can be traded for other items still in the group's possession.

Placing the Pot of Gold on a platform will encourage the group not to simply drag the pot. It also provides some additional challenge, as participants must have control of the pot before it begins to move from the platform, or else the gold is likely to spill out. A plastic hoop may also be used to mark the boundary beyond which the pot will sink into the mist or ashes.

Another variation which brings about considerably more effort and communication by the group, is to blindfold a third of the group. These are the only participants that can touch any of the equipment. Another third of the group are unable to communicate through verbal speech. These are the only participants that can make physical contact with the blindfolded participants. The final third of the group can see, and talk, and move about, but cannot touch anyone or anything. This particular variation typically lengthens the time required for this activity.

Important Points

One of the most potentially risky techniques for retrieving the Pot of Gold is to use several ropes to support a person, and then carry this person over the boundary circle to retrieve the Pot of Gold. In general, this situation can be avoided by using the stories above. Both the magical mist and the heat from the ashes makes it impossible for anyone to break the plane of the boundary circle.

For the variation mentioned above using blindfolds, consider when you wish for the group to become blindfolded and speechless. If you allow planning before these additional challenges, you will enable a greater involvement of the entire group in the planning process. One of the most often expressed emotions for participants that were blindfolded prior to the planning stages of this activity, is frustration due to lack of information, and the ability to make a contribution to the group.

Discussion and Debriefing Topics

Were there several techniques presented to solve this activity? How did the group decide which method to use? Were there any props which you chose not to use? Why? Do you think that there are similar props in your own life which really don't provide any service? Was there a single person that assumed the leadership of this activity, or were several leaders involved? If there was a single leader, was this person activity involved (i.e. holding a rope, helping to move participants into place), or was their role as a communicator? In the end, did your solution depend on hard work, good planning, or just luck?

Sequence

Pot of Gold utilizes teamwork, communication and problem solving skills. This activity does not require a great deal of trust or close proximity, and is suitable for all audiences, including those with limited mobility.

Activities Using Similar Skills and Follow-on Activities

Other activities which use ropes include Bull Ring and Extended Knots. Stretch It involves a similar set of skills and involvement of the group. Move It or Lose It II uses some similar surroundings with a slightly different challenge.

Notes

Activity 4.51

Raccoon Circles

At the T.E.A.M. Conference a few years ago, Tom Smith was co-leading some opening activities with Karl Rohnke. As Tom tells it, Karl was impressed with a variety of activities that he was leading using segments of 1 inch (25 mm) tubular webbing that had been tied with a water knot into a loop. Before the night was over Karl had helped name these webbing loops "Raccoon Circles." This title has a strong meaning in Native American tradition to Tom Smith. Here are just a sample of the things you can do with them. For more information, you can contact Dr. Tom Smith at The Raccoon Institute. The address is listed in Chapter 8.

Equipment

You'll need several 1 inch (25 mm) tubular webbing segments, each about 12 to 15 feet (3.5 to 4.5 meters) long. This style of webbing comes in a variety of colors and patterns.

The Challenge

Here are three samples. For more ideas, you'll need to request the Raccoon Circles handout from Tom Smith.

1. Let's Get Started—Using the knot in the Raccoon Circle as a pointer, begin this activity by revving up your motors, like a race car. Then squeel your tires (vocally) as the knot behaves like a race car going around a race track. Participants rapidly pass the webbing to the right. Slam on the breaks with a screech—and ask the person closest to the knot to answer a get acquainted question, such as "how did you get here today?" Then squeel the tires again, and you are off in the opposite direction.
2. Electric Fence 2000—In this version, two participants hold the Raccoon Circle so that it forms a long rectangular on the floor, about 1 foot (305 mm) wide and 5 feet (1.5 meters) long. Half of the remaining participants are on one long side of the rectangle, the other half are on the other long side. We'll imagine that there are 5 participants on each side. The first person from each side is requested to cross the electric fence without touching it, while the two positioners hold the Raccoon Circle about 1 foot (305 mm) off the floor. The second person from each side sill cross over with the Raccoon Circle about 2 feet (710 mm) off the floor. The final participant, no matter how many are on each side, will cross at a height of no more than 4 feet (1.2 meters).

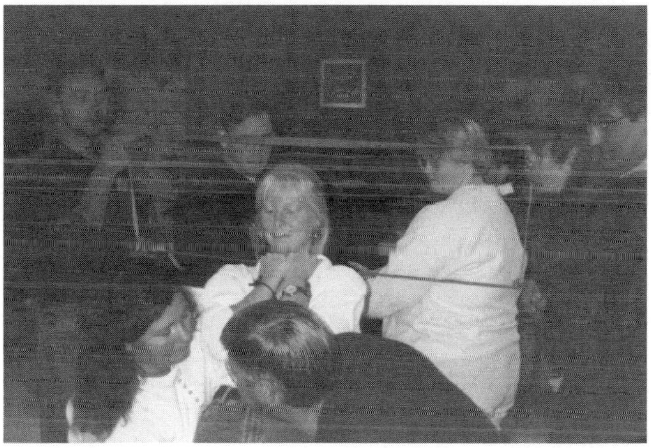

3. Balance—Finding a place where you are at balance with your life, your career, your coworkers, and your family is not easy in modern society. In this Raccoon Circle activity, the goal is to maintain a balance and awareness of the rest of the group in a quiet setting. For a single group, you can facilitate this activity from inside the Raccoon Circle. Begin by having each member of the group take hold of the Raccoon Circle with both hands about shoulder's width apart, and to gently pull the circle taut. Encourage them to balance their weight evenly on the right and left foot. Now encourage them to hold on, and lean back slightly, allowing the circle to support them. When the group can hold this balance, allow them to lower themselves to the floor, and then return

to a standing position. Try this again with eyes closed, offering commands for the lowering and raising portions of the event. Finally, allow them to descend twice with eyes closed, with no verbal commands at all.

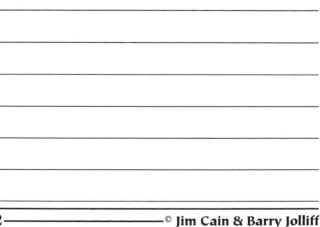

Variations

1. Using the Raccoon Circle as a get acquainted activity works well for nearly all of the groups we have ever worked with. Name games can be adapted using a Raccoon Circle. You can even establish a group Raccoon Circle by having group members write their names on the circle with permanent markers. At the completion of the program, consider cutting the Raccoon Circle into pieces, so that each participant can take home part of the experience with them.
2. This version of electric fence is terrific. It maintains participants on both sides of the fence at all times, which provides lots of spotting and support for participants. For a more difficult version, the horizontal Raccoon Circle can form a wider rectangle. For a different style, try holding the rectangle vertically, so that the activity becomes more like a portable version of Surfing the Web, or a larger version of Worm Hole.
3. The balancing exercise does require some deep knee bending, and may not be suitable for all participants. Stretching the Raccoon Circle into various patterns, and circling to the left and right may be a suitable alternative.

Important Points

Raccoon Circles are a terrific technique for focusing the attention of a group. This is especially important if you work with audiences that may tend to wander off during quieter moments. Processing can take place in such a circle, so can the planning stage of an activity.

Discussion and Debriefing Topics

Did you feel "connected" to the circle and the group? Did you feel supported by the rest of the group during these activities? What other events in your life have a circular meaning? How else could you use the Raccoon Circle?

Sequence

Raccoon Circles work well in low prop / no prop settings, or when you have minimal space to take along equipment. The community building that occurs with these events fits well into the opening of a challenge program.

Activities Using Similar Skills and Follow-on Activities

Many of the activities listed in this book can be accomplished with Raccoon Circles. 2B or KNOT 2B, Tree of Knots, Not Knots, and Traffic Circle can all be conducted with a few Raccoon Circles, instead of ropes.

Notes

Activity 4.52

Real Estate

Here is a giant-sized version of a classic puzzle, where the same pieces can be used to create a variety of shapes.

Equipment

Ten large wooden puzzles pieces in the standard geometric shapes shown on the following page. See Chapter 5 for directions on how to create these pieces. If you typically have more or less than 10 participants, considering cutting this puzzle into a different number of pieces. Paint or mark the top and bottom surfaces of each piece. It is also helpful to have a string or rope to mark the border of the puzzle.

The Challenge

For blindfolded participants to assemble their puzzle pieces in such a way that all pieces will fit into the specified shape. Participants can only touch their own puzzle pieces.

Typical Presentation, Storyline or Metaphor

Having won some really big bucks, you and your friends decide to move to a scenic island in the Pacific Ocean. Even before you leave, everyone has decided on the size property they would like to have, and so you all go looking for the perfect island. In this particular region, there are islands that are available in square, rectangular, triangular and X shapes. See if your group can incorporate their ideal property boundaries into each of these island shapes.

Variations

The primary technique for this activity is to blindfold everyone before passing out the puzzle pieces. Then allow a single person to remove their blindfold and to place their puzzle piece within the border outlined on the ground, starting the formation of the puzzle. They are not to look at the puzzle pieces that other participants are still holding in their hands. They now replace their blindfold. The next participant now removes their blindfold and places their piece. This continues until someone is unable to place their piece. At this point a conversation begins regarding which pieces should be moved to complete the puzzle.

Since participants are only blindfolded, they can still communicate through speech, although some may have forgotten this. So even before beginning the puzzle, participants could communicate the shape of the puzzle piece they are holding. This typically doesn't happen on the first round.

Since only the participant that placed a puzzle piece can move it, communication must occur between the sighted person now viewing the puzzle, and the person that originally placed the piece. At this point, this activity becomes a little like trying to tell someone how to solve a geometric puzzle over the telephone or internet, without being able to see what they see at the same time. This is the real strength of Real Estate. It promotes the use of visual descriptions that have meaning to both parties, and it let's us see that what is clear to us, may not be clear to others.

Important Points

This activity is very geometric, and some participants may not be able to visualize the boundaries described without some experience. It may be useful to conduct the first round of this activity without blindfolds, so that the group can begin to visualize what is expected of them. Later, when blindfolds are returned, only mention the shape of the island, such as a triangle, without giving any additional information. This will promote conversation within the group for this information, rather than seeking assistance from the facilitator.

Discussion and Debriefing Topics

Was the goal clear from the start of the activity? Did you converse with other group members before placing your piece? Were changes usually required? Was there communication between the sighted person placing their piece, and the blindfolded members of the group? Were there times when you could visualize the solution clearly, but had difficulties in explaining the solution to other participants?

Sequence

Real Estate is one of the few activities that blindfolds the entire group. It is a useful activity to expose the group to prior to Simply Amazing and other blindfolded activities.

Activities Using Similar Skills and Follow-on Activities

Simply Amazing requires the entire group to be blindfolded at one time.

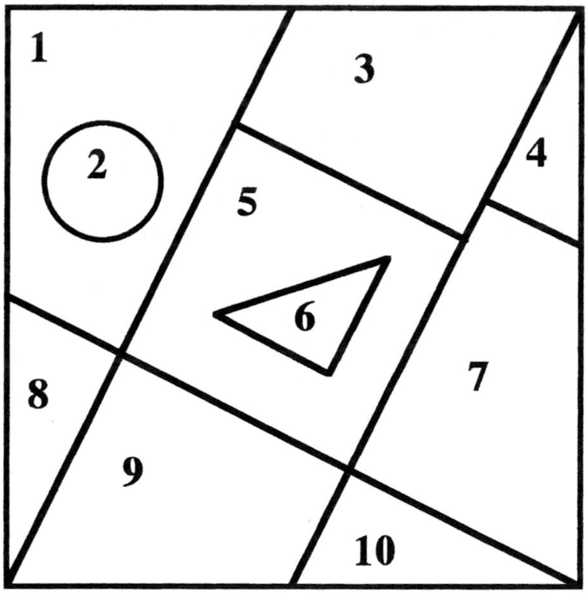

Notes

Activity 4.53

Right Where I Belong

Here is an activity that can be used as part of a trust sequence. It provides and opportunity to experience an awareness of the group, ourselves, and our neighbors.

Equipment

One blindfold for each participant, although this activity can also be completed with no props at all.

The Challenge

For a group standing in any pattern to blindfold themselves, mingle about a bit, and then return to their original position, using only the abilities granted by the facilitator.

Typical Presentation, Storyline or Metaphor

You are 7 years old, and your parents bring you to the country fair. It is a magical place with all kinds of sights and sounds, and thousands of people. When you arrive, your parents give you very careful instructions, "if you get lost, come right back to this spot, and we will come and find you here."

Variations

This is an activity which can be performed several times. Each time with a different ability granted by the facilitator. The first time through, try it without the blindfolds. Then ask the group what skills they used to find their original positions again. You may even have the group mark their positions with a golf tee, gym spot, or some other object.

Next, blindfolds on. Have the group mingle about slowly, with arms up to avoid collisions, and then to return to their original position. You can allow talking during this second journey. Ask what skills they used this time. Have them remove their blindfolds and check their position.

For the next try, blindfolds on first, and then inform the group that they have 2 minutes to plan a way to return to their original position without talking. After they mingle and attempt to return, have them again check their position.

Finally, with blindfolds on, have the group mingle, and then try to return to their original positions as quietly as possible, using only the surrounding environment for clues to their position.

Important Points

Any time you are working with blindfolded participants, it is important to choose a location that is free from any ground obstacles. Also watch the perimeter of the group to make sure that someone does not wander too far away during each mingling period.

Discussion and Debriefing Topics

We each use a series of clues to tell us where we are. A familiar road sign, a familiar looking house, and other clues, tell us when we are on the right road, and going in the right direction. There are a variety of metaphors here that can be used to discuss where we are in our lives, and where we are headed. Are we going there with our eyes closed?

What was different about finding your way back home the fourth time and the first time? Did you manage to come close, or were you off by a mile (1.6 km)? What other senses do we use to know about our surroundings?

Sequence

Right Where I Belong is a simple blindfolded activity that can be used before more blindfolded trust building activities.

Activities Using Similar Skills and Follow-on Activities

Another activity that utilizes blindfolds is Mine, Mine, Mine.

Activity 4.54

River Crossing

This is one activity that has been called by a variety of names. It takes a bit longer than many other challenge and adventure activities. It also requires a little more strength and balance.

Equipment

Four cedar 4x4's eight feet long, two long ropes for marking boundaries, and at least eight wooden platforms. The stackable wooden platforms used for All Aboard can be used for this activity, or the collection of the single sized platforms illustrated in Chapter 5.

The Challenge

To move the entire group from one side of the wooden platforms to the other without touching the ground, using only the 4×4's bridged between the wooden platforms.

Typical Presentation, Storyline or Metaphor

You've managed to guide your group through the jungle to the edge of a fast moving river. There are no bridges anywhere along the river, so your group grabs a few poles and starts planning a method for crossing the river. One of your group members scouts a location filled with rocks that can be used to support the poles. Can your group make it safely to the other side?

While vacationing with your hiking group near the ocean, you decide to each pitch your tents on some nearby islands. When morning comes, in comes the tide, blocking your path back to shore. A few brave group members begin building some bridges to rescue you. What can you do to help them?

Variations

The traditional technique for leading this activity, is to place the wooden platforms in such a way that the group moves from one bank of the river to the opposite bank by crossing the river with boards placed on top of stepping stones and rocks. Participant typically begin this activity with four 4×4's. An alternative is to only provide two or three 4×4's and place another 4×4 on one of the wooden platforms.

A second variation, is to place a participant on each of the platforms, and to have a rescue team attempt to build a system of bridges to allow them to reach the far side of the river. Every participant rescued from the river becomes a member of the rescue team, and assists with the recovery of other group members. This second version will typically take longer than the traditional technique. Some group members can also be in possession of a 4×4, which may allow the rescue to proceed quickly, as participants work from both the shore and the rocks to reach the other side.

Important Points

Anything touching the water is immediately swept downstream by the fast moving river, and can no

longer be used by the group. You can offer the group the opportunity to barter for additional equipment, or to recover a lost piece of equipment, by taking on an additional challenge.

Cedar 4×4's are very strong and substantially lighter than pressure treated materials. But even the cedar 4×4's can be awkward to handle, so encourage good lifting practices. As a spotter, some groups may require your assistance with the placement of a 4×4 from time to time.

During the journey to the other side, participants will soon discover that it is not possible to reach from some platforms directly to others. Assembling the 4×4's in a "T" shaped path may be required.

Discussion and Debriefing Topics

What was the biggest problem you encountered during this event? Did you try several different methods during the journey? What skills were required to accomplish this task? What is the minimum number of 4×4's needed to complete this activity? What choices that you made in this first attempt would you change if you were to repeat this activity?

Sequence

River Crossing is a strenuous activity, and typically a lengthy one. Do not begin this activity late in the program unless there is sufficient time to finish it completely. After this activity, most groups would probably appreciate some shade and some rest.

Activities Using Similar Skills and Follow-on Activities

Windmill can be constructed from some of the same equipment at River Crossing.

Notes

Activity 4.55

Shark Attack

This is a portable version of All Aboard that travels with the group during their adventure experience. It can be a very convenient technique for quickly assembling the group together. You can also use these props for makeshift tables, chairs, clipboards, presentation surfaces, and other adventure programming needs.

Equipment

You'll need one or more plywood cutouts made from the nautical patterns shown in Chapter 5. These patterns can be enlarged to fit the size of your group.

The Challenge

The challenge here is that whenever the facilitator yells, "Shark Attack," the entire group crowds aboard the plywood platform long enough to sing one verse of Row, Row, Row Your Boat, or a similar song with a nautical theme, without touching the surrounding ground.

Typical Presentation, Storyline or Metaphor

The local boating patrol takes great pride in the training each new recruit receives. One of the most important drills is the "Shark Attack" drill. Each team member must know how to safely execute this drill, without fail, in any condition, as quickly as possible.

Variations

The number of participants in the group determines the size of plywood cutouts typically needed. Some groups may require two or more. You may want to designate a participant to carry this prop with the group, or allow it to pass from person to person during the course of the program.

Important Points

This activity encourages the group to stay together, since a Shark Attack can occur at any time. It is also a means for quickly assembling the group to a very small area, so that you can proceed with your plans.

Discussion and Debriefing Topics

If someone is missing or far from the group, whose responsibility is it to make sure they are safe if a Shark Attack occurs? Does the group seem to improve each time the Shark Attack occurs, or not?

Sequence

Shark Attack can be used between any other adventure program activities, and especially when a facilitator needs to pull the attention of the group, and bring everyone together.

Activities Using Similar Skills and Follow-on Activities

All Aboard, Human Knot and Magic Carpet are also proximity activities. A Raccoon Circle can also be used to connect the group together in a fairly small space.

Notes

Activity 4.56

Simply Amazing

A simple activity in which the entire group is blindfolded. Directions for creating the maze are provided in Chapter 5.

Equipment

A grove of trees with level ground are ideal, although you can use wooden or metal stakes driven into the ground to form a similar pattern. You'll also need about 400 feet (122 meters) of ¼ inch (6.35 mm) poly rope to form the outline of the maze. Blindfolds for each participant. A unique toy or ball that can be attached to the rope serves as the object to be found during the search.

The Challenge

For the group to work as a whole to retrieve an object connected to the boundary rope of the maze, and to bring this object, and the entire group to the "exit" of the maze.

Typical Presentation, Storyline or Metaphor

One of the techniques used by deep-sea divers is to attach treasures and other artifacts that they find, to a rope which runs through the region in which they are diving. Your group finds themselves deep below the surface of the water, searching for one such treasure, tied to the surrounding rope. The turbulence of the water eliminates the ability for effective communication by talking, however, simple sounds, such as hand-clapping and foot-stomping can be heard. After finding the missing object, the entire group must then join together and find their way back to the surface.

Variations

The simplest way to begin this activity is with all group members blindfolded, and touching the rope boundary to the maze. Evenly distribute the group throughout the maze area. Then place the object to be found along the rope. Try placing the object onto the rope where the rope runs behind a tree. This will encourage the group to search carefully along the full length of the rope, not merely the portion of the rope running between each tree.

The "surface" or exit to the maze can be marked with a rope, bell or other tactile object. You can even mark the surface or exit location with aftershave lotion or perfume, to provide an aromatic solution to this challenge. It is a good idea to encourage participants to all reach the exit at the same time, and to make sure that they have all the members of their group. During the initial planning stages where communication is possible, it would probably be a good idea for the group to plan their exit strategy.

Important Points

The most obvious concern with this activity is to make sure that the zone defined by the rope is free from any hazards that a blindfolded person may encounter, such as tree roots, low branches, uneven footing, spider webs, etc.

A second, less obvious point, is to blindfold the group prior to reaching the maze, so that participants have no idea of the exact shape or size of the maze. Bringing the group into the center of the maze, and let the group "find" the rope. They can then decide whether to stay together or separate to find the object.

For safety reasons, no participant is allowed to climb under or over any rope. From the time of first contact, participants should always be in contact with the rope.

Discussion and Debriefing Topics

Was it difficult to keep from talking? Why? Were you able to keep track of the other members of your group? Did anyone lose their way? Do you think your search strategy was efficient? What would you do differently now that you have seen the maze?

Sequence

This type of blindfolded trust activity should follow some less intense activities, such as a partner walk with one participant blindfolded.

Activities Using Similar Skills and Follow-on Activities

Other blindfolded or sightless activities include Mine-Mine-Mine, and Line-Up.

Notes

Activity 4.57

Strange Attraction

In the field of chaos theory, there is an event that can occur near a critical point in phase space, that is, well, kinda cool really. That event is a strange attractor. And after you initiate this activity, it will probably remind you of pure chaos.

Equipment

A variation on the bull ring, but this time with unequal length strings and an additional metal ring at the end of every string. We call this device the connector. You'll also need a bunch of PVC marble tubes or 1 inch (25 mm) diameter wooden stakes that will stick out of the ground about 1 foot (305 mm). You'll need one string/ring and at least one stake for each person in the group. And finally, two ropes to mark the boundary at the beginning and end of phase space.

Directions are given in Chapter 5 for assembling the connector and placing the stakes for this activity.

The Challenge

To traverse a region filled with wooden or PVC stakes that have been pounded into the ground, using a connector with a central ring and additional rings at the end of each string. Each group member is responsible for their string/ring combination, and the group must be connected to at least one stake at all time (just to be safe in phase space). Each ring can only be placed on one stake during the journey.

Typical Presentation, Storyline or Metaphor

Your team has been chosen to journey through phase space, moving in both space and time. There are a series of critical contact points in this phase space (known as "critical points" actually) that your group must remain in contact with during the journey. Your goal is to reach the other side of phase space with at least one ring over a critical point at any given time. Your journey begins and ends with the central ring of the connector over the first (source) and last (sink) stakes. You can only make one connection during the journey with each of the outer connector rings.

Variations

Start by telling the group that they have 5 attempts to coordinate the smoothest passage across phase space. This is not a speed issue, but an attempt to create a smoothly flowing motion across the space.

Allow the participants to walk through phase space before beginning the activity, but once they pick up the connector, they must keep contact until reaching the other side of phase space.

You can choose to have participants change strings every time they pass through phase space. This will require a greater awareness of what everyone in the group is doing, and communication between participants as they discuss how they last moved through phase space.

If you want to add an opportunity for rescue in phase space, you can replace one of the strings with shock (bungie) cord. This elastic element will stretch to even the farthest stake, possibly saving the mission.

Important Points

Be sure to keep a few extra strings/rings that you can tie on just in case you have more participants than planned. Attaching the strings to the central ring with fishing snaps, miniature carabiners or even safety pins is one way to make quick additions or deletions to the total number of rings.

Make sure to pound the stakes well into the ground. There is likely to be some pulling and tugging on the strings, and a floppy stake (critical point) is just mathematically hard to deal with in phase space.

The location of the stakes is not critical (no chaos terminology humor intended). But it is desirable to place the stakes in such a way that the group must choose wisely which rings are placed on which stakes, or they will not be able to complete their journey. It is always possible to place a long string/ring, onto a nearby stake, but it isn't possible to stretch a short string/ring to reach a stake that is still a short distance away. Try to create two possible paths. One that has stakes appropriately placed so that participants can reach the other side, and the second path with two stakes that are just a little too far apart for any of the rings to reach.

One potential solution method is for the group to always use the shortest string/ring that reaches the stake. To confound this strategy, you simply need a few well placed stakes early in phase space that can only be reached by the two longest strings on the connector.

This is an activity in which the planning stage can go on for quite a while. Sometimes, it is best just to get on with it, and try finding some solutions by trial-and-error techniques. Given that the group has five attempts to make it through phase space, a little trial-and-error problem solving may provide some additional insight before more serious decision making and planning is warranted.

We've had this one on the back burner for quite a while, and the truth is, we've never actually played this one in public. If you come up with any suggestions or improvements, we'd love to hear them.

Discussion and Debriefing Topics

Did you have a plan that worked the first time? Did you plan for a lengthy period of time, or dive right into the activity? Were you able to identify a smooth technique for crossing phase space? What methods did you use to find your way across phase space? Is it OK to move backwards in phase space? Did you ever have to go back to the beginning of something and start all over? If you could go back in space and time, where would you go and what would you do there?

Sequence

This activity fits well into a series of problem solving activities.

Activities Using Similar Skills and Follow-on Activities

All the other Bull Ring activities utilize similar equipment to Strange Attraction. Gridlock is another activity that encourages trial-and-error problem solving techniques. Other problem solving activities include: The Danger Zone, Real Estate, 2B or KNOT 2B and Handcuffs and Shackles.

References

If you would like to read more about chaos theory and non-linear dynamics, here are a few interesting books that explain what is going on, without having to be a rocket scientist.

Does God Play Dice?—The Mathematics of Chaos
Ian Stewart, 1989, Basil Blackwell, Cambridge, MA

Chaos—Making a New Science
James Gleick, 1987, Penguin Books, New York, NY

Another Fine Math You've Got Me Into . . .
Ian Stewart, 1992, W.H. Freeman and Company, New York, NY

Chaotic and Fractal Dynamics—An Introduction for Applied Scientists and Engineers
Francis C. Moon, 1992, John Wiley & Sons, New York, NY

Notes

____

____

Activity 4.58

Stretch It

This activity requires at least five or six strong participants, although any ten people can probably complete the activity if they give it a good shot by first developing a good plan or strategy. More than ten and the new goal is to see that everyone is taking part in the activity. Stretch It can be a quickly achieved goal followed by an explosion of laughter from the shear excitement of accomplishment.

Equipment

You will need a 6 inch (152 mm) inner tube from a wheelbarrow tire. Eight to twelve pieces of soft rope, such as a cotton clothesline. Tie one end of the ropes so that they are evenly spaced around the tire. A sturdy plastic gallon jug, three fourths full of water, such as a bleach bottle or other gallon cleaner bottle. A gallon milk container will work but it is likely to get squashed during the activity. A tree stump, or wooden platform, or a five gallon bucket upside down, or a four gallon milk crate, or a 10 gallon hat (well, maybe not). A 50 foot (15 meter) length of rope for a boundary marker.

The Challenge

For the group to move the plastic jug from ground level to the top of the stump, bucket or platform, by using the rope and inner tube combination, without tipping over or dropping the jug. The long rope is used to form a boundary circle with the jug and the stump near the center.

Typical Presentation, Storyline or Metaphor

During the great ice-storm of the year, your lucky pig Gertrude manages to go for some skating lessons on the less than frozen farm pond. Wouldn't you know it, Gert goes for a swim, right in the middle of the pond. You've got an able team of rescuers ready, but Gert has been eating well this winter, and is about a foot larger than your biggest life preserver. Think fast, is there a way you can still save Gert, and get her to the small floating platform before she becomes frozen pork?

If you don't happen to be a pork fan, perhaps the jug represents the last 2 liter bottle of soda that has now floated out to sea during your latest picnic adventures. Can your group bring it back safely?

Variations

One of the first variations is to add various amounts of water to the jug, to alter the difficulty of the activity. Heavier jugs are somewhat more difficult to handle. For effect, you can remove the lid to the jug, so that any spills or drops will be immediately noticeable to the group.

If you happen to use a jug with the lid in place, partially filling the jug, and then placing it on its side to increase the difficulty of retrieving the jug initially.

Using blindfolds with some members will alter the skill of the entire group.

Important Points

Some groups may need to have two or three participants on a rope to create enough stretch to successfully place the inner tube over the top of the jug. Generally, the more evenly spaced the participants are around the inner tube, the easier it is to stretch the tube over the jug. Be sure that all group members are somehow involved in the activity.

Discussion and Debriefing Topics

Who offered ideas on how to accomplish this task? What ideas were tried? Were there any ideas that were not tried? Was anyone frustrated during this activity? What caused the frustration? Did completing the activity make you feel successful?

Sequence

This activity is one that can be used in the middle of a challenge program. It takes teamwork to accomplish and group decision making to come up with a plan of action.

Activities Using Similar Skills and Follow-on Activities

This activity is similar to both Pot of Gold and Bull Ring.

Notes

Activity 4.59

Stretching the Limit

Here is an activity that can be performed with or without props.

Equipment

Any combination of random props such as short segments of rope, broomsticks, dowel rods, sticks, string, etc. These objects can be placed in the vacinity of the playing field, so that they are reachable by the group. A pole or other "anchor" point is also useful, and you'll need a container to retrieve. On a hot day, a container filled with beverages will be appreciated by the group.

The Challenge

To create a continuous line using participants and various other equipment, so that an object can be retrieved, without breaking the contact of the group.

Typical Presentation, Storyline or Metaphor

Your mission into space has pretty much gone according to schedule, except for the part where the food supply just drifted out into space. At this rate of speed, you can't stop the spacecraft, and you have no other way to control the food container, so you'll just have to go and get it. You pull together all the equipment you can, and with the entire crew in space suits, you head out to retrieve the food supply. You'll need to stay linked to the spacecraft so that you can pull your team back in when you reach the food container. With so many crew members on this space walk, you'll only have enough oxygen for about a minute. If you don't happen to reach the container on your first try, come back to the ship, regroup, get some air, and try again. Be aware however, objects in space are seldom stationary.

Variations

Rather than attempting to retrieve an object you can divide the group in half and see which portion can form the longest line using only themselves and any spare equipment they have on them, such as belts, shoelaces, hats, etc.

Solar winds have a way of causing things to move in space. If you notice that the group has plenty of additional equipment left to reach their goal, consider moving the container slightly to additionally challenge them.

Important Points

Early in the development of this activity, participants would begin laying down at the beginning of the line, while other group members would keep stretching towards the goal. This technique doesn't keep the first participants fully involved in the process. Having the group quickly stretch to reach the object, and then return if they don't quite make it provides the opportunity for group members to change duties, and for the entire group to decide what to do next, rather than just the participants nearest the goal.

Modesty should dictate how many items of clothing can be used to extend the length of the line.

Discussion and Debriefing Topics

On the group's first attempt, how close were they to reaching their goal? Is it hard to estimate the distance? Did you know that you had the right length on the first try? How about the second try?

Sequence

Stretching the Limit uses some of the same props that are used for Pot of Gold, Handcuffs and Shackles, Tree of Knots and other rope related challenge activities.

Activities Using Similar Skills and Follow-on Activities

Tree of Knots uses some similar rope handling and problem solving techniques.

Notes

Activity 4.60

Stump Jumping

Here is an activity that requires minimal props, is simple to explain, and provides some real challenges to completing successfully.

Equipment

You'll need enough circular objects for each participant to stand on. These can be wooden disks (plywood works best), carpet circles, thin sections cut from a 12 inch (305 mm) log, paper plates, flying disks, or even the plastic lids from 5 gallon buckets. Place these disks in a circular pattern.

The Challenge

For the entire group to move completely around the circle, until they are back at their original location, without touching the ground, and with only one person on a disk at a time.

Typical Presentation, Storyline or Metaphor

Breakdown is a phrase used to describe the process by which a system or technique can no longer continue to function. Some systems can run for a short time, but eventually small defects in the technique multiply, causing the whole system to come crashing down. Stump jumping is a challenge of coordination and timing. See if your group can develop a technique for successfully completing this task. Begin one step at a time, and then see if you can complete a full revolution of the entire group without experiencing breakdown.

During your group's visit to a tropical rain forest, your guide brings you to the banks of a rapidly moving river. Pointing out a few small stepping stones, your guide requests that you hold onto each other, and place only a single person on each stone as you traverse the river.

Variations

To begin this activity, you might consider having one extra disk, so that participants can progress to a new spot without a great deal of difficulty. Removing this disk will require the group to rethink the problem, and create a new technique.

One constraint which may additionally challenge a group is to request that everyone use a two foot takeoff and a two foot landing (hopping). Yet another constraint would be to challenge the group after they have a plan, to complete the activity without talking.

Another slight variation that provides a considerable challenge to the group is to vary the spacing between each of the disks. This requires participants to vary their jump distances every step of the journey, rather than settling into a continuous pattern.

In addition to simply moving forward around the circle, have the group build a pattern of jumps, such as two jumps foreword, then one jump backwards.

Have every other participant around the circle face the opposite direction. This means that some participants will be jumping forewords while others are jumping backwards.

Important Points

Whether performed inside or outside, it is important to have disks that are not slippery. Wooden disks or segments of logs should be placed in a level location. Do not use plastic lids indoors on a tile floor, rather use non-skid carpets for indoor locations.

Encourage contact and spotting between participants.

Discussion and Debriefing Topics

What technique did you use to keep synchronized with each other? Were you able to use this technique without experiencing breakdown? What was hardest about this activity? What is the longest number of jumps that your group experienced without breakdown?

Sequence

Stump Jumping utilizes coordination and timing, and encourages an awareness of other group members. Contact with other group members is also encouraged. This may be a useful activity to conduct before using the Lycra Tube.

Activities Using Similar Skills and Follow-on Activities

Other activities which utilize coordination and timing include All Aboard and Boardwalking.

Notes

Activity 4.61

Surfing the Web I

The classic web pattern that has graced so many challenge courses around the world.

Equipment

100 feet (30 meters) of ¼ inch (6 mm) poly rope to form a framework between two trees or poles that are about 30 to 40 feet (9 to 12 meters) apart. 80 feet (24 meters) of 3⁄16 inch (4 mm) shock cord to create the web pattern. Project Adventure and Challenge Masters both provide stand-alone equipment for portable versions of this activity, trees not included.

The Challenge

For the entire group to travel through the web to the other side, without touching the web. Each participant must travel through a different opening in the web.

Typical Presentation, Storyline or Metaphor

You are trying to access your favorite web site, but there is a limitation on the number of users that can be simultaneously logged on. If you happen to connect with the wrong server, everyone in the group gets logged off.

Variations

There are a variety of ways that you can Surf the Web. In fact, four more variations of this activity follow this version.

For the classic web pattern, providing various size openings can challenge the group in different ways. Be sure to allow enough generous sized openings for the largest members of the group to pass through safely. If there are concerns about lifting participants, try placing plenty of openings near ground level. If there appear to be too many openings, instead of closing any, or altering the web, try having the participants pass through several objects, such as 4x4's, picnic coolers, storage boxes, stuff sacks, an open umbrella, an inflated beach ball, etc.

In addition to watching the web for contact, you can add a bell so that contact is more easily noted. In the event of contact, offer an option to the group, such as, "you can either start again from the beginning, or, you can pass two people through that are connected together." This allows the group to decide their fate, and involves a conscious choice, rather than a penalty or consequence.

You can consider allowing one participant to go underneath the web. This can be quite useful to a group member with limited mobility through the web.

Important Points

This is one challenge activity that requires the facilitator to say, "you have 5 minutes to plan your technique. At the end of that time, I would like to review your plan with you, BEFORE you begin." This review process encourages the group to plan, but more importantly, it provides the facilitator with every detail of movement, so that they may anticipate appropriate spotting positions before a participant begins their passage.

As with many challenges that have a visible sign of error, in this case that means contact with the web, allow the group to inspect their own movements, rather than setting yourself up as the judge. This places the responsibility directly on the group for their performance.

Be especially cautious near the roots of trees. The footing is uneven here and not suitable for passage. Encourage participants to stick to the middle regions of the web, far away from trees or support poles.

In many cases, participants may choose to lift other participants through the web. Encourage appropriate spotting techniques, especially focused on the shoulders and head region of the participant being transported. Discourage any passage through the web that does not involve contact with other participants. This will prevent jumping and unspotted movements.

Discussion and Debriefing Topics

At the beginning of the activity, did everyone know what their duties were? Were any of the original plans altered during the course of the activity? Why? Would additional planning have prevented these alterations? If contact occurred, what was the reaction of the group to the person that noted the contact?

Sequence

Surfing the Web requires some preliminary exposure of the group to spotting techniques (possibly from All Aboard), problem solving and a somewhat higher physical activity level than other challenge activities. As a warm up activity, consider using Worm Hole, and mentally note the response and respect of the group to each participant as they pass through the Worm Hole. A group that works together well with Worm Hole is ready for Surfing the Web.

Activities Using Similar Skills and Follow-on Activities

A single version of Surfing the Web is probably sufficient for any single day challenge program. If you happen to have repeat participants, try using a different style to additionally challenge the group. Worm Hole uses similar skills. You can even perform a similar activity using Raccoon Circles. See Electric Fence 2000 for a description of this activity elsewhere in this chapter.

Notes

Activity 4.62

Surfing the Web II

This inclined web is definitely the favorite pattern around the Teamplay office these days.

Equipment

100 feet (30 meters) of ¼ inch (6 mm) poly rope to form a framework between four trees or poles that for a square, and are about 15 to 20 feet (4.6 to 6.1 meters) apart. An additional 100 feet (30 meters) of poly rope or about 80 feet (24 meters) of 3⁄16 inch (4 mm) shock cord can be used to create the grid-like web pattern. Two tent stakes can be used instead of two trees for the lowest side of the web.

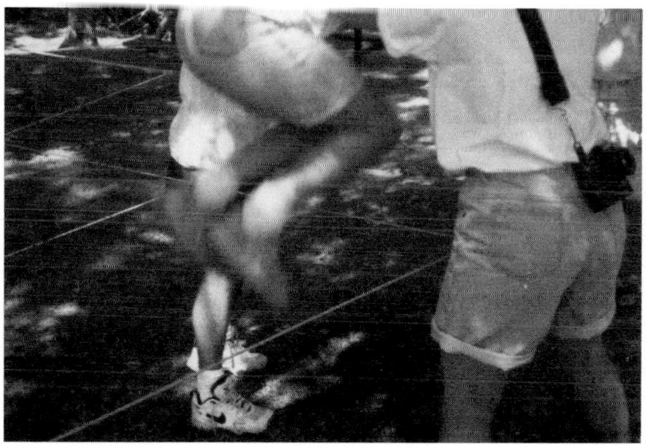

The Challenge

For the entire group to move from the lowest side of the inclined web to the highest side, without touching the web. A maximum of two participants can be in any one opening at a time. Each participant is allowed to burrow (crawl) under a web strand once during this event.

Typical Presentation, Storyline or Metaphor

Reaching your favorite website takes longer and longer, and gets harder and harder every time you go there. Finally you bring a friend along, and they help show you some techniques that make your journey a little easier.

Variations

There are a variety of ways that you can Surf the Web. In fact, four more variations of this activity can be found in this chapter.

For the inclined web, allow participants to trade their one burrowing move with other participants. This bartering can be an interesting point for processing after the event.

Construct the top of this inclined web so that one side is lower than the other. This will encourage taller participants to take the route with the taller web height.

There can be no diagonal movement between web openings in this version of Surfing the Web. Also, various paths can be restricted by taping off an opening, or only allowing participants to pass straight through the web.

Important Points

This is one challenge activity that requires the facilitator to say, "you have 5 minutes to plan your technique. At the end of that time, I would like to review your plan with you, BEFORE you begin." This review process encourages the group to plan, but more importantly, it provides the facilitator with every detail of movement, so that they may anticipate appropriate spotting positions before a participant begins their passage.

In many cases, participants may choose to lift other participants through the web. Encourage appropriate spotting techniques, especially focused on the shoulders and head region of the participant being transported. Discourage any passage through the web that does not involve contact with other participants. This will prevent jumping and unspotted movements. Do not allow participants to move diagonally between web openings.

Use spotters at the highest side of the web. The height of this side should not be more than 40 inches (1 meter).

Discussion and Debriefing Topics

At the beginning of the activity, did everyone know what their duties were? Were any of the original plans altered during the course of the activity? Why? Would additional planning have prevented these alterations? Was it helpful to be able to trade the burrowing movement with other group members? Did the same techniques that worked well at the beginning of the activity work well near the end?

Sequence

Surfing the Web requires some preliminary exposure of the group to spotting techniques (possibly from All Aboard), problem solving and a somewhat higher physical activity level than other challenge activities. As a warm up activity, consider using Worm Hole, and mentally note the response and respect of the group to each participant as they pass through the Worm Hole. A group that works together well with Worm Hole is ready for Surfing the Web.

Activities Using Similar Skills and Follow-on Activities

A single version of Surfing the Web is probably sufficient for any single day challenge program. If you happen to have repeat participants, try using a different style to additionally challenge the group.

Notes

Activity 4.63

Surfing the Web III

Here is a horizontal version of a web that can be made from the same materials as the other webs in this chapter.

Equipment

100 feet (30 meters) of ¼ inch (6 mm) poly rope to form a framework between four trees or poles that are in the shape of a large rectangle. An additional 100 feet (30 meters) of poly rope or about 80 feet (24 meters) of $^{3}/_{16}$ inch (4 mm) shock cord are needed to create the horizontal web pattern.

The Challenge

For the entire group to travel from one side of the web to the other while connected in some manner. Connections cannot be broken while inside the web. Several objects must be retrieved as the group travels to the far end of the rectangular horizontal web.

Typical Presentation, Storyline or Metaphor

You invite all your friends to join you on-line at your favorite web site chat room. The whole group decides to go on a web adventure and collect some cool stuff along the way. You must stay connected to your group so that they can see your web surfing trail and follow you through the web.

Variations

There are a variety of ways that you can Surf the Web. In fact, four more variations of this activity can be found in this chapter.

Requiring participants to always be connected during the activity works when the height of the horizontal web is between 12 and 20 inches (305 to 508 mm). Webs that are in the range of 20 to 30 inches (508 to 762 mm) requires additional spotting and the necessity for occasionally loosing contact as participants move from one square to the next.

Objects placed within the web should be lightweight and retrievable with one hand.

Important Points

This is one challenge activity that requires the facilitator to say, "you have 5 minutes to plan your technique. At the end of that time, I would like to review your plan with you, BEFORE you begin." This review process encourages the group to plan, but more importantly, it provides the facilitator with every detail of movement, so that they may anticipate appropriate spotting positions before a participant begins their passage.

As with many challenges that have a visible sign of error, in this case that means contact with the web, allow the group to inspect their own movements, rather than setting yourself up as the judge. This places the responsibility directly on the group for their performance.

Be especially cautious near the roots of trees. The footing is uneven here and not suitable for passage. Encourage participants to stick to the middle regions of the web, far away from trees or support poles.

In many cases, participants may choose to lift other participants through the web. Encourage appropriate spotting techniques, especially focused on the shoulders and head region of the participant being transported. Discourage any passage through the web that does not involve contact with other participants. This will prevent jumping and unspotted movements.

Discussion and Debriefing Topics

At the beginning of the activity, did everyone know what their duties were? Were any of the original plans altered during the course of the activity? Why? Would additional planning have prevented these alterations? How did your group decide which participants would pick up the objects in the group?

Sequence

Surfing the Web requires some preliminary exposure of the group to spotting techniques (possibly from All Aboard), problem solving and a somewhat higher physical activity level than other challenge activities. As a warm up activity, consider using Worm Hole, and mentally note the response and respect of the group to each participant as they pass through the Worm Hole. A group that works together well with Worm Hole is ready for Surfing the Web.

Activities Using Similar Skills and Follow-on Activities

A single version of Surfing the Web is probably sufficient for any single day challenge program. If you happen to have repeat participants, try using a different style to additionally challenge the group.

Notes

Activity 4.64

Surfing the Web IV

Here is a 3-D web that provides additional challenges for most groups.

Equipment

You'll need about 600 feet (183 meters) of ¼ inch (6 mm) poly rope to form the framework and web strands between four trees or poles that are about 10 to 20 feet (3 to 6 meters) apart. Some additional shock cord will keep this 3-D web under tension, and allow some latitude for when those four trees begin moving in the wind.

The Challenge

For the entire group to travel through the web to the other side, without touching the web.

Typical Presentation, Storyline or Metaphor

You are trying to access your favorite web site, but there is a limitation on the number of users that can be simultaneously logged on. If you happen to connect with the wrong server, everyone in the group gets logged off.

Variations

There are a variety of ways that you can Surf the Web. In fact, four more variations of this activity follow this version.

In addition to the various cords and ropes that are a part of this 3-D web, consider adding some additional strings with bells or other sound producing objects. Ask participants to retrieve some objects within the 3-D web. Some of these objects can be larger than the actual size of the web openings.

The entire group can pass through the web while connected, or smaller strands or chains of participants can attempt to retrieve specific objects within the web.

Important Points

This is one challenge activity that requires the facilitator to say, "you have 5 minutes to plan your technique. At the end of that time, I would like to review your plan with you, BEFORE you begin." This review process encourages the group to plan, but more importantly, it provides the facilitator with every detail of movement, so that they may anticipate appropriate spotting positions before a participant begins their passage.

As with many challenges that have a visible sign of error, in this case that means contact with the web, allow the group to inspect their own movements, rather than setting yourself up as the judge. This places the responsibility directly on the group for their performance.

Be especially cautious near the roots of trees. The footing is uneven here and not suitable for passage. Encourage participants to stick to the middle regions of the web, far away from trees or support poles.

In many cases, participants may choose to lift other participants through the web. Encourage appropriate spotting techniques, especially focused on the shoulders and head region of the participant being transported. Discourage any passage through the web that does not involve contact with other participants. This will prevent jumping and unspotted movements.

Discussion and Debriefing Topics

At the beginning of the activity, did everyone know what their duties were? Were any of the original plans altered during the course of the activity? Why? Would additional planning have prevented these alterations? Was the group able to retrieve all the objects? Did any objects present some particular problems? Which is more important, recovering all the objects, or making sure the group passes through the web without touching it?

Sequence

Surfing the Web requires some preliminary exposure of the group to spotting techniques (possibly from All Aboard), problem solving and a somewhat higher physical activity level than other challenge activities. As a warm up activity, consider using Worm Hole, and mentally note the response and respect of the group to each participant as they pass through the Worm Hole. A group that works together well with Worm Hole is ready for Surfing the Web.

Activities Using Similar Skills and Follow-on Activities

A single version of Surfing the Web is probably sufficient for any single day challenge program. If you happen to have repeat participants, try using a different style to additionally challenge the group. Worm Hole uses similar skills.

Notes

Activity 4.65

Surfing the Web V

Here is a final version featuring a combination of web configurations. In this variation of Surfing the Web, the group is split, and participants must decide when and where to enter, so that they can assist other members.

Equipment

Enough poly rope and shock cord for two or three different web configurations.

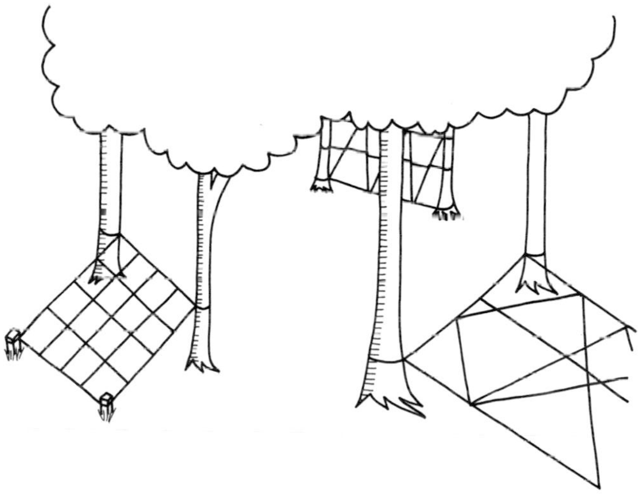

The Challenge

For each of the groups to pass through their web to the interior web domain, without touching the web. In order to escape from the web domain, they must assist another group member in some way, and pass back to the outside world via another web path.

Typical Presentation, Storyline or Metaphor

You are trying to access your favorite web site, but there is a limitation on the number of users that can be simultaneously logged on. If you happen to connect with the wrong server, everyone in the group gets logged off.

Variations

There are a variety of ways that you can Surf the Web. In fact, four more variations of this activity follow this version.

For the sketch shown, the group has been divided into three smaller groups, with each group entering the web domain via their web. In the case of the traditional vertical web, it would be helpful to have some spotters available, so perhaps some of the horizontal web group can enter first, and assist this second group. Those group members coming from the inclined web can also use some spotting at the very top, so perhaps the group coming from the vertical web can assist them.

Since each of the webs now becomes a two-way web, participants still need to plan which opening they will travel through to enter and escape. Using clothespins to mark closed web openings can be very useful. Place a clothespin on the opening when a participant enters the web domain, and remove this pin when a participant escapes via this same route.

Contact with the web can have a variety of effects, including the elimination of an entire web escape route, or the linking of two participants together.

Important Points

This is one challenge activity that requires the facilitator to say, "you have 5 minutes to plan your technique. At the end of that time, I would like to review your plan with you, BEFORE you begin." This review process encourages the group to plan, but more importantly, it provides the facilitator with every detail of movement, so that they may anticipate appropriate spotting positions before a participant begins their passage.

As with many challenges that have a visible sign of error, in this case that means contact with the web, allow the group to inspect their own movements, rather than setting yourself up as the judge. This places the responsibility directly on the group for their performance.

Be especially cautious near the roots of trees. The footing is uneven here and not suitable for passage. Encourage participants to stick to the middle regions of the web, far away from trees or support poles.

In many cases, participants may choose to lift other participants through the web. Encourage appropriate spotting techniques, especially focused on the shoulders and head region of the participant being transported. Discourage any passage through the web that does not involve contact with other participants. This will prevent jumping and unspotted movements.

Discussion and Debriefing Topics

At the beginning of the activity, did everyone know what their duties were? Were any of the original plans altered during the course of the activity? Why? Would additional planning have prevented these alterations? Were you able to choose the web route you liked, or did you go with the choice of the group? Did the team have a good plan?

Sequence

Surfing the Web requires some preliminary exposure of the group to spotting techniques (possibly from All Aboard), problem solving and a somewhat higher physical activity level than other challenge activities. As a warm up activity, consider using Worm Hole, and mentally note the response and respect of the group to each participant as they pass through the Worm Hole. A group that works together well with Worm Hole is ready for Surfing the Web.

Activities Using Similar Skills and Follow-on Activities

A single version of Surfing the Web is probably sufficient for any single day challenge program. If you happen to have repeat participants, try using a different style to additionally challenge the group. Worm Hole uses similar skills.

Notes

Activity 4.66

Target Specifications

This initiative was specifically created as a metaphor for the difficulty in achieving a specification target, such as: the number of correct invoices processed per week, a dimensional specification (31.05 +/− 0.4 mm), the number of completed orders per month, the number of chocolate chip cookies baked, etc. This activity works well for cross-functional organizations, engineering teams or other groups comprised of members with different talents or skills. Although it was developed for corporate technical teams, it also works with non-technical groups.

Equipment

A single blindfolded player (the "supplier") stands in the center of a 20 to 30 feet (6 to 9 meters) diameter circle. The remaining team members (ideally 4 to 8 people) each grasp "the target", a plastic hoop or soft rope loop about 3 feet (1 meter) in diameter. The supplier is given a series of items to throw towards the target. Typical items include beachballs, tennis balls, racket balls, water balloons, red playground balls, flying disks, hoseplay balls, paper airplanes, foam footballs, pillows, foam sections, paper plates and (the authors' favorite) a rubber chicken. The target team can move and attempts to position themselves so that the object thrown passes through the center of the target. Verbal communication is allowed (and encouraged) between the team and the supplier, even before the activity begins.

The Challenge

One player is blindfolded, the remaining team members each grasp the target circle. On a signal from the receiving members, the blindfolded player tosses one of the objects towards the other participants and they attempt to position themselves so that the object passes through the target circle, while remaining outside the large circle boundary. All participants holding the target circle must have both hands on the circle when the object comes through.

Typical Presentation, Storyline or Metaphor

Your engineering group has recently been assigned the task of designing a high-technology device (such as a disk drive) with tight specification tolerances on several critical components. In order to meet the challenging specifications of this product you must form a project team and closely interface with your supplier. Communication is largely verbal (analogous to using the phone as the primary communication tool) except for several prototypes which the supplier will be sending.

After several items have been tossed, offer the group a smaller target and report to them that research has indicated that a tighter specification tolerance is required on the remaining equipment to be shipped from the supplier. It is probable that additional communication and cooperation will be necessary to complete this design task.

Your team is supplying the parts for a new model of sports car. The factory has just called and wants you to ship your latest test models to them.

With just 5 seconds remaining in the championship basketball game, the lights go out in the arena. Your team attempts to tell you where to shoot the winning shot.

Variations

Here are a few variations involving some of the equipment used for Target Specifications:

Objects to be tossed—Always use soft items that will not cause injury if they happen to contact a team member rather than the target. Items typically include: party balloons, inflated beach toys, air filled garbage bags, weather balloons, knotted cloth rags, socks, gloves and pillows. You can also suggest throwing several objects at a time. This variation typically reduces the efficiency of the group.

The Rubber Chicken—For this object, the team can only provide information on their location to the supplier by "clucking" or making other chicken sounds. This is analogous to translating technical information in a foreign language.

Location—Try playing in a pool at various water depths. The team will have to react quicker and work harder to overcome the resistance of the water.

Blindfolds—Try blindfolding the target team and using a sighted supplier. This approach quickly shifts the responsibility for a successful catch from several players (the team) to a single individual (the supplier). This is analogous to a baseball pitcher trying to hit the bat with his pitch. Notice how easy it is to blame a single player (scapegoat) in this situation. This can be an interesting debriefing subject.

You can also try adding a blindfolded team member with each thrown object and notice how increasingly difficult it is to react. Also notice how dependent the team becomes on the remaining sighted players.

Target Size—Use a smaller hoop or rope circle to increase the difficulty of this initiative.

Important Points

This activity emphasizes the need for cooperation and communication between team members, especially in situations where one team member may be disadvantaged due to location, technical abilities, or familiarity with a successful technique. It also emphasizes the need for flexibility and perseverance when specifications or the situation changes.

Discussion and Debriefing Topics

The main debriefing issues here are the method of communication between the team and the supplier (one player vs. the entire team), the alterations made for various objects (weight of the object, avoidance of the water balloon, wind effects) and the effect of changing the specification target size. Additional discussion is appropriate for each of the variations presented above. You can also select the following global questions:

Was your group able to respond to changing conditions? Did you change techniques during the activity? If so, why? Would anyone from the receiving team have been more successful as the blindfolded delivery expert? How did it feel to be the person throwing the objects? What system did you use for moving the target circle? Which objects were easiest to catch? Could you catch more than one object at a time?

Sequence

Target Specifications is not a high energy activity, so an appropriate follow-on activity would typically have a higher level, or utilize more physical skills and motion. This activity does illustrate the positive effects and team rewards of working together successfully. As such, it can be used whenever a group is experiencing a lack of cooperation, and wants to improve.

Activities Using Similar Skills and Follow-on Activities

Additional activities that involve the coordinated effort of the whole group include Boardwalking and Bull Ring.

Notes

Activity 4.67

Tennis Ball Mountain

While this initiative is fairly simple, it provides the opportunity to process a variety of group interactions.

Equipment

150 or more clean, dry tennis balls. Many tennis clubs are willing to donate or sell used tennis balls at a reasonable cost. If tennis balls are unavailable, try using a variety of other sports balls. The more variety the better.

The Challenge

To stack as many tennis balls as possible on a single person. Generally this is accomplished without tucking any tennis balls inside of clothing and without supporting the tennis balls by other participants in the activity. The only part of the participant holding the tennis ball that can touch the ground, is their feet. Although they can choose to have no body parts touching the ground at all. The person holding the tennis balls can take any position they like, although reclining probably produces the most useful surface area for stacking tennis balls.

Typical Presentation, Storyline or Metaphor

Hard to believe that the whole ship could go down that fast. Now here you are, floating in the ocean. Luckily it is a nice day, and the water is warm. As you float about in the water, you gather up other floating objects, that you might need, and let them dry out by stacking them on top of your life preserver. How much of this stuff can you keep dry? Which of these objects is the most important to your survival? Which can you afford to lose?

Variations

Tennis balls are readily available and a good choice for this activity. Other objects, such as ping pong balls or packaging peanuts, can also be used. Whatever objects you have, you're going to need a lot of them.

Tennis Ball Mountain happens to be located along a major fault line, so after the completion of the activity, and earthquake can come along to shake the balls off the participant covered in tennis balls.

If the group happens to be lying on the ground, or supporting the person very near the ground, after placing all the balls, try to remove the supporting participants until the person covered with balls is lying flat on the ground, or until a great number of the balls have fallen off. Continue to spot the head and shoulders of this participant as supporters are removed.

During the activity, dropped balls can be removed from play—this encourages players not to throw them about.

Important Points

Encourage the group to support the person holding the balls in the most comfortable manner possible. While it seems logical to cradle the person with the rest of the group in a standing position, this same support can be offered with the support group sitting on the ground, supporting the ball receiver on their legs. This position also leaves the supporting group members with free hands to assist in the placement of the tennis balls.

Discussion and Debriefing Topics

Was the group able to successfully pile all the tennis balls onto one person? What qualities or talents did this person have that made them a good choice for this activity? How many tennis balls were dropped during the process? When you are keeping track of so many tasks at one time, is it easy to drop a few every now and then?

Sequence

This activity involves some contact between participants, in a supportive environment. It can also be used in a goal setting and problem solving environment.

Activities Using Similar Skills and Follow-on Activities

Community Juggling utilizes some of the same skills with tennis balls as Tennis Ball Mountain.

Notes

Activity 4.68

The Boardroom

This activity, which he calls The Wind-Mill, comes from the creative mind of Chris Cavert. You can find this and some other innovative and challenging activities in his book, Affordable Portables, and his newest book, 50 Ways to Use Your Noodle, co-authored with Feeding the Zircon Gorilla author, Sam Sikes. See Chapter 8 for information about these references. By the way, Chris also wins the award for being the most knowledgeable and nicest individual we met while writing this book. Two very admirable talents, and Chris has both of them. We have adapted a few attributes of this activity. Hope you like them.

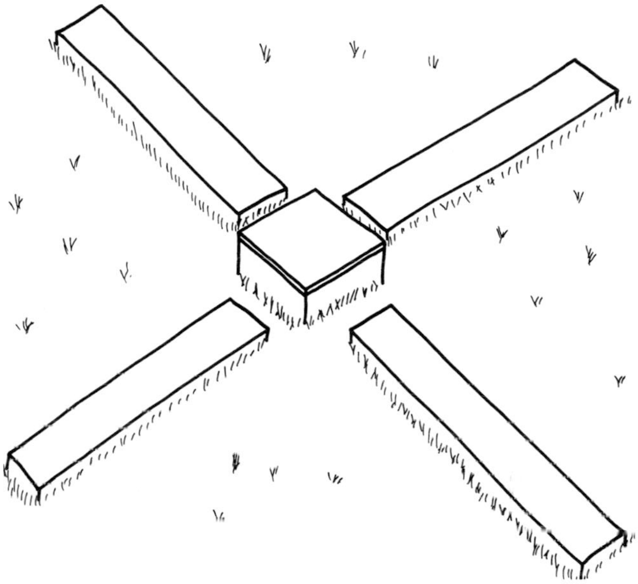

Equipment

A wooden platform or plastic hoop and a minimum of four 2x8 inch boards, at least 6 feet (1.8 meters) long.

The Challenge

For each group member to change the board they are standing on, so that they are not standing on a board with any original board members.

Typical Presentation, Storyline or Metaphor

In the fast pace world of international finance, where fortunes are made and lost in a single day, you can scarcely keep up with the mergers, corporate raiders, trading, partnering and flow of personnel in and out of the organization. Your resume is in hand, you have a plan, and you are ready for a change. You march right into The Boardroom, and demand a big raise or you're outta here. That takes about 5 seconds, and you are out on the street looking for your next position. Luckily there are at least three other organizations nearby that are looking for someone with your skills. Try to find a new position in an organization that doesn't have any of your original board members.

Variations

One very unique variation is to challenge the group to complete this activity without touching each other. This version still requires appropriate spotting. By using the space at the center, and shuttling participants around to various locations, it is possible to complete this challenge, even with only a single person in The Boardroom at a time.

Chris mentions having the participants carry a paper cup filled with water with them during the entire activity. Also, participants must make contact with the central platform with both feet at once while crossing, and they must always be in contact with either a board or a platform at all times.

To add some additional distractions to the group, and hopefully not to those spotting, try using beach ball resumes that you can send to other companies before going into The Boardroom. Any balls reaching the ground are lost, the others stay in play for as long as the activity continues.

For a slightly more difficult variation, require participants to change boards, and to end up in a board position that is different than their original board position. If they began the activity being last in line on their board, they must end up on another board, with none of their original board members, standing in any position other than the last position in line.

Important Points

This activity requires at least 9 participants. For 12 or less participants, use four boards. For 13 to 20 participants, use five boards. Having approximately 3 to 5 participants on each board is about right. This is not a speed activity. Encourage participants to stay in contact with the boards, and walk slowly.

Chris mentions that it is interesting to begin this activity with participants already standing on the boards. After offering them time to plan, some groups will leave the boards so that they can plan and see the activity from a better position. Other groups stay rigidly attached to their initial positions. This makes for an interesting topic to debrief.

Discussion and Debriefing Topics

Did you have any idea what was going on, or did other group members tell you where to stand? Were their comments helpful? How long did the planning stage and the actual activity stage of this challenge take? Were there any problems that you didn't foresee? What was most difficult about this activity?

Sequence

The Boardroom is a problem solving activity that has some balance issues. It works well with some personal contact for light spotting.

Activities Using Similar Skills and Follow-on Activities

Log Rolling uses some similar skills, as does All Aboard and River Crossing.

Notes

Activity 4.69

The Paper Chase

This activity has some definite business related metaphors, and you can use the new props for Community Juggling after The Paper Chase.

Equipment

A piece of paper for each person in the group.

The Challenge

Using primarily your non-dominant hand (participants can work together), create a paper airplane out of the large paper sheet. Be as creative as you like in forming your plane. You can even decorate it, again using your non-dominant hand. Then as a group, toss these airplanes high into the air. The goal is for everyone in the group to simultaneously catch an airplane thrown by someone else.

Typical Presentation, Storyline or Metaphor

You have a zillion things to do at work today, and you are already way behind. Luckily, you have an excellent team to work with, and they are all busy finishing up their assignments too. Just before lunch, you all decide to check each other's work, just to make sure everything is correct. At precisely 11:15, everyone passes their assignment to another person in the group. Did every assignment make it, or did some tasks get dropped?

Variations

Rather than making airplanes out of the paper, try making just a simple ball. You can use a variety of papers including wrapping paper, cardboard, newsprint, aluminum foil, old greeting cards, magazines or newspapers. You can also give participants more than one sheet of paper so that they can make one very large ball.

Another approach would be to use this activity as a teachable moment, and have the participants make a collection of origami animals to toss about. This may take a while longer to complete, but you won't be filling up any trashcans with left-over papers. Most folks will want to take home their creations.

Important Points

Paper balls have less sharp edges than paper airplanes, and are probably a better all around choice. Your group is likely to have a higher success rate catching paper balls than paper airplanes.

It is probably a good idea to have a trashcan or recycling bin ready at the completion of this activity unless you try the origami version above.

Discussion and Debriefing Topics

Even with other team members around to help, some problems just get out of hand. Which was easier to catch, a complex plane that took a while to create, or a simple ball that took only a few seconds? If someone handed you a project they were working on, would you rather it was a simple or complex one? What percentage of the objects were you able to recover each time? Did this match your goal? What skills would be necessary to increase the number of objects caught?

Sequence

Since The Paper Chase uses paper and possibly pens or other drawing instruments, this activity can be initiated while the group is seated around a table, or just finishing the debriefing session from a previous activity. Tables are especially useful for origami creations.

Activities Using Similar Skills and Follow-on Activities

Community Juggling is a typical follow-on activity. If you happen to have multiple sheets of paper for each group member, you could use these for a paper version of Tennis Ball Mountain.

Activity 4.70

Time Tunnel

Time Tunnel is a fun activity for a group that is willing to work together in a controlled manner and in some tight places. While many activities in this chapter can be approached with a great deal of enthusiasm, Time Tunnel requires some moderate restraint. Here the challenge, and the fun, comes from partners attempting to simultaneously exchange places at opposite ends of the Time Tunnel.

Equipment

The Time Tunnel is a section of lycra sewn into a long tube. Directions are presented in Chapter 5 for making the tunnel.

The Challenge

The challenge of Time Tunnel is for group members to enter one end of the tunnel and exit at the opposite end. This typically occurs while half of the other group members are simultaneously traveling within the Time Tunnel in the opposite direction. Having participants carry various objects with them, which cannot touch the walls of the Time Tunnel, increases the concentration of this activity. Other large items, such as inflatable beach balls, floating pool toys, water balloons, and even earth balls make for interesting shapes when viewed from outside the Time Tunnel.

Typical Presentation, Storyline or Metaphor

You have been chosen for a unique mission. Scientists have identified the location of the entrance to a Time Tunnel, and you have been selected to explore this phenomenon. Since balance is important in all regions of space and time in this universe, you will likely encounter another explorer as you pass through the Time Tunnel. Be careful, travel cautiously, and watch out for others that may be ahead of you! You will also be asked to take some equipment with you so that you can experience life in the future (or the past). Because this equipment is non-living, and from a different timeline, it cannot touch the walls of the Time Tunnel or it will be instantly transported to the beginning (or end) of time.

Variations

The walls of a lycra tube Time Tunnel are very elastic, and will allow quite a few participants to pass simultaneously. At first, you may wish to restrict Time Tunnel travel to two participants. Increasing the number of participants in the Time Tunnel increases the number of challenging passes that each person must make.

Lycra is very elastic. You can request that everyone must be inside the Time Tunnel before anyone can pass by another person on their way to the other side.

The objects carried in the Time Tunnel should be soft with no sharp edges to catch the lycra walls of the tunnel. Provide a wide variety of objects, with increasing size. See what the maximum size object the group can successfully pass through the tunnel.

If you wish to make a history lesson from this activity, consider having the travelers arrive in a specific location in time that you are reviewing in class, say France during the French Revolution, or Antarctica at the time of the first exploration of the South Pole.

Important Points

Lycra is very elastic, but can still rip or tear if confronted with a sharp object, pointed belt buckle, shoes with cleats, etc. Encourage participants to keep one hand above their head at all times as they pass through the Time Tunnel—this prevents a head-on collision with other time travelers. Since group members outside the Time Tunnel will be able to tell when two time travelers are approaching each other, it is fine to allow them to communicate with those travelers inside the Time Tunnel. It will probably be helpful to have a few group members hold the ends of the Time Tunnel while others are traveling inside.

Discussion and Debriefing Topics

Did you feel alone on your journey in the Time Tunnel or were you able to communicate with others in your own time zone? What experiences did you share with other travelers you encountered in the Time Tunnel? Were you able to transport your equipment successfully, without touching the walls of the Time Tunnel? How did you know when there was another time traveler coming your way?

Sequence

This activity encourages careful execution of a physical challenge. Some time in a Lycra Tube might be the next place to take the group. Time Tunnel also encourages communication between group members, and cooperation in transporting the equipment through the tunnel. Other activities utilizing these same elements would be useful.

Activities Using Similar Skills and Follow-on Activities

There are a variety of other Lycra Tube activities present in this chapter. Activities such as Bull Ring and Pot of Gold also require careful execution and communication between group members.

Notes

Activity 4.71

Tower Building

There are a variety of materials that can be used to create some pretty impressive structures.

Equipment

Several sets of any commercially available construction set equipment, usually found in toy stores. Other possibilities include plastic drinking straws & scotch tape, or cardboard tubes & masking tape, or uncooked spaghetti & marshmallows. Storage containers for each of these pieces.

The Challenge

To create the tallest tower possible using the pieces given. A variation on this challenge would be to include an object with the construction materials that the tower has to support, such as a book, stuffed animal, or ball.

Typical Presentation, Storyline or Metaphor

It is almost time for the holiday parade, and your group wants to be sure to see all there is to see that day. So you begin building the tallest tower you can, to give your group the best view possible.

You've discovered a box full of radio equipment on the desert island you're on. The only problem is that the transmitter is extremely heavy and you have limited materials to build a tower with. The higher the tower the longer your broadcast range, and time is running out.

Variations

There are a variety of building materials that can be used for this activity including, but certainly not limited to: spaghetti and marshmallows, toothpicks and gumdrops, drinking straws and cubes of cheese, pretzel sticks, and any of the non-edible toys and construction sets available in most toy stores.

Almost any combination of tubes, tape, clamps, string, construction paper, cardboard, staples and other household or shop supplies can be used. Commercially available construction sets can be reused, but the spaghetti, straws and tubes are generally used only once. Containers can include cups, plastic bags, food containers and tin cans.

Important Points

Wind can be a factor when attempting this activity outdoors. Make sure to have garbage cans ready if using disposable items to make the towers. Groups of about 4 participants are best for this activity. Consider having the group look at all the designs, and then rebuild their towers using the best technology from each of the designs.

Discussion and Debriefing Topics

Did your group have a specific design in mind, or were several different styles of towers tried before making a final decision? Could your group's tower have been higher if you didn't need to support the container weight? Which piece was the most important?

Sequence

Tower Building is a classic activity which incorporates elements of problem solving with creativity. This activity is often presented while participants are seated around tables or seated on the ground. This atmosphere creates a lower energy environment, and one that processing can immediately follow.

Activities Using Similar Skills and Follow-on Activities

Other problem solving activities using props include Pot of Gold, Wing It, and River Crossing.

Activity 4.72

Traffic Circle

Traveling in Great Britain, or Boston for that matter, can be challenging, thanks to the presence of a unique vehicular obstacle known as a Traffic Circle. Here is the challenge and adventure programming equivalent to that obstacle. This activity is simple to explain, but provides some real challenges.

Equipment

This activity can accomplished with a 2 foot (610 mm) diameter rope loop or plastic hoop, and also by making a double loop with a 12 foot (3.66 meter) length of 1 inch (25.4 mm) wide tubular webbing that Tom Smith calls a Raccoon Circle.

The Challenge

For group members standing in a circle to simultaneously change places with their opposites as quickly as possible. During the changing process, both partners (opposites) must simultaneously touch one foot in the center of the rope circle as they change sides of the circle. At no time can participants touch each other or the rope circle.

Typical Presentation, Storyline or Metaphor

This group problem is so simple that it seldom requires a story. However, if you are in need of a creative explanation, you can use the Traffic Circle analogy, or try suggesting that participants represent bits of data on a computer that need to transfer from the hard drive to a floppy disk. Any contact between data bits causes the system to crash. Ready, Go!

Variations

This activity is easily altered by the size of the group. More participants typically require more time. One of most unusual variations is to allow participants to touch anyone except their opposite partner. For this case, everyone can simultaneously touch one foot into the center of the rope circle, and then run around to the other side of the circle. Quick, easy, and it follows the rules.

Changing the size of the rope circle changes the speed of the activity. Smaller circles require more deliberate motions, larger circles allow lots of speed. Altering the geometry of the rope circle also changes the speed and path of the participants, particularly if you choose to use a long rectangular box rather than a simple circle.

Important Points

As a facilitator, do not set yourself up to be the quality inspector for this activity. Allow a member of the group or the whole group to judge whether or not the correct contact was made at the center circle. This allows the group to take ownership of their effort, and the responsibility for completing the activity successfully.

It can be very useful to have participants slowly walk through their plan, before attempting a full speed trial. After a slow motion walk through, allow the group to create a timing goal for themselves to complete the activity, before the first full-speed attempt.

Discussion and Debriefing Topics

Did each member of the group have a clear picture of what they were about to do? Was there any confusion regarding who your partner was? Did you manage to decide before trading sides, which side you would pass your partner on? Were there any traffic jams? Did your group try to decide on a successful plan before starting, or did your group just go for it? Were you able to meet your timing goal?

Sequence

Traffic Circle works well with other Raccoon Circle activities. This is a non-contact activity which can be useful for populations that are not comfortable with a great deal of personal contact during a problem solving activity.

Activities Using Similar Skills and Follow-on Activities

Community Juggling also establishes a pattern between participants, and occasionally produces a few traffic jams in the process. Having met the problem solving and timing goals of this activity, participants can move on to other timing goal activities, such as Alphabet Soup.

Notes

Activity 4.73

Tree of Knots

This activity provides an answer to the question, "what can I do with 30 feet (9 meters) of rope?"

Equipment

30 feet (9 meters) of rope approximately ⅜ inch to 1 inch (9 to 25 mm) in diameter.

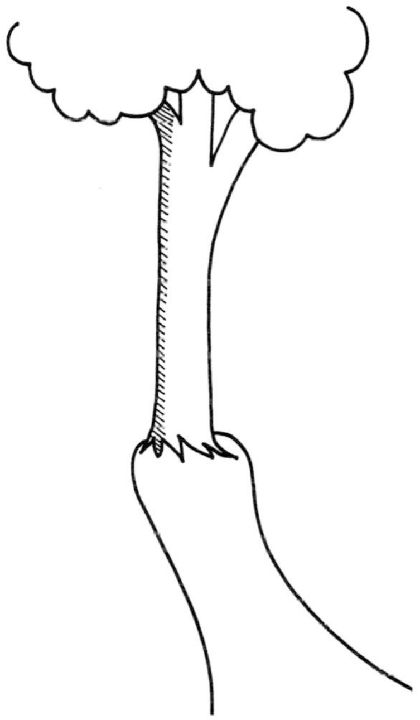

The Challenge

For the entire group to pick up a rope that has been passed around a tree and without letting go, tie a square knot in the rope against the tree.

Typical Presentation, Storyline or Metaphor

If you have heard the phrase, "when you reach the end of your rope, tie a knot in it and hang on," this is real 3-D version of that phrase. Your entire group has been exploring a cave, seeing some beautiful rock formations and underground geology in the process. Suddenly, an enormous wind comes sweeping through the cave. In an effort to keep your group together, you begin to tie a strong knot around a pillar using the safety line that you are all attached to.

Variations

The solution techniques can vary considerably depending on how the group chooses to pick up the rope. If the facilitator says the phrase, "where ever you touch the rope with your right hand must remain there throughout the activity," it is possible that some groups will realize that only using their left hands allows them to move anywhere they want. If half of the group picks up each side of the rope (which is very typical), both sides will usually complete about half the work. If a single participant chooses to hold the left side of the rope, and the rest of the group is on the right side, it is fairly easy for the single participant to do all the work of tying the knot.

Other variations include blindfolding every other participant and tying other types of knots and bows with the rope. A long segment of tubular nylon webbing could also be used to tie a water knot using this technique.

Important Points

Teaching basic knot tying is a teachable moment that can be used prior to this activity. If participants are not familiar with a square knot, having enough rope segments for each participant to create their own knot would be helpful. You can also tie a square knot using a brightly colored rope at eye level on the same tree, for the group to use as a model.

Discussion and Debriefing Topics

What was your contribution to the group's effort? Did you have a clear picture of what was needed to tie a square knot? Was it helpful to have an example of the knot to look at? What would have made this process easier?

Sequence

Tree of Knots involves problem solving with the ability to visualize the rope creating a knot. This ability to clearly see the solution to a problem is a useful skill that can be used with other problem solving activities, such as 2B or KNOT 2B, or Not Knots.

Activities Using Similar Skills and Follow-on Activities

A Collection of Knots can be conducted with the same rope used for Tree of Knots.

Notes

Activity 4.74

Under Cover

If you happen to use a cloth tarp or lycra tube to define the space for Danger Zone or Blackout, you can use that same prop for Under Cover. This activity nicely follows Danger Zone.

Equipment

A tarp, blanket, or a large square of cloth, at least 15 feet (4.5 meters) square. Lay this material perfectly flat on the surface of the ground or floor.

The Challenge

For the entire group to get under the cloth, so that it completely covers the group, without using their hands, arms or head in any way.

Typical Presentation, Storyline or Metaphor

During your latest climbing expedition, your group happens to be exposed during the beginning of a solar flare up. Against the white snow, the sunlight will be blindingly bright, so your group needs to relocate underneath the community ground cloth upon which you were previously sleeping. Since your hands are full of your possessions and equipment, you can only use your legs and bodies to accomplish this Under Cover attempt.

Variations

Consider including several nearby objects as part of the materials which must be included under the cloth. Other variations can include requiring all participants to stand beneath the cloth, or to be sitting down, or lying down.

A sometimes interesting, and frequently wet variation, is to have each participant carry a glass of water in each hand during this activity. Other props, such as tennis balls, also keep participants from unintentionally grasping the cloth with their hands.

Important Points

This is not a timed activity. For safety reasons, plastic cloth (such as a shower curtain, plastic bags or waterproof tarps) should not be used because these materials pose a safety risk for suffocation. Better to use any kind of open weave or breathable cloth.

Encourage participants not to squish any of the other participants under the cloth.

Discussion and Debriefing Topics

Did you have a plan before attempting to go Under Cover? Were you able to accomplish this task using that plan? Were there any difficulties that you didn't realize would occur? Would your plan have worked if you had 3 more participants?

Sequence

Under Cover works well immediately after Danger Zone, provided that a cloth is used and not a plastic sheet. Under Cover can also be used to bring the group into a Lycra Tube.

Activities Using Similar Skills and Follow-on Activities

Other activities which use a cloth and primarily the lower body include Gridlock and Magic Carpet.

Notes

Activity 4.75

Under the Doormat

In a gentler time, it was typical to leave an extra key to the house under the doormat on the front porch. This activity has more to do with personal space than with keys, but provides an interesting dilemma for two people.

Equipment

A piece of carpeting about 8 inches (200 mm) square. Two keys, coins or buttons. Place the keys below the carpeting before participants step on.

The Challenge

For two people to step on the carpet, and without stepping off, each collect one of the keys below the carpet.

Typical Presentation, Storyline or Metaphor

It has been raining all day, with no signs of stopping. You and a friends run from the car to the house through soggy puddles as the rain pelts you from above. You make it to the narrow front porch with a small roof that just barely blocks the rain. Somewhere during that mad dash to the house however, you dropped your keys. Oh well, you can find them after the rain stops, and besides, there should be a spare collection of keys under the doormat. The only problem is that you'll need to get them without stepping off the mat, or you'll be drenched by the downpour.

Variations

Changing the size of the carpets can make the difference between an easy activity and a difficult one. For starters, you can begin with a 12 inch (305 mm) square pad, and place the keys on top of the pad. Now all you have to do is bend down carefully, and have each partner collect one of the keys. Using smaller pads, and placing the keys initially under the edges of the carpet makes the difficulty level increase. The most difficult level is a very small carpet with both keys underneath and near the center.

If you enjoy making any activity a whole group activity, you can have the participants make a mad dash to any available carpet pad, forming partners when they arrive. By placing the carpets very near each other, you are likely to encourage some assistance from the "people next door." You are also likely to witness some unintentional bumping from groups that are very close together. This version is a little like trying to tie your shoe laces on a crowded subway car. In fact, forget the keys altogether and see if you can tie your shoelaces without stepping off the mat.

Important Points

The most obvious concern is that partners spot each other effectively during this activity. Prior to beginning the activity, some explanation of spotting techniques would be appropriate. It is also important to understand the limitations of invading someone else's personal space. There are many topics here that can be discussed during the debriefing.

Discussion and Debriefing Topics

One of the first issues that can be discussed with Under the Doormat, is the necessity or desire for "personal space." Did you feel that your personal space was compacted? Do you think your partner was helpful during your attempt to retrieve the key? Did the size of the doormat make a difference? Did having neighbors help? Did you have a plan for retrieving the key, or did you simply try a variety of techniques until one worked?

Sequence

Under the Doormat is an activity in which participants are clearly in close proximity to each other. This activity brings participants even closer than Handcuffs and Shackles. It might be a good idea to have partners working together prior to this activity.

Activities Using Similar Skills and Follow-on Activities

Other close proximity activities include: Handcuffs and Shackles, Magic Carpet, All Aboard, and Danger Zone.

Notes

Activity 4.76

Universe

More often these days, challenge and adventure activities are being incorporated into other educational settings. In some cases, students might be introduced to these activities in mathematics or science classes, not merely in physical education classes. Universe makes use of our solar system while also introducing group consensus building.

Equipment

Nothing is required to complete this activity other than the participants themselves. It may be useful however to have a long string with the exact locations of the planets marked, and a tent stake or pet stake (available at most pet stores) for anchoring the string.

The Challenge

To place 10 participants in the proper location for the nine planets in our solar system, and the sun. The height of each participant should be proportional to the diameter of the planet or the sun.

Typical Presentation, Storyline or Metaphor

Just as the members of our group each have a different height, so too all the planets in our solar system are a different size. Let's choose nine people to represent each of the planets in our solar system, and another person to represent the sun. Next, try to place each of the nine planets the exact scaled distance from the sun. Since the distances in space are really huge, we will scale the distance. For this problem 10 meters (about 32.8 feet) will be equivalent to 93,000,000 miles.

Variations

If you have a large group, you could always include the asteroid belt, the rings of Saturn, the moons of various planets. You might even illustrate just how far away the next nearest solar system is.

Important Points

As an educational activity, this activity is best presented after students have had the opportunity to learn about the solar system. One mnemonic technique for remembering the names of the planets in order is, Many Very Elderly Men Just Sit Upon Neat Pillows for Mercury, Venus, Earth, Mars, Jupiter, Saturn, Uranus, Neptune and Pluto.

With regard to choosing the size of the planets from various participants, height may be the best choice. Even the shortest class members representing Mercury are nearly 3000 miles in diameter. Avoid using weight or waist size as the measurement of planet size.

Discussion and Debriefing Topics

One of the most significant effects of this activity, is that student can visualize just exactly how big our solar system is. The distances are absolutely huge. In

Scaled Distances

(1 meter (m) = 9,300,000 miles)
(1 millimeter (mm) = 9,300 miles)

Object	Diameter	Distance from Sun
Sun	110 mm	0 m
Mercury	0.3 mm	4 m
Venus	0.8 mm	7 m
Earth	0.8 mm	10 m
Mars	0.4 mm	15 m
Jupiter	9.4 mm	52 m
Saturn	7.1 mm	95 m
Uranus	3.1 mm	192 m
Neptune	3.0 mm	301 m
Pluto	1.0 mm	395 m

many cases, the distance between the Sun and Pluto will be dramatically underestimated by the group. If you shine a flashlight on the group from the Sun's position, which is visible almost immediately, you can then relate the actual time that it takes sunlight to reach each of the planets. You can also incorporate the speed at which each planet spins, and the amount of time it takes for each planet to circle the sun.

Additional topics, such as the location of the asteroid belt, the present location of the Voyager space craft, Haley's Comet and other astronomical objects can be included.

Sequence

This activity should clearly come after a presentation on the solar system.

Activities Using Similar Skills and Follow-on Activities

Activities such as Stretching the Limit utilize similar skills.

Notes

Activity 4.77

Villages and Wells

This is a 3-D life-size version of the now classic puzzle. It also serves as a great early activity to reinforce group problem solving skills.

Equipment

Three objects to represent three villages, and three additional objects to represent the three wells. The wooden platforms from River Crossing or All Aboard can be used. Also needed are a total of nine ropes to connect the villages and wells, each rope at least 10 feet long.

The Challenge

Using the nine ropes, connect each of the three villages to the three wells, without allowing any of the ropes to cross each other.

Typical Presentation, Storyline or Metaphor

Fresh, clean water is one of the most valuable resources on the face of the earth. As environmental engineers, your task is to create a network of water lines which will connect three villages to three independent wells, using the nine pieces of ropes to represent these water lines. The ends of each rope represent a connection between a single village and a single well. Water lines cannot cross each other.

Variations

The orientation of the three villages and three wells can be altered to provide variety to this activity. The length of ropes can also vary (although the solution is typically not altered by this variation).

Facilitators can begin this activity with a single village and three wells, connected by three water lines. Then add a second village, and three more water lines. Adding a third village and three more water lines requires some deviation from previous methods. Adding a fourth well requires some additional outside the box thinking.

Important Points

For large groups, consider assigning two participants to each end of a rope, and allow only these two team members to decide on the ultimate location of this water line. This will allow each team member to have input to the final solution of the problem.

Discussion and Debriefing Topics

Which water lines were the most difficult to place?

Sequence

This activity is a quick initiation to the art of group problem solving, and is best used at the beginning of a challenge session, prior to other problem solving initiatives.

Activities Using Similar Skills and Follow-on Activities

Other problem solving activities using rope include: Pot of Gold, 2B or KNOT 2B and Bull Ring.

Notes

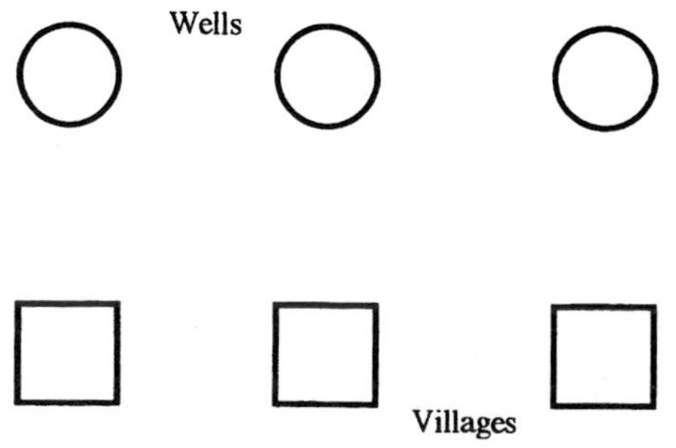

Activity 4.78

The Water Tube

Here is a fun and wet activity for a hot day. The water tube works well for groups of all sizes, especially around a source of water such as a pool, pond, fountain, or stream.

Equipment

You'll need either a 5 foot (1.5 meter) long section of PVC tubing (at least 4 inches in diameter, capped at one end, with a series of ¼ inch (6 mm) diameter holes drilled at random spacings), or one of the portable Water Tubes described in Chapter 5. The portable version has a wooden base stand which folds up into the tube for transport. In addition to the Water Tube, you'll

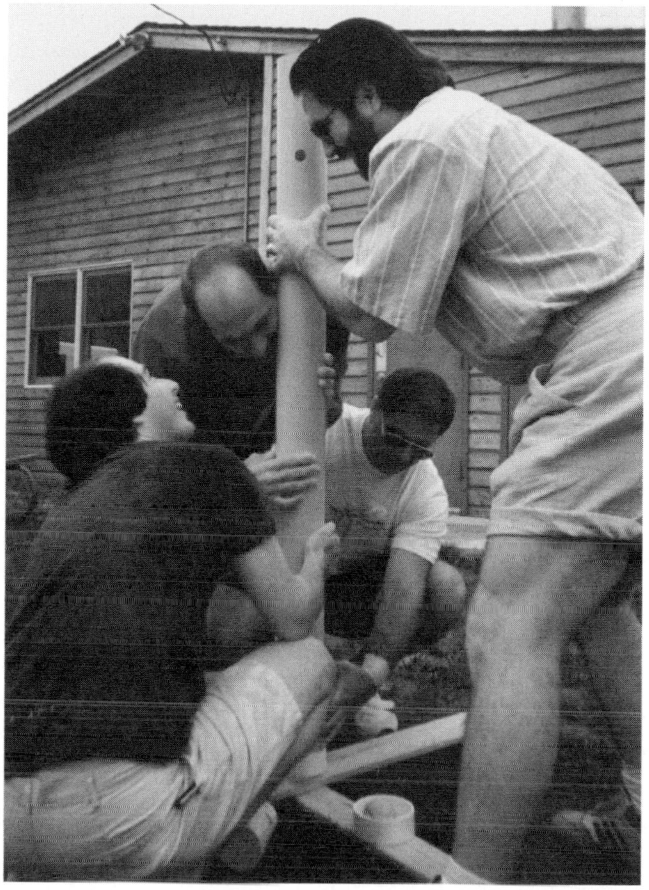

need a rubber ducky or some other floating toy, and a variety of cups, buckets, or containers in which to carry water. You may also wish to include some additional props that may or may not be of any assistance to the group, such as: plastic hoops, rope, dowel rods, garden hose, tennis balls, salad tongs.

The Challenge

To retrieve the object dropped to the bottom of the empty Water Tube using any available nearby props.

Typical Presentation, Storyline or Metaphor

You are busy negotiating a major business deal when your drop your all-weather cellular phone down an open pipe. What you were doing there in the first place is a mystery, but the phone at the bottom of the pipe is now a reality. You need to get it back quickly, because the phone is still on, and it is costing you big bucks in long-distance charges every minute.

While enjoying a pleasant dip in a remote wilderness pool high in the mountains, you are interrupted by not one, but three rather large, and hungry looking bears, who promptly take a bite out of your backpack, your suntan lotion bottle, your favorite hat, and who also have grabbed your favorite swimming companion, your rubber ducky. After regaining your composure, and most of your clothing, you go off looking to recover some of the goods. You discover that the bears are now gone, and they have deposited the rubber ducky at the bottom of an old hollow tree. There are a few items around—see if you can retrieve the rubber ducky before those pesky bears return.

Variations

One of the first variations in Water Tube, is to use different styles of containers to transport water. Film canisters are tiny, and require many trips. Buckets are large, and often times the water coming from them is transferred more to other participants than the Water Tube itself. One of the best water transport containers are the stadium sized plastic cups found in party stores. For an extra challenge, you can also drill some holes in these containers.

With regard to the Water Tube itself, the number of holes can be varied, as well as the diameter of these holes. A small hole at the bottom of the Water Tube can lose as much water as a large hole at the top. If you happen to have less participants than holes, try offering the group about 2 inches (51 mm) of duct tape, and let them "plug" a few holes. You can also vary the length of the Water Tube. A 5 foot (1.5 meter) height allows you to cut two tubes from a standard 10 foot (3.0 meter) length of PVC tubing. 7 feet (2.1 meters) is about the tallest Water Tube made so far, although anything is possible.

If you happen to work with groups that enjoy swimming, try making a water tube that can be sunk in a pool, with the PVC tubing sticking above the surface of the water by several feet. All holes drilled in the PVC tubing should be no more than 1 foot (305 mm) below the water line. Now participants can float up to the Water Tube as they pour water into it. This also works well to confine the spillage of water, but typically results in substantially wetter participants.

For floating objects, try using tennis balls, ping pong balls, rubber toys, or film canisters filled with secret information or directions to the next activity. You can also confound the group by placing an object that looks like it would float, but doesn't, into the Water Tube. This is an interesting way to process expectations vs. reality.

You can also ask participants to exchange roles when the water is about three quarters of the way to the top of the Water Tube (water carriers become hole pluggers, and vice-versa). You can also challenge the group not to spill any water during the activity.

Important Points

Do not allow participants to place more than one hand up to the wrist into the Water Tube to retrieve the rubber ducky. This will avoid the case where someone has their entire arm down the water tube, right up to their shoulder.

Discussion and Debriefing Topics

Did you have a plan when you started the activity? Did you stick to your plan, or change it as you went along? What technique did you use to recover the rubber ducky? Can you imagine other ways to accomplish this task? What roles did everyone play in the success of this project? Did you decide on your role at the beginning of the activity, or were you "volunteered." Did your idea work the first time, or did you add to it as you learned new things?

Sequence

Water Tube can be a wet activity, and so it fits just before a break in the program. It is also an activity that works well to refresh the group on a hot day. Once you are wet, consider trying other water activities.

Activities Using Similar Skills and Follow-on Activities

Waterfall I and Waterfall II are other activities that use water and PVC tubing. If you enjoy working with PVC tubing, you might try making some rain sticks using the directions provided in Chapter 7.

Notes

Activity 4.79

Waterfall I

Waterfall is a simple activity that works well in hot weather. Cool and refreshing if you happen to goof up.

Equipment

A long tube and enough water to fill the tube. A few towels might be nice.

The Challenge

To pass the tube around a circle, from person to person, loosing the least amount of water. For stability reasons, at least two participants must be in contact with the tube at all times.

Typical Presentation, Storyline or Metaphor

Centuries ago, fire was carried by swift runners between villages. In some countries, news was also carried using relay systems, much like the pony express system in the early days of the United States. In this case, your team is needed to relay clean water from a reservoir high in the mountains to a village located in a very arid region of the country.

Variations

The diameter and length of the tube are two sources of variation in this activity. Be careful though, a 10 foot long section of 1½″ diameter PVC tubing filled with water weighs about 8 pounds (3.6 kg).

Two variations in passing technique for the tube are possible. The first variation keeps the tube vertical as it is passed between participants. The second variation requires that that tube be turned over between players. This second version is substantially wetter than the first.

Some additional props, such as tennis balls, can be used as stoppers to hold the water in while transporting the tube.

Important Points

Size the tube and the amount of water to the ability of the participants. A 1½ inch diameter PVC tube about 8 feet long works well for teens and adults (and weighs about 6.4 pounds (3 kg). If you happen to use the version of passing where the tube is turned over between participants, have at least 4 people in contact with the tube during each transfer. The weight of the water can cause the tube to drop rapidly.

Discussion and Debriefing Topics

Were you able to create a plan and then stick to this plan throughout the entire activity? Did the group change the method for handing off the tubes once the activity started? Which handoffs were most efficient? Which handoffs were the driest?

Sequence

This activity works well on a hot day, or when the group needs a refreshing task. Better plan a little drying off time after this event.

Activities Using Similar Skills and Follow-on Activities

Other wet activities include Waterfall II and the Water Tube. The 2 liter pop bottle rockets described in Chapter 7 also use water.

Notes

Activity 4.80

Waterfall II

Waterfall II uses the same PVC tubes found in Marble Tubes and adds a unique and often wet variation to the traditional marble approach.

Equipment

Either of the two styles of PVC marble tubes described earlier in this chapter. A large bucket filled with water and a small measuring cup. A funnel is optional.

The Challenge

To pass as much water as possible from a large bucket at Point A to a measuring cup at Point B, using only the PVC tubes.

Typical Presentation, Storyline or Metaphor

Centuries ago, fire was carried by swift runners between villages. In some countries, news was also carried using relay systems, much like the pony express system in the early days of the United States. In this case, your team is needed to relay clean water from a reservoir high in the mountains down to a village in the flatlands. Water is a precious commodity, so try to transport as much as you can.

Your team has quite unexpectedly come across the fountain of youth. You have a change to transport some of the water back to your laboratory for analysis, for which you will need at one measuring cup full. You can use any of the equipment you now have in your possession for transporting this precious water.

Variations

Although not strictly in keeping with the cooperative nature of challenge and adventure activities in general, this activity does make an interesting relay race or competitive challenge.

If you happen to use the open half-tube version of Marble Tubes, you can also float a few ice cubes along with the water.

This activity becomes considerably more difficult if the location of the measuring cup is greater than the distance that the group can reach without moving. As an additional variation, you can allow movement when water is in the tube, but do not allow participants to hold the ends of the tube with their hands, or block these with any parts of their body.

Having the group decide on a goal or target amount of water to transport give them an opportunity to measure their abilities to successfully complete this activity.

Important Points

Plan to get wet. This is not an indoor activity.

Discussion and Debriefing Topics

Was the group able to meet their goal? Did you transport more or less water than you planned? What was the most effective technique for transporting the water? Where did you lose the greatest amount of water? How could you improve this situation? Did you change any techniques during the activity? Do you think you could transport evening more water without spilling it?

Sequence

Some hot days require refreshing water activities like Waterfall II. Plan some drying off time after this activity.

Activities Using Similar Skills and Follow-on Activities

Other wet activities include Waterfall I and the Water Tube. The 2 liter pop bottle rockets described in Chapter 7 also use water.

Activity 4.81

Wing It

Here is a simple initial problem solving activity that teaches some useful skills and provides some interesting debriefing opportunities early in the challenge program.

Equipment

You'll need one ¼ × 12 inch long threaded rod and 5 wingnuts for every group of 5 participants. You can creatively cheat and use 4 to 8 participants per threaded rod. This equipment is available at most hardware stores.

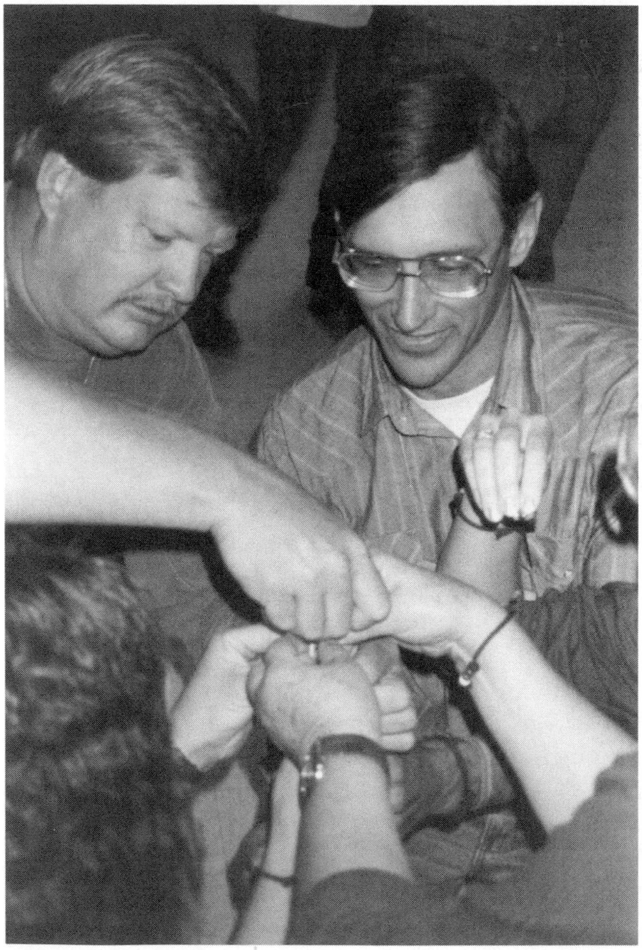

The Challenge

For each participant to place their own wingnut on the threaded rod, and then for the group as a whole to move all the wingnuts to the far end and off the rod as quickly as possible.

Typical Presentation, Storyline or Metaphor

You might be surprised to know that the solution to many of the problems presented in challenge and adventure activities, is in fact, NOT the goal of the activity. The goal is typically the ability of the group to function as a team, to work together, to be supportive of each other, and to have fun as a group. See if you can tell what the true goal of this activity is.

Variations

Rather than giving each participant their own wingnut, you can provide a bowl of wingnuts, and instruct the group to "take as many as you like." The group is then responsible for using each of the nuts they take.

In addition to providing a bowl full of wingnuts, you can also mix in some regular hex nuts. These are probably more difficult for some groups to spin effectively, but provide an interesting variation.

One of the sneakiest variations to play on a technical group of participants, is to intentionally damage two adjoining threads on the rod, which effectively stops the wingnut. This variation allows the processing point of what happens to your goals when you have equipment failures.

A final variation that brings about some interesting discussions during the post-activity debriefing, is to provide a variety of threaded rods, with slightly different lengths and diameters, and with 4, 5 or 6 wingnuts per rod. Group sizes for this activity will be different too. As a collective race begins between groups, it is easy to anticipate that the group with the least number of participants, or the shortest length rod will finish first. But in this activity, technique is generally more important than either the quantity of wingnuts or the length of the rod. This provides another opportunity for discussion during the debriefing process.

Important Points

Under the category of "famous mistakes we've made," the first time this activity was attempted, we choose to use 6 foot (1.8 meter) long ¼"×20 threaded rods. This meant that more than 20 minutes later, some groups were still winding their wingnuts down the length of the rod, and the enthusiasm level dropped considerably. The rods were simply way too long. Shorter lengths of rod are definitely better.

One of the typical techniques used to spin the wingnuts down the length of the rod is to have one group member hold the wingnuts, and have another group member spin the rod using their hands. This technique is efficient, but can produce some sore hands in a hurry. Caution participants about this method, and encourage them to use several people if this technique is employed.

Discussion and Debriefing Topics

Were you able to create a plan and then stick to it throughout the activity, or did you change techniques during the activity? Do you think that everyone in the group had an equal role? Did you feel pressured to perform? What do you think the true goal of this activity is?

If you happened to be racing against other groups, do you think that the equipment you were given was equally challenging? Did any groups appear to have the initial advantage because of the length of their threaded rod or the number of wingnuts they had in their group? Did these groups finish first? What else is important here?

Sequence

2B or KNOT 2B and Wing It are often times the mental and physical warm-up activities in Teamplay events. These two activities provide a quick exposure to building team consensus, group decision making, problem solving and working under pressure.

Activities Using Similar Skills and Follow-on Activities

After exposure to the problem solving process using Wing It, other physical problem solving activities, such as Magic Carpet and All Aboard, can be introduced.

Notes

Activity 4.82

Worm Hole

Worm Hole is a simply elegant initiative. It requires only a small amount of shock cord that can be obtained from a marine or hardware store. It is very inexpensive, very portable and provides an ideal warm-up activity for higher risk activities such as Surfing the Web. It can be used with many or few participants and is easily adaptable for populations with mobility limitations.

Equipment

The Worm Hole consists of a single piece of ⅛″ or ¼″ diameter shock cord, sometimes referred to as bungie cord, that has been tied into a loop with a strong knot. Shock cord is fairly elastic, so a strong knot must be used (see Chapter 5). A length of 50 inches is suitable for most populations, although a length of 100 inches will allow even the largest wheelchair to pass through—and the 100 inch version can be knotted at the midpoint to form two connected 50 inch Worm Holes.

The Challenge

The challenge of Worm Hole is to pass two connected participants through the shock cord, without touching the boundary of the Worm Hole (i.e. the shock cord). Other team members can hold the Worm Hole open by stretching the shock cord.

Typical Presentation, Storyline or Metaphor

In the far reaches of outer space, a Worm Hole is a unique place where space and time warp. In order to pass through such a phenomenon, it is necessary to always be connected to at least one other person. This connection can be in any form that is comfortable for you and your partners. While within the interior of the Worm Hole, partners must never contact the boundary of the Worm Hole. Other team members can hold the Worm Hole open for you as you pass through. You are responsible for safely navigating the Worm Hole, and helping your team members to join you on the other side.

Variations

There are a variety of ways that two people can be connected as they pass through the Worm Hole. Holding hands, standing back-to-back or face-to-face, holding the ends of a short piece of rope are all possible. To encourage creativity, suggest that each pair must travel through the Worm Hole while connected in a different method.

Participants may choose to stand still face-to-face as the Worm Hole is passed them. The Worm Hole can be stretched vertically, and participants can crawl

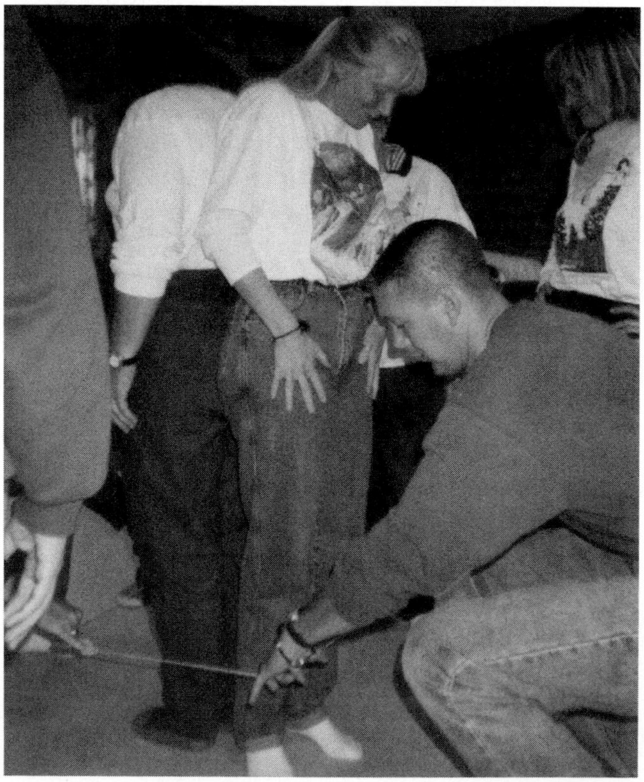

through the opening formed. Some participants may find that forming an arch with their partner and allowing the Worm Hole to be passed up one person and down the other provides the maximum space for movement.

The length of time that a person may hold the Worm Hole open is a function of their ability to withstand the warping effect. Holding the Worm Hole open for a maximum of 4 other participants is typically the maximum exposure recommended. The responsibility then must be passed to other team members to hold open the Worm Hole. Those holding the Worm Hole can further be restricted by allowing only a single point of contact, or one hand and one foot, or a maximum of three points of contact with the ground, etc.

For corporate groups, consider further reducing the size of the Worm Hole with additional knots, based on the groups projection of the minimum size they can successfully navigate. Ask the group to estimate the number of participants that will successfully make it to the other side of the Worm Hole.

Encourage group members to determine for themselves when contact has been made with the boundary of the Worm Hole. This allows the participants to *own* their failure and deal with the situation appropriately. In the event that contact is made with the outer perimeter of the Worm Hole, provide alternatives rather than penalties for the group to continue. Such alternatives may include having two points of contact between partners, only allowing three points of contact with the ground, blindfolding one partner, etc.

Instead of having both partners connected as they pass through the Worm Hole, consider having partners travel in opposite directions through the Worm Hole (so that energy and matter are balanced on both sides of the phenomenon!)

Instead of passing participants through the Worm Hole, consider passing a variety of objects, including some inflatable toys, large foam blocks, or other soft objects. Attaching a bell to the shock cord may encourage participants to handle the Worm Hole with greater care, so as to minimize the ringing of the bell.

Important Points

This initiative provides the opportunity for participants to creatively solve a problem, to judge their ability to meet group goals, and to cooperate with a partner in either a close proximity position or a more distant manner—as chosen by the participants. This initiative also provides the opportunity for the facilitator to observe such behaviors as coaching between participants, effective spotting, empathy and assistance, self-diagnosis by participants with respect to group goals, creativity, and as an assessment of the group's ability to follow through with an activity of higher risk, the Surfing the Web.

Encourage participants to choose a method of contact that is appropriate and suitable with their partner. For some audiences, holding hands can be emotionally threatening.

Discussion and Debriefing Topics

Debriefing issues include observations by the facilitator regarding the cooperation of the group in establishing a method for passing through the Worm Hole. Proximity issues can also be explored by the methods participants choose to pass through the Worm Hole. Allowing participants to judge for themselves when contact is made with the outer perimeter provides the opportunity for ownership of failure by the group—and how they accept this outcome. Involvement and adaptation for special team member needs can be discussed. Assessment of the group's involvement and spotting ability can also be discussed, especially if the next activity builds on these principles.

Sequence

Just as Willow in the Wind (See Cowtails and Cobras II by Karl Rohnke or More New Games by Andrew Fluegelman) serves as an excellent warm-up activity before conducting a trust fall with a group, so Worm Hole provides a warm-up activity before any of the various Surfing the Web challenges.

Activities Using Similar Skills and Follow-on Activities

Worm Hole utilizes some of the same skills found in activities such as Handcuffs and Shackles, and a variety of the Surfing the Web challenges. In some ways Worm Hole is a smaller version of Time Tunnel, also found in this chapter.

Notes

Activity 4.83

Yada Yada Yada

Yada, Yada, Yada, is not so much an activity in itself, but a way to challenge a group that is already communicating exceptionally well. Use this variation during your favorite challenge and adventure activity that requires some verbal communication and planning.

The Challenge

For participants to brainstorm, plan, and perform a challenge activity, only using the words Yada, Yada, Yada. Hand gestures, body language and other creative methods of non-verbal communication can be used, but the only spoken words can be Yada, Yada, Yada.

Typical Presentation, Storyline or Metaphor

During the early centuries, one civilization survived a variety of conquests from various barbarians. While sometimes brutal, these conquests did bring a variety of cultural and economic diversity to the region. After years of unrest, during which diverse civil groups offered a multitude of suggestions for a unified national language, the high council decided to put an end to all the verbal debate. They ruled that the official language of this civilization would consist of a single word, the word Yada, which to them simply meant "everything." Since their civilization was very expressive, their simplified language was augmented by flamboyant gestures, facial expressions, body language and a vast variety of poetic movements. This civilization was entirely verbal in their language, and so had no concerns about the small size of their dictionary, for in fact, they had no dictionary. And their lives progressed for weeks, and years, and decades, and centuries.

Unfortunately, with the invention of movable type, printing, and eventually email, the single word language did not really translate well into modern times, where printed language is often the only form of communication between cultures. As such, this simple one word language has been lost—that is, at least until video communication is available everywhere.

Variations

Feel free to substitute any appropriate single word to replace the nonsense word Yada. If you would like to significantly alter the planning of the group, rather than having participants say only a single word, have them use their full language, but only while they are looking straight up (i.e. not at any other person). This variation removes any visual feedback from other group members, and really makes the speaker wonder if anyone is listening to them. A less dramatic variation of this is to plan the activity with all group members lying flat on the ground looking up. The effect this has on the group planning process is profound. It also is a very visual method for showing the power in planning in a circle where everyone's views and opinions can be heard.

Important Points

While this activity appears whimsical and harmless, some groups can become very frustrated by the limitations of a one word language, especially after hearing it a hundred times and still having no idea what is being implied.

This variation on an activity should only be used with groups exhibiting strong communication skills. Use of this variation with a communicational challenged group may result more in frustration than in additional challenge.

Discussion and Debriefing Topics

Even with the limitations of this language, were you able to successfully plan and execute the activity?

What additions to the language were most useful in communicating with other group members? Can you think of words in your own language that have a variety of meanings depending on the context of the usage?

Sequence

This variation to a challenge activity is appropriate only after a group has been identified as having strong communication skills during earlier activities. Try using this variation with an activity that presents a simple problem or puzzle.

Activities Using Similar Skills and Follow-on Activities

We've never seen anything like this before. Try to follow with initiatives that explore the full range of words and language.

Notes

Section 4.84

More Ideas for the Future

There are a zillion variations on many of the activities in this book and those listed in the first section of references in Chapter 8. In additions to these variations, you can occasionally find some truly new and unique challenge activities in various places. Here are a few original gems and where to find them.

The Golf Course

Chris Cavert has the directions for making an 8 foot (2.4 meter) diameter plywood golf course that requires some real teamwork to complete successfully. You can find this activity for 6 to 8 people, on page PS-15 of his E.A.G.E.R. curriculum book, which is listed in Chapter 8.

Clap Together and Swattin' Flies

Here are two fun activities from the creative minds of Chris Cavert (EAGER Curriculum and Affordable Portables) and Sam Sikes (Feeding the Zircon Gorilla). You can find both of these activities, and more, in their newest book, 50 Ways to Use Your Noodle. See Chapter 8 for information.

The Squeeze Box

Here is a piece of installed ground level challenge equipment that we haven't seen in many places. It typically consists of four rigid walls that are used to contain the entire group. The Adventure Education Center near Worthington, Ohio was the first place we ever saw this initiative. Participants enter one at a time, and then can switch places, perhaps by birthdate or even height. Participants can also leave according to some prescribed order or plan. This activity will definitely invade most participant's personal space. This activity is not for the claustrophobic, or after a long sweaty day on the challenge course.

Flash Flood

Years ago at the Adventure Education Center near Columbus, Ohio, we learned about an activity using three 8 foot long cedar 4x4's and two lengths of rope. The object was to create some sort of structure that would hold the entire group up off the ground at least 12 inches (305 mm) to avoid the comming flood. Another version of this activity, contributed by Phil Costello of Project U.S.E., can be found in the book Into the Classroom: The Outward Bound® Approach to Teaching and Learning, by Mitchell Sakofs and George P. Armstrong. This book is definitely worth a read.

Ravine and Minefield

Here are two challenge activities that we have **never** seen on any North American challenge course. You can find both of these activities in The Pictorial Guide to Groupwork Activities, 1991, by Geoff Sanders. This book is available from Adventure Education in England. The ISBN is 0–9517302–0-7.

Minefield is a board and swinging tires initiative that involves some problem solving to complete successfully. Ravine is so unusual and interesting that it is worth buying the book for this activity alone. Ravine involves two telephone poles and about 8 planks. You'll have to check out page 64 of the book for more info.

Raccoon Circles

If we could include one piece of challenge equipment with this book, we would include a 12 foot (3.7 meter) length of tubular webbing that Tom Smith calls a Raccoon Circle. There are simply a bunch of things you can do with this single prop. When you need a ball, you roll it into a ball. When you need a hoop, you tie a water knot, and you have a hoop. We placed this topic in the future section, because as we go forward with the future of challenge and adventure programming, having a simple prop that can do so much, is going to be a great thing to know about. So go out there and find one, and make up your own collection of things to do with it.

Notes

Section 4.85

You'd Be Surprised!

The world is filled with some pretty creative people, and sooner or later, some of these folks are bound to end up in your challenge and adventure activity!

This section is entitled, "You'd Be Surprised !", but hopefully, after reading this section, you won't. Even with the best planning, the best training, good equipment and ideal surroundings, facilitators still have one major source of variation in leading activities, and that is the participants. The goal here is to heighten your awareness of some potential concerns that can occur while leading groups. This is not a complete list by any means, but serves as an example of some of the typical concerns that can occur while leading a challenge education program.

Since most challenge and adventure activities can be solved by a variety of techniques, it is important to let the group create their own solution. But the group's selected method should never disregard the safety of any group member. Knowing when unnecessarily risky methods are being proposed and discussing these risks with the group BEFORE problems arise is the responsibility of the facilitator.

On the following pages are several examples of situations that can occur while facilitating challenge and adventure activities. Review each photograph or paragraph of explanation and determine how a facilitator could improve the situation.

Boardwalking

In this case there may be two concerns. First, Boardwalking is probably not the ideal activity for barefoot participants. Does your program have guidelines or suggestions for footwear? Secondly, the technique of wrapping the Boardwalking ropes around the hands of the participants might be one that you would like to avoid.

Surfing the Web With Wire Rope

While visiting a challenge course that happened to be located along a section of a major hiking trail, we happened to notice a vertical web pattern that was made entirely of ⅜ inch (9 mm) multistranded metal cable, complete with some pretty beefy threaded anchors and saddle clamps at every intersection. It seems that many hikers had actually stolen previous rope and shock cord versions of the web that had been installed at the course. While there are some obvious concerns about passing participants over multistranded cables (not the least of which are snagging hair, broken strands, surface rust and the fact that wire webs are very difficult to tension), can you think of some alternatives to offer this challenge course, given their proximity to the hiking trail?

The Wall

Certainly one of the most impressive permanently installed ground level challenge is The Wall. Over the years, we've seen probably a dozen different styles. Of the designs shown here, which style is the best?

Stump Jump Indoors

Here's a short one. Stump Jump with plastic lids on an indoor tile floor. We don't think so!

should too. What do you think the most important piece of equipment is on the challenge course? Which ''tool'' do you value the most?

The Force of Nature

Here are just a few examples of challenge courses that have been altered by the force of nature. Frost heaving, snow loads, and freezing rain have a definite effect on permanently installed outdoor equipment in the northern regions. High temperatures effect the southern climates. Wind, which toppled this platform on a 40 inch (1 meter) diameter tree, can occur in any region. Wildlife also has a way of making an occasional appearance on the challenge course. Here a colony of woodpeckers has been busy modifying the pressure treated boards and poles of a southern ropes course.

The Wall Again

In this photo, you'll see what can happen to a challenge course that hasn't been recently inspected. In this photo, the construction technique for this wall did not allow for tree growth. A periodic inspection may have been able to identify this concern before the tree managed to destroy one of the major supporting beams of this wall. Obviously this wall has been retired.

The Tool Kit

Although this is only a sample of a challenge course builder's tool kit, it does remind us that if builders themselves use harnesses and helmets, perhaps we

Wing It

Under the category of ''famous mistakes we have made'', comes the first time we tried to lead Wing It using a 6 foot (1.8 meter) long threaded rod. After 20 minutes, the participants were still winding the wing nuts towards the far end of the rod, and the energy level of the group had dropped well into the negative value region. It is much better to keep the length of these rods short, and the energy level high. Threaded rods that are 12 to 18 inches (305 to 457 mm) long are about right.

Going to Extremes

In January of 1994, it was −24° F near Columbus, Ohio. In August of 1995 it was 110° F in Geneseo, New

York. That is a difference of 134° F! With outdoor challenge and adventure programs scheduled for both of these days, it was extremely important to inform participants how to properly prepare for the weather and the program. Do you have a plan in case the weather does not cooperate on the day of your program?

Pot of Gold

There are a few activities, such as the Blind Cure, that we have seen presented at both a Cradlerock and an Outward Bound program in the past year. This is a great activity, but requires some special equipment, such as a suitable climbing rope, and hopefully some protective head gear for the participant being transported by the ropes. The ropes suggested for the Pot of Gold activity in this book are not climbing ropes. They are largely decorative, and are not designed to support human cargo. This was actually the first of our "You'd Be Surprised" photos, and boy were we ever. You can bet that we changed the facilitation style for the next group. The idea here is to remove the Pot of Gold without touching the ground inside the circle. This group managed to do it, but in a manner that is clearly risky. What would you do to encourage the group to try a different technique?

Bull Ring I

Not all of the information presented here is risky business. At a recent program with the Venture program at the University of North Carolina at Charlotte, a participant did something so unique that it deserves to be mentioned here. At the beginning of the Bull Ring activity, the group was warned to keep the ball from falling off the metal ring in the center. So one of the participants, holding only the end of their string, wrapped it around the ball and ring, effectively "tying" the ball to the ring securely. And it work, the ball never fell off the ring. This group rates bonus points for creative thinking.

The Great Unknown

Occasionally you may be assisting with a program that has some equipment with which you are not familiar. For example, can you imagine what the objective of this challenge element might be? For those cases when you are not quite sure how a piece of equipment works, or how to properly facilitate an activity, be sure to check with local staff or knowledgeable personnel before attempting the activity. Not only may you be unaware of facilitation techniques that would be useful, you may not recognize the potential risks present.

What is This For?

If you are going to encourage participants to think creatively, and you have even gone as far as to encourage creative cheating, don't be surprised when you find them using equipment in a manner for which they were never intended. Here we find Stephen Gaddis and Tim Borton using both PVC and foam insulation Marble Tubes as "manual dexterity inhibitors." Try catching a lightweight ball when you've got these tubes to contend with.

Scoring Points with the Group

The second entry in our "famous mistakes we have made" contest comes from a simple gesture that had a dramatic negative impact on a corporate challenge program. For a corporate picnic, a series of six challenge activities were created, and teams were allowed to choose their own members prior to the event. As a way of encouraging a friendly competition to see which team could work the best together, nonsense amount of points were given for accomplishing various tasks. 23,015 points for having all team members on a small All Aboard platform. 15,063 points for retrieving the Pot of Gold successfully. Even though there were no significant prizes for this event, the teams became so focused on the point scoring system, that the true goal of the program was lost. Needless to say, we never used a public scoring system again.

Lycra Tube

A hard indoor floor is probably not the ideal place for this activity.

Lycra Tube or Lycra Rope?

In the photo shown here, you'll see that the red Lycra Tube has managed to fold over, and become more of a Lycra Rope than a Lycra Tube. The Lycra Tube activity in general needs supervision when in use.

Sign of the Times

While there are a variety of standardly available signs, such as this one that reads "Challenge Course—Keep Off—No Unauthorized Personnel," it

takes more than just a sign to keep your facility risk free. What are you doing to insure that unauthorized personnel are not using your course?

Worm Holes and More

The shock cord loop used for the Teamplay activity Worm Hole seems like it could have a variety of other purposes. Do you think that this loop would make a suitable replacement for the plastic hoop typically passed around a group of participants that are all holding hands?

In the activity which Karl Rohnke refers to as Circle the Circle in his classic text Silver Bullets, a plastic hoop is passed around a circle of participants that are all holding hands. Tom Smith proposes using a loop made from tubular webbing, which he calls a Raccoon Circle, for the same purpose. The replacement of either of these two articles by the shock cord Worm Hole presents a few problems for participants. First, the elasticity of the shock cord Worm Hole means that this prop is going to fit snugly around some participant's body. This alone is probably going to make some large participants a little self-conscious if not downright embarrassed. Secondly, the elastic shock cord Worm Hole can be stretched tightly, and quickly released, which can snap another participant. For any type of hoop passing, it is probably best to use a hoop that doesn't change size along the way.

Boardwalking with a Twist

Like we said, not all of the information presented here is about risky behavior. Here is another one of those classic events that happens when a group has no preconceived idea of what to do with a piece of portable ground level equipment. Here we find a group of young participants that when confronted with a jointed pair of Boardwalking boards, choose to use their own ingenuity and managed to hop these boards forward. We certainly were surprised.

Who's In Charge Here

A scenario to avoid. The phone rings and you are invited to present a program of challenge and adventure activities to an audience of 7th grade school children. Fine, you have all the stuff and you can do it. You work out the details of where, and when, and how, etc. Also fine. On the day of the program you realize, from four different sources, that four different people want you to perform four different (and by the way, incompatible) duties during your event. The event coordinator has one idea, the sponsors that provided the funds for this activity has another, the person that wrote the grant to obtain the funds has specified a variety of outcomes (none of which were ever presented to you), the students have some ideas of what you are going to present, and finally, the other speakers would just like you to run these children around a bit so that they stay awake during their classroom style sessions. Were we surprised? You bet! Our recommendation—have one contact for any organization, and make sure they are in charge.

Made in the Shade

This photograph of a picnic table made from some of the new plastic wood was taken just a few months before this book went to press. Do you notice anything unusual about this table?

Well, here are a few hints. Two of these tables are near College Park, Maryland. It is June. It is 90 degrees, in the shade, and it is only going to get hotter. Also, there aren't many students around in the summer. The tables are also not on level ground.

If you look hard, you'll be able to see that this table has begun to deform. It is actually bowing in the center. Not from a high loading condition, but from heat deformation and creep.

So even though you may be thinking about plastic wood as the ideal replacement for those rotting boards on your ropes course, better call in an expert, so that during next summer's heat wave, you don't have a melting challenge course.

How Long is Too Long?

You are facilitating a group that is working on the challenge activity known as 2B or Knot 2B. Nearly 20 minutes have gone by, and the group has not yet come to a decision. How long do you let the activity continue?

Typically you want to watch for the involvement of the group. If you notice that participants are all actively engaged in the process, certainly allow the activity to continue. If some participants have made up their minds, and are becoming increasingly detached from the rest of the group, consider providing some guidance for the group to reach a consensus. Hopefully you will never have to jump in with the solution. After all solving the puzzle is not the goal here, reaching a group consensus is.

So if you are a competent facilitator, how do you keep from being surprised during the activity? Well, here are a few ideas that will help to prepare you.

Notes

How Not to be Surprised

- One of the simplest techniques for evaluating the solution proposed by a group during a challenge program is to ask the participants to take a few minutes to plan their solution to the activity, and then, BEFORE THEY BEGIN, review their plan with you. This simple technique eliminates the element of surprise to the facilitator. If the group's solution at the Spider's Web is to throw the lightest person over the web first, many facilitators would want to know this in advance.

- Remember that not all risks are purely physical. A few years ago it seemed sufficient to provide the necessary physical safety during an activity, and this level was considered by most to be adequate. In recent years, and thanks to the enlightening authors and researchers that have shared their revelations with us, there is more to insuring the safety of an individual than merely addressing their physical safety. The emotional safety of an individual is equally if not more important than physical safety in many ways. Potential emotional injury can be just as painful as a physical injury, and unfortunately displays substantially less visible signs. In other cases, participants can be effected by gender issues that are improperly dealt with. Physical abilities vary between participants, and must be considered. Even such issues as smoking, interruptions due to pagers, cell phones, and the alarms of digital watches can alter the experience of the group. A good facilitator will know their audience, and take the necessary steps to insure an experience that sufficiently challenges the group, without pushing participants beyond their abilities.

- Read everything you can possibly read on the subject of interest. In Chapter 8 of this book, you find thousands of references that discuss the use of challenge and adventure related activities. Chapter 1 also provides a list of some recent periodical articles on the same subjects. There are also a variety of web-sites, home-pages, newsletters and organizations that publish additional information on the subject. Read, read, read.

- Consider some form of formal training. Many sites will require facilitators to attend an annual or periodic orientation session to reacquaint the facilitator with standard procedures, safety methods, and the physical layout of the program. For individual facilitators and adventure program providers, this type of periodic retraining is beneficial. In cases of insurance liability or injury, one of the prominent issues is whether the facilitator followed adequate and prescribed procedures—the kind typically found in a formal training session.

- Know your equipment. There are a variety of sources of information regarding the safe use of challenge related equipment. ACCT provides guidelines for challenge courses. REI provides technical information on strength and safe usage of climbing equipment. Climb Smart also provides climbing equipment information. Rope courses typically require periodic inspection by a qualified inspector. If you are in doubt of the safety of any piece of technical or challenge course equipment, don't risk it. Inform the owner of the equipment and choose another activity.

- Consider participating in a formal or informal peer review. One of the simplest forms of this technique is simply to network and find out what other professionals are doing in the field. A more formal approach is to review your techniques with trained professionals that can advise you on the suitability of your methods, and in many cases offer suggestions on how to improve your abilities. AEE and other organizations offer peer reviews at the program level.

Chapter Five
The Nuts and Bolts of Building Challenge and Adventure Equipment

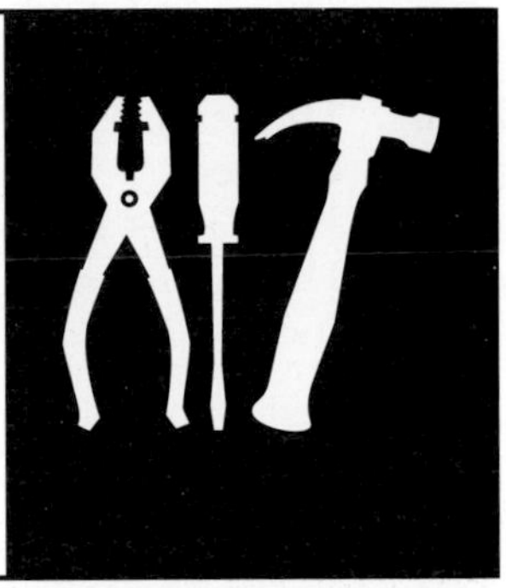

This chapter contains information for purchasing and constructing the portable challenge and adventure equipment presented in Chapter 4 of this book. In many cases, photographs or sketches are provided, along with instructions for assembling the necessary components. Where available, commercially supplied equipment is also mentioned in this chapter. A list of companies that sell a variety of challenge and adventure equipment is provided in Chapter 8. Finally, there are five sections in Chapter 7 that list the lightest, heaviest, most expensive, least expensive and most often used pieces of challenge and adventure equipment in this book. At the end of this chapter, concepts for creating and improving several classical challenge course elements are also provided.

What's Here

Here is a list of the construction directions that you'll find in this chapter, as well as some of the basic props that you will need.

No.	Activity	Basic Props
5.01	100 Words or Less	A copy of the page from Chapter 4
5.02	20 / 20 Vision	Wooden box, Transparencies made from Chapter 4
5.03	2B or KNOT 2B	5 ropes of different colors or patterns
5.04	63 / 64 / 65	Chapter 4 instructions made into a wooden puzzle
5.05	A Balanced Life	2 Oak planks and a large wood block base
5.06	A Collection of Knots	A long rope
5.07	A Work of Art	A variety of small props
5.08	All Aboard	A series of stacking wooden platforms
5.09	Alphabet Soup	Rope, stopwatch and 26 disks
5.10	Alphabetically	No props are required
5.11	Bag It	A stuff sack filled with familiar and unfamiliar objects
5.12	Blackout	The plastic cloth from Magic Carpet
5.13	Boardwalking—2 Styles	2×6's, screw eyes, quick links and rope
5.14	Bull Ring I	Metal ring, string or twine, tennis ball and PVC tubing
5.15	Bull Ring II	A Bull Ring and some magnetic objects
5.16	Bull Ring III—Write On!	A Bull Ring and a marking pen
5.17	Bull Ring Golf	A Bull Ring and a variety of balls, PVC tubes and cups
5.18	Cave In	A large cloth tarp, blanket, or Lycra Tube
5.19	Community Juggling	A variety of soft toys to throw
5.20	Community Jump Rope	One long rope
5.21	Danger Zone	The plastic cloth from Magic Carpet
5.22	Different Drum	A collection of music from various sources
5.23	Expansion and Contraction	Dowel rods, or flat end PVC tubes

No.	Activity	Basic Props
5.24	Film Can Group Formation	A bunch of film canisters
5.25	First Contact	No equipment is required
5.26	Funderbirds	Wooden spool, foam, feathers and leather
5.27	Gridlock	A large plastic sheet, or grid pattern
5.28	Handcuffs and Shackles	5 feet (1.5 meters) of soft rope per participant
5.29	Human Knot	No props are required, but rope is optional
5.30	Inch by Inch	Some small familiar objects (keys, paper clips)
5.31	Just One Word	A collection of letters on wood or paper
5.32	Life Raft	All the Boardwalking boards, four hoops, four sacks
5.33	Line Up	No props are required
5.34	Linearity	Two similar ropes, the plastic sheet from Magic Carpet
5.35	Living Ladder	Several hardwood dowel rods
5.36	Log Rolling	Pieces of 2×8's at least 12 feet (3.6 meters) long
5.37	Lycra Tube & Blindfolds	5 yards (4.5 meters) of lycra for a Lycra Tube
5.38	Magic Carpet	A plastic cloth about 5 feet (1.5 meters) square
5.39	Marble Tubes—2 Styles	PVC tubing galore
5.40	Midnight Sun	The plastic cloth from Magic Carpet or any large object
5.41	Mine, Mine, Mine	Blindfolds, trees, potatoes, oranges
5.42	Missing Page	Miscellaneous challenge equipment and props
5.43	Monumental	A set of Monumental Dice for the group
5.44	Move It or Lose It	A bunch of boxes, a bag full of bottles. . . .
5.45	Moving Towards Extinct	Several rope loops of various sizes
5.46	Not Knots	Several ropes about 10 feet (3 meters) long
5.47	Parade	No props are required
5.48	Plenty of Room at the Top	A wooden base and many large nails
5.49	Popsicle Sticks	Popsicle sticks, masking tape and marking pens
5.50	Pot of Gold	A plastic pot or container, rope, tennis balls
5.51	Raccoon Circles	12 feet (3.5 meters) of 1 inch (25 mm) tubular webbing
5.52	Real Estate	Some of the wooden puzzle pieces shown in this chapter
5.53	Right Where I Belong	Blindfolds
5.54	River Crossing	Wooden platforms, 4×4's, perhaps a rope or two
5.55	Shark Attack	Some plywood shapes with a nautical theme
5.56	Simply Amazing	Hundreds of feet of ¼ inch (6 mm) poly rope
5.57	Strange Attraction	A modified Bull Ring, PVC tubes
5.58	Stretch It	A plastic bottle, inner tube, rope and wooden platform
5.59	Stretching the Limit	Ropes and various other props
5.60	Stump Jumping	Wooden disks
5.61	Surfing the Web I	¼ inch (6 mm) poly rope and shock cord
5.62	Surfing the Web II	¼ inch (6 mm) poly rope and shock cord
5.63	Surfing the Web III	¼ inch (6 mm) poly rope and shock cord
5.64	Surfing the Web IV	¼ inch (6 mm) poly rope and shock cord
5.65	Surfing the Web V	A lot of ¼ inch (6 mm) poly rope and shock cord
5.66	Target Specifications	Two rope loops, a blindfold, soft throwable objects
5.67	Tennis Ball Mountain	Tons of tennis balls
5.68	The Boardroom	Long Boards and a wooden platform or hoop
5.69	The Paper Chase	Some paper for each participant
5.70	Time Tunnel	5 to 10 yards (4.5 to 9 meters) of lycra sewn lengthwise
5.71	Tower Building	Construction toys or food, or straws and tape
5.72	Traffic Circle	A single rope loop
5.73	Tree of Knots	One rope about 30 feet (9 meters) long
5.74	Under Cover	A cloth sheet, or blanket, or even a Lycra Tube

No.	Activity	Basic Props
5.75	Under the Doormat	A small carpet square or rug
5.76	Universe	93,000,000 miles of string (or less)
5.77	Villages and Wells	9 pieces of rope and 6 objects
5.78	Water Tube	A unique PVC tube with holes, a rubber ducky
5.79	Waterfall I	A PVC tube about 8 feet (2.4 meters) long
5.80	Waterfall II	The PVC Marble Tubes
5.81	Wing It	Wingnuts, hex nuts and threaded rods
5.82	Worm Hole	A shock (bungie) cord loop
5.83	Yada Yada Yada	No props are required

At the end of this chapter, you'll find our comments and opinions for constructing some classic challenge and adventure programming equipment, and where to find some additional new activities. This section includes information on trust fall platforms, tensioning the ropes used in Surfing the Web, a discussion on pressure-treated wood vs. standard dimensional lumber, a permanently installed version of Log Rolling, a telephone pole alternative for a ground level cable walk, and some additional creative equipment from Chris Cavert and the minds of Jim Cain and Barry Jolliff.

Also check out the last section in Chapter 4 entitled, "You'd Be Surprised." This section contains some actual situations that you may encounter when facilitating a group with the equipment in this chapter. Read it, and be prepared!

Building Challenge and Adventure Equipment to Last

- Make everything bombproof. Chances are you'll be using this equipment for a while, so you might as well make it sturdy the first time. Weather has a way of diminishing the strength of some materials, and so does frequent usage by even the most caring participants. Construct the props listed in this chapter from the strongest and best grade materials you can find. This includes building materials, ropes, fasteners, finishes and adhesives. You'll be making an investment that will last for a long time.

- Except for those items which are enhanced by looking natural, such as wooden platforms, try to use the brightest colors possible. This is especially true for nylon webbing, rope, plastic hoops, plastic tarps and Lycra Tubes. Participants will be able to visually locate this equipment during the activity, and you'll be able to find it in the grass at the completion of the program. If you have any small props that you want to keep track of, try tying a short segment of brightly colored nylon cord around them.

- While many of the activities in this book suggest specific equipment based on the functional requirements, many audiences will judge the quality of the program based on the visual appearance of both the challenge instructor and their equipment. Spend the extra time when you can to make the equipment you use more than just functional. This includes your selection of storage containers.

- Inspect your equipment periodically. Some challenge activity instructors inspect their equipment each time they put it away. Others choose to inspect before each use. Regardless of the time, have a periodic inspection planned for each piece of challenge equipment you have. This is especially true for any equipment which may be used to lift or support a person, such as the hardwood dowel rods for Living Ladder, or the 4×4 cedar beams for River Crossing. When your equipment becomes frayed, worn, cracked, torn or broken, replace it and keep the rest of your inventory up to high professional standards.

Activity 5.00

Sample Directions

In this chapter, the directions for purchasing or constructing the equipment for each of the activities in Chapter 4 is presented. For the Bull Ring activity shown in Section 4.14 of Chapter 4, the instructions for making this equipment can be found in Section 5.14 of Chapter 5. The following format is used throughout this chapter.

What You'll Need

This list of supplies is sometimes known as the Bill of Materials. Here you'll find exactly what supplies you'll need, and the quantity of each required. As a rule, most activities are planned for a group of 10 participants. If you plan to have more or less than this, you'll need to scale up or down the number of supplies you purchase.

Where to Find It

Most of the equipment featured in this book can be made from standard hardware store supplies, but in a few cases, you'll need to look a little harder than that to find the right stuff. In addition to any information you find here, there is also a list of organizations, book sellers, and equipment dealers in Chapter 8 that carry a wide variety of challenge and adventure related supplies and equipment.

How to Make It

For those props that require a bit more than just words, this section provides sketches, photographs and some sequential instructions for making this equipment.

Special Instructions

A few hints that should help you do the job right the first time.

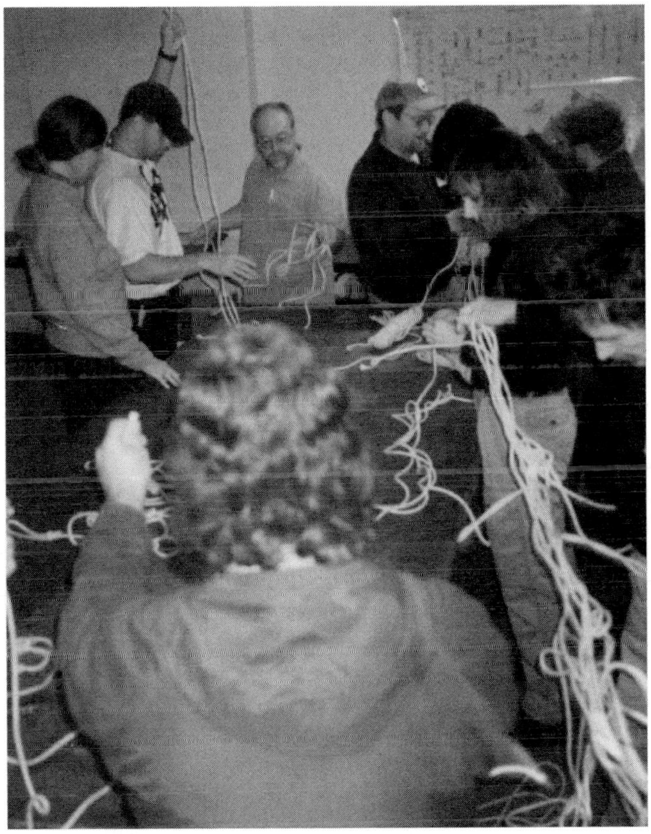

Activity 5.01

100 Words or Less

What You'll Need

Here is a copy of the 100 word counting sheet. Give a pencil and a copy of this page to the group, and ask them to write down each word spoken by team members as they plan how to accomplish the challenge confronting them. When the group is ready, or when all 100 words are filled in, the activity begins.

1 ______________________

2 ______________________

3 ______________________

4 ______________________

5 ______________________

6 ______________________

7 ______________________

8 ______________________

9 ______________________

10 ______________________

11 ______________________

12 ______________________

13 ______________________

14 ______________________

15 ______________________

16 ______________________

17 ______________________

18 ______________________

19 ______________________

20 ______________________

21 ______________________

22 ______________________

23 ______________________

24 ______________________

25 ______________________

26 ______________________

27 ______________________

28 ______________________

29 ______________________

30 ______________________

31 ______________________

32 ______________________

33 ______________________

34 ______________________

35 ______________________

36 ______________________

37 ______________________

38 ______________________

39 ______________________

40 ______________________

41 ______________________

42 ______________________

43 ______________________

44 ______________________

45 ______________________

46 ______________________

47 ______________________

48 ______________________

49 ______________________

50 ______________________

61 ______________________

52 ______________________

53 ______________________

54 ______________________

55 ______________________

56 ______________________

57 ______________________

58 ______________________

59 ______________________

60 ______________________

61 ______________________

62 ______________________

63 ______________________

64 ______________________

65 ______________________

66 ______________________

67 ______________________

68 ______________________

69 ______________________

70 ______________________

71 ______________________

72 ______________________

73 ______________________

74 ______________________

75 ______________________

76 ______________________

77 ______________________

78 ______________________

79 ______________________

80 ______________________

81 ______________________

82 ______________________

83 ______________________

84 ______________________

85 ______________________

86 ______________________

87 ______________________

88 ______________________

89 ______________________

90 ______________________

91 ______________________

92 ______________________

93 ______________________

94 ______________________

95 ______________________

96 ______________________

97 ______________________

98 ______________________

99 ______________________

100 ______________________

Activity 5.02

20/20 Vision

Here is a visual challenge that can be used to modify any of the activities in Chapter 4. By placing a transparency made from the geometric patterns shown in Chapter 4 over any text instructions, such as this page, you can effectively block the reader from seeing the text below. However, by quickly sliding the transparency over the surface of the text document, the eye's ability to sustain an after-image enables the brain to process the total image, and the text becomes instantly readable. This activity works with just a piece of paper and a transparent copy of the geometric patterns. For those that would like a little more formal presentation, a design for the 20 / 20 Vision box is presented here. By shaking the box, the underlying text document becomes readable.

Equipment

In Chapter 4, you'll find two geometric patterns to copy onto a transparency or clear piece of graphic film or plastic. You can also generate your own vision blockers by reproducing any of the designs shown here.

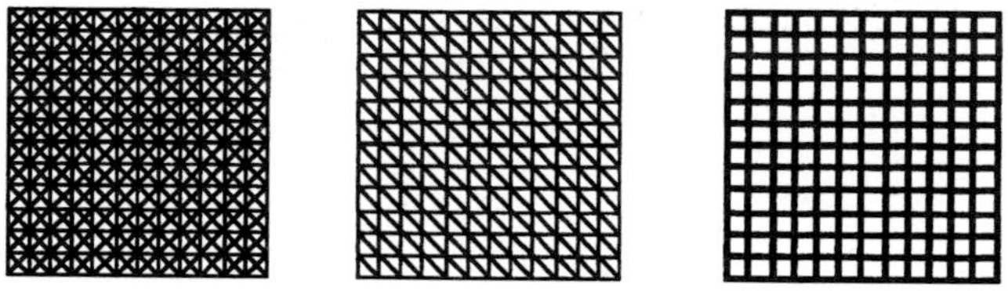

Have transparencies made from these patterns or any of the patterns shown in Chapter 4.

What You'll Need

A page of printed instructions using standard size 8 to 12 point typeface and a transparency with one of the patterns shown on it, is all that you'll need to perform this variation on presenting clear instructions to the group. Just let them know that the transparency must be touching the entire top surface of the text page at all times. If you would like a little more formal format for this activity, try making the wooden instruction box shown here. You'll need a ⅛ inch (3 mm) thick piece of clear plastic and a ⅛ inch (3 mm) thick piece of plywood. Both of these pieces are 10 inches (254 mm) wide and 12.5 inches (318 mm) tall. Next you'll need some ½ inch (13 mm) thick stock that is ¾ inch (19 mm) wide, to make a border to place between the plywood and clear plastic panels. The top and bottom pieces are 10 inches (254 mm) long. The side pieces are 11 inches (279 mm) long. These thin spacers are sandwiched between the plywood and clear plastic, and are held in place with glue and several small screws.

Where to Find It

Making transparencies from the patterns in this book can be done at many copy centers for a reasonable cost. The most unique component for the instruction box is the clear plastic sheet, which can be purchased at many hardware stores that custom cut materials for storm windows. You may also find this material in craft stores, and as the backing material for some stained glass patterns.

How to Make It

Before constructing the box, drill a series of small holes in the perimeter of the clear plastic sheet about every 2 inches. These holes will provide clearance for the small screws that will be fastened to the wooden spacers. Holes are needed so that the plastic will not crack near these regions. Screws are used to fasten the plastic sheet in place, so that they may be removed at a later time to either replace the printed instruction sheet or the transparency pattern. Small screws will typically not split the plywood, although this panel can be predrilled as well. Flat head wood screws that are no more than ½ inch (13 mm) long are needed for this project.

Apply a very thin layer of glue to all wooden spacers and attach these to the perimeter of the plywood. Fasten these spacers to the plywood securely with the flat head wood screws, and let dry.

Place the page of printed instruction inside the box, and lightly fasten this sheet to the plywood surface with a glue stick. Now insert the transparency that has been cut down to a size of 8 inches (203 mm) wide by 10.5 inches (267 mm) tall. The transparency should be free to slide about the interior of the box.

Now place the clear plastic cover on the box, and screw in place with approximately 16 to 20 wood screws placed every 2 inches (51 mm) around the perimeter of the box.

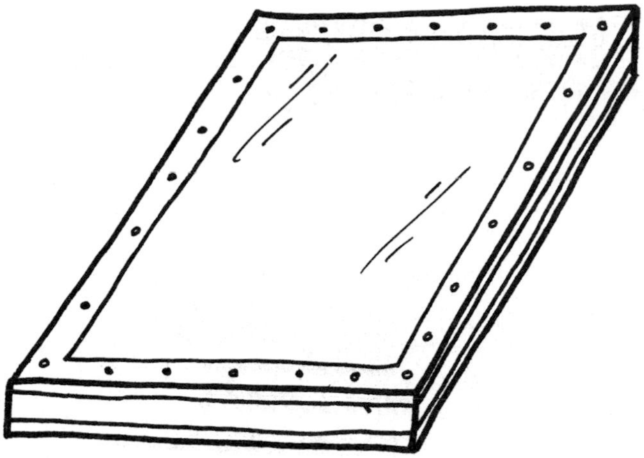

Special Instructions

Transparencies have a natural curl to them. Place the transparency so that the edges curl downwards, towards the plywood. If the transparency catches between the wooden spacers and the plywood back, try creating a fillet of glue around the entire interior of the box to prevent this condition.

Activity 5.03

2 B or KNOT 2 B

A few colorful ropes are all that is needed for this excellent consensus building activity.

What You'll Need

Four independent rope rings held together by a fifth rope ring. Tubular webbing, climbing ropes, shoe laces and even belts can be used in place of ropes. The Teamplay version of 2B or KNOT 2B has four separate sets of ropes, all made from 3/8 inch (9 mm) diameter ropes, in a variety of colors and patterns.

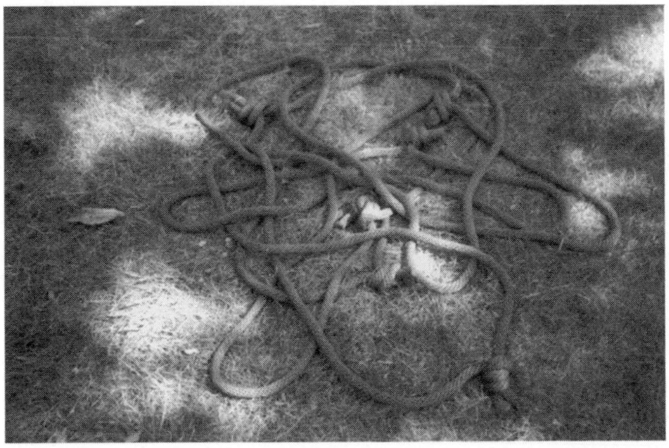

Where to Find It

Finding a wide variety of similar ropes is not easy. Bruce Smith of On Rope sells about a dozen different colors of webbing that can be used for this activity and also for Raccoon Circles. Wellington and Lehigh ropes are carried by some hardware stores. Some outdoor gear shops sells thinner ropes and cording that comes in a variety of colors and patterns.

How to Make It

Each of the ropes used for this activity are slightly different in length, so that they can also be used for other challenge and adventure activities. The shortest rope is 8 feet (2.4 meters) long, followed by 8.5 feet (2.6 meters), 9 feet (2.8 meters), 9.5 feet (3 meters) and finally about 10 feet (3.2 meters). After deciding which rope is holding all the other ropes together, have the group decide which rope is the shortest and which rope is the longest.

The easiest 2B or KNOT 2B puzzle has five ropes of five different solid colors, such as black, red, green, etc.

The next more visually busy version has five ropes of five different striped colors, such as red/white, blue/white, green/white, etc.

The next more difficult version has five ropes that are all the same solid color. Yes, the same exact solid color!

The most difficult version so far has five ropes that are all the same striped color.

Special Instructions

One variation in 2B or KNOT 2B is the number of ropes that can be included in the puzzle. Three ropes are generally not enough. Five ropes seem about right. Seven or eight ropes can be very challenging.

The length of the ropes used for 2B or KNOT 2B is typically somewhere between 7 and 15 feet. If you choose to use 165 foot (50 meter) climbing ropes, you can cover a much larger area, and include more twists and turns in the rope. This size may be appropriate if you happen to have more than 15 people in a single group.

Color or pattern changes in the ropes can also provide additional challenges to the activity. The Teamplay version of 2B or KNOT 2B uses four varieties of increasing difficulty. The first puzzle has five ropes that are different solid colors (blue, red, green, etc.) The second version has five ropes with different striped colors (blue and white, red and white, etc.) The third version has five ropes that are all the same solid color (blue). And the final version has five ropes that are all the same striped color (red and white).

If you happen to tie more than one knot in any single rope loop, you can add some difficulty to the challenge, and probably confuse the group a bit in the process. Another challenge would be to include a rope with not knots, by splicing the rope to form a single, seamless rope loop. Both of these variations are meant to unfocus or distract the group from their true mission, and as a result, provide excellent opportunities for discussion during debriefing.

Activity 5.04

63 / 64 / 65

What You'll Need

A checkerboard is probably the easiest object from which this puzzle can be made. But just in case you would rather not cut up your only checkerboard, or a hole in Mom's checkerboard picnic table cloth, here are a few patterns from which to make the puzzle. Paper or stiff cardboard works well for this activity. The small gaps that occur between pieces are easily seen if the puzzle is made from wood or thick plastic.

How to Make It

You can take this page to a photocopier (with our permission) and enlarge any of the patterns shown below. The puzzle works well when each square is approximately 1 inch (2.54 cm) square.

Special Instructions

You can cut the puzzle from any of the following patterns, just remember, the actual area of the puzzle is the area of whichever pattern you use.

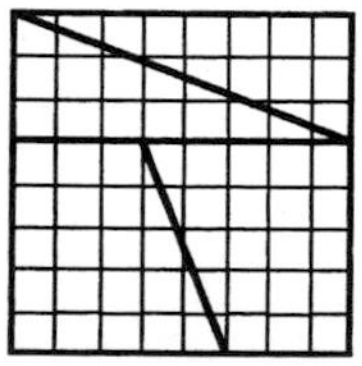

64 Squares from an 8 by 8 Square

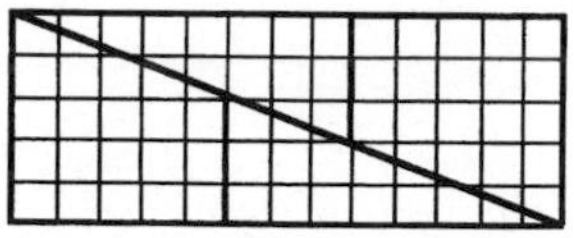

65 Squares from a 5 by 13 Rectangle

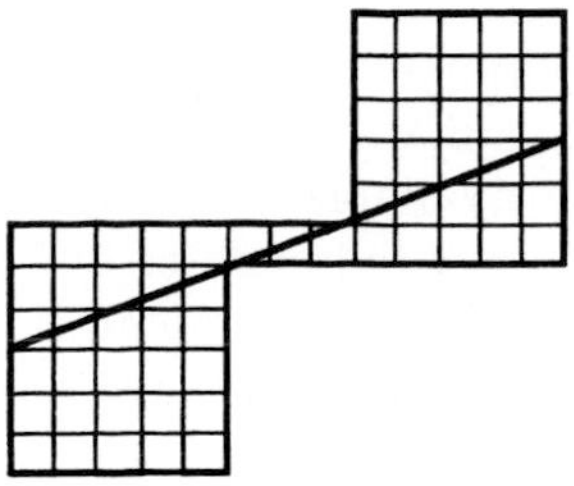

63 Squares from two 5 by 6
Rectangles with a 1 by 3 Bridge

After copying any of the above patterns, create the four puzzle pieces by cutting along the dark lines in each of the patterns.

Each of the above patterns will produce four puzzle pieces like these:

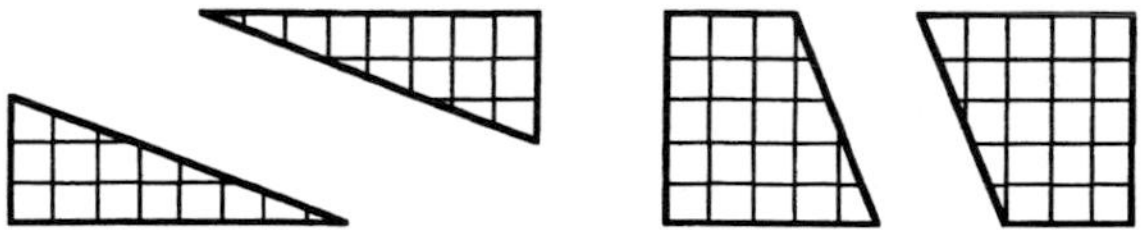

Activity 5.05

A Balanced Life

This activity requires two large oak planks. They are heavy, expensive and probably are going to be a pain in the neck to transport, but they do create a very interesting initiative.

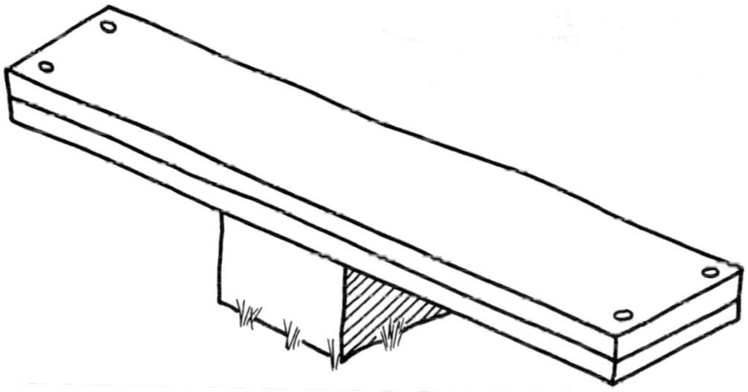

What You'll Need

There isn't much flexibility in this design. Supporting the weight of 10 average size adults on a single fulcrum is a tough job for any board. To do A Balanced Life right, you'll need two rough cut oak planks that are 2 inches (51mm) thick, 12 inches (305 mm) wide and 10 to 12 feet (3.0 to 3.7 meters) long. Four ½ inch carriage bolts, washers and nuts are required to join these boards together at the ends. You will also need a fulcrum constructed of a hardwood block, 12 inches (305 mm) square and 8 inches (203 mm) tall. This activity should be conducted on a flat surface.

Where to Find It

Forget the hardware store for this equipment, better head right to the lumber mill. You are going to need two oak planks (like barn floor decking) with a minimum of knots and other imperfections. You can be a little less discriminating for the hardwood fulcrum, but don't forget that this block is going to have to hold the weight of 10 adults. That is more than half a ton!

How to Make It

Align the two oak planks and hold them together with clamps. Drill two 9⁄16 inch (14 mm) diameter holes through both boards at least 3 inches (76 mm) in from each corner of the boards. Turn the boards over so that the bottom side is facing up, and with a counterbore or spade bit, drill a 1 inch (25 mm) diameter counterbore ¾ inch (19 mm) deep into the bottom of the bottom board, for each of the four holes. Now drop a ½ inch (12 mm) by 3.5 inch (89 mm) long carriage bolt through each of the four holes from the top side of these boards, attach a washer and a nut, and use a socket to tighten these four connections securely. This style of connection allows the two boards to be separated if necessary. If separation is not required, an exterior grade of glue can be added between these boards to additionally increase the strength.

Special Instructions

The length of the carriage bolts has been selected so that the ends of these bolts will extend past the thickness of oak boards. The counterbore is required so that the nuts do not extend past the thickness of the boards. Always use these boards with the heads of the carriage bolts facing upwards. Check the tightness of the connections on a regular basis. Do not add additional carriage bolts at the midpoint of these planks. The fulcrum position is the most highly stressed region of these boards, and any additional holes for fasteners only reduces the available support area.

It is possible for the ends of the planks to touch the ground, forming a pinch point. Be cautious when spotting in this region not to place your foot below the planks at any time.

Encourage the group to consider placing the lightest participants at the ends of the planks. This will reduce the stress on the planks, and also create the minimum imbalance at the fulcrum location.

Activity 5.06

A Collection of Knots

What You'll Need

A piece of rope, ⅜ inch (9mm) in diameter or greater, at least 30 feet (9.1 meters) long for a group of 10 participants. If you happen to have twenty or more participants, try making multiple ropes rather than placing more than twenty people on a single rope. The energy level of the group will be higher for two smaller groups than for one large group.

Where to Find It

Many of the large chain hardware stores and many marine stores carry a variety of large diameter, colorful ropes. While these ropes are not suitable for rock climbing, they are more than sufficient for activities such as A Collection of Knots. Climbing rope also works fine for this activity and can be found at many outdoor stores, or mail ordered from many of the equipment dealers listed in Chapter 8 of this book.

How to Make It

Directions for tying a variety of knots can be found in many of the books listed in Section 8.17 of Chapter 8. Try using a few different types of knots to add some variety to the activity. Try not to tie the knots too tight, or you'll have another activity called "#*@!!! Knots" for which the only solution usually involves either surgery with a knife or the less than popular flame removal technique.

Activity 5.07

A Work of Art

Here is a visual version of the children's game Telephone, using challenge and adventure props.

What You'll Need

Two sets of nearly identical equipment consisting of tennis balls, short segments of colorful rope, webbing, climbing hardware, marble tubes, Magic Carpets, dowel rods, wooden platforms and other available challenge equipment.

Where to Find It

It can be very useful and space saving to try to use some of the other equipment already in your challenge kit for this activity. If you need to pack special equipment for this activity, consider making up two Work of Art stuff sacks filled with nearly identical items.

How to Make It

Place the equipment for the original artist approximately 35 yards (32 meters) away from the equipment for the copying artist. Other group members stand between these two artists and pass information back and forth.

Special Instructions

The equipment used for Tower Building can also be used for Work of Art.

Activity 5.08

All Aboard

Here are directions for creating a series of four nesting All Aboard platforms. If you choose to create several sets of these platforms, you can also use them for River Crossing platforms. If this is the first time you've worked with dimensional lumber, you may be surprised to know that a 2×4 actually measures 1.5 inches by 3.5 inches (38 by 89 mm). Other dimensional lumber, such as 2×6's, 2×8's and 2×10's are also ½ inch (12.7 mm) smaller than the standard specification.

What You'll Need

Standard dimensional lumber, such as 2×4's, 2×6's, 2×8's and 2×10's, some ¾ inch (19 mm) thick plywood, 2 inch (51 mm) long exterior deck screws, exterior grade wood glue. A waterproof finish is optional depending on the use of this equipment.

How to Make It

The dimensions shown will create four nesting boxes that are about the right size for groups of 6 to 8 people. The dimensions for two optional larger boxes are given in the Special Instructions section on the following page.

Where to Find It

Nearly all of this material is available at most hardware stores. You may even be able to have the plywood cut to a more manageable size at the store.

Platform 4 One ¾ inch (19 mm) Plywood Top 19.5 inches (495 mm) square
Two 2×6's 19.5 inches (495 mm) long
Two 2×6's 16.5 inches (419 mm) long
Twenty-four 2 inch (51 mm) long exterior deck screws.

Platform 3 One ¾ inch (19 mm) Plywood Top 15.75 inches (400 mm) square
Two 2×6's cut to a 4.5 inch (114 mm) width by 15.75 inches (400 mm) long
Two 2×6's cut to a 4.5 inch (114 mm) width by 12.75 inches (324 mm) long
Twenty 2 inch (51 mm) long exterior deck screws.

Platform 2 One ¾ inch (19 mm) Plywood Top 12 inches (305 mm) square
Two 2×4's 12 inches (305 mm) long
Two 2×4's 9 inches (229 mm) long
Sixteen 2 inch (51 mm) long exterior deck screws.

Platform 1 One ¾ inch (19 mm) Plywood Top 8.25 inches (219 mm) square
One 2×10 cut into a 8.25 inch (219 mm) square
Four 2 inch (51 mm) long exterior deck screws.

Cut out each of these pieces before proceeding to the next step. It is convenient to perform all cutting operations prior to drilling and assembling the platforms. It is essential to make square cuts so that pieces join properly.

After cutting out these pieces, place each of the components in place, to verify that you have the correct number of each piece. Also try to place each piece so that any knots or defects are facing the interior of the platform.

With a countersink pilot drill, drill two holes ¾ inch (19 mm) from each end of the two longest boards of each platform size, except for Platform 1. These holes will allow the 2 inch (51 mm) long exterior deck screws to join the longer and shorter boards together for the box below the plywood top deck. The pilot holes will prevent the ends of these longest boards from splitting while inserting the deck screws. The countersink should be about ¾ inches (19 mm) deep.

Glue and attach eight deck screws to form the basic box shape with the dimensional lumber pieces of each platform, except Platform 1. Before gluing the plywood top in place, try placing it on the box in a variety of ways to hide any knots or imperfections, and to best match the exact shape of the box. Then glue this plywood top to the base box, and secure in place with the remaining deck screws. No countersinking is necessary for these top surface screws. Finish by sanding all edges of the platform.

Platform 1 simply uses a flat base that is the same size as the plywood top. Glue and fasten this platform together with four deck screws. Sand all edges.

Special Instructions

The slightly odd platform sizes will allow you to cut the plywood tops conveniently from a single piece of plywood, allowing room for the width of the saw blade.

These platforms will probably take quite a bit of abuse during their life as a challenge and adventure programming prop. Gluing the joints and top in place, and using good quality decking screws will help keep these platforms together longer than nails alone. Drywall screws generally have a smaller thread and can easily pull out of dimensional lumber—use only wide pitch deck screws for this job. The minimum thickness for the plywood top is ⅝ inch (16 mm) although ¾ inch (19 mm) is a much better choice.

If you would like to make larger platforms that will nest with the above four platforms, use the following dimensions.

Platform 5 One ¾ inch (19 mm) Plywood Top 23.25 inches (591 mm) square
Two 2×8's cut to a 6.5 inch (165 mm) width by 23.25 inches (591 mm) long
Two 2×8's cut to a 6.5 inch (165 mm) width by 20.25 inches (514 mm) long
Twenty-eight 2 inch (51 mm) long exterior deck screws.

Platform 6 One ¾ inch (19 mm) Plywood Top 27 inches (686 mm) square
Two 2×8's 27 inches (686 mm) long
Two 2×8's 24 inches (610 mm) long
Thirty-two 2 inch (51 mm) long exterior deck screws.

Activity 5.09

Alphabet Soup

With a rope and 26 lettered disks you have all the ingredients for Alphabet Soup.

What You'll Need

26 paper plates, wooden disks, carpet patches or flying disks on which to write each letter of the alphabet. A 30 foot (9.1 meter) long rope to outline a boundary around the 26 disks.

Where to Find It

Paper plates are certainly an inexpensive way of creating these 26 disks. If you would like a more professional set of equipment for a numerical version of this activity, Project Adventure sells the Keypunch kit complete with stuff sack, rope, plastic gym markers, and a stopwatch.

How to Make It

Draw a single letter on each of 26 different paper plates in large, bold printing.

Special Instructions

How about using disks with pictures of hands forming sign language letter, words or phrases. Another version would be to use Morse Code sequences instead of the more common letters or numbers. Yet another version would be to use a foreign alphabet—how's this for an opportunity in diversity and cultural education.

For corporate settings, how about disks that show a sequence in the manufacturing operation of the business, or in the marketing / distribution channel. Perhaps the disks can illustrate all the steps in correctly filling a purchasing requisition. For medical groups, or EMT's, WFR's, etc., how about disks that depict the correct sequence in providing care for an injured patient.

For elementary students, how about a version of this activity where each of the disks has the face of a clock, with various times illustrated. Students must touch the disks in the proper order as times range from 1 o'clock to 12 o'clock. As a history lesson, the disks could contain important historical events, and the students would need to touch the disks in chronological order.

If you happen to like the numerical version of this activity, consider using a large tarp or plastic sheet with a variety of shoeprints or footprints scattered about. Number the footprints upwards from 1. You can call this version "The Dance Studio." Yet another version using numbers would be to paint a series of lines disecting the tarp, and number each of the spaces. This could be the "Painting by Numbers" version.

Activity 5.10

Alphabetically

What You'll Need

No props are needed for this activity, although it does help to have a working knowledge of the local alphabet. Blindfolds are an optional prop. See the section on Lycra Tubes for instructions to make lycra blindfolds.

Activity 5.11

Bag It

Something fun to do with equipment and props you probably already have.

What You'll Need

A drawstring stuff sack, filled with about 6 or 8 small objects. The objects inside the bag should be unique, and have no sharp edges or corners. Caribiners, Figure-8 descenders, Community Juggling props, a rubber ducky, a round compass, a Worm Hole, a knotted piece of rope, a lycra blindfold, a film canister, a water bottle, a bird call, a popsicle stick and a few wing nuts all make suitable tactile objects to be placed in the stuff sack.

Where to Find It

Outdoor shops, camping and backpacking stores, mail-order gear catalogs and military surplus stores are good choices for a variety of stuff sacks. Hopefully you can find enough objects in your adventure kit to make an interesting Bag It activity.

How to Make It

Just place 6 to 8 objects in the stuff sack. You can either perform this activity with the stuff sack open or closed.

Special Instructions

There are a fair number of challenge related props such as z-balls, carabiners, figure 8 descenders, a rope with a square knot tied in it, half a tennis ball, etc. that will be familiar to the group. Consider using some not-so-familiar objects, such as turn of the century kitchen equipment (eliminate any items with sharp edges), an 8-track tape, a pet rock, a child's toy, etc. If you want to use a teachable moment, try filling the bag with small pieces of rope tied into various knots, and then asking the group to decide which knots are present.

It is probably better to have a stuff sack that is too big rather than one that is too small.

Activity 5.12

Blackout

Here is another activity that uses the same props as Magic Carpet, Midnight Sun and Danger Zone.

What You'll Need

The plastic sheets or tarps from Magic Carpet or the sheets or ropes from Midnight Sun or Danger Zone. A Lycra Tube will also work in a pinch.

Where to Find It

Hardware stores often carry plastic sheeting that can be cut to length. Fabric stores sell outdoor tablecloth materials by length, and waterproof fabrics too.

How to Make It

A rectangle of plastic or cloth is all that is needed. If you happen to have a corporate or academic group, consider cutting out a pattern to match their logo, corporate identity, name or mascot.

Special Instructions

Changing the shape of the plastic cloth will require the group to use various configurations to successfully cover the changing surface areas of the carpet. You can also try circles, triangles, letters and other significant shapes or symbols.

A completely different variation of this activity that requires almost no props at all is to have the group completely block out all the light between a well lit room and a closet or adjoining room with no windows, by blocking all the light coming through the entrance doorway. You may want to give the group a few pieces of foam to use as light insulation.

Activity 5.13

Boardwalking I

Next to the Water Tube, these Boardwalking boards are probably going to require the most work of any other equipment in this book. Lots of work, but worth it. This design is very portable, and a favorite of many portable challenge and adventure activity programmers.

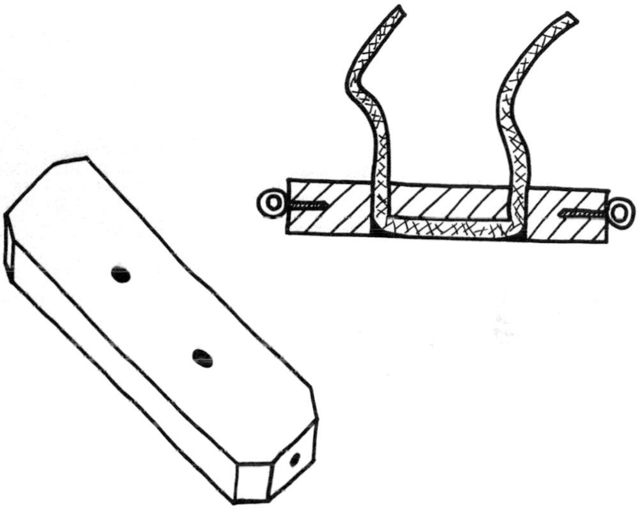

What You'll Need

For a set of jointed Boardwalking boards that will easily transport eight adult participants, and perhaps a few more if you squeeze, you'll need two 2×6's that are 12 feet (3.6 meters) long. These boards will produce a set of eight Boardwalking boards, each 36 inches (0.9 meters) long. You'll also need eight ⅜ inch (9 mm) ropes that are each 8 feet (2.4 meters) long, twelve steel screw eyes that are 5⁄16 inch (8 mm) by 4 inches (101 mm) long, and six 5⁄16 inch (8 mm) quick links (also known as rapid links).

Where to Find It

While you can find most of these items in any hardware store, you may want to try buy enough materials to make several Boardwalking board sets at one time. Sometimes if you are willing to purchase a whole box of screw eyes, or quick links, you may be able to negotiate a reduction in price. In most areas, the cost of the ropes, screw eyes and quick links will typically be higher than the cost of the wood itself!

How to Make It

Unless you have a heated rope cutting device on hand, try to cut rope at the store using a heated knife element. This seals the end of the rope and prevents it from unraveling. You can also use a flame to seal the ends, but this often leaves a black carbon residue. You'll need a total of eight ropes for these Boardwalking boards. You may choose to use different colors for each pair of Boardwalking boards.

Cut each of the 12 foot (3.6 meter) long 2×6's into four equal lengths of 36 inches (0.9 meters). Using the miter of a table saw, cut a 45 degree by 1 inch (25 mm) corner from each of the four corners of these 36 inch (0.9 meter) long boards. Draw a line down the center of each board, 2.75 inches (70 mm) from either edge. Make a mark along this line exactly 12 inches (305 mm) in from both ends. Drill a ½ inch (13 mm) hole at each of these two locations completely through the board. You can also drill a ¼ inch (6 mm) hole 3.5 inches (89 mm) deep at the exact center of each end of these boards. This is the pilot hole for the 5⁄16 × 4 screw eye. See the illustration below for the location of this hole. The four end Boardwalking boards only require a single pilot hole. The middle four Boardwalking boards have a pilot hole at each end.

With a router and a ½ inch (12 mm) core box bit (the kind that makes a complete round channel), connect these two holes with a ½ inch (12 mm) deep channel on the bottom surface of each Boardwalking board.

Using a rounding cove molding bit, round each of the four edges of each Boardwalking board using the router. Then sand all corners of each board.

Now install the screw eyes using a long handled screwdriver or rod to twist each screw eye into place. The circular eye should be just at the surface of the wood. Now you are ready to install the ropes.

Pass one end of each ⅜ inch (9 mm) rope downward though one hole in each board and upward through the other hole. Pull tightly on each end of the rope, and make sure that each end of the rope is the same length. Tie an overhand knot near the board with one end of the rope, then pull the other end of the rope tightly, and tie another overhand knot. This secures the rope to the board. Attach the other seven ropes to the remaining Boardwalking boards in the same fashion.

Now place the Boardwalking boards on the ground, so that the middle four boards each have two screw eyes in place, and the end four boards have a single screw eye. Use three quick links to connect each line of four Boardwalking boards together.

Special Instructions

For convenience, you may want to disconnect the quick links when transporting the Boardwalking boards.

One variation to this activity involves providing the group with individual boardwalkers and a supply of quick links, and having them create the most efficient configuration they can to transport the entire group. Be sure to mention that a safety inspection of the "vehicle" will be required before the journey can begin. This variation adds some construction activity to the event, and an additional level of problem solving as the group attempts to define the best way to join the boardwalkers together.

Another activity involves using two boardwalkers with a rope between them to travel and retrieve a bucket filled with water, or some other easily hooked object.

Activity 5.13

Boardwalking II

Here is a simple non-jointed technique for making Boardwalkers. This design is a little more difficult to transport than the jointed design, but happens to be substantially less expensive, and lighter than the jointed variety.

What You'll Need

For a non-jointed Boardwalker that will easily support eight participants at one time, you'll need two 2×6's that are 10 feet (3 meters) long and eight pieces of ⅜ inch (9 mm) rope that is 8 feet (2.4 meters) long.

Where to Find It

It is off to the hardware store for the dimensional lumber 2×6's and the rope. Before buying just the length of rope you need, you might consider buying a large spool of whatever style rope you'll need for all the activities you wish to construct in this book. You may save some money in the bargain. Other activities that can use this rope include Pot of Gold, 2B or KNOT 2B, Tree of Knots, Danger Zone, Midnight Sun, Community Jump Rope, River Crossing, Life Raft and the jointed Boardwalking boards.

How to Make It

2×6 boards are actually 5.5 inches (140 mm) wide. Draw a line down the center of each 2×6 board, 2.75 inches (70 mm) from either edge. From the end of the board, draw a mark at exactly 7.5 inches (190 mm) as the location for the first ½ inch (12 mm) hole to be drilled completely through the board. Mark the location for 7 additional holes, with 15 inches (381 mm) between each of these holes. The distance between the last hole and the other end of the board should be about 7.5 inches (190 mm). Drill a total of sixteen ½ inch (12 mm) holes completely through both boards.

Now using a router with a ½ inch (12 mm) core box bit (the kind that makes a completely circular channel), connect the first and second hole with a ½ inch (12 mm) deep channel on the bottom side of the board. In a similar fashion, connect holes number 3 and 4, 5 and 6, and finally holes 7 and 8.

With one of the lengths of rope, pass the end down from the top side of the first hole, under the board and up through the second hole. Pull so that the length of rope exiting both holes is the same. Not tie an overhand knot at the top surface of the board at the first hole. Then pull the rope tightly at the second hole, and again tie an overhand knot in this side of the rope. This captures the rope securely, while the rope rides in the carved channel at the bottom of the board. In a similar fashion, install the rest of the ropes on both of these Boardwalking boards.

Special Instructions

You can consider cutting a channel the entire length of the bottom of the boards to create room for the rope to connect each set of holes. Other methods are possible, but the routed channels sure looks the nicest.

Activity 5.14

Bull Ring I

The simple ring and string contraption known as a Bull Ring has to be one of the simplest portable challenge activities ever created.

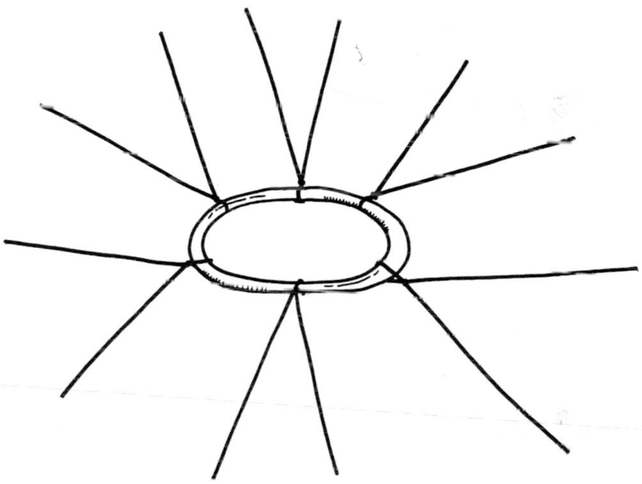

What You'll Need

The Bull Ring is made from a 1½ inch (38 mm) diameter solid metal ring. A large diameter key ring can also be used in place of the solid metal ring. Several brightly colored pieces of mason twine or string are attached to this ring. You'll also need a tennis or golf ball, and a single PVC Marble Tube works well as a ball holder.

Where to Find It

A variety of sizes of metal rings can be found in the fastener department of most hardware stores. Larger metal rings and embroidery hoops can be purchased at many craft stores. Plastic carnival rings can be purchased from the Oriental Trading Company (address in Chapter 8). Mason twine is also sold at most hardware stores, although any brightly colored string will work.

How to Make It

To create a Bull Ring for 12 participants, cut 6 pieces of twine that are each 20 feet (6 meters) long. After cutting each piece of twine, immediately tie a single overhand or figure eight knot at both ends of each piece, to keep the twine from unraveling. Pass a single piece of twine through the metal ring, until the ring is supported by the exact midpoint of the twine. Now, with both ends of the twine together, tie an overhand knot near the metal ring. An overhand knot will keep the Bull Ring from unraveling. A simple hitch is likely to unravel after some time, but an overhand knot will stay forever. There should be a little room for the knot to slide around the metal ring without binding. Now tie the other 5 remaining strings in the same fashion.

Consider making one or two of the twine lengths a different color from the rest of the twine attached to the metal ring. This will provide you with some options for the Bull Ring activity. See Chapter 4 instructions for more information about this.

The technique mentioned above creates a Bull Ring where each participant is at approximately the same distance from the metal ring. For variety, you may wish to use 12 pieces of twine that are each a different length.

Special Instructions

The metal ring used for this activity can be altered both in size and material. Plastic shower curtain rings work well. Plastic carnival rings can also be used. In a pinch, the plastic locking rings on gallon milk containers in North America can be used for a ring.

After making the Bull Ring, store it by wrapping the ring and strings around a PVC Marble Tube and secure it with a rubber band. You can also create a daisy chain with the strings.

Additional Bull Ring variations include using a rubber band instead of the metal ring. Using various lengths of string attached to the Bull Ring may also allow the group to successfully naviagate some more interesting and challenging obstacles. Participants should hold only the very ends of each string.

If your group has any participants in manual wheelchairs, you can use a short segment of shock (bungie) cord to tie the Bull Ring string onto a railing of the wheelchair. This will leave both of this participants hands free to maneuver the chair and provides some shock resistance to the movement of the ball.

A final variation is to replace the string or twine with dental floss. Because the floss is easily broken, participants must not be overly aggressive or they will physically eliminate themselves from the activity.

Activity 5.15

Bull Ring II

This first variation of Bull Ring replaces the transportation of a ball with the acquiring of various objects while participants are in a seated position.

What You'll Need

You'll need one of the Bull Rings created with the instructions from Section 5.14 of this chapter. You'll also need a variety of magnets, cones, marbles and other small objects to move around on the surface of a large table at the center of the group. Chairs are typically needed for all participants.

Where to Find It

Many discount stores carry a variety of magnetic objects, such as refrigerator magnets, magnetic marbles, and children's toys.

How to Make It

Same Bull Ring as before, but instead of transporting a ball, this Bull Ring is used to collect various objects, and move them to a collection location.

Special Instructions

A variety of objects present difference challenges for the group. Marbles are best contained by the Bull Ring as it drags along the surface of the table, and can be moved to the collection can pulling on the strings at one side of the group, and releasing the strings on the other side. Cone shapes made from wood or plastic can be captured by the Bull Ring, and the slid towards the collection can. Magnetic objects can be picked up by the metal ring, and removed by the bait shop owner. Challenge the group with several higher difficulty objects, such as a crumpled piece of paper, a suction cup dart stuck to the table, a brand new pencil, a paper clip, a piece of duct tape, or a magazine. Perhaps, in this case, picking up the piece of tape might enable the group to pick up the paper clip more easily. Producing what is commonly referred to as "complex tool-building behavior" within the group.

You can also add some obstacles by spacing two tables almost together, so that a small gap is present. Any obstacles reaching the gap must be carried, or forever lost to the depths of the sea. Folded duct tape can also be used to create barriers or fences.

Do not allow particpants to tie the string around

their fingers or wrists, because a sudden movement may cause rope rash rather quickly. Use of a larger diameter string or rope may be more appropriate for the dexterity level of your group. Visual perception skills may also require the use of a larger ring, or high contrasting colored objects. If gross motor skills in the group are limited, using all shock cord or elastic for the Bull Ring strings produces some interesting effects. With this system, a single quick pull or erratic movement has less effect on the group than with non-elastic strings.

This version of Bull Ring requires some depth perception skills.

Activity 5.16

Bull Ring III—Write On!

Yet another activity you can accomplish with a Bull Ring. This version adds a pen or marker to the center of the Bull Ring.

What You'll Need

A Bull Ring, a wide-tipped marker, some masking tape, a few rubberbands, and a large piece of thick paper or posterboard taped to the floor or the top surface of a table.

Where to Find It

Directions for making the Bull Ring are found in Section 5.14 of this chapter. Most of the other materials are probably already in your desk or office supply cabinet.

How to Make It

First attach the marker to the Bull Ring using the masking tape and rubber bands. Your group can then use this apparatus to write on the paper. For balance reasons, it is best to center the marker in the metal ring of the Bull Ring. Attaching the marker to the metal ring of the Bull Ring is no easy task, and the final result probably won't look very pretty, but try to make a secure attachment that doesn't wobble, even if it means using plenty of masking tape.

Special Instructions

One of the simplest challenges is to have the group fill in a coloring book page with different color markers, or to completely fill in a geometric shape without going outside the lines. Another activity is to have groups quickly spell words and for an observer to guess what they are spelling. A third challenge could be a king-sized tic-tac-toe game using two different teams. A fourth activity would be for the group to create a visual work of art, either in the form of a painting or perhaps a poem. A fifth variation would be to allow one, two or three people to control the motion of the Bull Ring, and for others in the group to simply allow the Bull Ring to move easily about.

A final activity would be to create a king-sized computer graded test sheet, with squares for answers (A) (B) (C) (D) and (E), and to have the group read a short quiz question and then mark the correct answer using the Bull Ring Universal Writing Tool—Mark 3.0.

Probably the most important point is to find a way to adequately fix the marker or pen to the Bull Ring. Next, try to use a thick enough piece of paper or posterboard so that the marker or pen does not soak through, or puncture the paper, causing damage to the table or floor surface below. If your group will be coloring a page from a coloring book, be sure to fashion a quick way to replace the marker, and to have a variety of colors available.

Notes

Activity 5.17

Bull Ring Golf

It is simply amazing how many things you can do with a Bull Ring. Here is a nine hole golf course plan using a variety of balls and golf course green designs.

What You'll Need

A Bull Ring with enough strings for every member of the group. A variety of balls, tubes, cans, cups, buckets, and obstacles. See Chapter 4 for different hole ideas.

Where to Find It

Standard athletic balls are fairly easy to find, but finding an extra billard ball or a 2 inch (51 mm) diameter steel ball bearing is probably a little more challenging. Check garage sales, industrial sales, junk yards and let all your neighbors and friends know. You'll probably collect a few interesting balls this way. Perhaps a croquet ball, a horse polo ball, or even a burma ball.

Special Instructions

Another Bull Ring Golf variation involves using a wide rubber band instead of the metal ring. With this prop you can play a more traditional version of golf. Begin with a golf ball placed on a golf tee. Stretch the rubber band Bull Ring over the golf ball, and either capture or cradle the ball. Every time the golf ball hits the ground counts as one stroke. The various holes can be tin cans placed around strategic obstacles. Each hole can still use a different ball. Suitable choices include, golf balls, tennis balls, ping pong balls, super bounce balls, whiffle balls, baseballs, etc. This activity can even be played inside by placing the golfing tees into small blocks of wood.

Here is a final variation that can be used during a Bull Ring Golf game. Any time the ball is dropped, one participant must let their string go slack, or let go completely of their string, until the ball reaches the hole.

Activity 5.18

Cave In

Cave in can be an emotionally intense experience. This activity is intended for groups that have a long-term relationship and have intimate knowledge and respect for each other.

What You'll Need

It is useful to have a tarp, table cloth or blanket that is large enough to completely cover the group. Use a material that is open weave and allows air movement. Plastic cloth is not a suitable material. One material that is perfect for this initiative is the military screening material suggested for the challenge activity Under Cover. Other materials can be used, but be sure to allow for adequate ventilation.

Where to Find It

Most tarps and screening material can be found at hardware stores, military surplus stores and occassionally at upholstery shops. Some mail order tool catalogs offer cloth tarps at reasonable prices.

How to Make It

Just a large rectangular cloth is all that is needed here.

Special Instructions

Make sure that there is adequate ventilation for the group.

Activity 5.19

Community Juggling

If your group has ever felt like they were juggling too many jobs at one time, this activity is probably ideal for them.

What You'll Need

A variety of soft, colorful, diverse objects that can be tossed without hurting anyone. Useful objects include: tennis balls, hoseplay balls, beanbags, plastic fruit, flying disks, pieces of upholstery foam, stuffed animals, pet toys, inflatable pool toys, rolled-up socks, pillows and balloons.

Where to Find It

Try looking at the bargain store for soft plastic toys. Craft stores often have plastic fruit that can be used. Pet stores sell a variety of soft and squeeky pet toys.

How to Make It

The only organization needed is to begin the activity with participants standing in a circle.

Special Instructions

In addition to varying the size, shape and texture of the objects, this activity can be greatly altered by having the participants wear gloves. Provide a variety of gloves such as new medical examination gloves, cotton work gloves, knitted mittens, slick ski gloves, cycling gloves, welding gloves, etc. Even the best athlete will be humbled by their performance using gloves. Playing with your non-dominant hand is also a challenge.

You might want to consider the members of your group before attempting to juggle anything unusual, like a giant plastic spider, rubber snake or other icky object.

Encourage participants not to toss objects near the face of the receiver is a good idea. Introduce additional objects only when the group has demonstrated proficiency with a single object.

Activity 5.20

Community Jump Rope

Just another reason for having a long piece of rope in your adventure equipment kit.

What You'll Need

One rope at least 30 feet (9 meters) long, suitable for twirling as a jump rope.

Where to Find It

You can use this same rope for Tree of Knots, Pot of Gold, A Collection of Knots, River Crossing and Life Raft.

Special Instructions

Twirling a jump rope on any hard floor surface, playground lot, or paved surface is sure to cause wear on the rope from abrasion. Select a rope that can handle this abrasion without fraying, or consider wrapping the middle section of the rope with duct tape.

Notes

Activity 5.21

Danger Zone

A large plastic sheet from Margic Carpet or a long rope can be used to define the space for Danger Zone.

What You'll Need

A long rope can be used to create an irregular boundary, or a large blanket, tarp or plastic sheet can be used to define the limited space available. Some additional "equipment" such as plastic containers, boxes, or other adventure stuff can be used as examples of expedition equipment that also must be stored on the ledge.

Where to Find It

Nearly all of these items are hopefully already in your adventure kit. A long length of rope can be used here, and has a variety of other useful challenge and adventure programming activity purposes. So does a large plastic sheet which can be used for Magic Carpet, Danger Zone, Midnight Sun, and Cave In.

How to Make It

Any rectangular or irregular shape works fine for this activity. Try to select a size that will challenge the group the very first time they attempt it.

Special Instructions

Choose a location this is comfortable for participants to lie down. A grassy field is fine, but a gravel parking lot or a hardwood gym floor is probably not the best location for Danger Zone.

If this activity is used indoors, try placing the ledge near a wall, or even in a corner. This produces additional variations since participants can now lean against the walls.

After participants are in place, have them all turn over (as many people do when they are sleeping) one person at a time. A second variation would be to have all participants turn over at the same time (slowly!) After order is restored, ask for a volunteer to be a "snorer", and have this person change places with another person in the group.

Activity 5.22

Marching to the Beat of a Different Drum

This simple activity builds energy within a group. It offers the chance for every participant to take the leadership role, even if only for a short time.

What You'll Need

The most simple equipment is a cassette tape player and a cassette tape with a variety of musical segments, each approximatly 30 to 60 seconds long. Use a variety of music styles, and have at least as many segments prepared as the number of participants in the group. Records can also be used effectively, but the transition between songs is generally less subtle.

Where to Find It

Many libraries now carry selections of music on cassettes, CD's and even a few rare vinyl albums. Try checking out your parent's music library. Even the oldies work well for this activity. Or if you happen to be an oldie but goodie, try some of your children's head banging music. You might just find something you like!

How to Make It

A single cassette tape is easiest to transport, and allows for smooth transitions between songs. Don't forget to bring along a cassette tape player. A collection of 10 to 15 songs is probably adequate for most groups. If you have more than 15 participants in a single group, consider splitting the large group into two smaller groups for this activity.

Special Instructions

Choose musical segments that are appropriate for the group. Marches and dance music usually produce bold movements, while classical and folk music typically produce smaller, quieter movements. For children, consider using cartoon music or songs from children's programs. For a western theme, consider using a collection of cowboy tunes, country and western music. For an audience discussing diversity issues, consider using music from a variety of countries. Occasionally include an energetic musical selection, such as a march, college fight song, or national anthem.

The length of the musical selection should be approximately 30 to 60 seconds, with a short pause in between segments. If you wish to use this activity as an energizer, the last musical segment should be a high energy selection. If you wish to address the group and hold their attention after this activity, the final two segments should be more reflective and peaceful, so that the participants complete the activity in a refreshed, but relaxed mood. Music is a great motivator for many populations, and the choice of music selected for this activity will directly affect the energy level of the group, and their response to this activity.

One of the most significant experiences that challenge and adventure activities provide is the opportunity to move participants outside of their comfort zone into an area of growth and self discovery. For some participants, movement to music is not an easy thing to participate in, let alone provide a leadership role. By simply asking participants to be willing to try new things at the beginning of a challenge and adventure programming session, a facilitator can set the stage for this activity. And remember, if a participant is self-conscious about their movements, they can simply close their eyes, and everyone else can watch them.

One of the most powerful uses of this activity is to expose participants to a diverse variety of other cultures, through their music. By choosing rhythms, musical styles, historically significant selections, and culturally diverse musical segments, the participants of this activity can begin to understand other populations.

Activity 5.23

Expansion and Contraction

This activity can be performed using Marble Tubes with flat ends or with dowel rods.

What You'll Need

If you happen to have some Marble Tubes that are cut squarely at both ends, you can use one of these for each participant. If you don't happen to have PVC tubes about 15 to 20 inches (391 to 508 mm) long, you can use ⅜ or ½ inch (9 or 13 mm) dowel rods about 18 inches (457 mm) long. Again, you'll need one dowel rod for each participant.

Where to Find It

It is a toss-up between hardware and craft stores to see where the least expensive dowel rods are going to be.

How to Make It

Dowel rods generally come in 36 inch (about 1 meter) lengths. These rods simply need to be cut into two equal lengths. Only PVC tubes with square ends should be used, since angled PVC tubes have a sharp edge that will be uncomfortable for participants.

Special Instructions

Choosing suitable connection rods is very important. Smooth ended marble tubes work well, so do smooth dowel rods, and even the smallest diameter floating foam pool sticks now available.

Asking the group to form different configurations, such as circles, squares, modern art, a beating heart, or an orchestra can be an expressive experience. Shrinking or contracting the size of the group is a good first activity.

The expansion of the group, which can be interpreted as an event of rapid growth, should push participants to hold both hands well away from their bodies. If the group simultaneously reaches their complete limit, all the connection rods should drop at exactly the same moment.

You can ask the group to create a goal for the size of circle they can create. Another goal may be the total number of connection rods dropped during the activity.

Look for a version of this activity entitled DNA on page 124 of the book, 50 Ways to Use Your Noodle, by Chris Cavert and Sam Sikes.

Activity 5.24

Forming Groups With Film Canisters

Here is an interesting method for forming groups that also involves recycling.

What You'll Need

You'll need a collection of 25 plastic film canisters and a stuff sack to hold them. Choose the classic film canisters that have a black base and a gray cap. You'll also need five pieces of five different objects (coins, paper clips, rubber bands, beans, marbles) to place in the canisters, and three different colors of permanent markers.

Where to Find It

Most film processors will donate film canisters to groups. Check out the film processing center at your local store, shopping plaza or camera shop.

How to Make It

Directions are given below for constructing a kit of film canisters that will group 25 participants into groups of five a total of three different ways, where none of the same members are ever in the same group twice. The technique shown also will work for six groups of six, or eight groups of eight, or. . . .

Begin by placing the black canisters in a 5 by 5 pattern as shown in the illustration below. Next to this pattern, place the 25 gray lids, upside-down also in a 5 by 5 pattern. Notice that both the lids and canisters have been numbered in the illustration for your information. With a permanent marker, begin labeling the inside of the gray lids, by row. The first row of five lids is "A." This includes lids 1, 2, 3, 4 and 5. The second row is "B", the third row is "C", the fourth row is "D" and the fifth row is "E." With a different color permanent marker, label the inside of each gray lid with a Roman numeral, this time by column. The first column of five lids is "I." This includes lids 1, 6, 11, 16 and 21. The second column is "II", the third column is "III", the fourth column is "IV" and the final column is "V."

Now for the tricky part. In order to create the 3 different groups of 5 participants, the contents must be added to the canisters in a precise way. In this case, that means adding the objects diagonally from the upper left to the lower right. For this explanation, the objects will be marbles, coins, 2 paper clips, a large rubber band, and a dozen beans. You can choose any objects you like, although it helps if each objects sounds different when shaken in the canister.

Begin by placing a marble in the upper left-hand canister which is number 1. Now move one canister to the right, and one canister down and place another marble in canister 7. Continue in this pattern until you have deposited the fifth marble in the lower right-hand canister number 25. Marbles now fill the diagonal line between the upper left and lower right canisters. The next object is a penny or other small coin. Begin placing this coin in canister number 2 followed by canisters 8, 14, 20. At this point the diagonal runs out, and the final coin is placed in canister 21. The next objects are 2 paper clips, placed into canisters 3, 9, 15, 16 and 22. The next object is a large rubber band placed into canisters 4, 10, 11, 17 and 23. Finally, a dozen or so beans are placed into canisters 5, 6, 12, 18 and 23. Congratulations, you have made it through the tricky part.

Now place the lid number 1 onto canister number 1, lid number 2 onto canister number 2, and so on. You'll now have 25 identical looking canisters that can subdivide a group of 25 participants into groups of 5 three different ways, with new members in every group formation.

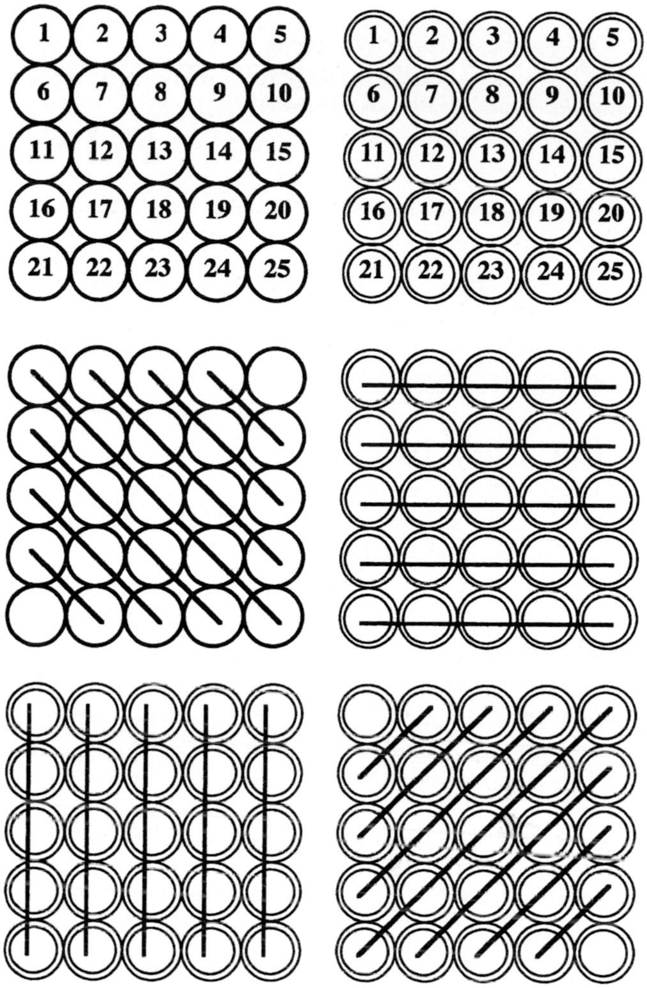

Special Instructions

If you number the lids with another letter, symbol or color, diagonally from the upper right to the lower left, you can create a 4th grouping.

Activity 5.25

First Contact

For those groups willing to risk some amount of contact, here is a simple activity that requires no equipment, and that has a variety of solutions.

What You'll Need

First Contact requires no props. See Chapter 4 for an explanation of this activity.

Activity 5.26

FUNderbirds

Here is one of the most unique looking pieces of equipment in the Teamplay challenge and adventure equipment kit. A special thanks to Bill Henderson for allowing us to share this with you.

What You'll Need

You'll find several illustrations below that may be helpful in creating your funderbird.

You'll need a large wooden spool (which are surprisingly hard to find these days) or a lathe turned wooden cylinder, several small pieces of carpet padding, two 4 inch (102 mm) disks made from thin leather, suede or synthetic vinyl, three long feathers, sewing thread and about 12 inches (305 mm) of artificial sinew from a leather store.

Where to Find It

Carpet installers typically have left over and scrap pieces of carpet padding. Wooden spools are hard to find these days, but may be available at craft stores, along with leather, vinyl, feathers and artificial sinew (used to make dream catchers). If you have access to a lathe, the individually turned wooden cylinders are our favorite.

How to Make It

With either the wooden spool, or the turned wooden cylinder, you'll need to create a groove around the base. A V-shaped tool on the lathe works well for this operation. You'll also need to drill a ⅜

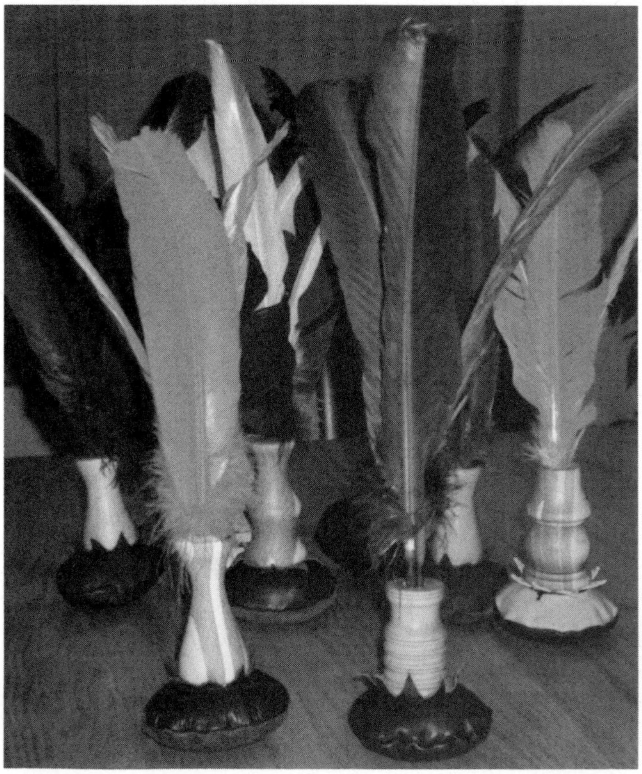

inch (9 mm) hole about 1.5 to 2 inches (38 to 51 mm) deep into the top end of the spool or wooden cylinder for the feathers.

Next, cut out two 4 inch (102 mm) diameter disks from the leather, suede or vinyl. One disk will remain solid, while the other has a series of 4 diagonal cuts near the center of this disk. See the illustration below. These four cuts can be made with a razor knife or sharp scissors. Sew the perimeter of the two disks together with the back side of the leather, suede or vinyl facing out. After sewing a circle around these disks, turn this assembly inside out by inverting the disks through the region with the diagonal cuts.

Stuff the interior of this pouch with carpet padding. Now use the artificial sinew to stitch through each of the 8 triangular shaped tabs near the bottom of each tab. Insert the spool or lathe turned cylinder into the pouch and tightly pull the sinew into the groove. Tie several knots to secure the pouch to the wooden cylinder. Cut off any excessive sinew.

Now insert the feathers into the top hole of the spool or wooden cylinder. Save the feather with the best point for last. These feathers may be glued in place, but we choose to only use friction, so that they can be pulled out easily when transporting them. In case you didn't realize this, feathers come in both right and left sided version (depending on which side of the bird they came from!) If you use feathers from the same side of the bird, the Funderbird will spin in the air.

Special Instructions

The book, Folk Arts Around the World, has directions for making another Funderbird-like object, known as a Brazilian peteca toy.

Activity 5.27

Gridlock

The grid pattern for Gridlock can be made from ropes, webbing, tarps, stepping stones, and masking tape.

What You'll Need

Gridlock requires a giant checkerboard pattern with each grid approximately 1 foot (305 mm) square. This can be accomplished by taping a grid pattern to a floor with masking tape, or marking a pattern on a tarp or cloth, or creating a grid with either ropes, flat webbing or a large open-weave net. You can also create a stepping stone pattern for Gridlock by using circular disks or flat stone.

Where to Find It

You can use one of the plastic sheets from Magic Carpet and paint, tape or permanently mark a grid pattern onto it. Ropes from the hardware store, or webbing can also be used. You can use the plastic disks from Stump Jumping for the stepping stone variety of this activity.

How to Make It

Construct a series of 1 foot (305 mm) square boxes in a pattern six square wide and ten squares long. For a tarp or plastic sheet, use permanent markers, paint

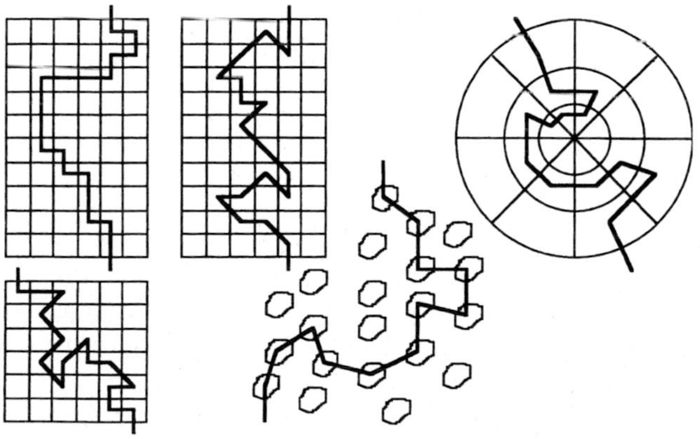

or duct tape to create the pattern. Masking tape can be used for an indoor program. Stepping stones can be placed in the traditional rectangular pattern, or used in any random fashion. A grid pattern can be made from 155 feet (47 meters) of rope or webbing by wrapping the rope in the pattern of the grid, and securing each intersection of ropes with a twist tie.

Special Instructions

Create two patterns through the Gridlock that are slightly different. One pattern should involve only moves forward or to the left or right (the simplest pattern). The other pattern can involve diagonal moves, backward moves, and moves to unconnected spaces.

Activity 5.28

Handcuffs and Shackles

Certainly one of the easiest get acquainted activities ever invented. But don't be surprised if some folks have still not experienced this activity yet. Even the most familiar activites are new to every generation.

What You'll Need

Handcuffs and Shackles are constructed from 5 feet (1.5 meter) of soft clothesline rope. The Handcuffs and Shackles are identical, so that the same rope can be used for either activity. You'll need one piece of rope for every participant. Any diameter soft rope can be used for this activity, althought the clothesline variety is probably the easiest to find and least expensive. A 100 foot (30 meter) length of rope will make 20 Handcuffs or Shackles.

Where to Find It

Back to the hardware store for this item. You may also find some soft sash cord at fabric stores.

How to Make It

For most audiences, the length of the rope for either Handcuffs or Shackles is identical. If you happen to have some participants with mobility limitations, consider using longer ropes to provide more movement between participants.

First cut a 5 foot (1.5 meter) length of rope. Immediately tie an overhand knot at each end of the rope to keep the cloth covering of the rope from unraveling.

Now form a loop at each end of the rope, and tie an overhand knot around the middle portion of the rope, as shown in the illustration below. This forms a slip knot so that the rope can be adjusted to the wrist or ankle size of any participant.

Special Instructions

Cloth ropes are the most comfortable for this activity. Poly ropes and small diameter ropes can be uncomfortable for participants. Yarn knots can be difficult to untie and often require a visit from the Knot Doctor and surgical removal.

You may want to consider adding some color to these ropes by using fabric dye. Different colors could signify different lengths.

Activity 5.29

Human Knot

For many participants, Human Knot is one of the first challenge and adventure activities they have ever seen.

What You'll Need

Nothing, unless you plan to use this activity with a population with limited mobility or limited upper arm movement. Then you might want to consider using the ropes from Handcuffs and Shackles or other ropes to extend the reach of the participants. These rope extensions also work well when there are more than ten participants in a group.

Where to Find It

You can use the ropes from Handcuffs and Shackles, 2B or KNOT 2B, Not Knots or the webbing from Raccoon Circles to extend the reach of the group.

Special Instructions

See Chapter 4 for a list of some useful variations to this classic activity.

Activity 5.30

Inch By Inch

Inch By Inch turns a searching mission into a team-based activity. Whether you're looking for a lost contact lens, the car keys, or the remote control for the television, this activity requires only a few simple props, and really focuses the attention of the group.

What You'll Need

Something familiar to search for, and a method for identifying the boundary of the search area, such as a rope boundary, wooden stakes or simply the walls at the edge of a room. Familiar searching objects can include a key, a paper clip, an earring. You can also use the camouflage creatures mentioned in Chapter 7 for this activity.

Where to Find It

Better use keys, earrings and other objects that no one is particularly fond of. Some of the lost items might just stay that way!

How to Make It

Define the searching area with ropes, stakes or room boundaries. You may even want to include some treasure maps for the group to point them in the right direction.

Special Instructions

Consider using an audio transmitter, such as a beeping pager or transistor radio, and finding this device with the group blindfolded. This encourages the use of listening skills.

If you happen to select a metallic object, such as a paperclip in the grass, you can consider giving the group some extra equipment, such as a few magnets.

Rather than placing an object, consider spraying a perfume or cologne on a tree and having the group use their sense of smell to find it.

Blindfolded searches should only take place in an environment free from obstacles. The size of the search area should be fairly small initially. After the group has perfected their searching techniques, larger areas can be used.

Activity 5.31

Just One Word

Here is a classic puzzle that groups often have difficulty solving, even when the solution is right in front of them.

What You'll Need

You will need 11 pieces of blank paper or blocks of wood. Print just one of the following letters in bold print on each of the 11 pages: D, E, J, N, O, O, R, S, T, U, W.

Where to Find It

If you choose to use a foreign language, Morse code, or manual sign language, you can find the appropriate information for creating these words, dot and dash patterns, or symbols at many public libraries. There are even a few internet sites for some of these languages.

How to Make It

Standard size paper (about 8½ inches by 11 inches in North America or A4 in Europe) works fine for this activity. Make the letters bold and large so that all members of the group can clearly see them.

J	U	S	T		O	N	E		W	O	R	D

Activity 5.32

Life Raft

Here is another activity that makes use of the jointed boards from Boardwalking.

What You'll Need

You'll need all eight of the Boardwalking boards for Life Raft. Four hoops or rope circles are used as islands. Four objects, such as flying disks, stuff sacks, etc. are used for supplies. A long rope can be added to mark some dangerous channel currents in the ocean. A few nautical props, such as a life preserver or a sharks fin add some comical realism.

Where to Find It

Time for yet another trip to the hardware store. This time for 2×6's, screw eyes, quick links, and rope Look for plastic hoops and flying disks at various discount stores and end-of-season sales at toy stores.

How to Make It

Directions for making the boards can be found under Boardwalking in this chapter. To construct the shape of the Life Raft, the four inner Boardwalking boards (the ones with screw eyes at both ends), are joined together to form a square, with four quick links. The four remaining Boardwalking boards are placed parallel to the four outside edges of this square. This completes the Life Raft.

The four plastic hoops, or Raccoon Circles, are placed 20 to 40 feet (6 to 12 meters) away from the Life Raft. The rope marker that signal a dangerous channel should be placed directly between the Life Raft and one of the plastic hoop islands.

Special Instructions

Encourage participants not to disassemble the Life Raft to complete the activity. This includes unlinking the quick links, removing the screw eyes, or removing the rope. You may want to carry along a pair of pliers to loosen the quick links. These devices can sometimes be accidently overtightened, and it takes a wrench or pliers to loosen them.

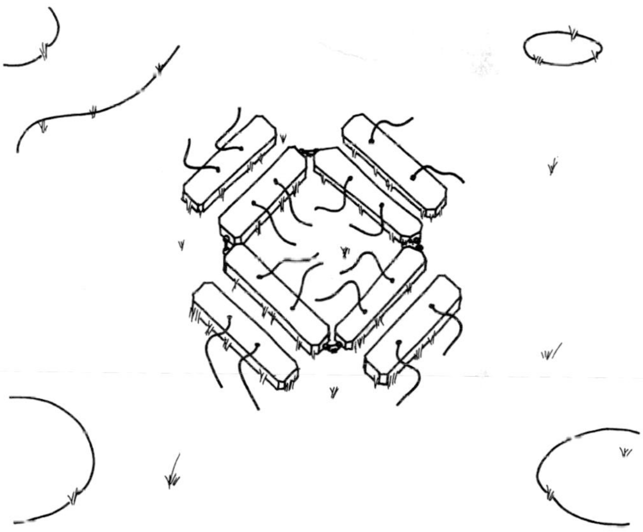

Activity 5.33

Line Up

Here is a simple activity that can be accomplished with no equipment at all.

What You'll Need

Nothing! See Chapter 4 for activity instructions.

Activity 5.34

Linearity

Just borrow a few ropes from 2B or KNOT 2B or Not Knots and the plastic cloth from Magic Carpet and you'll have all the supplies you need for Linearity.

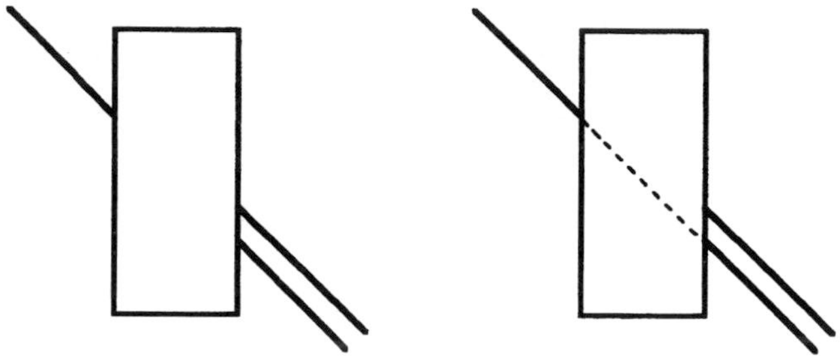

What You'll Need

Two ropes that are the same color and a large item with which to partially cover them, as in the illustration below. For the optimum optical illusion, select two ropes. One 5 foot (1.5 meter) long and a second rope 10 foot (3 meter) long.

The plastic cloth from Magic Carpet or the largest All Aboard platform will adequately cover the ropes.

How to Make It

The distance between the two ropes should be about 3 inches (76 mm).

Special Instructions

You'll need to pull the long rope tightly, so that it forms a straight line. The upper rope generally looks like the continuation of the rope on the left, when in fact, it is the lower one. As a facilitator, you can decide if you'll let the group use any outside resources to check the straightness of the lines. It is probably best not to allow them to touch either the ropes or the covering carpet, box, or board.

Activity 5.35

Living Ladder

Living Ladder is an excellent technique for showing how a group can support a single person in their efforts without overburdening any single member of the group.

What You'll Need

Six to eight hardwood dowels, 1¾ to 2 inches (44 to 51 mm) in diameter and 36 inches (about 1 meter) long. Oak or ash hardwood dowels are recommended. These materials are typically used for traditional wooden ladder rungs. Other equipment, such as broom handles, smaller dowels and PVC tubing are not recommended.

Where to Find It

Clearly the best place to find specialty wood, such as oak or ash hardwood dowel rods is at a lumber supply store, or sawmill. You'll need furniture grade materials, not standard decorative moldings for Living Ladder rungs. These dowels are not cheap, but will last for years if properly cared for.

How to Make It

The longer the length of the dowel rod, the greater the bending when a participant's weight is being supported. A length of 36 inches (0.91 meters) is adequate for both children and adults.

Special Instructions

For the 1996 ACCT National Conference, author Jim Cain performed a structural analysis on both 1¾ inch oak dowel rods and 1½ and 2 inch PVC tubing for Living Ladder rungs. You can find these calculations in the 1996 ACCT Conference Proceedings. The 1½ inch PVC tubing was clearly inappropriate for this activity for any audience. For participants less than 100 pounds in weight, both the 2 inch diameter thick-walled PVC tubing and the 1¾ inch oak dowel rods exhibited an acceptable factor of safety, although the 1¾ inch oak dowel rods are clearly the best all-around choice.

The technique for holding the hardwood dowels is important. Participants should hold the dowel firmly in one hand, and use the other hand to support this hand. Allow the shoulders and elbows to drop, so that the dowel is comfortably held with arms in an extended and relaxed position. Feet should be shoulder width apart, and participants should be standing vertically or leaning slightly backward. The next two partners should stand as close as possible to these first two partners. At any time when a climber is present on a dowel rod should partners attempt to move. Once the climber has gone past the last partners in line, they may carry the dowel rod to the front of the line, and again form another rung of the living ladder.

The technique for climbing is very much a matter of individual taste and preference. One simple technique is to crawl on hands and knees over the ladder rungs. For some participants, this may be a little difficult. Another technique involves using the hands to pull the lower body over the ladder rungs. A different technique is to sit on the first set of rungs, and then pull yourself backwards over the remaining rungs in a seated position. Encourage the climber to distribute their own weight over several dowels at a time.

Activity 5.36

Log Rolling

Here is another classic activity that can be a permanent or portable element for your challenge and adventure program. You can use the same boards needed for A Balanced Life or The Boardroom.

What You'll Need

For a portable challenge event, several boards or planks can be placed end to end on a flat surface, although a single continuous board works best. You'll need at least one foot (305 mm) of board length for each participant. 2×8 dimensional boards should be used for this activity. At the end of this chapter, you'll find instructions for creating a permanent Log Rolling element using telephone poles.

Where to Find It

Hardware stores and lumber yards carry dimensional lumber. Some stores will even cut this lumber to the exact length you need for a minimal charge.

Special Instructions

Dimensional lumber can be slippery when wet. Use these boards only in dry conditions, and be sure to place them on a level surface where they will not move while participants are on board.

If you happen to use several boards for your group, consider placing these boards in a slightly zigzag pattern rather than a straight line. This may make the activity easier for participants to change positions.

Activity 5.37

Lycra Tubes

Probably the most fun piece of equipment in this whole book, made from one of the coolest fabrics ever invented.

What You'll Need

5 yards (4.6 meters) of 36 to 60 inch (0.9 to 1.5 meters) wide nylon lycra. Color is really unimportant, although darker colors will hide grass stains better than lighter colors. Patterns are fine too, but try to avoid vertical stripes (these tend to make participants dizzy). 36 inch (0.9 meter) width lycra is perfect for young children. 48 to 60 inch (1.2 to 1.5 meter) width lycra is fine for adults, but for some activities, the 60 inch (1.5 meter) wide fabric is almost too wide. 5 yards (4.6 meters) is an ideal length for groups of 7 to 10 participants.

Where to Find It

Lycra is a fairly expensive material. You can often find it on sale during the fall and winter months at fabric stores. Look for stores that sell end bolts and remnants.

How to Make It

A Lycra Tube can be created from a length of nylon lycra by connecting the two ends of the fabric with a french seam. A sketch is presented below showing the three steps to creating this seam. First make a seam about ⅜ inch (9 mm) in from the end of the lycra, the full width of the Lycra Tube. There is no need to use elastic thread if you simply stretch the lycra as it is being sewn. For this first pass, the Lycra Tube is right side out.

For the second step, turn the Lycra Tube inside-out. Now sew a second seam the full width of the tube about ½ inch (12 mm) from the edge, stretching the lycra as the seam is created.

Finally, turn the Lycra Tube right side out, and from the inside of the tube sew the flap flat against one side of the Lycra Tube. This completes the stitching for the Lycra Tube.

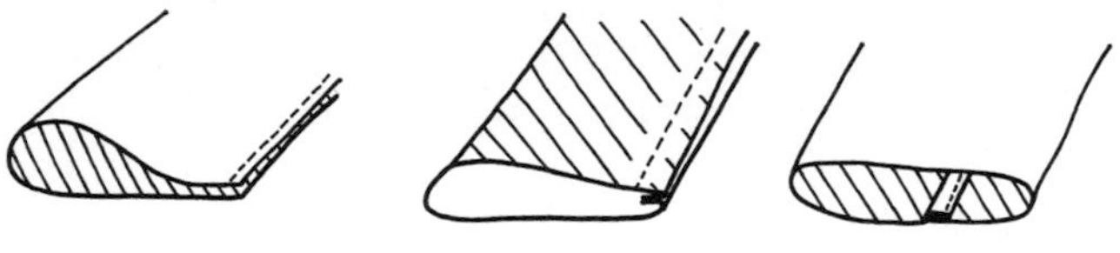

Special Instructions

Cotton lycra is not a suitable replacement for nylon lycra. Be sure to stretch the lycra while sewing each portion of the seam.

If you happen to have any left-over lycra, try making blindfolds using 7 by 21 inch (178 by 534 mm) pieces. Directions for lycra blindfolds can be found in the next section of this chapter.

Notes

Activity 5.37

Lycra Blindfolds

Lycra blindfolds are colorful, washable, and easy to make.

What You'll Need

Patches of lycra that are 7 by 21 inches (178 by 534 mm) in size. Make sure that the 21 inch (534 mm) dimension is running in the lycra direction that has the greatest amount of stretch. Color is unimportant, although darker colors will block more sunlight than lighter colors.

Where to Find It

Lycra is a fairly expensive material. You can often find it on sale during the fall and winter months at fabric stores. Look for stores that sell end bolts and remnants.

How to Make It

Lycra blindfolds require just two simple seams. First fold the long ends of the lycra together so that the back side of the material is facing outwards. This creates a long flat tube with the lycra. Sew a seam the full length of this lycra, about ⅜ inch (9 mm) from the edge.

Now turn this tube inside-out, so that the correct side of the material is visible, and the previous seam is at the bottom of the blindfold. Sew a final seam to join the ends of the blindfold together.

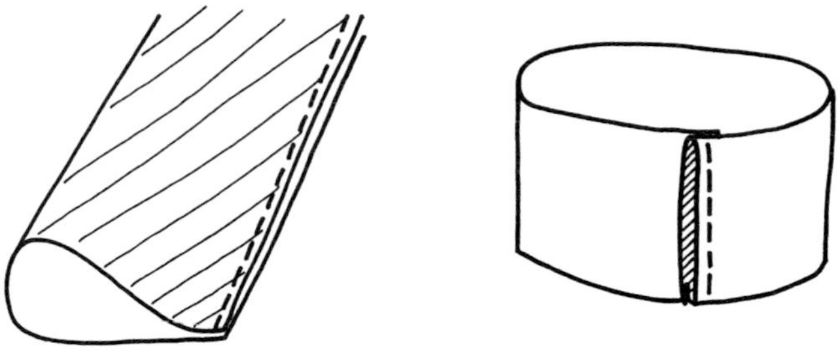

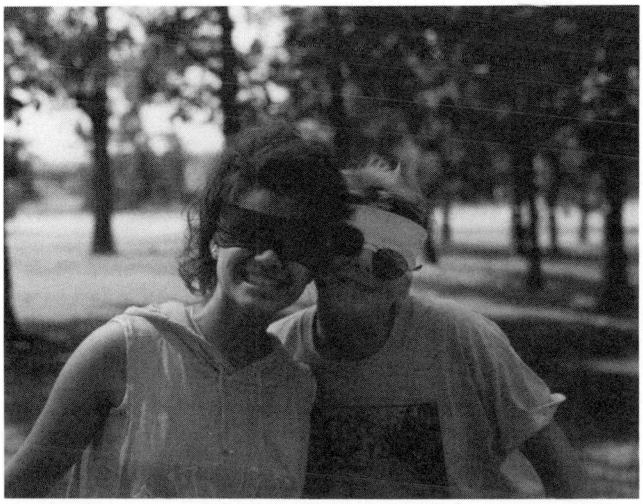

Special Instructions

Be sure to stretch the lycra while sewing each seam.

Notes

Activity 5.38

Magic Carpet

Magic Carpet requires a minimal amount of equipment and provides a challenging initiative to solve.

What You'll Need

The Magic Carpet consists of a single piece of tarp or plastic cloth. Other options include a plastic shower curtain, plastic tablecloth, or blanket. For groups of 8–12 participants, the Magic Carpet should be approximately 4 feet by 5 feet.

Where to Find It

Hardware stores carry a variety of plastic tarps. A better choice might be some of the colorful plastic table cloth covering materials available in many flooring and upholstery shops. These fabrics often have a different pattern on each side, so it is easy to see when the Magic Carpet has been completely turned over.

Party stores often sell festive plastic table cloths by length. These plastic cloths are colorful and very lightweight to carry. They won't last forever though.

How to Make It

Rectangular Magic Carpets are typical, but why not try a Magic Carpet in the shape of an oval or star. If you happen to be working with a corporation or academic institution, how about a Magic Carpet in the shape of their logo, mascot or name.

Special Instructions

The size of the Magic Carpet and the size of the group greatly effects the difficulty in accomplishing this initiative. Minimize risk by requiring all participants to be in contact with the carpet at all times.

Oddly enough, carpet is not a good choice for the Magic Carpet initiative. It is difficult to fold and is generally too thick to twist easily. Plastic sheets are a better choice, and take up much less space in the equipment storage container. Flexible materials generally make the best choice, although garbage bags are too thin, and tend to rip easily.

Activity 5.39

Marble Tubes

To a challenge education programmer, PVC tubing is worth it's weight in gold!

What You'll Need

Two types of Marble Tubes are presented here. The simplest style involves cuting 15 inch (381 mm) long pipes from 1 inch (25 mm) diameter cold water PVC tubing. These are described as standard Marble Tubes below. A second style uses 1½ (38 mm) diameter PVC tubing that has been cut to length, and then split into two pieces lengthwise. This style of Marble Tubes are described as open channel Marble Tubes.

You'll need at least one Marble Tube section for each participant, along with a few marbles, golf balls, and other small rolling objects. Find a stuff sack large enough to hold a complete set of Marble tubes.

Where to Find It

Back to the hardware or plumbing store for more PVC tubing. Also pick up some sandpaper, steel wool, a device for cutting PVC tubing, and one of the steel brushes designed especially for cleaning out the ends of PVC tubes that have been cut with a saw.

How to Make It

PVC tubing typically comes in 10 foot (3 meter) lengths. Begin making the standard Marble Tubes by cutting these 10 foot (3 meter) lengths of PVC tubing into 4 equal pieces, each will be 30 inches (762 mm) long. The cleanest technique for cutting this PVC tubing is by using one of the handheld scissor style cutters specifically designed for cutting PVC tubing. This style of cutter will leave a smooth square cut, with no dust or loose particles. A saw will also work, but leaves a rougher edge to clean up after the cut.

By making a diagonal cut, these standard Marble Tubes can also be used for stakes, Bull Ring ball holders, and other challenge activity props. Cut each one of the 30 inch (750 mm) lengths of PVC in half at a 30 degree angle with a bandsaw or miter box. 30 degrees is the optimal angle. Any steeper angle will produce a sharp tip that can be dangerous, and that breaks easily. After making this cut, clean out both ends of the PVC tubing with the wire brush, sandpaper or steel wool. This technique will produce eight Marble Tubes that are approximately 15 inches (381 mm) long, from each 10 foot (3 meter) length of PVC tubing. Consider making a variety of lengths. Participants using wheelchairs find that having a Marble Tube the same width as their wheelchair, about 23 inches (584 mm), is very helpful.

The open channel Marble Tubes are made from 1½ inch (38 mm) PVC tubing. Sixteen tubes, each 15 inches (381 mm) long can be made from a single 10 foot (3 meter) length of PVC tubing. After cutting these tubes to the proper length (with square edges at both ends), use a bandsaw to cut each of these tubes in half lengthwise. A wire brush can be used to clean up this edge. A file or sandpaper is helpful for creating a small radius at each end of the open channel tubes.

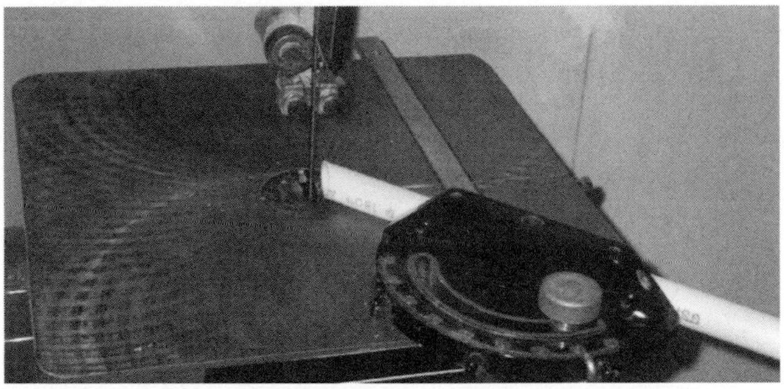

Special Instructions

Attach a variety of colored tape to the ends of the marble tubes, so that only similar colors can be partners. You can also add some of the various connections found in hardware stores, such as elbows, tees, Y sections, etc.

Drilling a few holes in some marble tubes will additionally challenge the participants having those tubes. We call these the "swiss cheese tubes."

For a truly unique open channel Marble Tube, twist the PVC tube as it is passed through the band saw blade. This will produce spiral tubes, that look a little like DNA strands. These tubes must be twisted as the marble moves from end to end, to keep the marble from falling off.

Notes

Activity 5.40

Midnight Sun

Midnight Sun requires what can sometimes be the most unreliable piece of equipment of all—the sun itself.

What You'll Need

You'll need something to place on the ground, such as a large beach towel, or the plastic tarps from Magic Carpet or Danger Zone, or a long rope to create an outline or a large familiar shape.

The second thing you'll need is bright sunlight, and the shadows that are cast by this light. If you happen to use this activity indoors, a single bright halogen spotlight can be used to cast shadows from each participant. If you will be performing Midnight Sun outdoors, the ideal time is early in the morning, or later in the day when shadows are significantly longer than at noon.

Where to Find It

The sun is that bright shiny thing that shows up in the sky every day, unless you happen to live in a place where rain isn't just an event, it is a way of life.

How to Make It

The size of the object to be completely shadowed should not be significantly larger than the members of the group. Begin with some smaller objects and increase the size of these objects and the difficulty level of the activity gradually.

Special Instructions

After the group creates a way to completely block the sunlight reaching the object, have them move back about 20 yards and then come forward quickly to recreate the shadow again.

A slightly more difficult challenge would be to have participants block the sun without touching each other. This typically involves several rows of participants, but can add an interesting and substantially more difficult variation to the process.

It takes a fair amount of contact to keep holes from opening up between participants and allowing sunlight to reach the object. Be prepared for some participants to incorporate their clothing into this activity.

Activity 5.41

Mine, Mine, Mine

Here is an activity that you can create with only a few similar objects.

What You'll Need

You will need one blindfold for every two people. As an outdoor activity, a grove of similar trees is ideal. For an indoor version, or when a grove of trees is not immediately accessible, try using potatoes, lemons, oranges, peanuts still in the shell, large woodchips or rocks.

Where to Find It

In natural settings you can probably find most of the trees or rocks nearby. Just in case though, you may want to stop by the grocery store and pick up some lemons, oranges, potatoes or peanuts.

Special Instructions

One of the most significant variations in this activity would be to have the blindfolded participant also wear any type of gloves (surgical, rubber, household cleaning, cotton gloves, mittens, an oven mit, welder's gloves, or (our favorite) the chain mail gloves worn by workers handling scrap metals and other sharp objects (typically sold only in specialty equipment stores—but really cool).

Nearly any objects that are similar, but unique will work for this activity. Pumpkins in the fall are another good choice. Tennis Balls however, would not be easily discernable. What about a sighted version of this activity where participants study a leaf, and then try to identify their leaf when it is mixed with other (numbered on the back) leaves? There is even another activity called Naturally Mine, where participants study a natural object, such as an orange, leaf, twig, blade of grass, pebble or wood chip, and try to recover this same object when it has been placed in a pile with other similar objects.

Any time a participant is blindfolded, it is a necessity to have another sighted person working directly with this individual during every phase of the activity. Wooded areas are typically filled with uneven footing, roots, rocks and other objects which can additionally challenge a blindfolded participant. If there is any concern about the risk involved, simply have participants close their eyes rather than blindfolding them. Then if the terrain becomes unsteady, the participant can simply open their eyes to regain their footing.

Activity 5.42

The Missing Page

The Missing Page is simply an interesting method for allowing the group to create their own initiative event, using whatever props are available. This activity should only be used with groups that have already experienced a variety of challenge activities, and can base a new activity on this experience. You may want to set the theme for the challenge as a problem solving, trust building, resource management, communication or physically challenging activity.

What You'll Need

For starters, you may want to have a page printed up in advance that has a portion of the challenge written on it, with a very big smudge, stain, hole or tear that effectively eliminates the ability of the participants to read this portion. The theme of the activity can be stated, as well as the intensity level. These two suggestions are typically all that experienced challenge participants need to begin creating their own activity.

Provide a collection of some standard challenge and adventure programming equipment (such as tennis balls, hoola hoops, rope, pvc tubing, short segments of 2×4's, carabiners, beach balls, blindfolds and anything else you typically carry with you) and some unique props (rubber chicken, mouse traps, a plastic halloween pumpkin, a birthday candle, dice, balloons, 100 feet of string). Be sure to include a clipboard, paper and pencil for the group to write down the activity (you never know what wonderfully creative activity may occur).

Where to Find It

Try using some (but not all) of the standard equipment that you already have in your equipment kit. This way you won't have to stock another set of "one activity" equipment.

Special Instructions

Rather than using typical challenge equipment, you might consider using some simple household items that could easily be recycled. Plastic milk jugs can be cut to create funnels, scoops and storage containers. Cardboard boxes can become signs, stepping stones or obstacles.

Be sure to keep a few unusual props ready, just in case the group needs some additional ideas to get going.

This type of free-form challenge requires the group to be familiar with challenge activities in general. Obviously this is not one of the first activities to present to your group. If you choose to include familiar objects that the group has seen used before, don't be surprised to see them using these props again in a similar way.

One of the most important moments in this activity comes when the group is asked to identify any safety related concerns with their proposed activity. It is a unique experience to watch a group work together to identify safety concerns, and then to work to eliminate any unnecessary risks.

Activity 5.43

Monumental

Monument + Mental = Monumental

The purpose of Monumental is to provide a structured method for learning spotting techniques within a group.

What You'll Need

You'll need one of the Monumental Dice for each member of the group. A stuff sack for transporting the dice would be helpful.

Where to Find It

Craft stores often supply various wooden shapes for projects. Choose the biggest hardwood cubes that you can find. You can also make your own Monumental Dice by cutting a 3.5 inch (89 mm) length from a standard cedar 4×4.

How to Make It

You can use a variety of techniques to place various Monumental patterns onto each die. An ink pen works fine, although markers will typically run and smear with the grain of the wood. A router or carving chisle comes in handy if you would like to carve these details. A woodburning pen can also be used. If you happen to choose the cedar 4 × 4 technique for making your own Monumental Dice, be sure to round all the edges to avoid splitting or chipping this soft wood.

Special Instructions

Consider some of the shapes shown below for your set of Monumental Dice. All patterns are shown only for the arm, leg and body positions. The head should always be in a natural and comfortable position. Demonstrating proper spotting techniques is essential.

Standing or lying straight 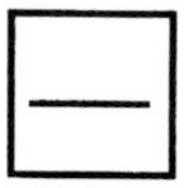

X position 

Kneeling with arms out 

Seated 

Participant can assume any position 

Spotter 

Bend at waist 

Lunge position 

Diving position 

U shape 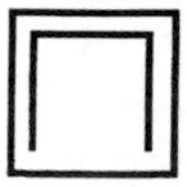

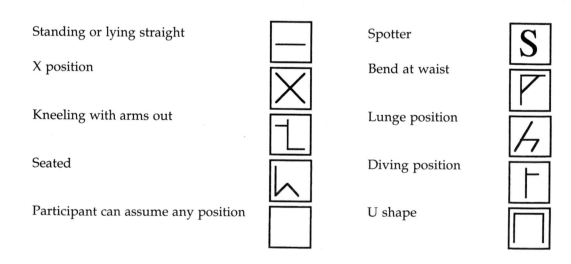

Activity 5.44

Move It or Lose It

Whatever objects you plan to use for this activity, you are going to need a whole bunch of them! If you happen to find objects that stack together or that can eventually fit into a smaller space, you will probably appreciate storing these more than 100 large boxes.

What You'll Need

You'll need quite a few identical lightweight containers. Some of our favorites are empty 2 liter soda bottles with the caps (you can use these later for making terrariums or bottle rockets—see Chapter 7), copier paper boxes and their lids (always useful for storing your stuff), or plastic film canisters with lids (which can also be used for holding small items, and for organizing large groups into smaller groups—see Chapter 5). In many places, all of these items are generally low cost or even free—but you need to start saving them now, to insure that you'll have enough when the date of your challenge program rolls around. You'll need about 100 containers total for a group of 10–12 participants. By the way, probably the most space conscious object is any type of inflatable toy. Beach balls are especially easy to find, inexpensive, and can be deflated for transport.

It is also helpful to have three ropes to mark the boundaries of the present container location, a transfer location, and the final destination location.

Where to Find It

Many photofinishing stores will donate film canisters for free. Two liter bottles carry deposits in some states, but can be collected or obtained from recycling centers.

Special Instructions

By choosing lightweight objects the risk of injury is minimized. The corners of the boxes are probably the most likely risk in this activity, and a few spotters watching the stack of swaying boxes is a good idea. These same spotters can also remove any dropped film cannisters or bottles from the path of the group as they move towards the next location. Encourage participants to pick up as many containers as they can before leaving the train, transfer zone, or the final helicopter location. If you make the rope surrounding the containers fairly small, participants will need to be more careful not to drop the containers outside the storage space.

This activity takes on a completely different character on a windy day!

Activity 5.45

Moving Towards Extinction

Moving Towards Extinction illustrates the difficulty than an organization or a society experiences when the environment changes, but their culture and methods do not.

What You'll Need

A dozen rope loops, plastic hoops, carpet circles, Raccoon Circles or plywood disks of various diameters from 1 foot (305 mm) to 3 feet (about 1 meter). No question about it, the easiest props to carry around would be either the rope loops or various size Raccoon Circles. You can squish a dozen of these into a stuff sack rather than carrying around a dozen plastic hoops or plywood disks.

Where to Find It

Use the ropes from 2B or KNOT 2B, Not Knots, Handcuffs and Shackles or even the webbing from Raccoon Circles for this activity.

How to Make It

Just tie a square knot (reef knot) to form a circle from the rope. Place these circles in a small space, allowing room for participants to walk in-between the ropes.

Special Instructions

Try to use ropes that contrast well with the surrounding ground or floor. Participants will find these more easily, and you'll be able to locate them in the grass after the activity or program is over.

Activity 5.46

Not Knots

The ropes used in the activity 2B or KNOT 2B can also be used for Not Knots. You may even want to have a rope for each participant to create a knot.

What You'll Need

Several colorful pieces of rope at least 10 feet (3 meters) long.

Where to Find It

Check out a large hardware store for a variety of different colors, diameters and textures of rope. You can also try using cable, shock cord and perhaps even chain for this activity.

How to Make It

Shown below are several ideas for Not Knots, including the devious Magician's Knot.

Special Instructions

This activity might be the perfect warm-up activity for Handcuffs and Shackles.

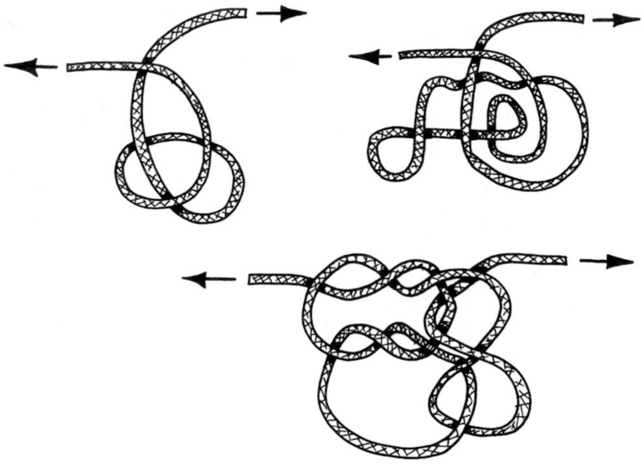

Notes

Activity 5.47

Parade

Parade is a ground level challenge activity that requires no equipment at all.

What You'll Need

Just the instructions from Chapter 4.

Activity 5.48

Plenty of Room at the Top

Back to the hardware store for the most basic of building supplies, wood and nails.

What You'll Need

20 large nails and a piece of wood.

Where to Find It

Hardware stores that also sell fencing materials or decking materials sometimes have the really large nails that make Plenty of Room at the Top a life-sized activity. Construction supply companies may also stock these extremely large nails.

How to Make It

You'll probably want the equipment for this activity to be portable, so we suggest drilling a hole that is the same diameter as the shaft of the nails you have chosen into the block of wood. Do not drill completely through the block. Now gently slide one nail into this hole, and you are ready to begin.

Special Instructions

Varying the size and quantity of nails does little to change the basic solution to this unique problem, but having several sizes of nails present at the same time can certainly add a degree of confusion. Consider using knitting needles rather than nails.

If you really want to boggle the minds of your group, give them about 70 decking nails (the really long variety), and challenge them to place all of these on the head of the single nail.

Several wild variations are also possible. In addition to the classic roof truss solution to this problem, rings can be formed from the nails to create a chain that can be hung off the solitary straight nail. Technically speaking, this solution works. It doesn't involve any external adhesives. A single ring can also be used to bundle the remaining straight nails. Finally, even without attempting this solution on the day of the equinox, one group was able to balance two large nails on the head of another, and then pile most of the remaining nails upon these two. Well done.

So if you are thinking that there is only one solution to this problem, think again. And we haven't even considered some really fun ideas like magnetizing the nails, or melting them down, or splitting the head of the single nail to form a cradle. What else can you do?

If you happen to want to use Bull Ring I as an indoor activity, you can also drill a hole in this wooden block to receive a PVC Marble Tube, on which you can rest a tennis ball for an indoor version of the Bull Ring activity. One block of wood with several functions.

Activity 5.49

A Closing Activity With Popsicle Sticks

Next time you visit your local craft store, buy a big box of these handy items. They come in boxes of 1000.

What You'll Need

Two or three popsicle or craft sticks for every participant. Something to write with such as a pen, marker or pencil. A roll of masking tape. Plan to have plenty of writing tools and popsicle sticks available at the beginning of the activity.

Where to Find It

Craft stores sells these inexpensive rounded sticks by the 1000's. You can also use medical tongue depressors.

How to Make It

The participants provide the assembly for this activity.

Special Instructions

Craft and popsicle sticks work terrific for this activity and are not very expensive. You can probably substitute other kinds of tape or string, but masking tape works just fine.

Activity 5.50

Pot of Gold

Pot of Gold involves the use of available props to retrieve a Pot of Gold which is located within a region that cannot be entered by the group.

What You'll Need

A plastic pot or bucket to use as a the Pot of Gold. The best choice is the plastic container that looks like a large metal boiling caldron, and is available at many garden centers, especially in the springtime.

Some tennis balls or brightly painted rocks can be used for the gold in the Pot of Gold. One 100 foot (30 meter) rope is need for a boundary circle. Six or more ropes roughly 6 to 20 feet (2 to 6 meters) long, that can either reach across the diamter of the boundary circle, or be tied together to reach this same distance.

A variety of additional props can be used, such as

plastic hoops, dowel rods, rubber deck rings, short boards, etc., although these props are typically of little value to the solution.

Where to Find It

While you can probably find the ropes and other equipment fairly easily at most hardware stores, the perfect Pot of Gold container is typically only sold in the springtime at most garden centers. When you find the right style for sale, consider buying several.

How to Make It

Create a large circle with the long rope. Place the Pot of Gold with gold nuggets at the center of this large circle. Place all remaining props outside the circle for the participants to use.

Special Instructions

Placing the Pot of Gold on a platform will encourage the group not to simply drag the pot. It also provides some additional challenge, as participants must have control of the pot before it begins to move from the platform, or else the gold is likely to spill out. A plastic hoop may also be used to mark the boundary beyond which the pot will sink into the mist or ashes.

Activity 5.51

Raccoon Circles

A special thanks to Dr. Tom Smith for allowing us to share this uniquely simple challenge prop that has so many uses. For more information, you can contact Dr. Tom Smith at The Raccoon Institute. The address is listed in Chapter 8.

What You'll Need

You'll need several 1 inch (25 mm) tubular webbing segments, each about 12 to 15 feet (3.5 to 4.5 meters) long. This style of webbing comes in a variety of colors and patterns.

Where to Find It

1 inch (25 mm) tubular webbing can be purchased at many outdoor shops that also stock climbing gear. There are several mail order catalogs listed in Chapter 8 that sell tubular webbing. Bruce Smith of On Rope can custom cut more than a dozen colors and patterns of Raccoon Circles.

How to Make It

A technique for tying a water knot is shown below. First tie an overhand knot at one end of the tubular webbing. The flat webbing allows the overhand knot

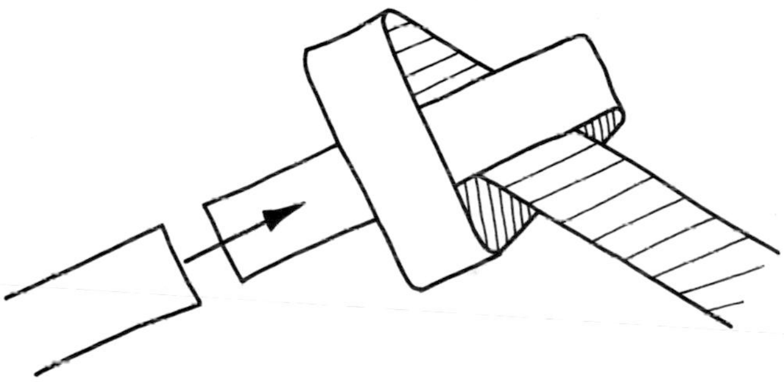

to lay flat. The other end of the rope follows the original knot in reverse. If you consider this first knot the "mentor" or model, the other end of the webbing can be used as the "student" that follows their instructor's teachings. Each end of the webbing should extend past the knot by about 2 inches (51 mm).

Special Instructions

It is useful to have a few different colors for Raccoon Circles. You may even decide to have a few different lengths, so that you may facilitate groups from 4 to 20 using the appropriate sized Raccoon Circle.

Activity 5.52

Real Estate

Here is a giant-sized puzzle, where the same pieces can be used to create a variety of shapes.

What You'll Need

Ten large wooden puzzles pieces in the geometric shapes shown below. Paint or mark the top and bottom surfaces of each piece. It may be helpful to have a string or rope to mark the border of the puzzle.

Where to Find It

Both lumber and hardware stores typically carry a variety of plywood, softwood and hardwood boards suitable for making these puzzle pieces.

How to Make It

We suggest making a cardboard version of this puzzle first, and then using these cardboard pieces as patterns for a wooden version. You can scale the illustration shown below. 1 inch equals 25.4 mm. The ten pieces shown in this first square pattern can also be used to create four other unique patterns, including a parallelogram, four bladed cross, rectangle, and a right triangle. Experiment with these pieces after cutting them out, and see what unusual shapes you can produce with them yourself.

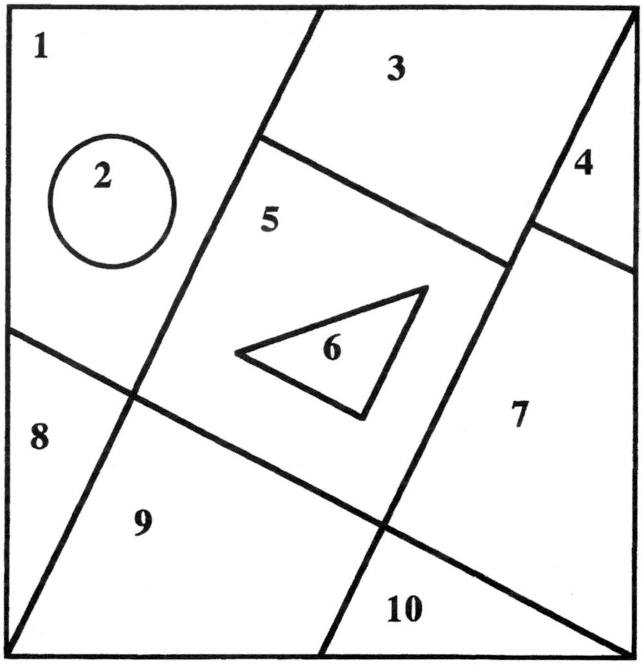

Special Instructions

If you happen to travel light, a cardboard or pine version of this puzzle will probably be the lightest.

Activity 5.53

Right Where I Belong

Here is an activity that can be used as part of a trust sequence. It provides an opportunity to experience an awareness of the group, ourselves, and our neighbors.

What You'll Need

One blindfold for each participant, although this activity can also be completed with no props at all.

Where to Find It

Directions for making blindfolds from lycra can be found in Chapter 5 just after the directions for making Lycra Tubes. These blindfolds are colorful, fit all sizes of participants, and can be washed many times without fading.

Another interesting blindfold can be made from a sleeping mask. Just use fabric paint or markers to paint eyes on the surface of the mask, and you not only have a technique for blindfolding the group, but you can group participants together by the eye colors shown on their blindfolds. Try a variety of styles (blue eyes, green eyes, brown eyes, bloodshot eyes, one eye winking, etc.)

Special Instructions

Any time you are working with blindfolded participants, it is important to choose a location that is free from any ground obstacles. Also watch the perimeter of the group to make sure that someone does not wander too far away during each mingling period.

Activity 5.54

River Crossing

The equipment for this activity takes up quite a bit of room, and is fairly heavy.

What You'll Need

Four cedar 4x4's eight feet long, two long ropes for marking boundaries, and at least eight wooden platforms. The nesting wooden platforms used for All Aboard can be used for this activity, or a collection of single sized platforms (which are just the 12 inch (305 mm) square platforms from the All Aboard nesting platforms).

Where to Find It

Probably the most difficult to locate item in this activity are the four finished cedar 4x4's. These items are fairly expensive, but necessary for this activity. The light weight and strength of these beams is needed to support the weight of several participants at one time. Pressure treated beams are simply too heavy for most participants to handle conveniently. If you happen to locate only rough cut cedar 4x4's, you can sand these smooth with a portable belt sander. Be sure to round off all the edges of these 4x4's. Participants will be handling these with their bare hands, and all sharp or split edges must be made smooth. Not all hardware stores carry cedar 4x4's, so try looking at a lumber supply center or your nearest sawmill.

How to Make It

The directions for making the wooden platforms are found in the All Aboard section of this chapter. If you choose to use only the smaller single sized platforms, you'll need to make at least 8 of the platforms named Platform 2 in Section 5. 08.

A layout for the minimum number of platforms (eight) is shown below. Participants must move from the lower left-hand side of this layout, to the upper right-hand side, using only the 4x4's for connecting the platforms.

Special Instructions

Cedar 4x4's are very strong and substantially lighter than pressure treated materials. But even the cedar 4x4's can be awkward to handle, so encourage good lifting practices. As a spotter, some groups may require your assistance with the placement of a 4x4 from time to time. Consider using shorter 4x4's to additionally lighten the weight of these props.

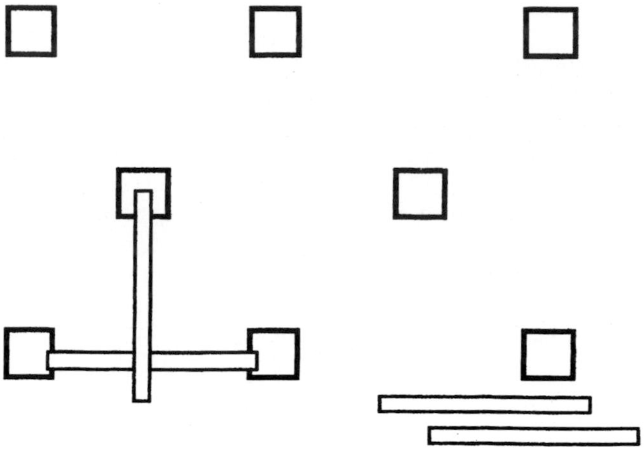

Activity 5.55

Shark Attack

This is a portable version of All Aboard that travels with the group during their adventure experience. You can also use these props for makeshift tables, chairs, clipboards, presentation surfaces, and other adventure programming needs.

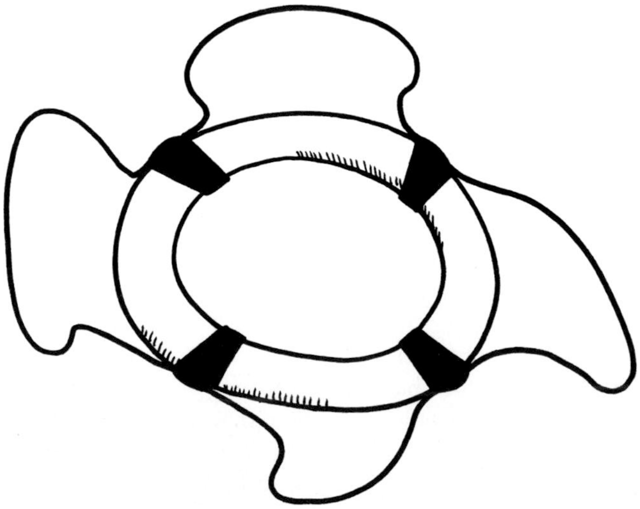

What You'll Need

You'll need one or more plywood cutouts made from the nautical patterns shown below. These patterns can be scaled to any size to fit the requirements of your group. ¾ inch (19 mm) plywood is heavy, but will hold up the longest for these shapes. Include a slot in each pattern for a carrying handle. You can use the ropes on the ring buoys design for carrying handles.

Where to Find It

You can make two ring buoys, the boat profile and the fish profile from a single 4 by 8 foot (1.2 by 2.4 meter) piece of ¾ inch (19 mm) plywood. Check your hardware store for this material. Some stores will even cut the plywood to a more easily managed size for a modest fee.

How to Make It

The shapes shown below are simply suggestions for this activity. None of the dimensions are critical, although it is probably a good idea not to cut any fine details or thin shapes that could easily break off under the weight of 8 participants. The patterns shown here are scaled so that 1 inch (25.4 mm) is equal to 1 foot (305 mm).

Place a slot in the boat and fish patterns for easy handling. This slot should be an oval shape that is 2 inches (51 mm) wide by 5 inches (127 mm) long, with rounded ends. You can begin this slot by drilling two 2 inch (51 mm) diameter holes exactly 3 inches (76 mm) apart. Then use a keyhole or scroll saw to remove the middle portion of the slot. Be sure to round all corners and smooth all exposed edges to form a comfortable handhold.

Painting the ring buoy two contrasting colors and attaching a rope gives this prop a true nautical feeling.

Special Instructions

Smooth all edges of these profiles, and provide handholds where necessary for carrying these props. You may even want to include other features on these boards that you can use with other challenge and adventure activities.

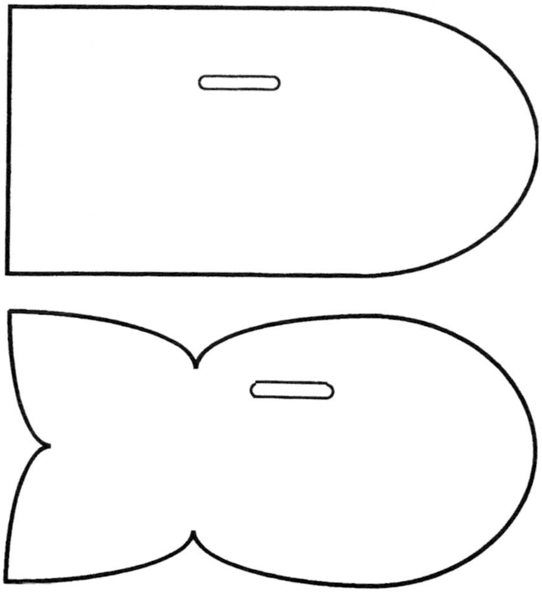

Activity 5.56

Simply Amazing

A simple activity in which the entire group is blindfolded.

What You'll Need

For starters, you'll need a grove of trees with fairly level ground. There just isn't a decent replacement for this setting. Somehow poles and fenceposts just don't work as well as a real forest. Next you'll need about 400 feet (122 meters) of ¼ inch (6 mm) poly rope to form the outline of the maze. You also need blindfolds for each participant, and a unique toy or tactile object that can be attached somewhere along the rope.

Where to Find It

Hardware, marine and construction equipment stores may sell poly rope by the spool. Spools typically come in lengths of 500 to 2500 feet (152 to 762 meters).

How to Make It

Create a border around the perimeter of the grove with the poly rope, about 40 inches (1 meter) off the ground. You can also add some interior paths for the group to follow. Attach the object to be found to the rope in a location where it will not be immediately found.

Special Instructions

The simplest way to begin this activity is with all group members blindfolded, and touching the rope boundary to the maze. Evenly distribute the group

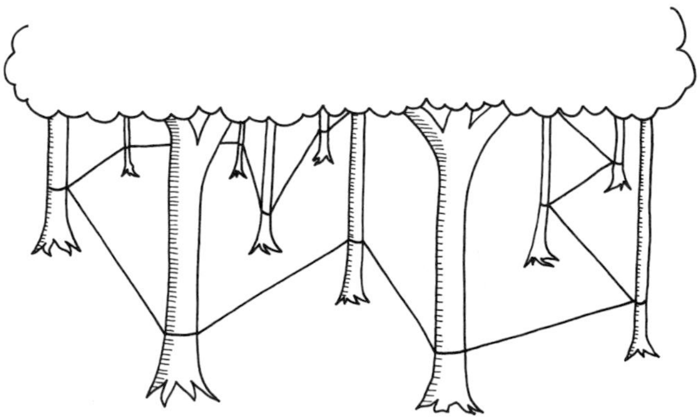

throughout the maze area. Then place the object to be found along the rope. Try placing the object onto the rope where the rope runs behind a tree. This will encourage the group to search carefully along the full length of the rope, not merely the portion of the rope running between each tree.

The "surface" or exit to the maze can be marked with a rope, bell or other tactile object. You can even mark the surface or exit location with aftershave lotion or perfume, to provide an aromatic solution to this challenge. It is a good idea to encourage participants to all reach the exit at the same time, and to make sure that they have all the members of their group. During the initial planning stages where communication is possible, it would probably be a good idea for the group to plan their exit strategy.

The most obvious concern with this activity is to make sure that the zone defined by the rope is free from any hazards that a blindfolded person may encounter, such as tree roots, low branches, uneven footing, spider webs, etc.

A second, less obvious point, is to blindfold the group prior to reaching the maze, so that participants have no idea of the exact shape or size of the maze. Bringing the group into the center of the maze, and let the group "find" the rope. They can then decide whether to stay together or separate to find the object.

For safety reasons, no participant is allowed to climb under or over any rope. From the time of first contact, participants should always be in contact with the rope.

Activity 5.57

Strange Attraction

Strange Attraction uses a modified version of a Bull Ring.

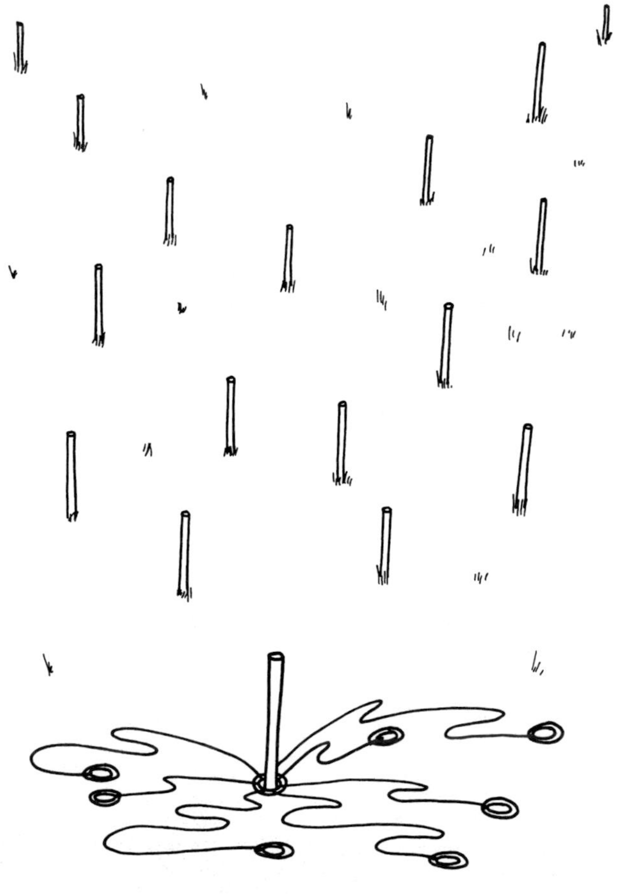

What You'll Need

A variation on the Bull Ring, but this time with unequal length strings and an additional metal ring at the end of every string. This device is called the connector.

You'll also need about 2 dozen PVC marble tubes or 1 inch (25 mm) diameter wooden stakes that are 15 inches (380 mm) long.

You'll need one string/ring attached to the connector and at least one stake for each person in the group.

Finally, you'll need two ropes to mark the boundary at the beginning and end of phase space.

Where to Find It

Most hardware stores carry both metal rings and mason twine for making the connector. One piece metal rings, key rings, and even larger metal washers can be used to create the connector. PVC marble tubes can be used in areas where the ground is soft enough to allow insertion. Wooden stakes or dowel rods with a sharp end can be used in tougher ground.

How to Make It

To make the connector, begin with a single metal ring at the center, just like the ones used to make a Bull Ring. Attach as many pieces of string to this middle ring as there are participants in the group. The length of each piece of string should vary from 2 feet (610 mm) to 12 feet (3.5 meters). If the size of the groups vary, permanently attach only a few strings to the middle ring, and attach all other string/rings with a snap swivel, paper clip, safety pin, miniture caribiner or other quick attachment device.

Special Instructions

This activity doesn't work well indoors, unless there is a technique for attaching the stakes to the floor so that they do not slide or move.

Be sure to keep a few extra strings/rings that you can tie on just in case you have more participants than planned. Attaching the strings to the central ring with fishing snaps, minature carabiners or even safety pins is one way to make quick additions or deletions to the total number of rings.

Make sure to pound the stakes well into the ground. There is likely to be some pulling and tugging on the strings, and a floppy stake (critical point) is just mathematically hard to deal with in phase space.

The location of the stakes is not critical (no chaos terminology humor intended). But it is desireable to place the stakes in such a way that the group must choose wisely which rings are placed on which stakes, or they will not be able to complete their journey. It is always possible to place a long string/ring, onto a nearby stake, but it isn't possible to stretch a short string/ring to reach a stake that is still a short distance away. Try to create two possible paths. One that has stakes appropriately placed so that participants can reach the other side, and the second path with two stakes that are just a little too far apart for any of the rings to reach.

Activity 5.58

Stretch It

Some rope, an innertube and an empty bleach bottle and you have the basics for Stretch It.

What You'll Need

You will need a 6 inch (152 mm) inner tube from a wheelbarrow tire. Eight to twelve pieces of soft rope, such as a cotton clothesline or 3/8 inch (9 mm) derby rope. A sturdy plastic gallon jug, three fourths full of water, such as a bleach bottle or other gallon cleaner bottle. A tree stump, or wooden platform, or a five gallon bucket placed upside down, or a four gallon milk crate. A 50 foot (15 meter) length of rope for a boundary marker.

Where to Find It

The pointed style bleach bottle is the perfect shape for Stretch It. The plastic bottles that contain windshield wiper fluid also are a good shape. If your hardware stores doesn't have an innertube for a wheelbarrow, try a lawn tractor store, or even a garden supply shop.

How to Make It

Tie one end of each rope securely around the innertube. Fill the bottle about half full with water, and replace the cap. Place the bottle on top of the wooden platform, tree stump or crate. With the 50 foot (15 meter) long rope, create a boundary circle with the bottle and platform at the center.

Special Instructions

The participants will be tugging on the ropes with quite a bit of force, so securely tie these ropes to the inner tube.

Activity 5.59

Stretching the Limit

Here is an activity that can be performed with or without props.

What You'll Need

Any combination of random props such as short segments of rope, broomsticks, dowel rods, sticks, string, etc. These objects can be placed in the vacinity of the playing field, so that they are reachable by the group. A pole or other "anchor" point is also useful, and you'll need a container to retrieve. On a hot day, a container filled with beverages will be appreciated by the group.

Where to Find It

Most of this equipment is probably already in your equipment kit. Try to use any of the props already available.

How to Make It

Scatter the objects throughout the playing field, including in the opposite direction of where the group is headed. Wasn't Christopher Columbus one of the first challenge and adventure participants to head west to get east?

Special Instructions

Discourage participants from attempting to utilize any natural objects, such as tearing branches from small trees and bushes.

Activity 5.60

Stump Jumping

A circular challenge, with circular disks.

What You'll Need

You'll need enough circular objects for each participant to stand on. These can be wooden disks (plywood works best), carpet circles, thin sections cut from a 12 inch (305 mm) diameter log, paper plates, flying disks, or even the plastic lids from 5 gallon buckets. Place these disks in a circular pattern on the ground where they will not slide. Do not attempt this activity on pavement, hardwood floors, or other surfaces which may allow the disks to move.

Where to Find It

While logs are certainly the most natural looking disks, the lids from 5 gallon buckets are our favorite. You can find these lids on drywall compound containers (make friends with your local carpenter or building contractor), and also on the storage containers of many types of food service supplies (make friends with your local restaurant, cafeteria, hospital or school). We happen to use the lids from large pickle containers. You can drill a ½ inch (12 mm) hole in the center of each disk and pass a rope through to carry them away and to keep them together during storage, after the activity is completed.

How to Make It

Create a circular pattern with the disks. The distance between each disk should be no more than about 18 inches (450 mm).

Special Instructions

It is essential to use disks that have a non-skid surface, and that won't slide along the surface of the floor or ground where they are placed.

A variation that provides a considerable challenge to the group is to vary the spacing between each of the disks. This requires participants to vary their jump distances every step of the journey, rather than settling into a continuous pattern.

In addition to simply moving forward around the circle, have the group build a pattern of jumps, such as two jumps foreword, then one jump backwards.

Have every other participant around the circle face the opposite direction. This means that some participants will be jumping forewords while others are jumping backwards.

Activity 5.61

Surfing the Web I

The classic vertical web pattern that has graced so many challenge courses around the world.

What You'll Need

100 feet (30 meters) of ¼ inch (6 mm) poly rope to form a framework between two trees or poles that are about 30 to 40 feet (9 to 12 meters) apart. 80 feet (24 meters) of 3⁄16 inch (4 mm) shock cord to create the web pattern.

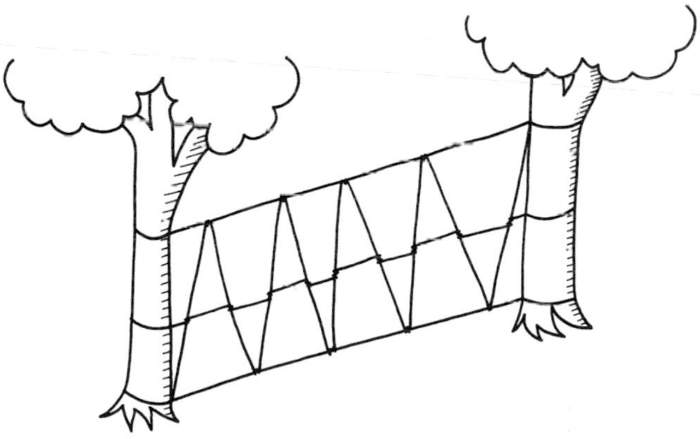

Where to Find It

While hardware stores typically carry a variety of ropes, you may need to visit a marine (boating) store to find shock cord in long lengths. Sometimes shock cord can also be found at stores that carry climbing equipment, and at military surplus stores.

How to Make It

First create a frame for the web with the ¼ inch (6 mm) poly rope. This frame should extend between the two trees, and be pulled tightly. The bottom rope should be very near the ground, and the top rope no more than 7 feet (2.1 meters) high. At the end of this chapter you'll find a unique technique for tensioning this rope frame for the web.

Next begin to make a series of triangular shapes with the shock cord between the upper and lower frame ropes. Complete the web by passing the shock cord through the middle height of the web. See the illustration below for details.

Special Instructions

Directions for tensioning this web can be found at the end of this chapter.

There are a variety of ways that you can Surf the Web. In fact, four more variations of this activity follow this version.

For this classic vertical web pattern, providing various size openings can challenge the group in different ways. Be sure to allow enough opening for the largest members of the group the pass through safely. If there are concerns about lifting participants, try placing plenty of openings near ground level. If there appear to be too many openings, instead of closing any, or altering the web, try having the participants pass through several objects, such as 4x4's, picnic coolers, storage boxes, stuff sacks, an open umbrella, an inflated beach ball, etc.

In addition to watching the web for contact, you can add a bell so that contact is more easily noted.

You can consider allowing one participant to go underneath the web. This can be quite useful to a group member with limited mobility through the web.

Be especially cautious near the roots of trees. The footing is uneven here and not suitable for passage. Encourage participants to stick to the middle regions of the web, far away from trees or support poles.

Activity 5.62

Surfing the Web II

An inclined version of the web that can be made from the same materials.

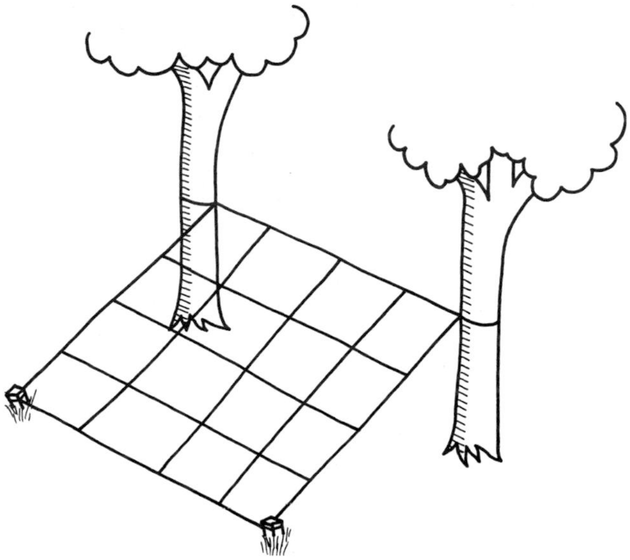

What You'll Need

100 feet (30 meters) of ¼ inch (6 mm) poly rope to form a framework between four trees or poles that form a square, and are about 15 to 20 feet (4.6 to 6.1 meters) apart. An additional 100 feet (30 meters) of poly rope or about 80 feet (24 meters) of 3⁄16 inch (4 mm) shock cord can be used to create the grid-like web pattern. Two tent stakes can be used instead of two trees for the lowest side of the web.

Where to Find It

While hardware stores typically carry a variety of ropes, you may need to visit a marine (boating) store to find shock cord in long lengths. Sometimes shock cord can also be found at stores that carry climbing equipment, and at military surplus stores. Pick up a few tent stakes while you are there. There may be times when you don't have four trees for this activity, but you can still create this inclined web with two trees and two tent stakes.

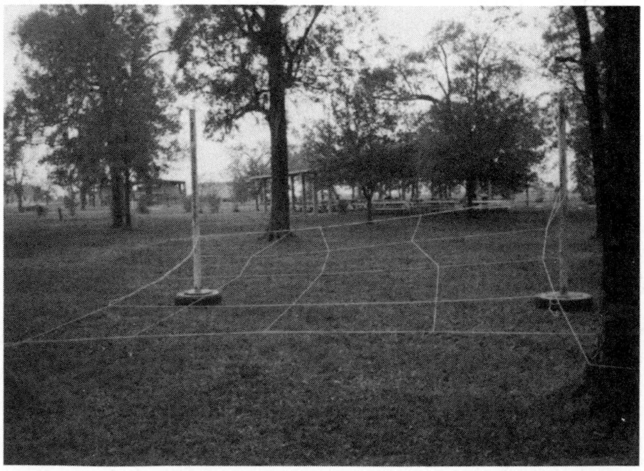

How to Make It

First create an inclined frame for the web with the ¼ inch (6 mm) poly rope. This rope frame should extend between the four trees, and be pulled tightly. See the illustration below for details.

Next make a series of square grids in the web with either more ¼ inch (6 mm) poly rope, or the shock cording. Each square opening should be about 27 inches (685 mm) square.

The starting side of the inclined web should be near ground level, and the top exit side of the inclined web should be no more than 40 inches (1 meter) high. If you happen to have a group where the height of the participants changes dramatically, consider making the top side of the inclined web at a slight angle. So that one side is higher than the other, and participants can choose which side to enter, based on their abilities to exit successfully.

Special Instructions

There are a variety of ways that you can Surf the Web. In fact, four more variations of this activity follow this version.

In addition to watching the web for contact, you can add a bell so that contact is more easily noted.

For the inclined web, allow participants to trade their one burrowing move with other participants. This bartering can be an interesting point for processing after the event.

There can be no diagonal movement between web openings in this version of Surfing the Web. Also, various paths can be restricted by taping off an opening, or only allowing participants to pass straight through the web.

Use spotters everywhere, but especially at the exit side of the web. The height of this side should not be more than 40 inches (1 meter) tall.

Activity 5.63

Surfing the Web III

Here is a horizontal version of a web that can be made from the same materials as the other webs in this chapter.

What You'll Need

100 feet (30 meters) of ¼ inch (6 mm) poly rope to form a framework between four trees or poles that are in the shape of a large rectangle. An additional 100 feet (30 meters) of poly rope or about 80 feet (24 meters) of 3/16 inch (4 mm) shock cord are needed to create the horizontal web pattern. A few objects can be placed in the web for the group to retrieve as they navigate the web.

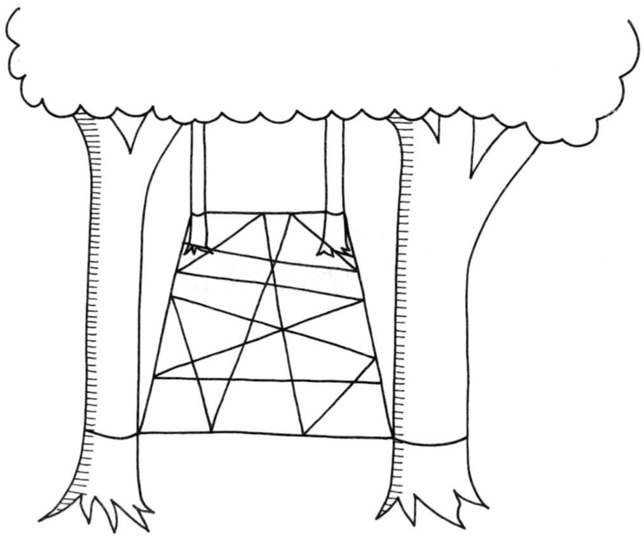

Where to Find It

While hardware stores typically carry a variety of ropes, you may need to visit a marine (boating) store to find shock cord in long lengths. Sometimes shock cord can also be found at stores that carry climbing equipment, and at military surplus stores.

How to Make It

First create a frame for the web with the ¼ inch (6 mm) poly rope. This frame should extend between the two trees, and be pulled tightly. This frame should be between 12 and 20 inches (305 and 508 mm) off the ground.

Next begin making a grid or web pattern with either more poly rope or the shock cord. See the illustration below for details.

Special Instructions

There are a variety of ways that you can Surf the Web. In fact, four more variations of this activity follow this version.

See the techniques at the end of this chapter for tensioning the rope framework of this horizontal web.

In addition to watching the web for contact, you can add a bell so that contact is more easily noted.

Requiring participants to always be connected during the activity works when the height of the horizontal web is between 12 and 20 inches (305 to 508 mm). Webs that are in the range of 20 to 30 inches (508 to 762 mm) requires additional spotting and the necessity for occasionally losing contact as participants move from one square to the next.

Objects placed within the web should be lightweight and retrievable with one hand.

Activity 5.64

Surfing the Web IV

Here is a 3-D web that that provides additional challenges for most groups, and still uses the same equipment to create as the other webs in this chapter.

What You'll Need

You'll need about 600 feet (183 meters) of ¼ inch (6 mm) poly rope to form the framework and web strands between four trees or poles that are about 10 to 15 feet (3 to 4.6 meters) apart, and roughly in the shape of a square. Some additional shock cord will keep this 3-D web under tension, and allow some latitude for when those four trees begin moving in the wind.

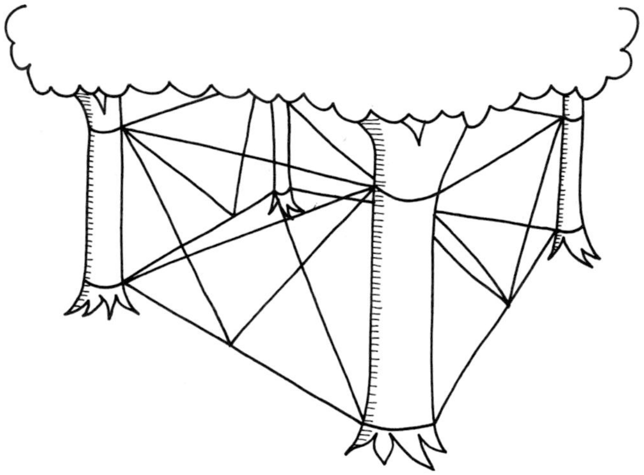

Where to Find It

While hardware stores typically carry a variety of ropes, you may need to visit a marine (boating) store to find shock cord in long lengths. Sometimes shock cord can also be found at stores that carry climbing equipment, and at military surplus stores.

How to Make It

First create a room-sized frame for the web with the ¼ inch (6 mm) poly rope. This frame should extend between the four trees, and be pulled moderately tight. The lower frame rope should be at ground level, while the upper frame rope should be about 8 feet (2.4 meters) high. See the sketch below for details.

Next, use more poly rope or shock cord to create a series of internal web fibers, filling much of the interior space in this 3-D version of the web.

Special Instructions

There are a variety of ways that you can Surf the Web. In fact, four more variations of this activity follow this version.

In addition to watching the web for contact, you can add a bell so that contact is more easily noted.

Be especially cautious near the roots of trees. The footing is uneven here and not suitable for passage. Encourage participants to stick to the middle regions of the web, far away from trees or support poles.

In addition to the various cords and ropes that are a part of this 3-D web, consider adding some additional strings with bells or other sound producing objects. Ask participants to retrieve some objects within the 3-D web. Some of these objects can be larger than the actual size of the web openings.

The entire group can pass through the web while connected, or smaller strands or chains of participants can attempt to retrieve specific objects within the web.

Notes

Activity 5.65

Surfing the Web V

Here is a final version featuring a combination of web configurations. In this variation of Surfing the Web, the group is split, and participants must decide where and when to enter the web, so that they can assist other members of their group.

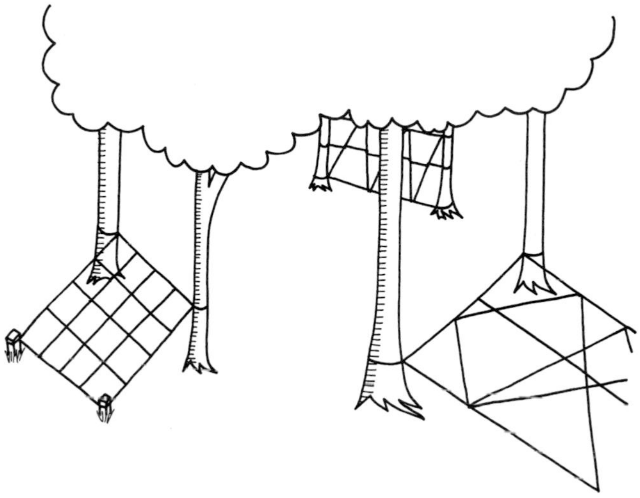

What You'll Need

Enough poly rope and shock cord for two or three different web configurations. See the illustration below, and see the previous pages for instructions on how to make each of the individual web patterns.

Where to Find It

While hardware stores typically carry a variety of ropes, you may need to visit a marine (boating) store to find shock cord in long lengths. Sometimes shock cord can also be found at stores that carry climbing equipment, and at military surplus stores.

How to Make It

See the previous pages in the chapter for instructions on how to make each of the individual web patterns.

Special Instructions

Finding a group of trees that is ideally spaced can be a real problem when facilitating a portable challenge and adventure program. Don't forget to pack a few wooden stakes just in case, for the inclined and horizontal web patterns.

Activity 5.66

Target Specifications

Here is another activity that only requires a few simple props.

What You'll Need

A blindfold, two rope loops, a long rope, and a variety of soft items such as beachballs, tennis balls, racket balls, water balloons, red playground balls, frisbees, hoseplay balls, paper airplanes, nerf footballs, pillows, foam sections, paper plates and the authors' favorite: a rubber chicken.

Where to Find It

Raccoon Circles work well for both the loop that the blindfolded participant stands in, and the flexible loop carried by the receiving team. Have several diameters of rope loops for the receiving team. Smaller loops make this activity significantly more challenging. The long rope used for A Collection of Knots, Tree of Knots, Pot of Gold or Community Jump Rope can be used to define the boundary circle. Other props probably can already be found somewhere in your equipment box, or in any nearby toy box.

How to Make It

The blindfolded participant stands inside a small rope circle which is surrounded by a 20 to 30 foot (6 to 9 meter) boundary circle. The receiving team grasps their rope loop and must stay outside the boundary circle. The size of the receiving team's rope loops can range from a maximum of 4 feet (1.2 meters) in diameter down to a minimum size of about 1 foot (305 mm) in diameter. The collection of soft throwable props should be near the blindfolded participant.

Special Instructions

Never use an object which could cause an injury to the receiving team if a participant happened to connect with the object.

Have several loops ready, including some very challenging small diameter loops. See if the group can successfully handle the smallest diameter loop available.

Activity 5.67

Tennis Ball Mountain

Make friends with your local tennis club manager. Eventually you are going to need about 150 tennis balls.

What You'll Need

150 or more clean, dry tennis balls. If tennis balls are unavailable, try using a variety of other sports balls. The more variety the better. A reasonable alternative to tennis balls are plastic whiffle golf balls.

Where to Find It

Some tennis clubs are willing to donate or sell used tennis balls at a reasonable cost. One of the best times to approach a tennis club for tennis ball donations is just after a major tournament or class session. Some tennis clubs have a special collection box for "dead" tennis balls.

Activity 5.68

The Boardroom

The Boardroom requires some fairly heavy equipment for a portable activity. Hope you have room in your vehicle for all this stuff.

What You'll Need

A wooden platform or plastic hoop or Raccoon Circle for the central Boardroom of this initiative. You'll also need a minimum of four 2×8 inch boards, at least 6 feet (1.8 meters) long. If you happen to have two sets of Boardwalking boards, you can use these. You can also use the oak planks recommended for A Balanced Life. You can also design these boards so that you may also use them for Log Rolling. The 4×4's used for River Crossing are probably too narrow for this activity, unless you can use two of these 4×4's placed side-by-side for each row of participants.

Where to Find It

Use standard dimensional lumber from a hardware or lumber store. Unless you plan to leave this equipment out in the weather, there is no need for utilizing the more expensive and heavier pressure or salt-treated woods.

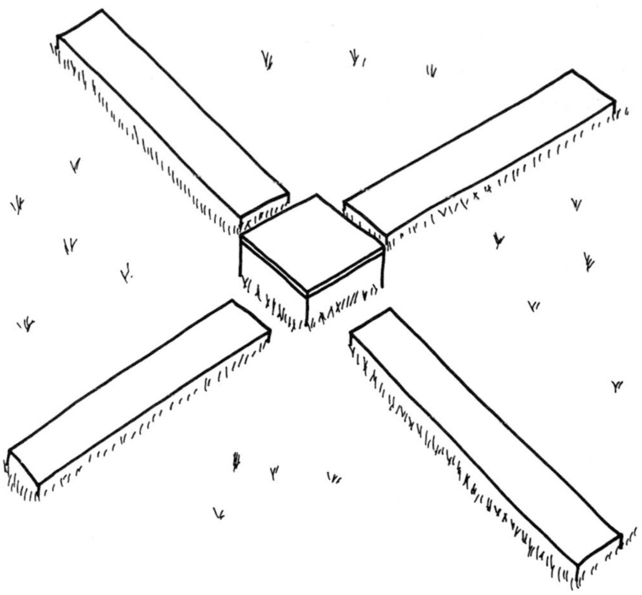

How to Make It

While most dimensional lumber boards come in a variety of lengths, you may want to choose a length that conveniently fits into your vehicle. 6 foot (1.8 meter) long boards are a recommended minimum length for this activity. 2×8's are also recommended rather than narrower 2×6's. You can use one of the larger All Aboard platforms for the central Boardroom.

If you happen to be using a total of four boards for your version of The Boardroom, place these boards at the 3, 6, 9 and 12 o'clock positions around the central platform or hoop, as shown in the illustration.

Special Instructions

Dimensional lumber can be slippery when wet. Be sure to use this activity only with dry surfaces.

Activity 5.69

The Paper Chase

Here is an activity you can lead at the office or school, even if you happen to forget the rest of your challenge and adventure programming equipment.

What You'll Need

A piece of paper for each person in the group. Size is not critical, but an averaged size 8½ by 11 inch (A4) page is fine.

Where to Find It

Even pages from a magazine or newspaper will work in a pinch.

How to Make It

The participants do most of the work here.

Special Instructions

Rather than making airplanes out of the paper, try making just a simple ball. You can use a variety of papers including wrapping paper, cardboard, newsprint, aluminum foil, old greeting cards, magazines or newspapers. You can also give participants more than one sheet of paper so that they can make one very large ball. Paper balls have less sharp edges than paper airplanes, and are probably a better all-around choice. Your group is likely to have a higher success rate catching paper balls than paper airplanes.

Another approach would be to use this activity as a teachable moment, and have the participants make a collection of origami animals to toss about. This may take a while longer to complete, but you won't be filling up any trashcans with left-over papers. Most folks will want to take home their creations.

Activity 5.70

Time Tunnel

First Lycra Tubes made from lycra, then really cool lycra blindfolds. Now a long tube made from this material for the activity Time Tunnel.

What You'll Need

The Time Tunnel is made from 5 to 10 yards (4.5 to 9 meters) of nylon lycra. While the Lycra Tube is made by joining the ends (width direction) of the lycra, the Time Tunnel is made by joining the top and bottom (length direction) of the lycra.

Where to Find It

Nylon lycra is a fairly expensive material. You can often find it on sale during the fall and winter months. Color is really unimportant, although darker colors will hide dirt and grass stains better than lighter colors. Use the 60 inch (1.5 meter) wide fabric for creating the Time Tunnel. 5 yards (4.6 meters) is the minimum length for this activity, 10 yards (9 meters) is more than long enough. Fabric stores, especially those featuring end bolts or remnants, are good choices for inexpensive lycra. Several shorter lengths of different color lycra fabric may be joined together to create a colorful Time Tunnel. These different colors may give participants some indication of how far along they are in the Time Tunnel.

How to Make It

Create the Time Tunnel from a length of nylon lycra by sewing a french seam. A sketch is presented below showing the three steps to creating this seam. First make a seam about ⅜ inch (9 mm) in from the long edge of the lycra, the full length of the tunnel. There is no need to use elastic thread if you simply stretch the lycra as it is being sewn. For this first pass, the lycra tunnel is right side out.

For the second step, turn the tunnel inside-out. Now sew a second seam the full length of the tunnel about ½ inch (12 mm) from the edge, stretching the lycra as the seam is created.

Finally, turn the tunnel right side out, and sew the flap flat against one side of the Time Tunnel. For this long length of lycra, it may be necessary to sew this flap from both ends of the tunnel.

This completes the stitching for the Time Tunnel.

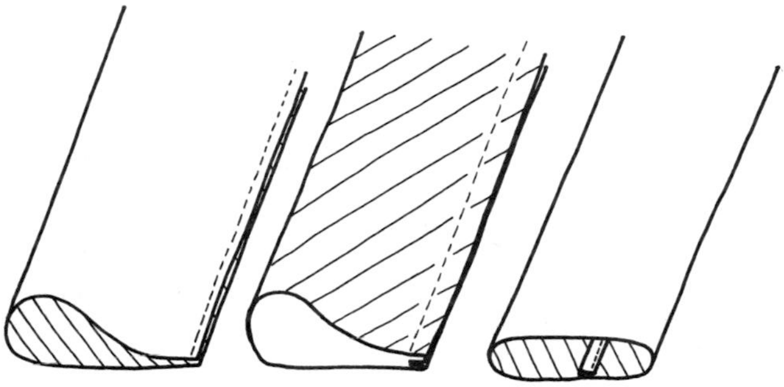

Special Instructions

Cotton lycra is not a suitable replacement for nylon lycra. Be sure to stretch the lycra while sewing each portion of the seam.

Notes

Activity 5.71

Tower Building

There are a variety of materials that can be used to create some pretty impressive structures.

What You'll Need

Several sets of any commercially available construction set equipment, usually found in toy stores. Other possibilities include plastic drinking straws and scotch tape, or cardboard tubes and masking tape, or uncooked spaghetti and marshmallows. Storage containers for each of these pieces.

Where to Find It

Well, for once you won't be going off to the hardware store. For this activity, you'll need to head for the toy store, the grocery store or the stationery store. If you plan to use the same equipment more than once, better use the wooden or plastic construction toys. If you only plan to use the equipment once, straws, spaghetti, cardboard tubes and tape are easy to find and not very expensive.

How to Make It

Lucky for the facilitator, the participants perform most of the assembly. You will need to supply the same number of components to each group. Having suitable storage bags, stuff sacks or plastic containers is convenient. These containers can even become part of the tower.

Special Instructions

Don't be afraid to try some unusual stuff. How about using large pretzel sticks? Or maybe using cooked spaghetti to lash uncooked spaghetti together with.

If you happen to be using commercial toys and construction sets, set aside a few extra pieces for spare parts. Every now and then you'll probably come up missing a piece or two. If you planned ahead, you won't need to buy a whole new set just to replace a few missing pieces.

Activity 5.72

Traffic Circle

You'll need just a single rope loop for this activity.

What You'll Need

This activity requires a 2 foot (610 mm) diameter rope loop or plastic hoop. If you make a double loop with a Raccoon Circle, you'll have the right size circle for the center of the group.

Where to Find It

Any rope loop or plastic hoop will work fine for this activity. No need to purchase a special prop just for Traffic Circle.

Special Instructions

You can also use a large plywood disk on non-slippery surfaces, sidewalk chalk on playgrounds or pavement, and masking tape to make a circle on an indoor floor.

Notes

___

___

___

Activity 5.73

Tree of Knots

This activity provides an answer to the question, "what can I do with 30 feet (9 meters) of rope?"

What You'll Need

30 feet (9 meters) of rope approximately ⅜ inch to 1 inch (9 to 25 mm) in diameter. This activity can be performed with a longer rope if necessary. This activity also requires a tree or pole.

Where to Find It

Some of the most colorful rope in the North American region is manufactured by Wellington and Lehigh. Hardware stores and marine (boating) supply stores typically carry a variety of ropes.

How to Make It

Not much to do here. Just make sure that the rope you choose is colorfast, and that the ends of the rope have been spliced or sealed so that the rope does not unravel with use.

Special Instructions

Larger diameter ropes work better than smaller diameter ropes for this activity.

Activity 5.74

Under Cover

If you happen to use a cloth tarp or lycra tube to define the space for Danger Zone or Blackout or Midnight Sun, you can use that same prop for Under Cover. This activity actually follows Danger Zone nicely.

What You'll Need

A tarp, blanket, or a large square of cloth, at least 15 feet (4.5 meters) square. Lay this material perfectly flat on the surface of the ground or floor.

Where to Find It

Large fabric tarps, blankets and cloth can be found at hardware, fabric and military surplus stores. One of the easiest to store materials, and one that is very breathable, is military netting or screening material. This material is lightweight, folds up easily, stores in a small space, and is sure to provide everyone Under Cover with adequate breathing room.

How to Make It

Not much to do here. Just have a large rectangle of fabric, and lay it flat on the ground before the group.

Special Instructions

For obvious safety reasons, plastic cloth (such as a shower curtain, plastic bags or waterproof tarps) should not be used because these materials pose a safety risk for suffocation. Only open weave cloths, fabrics or screening materials should be used for Under Cover.

Encourage participants not to squish any of the other participants under the cloth.

Activity 5.75

Under the Doormat

Under the Doormat has more to do with personal space than with keys, but provides an interesting dilemma for two people.

What You'll Need

A piece of carpeting about 8 inches (200 mm) square. Two keys, coins or buttons. Place the keys below the carpeting before participants step on. You may want to have a variety of carpet sizes if you happen to have a variety of participant sizes.

Where to Find It

Carpet stores often have extra carpet samples and scrap pieces that are perfect for Under the Doormat.

How to Make It

Rectangular carpets are probably the most reasonable shapes for this activity, although other shapes, such as circles, triangles, stars and ovals might create some interesting variations.

Special Instructions

Be sure to use a carpet or rug material that will not slip on the floor or ground.

Notes

Activity 5.76

Universe

Here is an activity that has some scientific content, perfect for a classroom setting.

What You'll Need

The chart shown below shows the relative sizes and distances between the planets and the sun in our solar system. You may want to construct a length of string with knots or labels at the location of each planet, and fasten this string to the ground with a tent stake at the location of the sun.

Where to Find It

Check your library for books on astronomy, the solar system, stars and space travel.

Special Instructions

For this challenge 32.8 feet (10 meters) will be equivalent to 93,000,000 miles. That means that the distance between the Sun and Pluto will be almost 400 meters or roughly one quarter mile apart. This distance will clearly show just how far apart objects in space really are. If that distance is too far for your group to conveniently use, just reduce the 395 meter value by a factor of ten, to produce 39.5 meters, which is a distance of about 130 feet.

Notes

Scaled Distances

(1 meter (m) = 9,300,000 miles)
(1 millimeter (mm) = 9,300 miles)

Object	Diameter	Distance from Sun
Sun	110 mm	0 m
Mercury	0.3 mm	4 m
Venus	0.8 mm	7 m
Earth	0.8 mm	10 m
Mars	0.4 mm	15 m
Jupiter	9.4 mm	52 m
Saturn	7.1 mm	95 m
Uranus	3.1 mm	192 m
Neptune	3.0 mm	301 m
Pluto	1.0 mm	395 m

Activity 5.77

Villages and Wells

Having 9 ropes is essential for this activity, but you can use about anything to represent the three villages and three wells.

What You'll Need

Three objects to represent three villages, and three additional objects to represent the three wells. The wooden platforms from River Crossing or All Aboard can be used. So can flying disks, plastic hoops, Raccoon Circles, or any other moderately large and flat objects. Also needed are a total of nine ropes at least 15 feet (4.6 meters) long, although ropes that are 20 feet (6.1 meters) long would allow for more creativity, and occassionally more creative cheating. If you really want to challenge the group, use a combination of ropes (which bend) and PVC tubing (which doesn't bend).

Where to Find It

Hopefully you won't have to carry additional equipment just to represent the villages and wells. Try using some of the other props already in your possession. Using a variety of colored ropes is beneficial for this activity. Wellington and Lehigh make a variety of colors of Derby style rope. Some hardware stores will order these brands directly on request, although you may have to buy quite a bit to make it worthwhile. You can also use old climbing ropes that have been retired for this activity.

How to Make It

Create a pattern of 3 villages in a row, and three 3 wells in a row, like the dots that signify the number 6

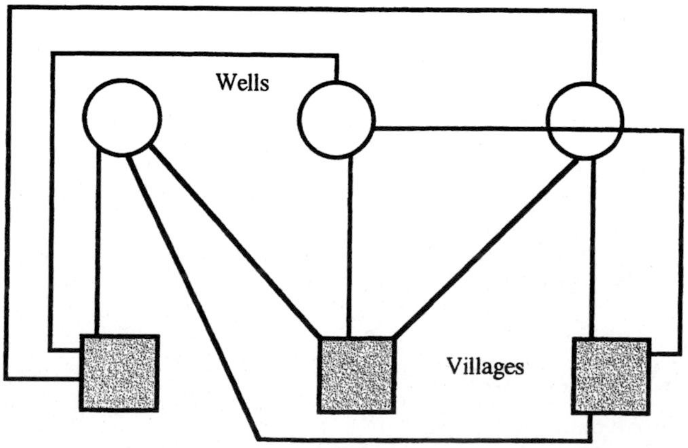

on the face of a die. The distance between neighboring houses and wells should be about 6 feet (1.8 meters).

Special Instructions

It is fairly easy to place eight of the nine ropes connecting the villages and wells. Placement of the ninth rope requires a bit of creative thinking. See the sketch below for one possible solution to this challenge. In this solution, the ninth rope does not touch any of the other ropes, per instructions, but does creatively pass through one of the wells to reach the other.

Activity 5.78

The Water Tube

No question about it, the collapsible, self-contained Water Tube is probably the most complicated piece of challenge and adventure equipment described in this book. But it is also very, very cool. Two other versions of this portable water-filled activity are described here, both of which are easier to construct.

What You'll Need

Free Standing Water Tube (the easy version)

You'll need a 5 foot (1.5 meter) long section of PVC tubing at least 4 inches (102 mm) in diameter, with a flat cap at one end, and with a series of ¼ inch (6 mm) diameter holes drilled at random spacings. Participants will need to hold this style of Water Tube upright as they complete the challenge, or you can suspend this tube from a tree branch with a section or rope for a hanging version.

Permanent Base Water Tube (not too difficult)

The Free Standing Water Tube from above, but this time with a 2×4 base. You'll need one 2×4 that is 8 feet (2.4 meters) long and fifteen 2 inch (51 mm) decking screws.

The Ultimate Water Tube (yes the really complicated one!)

For this version of the Water Tube, you'll need a 4 inch (102 mm) diameter thin-walled PVC tube that is at least 4.5 feet (1.3 meters) long. You'll also need two 4 inch (102 mm) solid flat end caps for this tube, one 2×4 that is 8 feet (2.4 meters) long, six 2 inch (51 mm) decking screws, one ¼-20 by 3 inch (76 mm) long carriage bolt with 2 washers and a ¼-20 wingnut, some exterior grade wood glue and a metal door handle to use as a carrying handle.

In addition to any of these PVC tubes, you'll need a rubber ducky or some other floating toy, and a variety of cups, buckets, or containers in which to carry water. You may also wish to include some additional props that may or may not be of any assistance to the group, such as: plastic hoops, rope, dowel rods, garden hose, tennis balls, salad tongs.

Where to Find It

PVC tubing comes in a variety of diameters and two typical thicknesses, schedule 40 and schedule 80. For any of these Water Tubes, the thinner wall thickness is adequate, and less expensive than the thicker tubes. You may want to use the thicker tubes however, if you happen to have a rather rough and tumble group to work with. The thicker PVC tubing makes a practically bullet-proof version of the Water Tube, and probably doubles the weight of this equipment compared to the thinner PVC tubes. End caps are usually available in both flat and rounded versions. Use the flat versions for all of the Water Tubes shown on this page. Most of the other required hardware can be found in the same store.

Grocery stores and party stores generally have plastic cups, pails and buckets that are suitable for the Water Tube activity.

How to Make It

Free Standing Water Tube

After cutting the PVC tubing to the desired length (5 feet is about right), drill 1/4 inch (6 mm) holes at random places all over the tube. For a group size of 12 participants, 20 holes is about right. Select a tight fitting flat end cap for the bottom of the tube. This end cap can be glued in place with PVC joint compound, or simply pressed on before each use.

When drilling holes in the PVC tube, consider placing several holes together, so that a single hand can be used to cover several holes at one, much like the openings on a musical flute or clarinet.

Permanent Base Water Tube

Create a similar PVC tube to that described above, but before securing the end cap to the PVC tube, create a base for this Water Tube using the 2×4. The first cut from the 2×4 is the top of the base, and is 42 inches (107 cm) long. The second cut is also 42 inches (107 cm) long for the bottom of the base. The remaining 12 inches (305 mm) of the 2×4 are cut in half to provide two pads to keep the base from tipping. Each pad will be 6 inches (152 mm). Assemble the two longest boards to form a right angle cross, and secure these boards at their midpoints with glue and decking nails inserted from the bottom side of the base. With the base turned over, so that the bottom side is facing upwards, attach the two pads to the bottom side of the top base board. These two pads will make this structure stable, when you turn over the base. Secure these two pads with glue and deck screws.

Now drill three holes near the center of the PVC flat end cap, and secure this cap to the 2×4 base with three deck screws. You can use waterproof glue or sealant around these screws to make the tube water tight. Now slide the 4 inch (102 mm) PVC tube into place, wait for the glue to dry, and the job is complete.

The Ultimate Water Tube

From a 10 foot (3 meter) length of 4 inch (102 mm) PVC tubing, first cut off the larger diameter (flared) joint section at one end of the tube. Now divide the remaining length in half, to produce two pieces about 56 inches (1.4 meters) long. Attach the handle to the PVC tube at the midpoint. You can either attach this handle with bolts that have been placed through the handle clearance holes from inside the tube (difficult) or you can drill two holes directly behind the handle so that these bolts can be dropped into place with a magnetic tipped screwdriver. Place the heads of the handle bolts inside the tube and secure the handle in position with hex nuts on the outside of the tube.

Next drill a variety of holes randomly around the exterior surface of the tube. Use drill diameters from 1/32 inch (0.8 mm) to 1/2 inch (12.7 mm). Drill a total of 25 holes in the tube.

Next drill a 5/16 inch (8 mm) hole in the center of each flat end cap. This completes the work on the PVC portions of the Ultimate Water Tube. Now for the wooden base.

The first operation on the 2×4 base board is to cut two 30 degree bevels down the full length of the board with a table saw. These bevels, as shown in the photograph, will enable the base to be stored inside the 4 inch (102 mm) diameter PVC tube. It might be a good idea to experiment with two short scrap pieces of 2×4 to make sure the bevel you have selected actually allows these two boards to fit snugly into the PVC tube.

Next, cut the 8 foot (2.4 meter) long 2×4 into four pieces. The top board of the base is 49 inches (1.2 meters) long. The pivoting bottom board of the base is 36 inches (914 mm) long. And the two attached base pads are each 4.5 inches (114 mm) long. Glue and screw the two base pads to the bottom of the top base board. The beveled edges of these two base pads will be facing down, while the beveled edges of the top board will be facing upwards. Double check to make sure that this assembly will fit into the PVC tube.

Now drill a 5/16 inch (8 mm) hole through the top base board at the exact center (which will be 24.5 inches (622 mm) from either end and 1.75 inches (44.5 mm) from either edge). Center the lower base board between the two base pads. There should be about 1 inch (25 mm) of clearance at both ends. Using the hole drilled in the top base board as a guide, drill a 5/6 inch (8 mm) hole completely through the lower base board. The final step is to drill a 1.5 inch (38 mm) diameter counterbore ¾ inch (19 mm) deep into the 5/16 inch (8 mm) hole of the lower base board on the same side of the board that has the two beveled edges.

To assemble the Ultimate Water Tube, pass the ¼ by 3 inch (76 mm) long carriage bolt through one washer, then through one of the flat PVC end caps, through the 5/16 inch (8 mm) hole of the top base board, and finally through the 5/16 inch (8 mm) hole of the lower base board. In the counterbored region of the lower base board, place another washer onto the carriage bolt, and secure this bolt with a wingnut. Rotate the lower base board so that it is at 90 degrees to the upper board, and you'll have a sturdy cross-shaped stand to support the Water Tube. Now insert the PVC tube into the end cap and the Water Tube is ready to go. The other end cap can be used as a spare.

To fold the Ultimate Water Tube for storage and transport, unfasten the wingnut, remove the PVC end cap, and reassemble the carriage bolt to the upper and lower base boards. Rotate the lower base board to align with the upper base board, tighten the wing nut, and slide this entire assembly into the PVC tube. Now install the end caps and carry the tube away.

After sliding the folded base assembly into the Water Tube, there should be sufficient space left for a rubber duckie, a tennis ball, and a few of the plastic cups.

Special Instructions

While the flat end caps for the ultimate Water Tube must be pressed in place, these caps are probably not sufficient for keeping the Water Tube together for long journeys. A little duct tape will insure that the caps stay in place on long road trips.

A word of warning: The first time you carry your new ultimate Water Tube to the airport for a trip, you will notice that airport security personnel are generally very interested in talking to you, immediately, right now, come with us please! You may find that carrying your water tube in one of the long zippered bags that cross-country and downhill skis are carried in is just the right thing.

One of the first variations in Water Tube, is to use different styles of containers to transport water. Film cannisters are tiny, and require many trips. Buckets are large, and often times the water comming from them is transferred more to other participants than the Water Tube itself. One of the best water transport containers are the stadium sized plastic cups found in party stores. For an extra challenge, you can also drill some holes in these containers.

With regard to the Water Tube itself, the number of holes can be varied, as well as the diameter of these holes. A small hole at the bottom of the Water Tube can lose as much water as a large hole at the top. If you happen to have less participants than holes, try offering the group about 2 inches (51 mm) of duct tape, and let them "plug" a few holes. You can also vary the length of the Water Tube. A 5 foot (1.5 meter) height allows you to cut two tubes from a standard 10 foot (3.0 meter) length of PVC tubing. 7 feet (2.1 meters) is about the tallest Water Tube made so far, although anything is possible.

Activity 5.79

Waterfall I

Probably one of the wettest activities in this book. The props are very simple to make.

What You'll Need

An 8 foot (2.4 meter) length of 1½ inch (38 mm) PVC tubing. When this tube is completely filled with water, it will weight about 6.4 pounds (3 kg). Smaller diameter and shorter tubes can be used to reduce the weight, or you can simply fill the tube with less water. It is easier to block the end of a smaller diameter tube. It is also a good idea to have a few towels around during this activity.

Where to Find It

Most hardware stores carry a variety of PVC tubing.

How to Make It

Many hardware stores will cut PVC tubing to length for little or no cost. Make sure that each end of the PVC tube is smooth and free from any sharp edges.

Special Instructions

You may want to size the length of the PVC tube for Waterfall II so that it can conveniently fit into your vehicle.

Activity 5.80

Waterfall II

Waterfall II uses the same PVC tubes found in Marble Tubes and adds a unique and often wet variation to the traditional marble approach.

What You'll Need

Either of the two styles of PVC Marble Tubes described earlier in this chapter. A large bucket filled with water and a small measuring cup. A funnel is optional.

Where to Find It

Check out the instructions for making PVC Marble Tubes earlier in this chapter. You probably already have the remaining supplies, such as the bucket and measuring cup, somewhere around the house.

Special Instructions

Less water will typically be spilled with the larger, open PVC channels than the closed PVC tubes.

Activity 5.81

Wing It

It is off to the hardware store for some standard hardware from the fastener department.

What You'll Need

You'll need one ¼-20 threaded rod that is 12 inches (305 mm) long and 1 wingnut for each participant. Five participants per rod is about right, although you can use anywhere from four to eight participants. You can use standard hex nuts instead of wingnuts for this activity as well.

Where to Find It

Threaded rods come in a variety of diameters, materials and lengths. The ¼-20 rod is ¼ inch (6 mm) in diameter and has 20 threads per inch. This is a common size, and fairly inexpensive. Try to select a material that will not easily rust or dent. Plated steels are best. Carbon steels will eventually rust, and brass is both expensive and soft in comparison to steel. The 12 inch (305 mm) length is a standard size, and a perfect length for this activity.

How to Make It

If you are able to purchase the wingnuts or hex nuts and a threaded rod of the correct length, there is no additional work involved in preparing the equipment for the activity. If 12 inch (305 mm) precut stock is not available, you may need to purchase longer threaded stock, and cut this to the desired length. Most precut threaded rods come with factory finished ends, which means that wingnuts will easily wind onto the threads. If you use a hacksaw or other form of metal saw to cut the threaded rod to length, try this technique. Before cutting the threaded rod, wind several wingnuts or hex nuts onto the threaded rod, on both sides of where the cut will be made. After cutting through the threaded rod, remove the nuts from each piece. The removal of these nuts will crush any malformed threads. Now take a file or grinding wheel and carefully polish the ends of the threaded rods, so that no sharp edges are present. Practice winding a few nuts onto each rod, just to make sure that each one works smoothly.

Special Instructions

Better keep a few extra wingnuts and hex nuts on hand. These tiny pieces manage to get lost every now and then during a challenge program.

Activity 5.82

Worm Hole

You can use the same type of shock cord that is required for Surfing the Web to create a Worm Hole.

What You'll Need

The Worm Hole consists of a single piece of ⅛ inch to ¼ inch (3 to 6 mm) diameter shock cord, sometimes referred to as bungie cord, that has been tied into a loop with a strong knot. Shock cord is fairly elastic, so a strong knot must be used. A length of 50 inches is suitable for most populations, although a length of 100 inches will allow even the largest wheelchair to pass through—and the 100 inch version can be knotted at the midpoint to form two connected 50 inch Worm Holes.

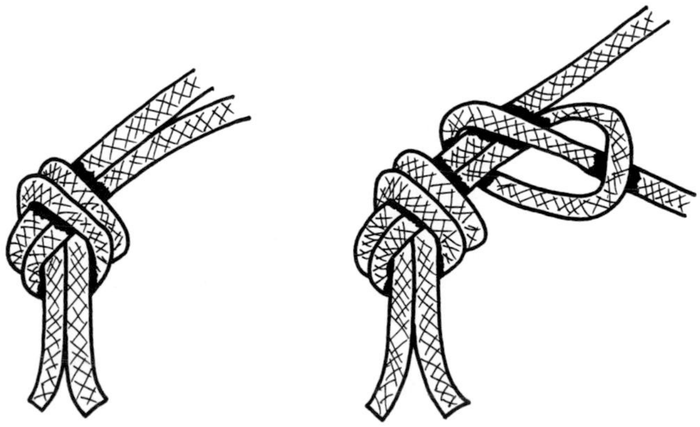

Where to Find It

Hardware stores may stock only a single size of shock cord, but many marine stores carry a variety of sizes and possibly even a few different colors.

How to Make It

The most difficult task in constructing the Worm Hole is to tie a knot that is secure and will not pull out, even when the Worm Hole is completely stretched. Begin by tying an overhand knot with both ends of the shock cord held tightly together. See the sketches below. Now tie an additional overhand knot by passing this first knot around one strand of shock cord. This second knot will effectively compress the original knot, forcing it more tightly closed, rather than attempting to unravel it.

Special Instructions

The ⅛ inch (3 mm) shock cord is fine for this activity. There is no need to use the larger ¼ inch (6 mm) shock cord unless you can't find the smaller diameter material. If you happen to have a Worm Hole that seems too large for your group, you can tie additional knots in it to shorten the length. Make sure that any knots in the Worm Hole are very secure, and will not slip when the Worm Hole is stretched.

Activity 5.83

Yada Yada Yada

Yada, Yada, Yada, is not so much an activity in itself, but a way to challenge a group that is already communicating exceptionally well. Use this variation during your favorite challenge and adventure activity that requires some verbal communication and planning.

What You'll Need

No equipment here, but you may want to have a few other words, in addition to Yada, for the group to use.

Where to Find It

Try finding other words in foreign dictionaries, ancient language texts and the languages used in science fiction novels and movies.

Special Instructions

While this activity appears whimsical and harmless, some groups can become very frustrated by the limitations of a one word language, especially after hearing it a hundred times and still having no idea what is being implied.

This variation on an activity should only be used with groups exhibiting strong communication skills. Use of this variation with a communicationally challenged group may result more in frustration than in additional challenge.

Notes

Activity 5.84

Some Ideas for Other Challenge Course Equipment

Having seen at least 70 challenge courses throughout North America, we would like to suggest some ideas for additional activities not presented in Chapter 4. No detailed instructions here, just a few comments regarding some common and some not-so-common activities encountered at various challenge courses.

If you plan to construct any of these activities for your challenge course, we recommend that you discuss your plan with a knowledgeable challenge course builder. While most of the activities listed in this book are exceptionally safe, a few of the following activities have higher levels of risk. Seek the appropriate information from a challenge course builder for these and other permanently installed challenge course activities.

Trust Fall Platforms

Trust fall platforms must be like snowflakes, seldom do you find two that are the same. Differences include the size of the platforms, the materials used to construct them, the platform height from the ground, the attachment methods to the tree or pole, and the occasional free-standing trust fall platform. In any event, many of these platforms have one critical difference from the one shown below—the method for reaching the platform generally involves climbing from the ground, over the tree roots, up a series of angled platform supports, and then onto a rather small platform. Even before the participant is in position for the trust fall, they have already had an ordeal reaching this point.

Some folks may argue that this initial effort provides additional opportunities for spotters to have positive contact with the participant prior to the trust fall, and generally speaking, that is probably true. But occasionally, over the years, we have seen some participants never reach the platform because of difficulties climbing it. There are also some populations that are perfectly capable of safely participating in a trust fall, but lack the mobility to safely ascend to the platform with the design presently used by many programs.

In the interest of making a traditional trust fall platform slightly more accessible, here is a design which incorporates a simple set of steps to the platform. The total increase in cost above the standard platform design was only the cost of 3 additional boards.

Tensioning Ropes for Surfing the Web

One of the standard methods for tightening the boundary rope for a maze or web pattern is a standard turnbuckle available at most hardware stores. This works fine for a while, but eventually the rope becomes

slack, and most standard sized turnbuckles will eventually need to bedisassembled and retied. There is an other device, that is inexpensive and works even better for tensioning these ropes.

What You'll Need

The device used to tension electric fences for farm animals is just great for tensioning the boundary rope in a maze or web pattern. It works well with ¼ inch (6 mm) poly rope, and can take up several feet of slack. It has a ratchet wheel that can be reversed for disassembly of the initiative. There is also a separate handle for tightening the ratchet wheel which makes the tensioning process very simple.

Where to Find It

This is not a typical item for most hardware stores, but it is available in most farm-based product stores. You may also be able to find these tensioners in fence or tack shops.

How to Make It

The fence tensioner comes with a hole that can either be attached to an open hook or screw eye, or the opposite end of the rope you wish to tension. The other end of the rope is attached to a hole in the ratchet wheel. Use the optional handle to turn the wheel and tighten the rope. You will hear a series of clicks as each tooth of the ratchet wheel moves past the ratchet pawl.

Special Instructions

This device can create a serious amount of tension in a rope, sometimes even enough to pull short screw eyes completely out of trees. Be careful not to over-tighten the rope the first time. Besides, with this device, you can always come back and easily add a few more clicks to the tensioner any time you want.

Pressure and Salt Treated Dimensional Wood

You'll notice that none of the building supplies mentioned in this book includes pressure-treated or salt-treated lumber, mostly for two reasons. First, all of the equipment described here is portable, which means that light weight is a priority. It also means that this equipment will typically not be exposed to the weather for any length of time. Secondly, pressure-treated materials are more expensive, heavier, and create much more of a safety concern from sawdust and slivers than standard dimensional lumber. If you have a concern about the weatherability of any of the wooden equipment in this book, consider apply a coating of waterproof sealant.

A Permanently Installed Version of Log Rolling

If you would like to create a more permanently installed version of Log Rolling, here is a simple design using telephone poles that works well.

What You'll Need

A uniformly shaped (non-tapered) telephone pole roughly 20 feet (6 meters) long. Two shorter telephone pole segments for supports, each 6 feet (1.8 meters) long. Two concrete reinforcement rods, ½ inch (12 mm) in diameter and 3 feet (914 mm) long. A chainsaw, a sledge hammer, and a ⅝ inch (16 mm) auger or drill bit that is at least 15 inches (381 mm) long.

Where to Find It

Concrete reinforcement rods are available in several lengths where masonry products, such as concrete block, bricks and paving stones are sold. Telephone poles of various lengths can sometimes be purchases or obtained by donation through local utility companies and building contractors. Some tool rental stores have augers and battery powered drills (and generators) for making even the most remote installations possible.

How to Make It

Cut a V-shape notch at the center of each of the 6 foot (1.8 meter) long supports. Place these supports into two shallow trenches so that they will not roll. Place the 20 foot (6 meter) long telephone pole onto these two supports. Each end of this long pole will overhang the V notched support logs by approximately 2 feet (610 mm). The long telephone pole should come to rest just slightly above the surface of the ground.

With the ⅝ inch (16 mm) auger, drill a single hole diagonally through both the main telephone pole and through each of the support poles. If your drill is not long enough to complete this operation in one step, drill the top pole first, and then remove this pole to finish drilling the support pole hole. After drilling these two holes, use a sledge hammer to insert the concrete reinforcement rod into each hole. Pound this rod well into the ground, and below the surface of the top telephone pole. You now have a structure that will not rock for the Log Rolling initiative.

Special Instructions

Telephone poles come in a variety of grades. Do not attempt to use just any old telephone pole lying around for this activity. Remember, the weight of a dozen or more adults may be on this pole someday. Use good quality poles for both the main top pole and the support poles.

A Telephone Pole Alternative to A Ground Level Cable Walk

If you have ever wanted to create the facilities for a ground level cable walk, but did not want to invest in the cables, tree augers, tensioning devices, and other concerns associated with permanently installed cables, consider using three of the telephone poles version of Log Rolling above to create a triangular telephone pole version of a cable walk.

Most participants find this apparatus a little easier to balance on, and the cost of installation is a fraction of that for a cable system.

A Portable Version of the Wild Woosey

For those times when "portable" means anything you can carry in the back of a 15 passenger van or pickup truck, you might be interested in a portable version of the Wild Woosey which Chris Cavert calls The Friendship Walk.

What You'll Need

Chris makes this portable challenge activity from 8 foot long 4×4's, bolts them together and uses eye-bolts, quick links and tubular webbing to space them apart.

Where to Find It

Most of the equipment is available in your local hardware store. You can find the plans for this equipment in Chris Cavert's E.A.G.E.R. Curriculum book, available form Experiential Products, P.O.Box 50191 Denton, TX 76206-0191 Phone (817) 566-1791

A Final Random Thought

This isn't so much a challenge and adventure tidbit, as it is just a really cool idea. In the box of activities we've collected is a special place for some really wildly creative activities, and here is our favorite: electric belt sander races!

Now, we know what you're thinking, Jim and Barry have gone over the edge with this idea (read the article in Chapter 7 to see if you want to join us in our madness). But the truth is we spend so much time making things in our shop, and sanding is almost second nature to us, that the thought of using our sanders for something a little more play-like is really exciting. Now granted, we have never actually seen a belt sander race, but from what we hear, they go like this:

Belt Sander racing is like a drag race. Two belt sanders, side-by-side, in a wooden track 20 feet (6 meters) long with 2×4 sides and a clear plastic top (for safety). Attach a long extension cord, turn that baby on, lock the on-switch, and let 'er go. First sander to the far end of the track wins.

Now if we can only find some other fun challenge and adventure things to do with the rest of the tools in our workshop.

Basic Training

A Few Words on Equipment

- Sooner or later, everything you have in your adventure kit is likely to be exposed to the weather. Choose fabrics and ropes that won't fade with sunlight, webbing and twine that will not rot with moisture, plastic props that will still work at temperatures below freezing, and expect everything to get soaking wet at least once. Be sure to thaw or dry out your equipment after any severe weather. Remember to use galvanized or plated metal parts, nails and screws on all equipment, unless you plan to invent a new challenge activity called "The Rust Bucket."

- If you intend to make equipment for a summer program or camp, consider making this equipment with the staff that will be using it. Then, when a piece turns up missing, the staff will know how to make a new one. This is also a great way of creating ownership for this equipment with the staff. Then, when some over-enthusiastic campers begin really hammering on one of the props they made, they can step in and show the correct techniques for using the equipment. This pride and ownership is essential to keeping your equipment in good shape.

- If you are not sure—ask! If any of the directions in this section are not clear to you, drop us a line at Teamplay. We have staff available to assist you in your staff training and equipment needs. You may even be able to buy some of this equipment commercially in the near future from several of the challenge course builders located in the United States. Stay tuned for more information about this from Teamplay.

Chapter Six

Processing: The Need for Discussion

Basic Training

A Few Words About Processing Challenge and Adventure Activities

It is a completely humbling experience to attempt to write even a modest few words about processing or debriefing challenge and adventure activities when there are, in our opinions, several significant works already available on this subject. Consider reading these classic texts, and many of the references listed in Section 8.12 of Chapter 8:

Processing the Adventure Experience Theory and Practice
Reldan S. Nadler and John L. Luckner, 1992, Kendall / Hunt ISBN 0-8403-7028-8

Processing the Experience—Strategies to Enhance and Generalize Learning
John L. Luckner and Reldan S. Nadler, 1997, Kendall / Hunt ISBN 0-7872-1000-5

The Skilled Facilitator: Practical Wisdom for Developing Effective Groups
Roger M. Schwarz, 1994, Jossey-Bass ISBN 1-55542-638-7

Notes on Processing Challenge/Adventure Experiences
With Clients From Business and Industry.
Tom Smith, 1992, Raccoon Institute P.O.Box 695 Cazenovia, WI 53924

Lasting Lessons: a teacher's guide to reflecting on experience
Clifford E. Knapp, 1992, ERIC/CRESS Clearinghouse, Charleston, WV
ERIC Document Number ED 348204.

In addition to these classic references, you will find a variety of techniques that have proven themselves to be effective in this chapter. Processing, debriefing and reflecting on the challenge and adventure experience is the part of adventure programming that allows the participant to incorporate new understanding into their knowledge base. Without this important step, many of the activities listed in Chapter 4 would be reduced to the level of simple games. Processing the events that occurred while the participants were engaged in the activity allows the knowledge gained by a single participant to be available to the entire group. Effective facilitation and processing skills are some of the most difficult skills to learn, and they require a great deal of patience and practice. Hopefully some of the information presented in this chapter, and in the suggested references, will help provide the reader with a better understanding of this very important element of challenge and adventure programming.

Going Beyond the Game

While a challenge program for a corporate group of regional managers probably differs significantly from that delivered to a group of 13 year old campers, there are a few significant elements which are similar for each program.

Step 1 The Assessment of Needs and Goals Some initial investigation and evaluation of the needs of the group is required to answer the question, "Why are we doing this?" This step helps to identify the underlying rationale for the program and the criteria for achieving the goals of the group.

Step 2 The Identification of Challenge Activities to Address these Needs and Goal. The needs and goals of the group identified in Step 1 suggests which activities might be best for the group (i.e. those activities with a problem solving focus, or trust building, or communication based, or confidence building, or creativity enhancing).

Step 3 Presenting the Challenge and Adventure Program The actual presentation and facilitation of the activity. This is the step where you drag out all that equipment and lead the group through a well sequenced series of activities to accomplish the goals identified in Steps 1 and 2 above.

Step 4 Processing the Adventure Experience with the Group The processing, debriefing, or reflecting time in which the group as a whole and as individual members begins to relate events encountered during the adventure experience to situations in their own environments.

Step 5 Post Event Follow-Up and Extensions of the Lessons Learned Follow-up after the event to reinforce and revisit the skills learned during the adventure experience and the application of these skills to the participants personal environment.

It is in Step 3 that the adventure experience becomes more than just a series of games. By discussing the actions and reactions of the group during the activity, participants can identify situations and circumstances in their own environments which can be improved using similar techniques. Processing also helps to reinforce how specific behaviors either assisted or resisted the efforts of the group.

What is the Role of the Facilitator?

The impact of the facilitator is critical in a processing or debriefing session. But it is important to note that the role of the facilitator is to assist the group in discovering what they have experienced, not telling them what they have experienced. The facilitator's role includes clarifying and focusing the comments of the group, providing helpful information, and calling attention to details that may be overlooked by the group. The facilitator is constantly looking for opportunities for participants to understand how their behavior effects the performance of the group. They look for teachable moments, where guidance and support can encourage participants to be more than they thought possible, or to think in new ways, or to consider additional factors. Facilitators encourage, support, and provide helpful assistance where possible, but they do not lead the group. Their role is that of consultant, not chairman of the board. They are a vocal resource to the group. In the end, the performance of the group belongs to the group, not the facilitator.

Is there such a thing as too much facilitation? Yes, and here are some of the symptoms:

1. Providing too much information at the beginning of the activity so that participants have little left to discover for themselves.
2. Talking more than listening.
3. Leading participants to the classic solution instead of allowing them to reach the goal in their own manner.
4. Processing the experience in more detail than required.
5. Stopping the activity too frequently. Not waiting for a teachable moment.
6. Encouraging the group to be creative and then restricting this creativity by unnecessary rules or guidelines.

Ground Rules for Processing and Debriefing

Before conducting a processing or debriefing session, it is typically helpful to establish some basic rules for the group to consider when expressing their feelings during this portion of the challenge and adventure experience.

1. Your comments are welcome here. Participants must feel that their comments are valued, even if they feel the need to voice a concern or explore an issue which may be sensitive to the group.
2. Respect the comments of others. In order to create an atmosphere where participants feel free to express themselves, they need to know that their comments will be received by the group.
3. Encourage participants to take ownership of their comments. "I feel this way . . .", "This is what I believe . . .", "The ball was dropped because I wasn't sure what to do next."

Given these ground rules, let's explore a few questions on the topic of discussion and debriefing.

1. When do you process? When you can have a positive impact on the direction of the group. This may be during a difficult challenge, at the end of a successful attempt, after a particularly intense experience by a member of the group, at the end of the activity, and at the end of the program.
2. What is the ideal setting for processing? First and foremost, processing should take place when the entire group is present. It is ideal to have participants in a comfortable position where they can see the other members of the group. It may also be helpful for the group to be near the area where the activity they are processing took place.
3. How do you know when processing is complete and it is time to move on? One of the first indications may be a rapid increase in the number of group members becomming detached from the processing event. They have learned the lesson and are ready to move on. If there are any pressing issues left unresolved however, it can be valuable to at least voice these issues, and let participants consider them as they move on. Just because the conversation has stopped doesn't mean that processing has ceased. Many participants need a few moments after hearing comments and suggestions during processing to internalize these remarks. If the group has gained something of value from the processing event, it is time to move on.

Techniques for Processing the Challenge and Adventure Experience

Near the end of each activity in Chapter 4, there is a section entitled "Discussion and Debriefing Topics" which provides some processing information specifically relevant to the challenge activity presented. Many facilitators find it useful to process after each activity, so that positive behaviors can be reinforced, and so that group members are reminded that their opinions and comments do matter.

At the completion of the adventure experience, a final processing session is generally presented. In many cases, this is the last opportunity for the facilitator and the participants to have direct contact. In addition to the debriefing topics presented with each activity in Chapter 4, the following techniques are provided for a final processing event at the completion of the challenge and adventure program.

1. **The Journal.** An individual or group journal can be kept by the group as they encounter each of the challenge activities during the program. Significant events can be noted and a critique of the problem solving method and final solution can be included. At the completion of the day's events, a review of the journal can reveal the progress experienced by the group. If a group journal is selected, choose a different participant to chronical each challenge activity.
2. **The Virtual Slideshow.** This is one of our favorite processing techniques, and it requires no equipment at all. During the closing processing event, the facilitator can prepare the virtual slideshow by asking the group to look at the large imaginery slide screen in front of them. Making a clicking sound, the facilitator begins the virtual slide show by describing a scene from the day's events. After a slide or two, the facilitator passes the remote control of the slide projector to the next person. Participants can either describe their favorite or most significant scene from the day's activities or pass the remote control to the next person.
3. **On Target.** This processing or evaluation tool is best used three or four times during the adventure experience. Using either a real or imaginary bullseye target, with the facilitator at the center, ask team members to place them-

selves on the target according to the following criteria:

- ♦ How well do you understand the goals of the activities you are about to experience?
- ♦ How do you feel about the way the group is working together?
- ♦ How effective do you feel your group is?
- ♦ How personally invested do you feel the other members of your group are?
- ♦ How effective do you think the communication is within your group?
- ♦ Where would you like to be at the end of the day's activities?

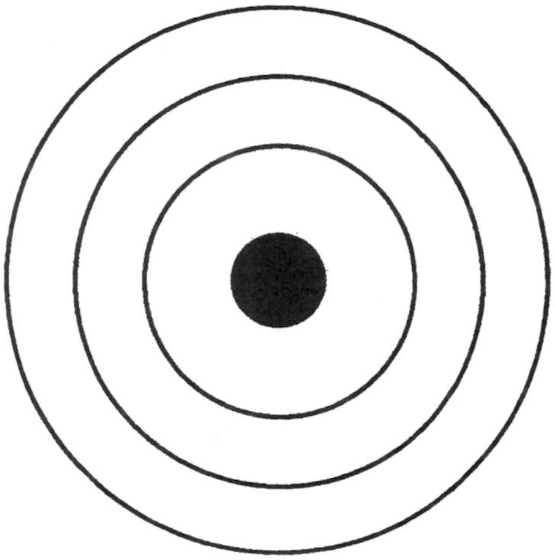

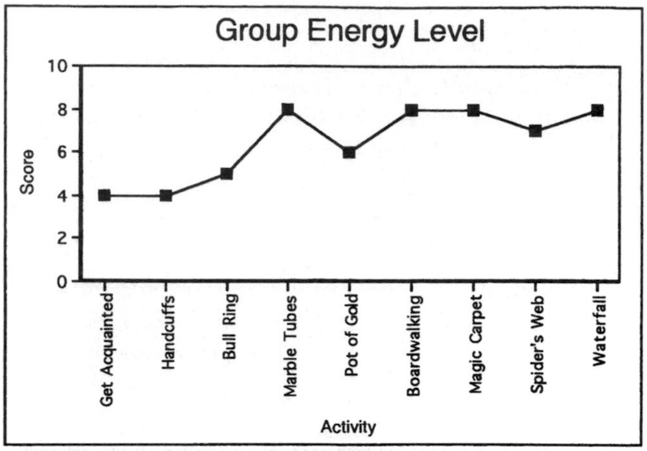

Energy Level for a Challenge Group with 8 Participants

4. **Great Graphics.** Using the standard picnic variety of white paper plates and some colorful markers, ask participants to draw a face illustrating how they felt during a particular activity or during a significant event.

5. **Great Graphics—Part II.** Using a large blackboard or poster board, create a graph of the days events, and the energy level of the group during each activity. Allow each person a single vote of 1 for high energy or zero for low energy. Discuss those events which demonstrated the highest and lowest energy levels. Look for significant trends. Did the energy level pick up during the day, or diminish? Which activity was the highest? What made this activity such a high energy event?

6. **Just One Word....** Have participants complete any of the following phrases with a single word:
   - ♦ I began the day feeling.....
   - ♦ The first time I was challenged I felt.....
   - ♦ I felt..... by the rest of the group.
   - ♦ One word that describes how I feel right now is......

   Author's note: We once witnessed this style of processing with a group of approximately 70 foreign college students. After using a single word in the English language, participants were asked to express the same feeling in their native languages. More than 25 different languages and dialects were represented and in many cases, the single English word could only be interpreted using a collection of words in other languages. This activity produced an on-the-spot appreciation of the diversity of this group.

7. **Communication Dice.** Communication dice consist of two dice that have a variety of subjects printed on their 6 faces. As a get acquainted activity, the first dice has the words: home, school, work, hobby, family and friends. The second dice has the words: happy, difficult, holiday, vacation, love and challenging. By rolling the two dice together, participants are asked to express something in their life that can be described by the dice, such as a happy moment with friends, a challenging school situation, or a family vacation.

   As a facilitation activity, the first dice can contain words like challenging, difficult, helpful, conflict, teamwork, frustration and success. The second dice can contain words such as the names of various challenge activities, specific portions of the program, emotions, learning events, and overall perceptions about the program in general. By rolling the two dice together, participants are asked to express something they experienced that day that can be described by the dice, such as a moment of frustration while Surfing the Web, a successful learning experience, or a feeling of teamwork at the end of the program.

In Chapter 5, directions are given for constructing the wooden dice for the challenge activity known as Monumental. These same directions can be used to create communication dice for debriefing and processing after the event. You can also create your own dice from the pattern shown below.

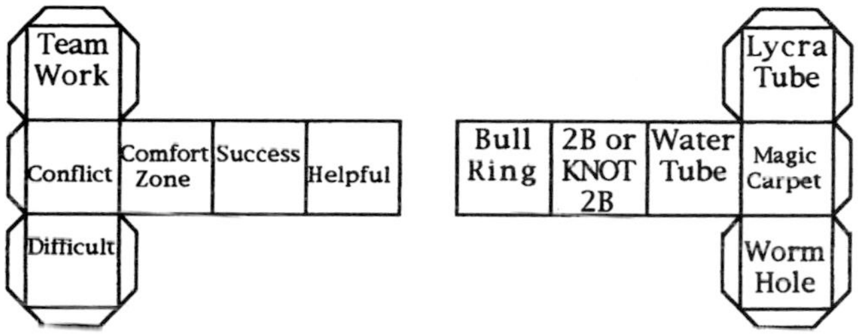

8. **Global Commentary.** Some comments are not necessarily directed towards a single activity or event, but rather at the global perception of the day's experience. This type of processing typically requires a longer amount of time, but allows participants to express themselves completely.
   - So, what did you learn today?
   - In general, how many ideas were required to solve the problems presented?
   - Did you feel challenged outside of your comfort zone?
   - What was the most unusual sensation you experienced today?
   - Which activity would you like to go back and do better?
   - Did you experience pressure from the group during any activity?
   - Would it have made a difference to have had more time?
9. **Creative Comments.** You'll find instructions and a blank comment sheet for an additional feedback activity entitled Creative Comments, at the end of this chapter.

The Final Wrap-Up

Remember to let participants know at the end of the program, that the goal wasn't simply to place the bull ring ball back on the stake, the goal was to form a team that could meet that challenge. If you measure the success of the group by whether or not they completed a challenge successfully, you are likely to fall short in some areas. Better for the group to realize that placing the ball on the stake was not the goal, communication, teamwork, creative problem solving and other skills encountered during the day were.

If you would like a final technique for demonstrating the power of a well functioning team, consider using the Popsicle Stick Closing Activity presented in Section 4.49 of Chapter 4. Or, if you happend to have used the Raccoon Circles throughout the day, and you can afford to spare the cost of the webbing, consider cutting this webbing loop into pieces for the group so that they can take back with them a piece of the experience.

After the Final Curtain—The Post Event Follow-Up

While it is not always possible to perform, the post event follow-up is generally regarded as a significant event which helps participants integrate skills and experiences they gained during the challenge and adventure program into their lives. If they participated as a professional group, the post event follow-up is generally focused on integrating skills which are useful in the work environment. If the group consisted of a sports team, the post event follow-up helps to reinforce team qualities.

The post event follow-up provides two significant benefits. First, it extends the skills and lessons learned during the challenge and adventure program and brings these lessons into the familiar environment of each group member. Secondly, the post event follow-up provides a valuable opportunity for the facilitator to see the results of their work. Participants will often provide information on which activities and events were most significant and memorable. They'll discuss how they've applied the skills and experience they've gained, and they can provide valuable feedback on how they feel about the original challenge and adventure program from their not so distant past.

These comments can be used by the facilitator to evaluate the effectiveness of the challenge and adventure program in meeting the needs and goals initially established during the planning stages of this program.

Creative Comments

On the following page is a creative post-activity survey form. By the end of the program, many participants are frazzled, and would rather not bother with any post-activity rhetoric, but your chances of gaining some valuable information diminishes with time after the completion of the activity, so you need to move quickly. Providing a form that is useful, and does not look like some sort of government application form or advanced math test is probably going to work well in your favor. Here is once such form. If you want to read more about the details of preparing a questionnaire form, read the text entitled:

Asking Questions—A Practical Guide to Questionnaire Design
Seymour Sudman and Norman M. Bradburn,
1989 Jossey-Bass, San Francisco, CA
ISBN 0-87589-546-8

Creative Comments

Please take a few moments to tell us about your adventure experience today.

Do you think anything will change in your life, now that you have had this experience? What?

What experience made you feel challenged today?

What new experiences did you have today?

Did any experience in particular push you outside your comfort zone?

Tell about something cool that happened today

What was the best thing that happened today?

I would just really like to say...

I never thought that I could . . .

I never thought that I would . . .

I was really surprised . . .

I will never forget . . .

I hope . . .

Please circle the number that reflects your overall experience today
1 = low, 5 = average, 10 = outstanding

1 2 3 4 5 6 7 8 9 10

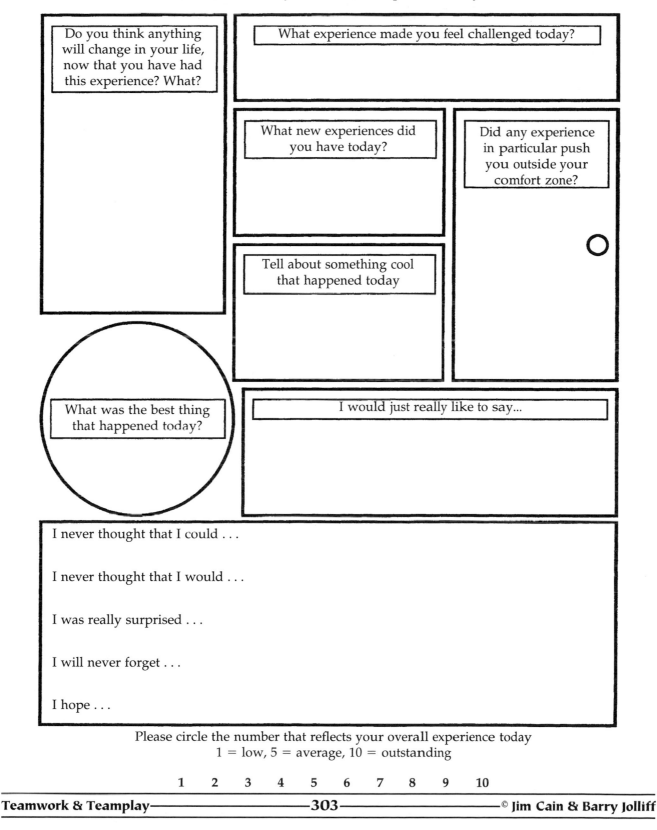

Chapter Seven

Beyond Adventure: Games and Activities Just for Fun

In addition to all the challenge and adventure activities we've collected over the years, we just happen to know all sorts of other cool things, and this is the chapter in the book where we tell you about them. All kinds of things show up here. Great programming ideas we have seen over the years, some cool equipment, some interesting educational programs, some phenomonal resources, and a few of our own random thoughts just for fun. If you remember from the introduction to this book, we promised to share with you some of the best information we know about leading successful challenge and adventure programs, and outdoor education programs in general. Here are a few of the gems we have encountered in our collective 50+ years of working in this field.

What's Here

Activity 7.01

ACCT

With all the recent interest in challenge course building, insurance, risk management and liability issues, and the need for uniformity and integration of the challenge course building network, we are lucky to have the organization known as the Association for Challenge Course Technology. ACCT was formally organized in 1993 and offers guidelines, a code of ethics and information related to designing, building, inspecting and maintaining a challenge course. Some of the principal members are associated with various challenge course building organizations throughout the North American continent, and around the world. This organization also coordinates an annual conference that is held at various sites throughout the United States. For more information, contact the ACCT at:

Association for Challenge Course Technology
P.O. Box 255
Martin, Michigan 49070-0255 USA
Phone (616) 685-0670 Fax (616) 685-7015
Email: acct@net-link.net
Internet: www.acctinfo.org

Notes

____

____

____

____

Activity 7.02

Bird Call

There are a variety of ways to call birds. Being a mechanical engineer however, means that Jim Cain was generally interested in the various kinds of mechanical devices that can be used to make bird sounds. The Audubon bird call is one of the simplest and well known calls. Here is a simple way to make a similar bird call device. Cut a 2 inch (51 mm) length from a hardwood dowel rod that is ¾ inch (19 mm) in diameter. Drill a hole 9⁄32 inch (7 mm) diameter hole completely through the length of the dowel pin. Now place the dowel pin in a vise or clamp, and thread a 5⁄16 × 1½ inch (9 × 40mm) long bolt into this hole. It will be a tight fit. Use a wrench to make the job easier. Now completely remove the bolt using the wrench, and once again thread the bolt back into the dowel pin, this time using your hands only. After about three or four threads are in place, you'll notice that it takes more effort to turn the bolt, and that by reversing directions at this point, a squeeking sound comes from the dowel pin. You may need to thread the bolt into the dowel pin a few times before enough clearance appears to create the squeeking sound.

Some folks think that this device has the same effect as fingernails on a chalkboard, but I think the sound is very much like the commercial bird calls available in many environmental and nature-oriented stores, and you won't need any violin bow rosin for this one!

Notes

____

____

____

____

____

Activity 7.03

Boomerangs

A few years ago at the Buckeye Leadership Workshop, World Champion Boomeranger Chet Snouffer offered a series of workshops on making, tuning, throwing and catching these unique objects. To say that Chet is an expert is putting it mildly. We made booms from everything we could find, including pizza boxes, paint sticks, tongue depressers, cardboard, plastic, and baltic birch plywood.

Here is a simple boomerange design that uses the wooden paint paddles available at most hardware and paint stores. If flies a 20 foot (6 meter) diameter circle and has a gentle floating return. Bevel the top four edges of each paint paddle, then connect both paddles together with the beveled edges up using hot glue and two ½ inch (12 mm) hardware staples. Fold the points of the staples over with a hammer, let the glue dry, and you have a boom almost ready to throw. All that is missing is some simple instructions on wind, throwing technique, and the most important of all, how to tune your boomerang. Chet Snouffer has an excellent handout on these final boomerang topics, or see the book by Mason listed below.

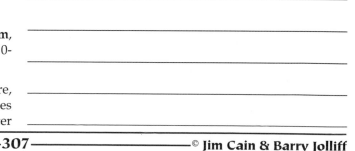

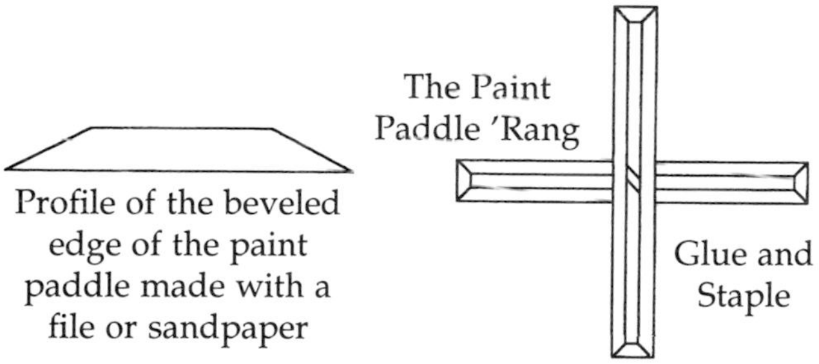

For more information on 'rangs, read or contact the following resources:

Boomerangs: How To Make and Throw Them, Bernard S. Mason, 1974, Dover Publications, ISBN 0-486-23028-7

U.S. Boomerang Association, P.O.Box 182, Delaware, OH 43015, Fax (614) 363-4414. Your membership dues also get you a copy of the USBA quarterly newsletter Many Happy Returns. The USBA also maintains a web page on the internet.

OZWEST, Inc., P.O.Box 6655, Aloha, OR 97007 USA. Phone (503) 643-6128 Fax (503) 643-1551. Custom printed foam boomerangs.

The Boomerang Man, Rich Harrison, 1806 North Third Street, Monroe, LA 71201, Phone (318) 325-8157. Probably the best selection of booms in North America.

Leading Edge Boomerangs, Chet Snouffer, 1868 Panhandle Road, Delaware, OH 43015, Phone/Fax (614) 363-8332.

Notes

Activity 7.04

Camouflage Critters

Some animals have the ability to blend into their environments by protective colorations of their skin. Here is a technique for teaching students about camouflage. You can also use these creatures for the challenge activity Inch by Inch described in Chapter 4.

Begin by giving each student or group one standard one-piece wooden clothespin. This is the body of their critter. Also supply a variety of markers, crayons, pencils, paper, tape, glue, paints, pipe cleaners, wire and other natural colored objects that each group can attach to their critter.

The object of this activity is to create a critter that blends so well into the habitat that any predator would never find it. When all critters have been assembled, have group members place these in an enclosed space, and then see which critters you can find the easiest, and which ones are more difficult to locate.

Notes

Activity 7.05

If you can hear me, clap once . . .

One of the most effective and amazing feats I ever witnessed was a facilitator gaining the attention of an extremely loud group, using a very simple and surprisingly effective technique. Imagine yourself in a classroom, or on a challenge course, or in the cafeteria of your local high school at lunchtime (you get the picture). Noise, confusion and chaos reign. You have an announcement that is vital to the group. With no public address system or bullhorn, you have to get their attention quickly, but how?

First you gain the attention of just a few members of the group, perhaps only a single person, and you say in an ordinary speaking voice, "if you can hear me, clap once." And you and your only attentive group member clap once together. This will gain the attention of a few other group members, to which you say, "if you can hear me, clap twice." You are now building numbers and volume, as more folks wonder what is going on. With the newest group, and keeping your voice at an ordinary speaking level, you say, "if you can hear me, clap three times." Clap, clap, clap. By now you'll probably have the attention of most of the group, but you can try a fourth or fifth round if you really want to pull folks in. At this point they will be listening so intensely that you can practically hear a pin drop. It really works!

If you happen to need this activity more than a few times during a single program, try switching from hand clapping to other visible and audible motions, such as finger snapping or foot stomping. "If you can hear me, stomp once . . ."

Notes

Activity 7.06

Core Groups

In Chapter 3, there are many suggestions for creative ways to form smaller groups from a large audience. If you happen to be coordinating a conference or some other event which will cover several days, and you wish to create small groups that stay together for the entire event, try using the Core Group method.

You can begin to create core groups using any of the methods listed in Chapter 3. After you have the groups established, ask each group to create a unique motion and a sound. Some groups may decide to make moose ears using their hands for the motion and their version of a moose call for the sound. Other groups can use hand motions along with whistling a familiar tune.

The utility of Core Groups is that at any point in the program where you need familiar groups to work on a problem together, you can simply call out "find your core groups," and after some initial chaos, you'll have all the groups together again.

Practicing this Core Group formation a few times on the first evening will help the groups remember their identifying sounds and motions. Often times, you'll find Core Groups eating together, attending the same workshops and building a real sense of community for their group.

Activity 7.07

The Concept of Creative Cheating

Most activities in life have directions, or instructions, or rules. The concept of creative cheating adds a little artistic license to those rules which may alter the activity, but do not in any way alter a direction intended for safety reasons. Simply stated, the only time creative cheating does not apply, is when an issue of personal or group safety is involved. With that said, here is how you can go about creatively cheating.

First of all, any time someone asks you to form groups of four, and there are only a few people left, and your group has either three or five, that works. You are creatively cheating. If the initiative asks that your group proceed as quickly as possible, and your group wishes to slow down the activity, and instead deliver a slower but higher quality result, that too is creative cheating.

Sometimes, especially when two groups are competing against each other, you'll hear the second place team say, "yes, they won, but they cheated." To avoid running into this situation, first of all, don't utilize activities that force groups to compete against each other. Secondly, encourage the concept of creative cheating from the beginning, so that the above phrase will become, "yes, they won, they cheated more creatively than we did."

About 90% of what we are attempting to do as facilitators is to ask our participants to think outside the ordinary boundaries. Why then should we act as a boundary to their creativity when they are suggesting techniques for potential solutions? The answer is never, unless there is a violation of a rule placed there for safety reasons. Almost none of the activities in this book have the sole goal of merely completing the task. It is the process by which the group completes the task that is critical. What better way then to expound on this process, than by letting participants join in the requirements and outcomes for that process?

An interesting by-product of creative cheating is that as a facilitator, you are more likely to witness a new variation to a traditional challenge activity from a group that has been encouraged to cheat creatively.

Activity 7.08

On the Issue of Diversity

Occasionally you find someone out there making a difference in the world. In this case, making a very big different. Part of our goal for this publication was simply to tell you some neat ideas, how to use them, and where to find them. In this case, we just wanted to say that Maggie Finefrock is one of the most talented resources we have ever experienced, especially when dealing with issues involving diversity. She is a talented facilitator, a knowledgeable professional trainer, and challenged us to be more than we are.

You can reach Maggie at the address shown below. We just thought you might appreciate knowing where to find some top-notch talent the next time your organization wants to take a critical look at diversity issues.

Maggie Finefrock
2615 Martha Truman Road
Kansas City, MO 64137
Phone (816) 765-9685

Notes

____

____

Activity 7.09

". . . Do as I Say, Not as I Do . . ."

The role of a mentor is an important one, and this interesting demonstration came from Dr. Dennis Elliott of Ohio State University, our mentor and friend. It demonstrates that most of the time, people will watch and do exactly what you do, rather than listening to the instructions you are trying so hard to present. Good advice for a facilitator to know, especially when you are trying to prevent unnecessary risks on your adventure course. This demonstration only takes about 10 seconds to perform. Once you have the attention of the group, proceed quickly.

"Please follow and do exactly what I do. Take your right hand and hold it out away from your body about face level, and make the "OK" sign with it.	*The presenter holds their hand out, showing the OK sign*
Now, as quick as you can, touch this hand to your CHIN.	*The presenter takes the OK sign in their right hand and touches it to their right CHEEK!*
If you notice, most folks will find their chin is located here."	*The presenter gazes at the audience most of whom have their right hand touching their right cheek. The presenter then uses his left hand to indicate where the CHIN is located.*

This is a quick demonstration that audiences, including challenge and adventure programming audiences, will often receive more information visually than from any amount of verbal communication. Action speak louder than words, in this case.

Notes

____

____

____

____

Activity 7.10

Energy Ball

I first experienced this activity at the Bradford Institute on Americans Outdoors a few years ago. About 14 people were playing while another 200 watched in amazement. Let your imagination run wild with this one.

Energy Ball is a circle game without props where players pass an imaginery object around the circle by using a unique collection of throws, bounces, passes, reverses and the ultimate "schwa' maneuver.

Begin the activity with the group seated in a circle. One member of the group creates the imaginary energy ball by a similarly imaginary method, such as inflating the energy ball like pumping up the tire of a bicycle, or blowing up a balloon, or making an energy snowball.

The simplest motion to begin moving the energy ball around the group is the "pass." This is a simple one-handed passing motion in which the person possessing the energy ball takes their right hand and moves it in front of themselves towards their left, palm up, saying "pass" as the imaginary energy ball moves to the next person, who then says "pass" as they motion with their right hand, and the energy ball moves around the circle to the left. When the ball has returned to the originator, stop the motion, and demonstrate how a left to right pass can be made using the left hand to pass the energy ball to the next person on the right.

After this motion has moved around the circle one complete time, the leader can demonstrate a technique for reversing the direction of the energy ball, known as the "bink." The bink move sounds like the original TV video game that displayed a paddle and a bouncing ball. If the energy ball is moving towards you from your right, and you hold up your left hand in a fist, bent at the elbow with forearm straight up, and say "bink," the energy ball reverses direction, and starts moving to the right. To reverse the energy ball comming your direction from the left, hold up your right hand, say "bink" and the energy ball reverses direction and goes back to the left.

This completes Level 1 of energy ball, and beginning groups can play here for a while. Level 2 involves two more complex moves. The first move is the "bounce." As the energy ball moves towards you from the right, you can use the bounce move to continue the ball in the same direction, but skip the person immediately to your left. The bounce motion is a chopping motion, with the hand held flat like a blade, pointed down at the feet of the person next to you on your left. As in all energy ball motions, the person handling the ball says the motion and demonstrates the motion at the same time. Bounce can be used to skip a person, but does not change the direction of the energy ball.

There is a two handed version of "pass" that allows a person to pass the energy ball across the circle to another person. The motion for this move is bending the elbows of both hands and then pointing directly at the person to receive the energy ball, and saying "over." The receiver of the energy ball can only pass left or right after catching the ball from an "over" pass across the circle. This is a great move in case the energy ball becomes stagnated in one portion of the circle.

The final Level 2 move is the "pop." In this move, a person can explode the energy ball, like popping a balloon with a pin, and then has the duty to create a new energy ball. The new imaginary energy ball may be a heavy medicine ball, so that all the motions become heavy and the associated names spoken in a deep voice. The new energy ball may be a snow ball that leaves players chilled after it passes. The new energy ball may really be an imaginary porcupine that requires some special handling.

Level 3 is the highest and most accomplished level of energy ball. There is but a single, highly polished move in Level 3. It is the "Schwa." The schwa is a one-handed, behind the back pass, like some basketball players use, that reverses the direction of the energy ball, and skips a person. As the energy ball approaches you from the left, take your right hand, catch the ball, and pass it behind your back towards the left. The ball now skips your immediate neighbor to your left and lands in the lap of the person to their left. The only penalty in Energy Ball is that only two schwas can be made in a row. Anyone choosing to schwa a third consecutive time can be asked to perform some classic penalty, such as singing out loud, performing a reasonable stunt, or some other harmless act of humility.

There is also the possibility of allowing the group to create their own movements and names for energy ball motions. In summary:

Pass	A one-handed scooping motion that moves the energy ball to the left or right
Bink	A one-handed vertical forearm motion that reverses the direction of the energy ball
Bounce	A one-handed motion with bladed hand that skips a person by bounding the energy ball at their feet, and then on to the next person
Over	A two-handed pointing motion that transfers the ball across the circle. The receiving person can only pass right or left.
Pop	A pin popping motion that breaks the energy ball. The instigator of this move must then create a new energy ball.
Schwa	An advanced move of the highest skill, in both the artistic display of movement, and the unique vocal screeching associated with saying "sssssccccchhhhhwwwwwaaaaaaaaaaaaaaahhhhhhhhh!" This motion reverses direction and skips a person.

Notes

Activity 7.11

The Heavyweights

In the interest of informing facilitators just how heavy some challenge and adventure equipment is, the following list of the seven heaviest pieces of challenge and adventure equipment is provided. You won't find any weight specified here however, because the density of wood varies with age, and even new wood has substantial variations in weight, for the same style of board. But rest assured, these are the heaviest props listed in this book.

As a general rule, the weight of many of the wooden platforms could be substantially reduced by replacing pressure treated wood with standard dimensional pine lumber, and further by replacing dimensional pine lumber with cedar. The cost for cedar however is considerably higher than pine in most geographic regions.

The Seven Heaviest Collections of Challenge and Adventure Equipment in this Book

Rank	Activity
1	River Crossing (Four 4x4's, 12 stacking platforms)
2	A Balanced Life (base plus hardwood lever)
3	Windmill (A platform and four long planks)
4	All Aboard (One set of four stacking platforms)
5	Life Raft or Boardwalking (One set of 8 jointed boardwalking segments)
6	Water Tube (all contained)
7	Living Ladder (hardwood dowel rods)

Activity 7.12

Hoseplay

A few years ago Glenn Bannerman was challenged by Dick Porter of L'eggs to find some creative use for waste nylon stocking from the production facility in South Carolina. And so he did. The result is a collection of nifty toys and colorful activities that use these inexpensive materials. Glenn even managed to make a video showing how to create these props from the hose. Many of the balls, donuts, flying disks, jump ropes, tether balls, and other props are perfect for challenge and adventure activities. Recently, Group Publishing has even published a book and a cylinder filled with already dyed hose for making these unique props, toys and games.

To obtain a shipment of waste hose, send a check or money order for $10.00 US to the Sara Lee address shown below. This amount is intended just to cover postage and handling by the corporation. Any funds lefts at the end of the fiscal year, beyond shipping costs, are donated to charitable organizations by the Sara Lee corporation. A noble effort, and an interesting and creative way to recycle these products. The waste hose you receive will typically be a variety of styles and colors, but a little fabric dye can turn them into a rainbow.

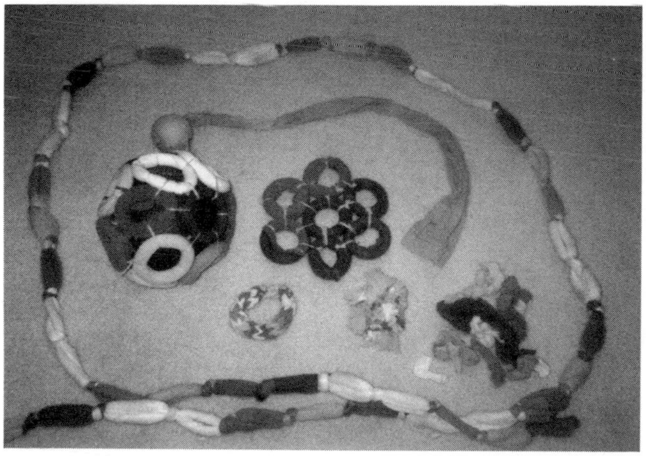

Sara Lee Hoisery
Waste Hose
P.O.Box 719
Marion, SC 29571

Creative Nylon Hoseplay © Video
Bannerman Family Celebration Services, Inc.
P.O.Box 399
161 Virginia Road
Montreat, NC 28757
Phone (704) 669–7323

Brite-Tite Book O' Fun
by Glenn Q. Bannerman, Beth B. Gunn and Lee Ann B. Konopka, 1996, Group Publishing 2890 North Monroe Box 366 Loveland, CO 80539 ISBN 1-55945-626-4 Creative Nylon Hoseplay © games and activities for all ages.

Activity 7.13

Hot Dice

One year at the Buckeye Leadership Workshop, a gang of late nighters were gathered at a table in the corner of the dining room, playing some sort of game. From a distance, an amazing amount of sound was generated as the players screamed, laughed and cried their way through the game. It didn't take long before Hot Dice became the official late night game. Bill Henderson, District 4-H Specialist in northwestern Ohio, created these instructions. Hot Dice works with groups of all sizes, but groups of six to eight people is probably the best. The object of the game is to be the first person to score 5000 points.

Points are scored by the following system, using a total of six cube shaped dice with values from one to six:

Single Dice

Any single dice showing a value of 1 is worth 100 points
Any single dice showing a value of 5 is worth 50 points

Three of a Kind Dice

Any group of three dice, each showing a 2 is worth 200 points
Any group of three dice, each showing a 3 is worth 300 points
Any group of three dice, each showing a 4 is worth 400 points
Any group of three dice, each showing a 5 is worth 500 points
Any group of three dice, each showing a 6 is worth 600 points

Any group of three dice, each showing a 1 is worth 1000 points

Straight Dice

A straight of six showing 1, 2, 3, 4, 5, and 6 is worth 1000 points.

To begin accumulating points, a player must first accumulate 500 or more points in a single roll. After achieving this beginning value, this player can accumulate additional points in any quantity.

A player's turn begins by rolling all six dice at onetime. At least one dice must be set aside on each roll. If no scoring points are accumulated on a roll, the players turn is over. For example, if a player already possessing 500 points rolls a 6 6 4 3 2 1 in the first roll, they can remove the two 6's and the 1. On the second turn, with the remaining 3 dice, they roll a 6 3 2, and set the 6 aside. On the third turn, they roll a 2 and a 4. Since no additional points are rolled on this turn, this players turn is over, and the dice are passed to the next player.

A unique scoring feature about Hot Dice is that points are not counted until one of three things happen:

1. The player stops rolling and decides to keep the points they have accumulated up to that point.
2. The player rolls a turn that produces no scoring points, and they lose all the points accumulated so far in that turn.
3. The player scores points with all six dice, and has "HOT DICE."

If on the third turn of the player mentioned above, instead of a 2 and a 4, they roll a 1 and a 5, both of which are scoring dice, they have "HOT DICE," which simply means that they have managed to score points will all six dice during a turn. A player with HOT DICE can now continue to roll again using all six dice, or keep the score they have. If they choose to roll again, they must set aside at least one scoring dice each roll. If they fail to throw a scoring point on any roll, they lose ALL points accumulated in that turn. This is probably the part where the late night crowd mentioned above does most of the screaming and laughing, when a high roller almost makes it, but not quite.

Play continues with each player taking their turn, and recording points they have accumulated. When any player reaches 5000 or more points, all remaining players have one more turn to try to top this score. This is typically the going-for-broke round, and players keep going no matter what the odds, trying to get HOT DICE and stay in the game.

Activity 7.14

Houdini

One good thing about challenge and adventure activities, is that there is usually a good piece of rope laying around somewhere when you need one. After your group has practiced their knots, try this puzzling activity just for fun. This activity, named after the famous American magician, encourages some creative thinking, and perhaps even an opportunity for some creative cheating.

The challenge is to see if participants can pick up the 3 foot (1 meter) long rope, and tie an overhand knot in it, without letting go of the rope. For many folks this is a familiar activity, with a tricky, but known solution. Don't forget though, that many others may not have experienced this activity yet, and appreciate the sort of outside-the-box thinking required to complete this activity.

The familiar solution is to cross your arms before picking up the rope. Then when you uncross your arms and pull on the rope, a single overhand knot will form.

After this activity, you can teach the group to make their own Handcuffs and Shackles from the same rope.

Activity 7.15

The Least Expensive Challenge Equipment

You can construct a fairly impressive collection of challenge equipment, including many of the items shown in this book, for a very reasonable amount of money. Here are some of the least expensive pieces of challenge and adventure programming equipment in the Teamplay supply box.

The Least Expensive Challenge and Adventure Equipment in this Book

Film Canisters for Group Formation—generally free at the photo shop

Tennis Balls for Tennis Ball Mountain—used balls are free or low cost at many tennis clubs

Hoseplay Balls, etc.—you can make a bunch of equipment from one box full of hose

Magic Carpet, Blackout, Midnight Sun—a plastic tablecloth or shower curtain works fine

Bull Ring—there are many things you can do with this little wonder

MarbleTubes—a few pieces of PVC from the local hardware store

63 / 64 / 65—just a piece of graph paper and a few copies

Popsicle Sticks for Closing Activity—1000 for a few bucks at the craft store

Raccoon Circles—worth every penny

and finally . . .

Free Flying Discs—Mattel Sports Promotions gives away free Frisbee® Discs to youth programs. Write them at:

World Jr. Frisbee® Disc Contest M1-0836
333 Continental Blvd.
El Segundo, CA 90245-5012
Phone (310) 252-4762

Activity 7.16

Modern Archeology

We're not sure if it is the activity, or the name of the activity we like, but both are pretty neat. Modern Archeology makes for an interesting theme or activity within a program. It is not a challenge or adventure activity, although it does require some creativity and group problem solving skills.

The first thing you'll need for Modern Archeology is a collection of the kinds of farm tools, kitchen devices, and home or industrial equipment that you typically find at auctions, flea markets, and garage sales. Give an object to each group of about eight or so participants. Their objective is to come up with five reasonable purposes for the object, and one guess at what the true purpose is. Other groups can then vote their approval by clapping as various purposes are proposed.

You'll want to make sure that you actually know the real purpose of each of the items you have available—although a truly unknown item makes for an interesting final object that the whole group can attempt to solve.

Farm items make for interesting items, as do 19th and 20th century kitchen utensils, unique industrial tools or widgets, unusual electronic components (unplugged of course), and various parts from household objects.

Activity 7.17

The Most Expensive Challenge Equipment

Not surprisingly, some of the most expensive challenge equipment is also the heaviest. So you'll see a few repeats between this list and the Heavyweight List also given in this chapter. This list is presented based only on the cost of the materials for each activity. No consideration was given for manufacturing costs, time, special tools, etc.

The Most Expensive Challenge and Adventure Equipment in this Book

River Crossing—the cedar 4x4's are expensive

A Balanced Life—expect to pay big bucks for the oak planks

All Aboard—it takes a while to assemble all the pieces

Life Raft or Boardwalking—hardware and nice ropes cost the most

Living Ladder—hardwood dowel rods are not cheap

Lycra Tube—wait for a sale or winter, new summer materials cost a bunch

Time Tunnel—more lycra costs

Water Tube—simple, but many pieces to assembly

2B or KNOT 2B—nice ropes can cost a bunch, use whatever you already have

Pot of Gold—Again, nice ropes can cost a bunch, look for an inexpensive supplier

Rainbow Writers—the telescoping poles can be expensive

2 liter pop bottle rocket launchers—costs a few bucks, but worth it

Activity 7.18

The Most Often Used Challenge Equipment

There are a few activities that always seem to be used at every challenge and adventure programming event we facilitate. These are the star performers in our challenge kit.

The Most Often Used by a Teamplay Staff Member Challenge and Adventure Equipment in this Book

Bull Rings—at least one of the many variations

Lycra Tube—always seems to make an appearance at some point in the day

2B or KNOT 2B—really enforces the need for group consensus

Funderbirds—just a fun way to start the day

Raccoon Circles—for warm-ups, processing, closing

Magic Carpet—still new to many folks and easy to carry

Marble Tubes—both varieties work great

Worm Hole—light, easy to carry, useful before Surfing the Web

Surfing the Web—at least one of the many variations

Marching to the Beat of a Different Drum—never fails to build enthusiasm

Life Raft and Boardwalking—heavy, but worth the effort

Waterfall I—especially on a hot day

Notes

Activity 7.19

Needle and Thread Tag

Of all the various tag games we have played, this is our favorite version. Begin with a circle of people standing about 2 feet apart, hands at their sides, and two additional players on opposite sides of the outside of the circle. In this case, we'll let the "cat" chase the "mouse." Each time either the cat or mouse runs between two people in the circle, they join hands, and the space between them is no longer a passageway. Continue until all hands are joined, or until the cat has caught the mouse. New players can then be chosen by the cat and mouse.

You can add some variation to this game by having the circle move slowly to the left or the right.

Notes

Activity 7.20

Nuts & Bolts

Next time you are organizing a gathering, conference or challenge event, try forming groups by using a variety of nuts and bolts. Place a variety of bolts and nine matching nuts in a large bowl or similar container. When participants arrive, have them select either a nut or bolt, and then find the other 9 members of their group that match the threads on the bolt in their group. This collection will form groups of ten, one member for the bolt, and nine nuts (no pun intended, really!). You can form different size groups by having different numbers of nuts for each both.

Another variation for this activity, is to form groups using all the same size nuts and bolts. When a bolt has enough nuts to fill the full lenght of its treads, that group is complete.

Better be sure to have a few extra nuts and bolts for this activity. You are likely to lose a few every now and then.

Activity 7.21

Packing Light

For some challenge and adventure facilitators, the equipment used during an adventure program is only limited by the size of the facilitator's vehicle. Occasionally however, it is necessary to pack everything needed for a challenge program into a very compact container, such as a single backpack. This is often the case when facilitators need to travel by air, and occasionally for such adventures as white water rafting expeditions. It is also useful to have a lightweight collection of equipment when attempting to incorporate challenge and adventure activities into wilderness programs where backpack space is at a premium, and every pound of equipment must be carried for the duration of the program.

Creating a Lightweight Kit of Essential Challenge Equipment

In the interest of suggesting the most lightweight, multifunctional and useful equipment for wilderness and portable challenge and adventure programs, the following list is provided. As always, the ultimate suitability of this list should be evaluated by the facilitator with regard to the structure of the group involved. This equipment however represents a very lightweight collection of some of the most useful portable challenge equipment for bringing out the best skills in a group.

Two Blindfolds—lightweight

One Bull Ring—versatile, compact and lightweight

One Worm Hole—lightweight, and you can use it tie items to your pack

Two Raccoon Circles—because there are a zillion things you can do with one

Several tennis balls—Community Juggling, name games, other activities

One 40 foot (12 meter) Rope—Tree of Knots, Jump Rope, boundary markers

One Plastic Tarp—Danger Zone, Under Cover, Magic Carpet, and to keep your pack dry

One 5 foot (1.5 meter) long rope for every group member—Handcuffs and Shackles, Linearity, Extended Human Knot, plus knot tying practice, and camp utility

Activity 7.22

Paper Bag Skits

One of the best rainy day activities we have ever seen was presented by Jayne Roth, a 4-H Extension Agent in northwest Ohio. Jayne probably has as many rooms in her house filled with boxes of programming materials as Barry Jolliff and Jim Cain put together, and that would be quite a bit.

Anyway, paper bag skits involve a little preparation. Namely, filling several paper bags with a variety of cool and colorful items, such as: big sunglasses, funny hats, party supplies, string, construction paper, tape, tennis balls, a rubber chicken, stuffed animals, magazines, kitchen utensils, and more.

The object is to create a skit, song, television commercial or story using all the props including the bag. Providing a wide variety of objects helps create a wide variety of skits. If you desire, you can use props with a nautical theme, or a tropical theme, or an artic theme, or a desert theme, or a carnival theme, or a beach theme. . . . .

Activity 7.23

Pulse

There is something exciting about an activity that requires absolutely no equipment, and can easily keep a group busy for 20 minutes or more.

You'll need a suitable table and chairs for pulse. There are variations however that can be played by slapping hands on neighboring players knees, or even on the floor.

Begin by having each player place their right hand palm down in front of the person on their right. Next have everyone place their left hand palm down, in front of the person on their left, crossing over the right hand in front of them. You'll now have a series of crossed arms going completely around the table.

As the leader, first demonstrate that a pulse is just a slap with the hand, that keeps the wrist of the player in contact with the table, somewhat like a hinge.

Begin by passing the pulse to the right around the group. The leader demonstrates this move, and the next hand (not the next person) to the right goes next. Continue this motion until the pulse is passed completely around the circle and returns to the right hand of the leader.

Next practice this motion by passing the pulse to the left around the circle, until is again reaches the left hand of the leader. These two practice rounds are important, and help to acquaint the group with the activity.

Next demonstrate with a quick double slap, that a double pulse reverses the direction of the pulse as it travels around the circle.

Now you are ready to play pulse in its full contact mode. Have a new leader begin the activity. Any time a hand is lifted out of turn, or someone slaps the table when it is not their turn, they must remove that hand from the table. The person removing one of their hands from the table then begins the game again with a single pulse to the right.

This activity plays quickly. It is not necessary to play to the very last hand, especially when some players have been completely eliminated. After seven or eight hands have been removed, begin a new game.

A third motion that is available is to make a quick fist with the hand, and thump the table instead of slapping it. This motion means that the pulse skips the next hand, and continues moving in the same direction. This also means that you can make up additional motions to suit the skill and needs of your group, such as

a thumping a fist motion twice to reverse directions and skip the next hand.

Finally, this is one activity, however briefly, that eliminates players during the contest. Perhaps there could be a way that participants could regain a position at the table, such as every third time the pulse comes by them, they can rejoin with one hand. This would keep the game constantly changing, and include everyone, all the time. Players could even work together to regain a participant that had just lost a hand position at the table.

If you find this activity a little too confusing because of crossing arms with neighboring players, try the same motions without crossing arms.

Notes

Activity 7.24

Rainbow Writers

A few years ago at the national conference of Recreation Laboratories and Workshops (RLW) in Colorado Springs, Warren Bailey, a long-time kitemaker and kiteflyer, brought along a flexible fiberglas fishing pole and attached a 40 foot (12 meter) multicolored plastic ribbon to it with a fishing snap-swivel. He then proceeded to paint the afternoon sky with a rainbow of colors as the ribbon waved in the breeze and took on endless shapes, spirals and patterns. In Chapter 8, you can find the address for the High Fly Kite Company near Philadelphia, PA that sells these telescoping fiberglas poles in a variety of lengths. You'll also find Warren's address in Chapter 8, under Wind Dance, Inc. The poles are imported by Walker International of Detroit, Michigan, and come in lengths from 10 to 20 feet long. Walker only distributes to other businesses, not individuals, so you'll need to check with either your local fishing gear supplier, or perhaps even your local kite shop to purchase these poles.

One of the easiest sources of ribbons, is to wait for the after Christmas sales in late December, and buy the red plastic outdoor decoration ribbon. If you happen to have a sail maker in your neighborhood, scrap pieces of kite or sail fabric can be sewn together to form

a colorful ribbon. In either case, you'll need to fold over the end and fix an ordinary tarp grommet, available in most sewing or fabric stores, in the center. Now attach a short section of string to the grommet, and fix to the fiberglas pole using a fishing snap-swivel. You are now ready to fly your creation.

This device is a sure crowd pleaser, and keeps even the youngest or oldest participants interested. But be sure to leave plenty of room between the pole artist and the spectators. You don't want to bonk anyone in the head.

Activity 7.25

Rain Sticks

We have managed to invent a thing or two in our time. Jim Cain has even managed to collect two U.S. Patents along the way. But the day we figured out how to make a decent sounding rain stick from PVC tubing was a landmark. Here is what you'll need:

Materials

One 2 foot (610 mm) length of 1.5 inch (38 mm) white PVC tubing

Two end caps for this diameter PVC tubing

About a dozen bamboo kitchen skewers

Navy beans, dried rice or aquarium gravel for inside the tube

PVC adhesive to keep the end caps in place

Wood stain to finish the outside of the tube

Supplies

A razor knife or scroll saw to cut the bamboo skewers to size

A drill just slightly smaller than the diameter of the bamboo skewers

A small hammer to pound the bamboo skewers in place

Some sandpaper to sand the outside of the tube before staining

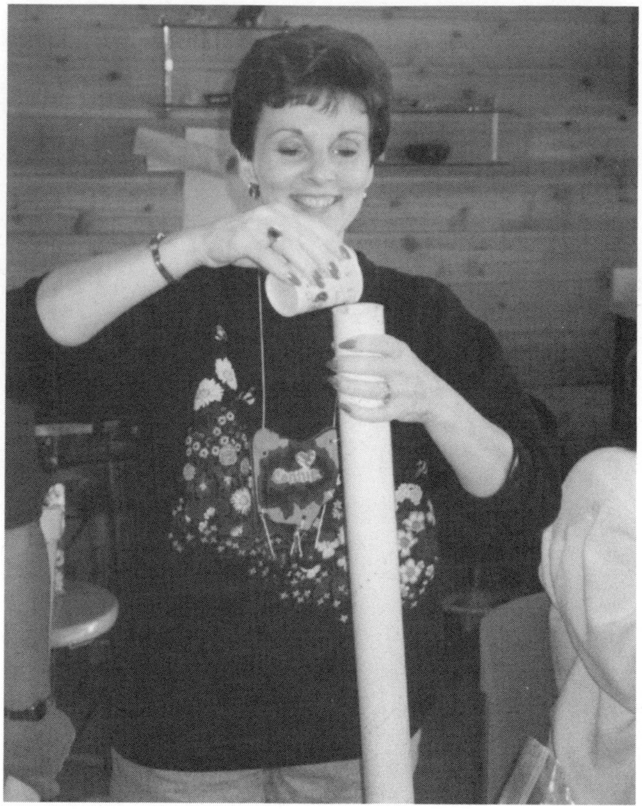

Instructions

Begin by drilling a series of holes in a spiral pattern down the length of the tube. This pattern will resemble a spiral staircase, and make about 3 revolutions within the length of the tube. The diameter of the hole should be slightly smaller than the bamboo skewers so that they must be hammered into the holes. Using this type of force fit means that no glue will be necessary to hold these bamboo skewer pins in place. Drill holes about ⅜ inch (9 mm) apart the entire length of the tube. There will typically be a total of between 70 and 100 holes.

For a really interesting rainstick, and a useful teaching aid, try making a sample rainstick from a clear piece of plastic tubing, so that your students can see how the bamboo pins are positioned inside the rainstick.

Cutting the bamboo skewers individually can take a long time, so band about a dozen of them together with masking tape, and then cut the whole bundle on a power scroll saw with a fine blade. Bamboo skewers come 100 to a package, so you'll have enough pins for about 14 rainsticks from one package. You'll need to cut these bamboo skewers into pins that are equal in length to the inside diameter of the tube plus the thickness of one side minus a bit for clearance. This means that when you hammer these pins into place, they will go through one side of the tube, and stop just short of the far side of the tube. These cantilevered pins will then vibrate as the contents of the rainstick dance over them.

Use a small hammer to pound the pins into each of the holes along the length of the PVC tube. If you happen to be teaching this project to a classroom full of students, give all the instructions before this part. Once the hammering begins, it will be noisy for quite a while.

After pounding in the bamboo pins, sand the outside of the tube smooth, removing all lettering and markings. You can use an old saw blade to gouge the surface of the PVC tubing, making a grain in it. Later, when you add wood stain to this surface, the scratches and gouge marks will appear like a wood grain in the surface of the tubing.

Now place one end cap onto the tube, and pour various quantities of particles, pellets and powders into the open end of the tube. Place your hand over this open end, and invert the tube, listening to the sound created by the mixture you have just added. When you are satisfied with the sound comming from your rainstick, you can use PVC glue to secure the end caps in place. Work quickly, PVC glue dries very fast.

When your rainstick is full assembled and sanded, you can apply a coating of wood stain to the PVC tube. You can also add other decorations, such as brightly colored twine, yarn or leather lacing.

Activity 7.26

Rockets

A few years ago, Bob Horton, Extension 4-H Specialist at Ohio State Univeristy helped to develop an alternative to the more traditional solid fuel rockets used by many youth programs. His work included a partnership with Wayne Versey, the inventor and fabricator of a unique air powered rocket launcher. The Extension Publications office at OSU also provides an extensive manual for teachers and students in the art and assembly of rockets, and a PC -based computer program for analyzing your rocket designs.

The results are an interesting and fun activity that works well with both youth, teen and adult groups. The two liter bottle rocket launchers shown here are manufactured by Wayne Versey. Several other rocket resources are listed here, and there are many pages of information available on the internet. Try looking under: rockets, water rocket and launch.

Teamplay also has a variety of designs for constructing bottle rockets, and building safe rope-activated and foot-stomping rocket launcher bases.

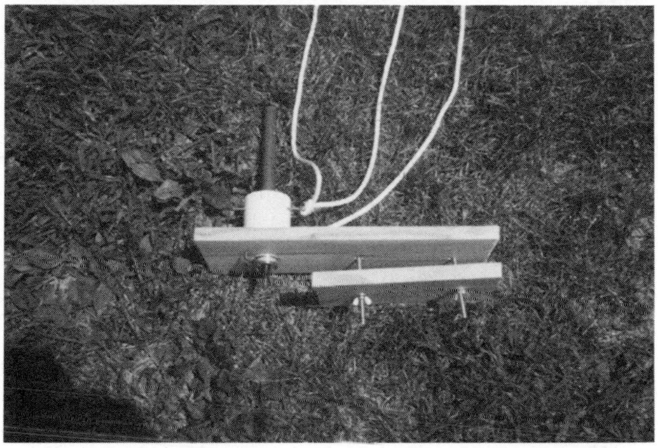

Two Liter Bottle Rocket Launchers
Wayne Versey
Versey Enterprises
1258 North 1100 East
Shelley, ID 83274
Phone (208) 357-3428
Email: versey@juno.com

Rockets Away! Manual
Extension Publications Office
The Ohio State University
Phone (614) 292-1607
Email: pubs@agvax2.ag.ohio-state.edu

Rocket Launch Base Plans
Teamplay
468 Salmon Creek Road
Brockport, NY 14420

Additional Rocket Resources:

National Association of Rocketry (NAR)
P.O.Box 177, 1311 Edgewood Drive
Altoona, WI 54720
Phone (800) 262-4872

Estes Industries
P.O.Box 227
1295 H Street
Penrose, CO 81240-0227
(800) 525-7563

Quest Aerospace Education, Inc.
P.O.Box 42390
Phoenix, Arizona 85080-2390
Phone (800) 800-858-7302

Suggested reading:

Handbook of Model Rocketry—Sixth Edition
George Harry Stine, 1994, John Wiley & Sons, NY
ISBN 0-471-59361-3

In addition to using 2 liter bottles for rockets, there are a variety of scientific, environmental and biological experiments that can be performed using 2 liter bottles. Check out the Bottle Biology book listed in Chapter 8. The Wisconsin Fast Plants project at the University of Wisconsin-Madison provides several activities which utilize 2 liter bottles. General inquiries can be directed to:

Coe Williams, Program Manager,
Wisconsin Fast Plants
University of Wisconsin-Madison,
Dept. of Plant Pathology
1630 Linden Drive, Madison, WI 53706
Phone (800) 462-4717 or (608) 263-2634
Fax (608) 263-2626
Email: fastplants@calshp.cals.wisc.edu

Notes

Activity 7.27

An Interesting Lesson in Physics

Does the phrase, "what goes up, must come down," apply in reverse? Does, "what goes down, must come up," really work? Here is a simple activity to take up some time. Actually the activity will only take a minute or so, but there will probably be people trying to figure it out for much longer than that.

Take a basketball in your left hand and a tennis ball in your right. Lift them up to shoulder height, and the drop them onto a hard surface. Note the height that each ball bounces. This next part is even more effective if you happen to begin with a tired old tennis ball that doesn't have much bounce left in it.

Now take the tennis ball, and place it so that it touches the top of the basketball. Now drop these two balls together, and see what happens! If you manage to keep the tennis ball vertically above the basketball, the tennis ball bounces way above your head, while the basketball barely comes up to your knees. Why?

If you really want to know, it is a neat example of potential energy and something called the coefficient of restitution (which is just a fancy way of saying that different objects bounce off the ground differently). In the first case, you'll see that the basketball and the tennis ball both bounce by themselves, probably to about waist height or so. By placing the tennis ball above the basketball, all the energy that is stored in the basketball when it deforms by hitting the ground, is transferred into the tennis ball. As a result, the tennis ball soars, while the basketball, having lost most of its energy, barely makes it off the ground.

So the next question is, "what happens if you put the basketball on top of the tennis ball?" We will leave this up to you to find out, but the answer has something to do with the mass of each ball. Have fun.

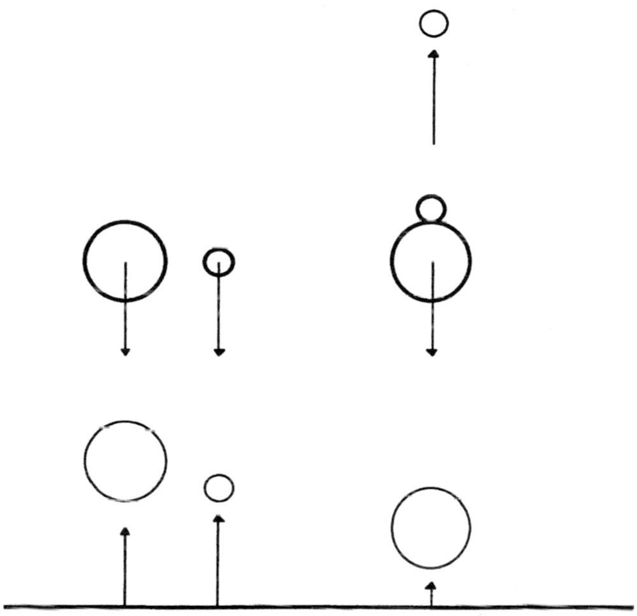

Activity 7.28

Something New To Do

If you are looking for something new to try, here are a few ideas to kickstart your imagination. . . .

find out how tall you are in centimeters—look in the phone book and find all the other people with your same last name—sit someplace new in the lunchroom tomorrow—learn the names of the flowers growing in your neighbor's garden—color a picture with crayons—learn to write your name with both hands—learn the name of your postal carrier—try a new food—read the name from someone's name tag and say hello to them by name—find out what the two dots above a German "a" are for—learn a new word in a foreign language—write a letter to the editor—find out where sesame seeds come from—buy a new food at the grocery store and learn how to cook it—buy a magazine you have never read before—watch a different channel for the evening news—read a foreign newspaper—save enough box tops or proof of purchase seals to buy a gift for a friend—think about all the things that would be different if snow were black instead of white—listen to national public radio—find a new book in the library and read it—count the steps from here to there—change oil in your car yourself—listen to a new radio station—find out who invented the ball point pen, the tennis ball, roller skates, popcorn—ask a friend what books they really enjoy and then read one of them—find out the ingredients of one of your favorite foods—listen to the shortwave band of the radio—recycle something—eat off of the good dishes for no special reason—plant a new type of flower or tree in your yard—donate something to a charity—write a letter to an old friend—get up a half hour earlier and have a really good breakfast—drive the back roads instead of the freeway—visit your local general store instead of the mall—walk through the hardware section and see if you identify what all the tools and hardware are for—listen to the wind blowing through the trees with your eyes closed—visit a relative—take food into work for your group—give someone else the close parking spot—take the stairs on the way down, instead of the elevator—take the elevator and talk to people inside, instead of staring at the numbers above the door—give a child a toy, or better yet, help a child make a toy—invent a new word—close your eyes and identify all the things you can smell—try a new toothpaste—volunteer for something—teach a child to tie their shoes—discover something—listen to your heart beating through a stethoscope—be kind to an animal—really listen to what someone is saying—share a newspaper article or cartoon—forgive someone—teach an old dog some new tricks—walk with a friend—share something—listen when a child tells a story—take a few minutes for yourself—watch a movie in black and white—buy a new tool and make something with it—start something all over again—hold hands with someone—remember a kind deed—send a card to someone for no reason at all—write a letter in green crayon instead of pen—compose a symphony using household items as instruments

by Jim Cain

Activity 7.29

Star Gazing
Making Film Canister Constellations

Here is something else to do with those tiny little film canisters. Learning about stars, constellations and their mythological names can be a fun classroom activity.

What You'll Need

A black film canister and gray lid for each student. It is probably a good idea to have a few extra gray lids, just in case any mistakes are made. You'll also need 40 inches (1 meter) of string, some construction paper, a ¼ inch (6 mm) drill and a few plastic push pins.

Where to Find It

Most photofinishing and camera shops will donate empty film canisters to groups. Plastic push pins can be found at most office supply or stationery stores.

How to Make It

First take a trip to the science library for a little celestial research. Have each student find a different constellation to research if possible. Their assignment is to research the constellation and then reduce the information they find into three of four sentences. Have each student write this information neatly on half a sheet of lined paper and then frame the paper with one half sheet of construction paper. Place one end of the string between the pieces of paper and glue them together.

Next make a paper circle about the size of a quarter. Sketch the location of each star in the constellation onto this circle, or use a photocopier to reduce the size of the constellation description from the reference to the size of the film canister lid. Using a push pin, transfer the drawing from the paper to the inside of a film canister lid. Once you have all the stars plotted on the lid, force the push pin completely through the lid to make a small hole representing each star. It is a good idea to use a piece of plywood underneath the lid when forcing the push pin through.

Next drill a ¼ inch (6 mm) hole in the bottom of a black film canister. This will become the eyepiece for the constellation viewer.

Finally, tie a small knot in the loose end of the string, and place this into the film canister, and press on the lid. With a permanent marker, draw an arrow on the outside of the lid to indicate the North or upwards direction of the constellation.

Special Instructions

Don't forget to consider the star constellations that show up in the opposite hemisphere from your location. Sailors and other navigators can't use the North Star if they can't see it from where they are sailing!

Activity 7.30

The Rope Kit

Sooner or later while cutting a piece of rope, you'll end up with a short section and rather than tossing this remnant into the scrap pile, you'll save it, just in case you ever discover an initiative or activity that could use just this one special piece of rope. For those of you that have experienced this event, this section is for you! The following ideas for challenge and adventure activities all use rope as the primary piece of equipment. You can use this list of materials for building your own Rope Kit. It is also likely that you will be able to purchase such a kit from some of the national challenge course builders in the near future. Either Project Adventure and/or Inner Quest may stock this item after December 1998.

A few years ago, Patrick English-Farrell of the Cradlerock Group gave a terrific workshop at a joint conference sponsored by the Middle Atlantic region of the Association for Experiential Education and the Virginia Council of Outdoor Adventure Education entitled, "90 Minutes and a Rope." The best part of the whole wonderful class was the realization that a single piece of rope is more than enough equipment to lead dozens of activities.

Listed below are some of the challenge and adventure activities listed in this book (shown with an *) and others that can be facilitated using rope or tubular webbing as the primary equipment. For metric conversion: 1 inch = 25.4 mm and 10 feet = 3.05 meters.

Activity	Equipment Needed
Tree of Knots*	One rope, 25 to 100 feet long
2B or KNOT 2B*	Five ropes, each 7 to 15 feet long
Pot of Gold*	One rope 100 feet long, three ropes 30 feet long
Blind Target*	One boundary rope 30 to 50 feet long, two ropes 12 feet long made into loops
Worm Hole*	One section of shock cord 50 to 100 inches long
Extended Knots*	Use the ropes from 2B or KNOT 2B
Bull Ring*	10 pieces of string, each 10 feet long and one metal ring
Stretching the Limit*	Rope segments, any number and length
Handcuffs and Shackles*	2B or KNOT 2B ropes, or cloth clothesline 5 feet long
Not Knots*	Any rope segments, 5 to 15 feet long
Raccoon Circle Activities*	1″ tubular webbing, 12 to 15 feet long
Traffic Circle*	A rope loop made from 7 to 10 feet of rope
3 Houses / 3 Wells*	9 pieces of rope, each at least 10 feet long
Trust Walks	A rope at least 4 feet long for each person in the group
Yurt Circle	A rope circle made from at least 50 feet of rope
Blind Polygon	A segment of rope 50 to 100 feet long
Group Jump Rope	A rope at least 30 feet long
Circle the Circle	10 to 15 feet of tubular webbing or rope, tied into a loop
A Work of Art*	Many short pieces of rope, two of every kind

Activity	Equipment Needed
Surfing the Web*	100 feet of ¼ inch poly rope plus 80 feet of shock cord
A Collection of Knots*	30 feet of ½ inch diameter rope
Traffic Circle*	7 to 10 feet of rope tied into a loop
Moving Towards Extinction*	Rope loops of various sizes

Where to Find the Right Ropes

Finding the right ropes for challenge and adventure activities is essential. If you don't happen to find what you need at your local hardware store, several sources for ropes and other challenge course materials can be found in Chapter 8.

Activity 7.31

Theatre Sports

Here are a few theatre improv activities that can be quite a bit of fun with an uninhibited group. While these activities appear mostly as games, they offer some valuable insights for the group. Learning how to read the emotions of others within the group is indeed useful. Learning how to participate as part of a group, and where to fit in, is also a useful life skill. In Arms Expert, learning how to work effectively with a partner is a matter of timing and skill, both of which can be transferred back to the workplace or community of the group.

The Hitchhiker

Place four chairs in front of the audience, two in front and two behind (just like the four seats in a car). The activity begins with four people in the car, driving, engaged in typical commuting conversations. Up ahead, they see a hitchhiker. Should they stop? Should they pick them up? Should they drive on?

They stop and pick up the hitchhiker, who gets into the front passenger seat, the front passenger moves to the driver's seat, the driver moves to the seat behind them (becoming the backseat driver), the backseat driver moves to the other side of the back, and the final passenger leaves the vehicle and rejoins the audience.

After this quick switch, everyone in the car takes on the personality of the hitchhiker. If the hitchhiker is quiet, the car becomes quiet. If the hitchhiker starts singing, so does the rest of the car.

Encourage the passengers to mimic the hitchhiker, but not to outperform them. After a minute, a new hitchhiker comes from the audience to change the mood of the vehicle.

Arms Expert

This is probably one of the funniest activites we have ever seen, especially if you happen to have two partners that can really work well together. Arms Expert begins with one person standing in front with their arms straight down at their sides. The partner stands behind them, and places their arms around the person towards the audience. You now have the "expert" (the person in the front) and the "arms" (the person in the back).

The audience can now ask questions of this learned and knowledgeable expert. As the expert provides the infinite knowledge they possess, the "arms" provides a series of appropriate arm and hand movements to accent the answer from the expert. Occasionally, the hand motions seem to go off in new directions, pulling the expert to follow. Here is a brief example:

Question from the audience:	"I always wondered, how does a bee tell other bees where the flowers are at?"
Answer from the Arms Expert:	"Well, as you know, there are two ways this happens." (The arms person holds up two fingers) "The third way (arms holds up three fingers and then begins flapping his arms wildly) is that the bee performs a wild dance to attract the attention of other bees. . . ."

Activity 7.32

The Three Minute Challenge

NAME ______________________________ A Three Minute Challenge—Just for Fun

1. Read each of the following instructions carefully before doing anything else. Work quickly, you have just three minutes. Don't worry about being neat.
2. Put your name in the upper right hand corner of this paper.
3. Circle "name" in instruction number two.
4. Draw five small squares in the upper left hand corner of this paper.
5. Put an "X" in each square.
6. If you are the first person to get this far, call out loudly, "I am the first person to this point! I am the leader in following directions !"
7. After instruction number six write "yes, yes, yes".
8. Put an "S" in the lower left hand corner of this page.
9. Draw a triangle around the S you just made.
10. On the back of this paper, multiply 4 by 51.
11. Draw a square around the word "paper" in instruction number four.
12. If you have followed directions carefully to this point, call out "I have".
13. On the reverse side of this paper add 8950 and 9805.
14. Put a circle around your answer and put a square around the circle.
15. Punch three small holes in the top of this paper with your pencil or pen.
16. Say out loud, "I am nearly finished ! I have followed directions !"
17. When you are finished reading carefully, perform only instructions one, two, twelve and eighteen.
18. Write the words "ICE BREAKERS" in capital letters across the bottom of this paper.

Activity 7.33

Two Truths and a Lie

You can learn a great deal about a person by what they truthfully say, but sometimes you can learn even more when they lie. Here is a quick little activity to expand the amount of information you'll typically hear from someone during an introduction. This works especially well for small groups.

The activity is called, Two Truths and a Lie, and is played like this: As each person in the group introduces themselves, they also mention two things about themselves that are true, and one which is not. For example, Bob says, "Hi, my name is Bob, and I have been to Paris. I have taken a raft down the Colorado River, and I have three daughters, all named Sarah."

What is surprising about Two Truths and a Lie, is that sometimes, the answer that is most incredible, and least believable, is actually one of the truths! Play this activity when you have a creative bunch of folks, and a little bit of time for introductions.

Activity 7.34

Up Jenkins

We've been told that Up Jenkins was played as far back as the American Civil War. It is not that we doubt it, we just have no way to prove it!

For those times when you find your group sitting around a rectangular table, here is a fun activity to pass the time. Let's imagine that you have a total of eight people in your group. Four people, Team A, are seated on one of the long sides of the table, and four people, Team B, are seated on the other. Team A begins with a coin, such as an American quarter, or a British pound, or a Canadian two-dollar coin (games can be so international). They place their hands below the table, and begin passing the coin up and down their line of players, so that Team B cannot see who has the coin. At some point in the passing, Team B say, "Up Jenkins," at which point all of Team A simultaneously lifts their arms up, with hands closed tightly into fists, and places their elbows on the table. On the count of three, all the members of Team A slam their hands down on the table with hands open, palms down, fingers together. If their technique is good, it will be hard for Team B to tell who has the coin. Team B now begins choosing hands based on where they think the coin is. Each guess counts as a point. Team B keeps guessing until they find the coin. It is not uncommon for the

coin to be under the very last hand chosen. Team A now gives the coin to Team B, and the fun begins all over.

Another version of Up Jenkins is called Slammers

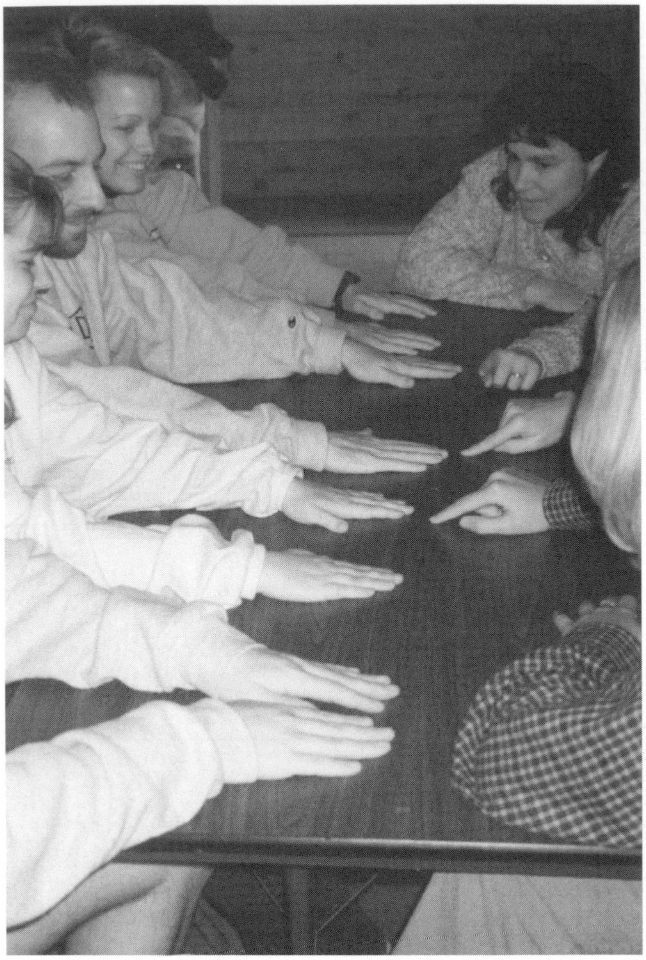

and Creepers. After the opposite team has called Up Jenkins as mentioned above, they can also call for slammers, or they can call for creepers. If they call for slammers, the opposite team slams down their hands, just as they did in the above version. If however, they call for creepers, the opposite team must slowly lower their hands to the table, keeping their fists closed, until they touch the table. Now they must slowly open their fingers until their hands are completely open, fingers together, palms down on the table. It is usually somewhere in this slow creeping motion that the coin makes a loud entrance, but some players become masters, and even in creepers mode, can conceal the coin successfully.

Although it is easy to keep score in this game, it is far more fun just to see how many guesses it takes during each round to find the coin. You can even reverse this game and try to make the last hand the one with the coin.

Notes

Activity 7.35

Where Do We Put All This Stuff?

"In Level One of a Teamplay workshop, we typically acquaint participants with a variety of challenge and adventure activities. In Level Two, we teach participants how to build this equipment. In Level Three, we teach participants how to pack their cars with all this stuff. Level Three is the hardest level!"

Jim Cain and Barry Jolliff

Considering that two or three different rooms in each of our houses are filled with challenge and adventure equipment, we thought we should probably say a few words about how we store all this stuff. Technically speaking, we use any container we can find depending on the exact need of the activity, or where we are taking the equipment.

Making Friends At the Rubbermaid® Store. Barry Jolliff lives in Wooster, Ohio. Rubbermaid® headquarters are in Wooster, Ohio. Three guesses what we put most of our challenge equipment into!

The good news is that the large Rubbermaid® storage containers for sporting equipment are exactly the maximum size that you can transport onto most commercial airlines in the United States. They also have locking handles to keep your stuff inside them. Just be careful, you can easily pack a few hundred pounds into one of these containers. Some of the newest designs from Rubbermaid® also have wheels—which makes moving the equipment for a portable program even easier. Thanks Rubbermaid®!

Making Stuff Sacks from Military Camouflage Pants. If you need a bunch of stuff sacks, try making friends with your local military surplus store. We found one that makes shorts from military pants, and then turns the lower leg portion of each pant leg into a stuff sack, simply by turning the leg inside-out and sewing the knee region closed. Then invert the pant leg, and use the draw-string ankle closures as the closures for your stuff sack. The material will last a long time, and the cost will probably be less than any commercial stuff sack you can buy.

A Trip to Home Depot®. If you are in search of the large waterproof metal construction site boxes made by Greenlee, you can find these at some of the bigger warehouse hardware stores such as Home Depot®. These boxes are great for storing and securing your ropes course equipment on-site. They are waterproof, weatherproof, and have some serious locking capabilities.

Activity 7.36

Who Is It?

Here is a simple game that promotes watching the eye contact and body language of others. After a volunteer has left the group, select a person to lead the motions. Even before the volunteer returns, the leader begins a motion, such as snapping their fingers together using their right hand. Once the person returns to the center of the group, they will attempt to guess which player is it, as they watch all the participants in the group. The leader should change motions several times every minute. Motions can be simple, such as hand clapping, or complicated, requiring the entire body.

When the volunteer correctly guesses the leader a new round begins. One variation that is extremely difficult is to change leaders with every new motion. This can keep the volunteer guesser in the center busy for a while.

Activity 7.37

Win, Lose, Cheat or Tie

As an interesting alternative to standardly competitive games, try this unique variation. Before the game commences, ask the players if they want to play to win, play to lose, cheat (playing outside the rules, except where safety is concerned) or play to tie. It is amazing how differently an activity can be when instead of fierce competition, players modify the goals of the game.

Playing to win is the standard scenario for most competitive games and sports. Playing to lose however does not necessarily mean playing poorly, but can mean playing in a manner that supports the other team. Playing to cheat is sure to raise the eyebrow of many an academic administrator, as we hear them say, "what values are you teaching these students." In fact, the simple act of blatantly cheating in front of so many witnesses brings about the ability to discuss integrity, honesty and truthfulness within the limits of trying to think outside of the box. If games really are a way of practicing and enforcing life values and skills, then experiencing cheating, and discussing this experience should help to reinforce the positive nature of playing fairly. Finally, playing to tie can be very challenging for a group. It requires a sense of where the other team is at, and also requires constant observation and timing.

Activity 7.38

Signs that you might be a little over the top in Challenge and Adventure Programming

1. If you have ever spent more than $100 on rope!
2. If the local hardware store owner knows your name, and calls you whenever there is a sale on PVC tubing. Bonus points if you have ever showed the owner how to balance 20 nails on the head of one nail!
3. If the only reason you learned to sew was so that you could make your own lycra tube, blindfolds, or funderbirds.
4. If you have ever called up another facilitator or presenter after midnight just to share a cool new activity you've just learned.
5. If you read the email from the aeelist before you read the email from your family.
6. If you have memorized the 800 number for your favorite carabiner supplier.
7. If you can name more than five of the registered voting members of ACCT.
8. If you have personally met or corresponded with more than three of the AEE Kurt Hahn or Michael Stratton award winners.
9. If you receive phone calls after 11pm or before 7am to lead challenge course activities for groups that you have never heard of.
10. If you have ever seen a prop for a challenge activity and said, "Gee, I could make that myself," and then did.
11. If you resist throwing out short segments of rope just in case you invent some new challenge activity that could use these segments.
12. If you can identify most of the following abbreviations: ACA, AEE, ACCT, PA, NSEE, NCOBS, AAHPERD, CAEL, and BLW.
13. If you watched the movies Cliffhanger and The River Wild just for the climbing and white water rafting scenes.
14. You have several rooms in your house that you close the doors to when company comes. These are the "my challenge and adventure stuff is in there" rooms, and they are continuously in a state of chaos.
15. You think that a lycra tube makes a perfectly acceptable wedding present.
16. You keep waiting for the trees in your backyard to be big enough for a ropes course.
17. You have ever tried to bring more than 100 pounds of challenge equipment onto an airplane.
18. You schedule your conferences, workshops, and training sessions up to a year in advance.
19. You have forgotten your first kiss, but can clearly remember your first zip line ride.
20. You have ever attended a challenge event instead of an important family function. This last one can be fatal!

Chapter Eight

Finding the Resources You Need

There certainly are no shortages to the information available on challenge and adventure activities specifically, and outdoor education and games in general. In this chapter you will find a comprehensive list of resources and reference materials from a variety of sources, on more than a dozen subjects related to challenge education.

Basic Training

Chapter 8 References

Resources in this chapter are provided in the following areas:

Books, Manuals, Texts and Guides

Additional Resources

Basic Training

The Wish List

Throughout Chapter 8, resources are listed alphabetically within each section. At the end of this chapter, in Section 8.28, a wish list is presented which provides a very concise listing of some of the best known and well regarded resources, organizations, vendors and information sources. While this list does not imply any endorsement by the authors, and indeed is the personal bias of the authors, it does provide a fairly concise view of some of the best resources in the field of challenge and adventure programming.

Books, Manuals and Guides

In the first 18 sections of this chapter, you will find several hundred references, listed alphabetically by lead author, relating to the field of challenge and adventure activities and a variety of related outdoor activities and pursuits. Some of these publications are available from the public library. If you have trouble finding a specific reference in print, try contacting the publisher directly or the book resources listed in Section 8.26 of this chapter.

8.01 Challenge and Adventure Activities, Initiatives, Groupwork and Ropes Course Materials

International Challenge Course Symposium Proceedings Association for Challenge Course Technology (ACCT), 1996, Purcellville, VA
Technical information related to building, inspecting and maintaining a challenge course.

Adventure Recreation—An Adventure in Group Building Sharon Baack, Hal Hill & Joe Palmer, 1989, Convention Press, Nashville, TN
Some familiar challenge activities revisited.

The Petrogrip Guide to Building Affordable Climbing Walls Jim Bowers, 1997, Petrogrips, 108 East Cherry Lane State College, PA 16803 Phone (814) 867-6870 Email: Petrogrips@penn.com

Project Cope Boy Scouts of America, 1991, Irving, TX ISBN 0-8395-4365-4

4-H/UOAC Adventure Ropes Course—Leader's Handbook Jim Brenner and Diane Nichols, 1981, 4-H/Urban Outdoor Adventure Center, P.O.Box 16156 San Francisco, CA 94116 also available as ERIC Document ED 255528.

Teamwork & Teamplay Jim Cain and Barry Jolliff, 1998, Kendall/Hunt Publishing Company, Dubuque, IA Winner of the Karl Rohnke Creativity Award from AEE! ISBN 0-7871-4532-1

Cooperative Group Problem Solving—Adventures in Applied Creativity Douglass Campbell, 1994, Frank Schaffer Publications, Inc., Torrence, CA ISBN 0-86734-557-8

Affordable Portables Chris Cavert, Experiential Products, Denton, TX

The E.A.G.E.R. Curriculum Chris Cavert, Experiential Products, Denton, TX 227 different experiential activities, games, and educational recreation activities.

Artificial Climbing Wall Design and Use Jerry Cinnamon, March 1985, ERIC Document ED256538

Changing Pace—Outdoor Games for Experiential Learning Carmine M. Consalvo, 1996, Human Resource Development Press, Amherst, MA ISBN 0-87425-354-3

Experiential Training Activities for Outside and In Carmine M. Consalvo, 1993, Human Resource Development Press, Amherst, MA ISBN 0-87425-962-2

Flow Mihaly Csikszentmihalyi, 1990, Harper & Row, New York, NY ISBN 0-06-016253-8 Some fairly high level information on creating an environment for personal growth.

Outdoor Adventure Activities for School and Recreation Programs Paul W. Darst and George P. Armstrong, 1980, Waveland Press ISBN 0-88133-583-5 Phone (708) 634-0081 Information on rope courses, ground level initiatives, climbing and more.

Challenge Course Manual—An Instructor's Guide for The Outdoor Education Center Julie A. Fassett, The Outdoor Education Center, Houston Independent School District, Route 2, Box 25B, Trinity, TX 75862 ERIC Document ED342749

Team Building Through Physical Challenge Donald Glover and Daniel Midura, 1992, Human Kinetics Books, Champaign, IL ISBN 0-87322-359-4 Useful activities for school and physical education classes.

Cooperative Games Book Sally Harms, 1997, National Farmers Union, Aurora, CO A collection of some tried and true activities.

Technical Tree Climbing Peter Jenkins, 1988 National Conference on Outdoor Recreation, Fort Collins, CO, ERIC Document ED357904.

On Course Adrian Kissler, 1994, Available through On Course and the ACA bookstore.

The Rock Climbing Teaching Guide J. Kudlas, 1979, AAHPERD, Reston, VA

The Book on Raccoon Circles Jim Cain and Tom Smith, 2002 Learning Unlimited, Tulsa, OK Phone (888) 622-4203 or www.learningunlimited.com

High Adventure Outdoor Pursuits J. F. Meier, T. Morash and C. Welton, 1980, Brighton Publishing Company, Salt Lake City, UT

High Adventure Outdoor Pursuits: Organization and Leadership Joel Meier, Morash and Welton, 1980, Brighton Publishing, Salt Lake City, UT

Experiential Activities for High Performance Teamwork Beth Michalak, Steve Fischer and Larry Meeker, 1995, Human Resource Development Press, Amherst, MA.

More Team Building Challenges Daniel W. Midura and Donald R. Glover, 1995, Human Kinetics Books, Champaign, IL ISBN 0-87322-785-9

Confidence Course Instructor's Guide Montgomery County Public Schools, 1984, Rockville, MD, ERIC Document ED 249033

Project Exploration: A Ropes Course Curriculum Guide Trish Nice, 1980, Project Exploration, Townsend, MA

North Carolina Outward Bound School Instructor's Handbook North Carolina Outward Bound School, 1979, Morganton, NC ERIC Document ED 209 046

Northwest Outward Bound School Instructor's Manual Northwest Outward Bound School, April 1981, Portland, OR ERIC Document ED 209 027

Ready, Set, Go !!! A Guide to Low Prop, No Prop Initiative Games and Activities Brenda Oberle and Sheri McClarren, 1994, Published by Direct Instructional Support Services, Inc. 123 West New England Avenue Worthington, OH 43085

Islands of Healing: A Guide to Adventure Based Counseling Dick Prouty, Paul Radcliffe and Jim Schoel, 1988, Project Adventure, Hamilton, MA ISBN 0-934-38700-1

Challenge by Choice—A Manual for the Construction of Low Elements and Ropes Courses Karl Rohnke, 1987, Project Adventure, Hamilton, MA

Cowtails and Cobras II—A Guide to Games, Initiatives, Ropes Courses & Adventure Curriculum Karl Rohnke, 1989, Kendall/Hunt Publishing Company Dubuque, IA ISBN 0-8403-5434-7 One of the best primers to challenge courses on the face of the earth.

The Bottomless Bag Karl Rohnke, 1988, Kendall/Hunt Publishing Company Dubuque, IA

The Bottomless Bag Again! Karl Rohnke, 1993, Kendall/Hunt Publishing Company Dubuque, IA ISBN 0-8403-8757-1

The Bottomless Bag Live! 60 Minute Video Tape Karl Rohnke, 1993, Kendall/Hunt Publishing Company Dubuque, IA ISBN 0-8403-9075-0

The Bottomless Baggie Karl Rohnke, 1991, Kendall/Hunt Publishing Company Dubuque, IA ISBN 0-8403-6813-5

FUNN STUFF—Volume I Karl Rohnke, 1996, Kendall/Hunt Publishing Company, Dubuque, IA ISBN 0-7872-1633-X

FUNN STUFF—Volume II Karl Rohnke, 1996, Kendall/Hunt Publishing Company, Dubuque, IA ISBN 0-7872-2316-6

Silver Bullets—Initiative Problems, Adventure Games & Trust Activities Karl Rohnke, 1984, Kendall/Hunt Publishing Company, Dubuque, IA ISBN 0-8403-5682-X
Probably, dollar for dollar, the best single book ever published on challenge and adventure activities.

Quicksilver A Guide to Leadership, Initiative Problems, Adventure and Trust Activities Karl Rohnke and Steve Butler, 1995, Kendall/Hunt Publishing Company, Dubuque, IA ISBN 0-7872-0032-8

The Pictorial Guide to Group Work Activities Geoff Sanders, 1991, ISBN 0-9517302-0-7

Feeding the Zircon Gorilla and Other Team Building Activities Sam Sikes, 1995, Learning Unlimited, Tulsa, OK, ISBN 0-9646541-0-5
A recent reference, filled with challenge and adventure activities.

It Is Outdoors—A Guide to Experiential Activities G. A. Simmons and E. C. Cannon, 1991, AAHPERD, Reston, VA ISBN 0-88314-499-9, ERIC Document ED330694.

Initiative Games Benjy Simpson, 1978, Colorado Outward Bound School, and also Butler Community College, College Drive, Oak Hills, PA 16001 Phone (412) 287-8711.
A collection of early activities, some of which also appear in Silver Bullets, New Games, and Cowtails and Cobras.

Raccoon Circles Tom Smith, 1996, Raccoon Institute P.O.Box 695 Cazemovia, WI 53924
A bunch of things to do with a single section of tubular webbing.

The Power of Team Building—Using Rope Techniques Harrison Snow, 1992, Pfeiffer & Company, San Diego, CA, ISBN 0-88390-306-7
An overview of teambuilding with a corporate perspective.

Ropes Course Procedural Manual Jim Wall, W. Delano and C. DeLano, 1991, Outdoor Institute Press, Pittsboro, NC

Ropes Course Manual Jim B. Wall and Catherine M. Tait, 1994, Kendall Hunt Publishing Company, Dubuque, IA ISBN 0-7872-0019-0
A very thorough description of all the information you need to conduct a ropes course activity.

Adventure Education David Wood and James Gillis, Jr., 1979, Published by National Education Association of the United States, Washington D.C., Stock No. 1677-7-00 ISBN 0-8106-1677-7
An interesting academic look at challenge related education.

50 Activities for Teambuilding Mike Woodcock, 1988, Gower Publishers, Aldershot.

8.02 Outdoor Activities and Outdoor Education

Are We Having Fun Yet? Enjoying the Outdoors with Partners, Families & Groups Brian Baird, 1995, The Mountaineers, Seattle, WA

Outdoor Education—A Resource guide to Outdoor Education in New England Elaine Barber and Will Phillips, Editors, 1978, Appalachian Mountain Club, Boston, MA

The Kids' Summer Handbook Jane Drake and Ann Love, 1994, Tickner & Fields, NY, ISBN 0-395-68709-8

The Camper's Guide to Outdoor Pursuits Jack Drury and Eric Holmlund, 1997, Sagamore Publishing, Champaign, IL ISBN 1-57167-74-2

Leadership and Administration of Outdoor Pursuits—Second Edition Phyllis Ford and Jim Blanchard, 1993, Venture Publishing, State College, PA ISBN 0-910251-60-6

University of New Hampshire Outdoor Education Program Manual Mike Gass, 1983, UNH, ERIC Document ED 242472

The Outdoor Leadership Handbook—A Manual for Leaders of Land-Based Outdoor Pursuits in the Pacific Northwest Paul Green, 1982, Emergency Response Institute, Tacoma, WA ISBN 0-913724-32-7 ERIC Document ED243612

Just Beyond the Classroom Clifford E. Knapp, 1996, Clearinghouse on Rural Education and Small Schools, Charleston, WV ISBN 1-880785-15-3

Outdoor Education: A Manual for Teaching in Nature's Classroom Michael Link, 1981, Prentice-Hall, Englewood Cliffs, NJ

The Complete Wilderness Training Book Hugh McManners, 1994, Dorling Kindersley, NY ISBN 1-56458-488-7

High Adventure Outdoor Pursuits: Organization and Leadership Meier, Morash and Welton, 1980, Brighton Publishing Co., Salt Lake City, UT

The Outside Play and Learning Book—Activities for Young Children Karen Miller, 1989, Gryphon House, Mt. Rainier, MD ISBN 0-87659-117-9

The Outdoor Action Leader's Manual Outdoor Action Program, 1995, Princeton University, Princeton, NJ 08544

Outdoor Programmers Resource Guide Outdoor Recreation Coalition of American (ORCA), Phone (303) 444-3353

Outdoor Pursuits: Guidelines for Educators G. Rawson, 1990, North Ministry of Education, Wellington, New Zealand.

Hug a Tree—And Other Things To Do Outdoor With Young Children Robert E. Rockwell, Elizabeth A. Sherwood and Robert A. Williams, Gryphon House, Inc. Mt. Rainier, MD ISBN 0-87659-105-5

Integrated Outdoor Education and Adventure Programs Stuart J. Schleien, 1993, Sagamore Publishing, Champaign, IL, ISBN 0-915611-59-7

Working Out Of Doors With Young People Alan Smith, 1989, ITRC, Glasgow, Scotland ISBN 1-85202-002-4

The Outdoor Programming Handbook Ron Watters, 1986, Idaho State University Press, Pocatello, ID ISBN 0-937834-12-2

The 2 Oz. Backpaker Robert S. Wood, 1982, Ten Speed Press, Berkeley, CA ISBN 0-89815-070-1

8.03 Educational Pursuits and Experiential Education Issues

In Their Own Way Thomas Armstrong, 1987, J. P. Tarcher
Discusses the seven areas of intelligence.

Schools and Colleges Directory Association for Experiential Education, 1995, Boulder, CO
Chronicals more than 200 programs related to experiential and outdoor education.

The Study of Games E. M. Avedon, 1971, John Wiley and Sons, Inc, NY

The Conscious Use of Metaphor in Outward Bound S. Bacon, 1983, Colorado Outward Bound School, Denver, CO

Relationship of Leadership Style, Gender Personality and Training of Outward Bound Instructors and Their Course Outcomes N. L. Bartley, 1987, Doctoral Dissertation, University of Utah, Salt Lake City, UT

Field Study—A Sourcebook for Experiential Learning Borzak, L., Editor, 1981, Sage Publications, Beverly Hills, CA

Schools of Thought: How the politics of literacy shape thinking in the classroom Rexford G. Brown, 1991, Josey-Bass, San Francisco, CA

100 Ways to Enhance Self-Concept in the Classroom J. Canfield and H. C. Wells, 1976, Prentice-Hall, NJ

Cooperative Education and Experiential Learning—Forming Community, Technical College and Business Partnerships Jeffrey A. Cantor, 1995, Wall & Emerson, Dayton, OH ISBN 1-895131-14-6

Differences Between Experiential and Classroom Learning Coleman, J., 1976, Jossey-Bass, San Francisco, CA

The Nature of Adventure Education Claude Cousineau, 1978, ERIC Document ED 171474

Fieldwork: An expeditionary learning Outward Bound reader—Volume I E. Cousins and M. Rodgers, Editors, 1995, Kendall/Hunt Publishing Company, Dubuque, IA ISBN 0-7872-0229-0

Fieldwork: An expeditionary learning Outward Bound reader—Volume I E. Cousins and M. Rodgers, Editors, 1996, Kendall/Hunt Publishing Company, Dubuque, IA ISBN 0-7872-2308-5

Kids Can Cooperate: A practical guide to teaching problem solving Elizabeth Crary, 1984, Parenting Press, Seattle, WA ISBN 943990-04-1

Experience and Education John Dewey, 1938, MacMillian Publishing, NY

Play with a Purpose—Learning games for children six weeks to ten years Dorothy Einan, 1985, Pantheon Books, NY, ISBN 0-394-54493-5

Outdoor Adventure Pursuits: Foundations, Models and Theories Alan W. Ewert, 1989, Publishing Horizons, Inc., Scottsdale, AZ ISBN 0-942280-50-4
An in-depth text for understanding the components of adventure activities.

Groupwork Skills—A Training Manual Fewell and Wolfe, 1991, Health Education Board for Scotland.

Frames of Mind: The Theory of Multiple Intelligence, 10th Anniversary Edition H. Gardner, 1993, BasicBooks, NY

More Than Activities Roger Greenaway, 1990, Save the Children Fund, Endeavour, Scotland Available from Adventure Education, Penrith, Cumbria, England ISBN 1-870322-21-5

Teaching in the Outdoors D. R. Hammerman, W. M. Hammerman and E. L. Hammerman, 1994, 4th Edition, Interstate Publishers, Danville, IL

Fifty Years of Resident Outdoor Education, 1930–1980: Its Impact on American Education William M. Hammerman, 1980, American Camping Association, Martinsville, IN ISBN 0-87603-055-X

Personal Growth Through Adventure David Hopkins and Roger Putnam, Adventure Education, England.

Cooperative Learning: Cooperation and Competition—Theory and Research Johnson, Johnson and Smith, 1989, Interaction Book Company, Edina, MN

Strengthening Experiential Education Within Your Institution Jane Kendall, John Duley, Thomal Little, Jane Permaul and Sharon Rubin, National Society for Experiential Education, Raleigh, NC

A Sourcebook for Teaching Problem Solving Stephen Krulik and Jesse A. Rudnick, 1984, Allyn and Bacon, Boston, MA ISBN 0-205-08106-1

The Challenge of Excellence, Volume I—Learning the Ropes of Change Scout Lee and Jan Summers, 1990, Metamorphous Press, Portland, OR ISBN 1-5552-004-9

Outdoor Education—A Manual for Teaching in Nature's Classroom Michael Link, Prentice-Hall, Inc. Englewood Cliffs, NJ

Handbook of Alternative Education Jerry Mintz, Editor, 1994, Macmillan Publishing Company, Riverside, NJ ISBN 0-02-897303-5

Adventure Education C. J. Mortlock, 1978, Keswick Ferguson Publishers, London, ERIC Document ED 172994

American Higher Education: A Guide to Reference Sources Peter P. Olevnik, 1993, Greenwood Publishing Group, Westport, CT ISBN 0-313-27749-4

Feeling Great—Teaching Children to Excel at Living Terry Orlick, 1996, Creative Bound, Carp, Ontario, Canada ISBN 0-921165-43-9

Group Dynamics in the Outdoors—A Model for Teaching Outdoor Leaders Maurice Phipps, ERIC Document ED356935

Into the Classroom: The Outward Bound® Approach to Teaching and Learning Mitchell Sakofs and George P. Armstrong, 1996, Kendall/Hunt Publishing Company, Dubuque, IA ISBN 0-7872-1972-X

Where Colleges Fail N. Sanford, 1967, Jossey-Bass, San Francisco, CA

Learning After College N. Sanford, 1980, Montaigne, Inc., CA

The Fifth Discipline Fieldbook Peter M. Senge, Art Kleiner, Charlotte Roberts, Richard B. Ross, Bryan J. Smith, 1994, Currency, NY ISBN 0-385-47256-0

Handbook of Cooperative Learning Methods Shlomo Sharan, 1994, Greenwood Publishing Group, Westport, CT ISBN 0-313-28352-4

The Theory and Practice of Challenge Education Thomas E. Smith, Christopher C. Roland, Mark D. Havens and Judity A. Hoyt, 1992, Kendall/Hunt Publishing Company, Dubuque, IA ISBN 0-8403-8042-9

Leisure Education: A Manual of Activities and Resources Norma J. Stumbo and Steven R. Thompson, 1988, Venture Publishing, State College, PA ISBN 0-910251-25-8

Leisure Education II: More Activities and Resources Norma J. Stumbo, 1992, Venture Publishing, State College, PA ISBN 0-910251-54-1

Tips and Tricks in Outdoor Education Malcolm Swan, Editor, Interstate Printer & Publishers, Danville, IL

Making Sense of Experiential Learning: Diversity in Theory and Practice Susan Warner Weil and Ian McGill, Editors, 1989, Open University Press, Philadelphia, PA ISBN 0-335-09549-6

The Theory of Experiential Education Karen Warren, Jasper Hunt and Mitch Sakofs, 1995, Third Edition, Association for Experiential Education, Kendall/Hunt, Dubuque, IA ISBN 0-7872-0262-2

A Simpler Way Margaret J. Wheatley and Myron Kellner-Rogers, 1996, Berrett-Koehler Publishers, Inc., San Francisco, CA ISBN 1-881052-95-8

8.04 Corporate Interests

Outdoor Development for Managers John Bank, 1985, Gower, Aldershot, England.

Experiential Training Activities for Outside and In Carmine M. Consalvo, 1994, Human Resource Development Press, Amherst, MA
Team building with a corporate focus.

Experiential Activities for High Performance Teamwork Beth Michalak, Steve Fischer and Larry Meeker, 1994, Human Resource Development Press, Amherst, MA
Corporate Training and Personnel Development Materials, priced for corporations.

Team Players and Teamwork Glenn M. Parker, 1990, Jossey-Bass Publishers, San Francisco, CA

Do It and Understand the Bottom Line on Corporate Experiential Learning Christopher Roland and Richard Wagner, 1995, Kendall/Hunt, Dubuque, IA ISBN 0-7872-0308-4
Articles by educators and trainers from around the world discussing experienced based training.

The Team Handbook—How to Use Teams to Improve Quality Peter R. Scholtes, 1988, Joiner Associates Madison, WI.
A corporate perspective on building teams in the workplace.

The Power of Team Building—Using Rope Techniques Harrison Snow, 1992, Pfeiffer and Co., San Diego, CA 92121 ISBN 0-88390-306-7

8.05 Bringing a Group Together and Teambuilding

Random Acts of Kindness The Editors of Conari Press, 1993, Conari Press, Emeryville, CA 94608 ISBN 0-943233-44-5

52 Simple Ways to Build Your Child's Self-Esteem & Confidence Jan Dargatz, 1991, Oliver-Nelson Books, Nashville, TN ISBN 0-8407-9587-4

Teamwork in Programs for Children and Youth: A Handbook for Administrators Howard G. Garner, 1982, Charles C. Thomas Publisher, ISBN 0-398-04655-7

Tribes—a process for social development and cooperative learning Jeanne B. Gibbs, 1987, Center Source Publications, Santa Rosa, CA ISBN 0-932762-08-5

Warm Ups & Wind Downs: 101 Activities for Moving and Motivating Groups Sandra P. Hazouri and Miriam S. McLaughlin, 1993, Educational Media Corporation, Minneapolis, MN ISBN 0-932-796-52-4

Joining Together—Group Theory and Group Skills David W. Johnson and Frank P. Johnson, 1994, Allyn and Bacon, Boston, MA ISBN 0-205-15846-3

Telltale Trees—What the Tree You Draw Reveals About You! Ethel Johnson, 1984, Maple Terrace Enterprises, Inc. 1217 West Market Street Orville, OH 44667 ISBN 0-9613738-0-6
A fun and informative group activity, especially for new groups.

If . . . (Questions for the Game of Life) Evelyn McFarlance and James Saywell, 1995, Villard Books, NY ISBN 0-679-44535-8
Questions for discussion in pairs or in groups. Contains some material that is only appropriate for adult issues.

Learning to Work in Groups M. Miles, 1970, Teachers College Press, Columbia University.

Groups—Theory and Experience Rodney W. Napier and Matti K. Gershenfeld, Fifth Edition, Houghton Mifflin Company, Boston, MA

Organizational Development Through Teambuilding T. H. Patten, 1981, John Wiley, NY

The Delicate Art of Dancing With Porcupines—Learning to Appreciate the Finer Points of Others Bob Phillips, 1989, Regal Books Ventura, CA 93006 ISBN 0-8307-1333-6

Working Effectively in Groups and Teams: A Resource Book R. Posner, Editor, 1990, Mid-Atlantic Association for Training and Consulting, Washington, DC.

Building Assets Together—101 Group Activities for Helping Youth Succeed Jolene L. Roehlkepartain, 1995, Search Institute, Minneapolis, MN ISBN 1-57482-333-7

Youth Group Trust Builders Denny Rydberg, 1993, Group Publishing, Inc. Box 481 Loveland, CO 80539 ISBN 1-55945-172-6

Energizers and Icebreakers—For All Ages and Stages Elizabeth Sabrinsky Foster, 1989, Educational Media Corporation Minneapolis, MN ISBN 0-932796-25-7

More Energizers and Icebreakers—For All Ages and Stages—Book II Elizabeth Sabrinsky Foster-Harrison, 1994, Educational Media Corporation Minneapolis, MN ISBN 0-932796-64-8

The Book of Questions Gregory Stock, 1987, Workman Publishing Co, Inc. New York, NY 10003 ISBN 0-89480-320-4

The Kids Book of Questions Gregory Stock, 1988, Workman Publishing Co, Inc. New York, NY 10003 ISBN 0-89480-631-9

The Book of Questions: Business, Politics and Ethics Gregory Stock, 1991, Workman Publishing Co, Inc. New York, NY 10003 ISBN 1-56305-034-X

Cooperation: Learning Through Laughter—51 Brief Activities for Groups of All Ages Charlene C. Wenc, 1993, Educational Media Corporation Minneapolis, MN ISBN 0-932796-51-6

Playful Activities for Powerful Presentations Bruce Williamson, 1993, Whole Person Associates, Inc., Duluth, MN ISBN 0-938586-77-7

8.06 Leadership

On Becomming a Leader Warren Bennis, 1989, Addison-Wesley, Reading, MA

Leadership and Administration of Outdoor Pursuits Phyllis Ford and Jim Blanchard, 1993, Second Edition, Venture Publishing, State College, PA ISBN 0-910251-60-6

How to make the world a better place—A guide to doing good—Over 100 quick and easy actions Jeffrey Hollender, 1990, Quill William Morrow, NY

8.07 Universal Access, Youth-At-Risk, Adapted Activities and Special Populations

Games, Sports and Exercises for the Physically Handicapped Ronald Adams, Alfred Daniel and Lee Rullman, 1972, Published by Lea & Febiger ISBN 0-8121-0352-1

Therapeutic Recreation: An Introduction D. Austin and M. Crawford, Editors, 1991, Prentice Hall, Englewood Cliffs, NJ

Principles and Methods of Adapted Physical Education and Recreation David Auxter and Jean Pyfer, 1985, Times Mirror/Mosby College Publishing, St. Louis, Missouri, ISBN 0-8016-0378-1

Sports and Recreation for the Disabled: A Resource Manual Benchmark Press, Inc. 8435 Keystone Crossing Suite 175 Indianapolis, IN 46240

Recreation for the Disabled Child Donna B. Bernhardt, Editor, 1985, Haworth Press, NY ISBN 0-86656-263-X

Activities for Adolescents in Therapy Susan T. Dennison, 1988, Charles C. Thomas Publisher, Springfield, IL ISBN 0-398-05409-6

Adapted Adventure Activities—A Rehabilitation Model for Adventure Programming and Group Initiatives Wendy Ellmo and Jill Graser, 1995, Kendall/Hunt Publishing Company, Dubuque, IA ISBN 0-7872-0334-3

The Adventure Book—A Curriculum Guide to School Based Adventuring with Trouble Adolescents Susan Erickson and Buck Harris, 1980, Connecticut State Department of Education, Wilderness School/Alternative Education Project, ERIC Document ED 200381

Therapeutic Recreation: Its Theory, Philosophy and Practice V. Fry and M. Peters, 1972, Stackpole Books, Harrisburg, PA

Directory of Experiential Therapy and Adventure-Based Counseling Programs J. Gerstein, 1993, Association for Experiential Education, Boulder, CO

Experiential Family Counseling: A Practitioner's Guide to Orientation, Warm-Ups and Family Building Initiatives Jackie S. Gerstein, 1994, Kendall/Hunt Publishing Company, Dubuque, IA ISBN 0-8403-9314-8

Backyards and Butterflies—Ways to Include Children with Disabilities in Outdoor Activities Doreen Greenstein and Naomi Miner, New York State Rural Health and Safety Council, 324 Riley-Robb Hall Cornell University Ithaca, NY 14853-5701 Phone (607) 255-0150

Bridge to Accessibility—A Primer for Including Persons with Disabilities in Adventure Curricula Mark D. Havens, 1993, Kendall/Hunt Publishing Company, Dubuque, IA ISBN 0-8403-7891-2

The Outdoor Programming Handbook Idaho State University Press Box 8118 Pocatello, ID 83209

A Study of the Therapeutic Benefits of the Summer Camp on the Handicapped Child M. A. Kawasaki, 1979, Unpublished research report, Indiana University.

The International Directory of Recreation-Oriented Assistive Device Sources Lifeboat Press, P.O. Box 11782 Marina Del Ray, California 90295

Research in Therapeutic Recreation: Concepts and Methods Marjorie J. Malkin and Christine Z. Howe, Editors, 1993, Venture Publishing, State College, PA ISBN 0-910251-53-3

Making School and Community Recreation Fun for Everyone—Places and Ways to Integrate M. Sherril Moon, Editor, 1994, Paul H. Brookes Publishing, Baltimore, MD ISBN 1-55766-155-3

Directory of Therapeutic Adventure Professionals Edited by Jim Moore, 1996, Association for Experiential Education, Boulder, CO

Resource Guide National Center on Accessibility, 5040 St. Rd. 67 N Martinsville, IN 46151 Phone 1-800-424-1877
Accessibility Sources and Publications for Recreation, Parks and Places of Tourism.

A Guide to Wheelchair Sports and Recreation Paralyzed Veterans of American, 1994. Includes a list of activities, organizations and ideas for activities involving individuals in wheelchairs.

Creative Play Activities for Children with Disabilities—A Resource book for Teachers and Parents Lisa Rappaport Morris and Linda Schulz, 1989, Human Kinetics, Champaign, IL ISBN 0-87322-933-9

An Introduction to Adventure: A sequential approach to challenging activities with person's who are disabled Christopher Roland and Mark Havens, 1981, Vinland National Center, Loretto, MN

Together Successfully—Creating Recreational and Educational Programs that Integrate People with and without Disabilities John E. Rynders and Stuart J. Schleien, 1991, The Association for Retarded Citizens of the United States Publications Department P.O.Box 1047 Arlington, TX 76004

Integrated Outdoor Education and Adventure Programs Stuart J. Schleien, Leo H. McAvoy, Gregory J. Lais & John Rynders, 1993, Sagamore Publishing, Champaign, IL ISBN 0-915611-59-7 An educational text on integrated programs.

Study of the Effects of Camping on Handicapped Children H. D. Sessoms, M. M. Mitchell, N. W. Walker and H.R. Fradkin, 1978, Unpublished Easter Seal Research Foundation report, University of North Carolina, Chapel Hill, NC

A Guide to Designing Accessible Recreation Facilities Special Programs and Populations National Park Service, Washington, DC 20240

The Outdoor Programming Handbook Ron Watters, 1986, Idaho State University Press, Pocatell, ID ERIC Document RC 019118

Adapted Physical Education and Sport Joseph P. Winnick, Editor, 1990, Human Kinetics Books, Champaign, IL ISBN 0-87322-258-X

Fitness Courses with Adaptations for Person with Disabilities Vinland National Center 3675 Ihduhapi Road P. O. Box 308 Loretto, MN 55357

A Guide to Outdoor Education Resources and Programs for the Handicapped Dennis A. Vinton, Project Director, 1982, Kentucky University, Lexington, KY ERIC Document ED 273401

8.08 Activities for Mature Populations

Recreation Programming and Activities for Older Adults Jerold Elliott & Judith Sorg-Elliott, 1991, Venture Publishing, State College, PA ISBN 0-910251-46-0

Grey Hair and I Don't Care Carlita Hunter, 1993, Hunter House Productions, Harrisburg, NC Phone (704) 547-0171

Adventure After 60: Working with Elders in the Outdoors Deborah A. Sugerman, 1983, ERIC Document ED 308995

Exercise Programming for Older Adults Kay A. Van Norman, 1995, Human Kinetics, Champaign, IL ISBN 0-87322-657-7

8.09 Environmental Issues

Project Learning Tree American Forest Foundation 1250 Connecticut Avenue NW Washington, D.C. 20036

The Northeast Field Guide to Environmental Education Antioch New England Graduate School, 1991, Box C Roxbury Street Keene, NH 03431
An extensive list of environmental organizations with educational information in the northest U.S.

Bottle Biology Bottle Biology Resources Network, February 22, 1990, 1630 Linden Dr. Madison, WI 63706 Phone (608) 263-5645
Great ideas for 2 liter bottles.

Keepers of the Earth—Native American Stories and Environmental Activities for Children Michael J. Caduto and Joseph Bruchac

50 Simple Things You Can Do To Save The Earth The Earth Works Group, 1989, The Earthworks Press Box 25 1400 Shattuck Avenue Berkeley, CA 94709 ISBN 0-929634-06-3

The New Complete Guide to Environmental Careers Environmental Careers Organization (formerly CEIP fund), 1993, Island Press, ISBN 0-933280-84-X

The Man Who Planted Trees (The Book) Jean Giono, 1985, Chelsea Green Publishing Co. Chelsea, VT 05038 ISBN 0-930031-06-7

The Man Who Planted Trees (The Recording) Written by Jean Giono, Narrated by Robert Lustsema, Music by Paul Winter Consort, 1990, Earth Music Productions P.O. Box 68 Litchfield, CT 06759 ISBN 0-930031-34-2

Soft Paths—How to enjoy the wilderness without harming it Bruce Hampton and David Cole, 1988, Stackpole Books, Harrisburg, PA ISBN 0-8117-2234-1

Walking Softly in the Wilderness John Hart, 1984, Sierra Club Books, San Francisco, CA

The Canadian Environmental Education Catalogue: A Guide to Selected Resources and Materials Wally Heinrichs, et. al., 1991, Pembins Institute, Alberta, Canada, ISBN 0-921719-07-8
Available in book form or on computer disk (dos or mac formats available).

The Nature Directory—A Guide to Environmental Organizations Susan D. Lanier-Graham, 1991, Walker and Company, NY ISBN 0-8027-1151-0

The Great Garbage Concert—Environmental Song and Activity Book Glenn McClure and Paula Stopha McClure, 1991, McClure Productions P.O. Box 293 Geneseo, NY 14454 Phone (716) 243-0324

This Planet is Mine—Teaching Environmental Awareness and Appreciation to Children Mary Metzger and Cinthya P. Whittaker, 1991, Simon & Schuster NY ISBN 0-671-73733-3
The perfect guide for concerned parents and teachers—includes dozens of fun and creative learning activities for kids from toddler to preteen.

Leave No Trace—Outdoor Skills & Ethics—Rock Climbing Developed by the National Outdoor Leadership School, 1996, Lander, WY

The Nature Directory: A Guide to Environmental Organizations ISBN 0-8027-7348-6

Mountaineering: The Freedom of the Hills Ed Peters, Editor, The Mountaineers, Seattle, WA

Project WILD 5430 Grosvenor Lane Bethesda, MD 20814 Phone (301) 493-5447 Fax (301) 493-5627

The Directory of National Environmental Organizations U.S. Environmental Directories, 1986, P.O.Box 65156 St. Paul, MN 55165

Just A Dream Chris Van Allsburg, 1990, Houghton Mifflin Co. 2 Park Street Boston, MA 02108 ISBN 0-395-53308-2

Acclimatization—A Personal and Reflective Approach to a Natural Relationship Steve Van Matre, 1974, American Camping Association, Martinsville, IN

Sunship Earth—An Acclimatization Program for Outdoor Learning Steve Van Matre, 1979, American Camping Association, Martinsville, IN

Earth Education—A New Beginning Steve Van Matre, 1990, Institute for Earth Education,

8.10 The Adventure Philosophy, Anthologies of Great Ideas and Historically Significant Publications

Of Play and Playfulness—Materials, Methods, . . . and Snacks at Ten. Nan Cope, Hal & Sy Kantor and Margaret Moyer, 1990 ISBN 0-944470-03-3
A Recreation Handbook of the Eastern Cooperative Recreation School.

The Well-Played Game—A Player's Philosophy Bernard De Koven, 1978, Anchor Books, Anchor Press/Doubleday, Garden City, NY ISBN 0-385-13268-9

Education as Experience J. Dewey, 1938, Macmillan Publishing, NY

The Omnibus of Fun—Volume I Larry & Helen Eisenberg, 1988, ISBN 0-87603-109-2
A Historically Significant Volume of Ideas.

A Call to Character Colin Greer and Herbert Kohl, Editors, 1995, Harper Collins, NY ISBN 0-06-017339-4

Directory of Programs in Outdoor Adventure Activities Alan N. Hale, 1975, Outdoor Experiences, Inc., Mankato, MN. May be out of print.

A History of Recreation Laboratories and Workshops Martha Hampton, 1988, Springville, IA Available from Recreation Laboratories & Workshops, Inc.

Impelled Into Experience James Hogan, 1968, Education Productions, London.

No Contest, The Case Against Competition—Why We Lose in Our Race To Win Alfie Kohn, 1986, Houghton Mifflin Co. Boston, MA 02108 ISBN 0-395-39387-6
A fascinating tutorial on our infatuation with competition and the opportunities that exist for cooperative adventures.

Punished by Rewards Alfie Kohn, 1993, Houghton Mifflin Co. Boston, MA 02108

Recreation Leader's Handbook Richard Kraus, 1955, McGraw-Hill, NY

Outward Bound USA: Learning through experience in adventure-based education
Joshua L. Miner and Joe Boldt, 1981, Morrow Quill Paperbacks 105 Madison Avenue, New York, NY 10016 ISBN 0-688-00414-8
The history of the Outward Bound movement from the very beginning. This edition may be out of print, but is also available on ERIC Microfiche, Document Number ED 215 811.

The Adventure Alternative Colin Mortlock, 1994, Cicerone Press, Cumbria, England ISBN 1-85284-012-9

Winning Is Everything and Other American Myths Thomas Tutko and William Bruns, 1976, Macmillan Publishing, NY ISBN 0-02-620770-2

8.11 Program Evaluation and Assessment

Many recent periodical references on this subject can be found in Chapter 1.

Three Approaches to Evaluation: A Ropes Course Illustration Marc Braverman, et. al., Journal of Experiential Education, Volume 13, Number 1, May 1990, pages 23–30.

Outdoor Leadership Competency: A Manual for Self-Assessment and Staff Evaluation
L. Buell, 1983, Environmental Awareness Publications, Greenfield, MA

An Alternative Feedback/Evaluation Model for Outdoor Wilderness Programs
R. Dawson, 1980, ERIC Document ED 207745.

Outdoor Leadership Competency—A Manual for Self-Assessment & Staff Evaluation
Environmental Awareness Publications, 1983, Greenfield, MA

Outdoor Adventure Pursuits: Foundations, Models and Theories Alan Ewert, 1989, Publishing Horizons, Scottsdale, AZ ISBN 0-942280-50-4

Working Effectively—A Guide to Evaluation Techniques Feek, 1987, Bedford Square Press (NCVO), England

Measuring Change, Making Changes—An Approach to Evaluation Graessle and Kingsley, 1986, London Community Health Resource, England.

Improving Evaluation in Experiential Education Bruce Hendricks, November 1994, ERIC Digest Document EDO-RC-94-8

Evaluating Training Programs—The Four Levels Donald L. Kirkpatrick, 1994, Berrett-Koehler, San Francisco ISBN 1-881052-49-4
Chapter 13, Evaluating an Outdoor-Based Training Program, includes commentary by Richard Wagner author of many significant challenged-based articles.

8.12 Processing, Debriefing and Review

A Manual for Group Facilitators B. Auvine, B. Densmore, M. Extrom, S. Poole and M. Shanklin, 1977, The Center for Conflict Resolution, Madison, WI

The Conscious Use of Metaphor in Outward Bound Stephen B. Bacon, 1983, Colorado Outward Bound School, Denver, CO

Listening: The Forgotten Skill Burney-Allen, 1982, John Wiley & Sons.

Theory and Practice of Group Counseling G. Corey, 1985, Second Edition, Brookes/Cole Publishing, Monterey, CA

Flow—The Psychology of Optimal Experience Mihaly Csikszentmihalyi, 1990, Harper & Row, NY ISBN 0-06-016253-8

The Book of Metaphors—A Descriptive Presentation of Metaphors for Adventure Activities Michael Gass and Craig Dobkins, 1991, Available from Michael Gass, University of New Hampshire

Book of Metaphors—Volume II Michael A. Gass, 1995, Kendall/Hunt Publishing Company, Dubuque, IA ISBN 0-7872-0306-8
Includes two activities by author Jim Cain.

Playback—A Guide to Reviewing Activities Roger Greenaway, 1993, Endeavour, Scotland.

Learning From Conflict—A Handbook for Trainers Lois B. Hart, 1981, Addison-Wesley.

Creative Reviewing Hunt and Hitchen, 1986, Groundwork Press.

Joining Together—Group Theory and Group Skills David W. Johnson and Frank P. Johnson, 1994, Allyn and Bacon, Boston, MA ISBN 0-205-15846-3

Lasting Lessons: a teacher's guide to reflecting on experience Clifford E. Knapp, 1992, ERIC/CRESS Clearninghouse, Charleston, WV ERIC Document Number ED 348204.

Adolescent Self-Disclosure: Its facilitation through themes, therapeutic techniques and interview conditions Marlene C. Mills, 1985, P. Long Publications, NY

Processing the Adventure Experience—Theory and Practice Reldan S. Nadler and John L. Luckner, 1992, Kendall/Hunt Publishing Company, Dubuque, IA ISBN 0-8403-7028-8
A classic.

Processing the Experience—Strategies to Enhance and Generalize Learning John L. Luckner and Reldan S. Nadler, 1997, Kendall/Hunt Publishing Company, Dubuque, IA ISBN 0-7872-1000-5
The second edition of the classic.

The Annual Handbook for Group Facilitators J. W. Pfeiffer and J. E. Jones, 1972+, University Associates, La Jolla, CA

How to Process Experience L.K.Quinsland and A. Van Ginkel, National Technical Institute for the Deaf, Rochester Institute of Technology, Rochester, NY

Debriefing: Its Effects on an Adventure Program P. Schempp, 1980, Unpublished manuscript, Boston University, Boston, MA

The Skilled Facilitator: Practical Wisdom for Developing Effective Groups Roger M. Schwarz, 1994, Jossey-Bass, San Francisco, CA ISBN 1-55542-638-7

A How-to Guide to Reflection Harry Silcox, Brighton Press, Holland, PA

Notes on Processing Challenge/Adventure Experiences With Clients From Business and Industry Tom Smith, 1992, Raccoon Institute P.O.Box 695 Cazenovia, WI 53924

The Backcountry Classroom The Wilderness Education Association, 1992, Fort Collins, CO.
Chapter 9 describes several group processing and debriefing methods.

8.13 Creativity

The Brain Game—27 Classic Intelligence Tests That Will Reveal Your Unique Abilities Rita Aero and Elliott Weiner, 1983, Quill, NY ISBN 0-688-01923-4
A wonderful variety of standardized tests in general mathematics, art, creativity, memory, reading, science, IQ and more.

Train Your Brain for Expressive Learning: Discover Your Multiple Intelligences Gabe Campbell, 1989, 39 Maplewood, Akron, OH 44313 Phone (216) 253-5109

Drawing on the Right Side of the Brain—A Course in Enhancing Creativity & Artistic Confidence Betty Edwards, 1989, Jeremy P. Tarcher, Inc. 9110 Sunset Blvd. Los Angeles, CA 90069 ISBN 0-87477-513-2

Magic Eye—A New Way of Looking at the World, Volumes I, II and III 3D Illusions by N.E.Thing Enterprises, 1994, Published by Andrews and McMeel Kansas City, KS ISBN 0-8362-7006-1

Thinkertoys—A Handbook of Business Creativity for the 90's Michael Michalko, 1991, Ten Speed Press Box 7123 Berkeley, CA 94707 ISBN 0-89815-408-1
An incredible collection of activities for enhancing your creative thinking.

A Whack on the Side of the Head—How to Unlock Your Mind For Innovation Roger von Oech, 1983, Warner Books, NY ISBN 0-446-38908-0
Brings out the creativity in all of us.

A Kick in the Seat of the Pants—Using Your Explorer, Artist, Judge and Warrior to be More Creative Roger von Oech, 1986, Harper & Row, New York, NY 10022 ISBN 0-06-015528-0

8.14 Games

Games for all Occasions—297 Indoor & Outdoor Games Ken Anderson & Morry Carlson, Youth Specialties Grand Rapids, MI 49506

Games We Should Play in School Frank Aycox, 1985, Front Row Experience ISBN 0-915256-16-9

Games for Social and Life Skills Tim Bond, Nichols Publishing Company, NY

Gamesters' Handbook—140 Games for Teachers and Group Leaders Donna Brandes and Howard Phillips, 1978, Hutchinson and Company, London ISBN 0-09-136421-3

Gamesters' Handbook Two Donna Brandes, 1982, Hutchinson and Company, London ISBN 0-09-159001-9

Creative Campfires Douglas R. Bowen, 1974, Thorne Printing, Nampa, ID 83651
Hard to find, but great to own.

Towards Togetherness: The Cooperative Games, Songs and Activities Book Richard Burrill, Anthro Company, Sacramento, CA ISBN 1-878464-12-4

50 Ways to Use Your Noodle Chris Cavert and Sam Sikes, 1997, Learning Unlimited, Tulsa, OK ISBN 0-9646541-1-3
A collection of games and problem-solving activities using the colorful floating pool toys.

Games (and Other Stuff) for Groups Chris Cavert, Experiential Products, Denton, TX

Games and Great Ideas Rhonda L. Clements, 1995, Greenwood Publishing Group, Westport, CT ISBN 0-313-29460-7

The New Games Book—Play Hard, Play Fair, Nobody Hurt Andrew Fluegelman, Editor, 1976, Doubleday & Company, Inc., NY ISBN 0-385-12516-X
A classic.

More New Games—Playful Ideas from the New Games Foundation Andrew Fluegelman, Editor, 1981, Doubleday & Company, Inc. NY ISBN 0-385-17514-0
Also a classic.

Outdoor Action Games for Elementary Children—Active Games and Academic Activities for Fun & Fitness David R. Foster & James L. Overholt, 1994, Parker Publishing Co., West Nyack, NY ISBN 0-13-009895-7

The Outrageous Outdoor Games Book—133 Group Projects, Games and Activities Bob Gregson, 1984, David S. Lake Publishers, Belmont, CA ISBN 0-8224-5099-2

The Incredible Indoor Games Book—160 Group Projects, Games and Activities Bob Gregson, 1982, David S. Lake Publishers, Belmont, CA ISBN 0-8224-0765-5

Great Games to Play With Groups Frank W. Harris, 1990, Fearon Teachers Aids, Parsippany, NY

Ground Loop William Hazel, 1995, Center for Active Education, Warminster, PA

A Compact Encyclopedia of Games, Games, Games for People of All Ages compiled by Mary Hohenstein, 1980, Bethany Fellowship, Inc. 6820 Auto Club Road Minneapolis, MN 55438 ISBN 0-87123-191-3

Elementary Teacher's Handbook of Indoor and Outdoor Games Art Kamiya, 1985, Parker Publishing Company, Inc. West Nyack, NY ISBN 0-13-260845-6
A strong focus on cooperation, group problem-solving and physical skill building. There is also a chapter on building low-cost recreation equipment.

New Games for the Whole Family Dale N. LeFevre, 1988, Perigee Books, Putnam Publishing Group, NY ISBN 0-399-51448-1

The Recreation Handbook Robert L. Loeffelbein, 1992, McFarland & Co., Jefferson, NC ISBN 0-89950-744-1

Hopscotch, Hangman, Hot Potato, and Ha, Ha, Ha—A Rulebook of Children's Games—More than 250 Gameso Jack Maguire, 1990, Prentice Hall Press, NY ISBN 0-13-631102-4

Learning through non-competitive activities and play B. Michaelis and D. Michaelis, 1977, Learning Handbooks, Palo Alto, CA

The Cooperative Sports & Games Book—Challenge Without Competition Terry Orlick, 1978, Pantheon Books, NY ISBN 0-394-73494-7
A classic.

The Second Cooperative Sports & Games Book—Over two hundred brand-new noncompetitive games for kids and adults both Terry Orlick, 1982, Pantheon Books, NY ISBN 0-394-74813-1

More Campfire Programs Jack Pearse, Jane McCutcheon & John Jorgenson, 1988, Cober Printing, Kitchener, Ontario, Canada

Clouds on the Clothesline Jack Pearse, Jane McCutcheon and Barrie Laughton, 1993, Cober Printing, Kitchner, Ontario, Canada ISBN 0-921155-03-4

Playing Smart—A Parent's Guide to Enriching, Offbeat Learning Activities for Ages 4–14 Susan K. Perry, Free Spirit Publishing

Bag of Tricks—180 Great Games (and Three More with Real Potential) Jane Sanborn, 1984, Search Publications ISBN 0-910715-02-5

Bag of Tricks II—More Great Games for Children of All Ages Jane Sanborn, 1994, Search Publications ISBN 0-910715-02-5

Everbody Wins—393 Non-Competitive Games for Young Children Jeffrey Sobel, 1983, Walker & Co. 720 Fifth Avenue New York, NY 10019 ISBN 0-8027-7237-4

Playfair—Everybody's Guide to Noncompetitive Play Matt Weinstein & Joel Goodman, 1980, Impact Publishers, San Luis Obispo, CA ISBN 9-915166-50-X
This should be on your bookshelf somewhere.

The Discourse—A Manual for Students and Teachers of the Frisbee® Disc Arts 1992, WHAM-O Sports Promotion 835 East El Monte St. San Gabriel, CA 91778-0004
A complete tutorial on the simple and complex skills of Frisbee enjoyment.

Play It—Great Games for Groups Mike Yaconelli & Wayne Rice, 1986, Youth Specialties, Grand Rapids, MI ISBN 0-310-35191-X

Play It Again!—More Great Games for Groups Mike Yaconelli & Wayne Rice, 1993, Youth Specialties, Grand Rapids, MI ISBN 0-310-37291-7

Super Ideas for Youth Groups Mike Yaconelli & Wayne Rice, 1979, Youth Specialties Zondervan Publishing House, Grand Rapids, MI 49506 ISBN 0-310-34981-8

Creative Socials and Special Events Mike Yaconelli and Wayne Rice, 1986, Zondervan Publishing House, Grand Rapids, MI ISBN 0-310-35131-6

8.15 Toys, Games and Activities

Awakening Your Child's Natural Genius—Enhancing Curiosity, Creativity and Learning Ability Thomas Armstrong, Jeremy P. Tarcher, Inc., Los Angeles, CA 90036 ISBN 0-87477-608-2

Brite-Tite Book O' Fun Glenn Q. Bannerman, Beth B. Gunn and Lee Ann B. Konopka, 1996, Group Publishing and Bannerman Family Celebration Services, Montreat, NC ISBN 1-55945-626-4
Creative Nylon Hoseplay games and activities for all ages.

The World of Games Jack Botermans, Tony Burrett, Pieter van Delft and Carla van Splunteren, 1989 Published by Facts on File, Inc. 460 Park Avenue South New York, NY 10016 ISBN 0-8160-2184-8
A beautifully illustrated book on the origins and history of board, table and outdoor games from around the world, including directions for making and playing these games.

Play Book Steven Caney, Workman Publishing Co., NY

How to Hold a Crocodile—Hundreds of Fascinating Facts and Wicked Wisdom Produced by "The Diagram Group", 1986, Treasure Press, Michelin House 81 Fulham Road London England SW3 6RB ISBN 1-85051-125-X
A collection of fun and fascinating things to do. This book may be out of print.

Recreation Leader's Handbook Richard Kraus, 1955, McGraw-Hill Book Company, NY

The Great American Depression Book of Fun—Growing Up in the 30's Toys, Games and High Adventures John O'Dell and Richard Loehle, 1981, Harper & Row Publishers, Inc. 10 East 53rd Street New York, NY 10022 ISBN 0-06-090898-X
A vast collection of simple toys and games, complete with dimensions.

Rise Up Singing—Sing Out Magazine's Group Singing Songbook Sing Out Corporation, 1988, P.O.Box 5253 Bethlehem, PA 18015 Phone (215) 865-5366 ISBN 0-86571-137-2
A great collection of music and songs.

Lollipop Grapes and Clothespin Critters—Quick, On-the-spot Remedies for Restless Children 2–10 Robyn Freedman Spizman, Addison-Wesley Publishing Company

Foxfire 6 . . . Toy & Games . . . and other affairs of just plain living Edited by Eliot Wigginton, 1980, Anchor Books, ISBN 0-385-15272-8

8.16 Puzzles and Games

Intelligence Games—Games from all over the world that test your powers of Reasoning, Imagination and Savvy Franco Agostini & Nicola Alberto DeCarlo, 1987, Simon & Schuster, NY ISBN 0-671-63201-9

Giant Book of Puzzles and Games Sheila Anne Barry, 1978, Sterling Publishing Co., Inc., NY ISBN 0-8069-9761-3

The Book of Ingenious & Diabolical Puzzles Jack Botermans and Jerry Slocum, 1994, Times Books ISBN 0-8129-2153-4

The New Book of Puzzles Jack Botermans and Jerry Slocum, 1992, W. H. Freeman and Company ISBN 0-7167-2356-5

Tricks, Games & Puzzles with Matches Maxey Brooke, 1973, Dover Publications, Inc., NY ISBN 0-486-20178-3

536 Puzzles & Curious Problems Henry Dudeney, 1967, Charles Scribner's Sons, Math and Geometry Puzzles & More

Mathematical Puzzles and Other Brain Twisters Anthony S. Filipiak, 1942, Bell Publishing Company, NY

Mathematical Magic Show—More Puzzles, Games, Diversions, Illusions & Other Mathematical Sleight-of-Mind From Scientific American Magazine Martin Gardner, 1977, Alfred A. Knopf, NY

Puzzlegrams Compiled by Pentagram, 1989, A Fireside Book published by Simon & Schuster, NY ISBN 0-671-68740-9

The Giant Book of Games from Games Magazine Edited by Will Shortz, 1991, Random House, NY ISBN 0-8129-1951-3

The Penguin Book of Curious and Interesting Puzzles David Wells, 1992, Penguin Books, NY ISBN 0-14-014875-2
One of most extensive collections ever.

8.17 Knots, String and Fun Things to do with Rope

String—Tying It Up—Tying It Down Jan Adkins, 1992, Charles Scribner's Sons, NY ISBN 0-684-18875-9

Rope Activities for Fun, Fitness and Fonics American Alliance for Health, Physical Education and Recreation (AAHPER), Practical Pointers, Volume 1, Number 11, May 1978, ERIC Document ED 160586

The Morrow Guide to Knots—For Sailing, Fishing, Camping, Climbing Mario Bigon and Guido Regazzoni, 1982, William Morrow and Company ISBN 0-688-01226-4

Arborist Equipment Donald Blair, 1995, International Society of Arboriculture.

50 Practical and Decorative Knots You Should Know Percy W. Blandford, Tab Book, Inc., Blue Ridge Summit, PA

Cowboy Roping and Rope Tricks Chester Byers, 1966, Dover Publications, Inc., NY ISBN 0-486-25711-8

Fiber Rope Technical Information Manual Gail P. Foster, The Cordage Institute, February 1993, 350 Lincoln Street, Suite 115, Hingham, MA 02043 Phone (617) 749-1016 Fax (617) 749-9783

Self-Working Rope Magic—70 Foolproof Tricks Karl Fulves, 1990, Dover Publications, NY ISBN 0-486-26541-2

Creative Rope Skipping—Official Competition Rules Lois Hale, 1985, Anchor Printing, South Lake Tahoe, CA

The Essential Know Book—The Seamanship Series Colin Jarman, 1986, International Marine Publishing Company, Camden, ME ISBN 0-87742-221-4

Fun With String Joseph Leeming, 1940, J. B. Lippincott, Philadelphia, also available from Dover Publications, Inc., NY

Chinese Jump Rope Sheree S. Marty, 1994, Sterling Publishing ISBN 0-8069-0352-X

Rope Skipping for Fun and Fitness Bob Melson and Vicki Worrell, Woodlawn Publishers, Wichita, KS

Forget Me Knots—A gentle reminder of the knots, ropes and lore used on a Challenge Ropes Course Karl Rohnke, 1992, Kendall/Hunt Publishing Company, Dubuque, IA ISBN 0-8403-7138-1

The Book of Rope and Knots Bill Severn, 1976, David McKay Company, NY ISBN 0-679-50674-8

On Rope—North American Vertical Rope Techniques Bruce Smith and Allen Padgett, 1996, National Speleological Society, Huntsville, AL ISBN 1-879961-05-9

Knowing the Ropes—A Sailor's Guide to Selecting, Rigging and Handling Lines Aboard Roger C. Taylor, 1989, International Marine Publishing Company ISBN 0-9887297-0-7

8.18 Safety and Risk Management Issues

Outdoor Education Safety and Good Practice—Guidelines for Guidelines 1988, Available from Adventure Education, England

Adventure Program Risk Management Report: Incident Data and Narratives 1989–1990 AEE and Wilderness Risk Managers Committee, 1990, Boulder, CO

An Introduction to Cable Roof Structures H. A. Buchholdt, 1985, Cambridge University Press, NY ISBN 0-521-30263-3
Information and engineering data on designing cable structures.

Search and Rescue Fundamentals—Third Edition Donald C. Cooper, Patrick La Valla and Robert Stoffel, 1990, Emergency Response Institute, Inc. and National Rescue Consultants, Olympia, WA

Rope Rescue Manual James A. Frank and Jerold B. Smith, 1987, Califormia Mountain Company, Santa Barbara, CA

Project Adventure 20 Year Safety Study Compiled by L. Furlong et.al., 1995, Available from Project Adventure.

The Rock Climbing Teaching Guide John Kudlas, 1979, American Alliance for Health, Physical Education, Recreation and Dance (AAHPERD), Washington, D.C. ERIC Document ED 188824

International Mountain Rescue Handbook H. McInnes, 1972, Charles Scribner & Sons, NY

Project Adventure 15 Year Safety Study Project Adventure, February 10, 1992, Available from Project Adventure.

Using Ropes, Chains and Slings Safely Module SH-14, 1981, Safety and Health Center for Occupational Research and Development, Inc, Waco, TX ERIC Document ED213848

On Rope: North American Vertical Rope Techniques—New Revised Edition Bruce Smith and Allen Padgett, 1996, National Speleological Society, Huntsville, AL
Phone (205) 852-1300 Email: manager@caves.org

High Angle Rescue Techniques—A Student Guide for Rope Rescue Classes Tom Vines and Steve Hudson, 1989, National Association for Search and Rescue, Kendall/Hunt Publishing Company, Dubuque, IA ISBN 0-8403-5433-9

Ropes Course Safety Manual—An Instructor's Guide to Initiative and Low and High Elements Steven E. Webster, 1989, Kendall/Hunt Publishing Company, Dubuque, IA ISBN 0-8403-6207-2

General Wire Rope Catalogue 1995, Wire Rope Industries Ltd., 5501 Trans-Canada Highway, Pointe Claire, Quebec, Canada H9R 1B7 Phone 1-800-361-6742 or (514) 426-6404 Fax (514) 697-6779
A current publication with serious technical information about cable and wire rope usage.

Wire Rope Users Manual—Third Edition Wire Rope Technical Board P.O.Box 286 Woodstock, MD 21163-0286 Phone (410) 461-7030 Fax (410) 465-3195 Orders: RGR/WRTB Fulfillment P.O.Box 14921 Shawnee Mission, KS 66285-4921
A great illustrated guide to using cable and wire rope correctly. This manual includes one of the best photographic collections of cable safety concerns available. Definitely worth reviewing if you have a ropes course.

Additional Resources

8.19 Organizations

Just a few years ago Training and Development magazine published a list of over 100 North American Outdoor Training Companies. Within just a few years, some of these organizations had changed their focus, moved their offices or no longer were involved with outdoor training. The Association for Experiential Education, mentioned in this chapter also has a directory of experience-based and outdoor training companies. Before you decide to enlist the assistance of an outdoor training company, consider the types of groups they typically work with and the length of time they have been involved. The following organizations are involved with outdoor education, challenge course construction and the leadership and management of adventure-based training, plus some other organizations with an outdoor, wilderness, sports or educational theme. Inclusion in this list does not imply an endorsement of these organizations.

At the time of publication, the contact addresses of the organizations listed in this chapter were confirmed. If you happen to be looking for additional organizations not listed here, try The Encyclopedia of Associations, a handy publication that can be found at many libraries. This is a useful reference when trying to find addresses, phone numbers and other information about local, regional, national and international organizations. The encyclopedia is published by Gale Research, Inc. of Detroit, Michigan. There are also a variety of internet resources for locating the phone numbers, email addresses and mailing addresses of these organizations.

As a final note, the proliferation of cellular phone lines, fax lines and computer modem lines has recently caused the need to renumber many of the area codes for United States based phone lines. At the time of this publication numbers listed here were correct, but be aware that some area codes may have changed by the time you read this section.

The Access Fund P.O.Box 17010 Boulder, CO 80308 Phone (303) 545-6772 Internet: AccessFund@aol.com
A non-profit organization dedicated to preserving the interests of climbers and wilderness participants.

Accessibility Consulting Group 5605 Monroe Street Sylvania, OH 43560
Telephone/TDD 419-885-5554 Fax 419-882-4813
Training, consulting and information about ADA compliance, facilities, planning and design.

Active Living Canada 601-1600 James Naismith Drive Gloucester, Ontario, Canada K1B 5N4
Phone (613) 748-5743 Fax (613) 748-5734 Internet: alc@rtm.activeliving.ca
A national organization promoting physical activity, recreation and active living in Canada.

Adirondak Mountain Club R.R. 3 Box 3055 Lake George, NY 12845-9523 Phone (518) 668-4447
Fax (518) 668-3746

Adventure Education 12 St. Andrews Churchyard, Penrith, Cumbria CA11 7LS United Kingdom
Phone 01768 891065 Fax 01768 891914 Email: enquiries@adventure-ed.edi.co.uk
Information, journals, training, maps and more on Brittish outdoor education issues.

Adventure Foundation of Pakistan (AFP) No. 1 Gulistan Colony, Coll. Road, Abbottabad, Pakistan
Phone 5921 5526 Fax 5121 2540
This organization promotes the Outward Bound philosophy and utilizes adventure sports and activities in educational programs.

Adventure Guide 382 King Street North Waterloo, Ontario, Canada N2J 2Z3 Phone (519) 886-3121

Adventure Huntington St. Mary's Hospital 2900 First Avenue Huntington, WV 25702
Phone (304) 526-6015

Adventure Learning 1326 North Fares Avenue Evansville, IN 47711
Consultants in challenge based programs.

The Adventure Network P.O.Box 273 Chalfont, PA 18914 Phone (215) 997-9270
Challenge based workshops, training, first aid certification and equipment.

Advice Adventure Consultancy Boyd Centre, Dykehead, Port of Menteith, Stirling, Scotland FK8 3JY
Phone 08775 293

Alliance for Environmental Education (AEE) 9309 Center St., No. 101 Manassas, VA 22110-5599
Phone (703) 330-5667 Fax (703) 253-5811
Environmental concerns, information and education.

Alpine Club of Canada Box 2040 Canmore, Alberta, Canada T0L 0M0 Phone (403) 678-3200
Fax (403) 678-3224 ACC Library Box 160 Banff, Alberta, Canada T0L 0C0 Phone (403) 762-2291
Fax (403) 762-8919 Canada's national mountaineering organization.

American Alliance for Health, Physical Education, Recreation and Dance (AAHPERD)
1900 Association Drive Reston, VA 22091-9989 Phone (703) 476-3400 Fax (703) 476-9527
Resource information on health, physical education, recreation and dance activities.

American Alpine Association 113 East 90th Street New York, NY 10128-1589

The American Alpine Club (AAC) 710 Tenth Street, Suite 100 Golden, CO 80401
Phone (303) 384-0110 Fax (303) 384-0111 Internet: amalpine@ix.netcom.com
More than 90 years of advocation for mountaineers and climbers, publications, an extensive library, expedition insurance.

American Alpine Institute, Ltd. 1515 12th Street, N-1 Bellingham, WA 98225 Phone (360) 671-1505

American Association for Leisure and Recreation 1900 Association Drive Reston, VA 22091
Phone (703) 476-3472 Fax (703) 476-9527

American Camping Associations, Inc. 5000 State Road 67 North Martinsville, IN 46151-7902
Email: aca@aca-camps.org Phone (800) 428-CAMP, (800) 428-2267 or (765) 342-8456 Fax (765) 342-2065
Books, educational materials & seminars for all types of camping & outdoor activities and 32 local chapters acrossed the United States.

American Education Research Association (AERA) 1230 17th Street NW
Washington, DC 20036-3078 Phone (202) 223-9485 Fax (202) 775-1824
Internet: aera@asuvm.inre.asu.edu

American Federation of Teachers 555 New Jersey Avenue Washington, DC 20001
Phone (202) 879-4400

American Hiking Society P.O.Box 20160 Washington, DC 20041-2160 Phone (703) 255-9304
Fax (703) 255-9308 Internet: ahsmmbrshp@aol.com

The American Mountain Foundation 1520 Alamo Avenue Colorado Springs, CO 80907
Phone (719) 471-7736 Internet: http://climb-on.com
A non-profit corporation dedicated to the preservation of America's mountains, crags and wilderness.

American Mountain Guides Association 710 Tenth Street, Suite 101 Golden, CO 80401
Phone (800) RU4-AMGA or (303) 271-0984

American Park and Recreation Society 2775 S. Quincy Street, Suite 300 Arlington, VA 22206
Phone (703) 578-5558 Fax (703) 820-2617

American Recreation Coalition 1331 Pennsylvania Avenue Northwest #726 Washington, DC 20004
Phone (202) 662-7420 Fax (202) 662-7424

American Society for Training and Development (ASTD) 1640 King Street P.O.Box 1443
Alexandria, VA 22313 Phone (800) 628-2783 or (703) 683-8100 Fax (703) 683-8103
Internet: astdic@capcon.net
Books, seminars, conference and journals.

American Sport Climbers Federation (ASCF) Hans Florine-Executive Director 35 Greenfield Dr.
Moraga, CA 94556 Phone/Fax (510) 376 1640
The governing body for competitive climbing within the United States.

American Sport Education Program P.O.Box 5076 Champaign, IL 61825-5076 Phone (800) 747-5698 or (217) 351-5076 Fax (217) 351-2674
Formerly the American Coaching Effectiveness Program (ACEP). Resource materials for coaching including books, videos, workshops.

American Therapeutic Recreation Association (ATRA) P.O.Box 15215 Hattiesburg, MS 39404-5215 Phone (800) 553-0304 or (601) 264-3413 Fax (601) 264-3337

Appalachian Mountain Club (AMC) 5 Joy Street Boston, MA 02108-1490 Phone (617) 523-0636 Fax (617) 523-0722

Appalachian Trail Conference 799 Washington Street P.O.Box 807 Harpers Ferry, WV 25425-0807 Phone (304) 535-6331

Association for Adventure Sports (AFAS) House of Sport, Longmile Road, Dublin 12, Ireland Phone 1 4509845 Fax 1 4502805
Courses on outdoor education, recreation and environmental activities.

Association for Business Simulations and Experiential Learning (ABSEL) Wayne State University Department of Marketing 5201 Cass Avenue, Suite 300 Detroit, MI 48202 Phone (313) 577-4551 Fax (313) 577-5486

Association for Challenge Course Technology (ACCT) P.O.Box 255 Martin, Michigan 49070-0255 USA Phone (616) 685-0670 Fax (616) 685-7015 Email: acct@net-link.net Internet: www.acctinfo.org
Challenge course building information, standards, and professional networking.

Association for Environmental and Outdoor Education 253 Johnstone Court San Rafael, CA 94903 previously at 915 West Dunne Avenue Morgan Hill, CA 95307

Association for Experience-Based Training and Development 131 Village Parkway, Suite 4 Marietta, GA 30067 Phone (404) 951-2173
Experiential training with a corporate focus.

Association For Experiential Education (AEE) 2305 Canyon Blvd. Suite #100 Boulder CO 80303-5651 Phone 303-440-8844 FAX 303-440-9581 Internet: info@aee.org
Internet: aeelist@pucc.princeton.edu
Memberships are available for individuals and corporations. Information on experiential education for corporate, educational, institutional and small groups.

Association for Quality and Participation 801-B West 8th Street Cincinnati, OH 45203-1607 Phone (800) 733-3310 or (513) 381-1959 Fax (513) 381-0070

The Association for Supervision and Curriculum Development (ASCD) 1250 North Pitt Street Alexandria, VA 22314-1403 Phone (703) 549-9110 Fax (703) 549-3891

Association for the Study of Literature and Environment (ASLE) David W. Teague ASLE Secretary University of Delaware Parallel Program 333 Shipley Street Wilmington, DE 19801 Phone (302) 573-5463 Voice-mail (302) 571-5395 Internet: teague@strauss.udel.edu

Association of Heads of Outdoor Education Centers Pendarren House, Llangenny, Crickhowell, Powys, NP8 1HE United Kingdom Phone 01873 810694

Atlantic Challenge Box B Rockland, ME 04841 USA Phone (207) 594-1800 Fax (207) 594-5056 and also 357 Lakewood Dr. Midland, Ontario, Canada L4R 5H4 Phone/Fax (705) 526-0228
Internet: woodsken@hookup.net
An adventure and experiential education program based on Kurt Hahn's philosophies utilizing tall ships and maritime activities for international youth development.

The Australian and New Zealand Association for Leisure Studies (ANZALS) Centre for Leisure Research, School of Leisure Studies, Griffith University, Queensland, Australia
Internet: D.Coleman@hbs.gu.edu.au

Australian Outdoor Education Council GPO Box 1896R Melbourne 3001 Victoria Australia Phone 61 3 9428 9920 Fax 61 3 9428 0313 Email: voea@netspace.net.au

Big Bear Adventures P.O.Box 5210-Dept B Whitehorse, Yukon, Canada Y1A 4Z1 Phone (403) 633-5642 Fax (403) 633-5630 Internet: bear@yknet.yk.ca
Hiking, biking and river trips in the Yukon wilderness of Canada.

Bradford Woods 5040 State Road 67 North Martinsville, IN 46151 Phone (317) 342-2915 Fax (317) 349-1086
The Outdoor Education Center for Indiana University, also has the National Center on Accessibility and the American Camping Association on site.

Breckenridge Outdoor Education Center (BOEC) P. O. Box 697 Breckenridge, CO 80424 Phone (303) 453-6422 Fax (303) 453-4676
Provides high adventure activities for persons of all abilities.

British Sports Association for the Disabled The Mary Glen Haig Suite, Solcast House, 13-27 Brunswick Place, London, United Kingdom N16DX Phone 0171 490 4919

Camp America 102 Greenwich Avenue Greenwich, CT 06830 Phone (800) 72STAFF
Providing internation staff for your program needs.

Camp Ohio 11461 Camp Ohio Road St. Louisville, Ohio 43071 Phone (614) 745-2194
The state 4-H camp featuring two seperate adventure courses (ground level and high-ropes) available to 4-H, educational, private and corporate groups.

Canadian Assoc. for Health, Physical Education, Recreation & Dance (CAHPERD) 1600 James Naismith Drive, Suite 809 Gloucester, Ontario, Canada K1B 5N4 Phone (613) 748-5622 Fax (613) 748-5737 Internet: CAHPERD@activeliving.ca

Canadian Outdoor Leadership Training (COLT) Center Box 2160 Campbell River Brittish Columbia, Canada V9W 5C9 Phone (604) 286-3122 Fax (604) 286-6010
Outdoor education training from kayaking to climbing of Vancouver Island.

Canadian Parks/Recreation Association (CP/RA) 1600 James Naismith Drive Suite 306 Gloucester, Ontario, Canada K1B 5N4 Phone (613) 748-5651 Fax (613) 748-5854 Internet: cpra@activeliving.ca
A national voluntary organization dedicated to leisure services.

Canadian Rehabilitation Council for the Disabled 45 Sheppard Avenue East, Suite 801 Toronto, Ontario, Canada M2N 5W9 Phone (416) 250-7490
Publications and information concerning program participation for those with special needs.

The Center for Active Education William M. Hazel, Director, P.O.Box 2055, Warminster, PA 18974-0006 Phone (215) 773-0885 Fax (215) 773-0885 Email: cenacted@aol.com

Center for Organization Effectiveness George Williams College—Lake Geneva Campus P.O.Box 210 Williams Bay, WI 53191 Phone (414) 245-5531 Fax (414) 245-5652

Centres International c/o James F. Keith, Jr. P.O.Box 9621 Greensboro, NC 27429-0621 Phone (910) 218-0023 Fax (910) 574-0509 Internet: JKeith8568@aol.com

Charlotte Outdoor Adventure Center (COAC) 2601 East Seventh Street Charlotte, NC 28204 Phone (704) 334-4631 Fax (704) 332-7551

Christian Camping International P.O.Box 62189 Colorado Springs, CO 80962-2189 Phone (719) 260-9400 Email: cci@gospelcom.net

Christian Wilderness Leaders Coalition Phone (503) 754-6001

Classic Field Adventures, Inc. 11515 Maze Road Indianapolis, IN 46259 Phone (800) 935-9909 or (317) 862-9409
Rock climbing, white water rafting and backpacking throughout North America.

Clearinghouse on the Handicapped Office of Special Education and Rehabilitative Services Room 3132 Switzer Building Washington, DC 20202 Phone 202-732-1245
Information, programs, publications and a service directory for issues regarding disabilities.

Climb Smart Phone (303) 444-3353
A public information program of the Climbing Sports Group, the trade association for the climbing industry.

Coalition for Education in the Outdoors Department of Recreation and Leisure Studies, State University of New York at Cortland, P.O.Box 2000, Park Center, Cortland, NY 13045
Phone (607) 753-4971 Fax (607) 753-5999

The Colorado Mountain Club Pikes Peak Group P.O.Box 2461 Colorado Springs, CO 80901 and also 710 Tenth Avenue, Suite 200 Golden, CO 80401 Phone (303) 279-3080

Colorado Outward Bound 945 Pennsylvania Street Denver, CO 80203-3198 Phone (800) 447-2627 or (303) 837-0880

Consortium for Problem-Based Learning Northern Illinois University—Center for Governmental Studies Dekalb, IL 60115 Phone (815) 753-0926 Fax (815) 753-2305

Cooperative Wilderness Handicapped Outdoor Group (C. W. HOG) Idaho State University, Student Union Box 8118 Pocatello, ID 83209
A challenge and adventure organization that persons of all abilities in outdoor pursuits.

The Cordage Institute 350 Lincoln Street, Suite 115, Hingham, MA 02043 Phone (617) 749-1016 Fax (617) 749-9783 Internet: RopeCord@aol.com
Technical information on fiber rope uses and applications.

Council for Adult and Experiential Learning (CAEL) 243 South Wabash Avenue Suite 800 Chicago, IL 60604 Phone 312-922-5909 Fax 312-922-1769 Internet: cael@interaccess.com

Council for Environmental Education (CEE) School of Education, University of Reading, London Road, Reading, Berkshire, RG1 5AQ United Kingdom Phone 1734 756061 Fax 1734 756264

Council for Outdoor Education Training and Recreation Muncaster Guest House, Muncaster, Ravenglass, Cumbria, United Kingdom
Covering the field of outdoor education in Wales, England and Northern Ireland.

Council of Outdoor Educators of Ontario (COEO) 1185 Eglinton Avenue East North York, Ontario, Canada M3C 3C6 1220 Sheppard Avenue East Willowdale, Ontario, Canada M2K 2X1 Phone 416-495-4264 Fax 416-495-4310
Promotes outdoor education in Ontario. Conferences, Journal and information.

Covey Leadership Center 3507 North University Avenue P.O.Box 19008 Provo, UT 84605-9008 Phone (800) 842-2388 or (800) 632-6839 or (801) 229-1333 Fax (800) 572-5551
Principle-centered leadership, training programs, best selling books and videos.

Cradlerock Outdoor Network PO Box 1431 Princeton, NJ 08542 Phone (609) 924-2919
Course builders, instructors certification & training and a world class adventure course.

Creative Think Box 7354 Menlo Park, CA 94026
Roger von Oech's organization specializing in innovation and creativity.

Cumbria Association of Residential Providers (CARP) 12 St. Andrews Churchyard, Penrith, Cumbria, CA11 7YE United Kingdom Phone 01768 891065 Fax 01768 891914
Workshops and training for outdoor educators and program providers in a variety of subjects, from risk management to outdoor education and adventure programming.

Direct Instructional Support Systems, Inc. 123 W. New England Ave. Worthington, OH 43085 Phone (614) 846-8946
Sponsors the Adventure Education Center, one of the finest outdoor adventure training facilities in the country.

Earth Watch 680 Mount Auburn Street P.O.Box 403 Waterton, MA 02272-9104 Phone (800) 776-0188 or (617) 926-8200 Fax (617) 926-8532 Internet: info@earthwatch.org
A non-profit organization which sponsors cultural and environmental research and studies.

Eastern Iowa Environmental Education 305 Second Street SE, Suite 509 Cedar Rapids, IA 52401 Phone (319) 362-5738 Fax (319) 362-5751 Internet: director@ecology.org

Easter Seals Camp Fairlee Manor Fairlee Manor Recreation and Education Center 22242 Bay Shore Road Chestertown, MD 21620 Phone (410) 778-0566
A beautiful facility for campers of all abilities, featuring: sailing on the Chesapeake Bay, an accessible adventure course and tower, fully accessible grounds and buildings.

Edie Greene Associates P.O.Box 453 Altamont, NY 12009 Phone (518) 861-6727
Group Games Plus. Using fun and games to achieve training objectives.

Education Commission of the States (ECS) 707 17th Street, Suite 2700, Denver, CO 80202-3427 Phone (303) 299-3600

The Environmental Careers Organization 286 Congress Street, Third Floor, Boston, MA 02210-1009

ERIC Clearinghouse on Teaching and Teacher Education American Association of Colleges for Teacher Education One Dupont Circle NW, Suite 610, Washington, DC 20036-2412
Phone (800) 822-9229 or (202) 293-2450

ERIC Document Reproduction Service (EDRS) ERIC Document Reproduction Service 7420 Fullerton Road, Suite 110 Springfield, VA 22153-2852 Phone (800) 443-3742
Internet: edrs@gwuvm.gwu.edu
Resource information on paper, microfiche and microfilms may be purchased through this organization using Master Card or Visa. All that is needed is the ED Accession Number for the publication, which can be obtained directly from ERIC.

Elderhostel 75 Federal Street Boston, MA 02110-1941 Phone (617) 426-8056 TTD (617) 426-5437
Provides a listing of courses, classes and events nationwide.

Elkhorn High Adventure Base Longs Peak Council Boy Scouts of America P.O.Box 1166 Greeley, Co 80632 Phone (970) 330-6305 or (800) 800-4052.
A spectacular program located on 3700 acres at 7000 feet elevation. For currently registered Boy Scouts only.

Enviros Wilderness School Association 5121 17th Avenue NW Calgary, Alberta, Canada T3B 0P8 Phone (403) 288-5104 Fax (403) 247-2746
Outdoor and experiential education for young people and families.

Folk Educators of American c/o J. Trader, 2606A 14th Street, Two Rivers, WI 54241

Foundation for Outdoor Adventure P.O.Box 191, Coventry, Warks, CV1 3YP United Kingdom Phone 01203 675575
Focus on educational research for youth programs in sports and outdoor adventure.

The Foxfire Fund, Inc.
Foxfire Teacher Network P.O.Box 541 Mountain City, GA 30562-0541 Phone (706) 746-5828 Fax (706) 746-5829 Internet: Foxfirefnd@aol.com

Glengarry The Scots College Jacks Corner Road Kangaroo Valley N.S.W. 2577 Australia Phone 044/651 089 Fax 044/651 458

Global Alliance for Transforming Education (GATE) P.O.Box 21 Grafton, VT 05146 Phone (802) 843-2382

Greenpeace 1436 U Street NW Washington, DC 20009 Phone (202) 462-1177 Fax (202) 462-4507 185 Spadina Ave. Toronto, Ontario, Canada M5T 2C6 Phone (416) 597-8408 Fax (416) 597-8422

Gregorc Associates, Inc. 15 Doubleday Road Box 251 Columbia, CT 06237-0351 Phone/Fax (203) 228-0093
Provides the Gregorc Style Delineator to profile various personality styles.

H.H. Owen & Company/Abbott Publishing 7808 River Falls Drive Potomac, MD 20854 Phone (301) 469-9269 Fax (301) 983-9314 Internet: http://www.tmn.com/openspace/index.html
Resources for open space technology, including the book "Open Space: A User's Guide."

Inner Quest Route 1 Box 271 C Purcellville, VA 22132 Phone (703) 478-1078 Fax (703) 668-6699
Safe Challenging Adventure, Ropes Course Design, Program Leadership

The Institute for Creative Living 3630 Fairmont Blvd. Cleveland, OH 44118

Institute for Earth Education (IEE) Cedar Cove Greenville, WV 24925 Phone (304) 832-6404 Fax (304) 832-6077
Formerly the Acclimatization Experiences Institute

International Association for the Study of Cooperation in Education (IASCE) Box 1582 Santa Cruz, CA 95061-1582 Phone (408) 426-7926 Fax (408) 426-3360

International Consortium for Experiential Learning (ICEL) c/o Dr. Argentine Craig 309 East Cold Spring Lane Baltimore, MD 21212 Phone (410) 433-6408 Fax (410) 433-0162
Global experiential learning opportunities.

International Society of Arborculture (ISA) P.O.Box GG, Savoy, IL 61874-9902

International Union of Alpinist Association (UIAA) c/o American Alpine Association, 113 East 90th Street, New York, NY 10128-1589
The UIAA governs the use and testing of climbing, adventure and mountaineering equipment.

I Will Not Complain International Beijing Lufthansa Centre 50 Liangmaiao Road, Cahoyang District, Beijing, China 100016 2072-3 Nakadaki Misaki-machi, Isumi-Gun, Chiba, Japan 299-46

Jumonville RR #2 Box 128 Hopwood, PA 15445 Phone (412) 439-4912
One of the best programs in western Pennsylvania, including an indoor center and video training.

Learning Unlimited Corporation 5155 East 51st, Suite 108, Tulsa, OK 74135 Phone (918) 622-3292 or (918) 664-3309 Fax (918) 622-4203

Mattel Sports World Jr. Frisbee® Disc Contest M1-0836 333 Continental Blvd. El Segundo, CA 90245-5012 Phone (310) 252-4762
The Sports Promotion Department sponsors yearly contests and makes frisbees, certificates and rules available to youth organizations, schools, camps and summer programs.

Medeba Adventure Learning Centre West Guilford, Ontario K0M 1S0 Canada Phone (705) 754-2444
A christian center with a variety of challenge related programs including ice climbing.

Michie Creek Mushing RR1, Site 20, Comp. 104, Dept. M Whitehorse, Yukon, Canada Y1A 4Z6 Phone (403) 667-6854 Fax (403) 668-2633
Wilderness dog sledding in the Canadian Yukon territory.

Mountain Direction Adventures P.O.Box 1927 Boulder, CO 80306-1927 Phone (303) 448-1098 Email: us027539@mindspring.com
Spiritual growth through mountain adventures and retreats.

The Mountaineers 300 Third Avenue West Seattle, WA 98119 Phone (206) 284-6310 Fax (206) 284-4977

Natahala Outdoor Center U. S. 19, Highway 41 Bryson City, NC 28713 Phone (704) 488-2175

National Arborist Association Inc. (NAA) Meeting Place Mall, Route 101, P.O.Box 1094, Amherst, NH 03031-1094 Phone (800) 733-2622 Fax (603) 672-2613

The National Association for Environmental Education (NAAEE) P.O.Box 400 Troy, Ohio 45373 Phone (513) 698-6493

The National Association for Outdoor Education (NAOE) 12 St. Andrews Churchyard, Penrith, Cumbria, CA11 7YE United Kingdom Phone 01768 65113 Fax 01768 891914
Supporting the development of outdoor education for all.

National Association for Search and Rescue (NASAR) 4500 Southgate Place, Suite 100, Chantilly, VA 22021 Fax (305) 666-6836

National Association for Sports and Physical Education (NASPE) Sponsored by AAHPERD. 1900 Association Drive Reston, VA 22091-9989 Phone (703) 476-3410 Fax (703) 476-8316

National Association for the Education of Young Children 1834 Connecticut Avenue, N.W. Washington, D.C. 20009-5786 Phone (800) 424-2460 or (202) 232-8777

National Association of People With Disabilities (NAPD) 2117 Buffalo Road, Suite 254 Rochester, NY 14624 Phone (716) 325-2540 Fax (716) 546-1225

National Association of Therapeutic Wilderness Camps, Inc. 174 Hiwatha Hills Road, Cleveland, GA 30528

National Consortium for Environmental Education and Training (NCEET) School of Natural Resources & Environment University of Michigan Ann Arbor, MI 48109-1115 Phone (313) 998-6726 Fax (313) 936-2195 Internet: nceet-info@nceet.snre.umich.edu Fostering environmental consciousness through education.

National Consortium on Alternatives for Youth at Risk, Inc. 5250 17th Street Suite 107 Sarasota, FL 34235 Phone (800) 245-7133 or (813) 378-4793 Fax (813) 378-9922 Alternatives for Youth at Risk, educational information, research, programming.

National Education Association 1201 16th Street NW, Washington, DC 20036 Phone (202) 833-4000

National Farmers Union 11900 East Cornell Avenue Aurora, CO 80014-3194 Phone (303) 337-5500 Fax (303) 368-1390

National Handicapped Sports and Recreation Association 1145 19th Street NW Suite 717 Washington, DC 20036 Phone (301) 652-7505

The National Information Center for Service-Learning University of Minnesota, R-290 VoTech Education Building, 1954 Buford Avenue St. Paul, MN 55108-6179 Phone (800) 808-SERV or (612) 537-6468

National Outdoor Education and Leadership Services Level 1, 17 Goble Street, Hughes, ACT 2605 Australia Phone 61 6 28 28 800 Fax 61 6 28 28 801 Email: noelsaust@msn.com

National Outdoor Leadership School (NOLS) 288 West Main Street Lander, WY 82520-3128 Phone (307) 332-6973 Fax (307) 332-1220 A variety of outdoor adventures, featuring extended sessions on land and water.

National Recreation and Park Association (NRPA) 2775 South Quincy Street, Suite 300, Arlington, VA 22206-2204 Phone (800) 626-6772 or (703) 820-4940 Fax (703) 671-6772 Email: info@nrpa.org or NRPA01@Delphi.com

National Safety Network P.O.Box 186 Bellefontaine, OH 43311

National Service-Learning Clearinghouse The Clearinghouse—University of Minnesota Vocational & Technical Education Building 1954 Buford Avenue, R-290 St. Paul, Minnesota 55108 Phone (800) 808-7378 or 612-625-6276 Serving teachers with information that connects community service and academic learning.

National Society for Internships and Experiential Education (NSEE) 3509 Haworth Drive Suite 207 Raleigh, NC 27609-7229 Phone 919-787-3263 Fax 919-787-3381 Promotes experience methods in learning.

National Speleological Society (NSS) 2813 Cave Avenue Huntsville, AL 35801-4431 Phone (205) 852-9241 or (205) 852-1300 Email: manager@caves.org

National Therapeutic Recreation Society (NTRS) 2775 South Quincy Street Suite 300 Arlington, VA 22206-2204 Phone (800) 626-6772 or (703) 578-5548 Fax (703) 671-6772

National Wheelchair Athletic Association (NWAA) 660 Capitol Hill Building Nashville, TN 37179

The National Wildlife Federation 1400 16th Street NW Washington, DC 20036-2266 Phone (703) 790-4483 Fax (703) 442-7332 Wildlife Camp (800) 245-5484 Leader training, classroom curriculums, camping and adventure programs, accessible trails.

National Youth Leadership Council 1910 West County Road B Roseville, MN 55113-1337 Phone (612) 631-3672

National Youth Sports Coaches Association 2050 Vista Parkway West Palm Beach, FL 33411 Phone (800) 729-2057

The Nature Conservancy 1815 North Lynn Street Arlington, VA 22209 Phone (703) 841-5300

New York State Recreation and Park Society, Inc. Saratoga Spa State Park 19 Roosevelt Drive Suite 200 Saratoga Springs, NY 12866 Phone (518) 584-0321 Fax (518) 584-5101
Email: nysrps@nysrps.org

New Zealand Outdoor Instructors Association P.O.Box 2551, Wellington, New Zealand Phone 04 728 058

North American Association for Environmental Education (NAAEE) P.O.Box 400 Troy, OH 45373 Phone (513) 698-6493 Email: BEager410@aol.com
Information, publication and networking for professionals in the environmental education arena.

North American River Runners Phone (800) 950-2585
Whitewater rafting in the New River Gorge region.

Nova Scotia Sport and Recreation Commission P.O.Box 864 Halifax, Nova Scotia B3J 2V2 Phone (902) 424-7670

NTL Institute for Applied Behavioral Science 1240 North Pitt Street Suite 100 Alexandria, Virginia 22314-1403 Phone (800) 777-5227 or (703) 548-1500 Fax (703) 684-1256
Offering a wide variety of corporate related training sessions and professional development seminars.

On Course, Inc. 23382 La Costa Court Auburn, CA 95602 Phone (916) 268-1259

Ontario Physical and Health Education Association (OPHEA) 1220 Sheppard Avenue East, Suite 414 Willowdale, Ontario, Canada M2K 2X1

Organization Development Network (ODNetwork) P.O.Box 69329 Portland, OR 97201 Phone (503) 246-0148
Networking, conferences and information on organizational development.

Orion International, Ltd. 555 Briarwood Circle, Suite 140 Ann Arbor, MI 48108 Phone (313) 663-2234 Fax (313) 663-3670
Management training, teambuilding simulations and role playing techniques.

Outdoor Education Association 143 Fox Hill Road Denville, NJ 07834 Phone (201) 627-7214

Outdoor Recreation Coalition of America (ORCA) P.O.Box 1319 Boulder, CO 80306 Phone (303) 444-3353
Publishes the ORCA Programmers Resource Guide.

Outdoors Wisconsin Leadership School (OWLS) George Williams College Box 210 Williams Bay, WI 53191 Phone (414) 245-5531 ext. 33 Fax (414) 245-5652
Professional development workshops for facilitation and ropes course management.

Outdoor Education Institute Department of Health & Kinesiology Texas A&M University College Station, TX 77843-4243 Phone (409) 845-3758

Outdoor Learning Center Utah State University Logan, UT 84322 Phone (801) 750-1879

Outdoor Recreation Council of British Columbia 334-1367 West Broadway, Vancouver, British Columbia, Canada V6H 1A4 Phone (604) 737-3058 Fax (604) 737-3666
Internet: outrec_council@sport.bc.ca
The voice for outdoor recreation in BC ! Publications, information and research in outdoor recreation.

Outward Bound National Headquarters Route 9D R 2, Box 280 Garrison, NY 10524-9757 Phone (800) 243-8520 or (914) 424-4000 Fax (914) 424-4280
Colorado School 945 Pennsylvania Street Denver, CO 80203-3198 Phone (800) 477-2627 or (303) 837-0880
Hurricane Island School P.O.Box 429 Rockland, ME 04841 Phone (800) 341-1744 or (207) 594-5548
North Carolina School 121 North Sterling Street Morganton, NC 28655 Phone (800) 627-5971 or (704) 437-6112

North Carolina Office 2582 Riceville Road Asheville, NC 28805 Phone (800) 754-8902
Internet: www. ncobs.org
A nonprofit educational organization offering a variety of programs for individuals, corporations, teachers, youth and couples in wilderness and urban settings throughout North America and around the world.

Pack, Paddle & Ski Corporation Box 82 South Lima, NY 14558-0082 Phone (716) 346-5597
Classes, courses and outdoor expeditions.

Participate in the Lives of America's Youth (P.L.A.Y.) NIke, Inc. One Bowerman Drive Beaverton, OR 97005
Making A Difference in Recreation Opportunities and Communities.

Pecos River Learning Centers P. O. Box 22279 1800 Old Pecos Trail Sante Fe, NM 87502 Phone 505-989-9101
Tailor-made adventure programs with a corporate focus.

Play for Peace Craig Dobkin 228 W. Sycamore Lane Louisville, CO 80027 Phone (303) 664-0830 Fax (303) 664-0395 Internet: chdobkin@aol.com P.O.Box 6205 Buffalo Grove, IL 60089 Phone (847) 520-1444 Fax (847) 520-6391
An initiative of the Association for Experiential Education, where children of conflicting cultures come to know each other through play.

Project Adventure P.O.Box 100 Hamilton, MA 01936 Phone (508) 468-7981 Fax (508) 468-7605
P.O.Box 2447 Covington, GA 30209 Phone (404) 784-9310 Fax (404) 787-7764
P.O.Box 14171 Portland, Oregon 97214 Phone (503) 239-0169 Fax (503) 236-6765
P.O.Box 1640 Brattleboro, VT 05301 Phone (802) 254-5054 Fax (802) 254-5182
Outdoor Education Programs, Training Seminars, Course Construction and Publications.

Project Adventure Australia 332 Banyule Road View Bank, VIC 3084 Australia Phone (03) 9457 6494 Fax (03) 9457 5438
Outdoor Education Programs, Training Seminars, Course Construction and Publications.

Project Learning Tree The American Forest Institute, Inc. 1619 Massachusetts Ave. N.W. Washington, D.C. 20036

Public Library Probably the most cost effective way of finding materials. Also check your local cooperative extension service (4-H), YMCA & YWCA centers, scouting council, colleges and mental health centers for information. Organizations that facilitate a summer camp often know about challenge and adventure activities.

Raccoon Institute P.O.Box 695 Cazemovia, WI 53924 Phone (608) 983-2327
Consulting and staff development for professionals in adventure education.

Recreation Laboratories and Workshops, Inc. Mary Lou Reichard—Registrar 21983 Crosswick Woodhaven, MI 48183 Phone (313) 676-1120
A non-profit network for sharing information and promoting the recreation laboratory experience.

Recreation Unlimited 7700 Piper Road Ashley, OH 43003 Phone (614) 548-7006
A premier facility specifically design for special-needs campers, featuring two adventure courses, in-ground pool, fully accessible grounds, building and nature trails.

Rocky Mountain Youth to Youth 6635 South Dayton Street, Suite 170, Englewood, CO 80111 Phone (303) 730-2905 P.O.Box 3413 Littleton, CO 80161-3413 Phone (800) 333-8673 or (303) 792-0951 Fax (303) 730-2905
A program of the Colorado Federation of Parents for Drug-Free Youth, Inc.

Karl Rohnke Box 328 Newfane, VT 05345
The Man, the Legend. Author of Silver Bullets, Cowtails & Cobras, FUNN Stuff.

Roland / Diamond Associates, Inc. 67 Emerald Street Keene, NH 03431 Phone (603) 357-2181 Fax (603) 357-7992
Corporate experiential learning methods, issues & research.

Search Institute Thresher Square West—Suite 210 700 South Third Street Minneapolis, MN 55415
Phone (800) 888-7828 or (612) 376-8955 Fax (612) 376-8956
Practical research benefiting children and youth.

Shepard's Ford Center Route 1, Box 496 Bluemont, VA 22012 Phone (703) 955-3071

Sierra Club 85 Second Street San Francisco, CA 94105 Telephone (415) 776-2211 Fax (415) 776-0350
Internet: http://www.sierraclub.org or dan.anderson0sierradub.org
A non-profit organization that promotes conservation and environmental issues through legislation.

Sir Edmund Hillary Outdoor Pursuits Centre (OPC) Private Bag, Turangi, New Zealand
Phone 07 386 5511 Fax 07 386 0204
Some programs (Hamilton Skills Group) incorporate Maori Tanga culture and language.

Skern Lodge Appledore, North Devon, EX39 1NG United Kingdom Phone 01237 475992
Fax 01237 421203
Outdoor adventure programs.

Smith and Boisclair Circus Camps 2045 Route 117 MontRolland, Quebec Canada J0R 1G0
Reaching New Heights — This traveling camp teaches circus tricks and confidence. Trapeze, tightrope, juggling, trampoline and more!

Society of Park and Recreation Educators (SPRE) 2775 South Quincy Street Suite 300 Arlington, VA 22206-2204 Phone (703) 820-4940 or (800) 626-NRPA Fax (703) 671-6772
A section of the National Recreation & Park Association (NRPA) serving the needs of park and recreation educators in North America.

Special Olympics, Inc. 1350 New York Avenue NW Suite 5M Washington, DC 20005
Phone (202) 628-3630
National and local sporting events for children and adults.

Special Populations Learning Outdoor Recreation & Education (S'PLORE) 27 West 3300 South Salt Lake City, UT 84115 Phone (801) 484-4128
Hosts a variety of high adventure outdoor programs for special needs populations.

Stonehearth Open Learning Opportunities, Inc. (SOLO) P.O.Box 3150 Conway, NH 03818
Phone (603) 447-6711 Fax (603) 447-2310
Outdoor Leadership Courses, Wilderness First Aid, WFR and EMF Training

Student Conservation Association P.O. Box 550 Charlestown, NH 03603

Sylvan Rocks—Climbing School & Guide Service Located at Granite Sports Box 600 Hill City, SD 57745 Phone (605) 574-2425
Some of the classic climbs in the west, including Devil's Tower, The Needles and Joshua Tree.

Teamwork & Teamplay 468 Salmon Creek Rd Brockport, NY 14420 Phone (585) 637-0328
Teambuilding activities, adventure education, staff training, equipment design and construction, adapting activities for special populations, challenge education consulting, workshops, seminars, engineering evaluation of challenge course equipment.

The Teamwork Challenge YMCA Camping Services 430 South 20th Street Omaha, NE 68102-2506
Phone (402) 341-4730 Fax (402) 341-8214
High and low ropes courses, teambuilding activities.

Tower Wood Outdoor Education Centre Windermere, Cumbria, LA23 3PL United Kingdom
Phone 015395 31519 Fax 015395 30071
Training and accreditation programs for a variety of outdoor adventure programs.

Tree Climbers International P.O. Box 5588 Atlanta, GA 30307 Phone (770) 377-3150

UIAA c/o American Alpine Association 113 East 90th Street New York, NY 10128-1589
The UIAA governs the use and testing of climbing, adventure and mountaineering equipment.

United States Snowshoe Association Cornith, NY 12882 Phone (518) 654-7648

United States Space Camp Foundation One Tranquility Base Huntsville, AL 35805-3399 Phone (800) 63 SPACE.

Victorian Outdoor Education Association 217 Church Street, Richmond, Victoria 3121, Australia Phone 03 9428 9920 Fax 03 9428 0313

Vinland National Center P.O.Box 308 3675 Ihduhapi Road Loretto, MN 55357 Phone (612) 479-3555 A healthsport and wilderness center.

The Watch Trust for Environmental Education Crawford House, Precinct Centre, Booth Street East, Manchester, MI3 9RZ United Kingdom

Wilderness Education Association (WEA) Department of Natural Resource Recreation and Tourism—Colorado State University Fort Collins, CO 80523 Phone/Fax (970) 223-6252
Internet: wea@lamar.colostate.edu
Information, training and certification for wilderness emergencies.

Wilderness Inquiry 1313 Fifth Street S.E. Box 84 Minneapolis, MN 55414-1546 Phone (800) 728-0719 Voice/TTY (612) 379-3858 Fax (612) 379-5972
Experience the Northern Minnesota-Canadian region via canoe, dogsled, skis & snowshoes.

Wilderness Medical Associates 189 Dudley Road #2 Bryant Pond, ME 04219
Phone (888) WILD-MED or (207) 655-2707 Canada (905) 522-4032 Email: wildmed@nxi.com
Training Specialists in emergency medicine and wilderness rescue, including WFA, WFR & WEMT.

Wilderness Medicine Institute P.O.Box 9 300 10th Street Pitkin, CO 81241 Phone (303) 641-3572

The Wilderness Society 900 17th Street NW Washington, DC 20006-2596 Phone (202) 833-2300 Fax (202) 429-3958

Wilderness Tourism Association of the Yukon P.O.Box 3960, Dept. C Whitehorse, Yukon Territory, Canada Y1A 3M6
Information on Yukon outfitters, guides and outdoor programs.

Wildwater P.O.Box 155 Lansing, WV 25862 Phone (304) 658-4007 Fax (304) 658-4008
Whitewater rafting on the New River Gorge National River.

Wind Dancer, Inc. Warren Bailey 2859 West State Route 37 Delaware, OH 43015-1375 Phone (614) 369-4153
The inventor of the rainbow writer and other fun kites and flying objects.

Wire Rope Technical Board P.O.Box 286 Woodstock, MD 21163-0286 Phone (410) 461-7030 Fax (410) 465-3195 Publications: WRTB Fulfillment P.O.Box 14921 Shawnee Mission, KS 66285-4921
Excellent technical information on ropes, cables and slings.

World Climbing Association 4120 Douglas Blvd #306-105 Granite Bay, CA 95746
Phone (888) 922-6362 Membership Office P.O.Box 2025 Cerritos, CA 90702-2025
Clip-In Climbing Insurance. Protecting climbers and climbing resources.

World Leisure and Recreation Association P.O.Box 309 Sharbot Lake Ontario, Canada K0H 2P0 Phone (613) 279-3172 Fax (613) 279-3372

World Leisure and Recreation Association International Centre of Excellence (WICE) Rengerslaan 8 8917 DD Leeuwarden, The Netherlands

The Worldwide Outfitter and Guide Association P.O.Box 520400 Salt Lake City, UT 84152-0400 Phone (800) 321-1493 or (801) 942-3000 Fax (801) 942-8095

Youth Challenge International (YCI) 11 Soho Street Tornonto, Ontario, Canada M5T 1Z6
Phone 416-971-9846 Fax 416-971-6863
Promotes programs for young people on environmental issues around the world.

8.20 Rope Course, Climbing Wall and Challenge Course Builders, Designers and Equipment Manufacturers

ABEE 39085 Foster Drive Oconomowoc, WI 53066 Phone (414) 474-7172

Accessible Adventures 250 N.E. Tomahawk Island Drive #309 Portland, OR 97217
Design, construction and adaptations for accessible challenge courses and play structures.

Adventure Systems & Designs, Inc. P.O. Box 31 Colorado Springs, CO 80901 Phone (719) 635-8667

Adventure Dynamics Well Cottage, Winskill, Penrith, Cumbria, CA10 1PD United Kingdom
Phone 01768 881096
Rope course design, development and construction.

Adventure Dynamics, Inc. P.O. Box 213 Nine Miles Falls, WA 99026 Phone (509) 467-0800
Adventure based leaming equipment, featuring the adventure in a duffle challenge kit.

Adventure Experiences, Inc. Route 2 Box 24J Trinity, TX 75862 Phone (409) 594-2945

Alpine Towers P.O. Box 69 Jonas Ridge, NC 28641 Phone (828) 733-0953
Certainly one of the most unique styles of high-element climbing towers in North America.

Blue Ridge Learning Centers, Inc. P.O. Box 606 DTS Boone, NC 28607 Phone (704) 265-0602 or (704) 963-4912 Email: blueridge@appstate.campus.mci.net
Challenge courses and climbing towers, equipment, program reviews, and training.

Challenge Masters Incorporated 821 Dock Street Box 1-16 Tacoma, WA 98402 Fax (206) 759-7548
Phone (800) 673-0911 or (206) 279-0052 Internet: 102047.2345@compuserve.com
Portable challenge program equipment and training.

Challenges Unlimited, Inc. 11730 Keele Street, Maple, Ontario, Canada L6A lSl Phone (905) 832-4787

Cradlerock Outdoor Network P.O. Box 1431 Princeton, NJ 08542 Phone (609) 924-2919
Fax (609) 466-0234

Direct Instructional Support Systems, Inc. P.O.Box 691 Worthington, OH 43085
Phone (614) 846-8946

Experiential Resources, Inc. P.O. Box 6584 Bloomington, IN 47407 Phone (877) 261-2890
Program development, course construction, facilitator training, course inspections.

Inner Quest Route 1 Box 271C Purcellville, VA 22132 Phone (703) 478-1078 or (703) 668-6699
Fax (703) 668-6699

Leahy & Associates, Inc. 1052 Artemis Circle Lafayette, CO 80026 Phone (303) 673-9832

Northeast Adventure Collaboration 12 Jennifer Lane Burlington, CT 06013-1705
Phone (860) 675-8734 Fax (860) 675-8736
Challenge course design, installation and training.

Pecos River Learning Centers P.O. Box 22279 Sante Fe, NM 87501 Phone (505) 989-9101 or (612) 925-2100 7600 Executive Drive Eden Prarie, N4N 55344 Phone (612) 975-2100

Pro Image 6390 Springmill Road Indianapolis, IN 46260-4242 Phone (317) 254-1815

Project Adventure P.O. Box 100 Hamilton, NM 01936 Phone (508) 468-7981 Fax (508) 468-7605
P.O. Box 2447 Covington, GA 30209 Phone (404) 784-9310 Fax (404) 787-7764
P.O. Box 14171 Portland, OR 97214 Phone (503) 239-0169 Fax (503) 236-6765
116 Maple Street Brattleboro, VT 05301 Phone (802) 254-5054 Fax (802) 254-5182

Project Adventure Australia 332 Banyule Road View Bank, VIC 3084 Australia Phone (03) 9457 6494
Fax (03) 9457 5438
Outdoor Education Programs, Training Seminars, Course Construction and Publications.

Radwall 2625 Alcatraz Avenue Suite 374 Berkeley, CA 94705 Phone/Fax (510) 655-3859
Email: radwall@well.com Internet: http://www.well.com/user/radwall
A founding member of the Climbing Wall Industrv Group (CWIG).

Rope Course Developments Ltd. Burnbake, Rempstone, Corfe Castle, Wareham, Dorset, BH20 5JH, United Kingdom Phone (01929) 480999 Fax (01929) 480001 Email: nmoriarty @Ids.co.uk

Rope Courses, Inc. P.O.Box 259 1344 12th Street Martin, NE 49070 Phone (616) 672-9173
Featuring a steel rope course!

Rope Works 551 Bluecreek Drive Dripping Springs, TX 78620 Phone (512) 894-0936

Signature Research Route 2 Box 666 1979 Moody Hollow Road Hiawassee, GA 30546
Phone (404) 896-1487

Teamwork & Teamplay 468 Salmon Creek Road Brockport, NY 14420 Phone (585) 637-0328
Consulting, staff development, equipment design, portable challenge programs.

Universal Builders Matthew Miller P.O.Box 12 Albrightsville, PA 18210 Phone (570) 722-3500

8.21 Colleges Which Offer Courses and Programs in Outdoor Education, Experiential Education and Related Fields

During the preparation of this section, the Association for Experiential Education published a listing of educational institutions that have outdoor programs. This publication is entitled, "The Schools and Colleges Directory" and contains nearly 300 listings of programs and degrees in the field of outdoor and experiential education. Contact information for AEE is located earlier in this chapter.

University of Alaska Alaska Wilderness Studies 3211 Providence Drive Building K Room 126
Anchorage, AK 99508 Phone (907) 786-1468 Fax (907) 786-1563

Aurora University Aurora, IL 60506-4892 Phone (708) 844-5406
Bachelor and Master programs in outdoor, therapeutic and commerical recreation and management.

Brown University Brown Outdoor Leadership Training Box 1960 Providence, RI 02912
Phone (401) 863-3476

California State University—Northridge Department of Recreation and Leisure Studies
Northridge, CA 91324 Phone (213) 885-3202

Colgate University Outdoor Education Program 211 Huntington Gym Hamilton, NY 13346
Phone (315) 824-7323

Colorado Mountain School at Colorado Mountain College P.O. Box 10001 Glenwood Springs, CO 81602-9989 Phone (800) 621-8559 or 303-945-8691
A variety of outdoor programs including mountain, desert and river training, snow ice and avalanche skills, wilderness, archaeology, travel studies and more.

Columbia University 206 Ferris Booth Hall New York, NY 10027 Phone (212) 854-3611

Cornell University Outdoor Education Box 729 Ithaca, NY 14851 Phone (607) 255-6415 or (607) 255-9791

Dartmouth College Office of Outdoor Programs P.O. Box 9 Hanover, NH 03755 Phone (603) 646-2428

Doane College Leadership Program Crete, NE 68333 Phone (800) 333-6263 or 402-826-2161

Eastern Washington University Phys. Ed., Health and Recreation Dept. Mail Stop 66 Cheney, WA 99004 Phone (509) 359-7097

Garrett Community College The Adventure Sports Institute, Mosser Road, McHenry, MD 21541
Phone (301) 387-6666 Fax (301) 387-7469
Adventure sports and economics, marketing, environmental science and events management.

George Williams College Outdoors Wisconsin Leadership School (OWLS) Box 210
Williams Bay, WI 53191 Phone 414-245-5531 Extension 33 Fax 414-245-5652
Adventure education courses, workshops and leadership training.

Latrobe University P.O.Box 199 Bendigo, Victoria 3550 Australia Fax (61-54) 447-777
B.A., M.A. and Ph.D. in Outdoor Leadership and Education.

Mankato State University Department of Experiential Education MSU Box 52 Box 8400
Mankato, MN 56002-8400 Phone (507) 389-1005

University of Michigan School of Natural Resources Ann Arbor, MI 48109-1115 Phone (313) 764-1404
Graduate studies in Natural Resources.

Norfolk College Tennyson Avenue, King's Lynn, Norfolk, PE30 2QW United Kingdom
Phone 01553 761144

Northern Arizona University Box 5619 Flagstaff, AZ 86011 Phone (602) 523-3530

Northern Illinois University Outdoor Education Program & Continuing Education Dekalb, IL 60115-2860 Phone (815) 753-6902 Lorado Taft Field Campus Box 299 Oregon, IL 61061
Phone (815) 732-2111 Fax (815) 753-9040
M.S.Ed in Outdoor Teacher Education.

Northland College Ashland, WI 54806 Phone (715) 682-1699
Environmental and Outdoor Programs.

Prescott College 220-A Grove Avenue Prescott, AZ 86301 Phone (520) 776-5180 or (520) 778-2090
Fax (520) 776-5137

Princeton University Princeton Education Center at Blairstown—The Amory Princeton, NJ 98544
Phone (609) 258-3340

Purdue University Recreation Studies Program West Lafayette, IN 47907 Phone (317) 493-9886

Queen's University Faculty of Education, Duncan McArthur Hall, Kingston, Ontario, Canada K7L 3N6

State University of New York at Cortland P.O.Box 2000 Cortland, NY 13045 Phone (607) 753-4941
Fax (607) 753-5999

Texas A & M University Outdoor Education Institute College Station, TX 77843-4243
Phone (409) 845-3758

University of North Carolina at Charlotte Venture Program, Cone University Center, Charlotte, NC 28223 Phone (704) 547-2486

University of Northern Iowa Recreation Division—School of Health, Physical Education & Recreation Cedar Fall, IA 50613 Phone (319) 273-2654

Univeristy of Waterloo Department of Recreation Waterloo, Ontario, Canada N2L 3G1
Phone (519) 885-1211 ext. 3529

Western Illinois University Dept. of Recreation & Park Admin. 103 Western Hall Macomb, IL 61455
Phone (309) 298-1967

8.22 Insurance Carriers and Information

Some of the following insurance carriers provide insurance for a wide range of camping and outdoor programs, including challenge and adventure programs. Inclusion in this list does not represent an endorsement.

American Income Life Insurance Company P.O.Box 50158 Indianapolis, IN 46250
Phone (800) 849-4820 or (317) 251-0199 or (317) 849-5545 Fax (317) 849-2793

American International Group 80 Pine Street New York, NY 10005 Phone (212) 770-2269

The American Alpine Club 710 Tenth Street, Suite 100 Golden, CO 80401 Phone (303) 384-0110
Fax (303) 384-0111
More than 90 years of advocation for mountaineers and climbers including world-wide rescue insurance, expidition sponsorships, an extensive library and publications.

Brotherhood Mutual Insurance Company 6400 Brotherhood Way P.O.Box 1525 Fort Wayne, IN 46801-1525 Phone (800) 876-4994 or 219-482-8668 John Strom, Ropes Course Inspector

The Camp Brokerage Company, Inc. 6 Port Imperial Blvd. Weehawken, NJ 07087
Phone (201) 902-0030

Chalmers Insurance 30 Main Street P.O.Box 189 Bridgton, ME 04009 Phone (207) 647-3311

Clip In Climbing Insurance World Climbing Association 4120 Douglas Blvd #306-105 Granite Bay, CA 95746 Phone (888) 922-6362 Internet: http://www.wca-climbing.org
Protecting climbers and climbing resources.

Fessenden and Sykes Insurance 1050 Waltham Street Lexington, MA 02173 Phone (617) 861-1560

K & K Insurance Group, Inc. 1712 Magnavox Way P.O. Box 2338 Fort Wayne, IN 46801
Phone (800) 553-8368
Comprehensive coverage for resident and day camps. An affiliate of SLE Worldwide, Inc.

R. F. Lyons Company 27576 Commerce Center Drive #111 Temecula, CA 92390-4839
Phone (909) 694-6194 Fax (909) 694-6129

Manion/Bell Insurance Associates P.O. Box 36186 Los Angeles, CA 90036 Phone (213) 387-8294
Fax (213) 389-5833

Markel Rhulen—Underwriters & Brokers 4600 Cox Road Glen Allen, VA 23060-9817
Phone (800) 416-CAMP or (800) 431-1270 or (800) 342-4841 Phone (804) 527-2700
Endorsed by the American Camping Association.

Morrow Insurance Agency, Inc. 800 Beverly-Hanks Centre P.O.Box 1109 Hendersonville, NC 28793
Phone (800) 228-3132 or (704) 693-5396

Non-Profit Risk Management Center (NRMC) 1001 Connecticut Avenue NW, Suite 900
Washington, DC 20036 Phone (202) 785-3891 Fax (202) 833-5747
Offers a publication entitled, "Am I Covered for . . . ? A Guide to Insurance for Non-Profits -Second Edition" and other publications.

Hibbs—Hallmark & Company P.O.Box 8357 501 Shelly Drive Tyler, TX 75711 Phone (903) 561-8484
Fax (903) 581-5988

Crump Insurance Services of Texas, Inc. 7557 Rambler Road, Suite 300 Dallas, TX 75231
Phone (214) 363-7636 Fax (214) 691-5460
Specifically handles challenge and ropes courses.

A. M. Skier Agency Hawley, PA 18428 Phone (800) 245-2666 Fax (717) 226-1105

Speare and Company, Insurance Brokers 30003 West Quail Run Drive Agoura Hills, CA 91301-4068 Phone (310) 914-9308 Fax (310) 914-9398

Carl Weil Insurance P. O. Box 909 Franktown, CO 80116 Phone (303) 688-5176
A division of Transamerica Insurance Group.

Worldwide Outfitter and Guides Association (WOGA) Box 520400 Salt Lake City, UT 84152-0400 Phone (800) 321-1493
Familiar with high adventure activities, can provide a risk management assessment.

In addition to the organizations listed above, the following references and resources are listed to provide further information about insurance and liability concerns. The ACCT newsletter has also published some more recent information regarding insurance for rope and challenge courses.

Avoiding a Lawsuit Jim Moss, Outdoor Network Newsletter, Volume 1, Number 9, Spring 1991, pages 6–7. ERIC Document EJ424948.

Risk and Hazard Management in High Adventure Outdoor Pursuits Joel Meier, ERIC Document ED356934

The Management of Risk Dan Meyer, Journal of Experiential Education, Volume 2, Number 2, Fall 1979, pages 9–14.

The Management of Risk K. Ogilvie, Journal of Adventure Education and Outdoor Leadership, Volume 6, Number 4, 1989, pages 30–34.

Outdoor Adventure Schools Need Specialized Coverage Carol Goodstein, Rough Notes, Volume 134, Issue 12, December 1991, pages 38–39.

Legal Liability—Adventure Activities Betty van der Smissen, March 1980, ERIC Document ED 187500

Minimizing Legal Liability Risks Betty van der Smissen, Journal of Experiential Education, Volume 2, Number 1, Spring 1979, pages 35–41.

Safety in Outdoor Adventure Programs (SOAP) Safety Policy Wayne MacDonald, et. al., May 14, 1979, ERIC Document ED 180728

Insurance and Risk Management at the National Outdoor Leadership School Lantien Chu, Outdoor Network Newsletter, Volume 1, Number 7, Fall 1990, pages 6–7. ERIC Document EJ424947.

Causation, assumed risk, and a failur to warn in sports suits J. D. Kozlowski, 1988, Parks and Recreation, Volume 23, Number 9, pages 18–21.

A Common Sense View of Liability J. D. Kozlowski, 1988, Parks and Recreation, Volume 23, Number 9, pages 56–59.

In Search of the Adequate Warning Sign: Communication is the Key J. D. Kozlowski, 1988, Parks and Recreation, Volume 23, Number 10, pages 20–25, 63.

Outdoor Adventure and Legal Liability Terri Helesic and Simon Priest, Pathways, Volume 3, Number 6, Octoboer 1991, pages 4–10.

Lawsuits: The Ins and Outs of Outdoor Education Cases Jim Moss, Outdoor Network Newsletter, Volume 1, Number 7, Fall 1990, page 7. ERIC Document EJ424946

8.23 Conferences, Seminars and Workshops

Many of the organizations listed earlier in this section also sponsor workshops and conferences. The following list provides the most recent information about these conferences.

One of the most unique methods for learning about challenge and adventure education, recreational leadership skills, camp skills and other craft and social forms of recreation is from a variety of recreational and leadership workshops held annually in more than 20 states and Canadian providences. Since the 1940's, these workshops have been providing wonderful opportunities to learn and share experiences and to gain new ideas and understanding. In the following list, these workshops are denoted with two asterisks (**). Additional information on these workshops is available from the national organization known as Recreation Laboratories and Workshops, Inc. This organization also hosts an internationally attended fall conference every few years.

AAHPERD National Convention An annual conference held throughout North America.
Lysa Price Director of Conventions 1900 Association Drive Reston, VA 22091 Phone (703) 476-3466 Fax (703) 476-9527

ACA National Conference 5000 State Road 67 North Martinsville, IN 46151-7902
Email: aca@aca-camps.org Phone (800) 428-CAMP, (800) 428-2267 or (765) 342-8456 Fax (765) 342-2065 The February 1998 conference is in Dallas, TX.

ACHPER National/International Conference ACHPER National Office 214 Port Road Hindmarsh, South Australia 5007 Australia Phone (08) 340 3388 Fax (08) 340 3399

Advanced Facilitator Development Training Held at various places and times during the year.
801-B West 8th Street Cincinnati, OH 45203-1607 Phone (800) 733-3310 or (513) 381-1959 Fax (513) 381-0070

Adventure Therapy Conference Petrie International P.O.Box 568 Kalamunda, Perth, Western Australia 6076 Phone (61) 9 291-9306 Fax (61) 9 291-9978 Internet: petrconf@iinet.net.au
Web site http://www.tas.gov.au/hahn/conference.html

Agusta A summer-long series of workshops festuring appalachian musicians, craftsmen, artists and educators. Augusta Heritage Center Davis & Elkins College 100 Campus Drive Elkins, WV 26241 Phone (304) 637-1209 Fax (304) 637-1317 e-mail: augusta@DnE.wvnet.edu

American Camping Association Regional and national annual conferences held at rotating sites throughout the United States. (1998 Dallas, 1999 Chicago, 2000 Albuquerque)
American Camping Association 5000 State Road 67 North Martinsville, IN 46151-7902
Conference Information Phone (317) 342-8456 ext. 336 Fax (317) 342-2065

Annual Recreation Workshop An annual workshop in early May, held near Montreat, North Carolina.
Kathy Emerson 1535 Alexander Road Rock Hill, SC 29732 Phone (803) 328-2764
Roger Maness 1750 Union Avenue Memphis, TN 38104 Phone (901) 722-5425

Teachers Playshop at Ashokan An August workshop featuring music, dance, storytelling and games for parents and professionals who enjoy working with children.
Fiddle & Dance Workshops RD 1 Box 489 West Hurley, NY 12491 Phone (914) 338-2996

Association for Challenge Course Technology (ACCT) Sponsor an international symposium on challenge course topics.
ACCT P.O. Box 255 Martin, Michigan 49070-0255 USA Phone (616) 685-0670 Fax (616) 685-7015

Association for Experiential Education (AEE) Sponsors an international conference in the fall and regional conferences in the spring.
AEE 2305 Canyon Blvd. Suite #100 Boulder CO 80303-5651 Phone 303-440-8844 FAX 303-440-9581
Internet: info@aee.org

The Association for Supervision and Curriculum Development (ASCD) 1250 North Pitt Street Alexandria, VA 22314-1403 Phone (800) 933-2723 or (703) 549-9110 Fax (703) 549-3891

Baptist Sunday School Board—Rec Labs** A January lab is held in Lake Yale, Florida and a February lab is held in the Southwest.
John Garner—Church Recreation Department 127 Ninth Avenue North Nashville, TN 37234
Phone (615) 251-2712

Black Hills Recreation Leaders Lab** The annual lab is held in September near Rapid City, South Dakota.
Ruth Moe 205 Corthell Road Laramie, WY 82070 Phone (307) 745-7227

The Bradford Woods Institute on Americans Outdoors An annual conference held in the fall near Indianapolis, Indiana.
5040 State Road 67 North Martinsville, IN 46151 Phone (317) 342-2915

Buckeye Leadership Workshop (BLW)** The annual workshop is held in Mid-March near Ashley, OH.
Dortha Mengert 204 Ambrose P.O.Box 217 Arcadia, OH 48804 Phone (419) 894-6976
Internet: teamplay@frontiernet.net or bjolliff@aol.com

John C. Campbell Folk School An annual winter dance week and classes throughout the year.
John C. Campbell Folk School Route 1, Box 14A Brasstown, NC 28902 Phone (800) FOL-KSCH or (704) 365-5724

Canadian Congress on Leisure Research Don Dawson University of Ottawa Department of Leisure Studies Ottawa, Ontario, Canada K1N 6N5 Phone (613) 564-5941 or (613) 564-9976
Internet: djdce@acadvm1.uottawa.ca

Chatcolab—Northwest Leadership Lab** The annual lab is held in June at various northwestern states.
Jean Baringer 520 South Maryland Conrad, MT 59425 Phone (406) 278-7716

Council for Adult and Experiential Learning Sponsors an annual conference in the late fall.
Contact: CAEL 243 South Wabash, Suite 800 Chicago, IL 60604 Phone (312) 922-5909

Country Dance and Song Society at Pinewoods and Buffalo Gap Camps Summer programs in a variety of dance, music, singing and storytelling styles.
Country Dance & Song Society 17 New South Street Northampton, MA 01060 Phone (413) 584-9913

Eastern Conference for Outdoor Leaders and Instructors (ECOLI) Annual conference held in the northeastern states.
For Information: Outdoor Leadership Program, Greenfield Community College, One College Drive, Greenfield, MA 01301 Phone (413) 774-3131 Extension 349.

Eastern Cooperative Recreation School** Hosts several workshop throughout the year in Eastern Pennsylvania and New York.
Ruth & Alex Sherman 27 Tappan Terrace Briarcliff, NY 10510 Phone (914) 941-7325
Arnie Zacharias 2210 Panama Street Philadelphia, PA 19103 Phone (215) 735-4523

Folklore Village Classes, Dances and Special Events throughout the year in Dodgeville, Wisconsin.
Folklore Village 3210 County Highway BB Dodgeville, WI 53533 Phone (608) 924-4000

Great Lakes Recreation Leaders Lab** Held annually in early May near Lexington, Michigan.
Daleine Eilers Route 1 Box 32 Mears, MI 49436 Phone (616) 861-4696

Great Plains Arts and Crafts Workshop Held in April near Cozad, Nebraska. Contact: LaRae Attebery 1906 West Third North Platt, NE 69101 Phone (308) 532-9559 or (308) 534-0404

Hawkeye Recreatory Mini Lab** Two annual labs in February and August near Dayton, Iowa.
Harriet Goslin Route 1 Ames, Iowa 50010 Phone (515) 233-1782

Hoosier Recreation Workshop** A long weekend held annually in April near Trafalgar, IN.
Charles Bradley 7262 18th Road Argos, IN 46501 or 112 West Jefferson Room 304 Plymouth, IN 46563 Phone (219) 935-8545

International Adventure Therapy Conference First Conference in July 1997 at Perth, Australia.
Petrie International P.O.Box 568 Kalamunda, Perth, Western Australia 6076 Phone (619) 291-9978 Fax (619) 291-9306 Internet: petroconf@iinet.net.au

International Experiential Learning Conference c/o Ann Becker and Associates, Inc. P.O.Box 94805 Chicago, IL 60690 223 West Jackson Blvd., Suite 510 Chicago, IL 60606 Phone (312) 263-2383 Fax (312) 263-4035

Kansas Recreation Workshop** Held in April near Junction City, Kansas.
Carmen Armantrout 2541 Raleigh Street Denver, CO 80212 Phone (303) 433-4548

Kentucky Heritage Institute Summer and Winter Dance Schools near Lake Cumberland, Kentucky.
Kentucky Heritage Institute P. O. Box 4128 Frankfort, KY 40604 Phone (502) 223-8367 or (502) 747-5700

Laurel Highlands Creative Life Lab (Western Pennsylvania)** Held annually in late April near Uniontown, PA.
Jack Harting, Registrar 1203 Malinda Road Oreland, PA 19075 Phone (215) 836-5309 or Nicki Jares 5930 Pinecrest Drive Erie, PA 16509 Phone (814) 864-9015

Leisure Craft Camp Held annually in September near Golden Pond, Kentucky.
Bonnie Ford 3869 Cairo Road Paducah, KY 42001 Phone (502) 443-5385

Leisurecraft and Counseling Camp Held annually in May near Monticello, Illinois.
Kathy Mason 1006 South Division Mahomet, IL 61853 Phone (217) 586-5784

Leisure/Recreation Workshop** Held annually in April near Gallant, Alabama.
Contact: Nina Reeves, United Methodist Ministries 898 Arkadelphia Birmingham, AL 35204 Phone (205) 251-9279

Lloyd Shaw Foundation A variety of workshops throughout the year.
Diane Burton 20 N.E. 47th Kansas City, MO 64116 Phone (816) 453-0157

Longhorn Recreation Laboratory Held at the Texas 4-H Center in Brownwood, Texas.
Danny Castro c/o Northwest Recreation Center 2913 Northland Drive Austin, TX 78731 Phone (512) 458-4107 or Faith Ballard Box 152 Hamilton, TX 76531

Midnight Sun Lab** A new lab first held in August of 1996.
Chris Pastro Box 83812 Fairbanks, AK 99708 Phone (907) 479-5903

National 4-H Camping Institute (NCI) Held in the fall at Virginia and other locations.
1997 Conference at Concordia Villages 9500 Ruppstrasse NE Bemidji, MN 56601 Tana Haugen-Brown Phone (320) 983-8317 Email: thaugen-Brown@mes.umn.edu

National Challenge Course Practioners Symposium (NCCPS) An annual conference held in the spring.
Thomas M. Leahy, Leahy & Associates 1052 Artemis Circle Lafayette, CO 80026-2840 Phone (303) 673-9832
A catalyst for the safe, ethical and effective use of challenge courses

National Service Learning Conference Sponsors an annual conference in the spring of each year.
The National Youth Leadership Council Phone (612) 631-3672

National Society for Experiential Education Sponsors an annual conference in the fall of each year.
NSEE 3509 Haworth Drive Suite 207 Raleigh, NC Phone (919) 787-3381

North American Society for Sport Management Dr. Garth Paton University of New Brunswick Faculty of PE & Recreation New Brunswick, Canada Phone (506) 453-5058 Fax (506) 453-3511 Internet: nassm@unb.ca

Northland Recreation Lab** Held annually in April near Lake Shakopee.
Jo Hecht 3420 48th Place Des Moines, IA 50310 Phone (515) 276-8045

Oglebay Institute Featuring programs throughout the year.
Stifel Fine Arts Center, 1330 National Road Wheeling, WV 26003 Phone (304) 242-7700

Ozarks Creative Life Lab** Workshop in October near Jefferson City, Missouri.
Ruth Jordan 115 W. Johnson Street Bonne Terre, MO 63628-1503 Phone (314) 358-2319 or Kathy Landers (314) 522-6416

Penland School of Crafts Penland, NC 28765-0037 Phone (704) 765-2359 Fax (704) 765-7389
Summer programs of crafts and fine arts.

Play Day Conference A yearly one day event in late May or early June held in the Rochester, New York area. Sponsored by the Cornell Cooperative Extension and local parks and recreation programs featuring a variety of programs and activities for those that work with youth.
Cornell Cooperative Extension of Monroe County 249 Highland Avenue Rochester, NY 14620 Phone (716) 461-1000

The Positive Power of Humor and Creativity An annual international conference held in Saratoga Springs, New York, in April. Sponsored by the Humor Project, Inc. and lead by Humor Project Director, Joel Goodman (known by many as co-author to PLAYFAIR).
The Humor Project 110 Spring Street Saratoga Springs, New York 12866 Phone (518) 587-8770
Fax (800) 600-4242

Presbyterian Annual Recreation Workshop** Annual Workshop in May near Montreat, NC
Glenn Bannerman P.O.Box 399 161 Virginia Road Montreat, NC 28757 Phone (704) 669-7323

Problem Solving Across the Curriculum An annual event in early summer in the upstate New York region.
Sheila Brady-Root St. John Fisher College 3690 East Avenue Rochester, NY 14618
Phone (716) 385-8452 Fax (716) 385-7311 Email: sroot@sjfc.edu
Internet: http://www.cs.oswego.edu/misc/psac

Recreation In Small Communities (RISC) Rick Harwell South Carolina Rural Recreation Project
Clemson University 263 Lehotsky Hall Box 341005 Clemson, SC 29634-1005
Email wharwel@clemson.edu

Recreation Laboratories and Workshops, Inc. (RLW)** The national rec lab organization, offers a national workshop every few years in the fall.
Mary Lou Reichard 21983 Crosswick Court Woodhaven, Michigan 48183 Phone (313) 676-1120

Redwood Recreation Leadership Lab** Annual Workshop in April near Fresno, California.
Rae Harn 385 Harn Ranch Road Soquel, CA 95073 Phone (408) 475-1802 or Monique Baca
Phone (818) 934-4228

Rocky Mountain Leisure Workshop** Annual workshop in April in Bailey, Colorado.
Lori Spearman P.O.Box 1934 Casper, WY 82602 Phone (307) 234-6127

Showme Recreation Leaders Lab** Annual Workshop in March near Jefferson City, Missouri.
Betty Mayo Route 2 Box 315 Huntsville, MO 65259 Phone (816) 277-4712
Betty Keys 516 Aldergate Farmington, MO 63640 Phone (573) 756-5545

Therapeutic Recreation Professional Development Sponsors a national forum in the spring.
NRPA Pacific Service Center 350 South 333rd Street #103 Federal Way, WA 98003
Phone (800) 796-NRPA Fax (206) 661-3929.

Thinking Outside the Box Presented by SkillPath® Seminars at a variety of locations in the United States.
SkillPath Seminars 6900 Squibb Road P.O.Box 2768 Mission, KS 66201-2768 Phone (800) 873-7545
Fax (913) 362-4241

Allison's Wells—School of Arts & Crafts P.O.Box 950 Canton, MS 39046 Phone (800) 489-2787 or (601) 859-5826 Fax (601) 859-5819
American's center for contemporary and traditional handicrafts, music and dance.

Winter Creative Life Lab** Annual Workshop in January near Onamia, Minnesota.
Jan Malone 3502 Larchwood Drive Minnetonka, MN 55345 Phone (612) 476-1413

National Society for Performance Instruction (NSPI) Conference and Expo Held annually in March. Phone (202) 408-7969

Society for Human Resource Management (SHRM) Conference and Expo Held annually in June. Orlando/Orange County Convention Center, Orlando, FL Phone (800) 283-SHRM

Teachers of Experiential and Adventure Education (T.E.A.M.) Conference An annual conference held in February featuring two days of classes, events and opportunities for learning and participating in experiential and adventure activities. Held at Northeastern Illinois University.
For information write to : TEAM Conference, Northeastern Illinois University 5500 North St. Louis Avenue Chicago, Illinois 60625-4699 Phone 312-794-2982

Thanksgiving Folk Dance Camp Four days of dancing, folk art, crafts and family activities. Bannerman Family Celebration Services P.O.Box 399 Montreat, NC 28757 Phone (704) 669-7323

Wilderness Education Association National Outdoor Leadership Conference Department of Natural Resource Recreation and Tourism—Colorado State University Fort Collins, CO 80523 Phone/Fax (970) 223-6252 Internet: wea@lamar.colostate.edu
A spring event.

Wilderness Risk Managers Conference An annual event sponsored by the Wilderness Risk Managers Committee with such organizational members as NOLS and Outward Bound.
John Gookin, National Outdoor Leadership School 288 West Main Street Lander, Wyoming 82520-3128 Phone (307) 332-8800 or (307) 332-6973 Fax (307) 332-1220
or Lewis Glenn, Outward Bound USA Route 9D R 2, Box 280 Garrison, New York 10524-9757 Phone (800) 243-8520 or (914) 424-4000 Fax (914) 424-4280

World Council of Comparative Education Societies (WCCES) Department of Education, University of Manchester, M13 9PL, United Kingdom Fax 44 (161) 275-3519 Email: r.ryba@man.ac.uk

World Leisure and Recreation Association International Congress Contact: Margaret Leighfield 91 Victoria Road Oxford, United Kingdom OX2 7QG Fax (44) 865 311887
Internet: af15@solo.pipex.com

8.24 Periodicals and Newsletters

The following is a listing of peridicals, journals and newsletters that frequently publish articles on outdoor pursuits, challenge education, and adventure programming. For a listing of more than 250 articles on these topics, see the references listed at the end of Chapter 1.

Alternative Education Resource Organization (Aero) Newsletter 417 Roslyn Road, Roslyn Heights, NY 11577 Phone (516) 621-2195

A New Day Gary Grimm & Associates, 82 South Madison Street, P.O.Box 378, Carthage, IL 62321-0378 Phone (800) 442-1614 or (217) 357-3401
A monthly magazine for activity professionals.

Accidents in North American Mountaineering American Alpine Club 710 Tenth Street Golden, CO 80401-1022 Phone (212) 722-1628

ACHPER National Journal ACHPER National Office 214 Port Road Hindmarsh South Australia 5007 Australia Phone (08) 340 3388 Fax (08) 340 3399

Adventure Education and Outdoor Leadership
Outdoor Source Book 12 St. Andrews Churchyard, Penrith, Cumbria CA11 7LS United Kingdom Phone 01768 891065 Fax 01768 891914 Email: enquiries@adventure-ed.edi.co.uk
Information, Journals, training, maps and more on Brittish outdoor education issues.

AEE Horizon
AEE Jobs Clearinghouse
Journal of Experiential Education AEE 2305 Canyon Blvd. Suite #100 Boulder CO 80303-5651 Phone 303-440-8844 FAX 303-440-9581 Internet: info@aee.org
Journal, newsletter and jobs listing of the AEE.

AMC Outdoors Appalacian Mountain Club 5 Joy Street Boston, MA 02108 Phone (617) 523-0636 Fax (617) 523-322
Subscriptions are available only to members of the Appalacian Mountain Club.

American Alpine Journal American Alpine Club 710 Tenth Street Golden, CO 80401-1022 Phone (212) 722-1628

Adirondac Adirondac Mountain Club, Inc. RR 3 Box 3055 Lake George, NY 12845 Phone (518) 668-4447 Fax (518) 668-3746
Published 6 times a year.

Alpine Journal: a record of mountain adventure and scientific observation Alpine Club 55 Charlotte Road London EC2A 3QT, England Phone 44-71-613-0755

American Alpine News American Alpine Club 710 Tenth Street Golden, CO 80401-1022 Phone (212) 722-1628
Published four times a year.

American Hiker American Hiking Society Box 20160 Washington, DC 20041-2160 Phone (703) 255-9304 Fax (703) 255-9308

American Trails Newsletter American Trails 1400 16th Street NW, Suite 300 Washington, DC 20036

ANZALS Leisure Research Series Department of Parks, Recreation and Tourism P.O.Box 84 Lincoln University New Zealand

Appalacia Journal Appalachian Mountain Club 5 Jay Street Boston, MA 02108 Phone (617) 523-0636 Fax (617) 523-0722

Appalacian Trailway News Appalacian Trail Conference Box 807 Harpers Ferry, WV 25425 Phone (304) 535-6331 Fax (304) 535-2667

Assets Search Institute P.O.Box 21652 St. Paul, MN 55121-9795 Phone (800) 869-6882 Fax (612) 686-4883
The magazine of Ideas for Healthy Communities and Healthy Youth.

Australian Journal of Outdoor Education c/o Margaret Nikolajuk, Administrator, Australian Outdoor Education Council GPO Box 1896R Melbourne 3001 Victoria Australia Phone 61 3 9428 9920 Fax 61 3 9428 0313 Email: voea@netspace.net.au

Backpacker Rodale Press, Inc. 33 East Minor Street Emmaus, PA 18098 Phone (215) 967-5171

Backpacking Newsletter Frank Ashley Box 79 Spickard, MO 64679-0079 Phone (213) 633-7821

Bag of Tricks Karl Rohnke c/o Project Adventure, Inc. P.O.Box 100 Hamilton, MA 01936
A quarterly publication for sharing new ideas in adventure and experiential education.

British Columbia Mountaineer British Columbia Mountaineering Club, P.O.Box 2674 Vancouver, British Columbia, Canada V6B 3W8 Phone (604) 737-3000

Council for Adult and Experiential Learning (CAEL) News 223 West Jackson Boulevard, Suite 510 Chicago, IL 60606

CAHPERD Journal
AVANTE 1600 James Naismith Drive, Gloucester, Ontario, Canada K1B 5N4
Phone (613) 748-5622 Fax (613) 748-5737

Camping Magazine American Camping Association 5000 State Road 67 North Martinsville, IN 46151-7902 Phone (800) 428-2267 Fax (317) 342-2065

Canadian Alpine Journal Alpine Club of Canada, Box 2040, Canmore, Alberta, Canada T0L 0M0 Phone (403) 678-3200 Fax (403) 678-3224

Challenge Magazine Published by The National Association of People With Disabilities (NAPD) 2117 Buffalo Road, Suite 254 Rochester, NY 14624 Phone (716) 325-2540 Fax (716) 546-1225
14 Franklin St. Suite 1320 Rochester, NY 14604-1504 Phone (716) 546-7710 Fax (716) 546-1225

Chicago Mountaineer Chicago Mountaineering Club, 22 South Thurlow Street Hindale, IL 60921

Climber and Hillwalker George Outram & Company Ltd., The Plaza Tower, East Kilbride, Glasgow, Scotland G74 1LW Phone 03552-46444 Fax 03552-63013

Climbing Elk Mountain Press, 1101 Village Road, Suite LLB1 Carbondale, CO 81623 Phone (303) 963-9449 Fax (303) 963-9442 Internet: climbing@infosphere.com
Climbing and outdoor pursuits.

Climbing Art Fairfield Communications, 5620 South 49th Street Lincoln, NE 68516 Phone (800) 755-0024 or (402) 421-2591 Fax (402) 421-1268
Mountaineering and Rock Climbing.

Colorado Outdoors Division of Wildlife, 6060 Broadway Denver, CO 80216 Phone (303) 291-7469

Cooperative Learning—The Magazine for Cooperation in Education Box 1582 Santa Cruz, CA 95061-1582
A publication of the International Association for the Study of Cooperation in Education (IASCE).

CRUX Northeast P.O.Box 149 Winsted, CT 06098 Phone (203) 738-4026
Ice and rock climbing information for northeastern United States and Canada.

Disabled Outdoors 5223 South Lorel Avenue Chicago, IL 60638 Phone (312) 284-2206
Articles and news items on living in the out-of-doors with special needs individuals.

Earth Work Earth Work, P.O.Box 550, Charlestown, NH 03603-0550 Phone (603) 543-1700

Environmental Education Report American Society of Environmental Educators Durham, New Hampshire 03824

Environmental Opportunities Newsletter P.O.Box 788 Walpole, NH 03608 Phone (603) 756-4553 ISSN 0736-9603

Experiential Education Newsletter National Society for Experiential Education 3509 Haworth Drive Suite 207 Raleigh, NC 27609-7229 Phone (919) 787-3263 Fax (919) 787-3381

Explore—Canada's Outdoor Adventure Magazine Thompson and Gordon Publishing Company, Ltd. #420, 301 14th Street NW Calgary, Alberta T2N 2A1 Canada Phone (800) 567-1372 or (403) 270-8890 Fax (403) 270-7922

The Forum 582 Baldy Hall SUNY/Buffalo Amherst, NY 14260 Phone 716-636-2451
A Publication of the New York State Federation of Chapters of the Council for Exceptional Children.

Foxfire News The Foxfire Fund, Inc., P.O.Box 541 Mountain City, GA 30562

Friends of Parks & Recreation National Recreation & Park Association 2775 South Quincy Street, Suite 300, Arlington, VA 22206 Phone (800) 626-6772 or (703) 820-4940 Fax (703) 671-6772
A quarterly publication for advocates of parks and recreation.

Frontload Roland/Diamond Associates, Inc. 67 Emerald Street Keene, NH 03431 Phone (603) 357-2181 Fax (603) 357-7992
A periodic review of corporate experiential learning methods, issues & research.

High Mountain Sports British Mountaineering Council High Magazine Ltd. 164 Barkby Road Leisester LE4 7LF, UK Phone 0533-460722 Fax 0533-460748 Internet: highmag@cix.compulink.co.uk also c/o Greenshires Print, Telford Way, Kettering, Northants, NN1 68 UN, United Kingdom Phone 01536 525 550 Fax 01536 518 721

Himalayan Journal Himalayan Club P.O.Box 1905 Bombay 400 001, India Phone 91022-494-0772 Fax 91-22-208-5977

Indian Mountaineer Indian Mountaineering Foundation Headquarters Complex Benito Juarez Rd. Anand Niketan, New Delhi 110 021, India

Impact Institute on Community Integration 6 Pattee Hall University of Minnesota 150 Pillsbury Drive SE Minneapolis, MN 55455 Phone (612) 624-4512.
Quarterly publication supporting disabilities.

Journal of Adventure Education and Outdoor Leadership Adventure Education, 12 Saint Andrews Churchyard, Penrith, Cumbria CA 11 7YE United Kingdom Phone 1768 891065 Fax 17768 891914

Journal of Applied Recreation Research Wilfrid Laurier University Press Waterloo, Ontario, Canada N2L 3C5 Phone (519) 884-1970 ext. 6123

Journal of Experiential Education AEE 2305 Canyon Blvd. Suite #100 Boulder CO 80303-5651 Phone 303-440-8844 FAX 303-440-9581 Internet: info@aee.org

Journal of Health, Physical Education and Recreation P.O.Box 6203 Te Aro Wellington, New Zealand

Journal of Leisure Research National Recreation & Park Association 2775 South Quincy Street, Suite 300, Arlington, VA 22206 Phone (800) 626-6772 or (703) 820-4940 Fax (703) 671-6772 Internet: NRPA01@Delphi.com

Journal of Outdoor Education Northern Illinois University, Lorado Taft Field Campus, Box 299, Oregon, IL 61061
Published once per academic year, with a variety of outdoor education topics.

Journal of Parks and Recreation Administration HPER 133 Indiana University Bloomington, IN 47405

Journal of Physical Education, Recreation and Dance (JOPERD) Published by the AAHPERD. 1900 Association Drive Reston, VA 22091-9989 Phone (703) 476-3477 or (703) 476-3400 Fax (703) 476-9527

Long Trail News Green Mountain Club Route 100 RR 1 Box 650 Waterbury Center, VT 05677-9735 Phone (802) 244-7037 Fax (802) 244-5867

Many Happy Returns The Quarterly International Publication of the United States Boomerang Association P.O.Box 182 Delaware, OH 43015 Phone/Fax (614) 363-4414

Mountaineer Mountaineers Inc. 300 Third Avenue West Seattle, WA 98119-4117 Phone (206) 284-6310 Fax (206) 284-4977

The Mountain Yodel P.O.Box 8753 Jackson, WY 83001 Phone (307) 734-1837
Internet: adrienne760@delphi.com
A grass roots publication on the art, photography, poetry and writings of climbing.

National Society for Experiential Education Quarterly National Society for Experiential Education 3509 Haworth Drive Suite 207 Raleigh, NC 27609-7229 Phone 919-787-3263 Fax 919-787-3381

The National Hookup 32 Margaret Drive Albany, NY 12211
Published by Indoor Sports Club for the Physically Disabled.

Northwest Wilderness Journal Northwest Wilderness Publications P.O.Box 25452 Seattle, WA 98125 Phone (206) 367-1355
Featuring outdoor activities and environmental issues of the Pacific Northwest.

Ocean Access National Ocean Access Project 410 Severn Avenue, Suite 107 Annapolis, MD 21403

Onsight!—International Climbing & Mountaineering Magazine 8516 West Lake Mead Blvd., Suite 104 Las Vegas, NV 98128 Phone (702) 255-8866 Fax (702) 228-4340 Internet: Onsight1@AOL.com

On The Edge The Climbing Company P.O.Box 21 Buxton, Derbyshire SK17 9BR, United Kingdom Phone 01778 393 652 Fax 01778 425 437 (Combined with Mountain Review)

The Outdoor Network Newsletter Once out of print, but now back in! The Outdoor Network, P.O.Box 4129 Boulder, CO 80306-4129 Phone (800) 688-6837 or (303) 444-7117 Fax (303) 442-7425

Outdoor Traveler WMS Publications, Inc. P.O.Box 2748 One Morton Drive, Suite 500, Charlottesville, VA 22903 Phone (804) 984-0655 Fax (804) 984-0656

Outdoors Forever P.O.Box 4832 East Lansing, MI 48823 Phone (517) 337-0018

Outside P. O. Box 54715 Boulder, CO 80321-4715
Outdoor pursuits and fitness articles.

PAEE Journal Pennsylvania Alliance for Environmental Education 225 Pine Street Harrisburg, PA 17101 Phone (717) 236-3599

Palaestra Challenge Publications, Ltd. P. O. Box 508 Macomb, IL 61455 Phone (309) 833-1902
Includes articles and reports on outdoor activities for disabled person.

Parallel Lines—The Newsletter of ACCT Association for Challenge Course Technology P.O.Box 970 Purcellville, VA 20134 Phone (540) 668-6634 Fax (540) 668-6634

Paraplegiia News/Sports 'n Spokes 2111 East Highland Avenue, Suite 180-B, Phoenix, AZ 85016-9611 Phone (602) 224-0500 Fax (602) 224-0507
Articles on fitness training and sports for wheelchair and other athletes with special needs.

Parks & Recreation Magazine National Recreation & Park Association 2775 South Quincy Street, Suite 300 Arlington, VA 22206-2204

Pathways—The Ontario Journal of Outdoor Education COEO 1220 Sheppard Avenue East Willowdale, Ontario, Canada M2K 2X1
COEO 1185 Eglinton Avenue East North York, Ontario, Canada M3C 3C6 Phone 416-495-4264 Fax 416-495-4310
Published six times a year by The Council of Outdoor Educators of Ontario.

Ravage—The Swiss Climbing Journal P.O.Box 1123, CH 8038 Zuerich, Switzerland
Phone/Fax: +1 481 68 56 Internet: alietha@gis.geogr.unizh.ch
The definitive rock climbing magazine of Switzerland. Published six times a year with a multitude of information about climbing in Switzerland. Also the first electronic climbing magazine on the internet.

Recreation Canada Canadian Parks/Recreation Association National Office 1600 Promenade James Naismith Drive Gloucester, Ontario, Canada K1B 5N4 Phone (613) 748-5651 Fax (613) 748-5854
Internet: cpra@activeliving.ca

Rock Wild Publications Pty. P.O.Box 415 Prahran, Victoria 3181, Australia

Phone 63 03 98368482 Australia's climbing magazine. Rock & Ice

Eldorado Publishing P.O.Box 3595 Boulder, CO 80307 Phone (303) 499-8410 Fax (303) 499-4131
Internet: RockandIce@nile.com
Serious climbing articles, equipment suggestions, routes and climbing information.

Rocky Mountain Sports Magazine 428 East 11th Avenue, Suite 104 Denver, CO 80203
Phone (303) 861-9229 Fax (303) 861-9209 Email: silverbco@aol.com

Schole Journal Leisure Studies & Recreation Administration CB #3185 Evergreen House UNC at Chapel Hill Chapel Hill, NC 27599-3185 Phone (919) 962-1222 Fax (919) 962-1223 Internet: moon@unc.edu
A yearly publication of the Society of Park and Recreation Educators.

Scottish Mountaineering Club Journal Scottish Mountaineering Club Cordee 3A De Montfort St. Leicester LE1 7HD, England Phone 0533-543579 Fax 0533-471176

The Server Published by the National Service-Learning Clearinghouse University of Minnesota Vocational & Technical Education Building, R-290 1954 Buford Avenue, St. Paul, MN 55108
Phone (800) 808-7378 or 612-625-6276

Sierra The Sierra Club 730 Polk Street San Francisco, CA 94109

Snowshoe United States Snowshoe Association Cornith, NY 12882 Phone (518) 654-7648

Summit: the Mountain Journal Summit Publications, Inc. 1221 May St. Hood River, OR 97031-1549
Phone (503) 387-2200 Fax (503) 387-2223

Taproot A publication of the Coalition for Education in the Outdoors, Dept. of Recreation & Leisure Studies, SUNY at Cortland, P.O.Box 2000 Park Center, Cortland, NY 13045 Phone (607) 753-4971 Fax (607) 753-5999
Dedicated to communication for the enhancement of education in the outdoors.

Technological Horixons in Education (T.H.E.) Journal 150 El Camino Real Suite 112 Tustin, CA 92680-3700 Fax 714-730-3739

Therapeutic Recreation Journal National Recreation and Park Association 3101 Park Center Drive Alexandria, VA 22302

Today's Team—The monthly newsletter for building and maintaining effective teams Wentworth Publishing Company 1858 Charter Lane P.O.Box 10488 Lancaster, PA 17605-0488 Phone (800) 822-1858 or 717-393-7317
The monthly newsletter to keep your team going strong.

Trail and Timberline Colorado Mountain Club 710 Tenth Street, Suite 200 Golden, CO 80401-1022 Phone (303) 922-8976 Fax (303) 922-7680

Training and Development [formerly Training and Development Journal] 1640 King Street Box 1443 Alexandria, VA 22313

Trends National Recreation and Park Association 2775 South Quincy Street Suite 300 Arlington, VA 22206 Phone (703) 820-4940
Park and Recreation Management, practical solutions to common problems.

United States Geological Survey Map Distribution Center Box 25286 Federal Center Denver, CO 80225

Universal Design Newsletter 1700 Rockville Pike Suite 110 Rockville, MD 20852 Phone (301) 770-7890 Fax (301) 770-4338
A quarterly newsletter with articles on designing with accessibility in mind.

Vertical Direct News and stories of interest to climbers—published bi-monthly by Climbers Choice International, Ltd. 1021 California Avenue Lamath Falls, OR 97601 Phone (800) 704-3891 Fax (541) 884-2681

Wilderness Trails Magazine Wilderness Trails, Inc. 712 Satori Drive Petaluma, CA 94954 Phone (707) 762-8839
Outdoor adventure, environmental issues and activism.

Youthworker Journal
Youthworker Update Newsletter Youth Specialties Periodicals P.O. Box 4406 Spartanburg, S.C. 29305-4406 Phone (800) 776-8008

Zip Lines—The Project Adventure Newsletter Project Adventure P. O. Box 100 Hamilton, MA 01936 Phone (508) 468-7981 P. O. Box 2447 Covington, GA 30209 Phone (404) 784-9310 Fax (404) 787-7764

8.25 Internet and World Wide Web Resources

Finding challenge and adventure related programs and homepages on the internet is not a difficult process with the many varieties of search engines available. Using key words such as adventure and outdoors will bring in more hits than you can possible read in a day, so try some specialty words like: rope course, challenge education, problem solving, and outdoor training. The following list is certainly not every source available, but is a pretty good introduction to the many types and styles of homepages that may contain just what you are looking for.

4-H Challenge Discussion List 4HCHALL Subscribe 4hchall your-real-name to: listproc@listproc.wsu.edu

Adventure Therapy discussion list ADVTHE-L Subscribe advthe-l your-real-name to: listserv@uga.cc.uga.edu

Arizona Challenge Discussion List AZCHALL Subscribe azchall your-email-address to: majordomo@ag.arizona.edu

Association for Experiential Education AEE aeelist@lists.princeton.edu
Association for Experiential Education Home Page *http://www.princeton.edu/~rcurtis/aee.html*
Subscribe aeelist your-real-name to: list@lists.princeton.edu

ClimbNET P.O. Box 905 Homewood, CA 96141 Phone (916)581-4147 Email: info@climbnet.com

Educational Resource Information Center—Clearinghouse on Rural Education & Small Schools—ERIC/CRESS P.O.Box 1348 Charleston, WV 25325 Phone (800) 624-9120
Internet address: lanhamb@ael.org
An excellent information center supported by the U.S. Government, which includes experiential and outdoor education topics. Check out the Clearinghouse Web page at: http://www.ael.org/~eric/eric.html

Not only does the Web page provide access to Clearinghouse resources in the field of challenge and adventure activities and ERIC system resources generally, but it also has links to nearly 80 related organizations.

ERIC Document Reproduction Service EDRS ERIC Document Reproduction Service 7420 Fullerton Road, Suite 110 Springfield, VA 22153-2852 Phone (800) 443-3742
Internet: edrs@gwuvm.gwu.edu
Resource information on paper, microfiche and microfilms may be purchased through this organization using Master Card or Visa. All that is needed is the ED Accession Number for the publication, which can be obtained directly from ERIC.

Educational Technology edtech@msu.bitnet

John Dewey Discussion List JDEWEY Subscribe jdewey-l your-real-name to: listproc@moose.uvm.edu

Leisurenet listproc@gu.edu.au
subscribe leisurenet your-real-name

National Service Learning Clearninghouse http://www.nicsl.coled.umn.edu or Phone (800) 808-SERV

Outdoor Education The outdoor education forum from Australia
Subscribe outdoor-ed your-real-name to: list serv@latrobe.edu.au

Problem Solving Across the Curriculum PSAC Internet: http://www.cs.oswego.edu/misc/psac
Listserve: subscribe psac to majordomo@cs.oswego.edu

Project Adventure's Homepage http://www.pa.org

Rock Goddess Gazette Information about climbing.
Email address: rockgddss@aol.com

The 'Ropes" List for information about building ropes courses subscribe your-email-address to: ropes-lserv@literati.com
questions to ropes-owner@literati.com

TowerTalk Some pretty high tech chat about towers—primarily for antennas
FAQ at http://www.contesting.com/towertalkfaq.html
subscribe your-email-address to: towertalk-request@contesting.com

Training and Development List TRDEV-L listserv@psuvm.psu.edu
subscribe trdev-l first and last name

Washington Challenge Discussion List WACHALL Subscribe wachall your-real-name to: listproc@listproc.wsu.edu

Wilderness Orientation Programs Subscribe wildornt your-real-name to: list@lists.princeton.edu

8.26 Sources for Books

Adventure Education 12 Saint Andrews Churchyard Penrith, Cumbria England C A 11 7 Y E
Phone (England) 01768 891065 Fax (England) 01768 891914 Internet: www.adventure-ed.co.uk
An international source for a variety of texts on ourdoor programs and activities.

Adventures Unlimited 5267 East Second Street Long Beach, CA 90803 Phone (310) 433-2204

Adventurous Traveler Bookstore P.O.Box 1468 Williston, VT 05495-1468 Phone (800) 282-3963 or (802) 860-6776 Fax (800) 677-1821 Internet: books@atbook.com

Alpine Adventures P.O.Box 921262 Sylmar, CA 91392-1262 Phone (800) 717-1919 Fax (818) 364-5257
Books, videos, tapes, CD's, maps and outdoor accessories.

Alpine Books 3616 South Road C-1 Mukilteo, WA 98275 Phone (206) 290-8587
A major distributor of outdoor books in North America.

Alpine Shop 601 East Lockwood Avenue St. Louis, MO 63119 Phone (314) 962-7715

American Camping Association Bookstore 5000 State Road 67 North Martinsville, IN 46151-7902
Email: aca@aca-camps.org Phone (800) 428-CAMP, (800) 428-2267 or (765) 342-8456 Fax (765) 342-2065
Books, educational materials & seminars for all types of camping & outdoor activities and 32 local chapters acrossed the United States.

Animal Town P.O.Box 485 Healdsburg, CA 95448 Phone (800) 445-8642 Fax (707) 431-0721
Childrens Books, Games and Fun Time Activities

Association For Experiential Education (AEE) 2305 Canyon Blvd. Suite #100 Boulder CO 80303-5651 Phone 303-440-8844 FAX 303-440-9581 Internet. info@aee.org
A variety of scholarly books on the use and application of experiential education.

Bannerman Family Celebration Services P.O.Box 399 Montreat, NC 28757 Phone (704) 669-7323
Creative Nylon Hoseplay games and activities for all ages.

CareerTrack MS20-13 3085 Center Green Drive P.O.Box 18778 Boulder, CO 80308-1778
Phone (800) 334-1018 Fax (800) 622-6211 Email: shop@careertrack.com
Books, tapes and videos for the professional on teambuiliding and more.

The Center for Active Education William M. Hazel, Director, P.O.Box 2055, Warminster, PA 18974-0006 Phone (215) 773-0885 Fax (215) 773-0885 Email: cenacted@aol.com

Champions On Film 745 State Circle Box 1941 Ann Arbor, MI 48106 Phone (800) 521-2832
Fax 313-761-8711
Sports Videos on a variety of subjects.

Chinaberry Book Service 2780 Via Orange Way, Suite B Spring Valley, CA 91978
Phone (800) 776-2242 or (619) 670-5200 Fax (619) 670-5203
Books and Other Treasures for the Entire Family (including tapes, videos and more).

Chessler Books P.O.Box 399, 26030 Highway 74 Kittredge, CO 80457 Phone (800) 654-8502 or (303) 670-0093 Fax (303) 670-9727
Mountaineering, exploration, rock climbing and adventure.

Chester Book Company 4 Maple Street Chester, CT 06412 Phone (203) 526-9887
A wide variety of craft and instruction books.

Chockstone Press, Inc. 32351 Horseshoe Drive Evergreen, CO 80439 Phone (303) 674-6888
Fax (303) 670-9190
Rock climbing, water sports and skiing guides, books, videos and maps.

The Clubhouse Bookstore/The Mountaineers 300 Third Avenue West Seattle, WA 98119
Phone (800) 284-8554 or (206) 284-8484 Fax (206) 284-4977

Creative Think Box 7354 Menlo Park, CA 94026 Phone 415-321-6775 Fax 415-321-0609
Books, cassette tapes, and supplies for being creative.

Crux Books 58 Ramsey Ave. Yonkers, NY 10701-5654 Phone (914) 969-1554
Internet: havranek@pipeline.com

Dover Publication, Inc. 31 East 2nd Street Mineola, NY 11501-3582
Includes many out-of-print titles, reprints and hard to find publications.

Educational Resources Information Center—Clearinghouse on Rural Education and Small Schools (ERIC/CRESS) Appalachia Educational Laboratory P.O.Box 1348 Charleston, WV 25325 Phone (800) 624-9120 Fax (304) 347-0487 Internet: lanhamb@ael.org also available on-line using "gopher ericir.syr.edu" The U.S. Department of Education Center filled with microfiche/film articles, publications, periodicals and information about education, including outdoor education and experiential education issues.

Educational Media Corporation P.O.Box 21311 Minneapolis, MN 55421-0311 Phone (612) 781-0088

Experiential Products P.O.Box 50191 Denton, TX 76206-0191 Phone (817) 566-1791 or (817) 591-0663
Experiential Activities, Games and Educational Recreation (E.A.G.E.R.), Games for Groups, and Affordable Portables by Chris Cavert.

Falcon Press P.O.Box 1718 Helena, MT 59624-1718 Phone (800) 582-2665 Fax (406) 442-2995
Adventure guides for hiking, biking, climbing, paddling and bird watching.

Ferron Teacher Aids (by Simon & Schuster) Box 280 1204 Buchanan Street Carthage, IL 62321-0280 Phone (800) 242-7272 or (217) 357-3900 Fax (217) 357-3908
For teachers and students through grade 8.

Free Spirit Publishing, Inc. 400 First Avenue North Suite 616-72 Minneapolis, MN 55401-1724
Phone (800) 735-7323 or (612) 338-2068 Fax (612) 337-5050 Email: help4kids@freespirit.com
Books, posters and games for teaching and enriching the lives of children and teens.

Group 2890 North Monroe Box 366 Loveland, CO 80539
Magazines, books, videos and events with a Christian theme.

Human Kinetics P.O.Box 5076 Champaign, IL 61825-5076 Phone (800) 747-4457 or (217) 351-5076
Fax (217) 351-1549
475 Devonshire Road Unit 100 Windsor, Ontario, Canada N8Y 2L5 Phone (800) 465-7301 or (519) 971-9500 Fax (519) 971-9500
P.O.Box IW14 Leeds, United Kingdom LS16 6TR Phone (0113) 2781708 Fax (0113) 2781709
Coaching references on a variety of subjects from dancing to mountain biking, kayaking to soccer.

The Humor Project, Inc. 110 Spring Street Saratoga Springs, NY 12866 Phone 518-587-8770
Fax (800) 600-4242
HUMOResources Jest for You! Books, videos, games, conferences, software and more.

Human Resource Development Press (HRD Press) 22 Amherst Road Amherst, MA 01002-9709
Phone (800) 822-2801 or (800) 466-4401 or (413) 256-1018 Fax (413) 253-3490
Corporate Training and Personnel Development Materials, videos, books, supplies.

Jossey-Bass Pfeiffer 350 Sansome Street Fifth Floor San Francisco, CA 94104 Phone (800) 274-4434
Fax (800) 569-0443
Books, resources and tools for success for the 21st century manager.

Kendall/Hunt Publishing Company 4050 Westmark Drive P.O. Box 1840 Dubuque, IA 52004-1840
Phone (800) 228-0810
A variety of educational publications and titles.

Kogan Page LTD. 120 Pentonville Road London, England N1 9JN Phone 0171-278-0433
Fax 0171-837-6348
Teaching and Learning Topics for Higher and Further Education.

Lark Books 50 College Street Asheville, NC 28801 Phone (800) 284-3388 Fax (704) 253-7952
Email: larkmail@larkbooks.com Internet: www.larkbooks.com
Books, crafts and equipment for fine art and crafts.

Learning Unlimited Corporation 5155 East 51st Street, Suite 108 Tulsa, OK 74135
Phone (918) 622-3292

MIG Communications 1802 Fifth Street Berkeley, CA 94710 Phone 510-845-0953 Fax 510-845-8750
A variety of publications featuring universal access, urban studies, safety and more.

Macmillan Publishing USA, a Simon and Schuster Company Phone (800) 716-0044 or (317) 361-5400

Metamorphous Press P.O.Box 10616 3249 N.W. 29th Avenue Portland, OR 97210-0616
Phone (800) 937-7771 or (503) 228-4972

National Recreation and Park Association Publication Center 2775 South Quincy Street, Suite 300, Arlington, VA 22206-2204 Phone (800) 626-6772 or (703) 820-4940 Fax (703) 671-6772

New Society Publishers New Society Educational Foundation 4527 Springfield Avenue Philadelphia, PA 19143 Phone (800) 333-9093 or (215) 382-6543

On Rope 1 6313 Jan Lane Drive Harrison, TN 37341 Phone (423) 344-4716 Fax (423) 344-9089
Bruce Smith is co-author of "On Rope: 2nd Edition", a great reference for rope techniques.

Parenting Press, Inc. 7750 31st Avenue NE Seattle, WA 98115

Pfeiffer & Company International Publishers 8517 Production Avenue San Diego, CA 92121-2280
Phone (800) 274-4434
Professional Tools for Managers, Trainers and Consultants—Definitely for the Corporate and Business World Client.

Project Adventure P.O.Box 100 Hamilton, MA 01936 Phone (508) 468-7981 Fax (508) 468-7605
P.O.Box 2447 Covington, GA 30209 Phone (404) 784-9310 Fax (404) 787-7764
P.O.Box 14171 Portland, Oregon 97214 Phone (503) 239-0169 Fax (503) 236-6765
P.O.Box 1640 Brattleboro, VT 05301 Phone (802) 254-5054 Fax (802) 254-5182
Excellent Programs, Training Seminars and Publications.

Project Adventure Australia 332 Banyule Road View Bank, VIC 3084 Australia Phone (03) 9457 6494
Fax (03) 9457 5438
Outdoor Education Programs, Training Seminars, Course Construction and Publications.

Ramblers and Climbers Book Society Readers Union Ltd. Brunel House Newton Abbot Devon, England TQ12 2DW

Resource Center for Redesigning Education P.O.Box 298 Brandon, VT 05733-0298
Phone (800) 639-4122 E-mail: resourcectr@vt.ngs.net
Books, journals and videos with a strong focus on educational alternatives.

St. Lucie Press 2000 Corporate Blvd., N.W. Boca Raton, FL 33431 Phone (800) 272-7737
Fax (800) 374-3401 Email: information@slpress.com Internet: http://www.slpress.com
Leadership, motivation, teamwork and human resources management books.

Sagamore Publishing P.O. Box 647 Champaign, IL 61824-0647
Phone (217) 359-5940 Fax (217) 359-5975 Internet: sagamore@prairienet.org

Frank Schaffer Publications, Inc. 10450 N. Lacañada Drive, Suite 120 Oro Valley, AZ 85737

Search Publications P. O. Box 167 2200 Old Stage Road Florissant, CO 80816

Search Institute 700 South Third Street, Suite 210, Minneapolis, MN 55415 Phone (800) 8887828 or (612) 376-8955 Fax (612) 376-8956

Speleobooks Emily Davis Mobley, P.O.Box 10 Schoharie, NY 12157 Phone (518) 295-7978

Stackpole Books 5067 Ritter Road Mechanicsburg, PA 17055 Phone (800) 732-3669
Outdoor books including several NOLS publications.

Venture Publishing, Inc. 1999 Cato Avenue State College, PA 16801-3238 Phone (814) 234-4561
Materials on Leisure Studies, Parks & Recreation and Planning.

Vertical Expressions Marc Gravatt 1070 North Mountain Road Gardiner, NY 12525
Phone (914) 255-9728 Fax (914) 256-0574 Email: VertExpres@aol.com and mgravatt@ix.netcom.com
Marc published a climbing clinic guide to climbing techniques.

Victorian Outdoor Education Association 217 Church Street, Richmond, Victoria 3121, Australia
Phone 03 9428 9920 Fax 03 9428 0313

Whole Person Associates, Inc. 210 West Michigan Duluth, MN 55802-1908 Phone (218) 727-0500
Programs on wellness, stress management, personal growth using media, audio and video tapes.

Youth Specialties—Zondervan Publishing House P.O.Box 4406 Spartanburg, SC 29305-4406
Phone (800) 776-8008
Youth Ministry Programs and Activity Ideas with a Christian Focus.

Zephyr Press 3316 North Chapel Avenue P.O.Box 66006-F Tucson, AZ 85728-6006 Phone (602) 322-5090
Fax (602) 323-9402
Books, guides and resource material on educational issues for teachers and parents.

8.27 Sources for Equipment

A5 Adventure, Inc. 1109 South Plaze Way #296 Flagstaff, AZ 86001 Phone (602) 779-5084

Action Haus Equipment (A.H.E.) 3200 Greenwich Road, Room 91, P.O.Box 1337 Norton, OH 44203
Phone (330) 825-7722 Fax (330) 825-1133 Email: ActionHaus@aol.com
Climbing gear galore, rescue equipment, specialty hardware and gear.

Adapt Ability—Products for Independent Living P.O.Box 515 Colchester, CT 06415-0515
Phone (800) 266-8856
Adapted games, tools and household equipment for those with physical limitations.

Advanced Base Camp 9325 S.W. Barber Street Wilsonville, OR 97070 Phone (800) 366-2666 or
(503) 685-9600 Fax (503) 685-9400
Camping, climbing and adventure education gear.

Adventure 16 4620 Alvarado Canyon Road San Diego, CA 92120 Phone (800) 852-2672 Fax (800) 854-6292
Camping, climbing and adventure education gear.

Alpine Adventures P.O.Box 921262 Sylmar, CA 91392-1262 Phone (800) 717-1919 Fax (818) 364-5257
Books, videos, tapes, CD's, maps and outdoor accessories.

Alpine Towers P.O.Box 69 Jonas Ridge, NC 28641 Phone (704) 733-0953 Fax (704) 733-3505
One of the most unique styles of high-element climbing towers in North American.

Anyone Can Whistle P.O.Box 4407 Kingston, NY 12401 Phone (800) 435-8863 Fax (914) 331-4475
A catalogue of musical discovery full of wonderful musical instruments, tapes, CDs and music boxes.

Bailey's P.O.Box 550 Laytonville, CA 95454 Phone (707) 984-6133 Fax (707) 984-8155
Arborist Equipment.

Beads and Beyond 35 Wall Street Asheville, NC 28801 Phone (704) 254-7927 Email: BODF@aol.com
Beads from around the world and through the ages. These folks have a wide variety of brightly colored feathers that can be used to make Funderbirds.

Berry Scuba Company 6674 North Northwest Highway Chicago, IL 60631 Phone (800) 621-6019 or
(312) 763-1626 Fax (312) 775-1815

Big Toys, Inc. 7717 New Market Street Olympia, WA 98501 Phone (800) 426-9788 and 206-943-6374
Designers and manufacturers of play structures and play areas.

Bike Nashbar 4111 Simon Road Youngstown, OH 44512-1343 Phone (800) NASHBAR or (330) 782-2244
Bicycles and equipment.

The Birds' Paradise 20835 Morris Road Conneautville, PA 16406 Phone (814) 587-3879
Birdhouses, feeders and information about a variety of birds.

Black Diamond 2084 East 3900 South Salt Lake City, UT 84124 Phone (801) 278-5533 Fax (800) 775-7625
Email: climb@bdel.com or bdmo@bdel.com
Rock climbing gear and equipment.

Blue Water 209 Lovvorn Road Carrolton, GA 30117 Phone (800) 533-7673 or (404) 834-7515
Fax (800) 836-1556
Known for their climbing ropes, but also carry climbing gear, webbing, harnesses.

Boomerang Man 1806 North Third Street Monroe, LA 71201 Phone (318) 325-8157
Probably the biggest collection of boomerangs in the world!

Brainstorms 8221 Kimball Skokie, IL 60076-2956 Phone (800) 231-6000
Wildly Creative Stuff.

Brewer's Ledge, Inc. 34 Brookley Road Boston, MA 02130 Phone (800) 707-9616 or (617) 983-5244
Fax (617) 983-5261
These folks make the Treadwall Fitness Climber.

Brigade Quartermasters 1025 Cobb International B1 Kennesaw, GA 30144-4300 Phone (800) 338-4327
or (404) 428-1234 Fax (800) 829-2999
Hunting, camping, backpacking, climbing & military supplies and equipment.

BSN Sports P.O.Box 7726 Dallas, TX 75209 Phone (800) 527-7510 Fax (800) 899-0149
School and Camp sporting gear.

Bumjo's 7445 East 22nd Street Tuscon, AZ 85710-6428 Fax (520) 751-4515 Phone (800) 649-0318 or
(520) 751-4212 Email: bumjos@ix.netcom.com
Caving, climbing, backpacking, and mountaineering equipment and supplies.

Cabela's 812 13th Avenue Sidney, NE 69160 Phone (800) 237-4444 Fax (308) 254-2200
Clothing, equipment and supplies for fishing, camping, hiking and hunting.

Campmor Store: 810 Route 17 North P.O.Box 997-P Paramus, NJ 07653-0997 Phone (800) 526-4784
Mail Orders: P.O.Box 700-J Saddle River, NJ 07458-0700 Phone (800) 226-7667 Fax (800) 230-2153
Internet Address: customer-service@campmor.com or info@campmor.com
Camping gear, equipment, footwear and supplies.

Camp Trails 1326 Willow Road Sturtevant, WI 53177 Phone (800) 848-3673

Canadian Alpine Manufacturing, LTD. 1140 River Road Richmond, Brittish Columbia, Canada
V6X 1Z5

Caribou Mountaineering P.O. Box 3696 Chico, CA 95927 Phone (800) 824-4153

Chime Time 2440-C Pleasantdale Road Atlanta, GA 30340-1562 Phone (800) 477-5075 Fax (800) 845-1535
Athletic Equipment and specialized movement accessories for all populations.

Chinook Medical Gear, Inc. 2805 Wilderness Place, Suite 700 Boulder, CO 80301
Phone (800) 766-1365 Fax (303) 444-8689
Medical necessities for the outdoors, wilderness and travel.

Climbers Choice International, Ltd. 1021 California Avenue Klamath Falls, OR 97601-2412
Phone (800) 704-3891 or (503) 883-3891 Fax (503) 884-2681
Climbing gear.

Climbing Distribution USA 3500 Clipper Road, Suite 201 Baltimore, MD 21211-1440
Phone (410) 243-6133

Climb High 1861 Shelburne Road Shelburne, VT 05482 Phone (802) 985-5056 Fax (802) 985-9141
Climbing equipment, ropes and gear.

CMC Rescue, Inc. P.O.Drawer 6870 Santa Barbara, CA 93160-6870 Phone (800) 235-5741 or (805) 967-5654 Fax (800) 235-8951
Search and rescue equipment, safety supplies, climbing rope and outdoor gear.

CMI P.O.Box 535 Franklin, WV 26807 Phone (800) 247-5901 or (304) 358-7041 Fax (304) 358-7991
Harness, Climbing Gear, Ascenders, Rescue Equipment, Repair Parts.

Colorado Cyclist, Inc. 3970 East Bijou Street Colorado Springs, CO 80909-9946 Phone (800) 688-8600 or (719) 591-4040 Fax (719) 591-4041 Internet: colcyc@rmi.net
A wide variety of racing and mountain bike gear.

Colorado Kayak USA P.O.Box 1 Nathrop, CO 81236 Phone (888) 265-2925 or (719) 395-6332 Fax (719) 395-2421

Colorado Mountain Equipment 29007 Richmond Hill Road Conifer, CO 80433 Phone (800) 635-6483

Company Spirit Clement Communications Inc. Concord Industrial Park Concordville, PA 19331 Phone (800) 345-3449 Fax (800) 459-1933
Motivation, safety and teamwork posters, displays and materials.

Cradlerock Outdoor Network P.O.Box 1431 Princeton, NJ 08542 Phone (609) 924-2919 Fax (609) 466-0234

Dive Rescue International, Inc. 201 North Link Lane Fort Collins, CO 80524 Phone (800) 248-3483 Fax (303) 482-0893

Don Gleason's Campers Supply, Inc. P.O.Box 87 9 Pearl Street Northampton, MA 01061-0087 Fax (413) 586-8770 Phone (800) 257-0019 or (413) 584-4895 Internet: cat96@gleasoncamping.com

Eastern Mountain Sports 1 Vose Farm Road Peterborough, NH 03458 Phone (603) 924-6154

Edelweiss, USA P.O.Box 110 Spencertown, NY 12165 Phone (800) 445-6664 or (518)392-3363

Edmund Scientific Company 101 E. Gloucester Pike Barrington, NJ 08007-1380 Phone 609-573-6250 Fax 609-573-6295
Scientific devices, toys and equipment for bringing the world of science alive.

Enterprises USA 20512 Nels Anderson Place or 550 N.W. Hill Street Bend, OR 97701 Phone (800) 580-5463 or (503) 388-5463 Fax (503) 388-3248
Supply a wide variety of climbing holds and equipment.

Eureka! 1326 Willow Road Sturtevant, WI 53177 Phone (800) 848-3673

Experiential Products P.O.Box 50191 Denton, TX 76206-0191 Phone (817) 566-1791 or (817) 591-0663
Experiential Activities, Games and Educational Recreation (E.A.G.E.R.), Games for Groups, and Affordable Portables by Chris Cavert.

Forestry Supplies, Inc. 205 West Rankin Street P.O.Box 8397 Jackson, MS 39284-8397 Phone (800) 647-5368 or (601) 354-3565 Fax (800) 543-4203
Tools and supplies for forestry, geology, environmental sciences and outdoor education.

Four Corners River Sports—The Whitewater Store P.O.Box 379 Durango, CO 81302-0379 Phone (800) 426-7637 or (970) 259-3893 Fax (970) 247-7819 Internet: 73003.304@compuserve.com
Whitewater rafting, kayaking and boating supplies.

Franklin Climbing Equipment P.O.Box 7465 Bend, OR 97708 USA Phone (541) 317-5716 Fax (541) 385-1821 Email: mail@fcehq.com
Climbing holds and clothing.

Gander Mountain, Inc. P.O.Box 248 Wilmot, WI 53192 Phone (800) 558-9410 Fax (800) 533-2828 TDD (800) 558-3554
Camping, hunting, fishing and hiking equipment.

Don Gleason's Campers Supply, Inc. 9 Pearl Street P.O.Box 87 Northampton, MA 01061
Phone (800) 257-0019 or (413) 584-4895 Fax (413) 586-8770

Guildcraft, Inc. 100 Firetower Drive Tonawanda, NY 14150 Phone (800) 345-5563 Fax (800) 550-3555
Internet: guildcraft@aol.com
Arts and crafts supplies.

Gulf Rope and Cordage, Inc. P.O.Box 5288 Mobile, AL Phone (800) 633-1805 or (205) 438-3159
A wide variety of ropes.

Hearth Song 156 North Main Street Sebastopol, CA 95472 Phone (800) 325-2502 TTD/TTY (800) 228-2589
Fax (309) 689-3857
Books, games, toys and activities.

High Adventure Sports P.O.Box 3756 Redding, CA 96049

High Fly Kite Company 30 West End Ave. Haddonfield, NJ 08033 Phone (609) 429-6260
Fax (609) 429-0142
Kite materials and supplies, and the fiberglas poles for rainbow writers.

Innovator of Disability Equipment and Adaptations, Inc. (IDEA) 1393 Meadowcreek Drive
Suite 2 Pewaukee, WI 53072 Phone (414) 691-4248 Fax (414) 691-8616
Accessories for independent living, adaptive sports and recreation for mobility impaired persons.

Into the Wind 1408 Pearl Street Boulder, CO 80302-5307 Email: kites@intothewind.com
Phone (800) 541-0314 or (303) 449-5356 Fax (303) 449-7315
Kites, boomerangs, flying toys and other kinds of fun stuff.

Indusco 1200 West Hamburg Street Baltimore, MD 21230 Phone (800) 727-0665 or (410) 727-0665
Fax (800) 666-0757 or (410) 727-2538
Cable, wire rope, chains and hardware for climbing walls and rope courses.

Inner Quest Route 1 Box 271C Purcellville, VA 22132 Phone (703) 478-1078 Fax (703) 668-6699
Challenge and adventure equipment, training, course construction and staff development.

International Mountain Equipment Box 494 Main Street North Conway, NH 03860
Phone (603) 356-7013

Jossey-Bass Pfeiffer 350 Sansome Street Fifth Floor San Francisco, CA 94104 Phone (800) 274-4434
Fax (800) 569-0443
Resources and equipment for the 21st century manager including the teams kit.

The Klutz Flying Apparatus Catalogue 2121 Staunton Court Palo Alto, CA 94306
Phone (800) 558-8944 or (415) 424-0739 Fax (800) 524-4075 or (415) 857-9110
Internet http://www.klutz.com
Some very cool and unusual stuff, for kids of all ages.

Kompan/Big Toys Northeast, Inc. RD 2 Box 249 Marathon, NY 13803 Phone (800) 345-6956
Fax (607) 849-6686

Leading Edge Boomerangs 51 Troy Road Delaware, OH 43015 Phone (614) 363-8332
Email: 103327.3123@compuserve.com
Some of the finest boomerangs around (including blanks to make your own).

L.L. Bean Casco Street Freeport, ME 04032 Phone (800) 221-4221

Long Island Rocks, Inc. 17-D Field Street West Babylon, NY 11704 Phone (516) 420-4026
Fax (516) 420-0754
Dynowall™ and Dynohold™ climbing wall systems, consulting and hardware.

Lowe Alpine P.P.Box 1449 Broomfield, Co 80038 Phone (303) 465-0522 or (800) 366-0223
Technical apparel, alpine packs, climbing hardware.

Map Distribution—U.S. Geological Survey Box 25286 Federal Center, Building 810
Denver, CO 80225

Map Express, Inc. P.O.Box 280445 Lakewood, CO 80228-0445 Phone (800) 627-0039 or (303) 989-0003 Fax (303) 969-8195
A wide variety of USGS, topographic, image and geological maps for North America.

Marmot Mountain Works 827 Bellevue Way NE Bellevue, WA 98004 Phone (800) 254-6246 or (206) 453-1515 Fax (206) 453-3176
Serious outdoor wear, sporting, kayaking, climbing, and mountaineering equipment.

Meisel Hardware Specialties P.O.Box 70 Mound, MN 55364-0070 Phone (800) 441-9870
Project plans and parts for the woodworking hobbyist! Plans, kits and supplies (including game pieces, dice, marbles, etc) Great for camps.

Merrel P.O.Box 4249 South Burlington, VT 05406 Phone (800) 869-3348

Metolius Mountain Products, Inc. 63189 Nels Anderson Road Bend, OR 97701 Phone (503) 382-7585 Fax (503) 382-8531 Email: metolius@empnet.com
Climbing pieces, harnesses and accessories.

Mid-Continent Mapping Center—NCIC U.S.Geological Survey 1400 Independence Road Rolla, MO 65401

Misty Mountain Threadworks Route 4, Box 73, 718 Burma Road Banner Elk, NC 28604 Phone (704) 963-6688 Fax (704) 963-6810
Climbing harnesses and equipment.

Mountain Equipment Co-op 1665 West 3rd Avenue Vancouver, British Columbia, Canada V6J 1K1 Phone (800) 663-2667 or (604) 876-6221 Fax (800) 722-1960 or (604) 876-6590

Mountain Gear 2002 North Division Spokane, WA 99207-2254 Phone (800) 829-2009 or (509) 326-8180 Fax (509) 325-3030 Email: sales@mgear.com

Mountain High 123 Diamond Peak Ave. Redgecrest, CA 93555 Phone (800) 255-3182

Mountain Safty Research (MSR) 4225 2nd Avenue South P.O.Box 24547 Seattle, WA 98134 Phone (800) 877-9677 or (206) 624-7048 Fax (206) 682-4184
Climbing, cooking, water purification and outdoor equipment.

Mountain Smith 18301 West Colfax Building P Golden, CO 80401 Phone (800) 426-4075

Nalgene Trail Products Nalge Company 75 Panorama Creek Drive Rochester, NY 14625
Makers of those great trail, sports, and fuel bottles that hold up to the elements.

Nantahala Outdoor Center—Outfitter's Store 13077 Highway 19 West Bryson City, NC 28713-9114 Phone (800) 367-3521 or (704) 488-2175 Fax (704) 488-2498 Email: storecatalog@noc.com Internet: http://www.nocweb.com

NASCO Arts and Crafts 901 Janesville Avenue Fort Atkinson, WI 53538-0901 Phone (800) 558-9595 and (414) 563-2446 Fax (414) 563-8246
A wide variety of craft supplies and equipment.

Nature Watch 9811 Owensmouth Avenue #2 Chatsworth, CA 91311 Phone (800) 228-5816 or (818) 882-5816 Fax (800) 228-5814 or (818) 882-5881 Email: Nature wat@aol.com

New England Camp and Recreation Supply P.O.Box 7106 Dallas, TX 75209 Phone (800) 343-0210
All types of recreation and sports equipment, camp furniture and supplies.

New England Ropes, Inc. 23 Popes Island New Bedford, MA 02740-7288 Phone (508) 999-2351 Fax (508) 999-5972 848 Airport Road Fall River, MA 02720-4735 Phone (508) 678-8200 Fax (508) 679-2363
One of the best and most cost effective places to purchase climbing ropes and equipment.

Nicros 519 Payne Avenue St. Paul, MN 55101 Phone (800) 699-1975 or (612) 778-1975 Fax (612) 778-8080 Internet: http://www.nicros.com
Absoutely cool holds, climbing walls, mounting hardware, and books.

The North Face, Inc. 999 Harrison Street Berkeley, CA 94710 Phone (800) 384-FACE Extension 500
Some serious equipment for extreme conditions, expeditions and outdoor pursuits.

Northwest River Supplies 2009 South Main Moscos, ID 83843-8913 Phone (800) 635-5202 or (208) 882-2383 Fax (208) 883-4787
Equipment for river and white water enthusiasts.

On Rope 1 6313 Jan Lane Drive Harrison, TN 37341 Phone (423) 344-4716 Fax (423) 344-9089
Climbing ropes, harnesses, specialty supplies for climbing and caving. Bruce Smith will also custom cut 1 inch webbing for "Raccoon Circles."

Oriental Trading Company, Inc. P.O.Box 2318 Omaha, NE 68103-2318 Phone (800) 228-2269 or (402) 331-6800 Fax (800) 327-8904 or (402) 596-2364
Plenty of inexpensive items for programs, prizes and play.

Paper Direct 100 Plaza Drive Secaucus, NJ 07094-3606 Phone (800) 272-7377 Fax (800) 443-2973
Tons of specialty papers, labels, certificates, binders, envelopes, VCR tape labels, etc.

Passion's Sports P.O.Box 49 Jenkintown, PA 19046 Phone (800) 523-1557
Equipment needs for varsity athletics and physical education programs and playgrounds.

Patagonia 1609 West Babcock Street Box 8900 Bozeman, MT 59715-2046 Voice/TDD (800) 638-6464 Phone (406) 587-3838 Fax (406) 587-7078
High quality outdoor wear.

PCA Industries, Inc. 5642 Natural Bridge St. Louis, MO 63120 Phone (800) 727-8180 or (314) 389-4140 Fax (314) 389-9034
Manufacturers of playground and recreation equipment.

Petro Grips 108 East Cherry Lane State College, PA 16803 Phone (814) 867-6870
Email: Petrogrips@penn.com
Natural granite and sandstone climbing holds, excellent climbing wall videos.

Pitsco 1002 East Adams P.O.Box 1708 Pittsburg, KS 66762-1708 Phone (800) 835-0686 or (800) 358-4983 Fax (800) 533-8104
Ideas and solutions for teachers. Equipment and information on problem solving, science & technology, electronics, inventions, robotics and engineering.

Performance Bicycle Shop P.O.Box 2741 Chapel Hill, NC 27514 Phone (800) 727-2453 or (800) 727-2433 Fax (800) 727-3291
Bicycles, cycling gear, equipment, tools, clothing and safety equipment.

Petzel—Pigeon Mountain Industries (PMI) P.O.Box 803 LaFayette, GA 30728-0803 Phone (800) 282-7673 or (706) 764-1437 Fax (706) 764-1531
World-Class Climbing Ropes, safety and climbing equipment.

Petrogrip Jim Bowers, 108 East Cherry Lane State College, PA 16803 Phone (814) 867-6870
Email: Petrogrips@penn.com
Modular climbing holds crafted from real rock.

Project Adventure P.O.Box 100 Hamilton, MA 01936 Phone (508) 468-7981 Fax (508) 468-7605
P.O.Box 2447 Covington, GA 30209 Phone (404) 784-9310 Fax (404) 787-7764
P.O.Box 14171 Portland, Oregon 97214 Phone (503) 239-0169 Fax (503) 236-6765
P.O.Box 1640 Brattleboro, VT 05301 Phone (802) 254-5054 Fax (802) 254-5182
Excellent Programs, Training Seminars and Publications.

Project Adventure Australia 332 Banyule Road View Bank, VIC 3084 Australia Phone (03) 9457 6494 Fax (03) 9457 5438
Outdoor Education Programs, Training Seminars, Course Construction and Publications.

Quest 569 Charcot Avenue San Jose, CA 95131 Phone (800) 875-6901 or (408) 433-1600 Fax (408) 433-1614
Tents, backpacks, storage bags and outdoor gear.

Raichle Molitor USA Geneva Road Brewster, NY 10509 Phone (800) 431-2204

Real Goods 966 Mazzoni Street Ukiah, CA 95482-3471 Phone (800) 762-7325
Everything under the sun! Environmentally friendly books and products with a focus on natural, organic and recycled products.

Recreational Equipment Inc. (REI) 1700 45th Street East Sumner, WA 98390 Phone (800) 426-4840
TTD (800) 443-1988
Quality Outdoor Gear and Clothing since 1938.

Rescue Technology P.O.Box 1465 Carrollton, GA 30117 Phone (800) 334-3368 or (404) 832-9694
Fax (404) 832-1676
Rescue and safety equipment for firefighters, police, military and industry.

Rescue Systems, Inc. Highway 95 Box RSI Lake Powell, UT 84533-0110 Phone (800) 552-1133 or (801) 979-4664 Fax (801) 979-4660

Robertson Harness P.O.Box 90086 Henderson, NV 89009-0086 Phone (702) 564-4286 Fax (702) 564-4287
Climbing harnesses, caving gear, ropes, helmets, and belay devices.

Round Trip Boomerang Gregg Snouffer 340 Troy Road Delaware, OH 43015 Phone (614) 363-4414
Email: 75574.2346@compuserve.com

S&S Arts & Crafts P.O.Box 513 Colchester, CT 06415-0513 Phone (800) 243-9232 Fax (800) 566-6678
Arts & crafts supplies, toys, games and sporting equipment.

Seda Products P.O.Box 997 Chula Vista, CA 91912 Phone (800) 322-7332 or (619) 336-2444
Equipment, kayaks, paddles and info for all types of paddlesports.

Shoreline Mountain Products 11 Navajo Lane Corte Madera, CA 94925 Phone (800) 381-2733 or (415) 924-5257 Fax (415) 924-1188
Climbing gear, harnesses, videos, clothing.

Signature Research Route 2 Box 666 Hiawassee, GA 30546 Phone (404) 896-1487
Challenge and adventure based programming equipment, course construction and training.

Smith Safety Products, Inc. P.O.Box 36 Petaluma, CA 94953 Phone (800) 772-5948 or (805) 681-1338
Fax (707) 526-5290 Internet: http://www.smithsafety.com
Climbing and rescue equipment and supplies.

Speleoshoppe P.O.Box 297 Fairdale, KY 40118 Phone (800) 626-5877 or (502) 367-6292
Internet: ian@speleo.com
Equipment and information for the caving enthusiast.

Sportime Select Service & Supply Company, Inc. One Sportime Way Atlanta, GA 30340
Phone (800) 283-5700 or (770) 449-5700 Fax (800) 845-1535 or (770) 263-0897 Email: orders@sportime.com
All the standard equipment for sports and recreation plus pages and pages of unique, innovative and one-of-a-kind equipment, including challenge and adventure equipment.

Sportime Abilitations One Sportime Way Atlanta, GA 30340 Phone (800) 845-1535
Development and restoration of physical and mental ability through movement.

Starlight Outdoor Education P. O. Box 96 Smoot, WV 24977 Phone (800) 845-5692 or (304) 392-6306
Fax (304) 392-6184
Equipment and accessories for adventure programs, climbing walls, challenge courses, including design, construction, inspection and maintenance.

Sterling Rope Company 181 Elliott Street, Suite 707 Beverly, MA 01915-3060 Phone (508) 921-5500 Fax (508) 921-5501
Ropes for climbing and adventure activities.

Successories, Inc. 919 W. Springer Drive Lombard, IL 60148-9751 Phone (800) 535-2773 Fax (708) 953-1229
A variety of motivational and insprirational posters, plaques, shirts and gift items.

Things From Bell, Inc. 230 Mechanic Street P.O.Box 206 Princeton, WI 54968 Phone 414-642-7337
All of the standard recreation and playground equipment. Unusual games, too!

Trails Illustrated P.O.Box 3610 Evergreen, CO 80439-3425 Phone (800) 962-1643 or (303) 670-3457
Topological Maps.

United States Boomerang Association P.O.Box 182 Delaware, OH 43015 Phone/Fax (614) 363-4414

U.S.Games P.O.Box 117028 Carrolton, TX 75011-7028 Phone (800) 327-0484 Fax (800) 899-0149
Meeting the needs of education, recreation, athletics, health & adaptive physical education.

United States Geological Survey (USGS) Map Sales Federal Center P.O.Box 25286
Denver, CO 80225 Phone (800) USA-MAPS or (303) 236-7447

Upper Limits Rock Gym and Pro Shop 1304 West Washington Bloomington, IL 61701
Phone (800) 964-7814 or (309) 829-8255 Fax (309) 829-2284 Internet: www.upperlimits.com
Climbing equipment, books, videos and guides.

Versey Enterprises Wayne Versey 1258 North 1100 East, Shelley, ID 83274 Phone/Fax (208) 357-3428
Email: versey@juno.com
Two liter bottle rocket launchers and inlaid award plaques.

Vertical Concepts 3225A N.W. Shelvin Park Road P.O.Box 1602 Bend, OR 97709
Phone (800) GO-CLIMB or (503) 389-5198
Climbing holds and more.

Wild Country 230 East Conway Road Center Conway, NH 03813 Phone (603) 356-5590
Essential equipment for sporting climbs.

Wild Things Inc. P.O.Box 400, 2955 Main Street North Conway, NH 03860 Phone (603) 356-6907
Fax (603) 356-3843
Climbing equipment and gear, including sewn webbing, etriers, and other specialties.

Wolverine Sports 745 State Circle P.O.Box 1941 Ann Arbor, MI 48106 Phone (800) 521-2832
Fax (313) 761-8711
All types of sports and recreation equipment, balls, parachutes, playground equipment.

Woodplay, Inc. 1108 New Hope Road Ext. P.O.Box 27904 Raleigh, NC 27610 Phone (800) 982-1822 or (919) 231-6080 Fax (919) 231-3074
Creative wooden play equipment for children.

The Woodworkers' Store 21801 Industrial Blvd. Rogers, MN 55374-9514 Phone (800) 279-4441
Hardware, wood, tools and know how! A great source for those hard-to-find woodworking supplies, fasteners, finishes, tools and instructional manuals.

Worldwide Games P.O.Box 517 Colchester, CT 06415-0517 Phone (800) 888-0987 or (800) 243-9232
Fax (800) 566-6678
A large variety of innovative games for camps, recreation programs and families.

XICOM 60 Woods Road Tuxedo, NY 10987 Phone (800) 759-4266 or (914) 351-4735 Fax (914) 351-4762
Email: Xicom@aol.com
Tools for Personal, Professional and Organizational Development.

Zend Holds P. O. Box 4575 Portland, ME 04112 Phone (207) 824-0596
Climbing holds.

8.28 The Wish List

The following list is provided, based heavily on the personal bias of the authors, as a concise list of some of the best regarded and useful resources for the field of challenge and adventure programming. A complete citing for each of these references can be found earlier in this chapter.

8.01 Challenge and Adventure Activities, Initiatives, Rope Courses

Silver Bullets by Karl Rohnke—Probably, dollar for dollar, the best book ever published on challenge and adventure activities.
Cowtails and Cobras II by Karl Rohnke—One of the best primers to challenge courses on the face of the earth.
Teamwork & Teamplay by Jim Cain and Barry Jolliff—Some of the finest ground level portable challenge and adventure activities ever collected, with building instructions and one of the best resource lists ever published for this field.
The Pictorial Guide to Group Work Activities by Geoff Sanders—Challenge and adventure activity publication from Great Britain.

8.02 Outdoor Activities and Outdoor Education

Integrated Outdoor Education and Adventure Programs by Stuart J. Schleien
Just Beyond the Classroom by Clifford E. Knapp

8.03 Educational Pursuits and Experiential Education Issues

Adventure Education by C. J. Mortlock
The Fifth Discipline Fieldbook by Senge, Kleiner, Roberts, Ross and Smith
Experience and Education by John Dewey
The Conscious Use of Metaphor in Outward Bound by S. Bacon
Into the Classroom: The Outward Bound® Approach to Teaching and Learning by Mitchell Sakofs and George P. Armstrong
Outdoor Adventure Pursuits: Foundations, Models and Theories by Alan Ewert

8.04 Corporate Interests

The Power of Team Building—Using Rope Techniques by Harrison Snow
Do It and Understand the Bottom Line on Corporate Experiential Learning by Christopher Roland and Richard Wagner

8.05 Bringing a Group Together and Teambuilding

Joining Together by David Johnson and Frank Johnson
Playful Activities for Powerful Presentations by Bruce Williamson
Telltale Trees by Ethel Johnson—A fun and interesting activity

8.06 Leadership

How to Make the World a Better Place by Jeffrey Hollender

8.07 Universal Access, Adapted Activities and Special Populations

Adapted Adventure Activities by Wendy Ellmo and Jill Graser
Together Successfully by John Rynders and Stuart Schleien
Bridges to Accessibility by Mark Havens

8.08 Activities for Mature Populations

Recreation Programming and Activities for Older Adults by Jerold Elliott and Judith Sorg-Elliott

8.09 Environmental Issues

Earth Education by Steve Van Matre
Project WILD
Bottle Biology by the Bottle Biology Resources Network
The Great Garbage Concert by Glenn McClure
Soft Paths by Bruce Hampton and David Cole

8.10 Adventure Philosophy and Historically Significant Publications

The Well-Played Game by Bernard De Koven
Winning is Everything and Other American Myths by Thomas Tutko and William Bruns
No Contest, the Case Against Competition by Alfie Kohn

8.11 Program Evaluation and Assessment

Evaluating Training Programs by Donald Kirkpatrick
Outdoor Adventure Pursuits: Foundations, Models and Theories by Alan Ewert

8.12 Processing, Debriefing, Reflection and Review

Processing the Adventure Experience by Nadler and Luckner—A classic reference.
The Skilled Facilitator by Roger Schwarz
A Manual for Group Facilitators by Auvine, Densmore, Extrom, Poole and Shanklin

8.13 Creativity

Thinkertoys by Michael Michalko
A Whack on the Side of the Head by Roger von Oech—Destined to be a classic.

8.14 Games

50 Ways to Use Your Noodle by Chris Cavert and Sam Sikes
The Cooperative Sports and Games Book by Terry Orlick—Definitely a classic.
Playfair by Matt Weinstein and Joel Goodman—This should be in your collection.
Creative Campfires by Douglas Bowen—Hard to find, but great to own.
Ground Loop by William Hazel
The New Games Book, and More New Games Edited by Andrew Fluegelman—Who can forget these two world changing classics.

8.15 Toys, Games and Activities

Brite-Tite Book O' Fun by Glenn Bannerman, Beth Gunn and Lee Ann Konopka—All the directions for creative Hose Play.
Play Book by Steven Caney—A book filled with fun stuff.

8.16 Puzzles and Games

The Penguin Book of Curious and Interesting Puzzles by David Wells—One of the most extensive collections of puzzles ever.

8.17 Knots, String and Fun Things to do with Rope

Fiber Rope Technical Information Manual by Gail Foster—All the technical information you will probably ever need.
On Rope by Bruce Smith and Allen Padgett
Forget Me Knots by Karl Rohnke

8.18 Safety and Risk Management Issues

High Angle Rescue Techniques by Tom Vines and Steve Hudson
Ropes Course Safety Manual by Steven Webster
Project Adventure 20 Year Safety Study complied by L. Furlong and others—Worth reading.
Wire Rope Users Manual by the Wire Rope Technical Board

8.19 Organizations

American Alliance for Health, Physical Eduation, Recreation and Dance **(AAHPERD)**
American Camping Association **(ACA)**
Association for Challenge Course Technology **(ACCT)**
Association for Experiential Education **(AEE)**

8.20 Rope Course, Climbing Wall and Challenge Course Builders

There are a variety of knowledgeable builders throughout the world. Your best choice is to find a builder that fulfills your needs, and one that you trust to do the job right.

8.21 College Programs

There are literally dozens of programs around the world that are available. A few, such as Mankato State University, have departments dedicated to experiential education programs. Others utilize existing educational departments to offer courses and degrees in this field.

8.22 Insurance Carriers and Information

Of all the topics in challenge and adventure education likely to change in the comming years, insurance and risk management issues are definitely at the top of the list. Check for new information from your local provider.

8.23 Conferences, Seminars & Workshops

The recreation workshops designated with (**) two asterisks are some of the most economical and unique conferences for learning a variety of recreational programming ideas. Other significant annual events include:

The **ACCT** event typically held in the late winter/early spring.
The Black Hills Recreation Leaders Lab held in September.
The Buckeye Leadership Workshop (our favorite) held in March.
The Bradford Institute on Americans Outdoors held in the fall.
Regional AEE Conferences held throughout the United States.

8.24 Periodicals and Newsletters

Journal of Adventure Education and Outdoor Leadership
Pathways—The Ontario Journal of Outdoor Education
Rock & Ice Magazine
Taproot

8.25 Internet Resources

AEE Homepage and Listserv
The 'Ropes' List
ERIC / CRESS

8.26 Sources for Books

Adventure Education
American Camping Association Bookstore
Association for Experiential Education
Kendall/Hunt Publishers
Youth Specialties—Zondervan Publishing House

8.27 Sources for Equipment

Franklin Climbing Equipment—Some very unique and good quality gear.
Into the Wind—for all kinds of things that fly. Visit the store when you're in Boulder, CO.
Misty Mountain Threadworks—Find a harness you can trust.
Mountain Gear—One of the most complete and inexpensive catalogs collected during the writing of this book.
New England Ropes—One of the most cost effective places to buy rope.
On Rope 1—Will custom make about anything with webbing including Raccoon Circles, and perhaps even a Gridlock pattern.

Notes

Chapter Nine

The Future of Challenge and Adventure Programming

The material collected and presented in this book has taken more than 25 years to assemble. As we were finishing, we began to wonder where the future would take us in another 25 years. What new activities will be invented? What new organization will spring up and development huge memberships? What new ways will challenge and adventure education be used in the 21st century? Who will be our leaders, our mentors, our authors, and our friends?

Given that we are at least as creative as some other futurists, we thought we would try looking ahead, and offering some ideas and suggestions for the future.

Basic Training

The Future

Don't Wait for the Future—Invent It!

Free Advice

Intelligent is when you only believe half of what you hear.
Brilliant is when you know which half to believe!

Considering all of the zillions of workshops, conferences, camps, meetings, planning sessions, training days, challenge programs, classroom activities and similar events that we have presented in the past 25 or so years, it is pretty likely that by now, we have formed some definite ideas about the nature of challenge and adventure programs, the program leaders that facilitate these activities, and the participants that come to be a part of it all. On the other hand, seldom does a day go by when we are not personally challenged by a thought or technique that we have heard for the very first time, causing us to constantly rethink what we know and value. So, given these experiences, and our personal thoughts as well, here are a few words of advice for those attempting to be a part of this wonderful adventure.

1. Read everything you can about challenge and adventure programming. It is no accident that there are hundreds of listings in this book for periodical articles, internet resources, books, manuals and other reading materials just waiting for your eyes to visit them. Why should the bookcases in your house be any less full than ours? Start leaving book lists, with author's name, title and ISBN number around the house near the holidays or your birthday. Go to the library before a long holiday break and pick up a few classic gems on challenge and adventure programming, experiential education, or groupwork activities.

2. Volunteer. There are many organizations that would love to have someone volunteer their time to share challenge and adventure related programs with their members. Summer camps, sport leagues, colleges, corporate groups, staff training sessions and many others are looking for program assistance on a continual basis. By volunteering, you establish yourself as a resource, and you will typically be exposed to a variety of activities that you may not have seen before. You will also have the chance to work with a variety of populations. All of this is valuable experience. The more opportunities you have for polishing your presentation of an activity, or for practicing your facilitation skills, the better you will be.

3. Share. Share your activities with others working in this field, share your stuff (your ropes, your props, your rubber chickens), share your worst nightmares and highest hopes for this field. Share your ideas in writing. There is probably not a newsletter editor out there that has enough material each month to fill their space. Write it down, and tell the world. When someone shows you a neat idea or activity, give them one back.

4. Give credit where credit is due. Even the most individual thought was probably generated as a result of exposure to someone else's ideas. Thank people when you borrow their ideas, or present an activity they created. A good friend once presented an activity at a conference and credited the author that had created it. Little did he realize that the author was in the audience at the time. Not only did he make a new friend that day, but he was asked to speak at the author's organization the next week. It takes so little to say, "here is a great activity that I first learned from Denny Elliott at an Ohio 4-H conference. . . . ." And the folks that gave you that gem are likely to give you others, knowing that you gave credit where credit was due.

5. Join professional organizations that promote challenge and adventure programming. There are a variety of local, state, regional, national and international organizations (AEE, ACCT, ACA, NSEE) that provide resources, conferences, workshops, professional accreditation, skill enhancement and networking opportunities. Attend a conference or a workshop and see what these organizations have to offer you, and what you may have to offer them.

6. Find out who else in your region is working in this same arena, and visit them. There are probably people in your neighborhood that work with programs utilizing challenge and adventure activities. Check out the membership listing of organizations to find them. Check out local day and resident camps.

Many schools and colleges also have challenge programs.

7. Find a mentor. Learn their philosophy, know what they know, and then make it your own. Find out what works, how they do it, who they based their opinions on. Read what they have read, go where they have gone, and invite them to see you in action. Most of us can benefit from the advice and critique of a kind mentor whose opinions we value. Not all mentors are alive however. If you can't happen to find a living mentor, you can still find quite a bit in print from some of the more prolific writers in the past 2 centuries.

8. Have lunch. Once a month, have a lunch somewhere and invite others working in your field to join you. One group we know meets once a month, and in order to join the group, you have to bring 3 new activities to teach the group. The membership is diverse, but driven by the love of adventure programming, and the quest for the perfect lunch.

9. Go outside of your own comfort zone. If you are asking your group to extend themselves and move outside of their comfort zone, you must be willing to do the same. This may mean that you volunteer to teach activities on a day when you know it is going to rain, or when the conditions are not ideal, or for a group that is a little bigger than the last group you worked with. The point is to grow, but never, never sacrifice the safety of the event. Remember creative cheating and rule bending doesn't apply when there is a genuine safety concern. But in matters of personal preference, as a facilitator, you can probably do more than you realize, so go out there, find your limitations, and push them further.

10. Be willing to learn from your mistakes. Face it, you are going to goof up. Your ability to handle it when you do will make all the difference. Aside from any obvious safety blunders, you are going to experience a variety of situations that really push you off balance. If the participants in your group are there to learn, why should the experience be any less for you? Admit it when you make a mistake. Learn from it, and then move on.

11. Get some training. While there remains no individual program that is the apex of challenge and adventure programming, there are quite a few organizations around the world that provide significant training opportunities. Some colleges offer classes for credit. Some camps and outdoor programs provide internships and study programs. Many rope courses offer seasonal training with yearly refresher courses. First aid and CPR certification are good to have. How about advanced skills such as WFA and WFR too?

12. Show some respect. As a challenge facilitator, you will be in the position to influence the thoughts and actions of everyone you work with. Some participants will appreciate a kind word of encouragement as they attempt a new activity. Some can use a useful hint or a friendly hand reaching out to help them. Everyone will appreciate your respect. Even when it is raining, and your group is in chaos, and 20 minutes have gone by and they are still only halfway throught River Crossing, even then, simple courtesy and respect will help you keep control of the situation, and maintain the confidence of your group.

Any Questions?

The person that knows HOW, will always have a job.
But the person that knows WHY, will be his boss!

John Fark as Father Time
Buckeye Leadership Workshop

Hopefully by the time you reach this point in the book, you will begin to know a little bit about how to use challenge and adventure programming activities to provide growth opportunities for your group. Beyond the activities listed here, the numerous references, articles and resources listed for your benefit, and the authors' own commentary on this uniquely wonderful experience, there is still much more to know. In an effort to encourage you to look farther than just these pages, the following questions are provided. Some are based on real-life experiences, others are simply fabrications of our minds. We will leave it up to you to determine which is which, the answers would truly surprise you! So dig deep into this world of challenge and adventure and experiential education, and for the final challenge in this book, see how many of the following questions you can answer.

1. Describe three different name games suitable for a group of 14 year old students.
2. Why process or debrief an activity?
3. Name three books that describe portable challenge and adventure programming ideas.
4. Name as many places as you can where you can buy ⅛ inch shock (bungie) cord.
5. What do the following abbreviations stand for:
   AEE, ACCT, ACA, AAHPERD, NCCPS, ASCF, BLW, WFR, PA?
6. What is the difference between a universal and an accessible challenge course?
7. Describe a challenge activity that can be physically safe, but emotionally risky.
8. How can you tell if a participant has suffered an emotional injury on your challenge course?
9. Name three publishers that frequently provide books with an experiential education theme.
10. If you need to find the telephone number of a business, but you don't know where it is located, how can you do it?
11. What role does the philosophy of John Dewey play in challenge and adventure education activities?
12. Name three periodicals or magazines that provide information on challenge and adventure programming.
13. You are allowed one athletic bag full of challenge equipment to carry on the airplane that will take you to a remote region to facilitate a full days worth of activities for 25 people. Remembering how cautious the airport security guards are at the metal detectors, what do you bring?
14. List 5 of the resources / websites that you can find if you search the internet on the following search parameters: challenge, teambuilding, rope course, experiential education, outdoor education.
15. List 5 other search parameters that can be used to locate experiential education and challenge and adventure programming ideas.
16. List at least one experiential education or challenge and adventure related website that is not presented in the English language.
17. Name three international organizations that provide challenge based educational programs.
18. You would like to have a peer review of your organization's program. Who can you contact to arrange such a peer review?
19. The 43 year old executive said, "you can't make me." What do you do?
20. Name three activities that you can lead using a 30 foot (9 meter) rope.
21. How much does it cost to join AEE? ACA? Do they offer discounts or student rates?
22. Take one of the activities in Chapter Four, and adapt this activity for each of the following situations:
    - The only available play area is on the hard pavement of a nearby parking lot.

- Weather has forced the activity to be held inside.
- Only four people show up.
- All eight of your participants are capable of moving, but require oxygen tanks to assist their breathing.
- One of the participants in the group has some lower back pain.
- You are leading the program for 4 marriage encounter couples (8 people total).

23. What does the concept of Challenge by Choice really mean?

24. The camp you are working for this summer has a trust fall platform that is 72 inches above the ground. Is this height appropriate for the college students attending your summer program? Where can you find out about the safety of this platform?

25. Name one really good closing activity for a group of corporate managers.

26. You are leading a program in an open grassy playing field. During a debriefing session, one of the participants in your group begin smoking a cigarette. What is your policy?

27. You've been asked to lead an on-site problem solving session for a company which allows smoking. You are in a closed classroom at the company's headquarters. You do not smoke. If you don't allow smoking, the company will hire someone else that does. What accomodation can you make for the smokers in this session?

28. You have a backpacking trip for the next 11 days. What lightweight challenge and adventure props can you bring to use with your 12 member group?

29. You are about to lead a high ropes course activity. As your group is checking out their gear, you notice that one of the participants is extremely large, and doesn't seem to be able to find a climbing harness that fits properly. What now?

30. You grew up in the north where 8 inches of snow is just a 'light dusting.' Now you've moved to the south, and when you ask the builder installing your ropes course if they are going to dig below the frost line, they say it doesn't matter. Are they right?

31. In ropes course terminology, what is a "near miss?"

32. You have 15 groups of 12 people that will be experiencing Raccoon Circles at the opening session of your next conference. Where can you find 15 different colors of tubular webbing?

33. The challenge course builder you are considering using is advocating the use of plastic wood, which they say is more expensive, but will last longer on your course. Is this a good idea?

34. You have a ropes course in the southern United States. Woodpeckers have taken up residence near the course, and are beginning to riddle your rope course poles with nesting holes. What do you do?

35. Ok, you've been to camp and you know that chomping down on a wintergreen Lifesaver® candy produces a kind of glowing spark. Why? Here's a hint, it has to do with triboluminescence. Check pages 146–153 of the July 1982 issue of Scientific American magazine for more information.

36. You are leading a challenge program for a corporate group, with a focus on communication and problem solving issues. After the lunch program, you notice that four of the 10 group members are experiencing balance problems, and may have been drinking alcohol. What do you do?

37. How do you tie a water knot?

38. As part of your acceptance to work at a local adventure program, you sign an agreement not to engage in private free-lance adventure programming. About a week after you start, your local youth club, of which you were a member, asks you to come by for the beginning meeting of the year, and invites you to lead two activities. What is the most ethical course of action?

39. Name at least one source for challenge and adventure books that is not on your continent.

40. Your local elementary school principal asks you to present a program on teambuilding for a group of second grade students? What questions would you like to ask the principal?

41. A national conference is going to meet in your community. One of the event sponsors asks you to lead a 1 hour teambuilding ex-

perience for 300 people on the first day. What is your plan?

42. After working with a few corporate groups this summer, you have just about had it with cellular phones, pagers, and beeping wristwatches in the middle of a critical activity or debriefing session. What is your policy on these devices during an adventure program?

43. You have an off-site teambuilding program planned, and quite a few of the participants show up in both waterproof sandles and open-toed shoes. Is this a problem?

44. Some researchers believe that there are at least seven different ways in which a person can learn, including: linguistically, mathematically, spatially, musically, kinesthetically, interpersonally, and intrapersonally. Choose one of the activities from Chapter 4 and discuss how you would teach this activity for groups consisting of each of the above types of learners? What would you do with a group that had some of each style?

45. What is the ideal number of participants for a single facilitator to work with during a ground-level challenge and adventure program?

46. Is there a recommended sequence of commands for a trust fall activity? If so, what are they? If not, what should they be?

47. If you had $100 to spend on challenge resources and equipment for your new camp program for 70 teenagers, what would you spend it on?

48. You work for a non-profit organization, and you need 150 tennis balls donated for the next challenge program event. Where do you find them?

49. Find the Comments sheet at the front of this book. Make a copy, fill it out, and send it in.

50. Consider this issue on technique: as a facilitator, you begin a workshop in complete silence, and only respond when someone asks you a question. Is this approach effective? Can you identify any concerns with this method?

51. Invent one new activity using a Raccoon Circle that requires one of the following skills: conflict resolution, decision making or communication between participants.

It is better to know some of the questions
than all of the answers.

James Thurber

Ideas for the Future of Challenge and Adventure Programming

Here are even more random thoughts, ideas, suggestions and inspirations for the future. Hopefully someone will pick up the ball and run with a few of these ideas, and the entire challenge and adventure programming community will benefit from their efforts.

Utilize all the knowledge and skill that currently resides in the occupants of our nursing and rest homes. Some of the challenge and adventure programs we have provided in the past few years have included folks that often have thoughts worth hearing, but few people to share them with. The knowledge base held by the elderly population is one of the greatest untapped resources in the world today.

Try organizing an adventure program power lunch. Everyone that comes brings along their favorite activity to teach the group. Network, share ideas, and eat. Or extend this concept by working with several groups to organize a play day, where various local resource personnel present activities and topics of interest to the local community recreation and adventure education population.

Imagine an underground adventure course to teach caving and climbing techniques. By using a series of tunnels and culverts, with plenty of locations for standing or escape, the term challenge course could be expanded to include caving techniques.

Consider taking on the task of republishing all the articles listed in the literature review of Chapter 1, in one expanded volume, or perhaps a volume a year for the next few years. This information, from more than 3 dozen sources, would be a sure classic to the adventure and challenge programming community.

Consider the publishing of a national guide on insurance and risk management issues related to challenge and adventure programming. This publication should include articles, recommendations, and guidelines, and hopefully be presented by eligible insurance companies that are interested in helping us all minimize the risk in our programming.

Create a national or statewide clearinghouse for recreational props, books and equipment. Many, if not all of the organizations that typically utilize challenge and adventure programming could use a little more funding. Instead of buying new and occasionally expensive equipment, why not organize a depository for recreational equipment. If your camp, or a member of your staff has extra copies of books, or multiple sets of equipment, they could donate these to the depository for a charitable tax deduction. Camps, schools and recreation programs could then contact the depository to see what equipment they have available, and only pay for shipping and processing costs to obtain it. We could set up a pick-up at major outdoor education events like the ACA, ACCT and AEE national conferences.

Make a wish for an entirely portable ropes course. Somewhat of a cross between an Alpine Tower and a carnival ride, so that it can be transported to a site with no facilities, set up, and used for a day, a week or for the summer.

Make it a mandatory requirement for all retiring challenge and adventure education programmers, that they write at least one article on their experiences for a journal, newsletter or publication. We need to recycle some of the vast knowledge that is out there from the past, and make it a part of our future.

How about a relationship between the companies that make plastic wood with schools and not-for-profit organizations to provide plastic wood for challenge course equipment in exchange for recyclable plastic materials?

Suggestions and guidelines from the ACCT, AEE or other organizations on how to make programs truly accessible and/or universal.

The Silo Project

The story is really very simple. A local farmer has a few silos, and like many modern farmers, he now has more than he needs. Throughout the North American countryside, and indeed many other locations around the world, agricultural silos can be seen everywhere. Recent improvements in agriculture, including the horizontal plastic film silo and modern automated silos are more the norm these days, as poured concrete and block silos begin to go the way of the steam engine and vacuum tube radios. The good news however in this change, is that there are an amazing number of structurally sound silos still out there, and they have the unique architecture that just cries out for an adventure based programming center, or climbing wall to be built within them. Early American farm silos are an elegant reflection of America's heritage. In a similar fashion to the technique in which the "Rails to Trails" program has helped to rejuvinate old rail lines in the United States, this project has the potential to "recycle" another item of our architectural heritage, the farm silo.

The reason for presenting this idea in Chapter 9, is that here is an idea that is just waiting for the right collection of people to work out the details to make it feasible. Few silos exist in a place where they can be immediately used by challenge and adventure based education programs. That means that something has to be moved. If your student population is not portable, that means having to move one of these monsters, piece by piece.

If this is beginning to sound like a script for a PBS mini-series called "This Old Silo," you are probably right. But the opportunity to have such a unique structure for a climbing center is certainly understandable. Many folks would probably donate the silo, just to have it removed from their property after years of standing empty.

Just thought you might like to consider the possibilities of this project. In the mean time, we are already figuring out how many yards of concrete we are going to need for the new foundation. Perhaps we'll show you some photographs in Teamwork & Teamplay II.

This is a real project being undertaken by Teamwork & Teamplay author Jim Cain. Luckily, he has a background in structural engineering. If you want to discuss the project in more detail, contact Jim Cain at the Teamplay address shown at the back of this book.

What Is Really Next?

We just wanted to throw out a few predictions of where we think challenge and adventure programming will be in the year 2000 and beyond. If we are totally wrong, at least these will be good for a few laughs in 20 or 30 years.

1. Insurance and Risk Management Issues. Expect to see some sweeping changes with this issue in the next few decades. Hopefully much of the change and regulation will come from within the insurance and challenge course building associations, and not from a third party regulation strategy.
2. Organizations. After a few more years of sorting things out, several major organizations are likely to emerge. Organizations that attempt to be all things to all members are likely to lose the memberships of participants that want hard skills and information in specific areas, not general knowledge on diverse issues.
3. More portable activities that utilize smaller, lightweight pieces of equipment.
4. Some completely "new" challenge activities.
5. Improved processing and debriefing techniques.
6. More utilization of challenge courses and programs by corporate groups, enabling the survival of not-for-profit challenge and adventured based programs.
7. A better understanding of the value of adventure programming and challenge-based education by corporations and academic institutions.
8. A nationally recognized training program for adventure educators in the United States.
9. Statistical analysis that documents the impact of challenge and adventure programs.
10. An accredited college curriculum and degree in the field of challenge education.
11. Additional expansion into non-traditional settings, such as marriage encounter programs, gang conflicts, youth at risk programs, spiritual enrichment, etc.
12. A national regulation of this industry in the United States.
13. National accreditation for facilitators and challenge education programmers.
14. An increase in the minimal level of first aid training from Basic First Aid and CPR to WFA and WFR certification levels.

"To know that even one life has breathed easier because you have lived. This is to have succeeded."

Ralph Waldo Emerson

Team Building Ahead

Teamwork
&
Teamplay

Hammermill

Teamplay

Training Events, Workshops, Resources and Equipment

Teamplay staff, including co-authors Jim Cain and Barry Jolliff, are available for on-site workshops, conferences, leadership events, keynote and playnote speeches, staff development, and training events.

If your group would like to construct the equipment for the activities listed in this book, and you would like a little assistance with the building process, Teamplay staff are available to help.

If you would like more information about the activities featured in Teamwork & Teamplay, or to schedule a member of the Teamplay staff for your next event, you can contact the authors at the following addresses. For staff training events, train-the-trainer programs, extending your bag of tricks workshops and conference sessions, Teamwork & Teamplay offers a variety of programs that are sure to please your staff and participants.

Jim Cain
468 Salmon Creek Road, Brockport, New York 14420
Phone (585) 637-0328 Fax (585) 637-5277
Email: jimcain@teamworkandteamplay.com
Website: www.teamworkandteamplay.com

Barry Jolliff
760 East Hutton Road, Wooster, Ohio 44691
Phone (330) 345-8492
Email: bjolliff@sssnet.com

If you are interested in obtaining additional copies of this book, the fastest method is by directly contacting the publisher, Kendall/Hunt at (800) 228-0810. They also maintain a website at www.kendallhunt.com. Copies of Teamwork & Teamplay can also be purchased from the companies shown below, and many of the suppliers listed in Chapter 8. In addition, the great folks at Alpine Towers International can provide the Teamwork & Teamplay book, trainers to teach and facilitate Teamwork & Teamplay activities, and most of the equipment described in this book (everything from Funderbirds and Bull Rings to Marble Tubes and Lycra Tubes).

Adventure Hardware
P.O. Box 69
Jonas Ridge, NC 28641
Phone (800) 706-0064
www.adventurehardware.com

American Camping Association
5000 State Road 67
Martinsville, IN 46151
Phone (800) 428-CAMP
aca@aca-camps.org

Sportime
One Sportime Way
Atlanta, GA 30340
Phone (800) 283-5700
www.sportime.com

Dr. Jim Cain was recently awarded the Karl Rohnke Creativity Award by the Association for Experiential Education for his contributions to the book Teamwork & Teamplay. *You can obtain a copy of this award winning adventure-based book directly from the publisher, Kendall/Hunt, at 1-800-228-0810.*

Teamplay

Training Events, Workshops, Resources and Equipment

Teamplay staff, including co-authors Jim Cain and Barry Jolliff, are available for on-site workshops, conferences, leadership events, keynote and playnote speeches, staff development, and training events.

If your group would like to construct the equipment for the activities listed in this book, and you would like a little assistance with the building process, Teamplay staff are available to help.

If you would like more information about the activities featured in Teamwork & Teamplay, or to schedule a member of the Teamplay staff for your next event, you can contact the authors at the following addresses. For staff training events, train-the-trainer programs, extending your bag of tricks workshops and conference sessions, Teamwork & Teamplay offers a variety of programs that are sure to please your staff and participants.

Jim Cain
468 Salmon Creek Road, Brockport, New York 14420
Phone (585) 637-0328 Fax (585) 637-5277
Email: jimcain@teamworkandteamplay.com
Website: www.teamworkandteamplay.com

Barry Jolliff
760 East Hutton Road, Wooster, Ohio 44691
Phone (330) 345-8492
Email: bjolliff@sssnet.com

If you are interested in obtaining additional copies of this book, the fastest method is by directly contacting the publisher, Kendall/Hunt at (800) 228-0810. They also maintain a website at www.kendallhunt.com. Copies of Teamwork & Teamplay can also be purchased from the companies shown below, and many of the suppliers listed in Chapter 8. In addition, the great folks at Alpine Towers International can provide the Teamwork & Teamplay book, trainers to teach and facilitate Teamwork & Teamplay activities, and most of the equipment described in this book (everything from Funderbirds and Bull Rings to Marble Tubes and Lycra Tubes).

Adventure Hardware
P.O. Box 69
Jonas Ridge, NC 28641
Phone (800) 706-0064
www.adventurehardware.com

American Camping Association
5000 State Road 67
Martinsville, IN 46151
Phone (800) 428-CAMP
aca@aca-camps.org

Sportime
One Sportime Way
Atlanta, GA 30340
Phone (800) 283-5700
www.sportime.com

Dr. Jim Cain was recently awarded the Karl Rohnke Creativity Award by the Association for Experiential Education for his contributions to the book Teamwork & Teamplay. *You can obtain a copy of this award winning adventure-based book directly from the publisher, Kendall/Hunt, at 1-800-228-0810.*

Index